# Contents

## PART IV The counter-Enlightenment



## PART V The twentieth century: four approaches

# Detailed contents

## PART II The two kingdoms



## PART III The rationalist Enlightenment

# Notes on the Contributors

**Terence Ball** is Professor of Political Science and the Public Ethics Scholar at the Lincoln Center for Applied Ethics at Arizona State University. He has held appointments at the University of Minnesota, the University of California, and Oxford University. He is the author of *Transforming Political Discourse* (Oxford University Press, 1988), *Reappraising Political Theory* (Oxford University Press, 1995), and a political theory mystery novel, *Rousseau's Ghost* (State University of New York Press, 1998), as well as co-editor of *Political Innovation and Conceptual Change* (Cambridge University Press, 1989), *Conceptual Change and the Constitution* (University of Kansas, 1988), *Thomas Jefferson: Political Writings* (Cambridge University Press, 1999), and *The Cambridge History of Twentieth-Century Political Thought* (Cambridge University Press, forthcoming).

**Deborah Baumgold** is Professor in the Department of Political Science, University of Oregon, where she teaches political theory. She is the author of *Hobbes's Political Theory* (Cambridge University Press, 1988) and other writings on seventeenth-century political thought.

**Kenneth Baynes** is Professor of Philosophy at the State University of New York at Stony Brook. He is the author of *The Normative Grounds of Social Criticism: Kant, Rawls, and Habermas* (State University of New York Press, 1992), and co-editor of *Discourse and Democracy: Essays on Habermas's 'Between Facts and Norms'* (State University of New York Press, 2002) and *After Philosophy: End or Transformation* (MIT Press, 1987).

**David Boucher** is Professorial Fellow in the School of European Studies, Cardiff University, and Adjunct Professor of International Relations at the University of the Sunshine Coast, Australia. He is also Director of the Collingwood and British Idealism Centre, Cardiff University. He was formerly Professor of Political Theory and Government at the University of Wales, Swansea. His publications include *Texts in Context* (Martinus Nijhoff, 1985), *Social and Political Thought of R. G. Collingwood* (Cambridge University Press, 1989), *A Radical Hegelian* (with Andrew Vincent; St Martin's Press, 1993), *Political Theories of International Relations* (Oxford University Press, 1998), and *British Idealism and Political Theory* (with Andrew Vincent; Edinburgh University Press, 2000). David Boucher has previously edited two books with Paul Kelly, *The Social Contract from Hobbes to Rawls* (Routledge, 1995) and *Social Justice from Hume to Walzer* (Routledge, 1998). He is currently working on varieties of human rights theory, and politics, poetry, and protest in the writings of Leonard Cohen and Bob Dylan to be published by Continuum (2003).

**Tony Burns** is Reader in Politics at Nottingham Trent University. He is convenor of the Hegel Panels of the annual conference of the Political Studies Association of Great Britain. He is the author of *Natural Law and Political Ideology in the Philosophy of Hegel* (Avebury, 1996), and co-editor of *The Hegel and Marx Connection* (Palgrave, 2000). He is currently working on *The Aristotelian Natural Law Tradition*.

**Joseph Canning** is Reader in History at University of Wales, Bangor. His major publications include *The Political Thought of Baldus de Ubaldis* (Cambridge University Press, 1987; repr. 1989 and 2002); *A History of Medieval Political Thought, 300–1450* (Routledge, 1996; repr. 1998); and contributions to J. H. Burns (ed.), *The Cambridge History of Medieval Political Thought, c.350–1450* (Cambridge University Press, 1988); also (ed. with Otto Gerhard Oexle) *Political Thought and the Realities of Power in the Middle Ages/Politisches Denken und die Wirklichkeit der Macht im Mittelalter* (Göttingen, 1998). He is currently writing a book entitled *Ideas of Power in the Late Middle Ages, c.1290–c.1420.*

**Jean Bethke Elshtain** is the Laura Spelman Rockefeller Professor of Social and Political Ethics at the University of Chicago. The author of many books, her most recent is *Jane Addams and the Dream of American Democracy* (Basic Books, 2002). Her 1995 book *Democracy on Trial* was a *New York Times* notable book for that year. 1996's *Augustine and the Limits of Politics* was named one of the top five books on religion for that year by *Christian Century*. Other of her books have been named by *Choice* as top academic books in the year of their publication. Professor Elshtain was elected to the American Academy of Arts and Sciences in 1996.

She is co-chair of the PEW Forum on Religion and Public Life in America and serves on many boards. She writes regularly for academic publications and journals of civic opinion.

**Joseph V. Femia** is Reader in Political Theory at Liverpool University. He has been a British Academy Visiting Professor at the European University Institute in Florence, and a Visiting Fellow at Princeton and Yale Universities. He is the author of *Gramsci's Political Thought* (Oxford University Press, 1981), *Marxism and Democracy* (Oxford University Press, 1993), and *The Machiavellian Legacy* (Oxford University Press, 1998). He is currently writing books on Machiavelli and varieties of anti-democratic thought.

**Yoshie Kawade** is associate professor of Tokyo Metropolitan University in Japan. A specialist in modern French political thought, she is the author of *kizoku no toku, shogyo no seisin,* which examines the ambivalent attitude of Montesquieu toward aristocratic virtue and the spirit of commerce. Her writings include *La Liberté civile contre la théorie réformiste de l'etat souverain* and *Will and Politics: The Theory of Sovereignty in Bodin and Rousseau.*

**Paul Kelly** is Senior Lecturer in Political Theory at the London School of Economics, and editor of *Political Studies.* He has written on the history of political ideas and modern political philosophy and his books include *Utilitarianism and Distributive Justice* (Clarendon Press, 1990), and, as editor, *The Social Contract from Hobbes to Rawls* (Routledge, 1994), *Impartiality, Neutrality and Justice* (Edinburgh University Press, 1998), *Social Justice* (Routledge, 1998), and *Multiculturalism Reconsidered* (Polity Press, 2002).

**Rex Martin** has held university appointments in both the United States and the United Kingdom. Currently he is Professor of Philosophy at the University of Kansas and Honorary Professorial Fellow at Cardiff University. His most recent books are *A System of Rights* (Oxford University Press, 1997) and a revised edition, with introduction, of R. G. Collingwood's *An Essay on Metaphysics* (Oxford University Press, 1998). Martin continues to work on Rawls's political thought and is currently working on two long-term projects as well: the nature and justification of human rights and the problem of providing a moral justification for a democratic system of rights.

**Cary J. Nederman** is Professor of Political Science, University of Arizona. He is the author of *Community and Consent* (Rowman & Littlefield, 1994) and *Worlds of Difference* (Penn State University Press, 2000). He is the editor of John of Salisbury, *Policraticus* (Cambridge University Press, 1991), and co-editor of *Medieval Political Theory* (Routledge, 1993), *Marsiglio of Padua, Defensor Minor* (Cambridge University Press, 1993), *Three Tracts on Empire* (Thoemmes Press, 2000), *Readings in Medieval Political Philosophy* (Hackett, 2000), and Marsilius of Padua, *Defensor Pacis* (Columbia University Press, 2000). He is currently completing an edition of fourteenth- and fifteenth-century European texts on empire (Thoemmes Press, forthcoming); and revising a monograph study of the medieval roots of religious toleration, for Cambridge University Press.

**Peter Nicholson** studied at the University of Exeter, and lectured at the University of Wales, Swansea, and the University of York, including a range of courses in the history of political thought; he retired as Reader in the Department of Politics in 2001. He has published papers on Protagoras, Plato, and Aristotle, and is the editor of *Polis,* the journal of the Society for the Study of Greek Political Thought. He is the author of *The Political Philosophy of the British Idealists: Selected Studies* (Cambridge University Press, 1990), and editor of an expanded edition of T. H. Green's *Works* (Thoemmes Press, 1997).

**Carole Pateman** was formerly a Reader at the University of Sydney and is Professor of Political Science at the University of California, Los Angeles. She has held numerous visiting fellowships in Australia and Europe and was President of the International Political Science Association in 1991–4. Her publications include *Participation and Democratic Theory* (Cambridge University Press, 1970), *The Problem of Political Obligation* (John Wiley, 1985), *The Sexual Contract* (Polity Press, 1988), and *The Disorder of Women* (Polity Press, 1989). She is the co-editor of *Feminist Interpretations and Political Theory* (Polity Press, 1991).

**Alan Patten** is Assistant Professor in the Department of Political Science, McGill University, Montreal. His research interests include contemporary Anglo-American political philosophy and the history of political thought, especially from the seventeenth to the nineteenth centuries. His book *Hegel's Idea of Freedom* (Oxford University Press, 1998) was awarded the Macpherson Prize of the Canadian Political Science Association in 2000. He is currently working on a book on language rights.

**Paul Patton** is Professor of Philosophy and Head of School at the University of New South Wales, Sydney, Australia. Paul Patton has published widely on aspects of twentieth-century French philosophy, political philosophy, and social and cultural theory. He is author of *Deleuze and the Political* (Routledge, 2000), and co-editor of *Political Theory and the Rights of Indigenous Peoples* (Cambridge University Press, 2000). His current research includes comparative work on the philosophies of Deleuze and Derrida and an Australian Research Council collaborative project funded by the ARC and directed at a naturalistic approach to rights and norms. He is currently a co-editor of *Theory & Event.* He has translated *Difference and Repetition* by Gilles Deleuze (Columbia University Press, 1995).

**David C.D.C. Reeve** is Professor of Philosophy at the University of North Carolina at Chapel Hill. He has published widely in the field of Greek philosophy and ethics and translated a number of classical Greek philosophical texts. His most recent books include *Philosopher Kings* (Hackett, 1998), *Substantial Knowledge: Aristotle's Metaphysics* (Hackett, 2000), and *Women in the Academy: Dialogues on Themes from Plato's 'Republic'* (Hackett, 2001).

**Jennifer Ring** is Professor of Political Science and Director of the Women's Studies Program, University of Nevada, Reno. She has published in the fields of women and politics, gender, and race. Her books include *Modern Political Theory and Contemporary Feminism: A Dialectical Approach* (State University of New York Press, 1991) and *The Political Consequences of Thinking: Gender and Judaism in the Work of Hannah Arendt* (State University of New York Press, 1997).

**Fred Rosen** is Professor of the History of Political Thought at University College London. He has written widely in ancient Greek political thought and particularly on the Socratic dialogues of Plato, was a founder of the Society for Greek Political Thought, and serves on the editorial board of *Polis.* He was for many years Director of the Bentham Project at University College London, and is joint general editor of *The Collected Works of Jeremy Bentham.* Among his books are *Jeremy Bentham and Representative Democracy* (Oxford University Press, 1983) and *Bentham, Byron and Greece* (Oxford University Press, 1992). He is currently completing a book entitled *Classical Utilitarianism from Hume to Mill.*

**Paul Thomas** is Professor of Political Science at the University of California, Berkeley. His publications include *Karl Marx and the Anarchists* (Routledge, 1985); *Alien Politics: Marxist State Theory Retrieved* (with Terrell Carver; Routledge, 1994); *Rational Choice Marxism* (with David Lloyd; Macmillan, 1995); and *Culture and the State* (Routledge, 1998).

**Jeremy Waldron** is Maurice and Hilda Friedman Professor at Columbia Law School and Director of Columbia's Center for Law and Philosophy. He has published numerous books, including most recently *The Dignity of Legislation* (Cambridge University Press, 1999), *Law and Disagreement* (Oxford University Press, 1999), and *God, Locke and Equality* (Cambridge University Press, 2002).

**Cheryl Welch** received her MA and Ph.D. from Columbia University in political theory. She taught at Harvard University for nine years as an Assistant and Associate Professor, and has also taught at Columbia, Rutgers, and Tufts. Professor Welch has received research grants from the National Endowment for the Humanities and the Mellon Foundation, and has been a fellow at the Bunting Institute and at the Harvard Law School. She is currently a Professor at Simmons College, where she chairs the Department of Political Science and International Relations. During the academic year 2001–2 she was a fellow in residence at the Carr Center for Human Rights Policy at the John F. Kennedy School of Government, Harvard University. Cheryl Welch is the author of *Liberty and Utility: The French Idéologues and the Transformation of Liberalism* (Columbia University Press, 1984), *Critical Issues in Social Theory* (with Murray Milgate; Vanderbilt University Press, 1989), and *De Tocqueville* (Oxford University Press, 2001), as well as numerous articles on French and British political thought, liberalism, and democracy. Her current work focuses on cosmopolitanism and the challenge to traditional ideas of citizenship.

**Nathan Widder** is Lecturer in Political Theory at the University of Exeter, having previously taught at the London School of Economics. His research interests span the history of Western political thought, contemporary continental philosophy, and feminist political theory. He is the author of *Genealogies of Difference* (University of Illinois Press, 2002), and is currently working on a book on Gilles Deleuze.

**Lawrence Wilde** is Professor of Politics at Nottingham Trent University. He is the author of *Marx and Contradiction* (Avebury, 1989), *Modern European Socialism* (Dartmouth, 1994), and *Ethical Marxism and its Radical Critics* (Macmillan, 1998). He is the joint editor of *Approaches to Marx* (with Mark Cowling; Open University 1989) and *Marxism's Ethical Thinkers* (Palgrave, 2001). He is currently completing a book on Erich Fromm.

# 1 Introduction

David Boucher and Paul Kelly

## Contents



## Introduction

Thinking about politics or political thought, which is an activity almost as old as politics itself, comprises a huge variety of styles and approaches. Political thinkers have sought to explain institutions and practices, advise rulers, defend values and principles, or criticize the world in which they found themselves. They have focused narrowly on institutions of government, law-making, and the exercise of coercive power, or more broadly on the character of a society or people. At its most general, political thought converges with what we now describe as ethics and moral philosophy, sociology and anthropology, as well as theology and metaphysics. Some political thinkers have sought to explain the nature of man as a political animal and the role of politics in an account of human flourishing and well-being, and thus assert the dignity of political activity in fully human life. Others have sought to explain why politics, though necessary, is secondary to more important human goals such as seeking salvation and eternal life. More recently other thinkers have sought to subsume political activity beneath realms of human activity such as 'society' or 'the economy'. This variety or plurality of styles, approaches, and presuppositions has made political thought an exciting intellectual activity for students and scholars alike, as well as making general surveys of the character of political thought a matter of deep and persistent conflict among them. As approaches to theorizing about politics differ, so do accounts of how and why we should continue to study political thought. It is therefore incumbent upon us, in presenting a new overview of some of the main Western political thinkers from ancient Greece to the present, to say something, by way of introduction, both about the activity and point of political thinking and about those thinkers we have included in this book.

This volume presents a canon of major political thinkers who in various ways have shaped the intellectual architecture of our modern conceptions of the scope of politics. Yet the very idea of a canon, which we have received and inevitably transformed in constructing this book, is itself deeply contested. What makes one thinker 'canonical' and another not? Clearly in constructing this volume we have had to be selective. But what are our criteria of selection? Does the canon of Western political thought embody a single progressive narrative that explains the emergence of 'natural law' or the triumph of some variety of liberal constitutional democracy as the ideal form of government? Or could we have provided a completely different canon of thinkers which would represent a very different account of the origin and nature of our contemporary conception of politics? All of these questions relate to the 'how' question facing the study of political thought. In this introductory chapter we will address some of these questions; in particular we will look at the emergence of the idea of a 'canon' of political thought. We will also address some of the 'why' questions that inevitably attach to the study of political thinkers from the past. Given the development of ever more theoretically sophisticated methods for the study of government and bureaucracy, why do we need to study what dead, white, and almost exclusively male thinkers had to say about politics in the past? Why does a politics major in the United States, or an advanced British or Canadian undergraduate student, need to know about Plato, St Augustine, Thomas Hobbes, or Karl Marx if he or she is interested in the study of politics itself and not merely the history of philosophy? In presenting an account of the emergence and character of political thought as an object of inquiry, we hope to provide an answer to this 'why' question as well as provide an interesting overview of the considerations underlying *how* one should study the canon of political thinkers.

This chapter begins with an account of the origins of the study of political thought as a distinct activity. We start with the emergence of political thought in order to show how the subject emerged in British and American universities to serve a variety of purposes, many of which are still of central concern to students and scholars of political thought. This variety explains the difficulty and undesirability of imposing a single common narrative structure and set of concerns on Western political thought, but it also undermines the point of constructing a single authoritative methodology for the study of political thought. Instead we offer four sets of considerations which shape approaches to the study of political thought and which contribute answers to why we should study it. Building on these pluralist considerations we provide an outline of the book and an account of our criteria of inclusion. The chapter concludes with a discussion of the problem of perennial questions and the attempt to explain and defend what it is that makes a book a 'classic' text. In this way we provide students with a companion and guide to the most important political thinkers of the Western tradition, but also with an advanced introduction into some of the issues that surround the activity of studying political thought.

## The study of political thought

The traditional canon of texts which comprise the subject matter for the study of political thought arose not in the use of one philosopher by another in the ideological exploitation of a text, although no doubt such use contributed to the canon, but in a quite different context. That context was the emergence of the academic discipline of politics in the United States and Great Britain, and in response to the demand for textbooks to teach a broadening curriculum meant to educate citizens and prepare them for public service.[1] There are a variety of factors that came to shape the character of the discipline of politics, and the study of political philosophy in particular. It is indeed a hybrid discipline accommodating the demands of philosophy, history, science, and practical political considerations. The tradition of political theory, composed of texts, is what John Gunnell calls the 'regulative paradigm in the study of politics', and it is largely the creation of historians of political thought themselves.[2]

## Philosophical considerations

Discussions of political philosophy first began to emerge in histories of philosophy and general literature. Literature then had a much broader meaning encompassing most forms of knowledge imparted through books. Multiple-volume studies generally included sections on political literature, as for example, in the general surveys of Henry Hallum (1838), and F. D. Maurice (1840s). The honour of producing the first history of political thought, a foretaste of which he supplied in *The Temporal Benefits of Christianity* (1849), is often attributed to Robert Blakey. His *History of Political Literature from the Earliest Times* (1855) is not obviously a forerunner of the genre because it lacks recognizable criteria of selection and principles of value. He is concerned to display the vast array of political discussion evident at all levels of discourse, and therefore included political ballads, plays, satires, popular songs, and poetry, as well as the more standard writings that have subsequently come to constitute the canon.

As the discipline began to take form at the end of the nineteenth century, philosophical idealism was the predominant fashion in philosophy with its emphasis upon the coherence theory of truth, according to which the truth of a statement did not rely on its correspondence with an external reality independent of mind, but instead upon its place in a world of ideas whose consistency and coherence were the criteria of the truth of the statement. Studying the history of political thought, on this view, was largely seen as a prelude to formulating one's own philosophy. It was not denied that the history of political philosophy had certain merits in its own right, but it was maintained that the only proper attitude to adopt in studying the great philosophers of the past was to use them to formulate one's own philosophical theories. This was an attitude that many British idealists displayed in their considerations of political philosophers. T. H. Green in his *Lectures on the Principles of Political Obligation* (1919) and Bernard Bosanquet in *The Philosophical Theory of the State* (1899) both examined the political theories of other philosophers before going on to develop their own philosophical positions.[3] Michael Oakeshott, a great believer in the autonomy of history, maintained that the philosopher in studying past political philosophy should do so with a view to bringing about a 'genuine renaissance'.[4] R. G. Collingwood attempted to bring about such a renaissance when his reading of Hobbes stimulated him 'to bring *Leviathan* up to date'.[5] Viewing the history of political thought as a stimulus to philosophy was by no means confined to idealists. Two of the most distinguished and recent exponents were Leo Strauss and Eric Voegelin.[6]

## Political thought as history

The second set of considerations that came to shape the study of political thought concerned the issue of what properly constituted a historical study. The term 'history' often appeared in the title of studies of political thought more as a courtesy than as an indication of the method. The study of both politics and political philosophy took place under the auspices of history departments in the universities. There was much serious scholarship produced in the early years that attempted to arrest tendencies that detracted from the historical character of the discipline. Many historians did not subscribe to the idea that canonical texts defined the discipline, and did not hesitate to pursue antiquarian and esoteric interests, while at the same time criticizing the tendency to produce textbooks that, for them, distorted historical scholarship. J. N. Figgis, one of the pioneers of political thought at Cambridge University, made no apology for the breadth of specialized literature with which he dealt, which was, he claimed, 'without charm or brilliance or overmuch eloquence, voluminous, arid, scholastic. . . . Yet it was once living and effectual.'[7] J. W. Allen despaired of much of the work carrying the title 'history of political thought'. He contended that 'The study of the history of political thought seems to me to exhibit still some of the characteristics of extreme youthfulness; its crudity, its haste, its readiness to jump to conclusions. A good deal of current generalisation would seem to represent guess-work or impressions derived one knows not how.'[8] The six volumes of the history of political philosophy produced by A. J. and R. W. Carlyle attempted to deal with medieval thought in a disinterested manner, and in which the present is not a constant reference point of the past.[9]

One may with plausibility claim that the Cambridge School of the 1960s and after, whose principal exponent in America was J. G. A. Pocock and in England, Quentin Skinner, was in a direct line of descent from the likes of Figgis, Allen, and the Carlyles in arguing for the disciplinary integrity of the historical study of political thought. What they all have in common, to use Skinner's words, 'might be summarised as a desire to stress the historicity of the history of political theory and of intellectual history more generally'.[10] Principally they had two aims. First they wanted to unravel the competing claims of philosophy and history. In Pocock's view the philosophical use of the past was perfectly legitimate, but it had no business in intruding on the historical. For him, it was the historian, and not the philosopher, who was the guardian of the truth, and protected society against the manipulation of the past for present ideological purposes.

There has been a tendency in criticism of the Cambridge School, or the New Historians as they are sometimes known, to take part of what they recommend for the whole. Although Pocock and Skinner were invariably lumped together in criticism of the Cambridge School, they do in fact have quite different arguments and therefore do not constitute a single target. For example, there are those who object to the retrieval of authorial intentions as the sole legitimate focus of historical inquiry on the grounds that the texts themselves have produced serious and sometimes catastrophic unintended consequences unthought of by their authors. In other words, it is the consequences rather than the intentions that matter.[11]

Pocock's argument gives priority to languages, particularly paradigmatic languages within which authors work, and which may comprise concepts and vocabularies drawn from a range of activities, carrying with them their authoritative import, as, for example, from the field of law. Pocock makes it quite clear that the historian chooses the level of abstraction at which to trace an idea, and this need not be at the level of intentions. Writers, in his view, cannot avoid performing linguistic acts in excess of their intentions.

Skinner gives priority, not exclusivity, to the retrieval of the intentions of the author in determining the meaning of an argument. From Pocock's point of view, it is the language itself and the constraints it imposes that provides the focus; for Skinner, it is the individual utterance as an intentional communication in relation to a context of conventions.[12] Gradually this took the form of concentrating upon the concepts that we use to describe and appraise morality and politics. In particular, evaluative descriptive concepts such as democracy and liberty which have both descriptive referents that change over time, and evaluative connotations that may remain the same or similarly change. 'Democracy', for example, during the early and late modern period changes from being a pejorative evaluative term to being one of commendation. Skinner's concern, then, was to show what could be done with concepts in argument.[13] What Pocock and Skinner have in common is positing a linguistic context as the appropriate unit of analysis that elicit the types of meaning that the historian makes intelligible.

## Political thought and the claims of science

A third set of pressures that the nascent discipline of the history of political thought had to accommodate was the demand to conform to scientific modes of explanation. After the publication of Charles Darwin's *Origin of Species* in 1859 evolution became a concept that captured the public imagination and held out great hope of becoming the unifying scientific theory, so much so that almost all modes of discourse were converging upon it, including not only the biological sciences, but also poetry, politics, and philosophy. History for its own sake in some quarters was viewed as little more than the collection of facts, and in order to raise its academic credibility needed to subject those facts to scientific consideration. The great nineteenth-century historian J. B. Bury, at Cambridge, presented physics and biology as exemplars that historical explanation should emulate.[14] Robert Blakey unsuccessfully took great pains to avoid producing something that would be only of 'antiquarian or historical curiosity' in order to advance 'our reasonings on political science' to reveal the 'progressive character' of the discipline.[15] J. R. Seeley succeeded in 1885 in changing the name of the political philosophy tripos at Cambridge to 'political science', and Sheldon Amos argued that in history observation served as a substitute for experimentation and had achieved some degree of success in the formulation of universal propositions about the human condition. Amos examined the now familiar canon of thinkers in the history of political thought in order to determine the contribution of each to the development of a true science of politics.[16] Finally, Frederick Pollock, in his *History of the Science of Politics* (1890), argued that a true sign of scientific analysis is 'patient analysis and unbiased research'; on this basis Aristotle made a much greater contribution than Plato, and Machiavelli greater than either, to the dispassionate scientific study of politics.[17]

This tendency towards scientific explanation as the only valid form of knowledge found its most forceful expression in behaviouralism in the United States and logical positivism in Britain. Here we need to remind ourselves of the distinction between the first-order activity of political philosophizing and the second-order activity of studying what political philosophers write. David Easton, the doyen of behaviouralism, launched an attack that was mainly, but not exclusively, directed at the second-order activity. He regretted the decline of political theory into historicism in the work of such American historians as W. A. Dunning and C. H. McIlwain. Instead of analysing and producing new value theory Easton convicted them of simply reiterating and retailing the meanings, logical consistency, and historical development of political ideas.[18] He criticized historians of political thought for being preoccupied with the narration of the intellectual events of the past, and suggested that the modern political theorist should use the history of values in order to discover the variety of moral outlooks 'with the hope that this would aid him in the construction of his own political synthesis or image of a good political life'.[19]

The first-order activity of political theory was dealt a severe blow by logical positivism, the most well-known exponent of which in the English-speaking world was A. J. Ayer, who had gone to Vienna in the early 1930s to learn about the group of philosophers gathered around Moritz Schlick, who were influenced by the early Ludwig Wittgenstein and Bertrand Russell. Ayer published *Language, Truth and Logic* in 1936, which was a devastating attack on traditional philosophy, rendering much of it meaningless, including metaphysics, and most of ethics and political philosophy. Philosophy seemed to many to be a series of interminable disputes with no agreement on the right answers. What exactly was preventing philosophy from arriving at truths that were generally acceptable? Was there some flaw in the whole enterprise? Ayer's bold claim was that philosophy was indeed seriously flawed, and identifying that flaw meant that philosophy could at last be transformed into an altogether more productive activity. This involved a clear account of what the legitimate purpose and method of philosophy was to be.

Like Hume, Ayer made a distinction between *analytic* statements that are true by definition, and therefore tautologies that do not depend upon sense-experience or empirical evidence for their truth, and *synthetic* statements that are propositions about reality and in principle subject to verification. Ayer goes on to contend that metaphysical statements are neither analytic nor synthetic and are in fact nonsense statements.

The book has been seen principally as an attack on metaphysics, but it was generally an attempt to diminish the epistemic authority of philosophy in general by demarcating its legitimate aims and objectives. Philosophy had no special insights to offer into the non-empirical world, nor could it offer any guidance to moral conduct. Politically, the book had a certain significance given the context of the rise of Fascism, Nazism, and authoritarianism on the Continent. It was, after all, in Germany during the rise of Nazism that Ayer formulated his position. Ayer was denying special authority to any claims about absolute knowledge, especially in the realms of metaphysics and morals. As the author of the introduction to *Language, Truth and Logic* suggests, 'A lot of anger and revolutionary zeal went into its writing and its arguments had very radical implications. If they were accepted, religion would wither away, ideology would perish, social hierarchies would collapse. Truth and, Ayer hoped, tolerance would flourish in their place.'[20] The book has to be seen as a contribution to the theory of truth, but at the same time it rejected the question 'What is truth?' A theory of truth, in Ayer's view, could only show how propositions were validated. Followers of Ayer, such as T. D. Weldon and Margaret MacDonald, reduced political philosophy to little more than the analysis of language into meaningful propositions that could be verified, or an analysis of the type of emotional response a statement was meant to elicit.

Subject to such hostile criticism, and with what appeared to be a less urgent need for political analysis at a time that most prominent intellectuals, with the notable exception of Friedrich Hayek, agreed was 'the end of ideology' and one of convergence upon consensus politics, political philosophy on both sides of the Atlantic by the mid-1950s was rendered moribund, and pronounced, by the likes of Leo Strauss and Peter Laslett, either dead or in the process of dying.

Almost immediately first- and second-order political philosophy was resurrected by distinguished historians of ideas such as John Plamenatz and Isaiah Berlin, and the activity underwent a renaissance when H. L. A. Hart generated serious thinking about the place of law in society and the conditions necessary to sustain it and John Rawls revived the social contract tradition to formulate a consensual theory of distributive justice.

## Political thought and practice

We have seen so far that the activity of studying past political thought emerged in the context of competing pressures: the philosophical, which tended to emphasize the timelessness of the ideas discussed; the historical, which emphasized the disinterestedness of the historian's task; and the scientific, which tended to emphasize the objectivity of the inquirer and the need to go beyond an antiquarian interest to formulate generalizations or testable propositions that might be of use to the political scientist. The fourth set of considerations we want to discuss is, perhaps, the most pressing. Because political questions are intensely practical, and political opinions potentially divisive and emotive, it is difficult, and perhaps not even desirable, for the inquirer to separate practical from philosophical considerations. Considerations of practical utility consider historical disinterestedness anathema to the ethos of political thinking. Thus McIlwain's view that the historian is not a partisan, and therefore it is not his or her task to decide between two positions, precipitated hostile responses from those who emphasized the practical value of studying the works of political philosophers.[21] Robert Blakey had set the precedent in being himself a political activist. He had been the editor of two English radical newspapers, *Black Dwarf* and *The Politician.* He was very much concerned to make judgements about what was good and bad in political theory in relation to pressing practical problems. W. K. Hancock, for example, suggested that Machiavelli could tell us a great deal about ourselves, and about the power and interest of the state and technical knowledge.[22] C. Deslisle Burns was even more forceful in his view that the study of the past must have a practical value. He argued that the history of political thought 'must show us how to change the present into a better future, by showing how the past became the present'.[23]

Some modern philosophers, among them T. D. Weldon, Ludwig Wittgenstein, and Michael Oakeshott, although holding quite different theoretical positions, nevertheless agreed that philosophy had nothing to contribute to the activities it took as its subject matter. In other words, there is a division between theory and practice that cannot be bridged. This in itself was a denial of the possibility of normative political theory. R. G. Collingwood, on the other hand, who did much to establish the autonomy of the historical mode of understanding, maintained that theory and practice overlap. One cannot be a utilitarian in theory without its having some bearing on how you view people and objects, namely, as means to an end, and each occasion as an opportunity for utility maximization. In Collingwood's view, all philosophical problems arise from practical problems, and their solutions return to practice. Collingwood's own major work of political philosophy was occasioned by the Second World War and was meant to instil in Europeans the importance of the values that underpinned their civilization and which had to be defended against Fascism and Nazism.[24]

After the so-called demise of political theory in the late 1950s and early 1960s it has been argued that among those factors that have contributed to its revival and flourishing are the fact that it very quickly became abundantly clear that ideological politics, far from having ended, made a resurgence, both between and within societies. Furthermore, the civil rights movement and the war in Vietnam confronted theorists with normative issues of political obligation, civil disobedience, conscientious objection, just war, and social justice.[25] It is no coincidence that these are the very issues addressed by the two leading theorists to have surfaced in 1960s America, Michael Walzer and John Rawls. In Britain in the same period political theory re-emerged under the influence of H. L. A. Hart and Brian Barry, as both set out to challenge the hegemony of utilitarian thinking in the field of political and social theory. Hart was an important scholar of Jeremy Bentham and John Austin, but was also a sophisticated critic of a crude utilitarianism in social and penal policy.[26] His critique of the limitations of utilitarianism had its roots in reflections on the emergence and development of utilitarian ideas in the late nineteenth century. Like a subsequent generation of Oxford political theorists including Alan Ryan, John Gray, David Miller, Gerry Cohen, and Jeremy Waldron, Hart's example showed that the engagement with the tradition of past political thinkers could inform, explain, and provide the intellectual resources to think beyond the limitations of contemporary political orthodoxy.[27] Barry also writes of the resurgence of political theory, since the publication of his *Political Argument* in 1965 and John Rawls's *A Theory of Justice* in 1971, as a return to a grand tradition of political theory that had ceased around the turn of the twentieth century.[28] The return to normative, or first-order, political theorizing mirrors the approach of the idealists in Britain at the end of the nineteenth and beginning of the twentieth century. A reflection on past thinkers provides a prolegomena to actual theorising. This is not intended in the simplistic sense of continuing a timeless conversation, nor of drawing simple lessons or arguments from past political thinkers. Rather it embodies a recognition that first-order political theorising cannot emerge from nowhere, but instead is a constructive enterprise that involves building, expanding, and developing the vocabularies that are inherent in great political texts.

This revival in first-order political theory has gone hand in hand with a renaissance in second-order political theorizing, some, as we saw, dedicated to historical authenticity, but a considerable amount passionate to address and contribute to the resolution of present political problems. The Straussians in the United States have been most vociferous about the dangers of devaluing the status of classic texts by the propagation of an insidious relativism that threatens to render moribund two of the most prominent characteristics of the stuff of political thought, namely philosophical criticism and practical relevance. The classic authors, despite being dismissed by feminists and multiculturalists as dead, white males, offer us visions of the good life, and it is our duty to take their claims to truth seriously. Allan Bloom complained of the marginalization and historicization of the study of political thought, which for him was symptomatic of the more general crisis of modernity in the loss of our capacity to value, marvellously diagnosed and regrettably accentuated by Nietzsche, who encouraged the rejection of the categories of truth and falsity in political and moral matters. In order to overcome the perversity of modernity we must, in Bloom's view, return to the contemplation of Socrates.[29] One does not have to be a Straussian to defend the value of studying classic texts. Indeed even those defenders of disinterested historical inquiry who are brought together under the heading of the Cambridge School do not avoid drawing substantive, albeit negative, lessons from the contemplation of the classical thinkers. This is most clearly exemplified in Quentin Skinner's proposal of a third, 'republican' defence of liberty as superior to the 'negative' liberty of modern liberal theory, and James Tully's extension of this approach to liberty and historical method to address problems of multiculturalism and national identity.[30] Despite the many objections to their unrepresentativeness, the classic texts are a series of reflections on the Western state experience, the domination of the many by the few, that has served to shape not only Europe and America, but also the whole world. In the words of Neal Wood:

> These texts reflect and comment upon the nature of the Western state with all its blemishes and deficiencies as well as benefits. Some of the texts call for radical reorganization of the state, others for its reform, and in so doing grapple with fundamental social and political problems which we share with the past. Whether we like it or not, these works have indelibly stamped our modern culture and the World today.[31]

## Political thinkers: an overview

This brings us to the task of justifying our particular conception of the canon and our account of those we include and those we deliberately exclude. It is important to state clearly and unambiguously that all accounts of the importance of a group or canon of political thinkers has to be constructed from the perspective of the present. Even if we set out to provide a purely historical account of the canon, those criteria we would have to use would still be located in the present. Which historical issues, debates, and events are singled out as of primary significance can only be judged from the perspective of the present. The historical past is not only 'another country' where they 'do things differently'; it is also something that is constructed by historians (albeit not arbitrarily) from material that is in the present. Given that all such criteria for an account of the canon are in the present, it is our contention that all of the thinkers we have chosen to include make a complex but significant contribution to the architecture of our moral and political universe. That is not to say that they set in train chains of cause and effect that lead inexorably to our moral and political institutions and practices. They do, however, provide part of the common resource out of which, and against which, we articulate our contemporary political aspirations. All political thinkers, no matter how minor, will to some extent make such a contribution to our present, but some do so in much more important ways than others. The thinkers we have included fall within this second category. They are all philosophically significant, though often for quite different reasons. We have not attempted to locate texts as exemplars of distinct vocabularies that might have lead us to include more of what are often considered minor thinkers. Instead we have chosen thinkers who are important for their philosophical subtlety and fecundity; thinkers who have extended the boundaries of the political; thinkers who have challenged prevailing philosophical paradigms and opened up new avenues of thought and inquiry; thinkers who present contrasting conceptions of the purpose of politics and the possibilities of theorizing politics. It is for this reason that we exclude Roman thinkers such as Cicero but do include the late Roman Christian thinker Augustine of Hippo. Although Cicero's influence is great, he is a highly eclectic thinker whose significance is through his application of Greek ideas to the institutional practices of the Roman republic. Augustine, on the other hand, is hugely influential because he transforms the way in which we see politics as part of the highest good for man, and provides us with a chastened vision of political life as a response to man's imperfection rather than as a condition of his perfectability. With Augustine we see a transformation from a Greek-inspired set of questions to a whole new vision of politics and its significance. In the modern period we have included Marx and Nietzsche, but not the host of post-Marxian socialist thinkers such as Lenin, Kautsky, Bernstein, or Trotsky, nor post-Nietzscheans such as Derrida or Lyotard. All of these latter thinkers are important, but they are important for working out the ideas of other more significant thinkers. Lenin is clearly an important political figure as theorist and leader of the October Revolution of 1917. But as we respond to the collapse of 'really existing' socialism after 1989, we can take a more impartial view of Lenin's significance as a theorist as opposed to an important political agent. It remains Karl Marx, from whom Lenin and Trotsky derived their ideas and political practice, rather than these secondary thinkers who still has a legitimate claim on our attention.

We have divided the book into five parts. Part I covers the birth of political theory in the context of the ancient Greek *polis*. It is from this very different world that many of our modern notions about the point of political life, the nature of citizenship and its virtues, and the idea of justice as the primary political virtue emerge. Although the ancient Greeks' answers to questions about the nature of the political, be they the demands of justice or the nature of citizenship, are either unfeasible or undesirable because of the dependence on a slave class and the subordination of women to the private sphere, the huge influence of Socrates, Plato, and Aristotle on all subsequent Western thinking makes them the obvious starting point for any conception of the Western canon. This section begins with an important chapter on the Sophists, that group of thinkers against whom Socrates developed his own political theory. The Sophists provide the earliest recognizable political theory in the Western tradition, and this chapter supplies the framework against which to make sense of Socrates and Plato. Aristotle is the other key source of classical political theorizing. His conception of political theory as political science is fundamentally different from Plato's and sets up a significant intellectual paradigm that is not only important for its impact on subsequent Christian theorizing in the case of Augustine and Aquinas, but also because it provides the foil for modern theorists such as Hobbes. It is also one of the key sources of communitarian understandings of politics and morality, and as such has a distinctly modern resonance in debates about the character of the contemporary political community.[32]

Part II, which we have entitled 'The Two Kingdoms', covers late Roman Christians such as Augustine of Hippo, extends into the medieval period with Aquinas and Marsiglio of Padua, and ends with Machiavelli, as the beginning of the modern period. Augustine and Aquinas are the two main representatives of Christian characterizations of politics. Augustine's conception of the limitation of politics and human imperfection shapes all modern understandings of political relationships. Aquinas was much less pessimistic, and develops a significant vocabulary of natural law and natural rights. His combination of the doctrines of political activity as a component of the good life with an appreciation of the limits of politics and a commitment to natural law and rights feeds into modern debates about the continuity of morality, politics, and law, against 'modern' conceptions of the autonomy of the political which are based on the very different approaches of Hobbes and Machiavelli. Although the high Middle Ages remains a significant period for thought about the relationship between politics, law, and morality (the intellectual vitality of this period is beautifully conveyed in Umberto Eco's novel *The Name of the Rose*), we have confined our attention to Marsiglio of

Padua. Marsiglio writes within the context of debates between empire and papacy, but his significance also extends beyond the politics of the high Middle Ages as a key source of constitutional ideas. Part II concludes with a chapter on Machiavelli, whose uniqueness and influence makes him very difficult to characterize. For some he is a backward-looking thinker who attempts to recover and apply a pre-Christian idea of politics as an autonomous realm of human action with its own distinct rules and conceptions of virtue which are opposed to the virtues of the good Christian. For other commentators, this defence of the autonomy of politics makes the Florentine republican one of the first modern theorists, who is able to think beyond the Christian natural law framework that has its origins in Augustine's rejection of the classical conception of politics.

The focus then shifts to the modern period from Hobbes to Marx and Nietzsche. The range of thinkers included in Parts III and IV are those that most clearly shape the architecture of modern politics and its conflicting institutional forms. All are theorists of the modern juridical state, but each approaches the emergence and justification of this peculiar form of political association in different ways. For some the state is the necessary solution to the problem of conflict in a pluralist world, whereas for others the state with its associated concepts of sovereignty and right is a problem than needs to be controlled and constrained. While the juridical state casts a shadow across subsequent political theorizing in the modern world, it would be wrong to see all the theorists of this modern political form as providing a straightforward celebration and explanation of this political form. In theorizing around the state many of these thinkers consciously reject traditional forms of justifying political power and authority. Against the authority of the Church, received tradition, or the divine right of kings, they counterpose the authority of the individual. This authority is both political and epistemological. Whereas the received authorities of divinely sanctioned monarchy, empire, or Church were closed, elitist, and peremptory, the search for justification in a pluralist world of different religious confessions required the exercise of individual reason and judgement. Out of this challenge to received authority emerges what we have characterized as the rationalist Enlightenment. The thinkers who fall under this category differ in subtle ways, but they all seek to justify and explain political obligation, the authority of the individual, the nature of the political community, and equality of concern and respect in terms of publicly accessible universal norms of natural law, justice, or utility. The only authority that is ultimately acceptable is the authority of human reason.

Part III begins with the dominant figure of Thomas Hobbes, who contributes to the modern notion of the state and its central concepts of sovereignty, right, and will. Hobbes also resurrects the language of contractualism but transforms it into the modern doctrine of the social contract as the source of political authority. These ideas of the contractual origins or political legitimacy, natural rights and the state of nature, the rejection of patriarchal power and the development of modern constitutionalism, are then taken up by Locke in his assault on political absolutism. The discussion of Locke is followed by a chapter on the Scottish philosopher David Hume, who marks a break with the classical contractarianism of Hobbes and Locke. Hume is a savage and largely effective critic of social contract theories and theorists of consent. He is also important as a source of speculative historical sociology and as a theorist of emerging commercial society as a condition of constitutional or soft government, rather than abstract philosophical theories about contract or natural rights. He is also a precursor of the utilitarian theories of Bentham and J. S. Mill. Montesquieu is another subtle critic of contractualism but who nevertheless champions constitutional government in opposition to the despotism of absolutism. He develops an anthropological theory of the state of nature that influences Rousseau. Yet he also develops a conception of political science that emphasizes the subrational or non-rational components in accounting for the development of political institutions and constitutional forms. He particularly emphasizes climate and geography, making him a precursor of modern political sociology and social history. This armed him with the resources to reject the moralized politics of traditional natural law theory. His dispassionate study of constitutional forms independently of morality makes him a precursor of utilitarians such as Bentham and the writers of the Federalist such as James Madison.

There then follows a chapter on Rousseau, who is both one of the most profound critics of the social contract tradition and one of its most influential theorists through his doctrine of the general will. Rousseau is also significant for his commitment to republicanism and popular sovereignty as well as the enormously influential view that human perfectibility is frustrated by human political institutions. This latter idea clearly leads on to the politics of total revolution as a condition of human emancipation—a doctrine that has its most significant statement in the works of Karl Marx. Following Rousseau we have chapters on the Federalist Papers, Mary Wollstonecraft, Alexis de Tocqueville, Jeremy Bentham, and two chapters on J. S. Mill. The chapter on the Federalist and their most important contributor, James Madison, is addressed primarily to the explanation and defence of the American Constitution, but also to the defence of a limited form of constitutional republicanism appropriate to a large-scale pluralist society. Alexis de Tocqueville is another key theorist of the American republic, particularly at the time of the presidency of Andrew Jackson, but he too is addressing broader themes about the nature of government in the new egalitarian democratic society exemplified by the United States.

Wollstonecraft is one of the few women authors who have a place in our canon. There were certainly other women writers on politics throughout the modern period, and indeed some before that time. However, it would be a mistake to play down the significance of women's exclusion from the public realm of politics and therefore pretend that there is a large but ignored canon of significant women theorists. The fact of the absence of significant women theorists from the canon is a function of their political exclusion and not simply the prejudices of contemporary defenders of the canon. That said, Wollstonecraft genuinely merits inclusion, not simply for her theoretical subtlety, for her arguments are often eclectically woven from a diverse variety of sources, but because of her significance as a founder of the modern feminist tradition. She is relentless in drawing the implication of the doctrine of the rights of man, but with her critique of the subjection of women she also challenges the gendered conception of the subject which underlies the doctrine. Part III ends with chapters on Bentham and Mill. Bentham provides an alternative rationalist foundation for political and moral norms with his doctrine of utilitarianism, and he provides an account of some of the key concepts of the modern juridical state such as sovereignty, law, and the concept of rights. His separation of analytical questions from normative or critical questions makes him not only a founder of analytical jurisprudence but also a precursor of modern positivist conceptions of political science. J. S. Mill is both a follower and critic of Bentham. His unique blend of philosophical naturalism, utilitarianism, and liberalism makes him a major source for contemporary political thought in modern Western liberal democracies. However, his eclecticism and significance are difficult to capture in one chapter devoted largely to his defence of liberty, so we have included a separate discussion of his increasingly important work *The Subjection of Women.*

Although the rationalist Enlightenment extends into our own political concepts and theories, there is a sense in which the momentous events of 1789 and the French Revolution marked a high point in the aspirations of rationalist Enlightenment thinkers to subordinate all authority claims to the tribunal of individual reason and judgement. Even those thinkers who continued to pursue the aspirations of the rationalist Enlightenment into the nineteenth century did so in a more chastened form, aware of the dangers of unleashing mass society. This is a tension particularly noticeable in J. S. Mill's writings. Yet 1789 marks an important change in the character and aspirations of political theory. At one level it initiates a new form of ideological political thought which is more concerned with mobilizing and directing classes, interest groups, or factions in an age of mass society. Yet alongside the initiation of this new age of ideological politics, the challenge of 1789 also initiates a strand of counter-Enlightenment thinking that was to have a most profound impact on the subsequent development and possibilities of political theory itself. In Part IV, 'The Counter-Enlightenment', we include discussion of Burke, Hegel, Marx, and Nietzsche. Each in their own way has a deeply controversial reputation, yet each also provides some of the most profound insights into the nature and possibilities of political life as well as into the character and status of the modern state.

Edmund Burke helps shape our understanding of the impact of the French Revolution on British political thought and the consequent political mobilization of the political masses. Burke's response to the rationalist Enlightenment and the French Revolution which it spawned is unrelentingly hostile, and he unleashes through his critique an exemplary statement of the modern conservative cast of mind. Yet the most challenging response to the rationalist Enlightenment is provided by Hegel. He is equalled only by Plato and Hobbes in terms of his significance. His complex and dense works have shaped the self-understandings of all modern theorists of politics. Even those who violently reject every component of his philosophical system cannot ignore him. His ideas have naturally been seen as a precursor of those of Marx, or modern nationalism, constitutional liberalism, conservatism, and at the more extreme Fascism and totalitarian-state worship. There is almost no modern ill that has not been attributed to Hegel's ideas by some thinker or other. Where Hegel challenges the ideal of abstract individualism that underpins the arguments of many Enlightenment thinkers, Karl Marx attacks the idealist conception of history that underpins Hegel's account of freedom in the modern state. Like Hegel, Marx has an ambiguous reputation. Undoubtedly tainted by the use to which his ideas were put by his defenders between 1917 and 1989, his real subtlety and challenge to the very notion of political theory is often overlooked. Yet Marx is an extraordinarily complex and controversial thinker even among those who identify themselves as Marxists. We have devoted two chapters to Marx to cover the conventional distinction between the early 'humanistic' thinker of the Paris Manuscripts and *The German Ideology*, and a second chapter to cover the later, mature Marx of Marx and Engels fame. The final thinker in Part IV is perhaps the most controversial of all, namely Nietzsche. Like Hegel, there is almost no bad thing that has not been attributed to his thought. Despite the work of many scholars he still retains in the popular imagination the tainted image created for him by his sister as a precursor of Nazism. For others, more sympathetic to his ideas, he is not really a political theorist at all. In one sense they are right, as Nietzsche does not theorize the state or any of the concepts that go with it. Yet his diagnosis of the consequences of the death of God transforms the moral resources from which we theorize about political and moral relationships. Nietzsche's challenge is not merely to find new foundations for political theory but to respond differently to the absence of foundations and the fact of nihilism. His potentially bleak view coincides with the bleak history of the first fifty years of the twentieth century. Although the thinkers of the twentieth century are not responding directly to Nietzsche, in the sense that he is the theorist of the end of morality and the ultimate liberation of power, all post-Nietzschean thinkers are responding to his legacy.

In the fifth and final part of the book we make perhaps our most controversial choices as we select just four representatives of the twentieth century. We have chosen four thinkers who have engaged both with the Nietzschean challenge of nihilism and with the legacy of the canon we have presented in the preceding sections. Each thinker draws on different aspects of that legacy to provide us with an account of the prospects for political theory in the future. With Oakeshott we have a chastened vision of politics that draws on Augustine's politics of imperfection as well as the cautious scepticism of Hume and historicism of Hegel. Rawls and Habermas offer two different ways of resurrecting the legacy of the rationalist Enlightenment without appealing to a conception of natural law. Foucault offers us a continuation of the ideal of radical critique that is derived from Marx and Nietzsche. Taken together these four thinkers offer us accounts of the continuing relevance of the great texts of political thought for the ongoing activity of political theorizing in a new century. As we saw in Part IV, the study of political theorizing is far removed from a dry antiquarianism, but is part of an ongoing activity that remains central to the activity of doing politics in our own times.

Our selection of canonical texts and authors is broadly conventional. That said, we will no doubt have raised important questions about who we have left out and how we conceive of the thinkers included and why we regard them as having canonical status. We have given general considerations behind the choices we have made, but in order to defend our criteria of inclusion in this section we need to address two sets of issues that have surrounded the study of political theory in the last few decades. The first set of debates touches on the methodology appropriate for studying the ideas of a past political thinker. The second issue addresses the idea of the canonical or classic status of a text. In order to further support our conceptions of the canon of political thinkers we turn to address those questions in the two remaining sections of this introductory essay.

## Perennial problems

We have deliberately refrained from calling this volume a history of political thought because we acknowledge that not all studies of the past assume the character of historical studies. The concept of history is deeply contested and suggests for many students a single disciplinary approach or set of methods which we have rejected in adopting our pluralist approach to the canon and to the thinkers in the individual chapters. Students of political thought were reminded of the variety of attitudes that one may adopt towards the past in the late 1960s, when the question of methodology almost eclipsed the study of past political texts itself. In reaction to the idea of a timeless, ongoing conversation conducted between philosophers, exemplified by Sheldon Wolin's *Politics and Vision* and Leo Strauss's *Natural Right and History*,[33] in what Paul Ricœur calls a quasi world of texts cast free of their contexts, and in which perennial questions were addressed over two and a half thousand years, the so-called New Historians pressed the claims of history as an autonomous discipline distinct from the philosophical character of its subject matter.

George Sabine, the author of one of the most famous histories of political thought, epitomized the basic assumption involved in positing the existence of perennial problems when he reiterated what Thucydides, the ancient Greek historian, and Machiavelli, the Italian Renaissance political thinker, maintained, that: 'Political problems and situations are more or less alike from time to time and from place to place.'[34] The political philosophers who addressed themselves to such problems, it was contended, used the same vocabulary, added their own personal nuances to concepts, and addressed themselves to arguments formulated by other philosophers. It was not uncommon for the historian of political thought to assume that there was one vast tradition of related ideas that stretched from Plato to the present day. Such a belief had no necessary implications for what it was considered appropriate to do with the ideas once they had been faithfully represented. C. H. McIlwain, an influential American historian of political thought, for example, believed that it was none of the historian's business to pronounce on the question of whether one theory was better than another.[35]

Historians such as Peter Laslett, W. H. Greenleaf, J. G. A. Pocock, John Dunn, and principally Quentin Skinner maintained that understanding the arguments of the political philosophers entailed reconstructing the language context in which they were formulated.[36] Much was made of contemporary philosophies of language, such as those of Ludwig Wittgenstein, J. L. Austin, and J. R. Searle, in the arguments for historical purism, but fundamentally the case rested on two seminal contentions of the English philosopher of history R. G. Collingwood in his *An Autobiography*.[37] He contended, first, that there are no perennial problems in philosophy, only individual answers to specific questions. And, secondly, that no two statements could be convicted of being contradictory unless they were shown to be different answers to the same question. The words in a question may remain the same, Collingwood argued, but the meaning changes with the context. When Plato talked of the Greek *polis*, or state, he meant something very different by using the concept than Hobbes did in seventeenth-century England. In this respect Plato and Hobbes were not addressing a perennial question. The two different concepts of the state are related, not as answers to the same question, but as part of the same historical process: the process by which the one conception of the state gradually became transformed into the other. The business of the historian is to trace and understand this process of change, and not to imagine a timeless question to which there are different answers.

Such views constituted an important corrective to a belief that the problems of political philosophy were somehow timeless, but it needs to be pointed out that the historians who are said to have held such views were never quite as naive as they are claimed to have been. For example, Quentin Skinner's famous denunciation of the practice of the history of political thought throughout the mid-twentieth century is mistaken in two important respects. In the first place, he associated the idea of perenniality and timelessness with what he called the 'textualist' approach. According to Skinner, contextualists took the text to be the sole determinant of meaning. He argued that to concede that the 'social context is a necessary condition for an understanding of the classic texts' constitutes a denial that they 'contain any elements of timelessness or perennial interest'.[38] This was not, in fact, how most historians viewed the matter. They did not distinguish between textualist and contextualist interpretation. Indeed, many argued that the social context enabled us to achieve a clearer understanding of the meaning of a text, and that this did not preclude a belief in the perenniality of the issues that the texts addressed. Paul Ward, for example, argued that 'the political and social theories of men always concern the problems of their own culture and age, and are to be understood only in that context'. He goes on to contend, however, that 'there are tides in the affairs of men, ebbs and flows of human events, which have been recurrent since human life began'.[39]

The second point at which criticism has been exaggerated is in the purposes attributed to historians who study the perennial issues. It is true that such historians as Ward contended that 'the solutions which men have given to their social problems in the past may be of help to men in contemporary society',[40] but it does nor warrant Skinner's contention that there is 'simply no hope of seeking the point of studying the history of ideas in the attempt to learn directly from the classic authors'.[41] In fact, there is no suggestion that we can pillage the past in order to learn directly from past political texts. Sheldon Wolin readily argues that philosophers address 'persistent ideas', but the reason for studying them is to familiarize ourselves with 'a continuously evolving grammar and vocabulary to facilitate communication and orient the understanding'.[42] Even Leo Strauss, the most stalwart adherent to the idea of perennial issues, contended that 'we cannot reasonably expect that the fresh understanding of classical political philosophy will supply us with recipes for today's use. . . . Only we living today can possibly find solutions to the problems.'[43] Finally, this attitude is confirmed in one of the most widely read college textbooks in the United States, *Political Thinking: The Perennial Questions*, in which Glenn Tinder contends that the purpose of studying past thought is to 'learn to consider questions with clarity and determination and an open mind'.[44]

While there are differences of emphasis, most historians of political thought agree with both Collingwood and Skinner that, while we do not learn directly from the past the solutions to our own present practical problems, we do nevertheless gain something of practical value. For Collingwood, history is self-knowledge of the mind. Knowing what people have thought and done makes us aware of human potentials and prepares us better for future action.[45] Skinner also held some such view when he maintained that studying how past thinkers have dealt with political concepts could enable us to see our way round seemingly intractable conceptual problems in the present.[46]

## What is a classic text?

Why should such issues have become so important and so potentially divisive in the discipline of politics? No other discipline has so inextricably defined itself in terms of past texts, and these texts are significant both for the political philosophers themselves in developing their own arguments, and for students of political thought interested in those arguments. We should not lose sight of the fact that these activities, though related, are nevertheless distinct, but they both rely upon a range of texts that have been afforded classic status. For philosophers they acquire this status because they are capable of exercising a degree of epistemic authority, which is a type of non-executive authority. This is quite different from executive authority, of which political authority is a species. Non-executive authority, such as epistemic authority, carries with it no right to command. Epistemic authority entails acceptance on the part of the subject that *A* is an authority, but does not oblige the subject to obey or act upon what *A* says. In other words, knowledge does not give anyone the right to impose the fruits of his, or her, labours upon anyone else.[47]

The implications of too heavy a reliance upon epistemic authority, the tyranny of the expert, have become all too evident in our modern technocratic societies, in which the fear is that our every decision will be made for us on the basis that those who make the decisions possess superior knowledge, or expertise, to us in their fields of specialization. The danger in modern society seems to be not only that epistemic authorities will come to impose their decisions upon us, like philosophers returning to the cave after having seen the sunlight, by means of the exercise of legitimate executive authority, but that they will come to wield undue influence over legitimate elected executive political authorities because of deference on the part of the latter to the superior knowledge of the former. We see in the realm of economic strategy, for example, the increasing dependence of governments upon the expertise of economists in formulating policy.

In the history of political thought we can clearly see the epistemic authority of Aristotle after the rediscovery of his work in the Latin West during the thirteenth century. From then until the seventeenth century he was cited as 'the philosopher'. Dante, for example, in both *The Banquet* and *Of Monarchy* frequently invokes Aristotle's authority to add weight to his argument. In recommending the necessity of temporal monarchy for the well-being of the world, Dante contended that 'there are very clear and strong arguments for it. The first argument enjoys the authority of the Philosopher, in his *Politics*.'[48] Similarly, Sir Robert Filmer, in his famous *Patriarcha*, which derived political authority from its first conferment by God upon Adam, constantly invoked the authority of Aristotle, who he thought came as close to the truth as was possible for a pagan. Had Aristotle been a Christian, the implication is, he would have got it completely right. In more recent times, of course, Karl Marx became an epistemic authority for many of those who purported to follow him. Scarcely any further argument was needed, other than clarification, if it could be shown that Marx had recommended it.

Epistemic authority should not, however, be equated with deference. The purpose of invoking an authority was not so much to defer to the text, but to associate one's own arguments with the favourable evaluative connotations of standard 'authorities'. The arguments of authorities in political theory are often exploited by other political theorists for their own political purposes, and the accuracy of what they claim 'the philosopher' said is often not uppermost in their minds. Furthermore, a theorist may wish to invoke the negative authority of an author in order to add a pejorative connotation to an argument he wishes to refute, as, for example, Sir Robert Filmer did with Cardinal Bellamine, a theorist of the state of nature and of natural equality, but also a Catholic, which in itself was enough to discredit the argument in Protestant England.

The appropriation of authors as authorities, or as so despised as to discredit any argument with which they are associated, is a constant feature of the history of political thought. The capacity of a text to be used in this way over a significant period of time, and in changing historical circumstances, signified for Conal Condren, a contributor to the methodological controversies, the key to what makes a text attain classic status. He argued that 'the safest generalisation appears to be that the status of *x* was a function of the rhetorical and ideological resonance that stemmed from his being effectively exploited as an authority'.[49]

Why can a text be used as an authority and be successfully exploited in a variety of ideological contexts? Condren makes the suggestion that it is because of the text's ambiguity, and goes on to make the rather remarkable claim that ambiguity is in fact an appraisive category in terms of which a text attains classic status. Ambiguity, for Condren, is in fact the foundation upon which such appraisive claims are made.[50] It is ambiguity that prevents a text from becoming so inextricably tied to one ideological context as to become emblematic of it, and which prevents it from losing its value to the broader political theory community.

Condren is claiming that what gives a text classic status is not a list of substantive virtues, but the triadic complex of authority, exploitation, and ambiguity. If this were the case, such appraisive categories would enable us to say nothing about the quality of argument, the forcefulness of its imagery, nor anything about the extent to which it contributed to our understanding. In fact, they are not appraisive categories at all. Take authority and exploitation. They point us not towards the text itself, but to its consequences. The value of the text, on these criteria, is judged in relation to the effect it has on its audience. It is what J. L. Austin, the analytic philosopher of language, called its perlocutionary effect. This is something quite different from the locution of a sentence, whose meaning is discerned in the dictionary definition of the words, their sense, and the things to which the words refer, their reference. To say that the officer was dressed in uniform is certainly intelligible, but to know that the reference of the sentence is Field Marshal Montgomery enhances its meaning. The illocution of a sentence is the particular action that a speaker is performing in uttering the sentence without the sentence itself specifying the action. For example, to specify that what you are saying is a joke detracts considerably from the act of joking. To gain what Austin called uptake, that is to understand what is being done, entails a knowledge of the context of conventions that enable the action to be comprehended.[51] Condren's appraisive categories do not allow us to say anything about these aspects of the text's meaning, but only about, in Austin's terms, the perlocutionary effect on the audience.

Furthermore, ambiguity is not in fact an appraisive category. We cannot use it to judge the quality of a text, nor can we use it as a standard with which to compare it with other texts. To say that one text is more ambiguous than another is hardly a recommendation. It is in fact a property of a text, that which allows variety of interpretation. Ambiguity is a condition of interpretation. All words are polysemic. They have multiple meanings, or nuances of meaning. This is what Paul Ricœur means when he talks of discourse and the surplus of meaning. Whatever the author may intend, the meanings the word carries are far greater, and surplus to what the author intends.[52]

Interpretation is not a matter of choice. We are unavoidably interpretative beings. Both Martin Heidegger and Hans-Georg Gadamer have underscored this point in modern philosophy. Interpretation for them is an ontological condition of our being. Interpretation is always from a standpoint because we are born into a world of inherited meanings, and we take with us a forestructure of meanings, or prejudices, when we read texts. There is no text independent of interpretation. The act of interpretation entails a fusion of horizons, that of the text and that of the interpreter, neither of which remains the same after the encounter. This is what Terence Balls calls 'the inescapability of interpretation'.[53]

The chapters in this volume are, then, unavoidably interpretations, personal readings of the thinkers who have attained importance in the study of the history of political thought. For the most part, each of the chapters tries to reflect the variety of interpretation, while pursuing its own line of argument. So far in this section the focus has been upon the use of political philosophers by other political philosophers. The authors in this volume are clearly doing something different from what Condren has claimed gives texts their classic status. The authors are not invoking the texts as authorities, nor seeking to exploit them for ideological purposes, although it is a matter of contention whether all interpretation has an ideological import. They are engaging in an activity of relatively recent origin, that is, the disciplined academic study of past political philosophers. It is an activity, to paraphrase Michael Oakeshott, that has emerged like the games that children play and always exhibited an unsettled surface owing to the different tensions and disciplinary pressures it was compelled to accommodate, both in Britain and in the United States. As such this volume is a contribution to that activity rather than an attempt to legislate for it. If we can succeed in helping new generations of students enter into that activity and find value in the study of great political theorists, we will have achieved our purpose.

## NOTES

1. See P. J. Kelly, 'Contextual and Non-Contextual Histories of Political Thought', in Jack Hayward, Brian Barry, and Archie Brown (eds.), *The British Study of Politics* (Oxford: British Academy, 1999).
2. John G. Gunnell, *Political Theory and Interpretation* (Cambridge, Mass.: Winthrop, 1979), 11.
3. T. H. Green, *The Principles of Political Obligation*, ed. Bernard Bosanquet (London: Longmans Green, 1919), 49–120, and id., *The Philosophical Theory of the State* (London: Macmillan, 1965).
4. Michael Oakeshott, 'Thomas Hobbes', *Scrutiny*, 4 (1935–6), 267.
5. R. G. Collingwood, *The New Leviathan*, rev. edn., ed. David Boucher (Oxford: Clarendon Press, 1992), p. iv.
6. Leo Strauss, *What is Political Philosophy?* (Glencoe: Free Press, 1959); Eric Voegelin, *Order and History* (Baton Rouge: Louisiana State University Press, 1956–74), vols. i–iv.
7. J. N. Figgis, *Studies of Political Thought from Gerson to Grotius* (Cambridge: Cambridge University Press, 1907), 3.
8. J. W. Allen, *A History of Political Thought in the Sixteenth Century* (London: Macmillan, 1928), pp. xvii–xviii.
9. A. J. Carlyle and R. W. Carlyle, *A History of Medieval Political Theory in the West*, 6 vols. (6th imp. Edinburgh: Blackwood, 1970).
10. Quentin Skinner, 'The Rise of, Challenge to and Prospects for a Collingwoodian Approach to the History of Political Thought', in Dario Castiglioni and Iain Hampsher-Monk (eds.), *The History of Political Thought in National Context* (Cambridge: Cambridge University Press, 2001), 176.
11. This was Sir Karl Popper's line of reasoning in *The Open Society and its Enemies* (London: Routledge, 1969), ii. 95–6. Ian Shapiro makes the argument against the New Historians in 'Realism and the Study of the History of Ideas', *History of Political Thought*, 3 (1982), 535–78.
12. James Tully (ed.), *Quentin Skinner and his Critics* (Cambridge: Cambridge University Press, 1988), and J. G. A. Pocock, *Politics, Language and Time* (London: Methuen, 1972).
13. Quentin Skinner, 'Rhetoric and Conceptual Change', *Finnish Yearbook of Political Thought*, 3 (1999), 61.
14. J. B. Bury, 'The Science of History', inaugural lecture (1903), in *Selected Essays of J. B. Bury*, ed. Harold Temperly (Cambridge: Cambridge University Press, 1930), 9.
15. Robert Blakey, *History of Political Literature* (London: Richard Bentley, 1855). vol. i, pp. vii and xxix–xxx.
16. Sheldon Amos, *The Science of Politics* (London: Kegan, Paul, Trench, 1883), 5 and 21.
17. Frederick Pollock, *An Introduction to the History of the Science of Politics* (1890; London: Macmillan, 1918), 2 and 43.
18. See Gunnell, *Political Theory and Interpretation*, 5.
19. David Easton, *The Political System: An Inquiry into the State of Political Science* (New York: Knopf, 1953), 237; cf. pp. 235–9 and 254. Also see David Easton, 'The Decline of Modern Political Theory', *Journal of Politics*, 13 (1951), 41, 42, and 52.

20. A. J. Ayer, *Language, Truth and Logic* (1936), with introd. by Ben Rogers (London: Penguin, 2001), p. xvi.
21. C. H. McIlwain, *The Growth of Political Thought in the West from the Greeks to the End of the Middle Ages* (New York: Macmillan, 1932), 314.
22. W. K. Hancock, 'Machiavelli in Modern Dress: An Inquiry into Modern Method', *History*, 20 (1935), 114.
23. C. Delisle Burns, *Political Ideals: Their Nature and Development* (London: Oxford University Press, 1915), 11.
24. Collingwood, *The New Leviathan*.
25. Terence Ball, 'Whither Political Theory?', in his *Reappraising Political Theory* (Oxford: Oxford University Press, 1995), 49.
26. H. L. A. Hart, *Essays on Bentham* (Oxford: Clarendon Press, 1982).
27. See Alan Ryan, *The Philosophy of John Stuart Mill* (Basingstoke: Macmillan, 1987); John Gray, *Mill on Liberty: A Defence* (London: Routledge, 1983); D. Miller, *Philosophy and Ideology in Hume's Political Thought* (Oxford: Clarendon Press, 1981); G. A. Cohen, *Karl Marx's Theory of History: A Defence* (Oxford: Clarendon Press, 1978); and Jeremy Waldron, *God, Locke and Equality* (Cambridge: Cambridge University Press, 2002).
28. See Brian Barry, *Political Argument*, 2nd edn. (Hemel Hempstead: Harvester, 1990).
29. Allan Bloom, *The Closing of the American Mind: How Education has Failed Democracy and Impoverished the Souls of Today's Students* (Harmondsworth: Penguin, 1988), 34, 198, 219, 312, and 344.
30. See esp. Quentin Skinner, 'On Justice, the Common Good and the Priority of Liberty', in C. Mouffe (ed.), *Dimensions of Radical Democracy* (London: Verso, 1992), 211–24, and James Tully, *Strange Multiplicity* (Cambridge: Cambridge University Press, 1995).
31. Neal Wood, *Reflections on Political Theory: A Voice of Reason from the Past* (London: Palgrave, 2002), 4.
32. See A. MacIntyre, *After Virtue* (London: Duckworth, 1981), and id., *Whose Justice? Which Rationality?* (London: Duckworth, 1988).
33. Sheldon Wolin, *Politics and Vision* (Boston: Little, Brown, 1960); Leo Strauss, *Natural Right and History* (Chicago: Rand McNally, 1963).
34. George Sabine, 'What is Political Theory?', *Journal of Politics*, 1 (1939), 4.
35. McIlwain, *The Growth of Political Thought*, 3 and 314.
36. For a discussion of the debates and an argument for methodological pluralism in the study of political thought, see David Boucher, *Texts in Context: Revisionist Methods for Studying the History of Ideas* (Dordrecht: Martinus Nijhoff, 1985).
37. R. G. Collingwood, *An Autobiography*, with new introd. by Stephen Toulmin (Oxford: Clarendon Press, 1978).
38. Quentin Skinner, 'Meaning and Understanding in the History of Ideas', *History and Theory*, 8 (1969), 5.
39. Paul W. Ward, *A Short History of Political Thinking* (Chapel Hill: University of North Carolina Press, 1939), 5 and 3.
40. Ibid. 5.
41. Skinner, 'Meaning and Understanding in the History of Ideas', 50.
42. Wolin, *Politics and Vision*, 26 and 27.
43. Leo Strauss, *The City and Man* (Chicago: University of Chicago Press, 1978), 11.
44. Glen Tinder, *Political Thinking: The Perennial Problems*, 6th edn. (New York: HarperCollins College Publishers, 1997), 21.
45. R. G. Collingwood, *The Idea of History*, rev. edn., ed. Jan van der Dussen (Oxford: Oxford University Press, 1993).
46. Quentin Skinner, *Liberty before Liberalism* (Cambridge: Cambridge University Press, 1998).
47. For a discussion of these distinctions, see Richard T. de George, *The Nature and Limits of Authority* (Lawrence: University of Kansas Press, 1985).
48. Dante, *On World Government*, trans. Herbert W. Schneider (Indianapolis: Bobbs-Merrill, 1957), 8.
49. Conal Condren, *The Status and Appraisal of Classic Texts: An Essay on Political Theory, its Inheritance, and the History of Ideas* (Princeton: Princeton University Press, 1985), 255.
50. Ibid. 181.
51. See J. L. Austin, *How to Do Things with Words* (Oxford: Oxford University Press, 1962).
52. Paul Ricœur, *Interpretation Theory: Discourse and the Surplus of Meaning* (Fort Worth, Tex.: Christian University Press, 1976).
53. Terence Ball, *Reappraising Political Theory: Revisionist Studies in the History of Political Thought* (Oxford: Clarendon Press, 1995). Also see Hans-Georg Gadamer, *Truth and Method*, trans. J. Weinsheimer and D. G. Marshall (London: Sheed & Ward, 1975).

# PART I

## The *Polis*

# 2 The Sophists

Peter Nicholson

## Contents



## Chapter guide

The Sophists were a new kind of professional intellectual and teacher in late fifth-century BC Greece. They debated fundamental moral and political issues, and especially the question of the origin and nature of justice, and the question whether it was better for the community, and better for the individual, to be just or unjust. Only fragments of their writings survive and there are problems of interpretation. Protagoras presented justice as an indispensable ingredient of political life, such that both the community as a whole and every individual benefited from its practice. Thrasymachus by contrast contended that every community really is controlled by some faction in its own interest, making laws which favour itself, so that being just is to that faction's advantage and every other individual's disadvantage. Antiphon's work stressed the problems of justice by highlighting other difficulties, costs, and dangers to the individual of being just. The arguments against being just cannot be answered satisfactorily on the assumptions used by the Sophists. A stronger case for justice was developed by Socrates, Plato, and Aristotle, who changed some of the terms of the debate.

## Biography

Even the most basic information is often missing or tentative (the ancient biographical material is gathered and discussed in Rosamund Kent Sprague (ed.), *The Older Sophists: A Complete Translation by Several Hands of the Fragments in Die Fragmente der Vorsokratiker edited by Diels-Kranz* (Columbia: University of South Carolina Press, 1972)). Protagoras, from Abdera in northern Greece, lived approximately from 490 to 420 BC. He is said to have been the first Sophist, or professional teacher, and was highly successful and the most famous and respected. He visited Athens several times, and became a close associate of the leading Athenian politician Pericles, who invited him to draw up the constitution for a new colony, Thurii, in Italy (444). Thrasymachus, from Chalcedon on the

Bosporus, was primarily known as a teacher of rhetoric and a stylist. He travelled extensively, and possibly lived in Athens for some time. Plato makes him a central character in his *Republic*, set in Athens in 427. Antiphon was an Athenian, perhaps roughly contemporary with Socrates (469–399), with whom he conversed, according to Xenophon. Some believe that Antiphon the Sophist is the same man as Antiphon the Orator, born about 480 and executed as one of the leaders of the failed oligarchic coup in Athens (411), but this identification remains controversial.

## Key texts

Antiphon, *Truth*, in Michael Gagarin and Paul Woodruff (ed. and trans.), *Early Greek Political Thought from Homer to the Sophists* (Cambridge: Cambridge University Press, 1995). (Pt. v of this collection contains the main fragments of all the Sophists.)

Plato, *Protagoras*, in Michael Gagarin and Paul Woodruff (ed. and trans.), *Early Greek Political Thought from Homer to the Sophists* (Cambridge: Cambridge University Press, 1995).

Plato, *Republic*, trans. G. M. A. Grube, rev. C. D. C. Reeve, in *Plato: Complete Works*, ed. John M. Cooper and D. S. Hutchinson (Indianapolis: Hackett, 1997).

Other dialogues by Plato are quoted in the translations in *Plato: Complete Works*, ed. John M. Cooper and D. S. Hutchinson (Indianapolis: Hackett, 1997).

## Key ideas

**Protagoras. Justice** is obeying the rules of society: is essential to the existence of a **community**, therefore a good benefiting the **individual**. Justice and **political skill** are taught. **Politics** is cooperative. Protagoras was a **social relativist**; hence any defence of **democracy** must be limited.

**Thrasymachus. Politics** is a struggle. The stronger dominate the weaker and make laws favouring themselves. **Justice** is the interest of the stronger, and sensible men avoid it. **The individual** is happy when he gains his own interest.

**Antiphon. Justice** is a **convention** opposed to **nature**, and the natural brings pleasure. **Law** is unable to uphold justice; therefore it is better to be unjust whenever one can.

---

# Introduction: the Sophists and their significance

There was a major intellectual awakening, an Enlightenment, in ancient Greece roughly in the second half of the fifth century BC, when fundamental questions concerning human life, and particularly morality and politics, were critically investigated and traditional ideas were challenged. The Sophists were an important element in this Enlightenment, along with dramatists such as Sophocles, Euripides, and Aristophanes, the historians Herodotus and Thucydides, and Socrates. The Sophists forged influential new methods of thinking and rational debating, setting out opposed positions so that they could be systematically tested, and themselves contributed significantly to the discussions. The most prominent were Protagoras (reputedly the first), Gorgias, Prodicus, Hippias, and Thrasymachus. The Sophists formed a distinctive group principally because they originated charging fees for teaching. There were some similarities in their methods of analysis and argument, and all of them claimed to be able to impart practical skills of communication and to enable men to make a success of their lives (justifying their charges), but they shared no set of beliefs and were not in that sense a 'school' of thought. They did agree, however, on the importance of certain issues. In particular, they examined the moral basis of political life, and debated the question whether or not it was better to be 'just', meaning by that, to follow the moral and legal rules of one's society—rules which they thought were man-made, conventions created by human agreement, rather than existing by nature (on nature and convention, see the penultimate section, on Antiphon). They differed, however, in their explanations of the origin and function of rules, and they gave widely divergent answers to the question whether one was better off or worse off if one followed them.

The Sophists, often leading citizens in their own *poleis* (politically independent city-states), came from, and taught in, *poleis* all over the Greek world, but tended to congregate in Athens, which was then at its height as a political power and commercial and cultural centre. They were in great demand, particularly for their lessons in public speaking, which was crucial for anyone pursuing a career in politics since power came to those able to persuade their fellow citizens in the council and assembly (where political decisions were taken) and in the courts (where political scores were often settled, and one's property or even one's life could be at stake). The Sophists were offering a kind of higher education for the first time in Greece, and they became famous and prosperous. This was one explanation of their general unpopularity in Athens, now a direct democracy where power had shifted from the rich into the hands of the majority of less well-to-do. The Sophists were, in effect, teaching wealthy young men how to become influential in politics, and that made some of the democrats hostile (a hostility Protagoras, as we shall see, sought to overcome). Moreover, many of their innovative ideas were controversial or suspect and shocking, and widely viewed as threatening the received wisdom, especially that embodied in customary morality and religion. The Sophists were ridiculed by Aristophanes in his comedy *The Clouds* (423 BC).[1] They were attacked by Plato, who frequently portrayed them in argument with Socrates. With the major exceptions of Protagoras and Gorgias, Plato painted the Sophists, and especially their customers and disciples, as showy talkers and muddled, shallow thinkers, peddling dangerous ideas. They appeared in his dialogues as the complete opposite of Socrates, who relentlessly pursued the argument wherever it led, regardless of its fee-earning potential. Aristotle defined a Sophist as 'one who makes money by sham wisdom' (*Sophistical Refutations* 165$^{a}$22), and remarked that the Sophists (excepting Protagoras) had to charge in advance because no pupil would have paid once he discovered what they were teaching (*Nicomachean Ethics* 1164$^{a}$30–2).[2]

There are, then, two reasons for beginning one's study of the history of Western political thought with the Sophists. First, they are of interest in themselves. They were the first serious and systematic political thinkers, reflecting on some of the perennial issues of morals and politics, and originating some distinctions of permanent importance.[3] Secondly, the Sophists were very influential on Socrates, Plato, and Aristotle, usually but not exclusively in a negative way, and consequently some knowledge of their ideas is a necessary background to understanding properly what Socrates, Plato, and Aristotle argued and why. In particular, Plato and Aristotle inherit the rich debate about justice conducted during the Greek

Enlightenment. They revise some of its terms and reach different conclusions—notably on the nature–convention issue—yet their positions are recognizable as contributions to the same discussion.

Accordingly I aim to set out the leading political ideas of some of the main Sophists, noting the range of different opinions; and finally to note briefly how they all, though in varying respects and degrees, differ from Plato. I give a schematic account in order to provide as clear an introduction as possible; further study will reveal that it needs both elaboration and qualification.

But first, problems about evidence must be mentioned. It is difficult to find out exactly, and in detail, what the various Sophists thought. Very little of their own writing has survived, often only in small fragments which are hard to interpret. Furthermore, our main source for the Sophists and their ideas is a biased witness—Plato. Even if Plato is not, as some hold, deliberately distorting them in his reports, he is giving selective accounts to suit his own purposes and to develop his own arguments. Nonetheless, most commentators judge that it is possible to get past Plato's bias and reconstruct the main ideas of some of the Sophists, although sometimes the interpretation must be tentative, and that it is important to do so because of the high quality of their thinking.[4]

## Protagoras and the politics of the community: the indispensability of justice

The bulk of the evidence for Protagoras' ideas comes from Plato, above all from his dialogue *Protagoras*, so it must be used cautiously.[5] However, Plato consistently treated Protagoras respectfully, even when he was disagreeing with him, and most scholars assume that Plato's representation of Protagoras' philosophy is basically accurate.

The *Protagoras* offers a substantial account of Protagoras' claims as a Sophist. He teaches political skill and makes his pupils good citizens: a pupil gains 'good judgment (*euboulia*) about domestic matters, so that he may best manage his own household, and about political affairs, so that in affairs of the *polis* he may be most able both in action and in speech' (*Protagoras* 318e–319b; Gagarin and Woodruff, 175).[6] Socrates probes this claim, doubting whether such a skill can be taught. He points out that Protagoras' claim apparently conflicts with what the Athenians believe:

> I observe that when we convene in the Assembly and the city has to take some action on a building project, we send for builders to advise us; if it has to do with the construction of ships, we send for shipwrights; and so forth for everything that is considered learnable and teachable. But if anyone else, a person not regarded as a craftsman, tries to advise them, no matter how handsome and rich and well-born he might be, they just don't accept him. They laugh at him and shout him down . . . This is how they proceed in matters which they consider technical. But when it is a matter of deliberating on city management, anyone can stand up and advise them, carpenter, blacksmith, shoemaker, merchant, ship-captain, rich man, poor man, well-born, low-born—it doesn't matter—and nobody blasts him for presuming to give counsel without any prior training under a teacher. The reason for this is clear: They do not think that this can be taught. Public life aside, the same principle holds also in private life, where the wisest and best of our citizens are unable to transmit to others the virtues that they possess. (*Protagoras* 319b–e; Cooper and Hutchinson, 755–6[7])

This challenge, resting on the important distinction between expert technical knowledge and general political competence, leads to a fuller explanation from Protagoras of what he can offer his pupils, and a justification of his ability to teach it, all provided with an eye to his situation in Athens as an outsider who might appear, as Socrates has hinted, to be subverting its democratic practices.

The explanation comes in two parts: first a story about the origin of the *polis*, then a reasoned analysis and interpretation of the story which develops an argument that political skill can be taught. Both the story and its explanation, probably closely following Protagoras' own, are full of fascinating detail and are presented with considerable rhetorical brilliance. The first essential point is that knowledge of how to behave politically, respecting other people, accepting obligations to them, and acting justly, is indispensable if people are to live together in a city; it must be possessed, and acted on, by everyone in the city. The second essential point is that the knowledge is not natural in the sense of innate, one is not born with it, but, like specialized knowledge such as medicine, it must be learned and it must be passed on. Thus the Athenians are right to believe that on technical matters only the expert few should be heard, whereas on issues concerning the general running of the city every citizen can be presumed to be qualified and should be allowed to participate. Here and elsewhere the Athenians assume that everyone knows about politics and justice (justice being one of the constituents of political skill). 'In fact, people say that everyone ought to call himself just, whether he is or not; and if someone doesn't pretend to be just, they say he's crazy, on the grounds that there cannot possibly be anyone who does not in some way or other share in Justice, or else he cannot exist among human beings' (*Protagoras* 323b–c; Gagarin and Woodruff, 179). It is because everyone thinks justice and political skill are neither naturally inherited nor innate, but teachable and can be acquired by diligence, that they rebuke and get angry with anyone who does not make the necessary effort (whereas they think pity, not blame, is appropriate for anyone who is poorly endowed by nature in their looks or size or strength). Again, the point of punishment is not vengeance 'for the wrong that is past, since what has been done cannot be undone'; instead punishment is inflicted 'so that both the wrongdoer and anyone who sees him punished will be deterred from doing wrong again' (*Protagoras* 324a–c; Gagarin and Woodruff, 180). Protagoras brings out what is implied in ordinary social practices: the very idea of deterrence implies that people can change their behaviour, can be educated through punishment to act justly.

How, then, does one account for the fact that men particularly good at politics, for example Pericles, fail to pass their skill on to their sons? Is that not a powerful counter-example? Protagoras notes that, if political skill is as basic as he claims, and everyone thinks it can be learned, it would be amazing if good men did not have it taught to their sons. And in fact they do. As soon as children can understand, parents and all concerned in bringing them up work hard to teach them to be as good as possible, using threats and blows if necessary. When the children are sent to school, the main concern is that they learn good conduct, and they are given edifying poems and stories to read, copy, and memorize. After school, 'the city in its turn requires them to learn its laws and to live by the example they set, so that they'll not do whatever they feel like, now that they're on their own', and punishes anyone who does not follow the laws (*Protagoras* 326c–d; Gagarin and Woodruff, 183). So political skill *is* taught, and successfully (even the most unjust person is seen to be actually just, indeed an expert in justice, when he is compared to people who have had no exposure to law at all). One must realize that *everyone* is a teacher of political skill—'it's as if you were looking for a teacher of the Greek language: you wouldn't notice a single one!' (*Protagoras* 328a; Gagarin and Woodruff, 184). The reason that many sons of particularly skilled fathers turn out poorly is that they differ in their natural ability: the sons may have all the education and training possible, but if they have not inherited the special talent, then their skill will not be as great. It is exactly the same as playing a musical instrument: people's ability differs, so that everyone is able—with the appropriate education and encouragement, already outlined—to reach a basic level, but some have greater talent and can excel.

From all this, Protagoras justifies his own position as a Sophist, an educator specializing in political skill. Everyone has enough knowledge of political skill to be able to teach it to the basic level, but it is hard to find someone competent to teach it at the higher levels. 'So if any one of us is even a little bit better at helping others advance . . . he should be welcomed. I believe that I am one of these, that I do a better job than others do in helping a person become fine and good, and that I am worth the fee I charge' (*Protagoras* 328a–b; Gagarin and Woodruff, 184).

Protagoras features, much more briefly, in another of Plato's dialogues, the *Theaetetus*. Here some version of relativism is attributed to him (precisely what version is in dispute among commentators). 'A human being is measure of all things, of those things that are, that they are, and of those things that are not, that they are not', and 'each thing is to me such as it appears to me, and is to you such as it appears to you' (*Theaetetus* 152a; Gagarin and Woodruff, 186). For example, the same wind may be perceived as cold by me but not cold by you. However, Protagoras also retains the idea of objective facts which are what they are whatever anyone thinks about them. For instance, a substance may be harmful to humans but beneficial to horses or vice versa, or beneficial if applied externally but harmful if taken internally; and someone who knows such facts is an expert, in this case a doctor (*Protagoras* 334a–c; Gagarin and Woodruff, 185). Crucially for our purposes, in the case of moral and political values Protagoras espouses *social* relativism. 'Whatever each city judges to be just and fine, these things in fact are just and fine for it, so long as it holds those opinions' (*Theaetetus* 167c; Gagarin and Woodruff, 186). It had long been observed that customs and laws varied greatly from one society to another. Herodotus gives many examples. In one famous passage, contrasting the Greek practice of cremating the dead with an Indian practice of eating them, he comments: 'If you should ask all people to select the best from among all the various conventional practices, each group would choose their own, even after examining them all; for they would consider their own practices to be by far the best' (*The Histories* 3. 38; Gagarin and Woodruff, 82). Protagoras is, in effect, providing an epistemological view to support this judgement. There is no right or wrong way of disposing of the dead, nor any 'correct' standard of justice, which some cities adopt and others fail to adopt; rather, each city establishes its own customs and laws, and determines its own conception of justice, and for each city those are what is 'right'. This is not inconsistent with his fundamental view that each man is the measure of all things, which must include values such as justice: rather, it may be precisely because each man is his own measure of justice that Protagoras thinks that, in order to live together as a single political entity, the members of the community must agree on a common measure and work constantly to ensure that it is effective. Thus Protagoras' relativism leads him to a strongly communitarian, indeed anti-individualist, political position. Nor is his social relativism inconsistent with his claim to be an expert with knowledge to teach the Athenians or any community of citizens. For a city may adopt conventions, rules, and laws (known collectively as *nomoi*) which are useless or disadvantageous, so that the city is not as successful as it might be. This is where the Sophist can bring improvement by persuading the citizens to change: 'the wise and efficient politician is the man who makes wholesome things seem just to a city instead of pernicious ones' (*Theaetetus* 167c; Cooper and Hutchinson, 186). This is Protagoras' definition of a wise man: 'when one of us has bad things appear and be to him, the wise man can change that and make good things appear and be to him' (*Theaetetus* 166d; Gagarin and Woodruff, 185), much in the way that a doctor can persuade a man to take unpleasant, beneficial medicine. This is the service that Protagoras can provide to any city; and it is a skill that he can teach to his pupils.

Protagoras has built up a complex, coherent, and attractive account of politics. By articulating and analysing what is presupposed in Athenian thinking about politics, he has shown that an understanding of justice and other virtues is indispensable and foundational to living with other people. In fact, if you lack it altogether, you have to be excluded (*Protagoras* 322d and 325a–b; Gagarin and Woodruff, 178 and 181). It 'is what everyone must share in . . . what everyone must follow in doing whatever else he wants to learn or do, or else not do it at all' (*Protagoras* 325a; Gagarin and Woodruff, 181). Every community inculcates its own particular rules (*nomoi*) in its citizens, trains them to obey them, and, as part of the educational process, punishes them if they do not. Protagoras' emphasis on the community is perfectly compatible with his position that some of its members will be better at politics than others and will get ahead. Whenever particular individuals are especially successful at politics, everyone benefits, since those individuals are practising an admired social skill which facilitates the smooth running of the city along its agreed lines (and they may sometimes bring improvements). Everyone gains from this. 'I think', says Protagoras, 'that practicing [political skill] and justice towards each other is to our advantage; that's why everyone is so eager to teach everyone else what is just and lawful' (*Protagoras* 327a; Gagarin and Woodruff, 183). This gives Protagoras the grounds for justifying his teaching. His pupils will excel at political skill, and as individuals become popular and prosperous; but the whole city benefits from their exercising their skill. Protagoras thus presents himself as simply continuing, at a higher level, the educational process of the Athenian democracy, which should reassure both the democrats and his potential pupils. His teaching was also well suited to what happened in Athens in practice. Though all citizens had equal status, with no official 'government' (no head of state, prime minister, leader of the opposition), and most administrative posts rotating and filled by lot, the Athenian democracy was led by a handful of outstanding men. In Pericles' day, in Thucydides' judgement, 'Athens was in name a democracy, but in fact was a government by its first man', Pericles (*History of the Peloponnesian War* 2. 65. 9; Gagarin and Woodruff, 102).

Some commentators claim Protagoras provides a justification of democracy. Kerferd, for example, stresses his importance in the history of political thought for producing 'for the first time in human history a theoretical basis for participatory democracy'.[8] But this needs the qualification that Protagoras' arguments are not exclusively pro-democratic, but have a more general application. Protagoras' social relativism entails that the 'right' constitution is whatever the members of the city have decided is right; so an oligarchy based on consent (where only the wealthy few have full political rights) is as legitimate as a democracy (where more citizens, and in Athens' case, even the poorest, have full rights). In effect, Protagoras is defending the idea of the *polis*, where the governing of the city is shared by all its citizens (what proportion of the adult native males are full citizens, making the difference between one constitution and another). Accordingly, any Greek city, even a monarchy, meets Protagoras' criteria, with the sole and significant exception of a tyranny—where a single individual has seized power for himself and rules by force and in his own interest. In other words, Protagoras does justify democracy but only because his position is a justification of any *polis* constitution: but it is indecisive as between a democracy and an oligarchy. Strictly speaking, Protagoras simply *explains* Athenian democracy, analysing what Athenian ideas and practices involve, what is implied by what the Athenians think. This is different from claiming that what they think is in some sense 'true'. He demonstrates that their beliefs are consistent with their actions. But he does not raise the question whether what they think is right: his relativism leaves no room for that.

Protagoras has strongly defended traditional values, and in particular the centrality of acting justly and obeying the law.[9] To be just yourself and to live in a just society are, for Protagoras, inseparable, so that not only does your acting justly benefit others and their acting justly benefit you; your acting justly benefits you yourself because unless you are just you cannot belong to a society and cannot gain the benefits of others being just to you. However, Protagoras' position is not free from difficulty, and it did not go uncriticized. Some Sophists found the traditional values problematic and attacked them directly—and by implication criticized Protagoras. I turn next to one of the fiercest attacks, from Thrasymachus.

## Thrasymachus and the politics of the individual: the disadvantage of justice

Once more, Plato is the principal source. His presentation of Thrasymachus early in the *Republic* seems designed to outline a set of assumptions and conclusions against which to contrast his own position. Many readers see the remainder of the *Republic* as Plato's response to Thrasymachus. How far the ideas Plato puts into Thrasymachus' mouth are those of the historical Thrasymachus, how fairly he represents Thrasymachus' position, cannot now be known; but even though he is fitting this view of justice into his own argument, it would have been a pointless distraction to attribute it to Thrasymachus unless Plato's readers would have accepted the general accuracy of his portrayal.

Although commentators disagree over many aspects of the interpretation of Thrasymachus' contributions in the *Republic*, especially their consistency, the main points are clear and coherent. Early in the dialogue Thrasymachus and Socrates are discussing the fundamental question 'which whole way of life would make living most worthwhile for each of us' (*Republic* 344e; Cooper and Hutchinson, 989), and specifically whether or not one should be 'just', meaning by that, follow the rules and laws of one's society. Thrasymachus contends that 'justice is nothing other than the advantage of the stronger'(*Republic* 338c; Cooper and Hutchinson, 983). The rules are made by the stronger in each society, by the tyrant in a tyranny, by the democrats in a democracy, and so on, and always made to their own advantage.[10] Thus, whatever the constitution, justice 'is the same everywhere, namely, the advantage of the stronger' (*Republic* 339a; Cooper and Hutchinson, 983). Hence if you obey the stronger's rules, you act to the advantage of the stronger, and against your own interests. Subsequently, Thrasymachus widens his claim to cover all relations between people, in private life too: in every case, 'justice is really the good of another' (*Republic* 343c; Cooper and Hutchinson, 988). Those who understand this, and have the sense to break the rules and take advantage of others, are in that sense the stronger, and gain from their impositions. Those who are so simple as to let themselves be imposed upon are the weaker, and by following the rules 'they make the one they serve happy, but themselves not at all' (*Republic* 343c; Cooper and Hutchinson, 988). Thus there are two kinds of people, pursuing two ways of life. Some people always rig rules in their own favour when they are in power or, when they have to knuckle under other people's rules, seize every opportunity to bend or evade them to suit themselves; generally they manipulate and exploit other people in order to gain more than their fair share. These are the strong, and they live the unjust way of life. The other kind of people follow the rules, and always lose by it. These are the weak, and they live the just way of life. Thrasymachus gives illustrations:

> A just man always gets less than an unjust one. First, in their contracts with one another, you'll never find, when the partnership ends, that a just partner has got more than an unjust one, but less. Second, in matters relating to the city, when taxes are to be paid, a just man pays more on the same property, an unjust one less, but when the city is giving out refunds, a just man gets nothing, while an unjust one makes a large profit. Finally, when each of them holds a ruling position in some public office, a just person . . . finds that his private affairs deteriorate because he has to neglect them, that he gains no advantage from the public purse because of his justice, and that he's hated by his relatives and acquaintances when he's unwilling to do them an unjust favor. The opposite is true of an unjust man in every respect. (*Republic* 343d–e; Cooper and Hutchinson, 988)

Thrasymachus' paradigm case is the tyrant, who wields despotic power and lives above the law. He is able to be completely unjust, thereby making himself the happiest man in the city, as everyone acknowledges (*Republic* 344a–c; Cooper and Hutchinson, 988).[11] The completely unjust man is clever and good: the just man exhibits 'very high-minded simplicity' (*Republic* 348c; Cooper and Hutchinson, 992). It seems to follow that, for Thrasymachus, justice is a mug's game which only the stupid play, while injustice is preferable and is chosen by anyone with their wits about them.[12]

The unstated assumptions behind Thrasymachus' position are obvious. He treats individuals as isolated beings, each with his own interests. Individuals are in pursuit of limited goods (e.g. money, material possessions, fame, honour), and therefore in competition with one another; thus, in any exchange or relationship between individuals, when one of them gains, the other or others must lose. The individual's interests are his exclusively, and opposed to every other individual's: individuals have no common interest. The sensible way to live your life is always to put yourself first as much as you can. Correspondingly, politics is viewed as a power relation between stronger and weaker (ruler and subjects), in which the parties have opposed interests and the stronger satisfy their interests at the expense of the weaker. The stronger are able to make the rules, and lay down as 'just' what advantages them, so that justice is what is against the interests of the weaker.

These assumptions involve a restricted view of human relationships and a narrow conception of one's interest or advantage; and they disregard all Protagoras' insights into the social nature of justice and its reciprocal benefits. One can see in Thrasymachus a whole series of contrasts with Protagoras' position, indeed a comprehensive repudiation of that position and its assumptions. From Thrasymachus' 'realist' perspective, Protagoras is naive and superficial, taking political ideals at face value instead of investigating whether they are put into practice, and who gains when they are. Above all, Thrasymachus' position entails denying that justice is reciprocally beneficial and in everyone's interest. It would be, if everyone were just: justice could be another's advantage, yet one could be just and not lose if everyone else acted to one's advantage in return. But, Thrasymachus would insist, not everyone is just. Those strong enough to be unjust benefit more from injustice and are unjust whenever they can get away with it, and then those who are just lose out because they do not gain from them in return but merely serve their interests. For Protagoras politics is a cooperative activity in which all citizens gain, using discussion and persuasion to reach agreement on their constitution and laws, and providing continuity and stability by training each succeeding generation in them; whereas for Thrasymachus politics is conflictual, another competitive arena in which some men control, exploit, and oppress others, manipulating and deceiving them and using force if necessary. Significantly, in Plato's portraits of the two Sophists, Protagoras uses the same word (*euboulia*), meaning 'good judgement', to describe the political skill he teaches, which includes being just oneself and teaching others to be just, as Thrasymachus uses for the stronger man's policy of injustice (*Protagoras* 318e; Gagarin and Woodruff, 175; *Republic* 348d; Cooper and Hutchinson, 992). So Thrasymachus seems to take the opposite view from Protagoras on the nature of politics and on how one should live one's life. Protagoras defends the traditional view of the *polis*: that, Thrasymachus objects, is unrealistic. It is hard to see how anyone taking the Thrasymachean perspective, and who proposes to act unjustly whenever he can, can be dissuaded by Protagorean arguments. The unjust man will be free-riding on the justice of his fellow citizens, but if he can free-ride, why should he not?

Nor is this the only objection to Protagoras. Plato clearly believes that many people share something like Thrasymachus' cynical view of the disadvantages of being just. Plato has Glaucon renew Thrasymachus' argument, observing that 'most people' think that justice is 'onerous' and 'to be practiced for the sake of the rewards and popularity that come from a reputation for justice, but is to be avoided because of itself as something burdensome' (*Republic* 358a; Cooper and Hutchinson, 999). According to Glaucon, most people think that

> to do injustice is naturally good and to suffer injustice bad, but that the badness of suffering it so far exceeds the goodness of doing it that those who have done and suffered injustice and tasted both, but who lack the power to do it and avoid suffering it, decide that it is profitable to come to an agreement with each other neither to do injustice nor to suffer it. As a result, they begin to make laws and covenants, and what the law commands they call lawful and just. . . . [Justice] is intermediate between the best and the worst. The best is to do injustice without paying the penalty; the worst is to suffer it without being able to take revenge. . . . People value [justice] not as a good but because they are too weak to do injustice with impunity. (*Republic* 358e–359b; Cooper and Hutchinson, 1000)[13]

If a just and an unjust man both had the freedom to do whatever they liked, then they would both behave unjustly because everyone naturally desires 'to outdo others and get more and more' (*Republic* 359c; Cooper and Hutchinson, 1000). Men are just because they have to be, because they cannot do whatever they like. But if they could do whatever they liked, they would be unjust, because they think the life of the unjust man is 'much better' (*Republic* 358c; Cooper and Hutchinson, 999). 'Indeed, every man believes that injustice is far more profitable to himself than justice' (*Republic* 360c; Cooper and Hutchinson, 1001). 'And any exponent of this argument will say he's right,' Glaucon adds, because anyone given the chance to be unjust with impunity who did not seize the opportunity 'would be thought wretched and stupid by everyone aware of the situation, though, of course, they'd praise him in public, deceiving each other for fear of suffering injustice' (*Republic* 360d; Cooper and Hutchinson, 1001). Someone who is good at being unjust, so that he is never caught but is actually thought to be just, has the best life:

> He rules his city because of his reputation for justice; he marries into any family he wishes . . . he has contracts and partnerships with anyone he wants; and besides benefiting himself in all these ways, he profits because he has no scruples about doing injustice. In any contest, public or private, he's the winner and outdoes his enemies. And by outdoing them, he becomes wealthy, benefiting his friends and harming his enemies. . . . He takes better care of the gods . . . (and, indeed, of the human beings he's fond of) than a just person does. Hence it's likely that the gods, in turn, will take better care of him than of a just person. That's what they say, Socrates, that gods and humans provide a better life for unjust people than for just ones. (*Republic* 362b–c; Cooper and Hutchinson, 1002)

This bears very significantly on Protagoras' position. On the view Glaucon summarizes (which echoes radical Sophist ideas), the ordinary opinion of justice is pretty much the opposite of what Protagoras claimed it was. Either Protagoras misreported what people thought, or there had been a major shift in public opinion in the intervening years, perhaps as a result of the stresses of the great war with Sparta and eventual heavy defeat.[14] Whatever the reason, the difference is vital. The basic weakness of Protagoras' position is precisely that he argues from what people think ('Whatever each city judges to be just and fine, these things in fact are just and fine for it, so long as it holds those opinions'; *Theaetetus* 167c; Gagarin and Woodruff, 186). Consequently, justice is valuable only so long as people think that it is, and want to practise it themselves and encourage it in others in the ways that Protagoras described. But if Glaucon is reporting correctly that most Athenians then thought that justice was *not* good, Protagoras' defence of it collapses. His relativism entails that, in a society where people think as Glaucon claims they do, justice is not a highly valued good but simply a necessary evil, a compromise which is accepted because there is no alternative and which will be evaded whenever opportunity allows.

## Antiphon and further doubts about justice

So far I have roughed out two views of politics and of justice, relying on Plato's versions of what Protagoras and Thrasymachus argued. In the case of Antiphon, unusually, we are not dependent on Plato (who never mentions him) but possess Antiphon's own words. This makes him highly significant, because his ideas can be used to check the historicity of other reports of Sophists' ideas. Unfortunately, there are other problems of evidence.

We have only small fragments of Antiphon's treatise *Truth*, and his intentions are not clear.[15] Nonetheless, these fragments establish that the ideas which Plato attributes to figures such as Thrasymachus, and those which Glaucon expresses, are not figments of Plato's imagination but were under discussion.

The overall structure of Antiphon's *Truth* and his purpose in discussing justice are not known, and commentators attribute different positions to him.[16] Possibly, in the surviving fragments, he was expressing his own view and attacking justice, or perhaps he was setting out sample arguments for teaching purposes without committing himself for or against them. So I shall follow a cautious path of minimal interpretation, and present what Antiphon writes as the exposure of features of justice which must raise doubts about whether one should be just. I do not claim the doubts are his own, nor that they led Antiphon himself to recommend acting unjustly: it is enough for my purposes that these were the kinds of arguments that the Sophists examined.

Antiphon uses the common distinction between nature (*phusis*) and convention (*nomos*). As standardly formulated, what is natural is the way it is innately, it is unchangeable, and it is the same everywhere, 'as fire burns both here and in Persia'; what is conventional is a human creation, it can be changed, and it varies from one society to another.[17] Antiphon is one of those who does not simply posit the natural as *different from* the conventional, but sees them as *opposed to* one another; and draws radical conclusions from the distinction.[18] He observes that we know and respect the conventions of nearby communities but not those of distant communities, and that this is barbarous behaviour because

> we are all at birth in all respects equally capable of being both barbarians [i.e. foreigners] and Greeks. We can examine those attributes of nature that are necessarily in all men and are provided to all to the same degree, and in these respects none of us is distinguished as foreign or Greek. For we all breathe the air through our mouth and through our nostrils, and we laugh when we are pleased in our mind or we weep when we are pained, and we take in sounds with our hearing, and we see by the light with our sight, and we work with our hands and we walk with our feet . . . (Gagarin and Woodruff, 244–5)

The next fragment applies the nature–convention distinction to justice. Justice, he says, using a common definition and one which both Protagoras and Thrasymachus could accept, is 'not violating the rules (*nomima*) of the city in which one is a citizen' (ibid. 245). Antiphon then states a radical conclusion which Thrasymachus would applaud but Protagoras would repudiate: 'a person would best use justice to his own advantage if he considered the laws (*nomoi*) important when witnesses are present, but the consequences of nature (*phusis*) important in the absence of witnesses' (ibid.).[19] The reasoning seems to be as follows. Nature requires us to do things which are necessary and unavoidable (perhaps an example would be, to eat and drink), whereas what the conventional rules of our city require are neither. So if we break the rules, we suffer harm (shame and punishment) only if we are witnessed doing it; but we necessarily suffer harm if we try to violate one of the inherent requirements of nature (e.g. if we do not eat or drink, we die) regardless of whether we are witnessed or not. This is an important matter, Antiphon stresses, because 'most things that are just according to law are inimical to nature', bringing pain rather than pleasure and life (ibid. 245–6). For example, if you follow the rules and treat your parents well even when you have been treated badly by them, you are acting contrary to nature and giving yourself 'more pain when less is possible and less pleasure when more is possible' (ibid. 246).[20] On this line of argument, the opposition between what nature and what convention require of the individual becomes a justification for the individual to disobey laws and other rules whenever he can get away with it.[21]

The analysis then turns to another consideration, that the rules fail to protect those who obey them. In the first place, the rules do not stop the unjust from breaking them, or prevent their victims from suffering. In the second place, when there has been an offence and it comes to punishing the aggressor, the law does not favour the victim: the victim must convince the court that the crime occurred and he suffered loss, and whatever means of persuasion he has are equally open to the perpetrator.[22] Antiphon notes that the alternative to persuading the court is to deceive it, and the implication surely is (though this is not stated explicitly) that the offender will have no compunction in lying, whereas the victim, if he is just, will tell the truth and once more disadvantage himself.

There is a change of tack in the final fragment, which draws attention to another aspect of the legal process, the obligation to appear in court as an eyewitness:

> To testify truthfully for one another is customarily thought to be just (*dikaios*) and to no lesser degree useful in human affairs. And yet one who does this will not be just if indeed it is just not to injure (*adikein*) anyone if one is not injured oneself; for even if he tells the truth, someone who testifies must necessarily injure another somehow, and will then be injured himself, since he will be hated when the testimony he gives leads to the conviction of the person against whom he testifies, who then loses his property or his life because of this man whom he has not injured at all. In this way he wrongs the person against whom he testifies, because he injures someone who is not injuring him; and he in turn is injured by the one against whom he testified in that he is hated by him . . . As a result he has an enemy who will do him whatever harm he can in word or deed. (ibid. 246–7)

Here Antiphon is pointing out a contradiction between two ideas of justice, that it is just to take part in the judicial process and that it is just not to injure someone who has not injured you, when telling the truth as an eyewitness involves harming someone who has not harmed you. It is impossible for both these to be just, and Antiphon apparently concludes that 'the judicial process, verdicts, and arbitration proceedings are not just, since helping some people hurts others' (ibid. 247). We observe that the argument works only on the assumption that the witness of an offence against someone else is not himself harmed. If, on the other hand, it is thought, as one might from Protagoras' perspective, that any offence breaches some community interest (such as an ordered society providing security of life and property), then the witness has been harmed, albeit indirectly, and the inconsistency disappears. So the argument Antiphon presents, and perhaps Antiphon himself, presupposes that there is no community interest in justice.

Antiphon's analysis here focuses on the inadequacies and failures of law (*nomos*). It highlights necessary limits to what law can achieve either for the individual or for the community, and thereby produces a powerful case against being just. First, the rules one follows if one is just are disadvantageous to oneself, and the disadvantages are natural and thus unavoidable. Secondly, such advantages as there may be from being just are highly contingent and may never be enjoyed. And thirdly, participating in the legal process, as justice requires, involves harming people who have not harmed one and hence is both inconsistent and very imprudent—especially in a world where a bedrock moral conviction was that a real man should bear grudges and get even with his enemies.[23] We may note that Antiphon is discussing fundamental and constitutive features of any legal system: so they are found in modern legal systems and remain problematic. His examination shows that there must be a choice between acting justly and maximizing one's own advantage, and at the very least he has raised extremely serious doubts about whether it is possible, and whether it is sensible, to be just. Everything seems to point towards acting unjustly whenever one can get away with it (and there are strong hints that the unscrupulous can get away with a great deal). Otherwise not only do you refrain from pursuing your own advantage, you also allow yourself to be the victim of others pursuing theirs.

## Conclusion: the Sophists and Plato

Something of the range and variety of the Sophists' political thought should now be apparent. The most significant feature is that justice is both applauded and defended, and queried and denigrated; old landmarks have been replaced by uncertainty. This was the state of the debate that Socrates engaged in, and that Plato joined after him. Plato cannot be seen simply as the opponent of the Sophists. Rather, he is in agreement with Protagoras on many matters, such as the value of community and the importance of education (socialization), and above all on the centrality and indispensability of justice. On the other hand, from Plato's perspective Protagoras built his case for justice on weak foundations and had no defence against the attacks mounted by the next generation of Sophists. Protagoras' great weakness is his narrow conception of the individual's interest. Protagoras measures the individual's success by his material achievements and his standing in his *polis.* But Thrasymachus and others claimed that the individual best serves his interest if he is *unjust* (when he can be), justice always being to the advantage of someone else and injustice being to one's own advantage. Protagoras' theory has no resources to generate a response. His relativism means that justice has no value in itself; it is merely useful as a means to serving one's own interest. And if one's interest is defined in terms of external goods, and one can serve it without being just, then Protagoras can offer no convincing reason why one should act justly.[24]

Plato follows Socrates in adopting a different strategy. The individual's interest is understood in non-material terms, and made internal to him, and justice is redefined as intrinsically valuable. From this new perspective, reasons can be offered for being just even when one might gain more wealth or reputation from not being just. The change of perspective also meets the doubts raised by Antiphon. If justice is good in itself, and brings the individual internal benefits, then it is worth acting justly even though the law is defective. The just man may not be effectively protected by the law, and crimes may go undetected or unpunished—but the just man remains better off in other ways. Thus law and justice are valuable and desirable despite their unavoidable operational limitations. The corresponding conception of politics sees it much as Protagoras did, that is, as the cooperative enterprise of a community of individuals who have a common interest in living under law and in acting justly, since everyone who is just benefits from it both communally and individually.

Of course, whether this strategy is successful, and what costs it incurs, are another matter. Modern readers jib, for example, at Plato's rejection of Protagoras' endorsement of the Athenian democrats' opinion that political skill can be learned by everyone. Plato agrees that there is a political skill, and that it can be taught—but argues it is specialist expertise which can be learned only by that tiny minority with the appropriate natural ability (though he includes women among them), and that politics should be controlled by these people exclusively. So it may put Plato's *Republic* in a different and more sympathetic light if it is located in relation to the discussions and disputes of the Sophists. Then the *Republic* can be understood as attempting to provide support stronger than Protagoras could, for the traditional idea of communal justice against the attacks of Thrasymachus and other radical individualists. Plato's aim is to reconcile the conflicts of interest between the community and the individual which the Sophists highlighted, by revealing the interdependence and harmony of true interest between community and individual.[25]

## FURTHER READING

Caizzi, Fernanda Decleva, 'Protagoras and Antiphon: Sophistic Debates on Justice', in A. A. Long (ed.), *The Cambridge Companion to Early Greek Philosophy* (Cambridge: Cambridge University Press, 1993).

Guthrie, W. K. C., *A History of Greek Philosophy, iii: The Fifth-Century Enlightenment* (Cambridge: Cambridge University Press, 1969); pt. I reissued as *The Sophists* (Cambridge: Cambridge University Press, 1971).

Kerferd, G. B., *The Sophistic Movement* (Cambridge: Cambridge University Press, 1981).

Romilly, Jacqueline de, *The Great Sophists in Periclean Athens*, trans. J. Lloyd (Oxford: Clarendon Press, 1992).

Schiappa, Edward, *Protagoras and Logos: A Study in Greek Philosophy and Rhetoric* (Columbia: University of South Carolina Press, 1991).

## NOTES

1. Interestingly, Socrates was the main figure of fun. This confirms Socrates' centrality in the Enlightenment, alongside the Sophists, and is revealing of the popular view of him. Aristophanes was otherwise completely unfair to him, because Socrates distinguished himself from the Sophists. He never charged a fee, being concerned to bring men to reconsider their lives and their characters in individual conversations rather than to market some expertise wholesale; moreover, he had a very different idea of what counted as a 'successful' life, and what was needed to live it.
2. See Plato, *Protagoras* 328b–c; Gagarin and Woodruff, 184, for Protagoras' system of charging fees, which satisfied his pupils (references are first to the standard pagination, common to all translations, and secondly to the translation in Michael Gagarin and Paul Woodruff (ed. and trans.), *Early Greek Political Thought from Homer to the Sophists* (Cambridge: Cambridge University Press, 1995), hereafter Gagarin and Woodruff).
3. For Greek political thought before the Sophists, which (on the little evidence which survives) tends to be much less explicit and developed, see Gagarin and Woodruff, pts. I–IV.
4. See in particular George Grote, *A History of Greece* (London: John Murray, 1846–56; new edn. 1869), ch. 67; Karl R. Popper, *The Open Society and its Enemies*, i: *The Spell of Plato* (London: Routledge & Kegan Paul, 1945; 4th edn. 1962); Eric A. Havelock, *The Liberal Temper in Greek Politics* (London: Jonathan Cape, 1957); and Jacqueline de Romilly, *The Great Sophists in Periclean Athens* (Oxford: Clarendon Press, 1992). Popper and Havelock mar their accounts through mistakenly believing that the case for the Sophists can be advanced only if Plato is denigrated.
5. I have used the selection of fragments and reports of Protagoras in Gagarin and Woodruff since this emphasizes his political thinking. A somewhat different selection, attending more to his philosophy, is offered with an enlightening commentary by Robin Waterfield, *The First Philosophers: The Presocratics and Sophists*, World's Classics (Oxford: Oxford University Press, 2000).
6. Protagoras automatically assumes that his pupils will be men. In the Greek cities only native adult males were full citizens with political rights, and almost no one questioned this (Plato being the most notable exception). Protagoras' teaching is targeted at men, as heads of households and as citizens. He recognizes in passing that political skill, the art of living together in a city, must be shared by literally every inhabitant, 'whether man, woman, or child' (*Protagoras* 325a; Gagarin and Woodruff, 181); but he does not pursue this and he does not infer, as we would, that it means women are qualified to be full citizens. (See too n. 23.)
7. *Plato: Complete Works*, ed. John M. Cooper and D. S. Hutchinson (Indianapolis: Hackett, 1997); hereafter Cooper and Hutchinson.
8. G. B. Kerferd, *The Sophistic Movement* (Cambridge: Cambridge University Press, 1981), 144.

9. Another Sophist who defends the traditional values is Prodicus; see 'The Choice of Heracles', which presents a case for preferring the path of virtue to the path of vice, in Gagarin and Woodruff, 211–14. See too the very conventional moral assertions in the Sophistic treatise *Anonymus Iamblichi*, in Gagarin and Woodruff, 290–5.
10. For examples of how democrats in a Greek city might organize their constitution to favour themselves over others, see *The Constitution of the Athenians*. Its unknown author, usually called the Old Oligarch, alleges that the Athenian democrats did precisely that. Extracts appear in Gagarin and Woodruff, 133–44.
11. On the popular opinion of the outstanding happiness of successful tyrants, see too Plato's *Gorgias*, 470d–472b.
12. I think Thrasymachus is recommending injustice. Others contend he is simply describing what people think and how they behave; see e.g. de Romilly, *The Great Sophists in Periclean Athens*, ch. 6.
13. Some commentators have seen here the first statement of social contract theory; e.g. J. W. Gough, *The Social Contract: A Critical Study of its Development* (2nd edn. Oxford: Clarendon Press, 1957). Glaucon's statements do indeed locate the origin of morality in an agreement between the members of a society, but he says nothing about politics, about obligation to obey the law, or the rights of subjects and limits on the law, or the role of a sovereign. Indeed, in Greece the sharp modern distinction between moral and legal rules did not exist (*nomos* covered both); there were no political institutions equivalent to the modern state to perform its role. Hence any Greek 'contract theory' is inevitably very different from the social contract theories of the 17th century and later. See further on the differences David Boucher and Paul Kelly (eds.), *The Social Contract from Hobbes to Rawls* (London: Routledge, 1994), 1–4.

    Again, an early contract theory may lie behind the Sophist Lycophron's remark, recorded by Aristotle, that 'law is the guarantee of just behavior (*dikaia*) among men' (*Politics* 1280$^{b}$12; Gagarin and Woodruff, 275). However, even in the context of Aristotle's objections to it, the remark is too brief to allow reliable reconstruction of Lycophron's social contract theory (if indeed he had one).
14. For examples of the wartime collapse of traditional civic and other moral standards, see Thucydides' accounts of the plague in Athens and of the civil wars in Corcyra: 2. 52–8 and 3. 81. 2–84; Gagarin and Woodruff, 102–8.
15. I take the fragments in the order followed by Gagarin and Woodruff, 244–7; see p. xliii on the text and its arrangement.
16. For instance, Antiphon is portrayed as an immoralist by Michael Nill, *Morality and Self-Interest in Protagoras, Antiphon and Democritus* (Leiden: E. J. Brill, 1985), ch. III, but as much more like Protagoras by de Romilly, *The Great Sophists in Periclean Athens*, 122–8.
17. I draw here on Aristotle, *Nicomachean Ethics* 1134$^{b}$18–1135$^{a}$6.
18. For instance, nature and convention are explicitly opposed, though with varying emphases, by Hippias (*Protagoras* 337d–338b; Gagarin and Woodruff, 216–17); in the theory Glaucon recounts (*Republic* 359c; Cooper and Hutchinson, 1000); and by Callicles—usually taken as working from Sophist ideas—in Plato's *Gorgias* (482c–4c and 488b–92c; Cooper and Hutchinson, 827–8 and 831–5). See generally, on the nature–convention distinction, W. K. C. Guthrie, *A History of Greek Philosophy*, iii: *The Fifth-Century Enlightenment* (Cambridge: Cambridge University Press, 1969); pt. I reissued as *The Sophists* (Cambridge: Cambridge University Press, 1971), 55–134, and Kerferd, *The Sophistic Movement*, ch. 10.
19. For Glaucon's account, too, whether or not one's unjust act will be witnessed makes a crucial difference: his graphic test case is to suppose one can make oneself invisible (i.e. unwitnessable), in which case he claims the just man and the unjust man would behave identically (*Republic* 359c–60c; Cooper and Hutchinson, 1000–1). Some thought religion plugged this gap in the human sanctions for justice. For instance, a fragment which may be by the Sophist Critias (or it may be by Euripides) suggests that after laws were invented, and people continued to break them secretly, 'some shrewd, intelligent (*sophos*) man invented fear of the gods for mortals, so that the wicked would have something to fear even if their deeds or words or thoughts were secret' (Gagarin and Woodruff, 261). However, this aid to justice was undermined by the common belief that the unjust could avoid their punishment by bribing the gods (see *Republic* 362d–366b; Cooper and Hutchinson, 1003–6).

    One implication of Antiphon's analysis in the rest of this section is that the unjust may well get away with their crimes even if they are witnessed, by suborning the witnesses or by discrediting them in court.

20. The assumption that it is natural and acceptable for the individual to pursue his own interests at the expense of others (also found in Thrasymachus and in Callicles, Callicles asserting that this is natural justice) is replicated at the level of the city according to Thucydides, who depicts the Athenians (then struggling to maintain their grip on their empire) arguing that it is a natural necessity that stronger cities rule by force over weaker, for their own advantage and disregarding what justice requires; see e.g. 1. 75–6 and 5. 89–105; Gagarin and Woodruff, 91–2 and 119–22. On Thucydides, see further David Boucher, *Political Theories of International Relations from Thucydides to the Present* (Oxford: Oxford University Press, 1998), ch. 4.
21. Contrast Havelock, *The Liberal Temper in Greek Politics*, who argues that Antiphon is not an immoralist but, in a society with a powerful group ethos where the individual's whole life is laid down for him, trying to carve out an area for private judgement: 'Antiphon's overall target is the grip of the group and its traditions' (p. 278). In this respect, as in others, Antiphon seems to be at the opposite extreme from Protagoras. Fernanda Decleva Caizzi structures her very helpful discussion of Sophist debates on justice around the assumption that Protagoras and Antiphon may plausibly be regarded as 'the exponents of two radically different views on human nature and the role of justice, elaborated probably within a decade of one another' ('Protagoras and Antiphon: Sophistic Debates on Justice', in A. A. Long (ed.), *The Cambridge Companion to Early Greek Philosophy* (Cambridge: Cambridge University Press, 1993), 317).
22. In Athens there was no body of police to enforce the law or detect or prosecute breaches, and no professional judiciary or lawyers to administer it. A wronged citizen stated his own case before a court (a large panel of fellow citizens) and the accused stated his in reply. (Hence the appeal of the Sophists' claims to be able to teach people to speak well and argue persuasively.) For examples of prosecution and defence speeches, see the 'Tetralogies' of Antiphon the Orator (who may or may not be the Sophist) in Gagarin and Woodruff, 219–44.
23. To do good to one's friends and harm to one's enemies is of course the idea of justice espoused by Polemarchus (*Republic* 331d–332c; Cooper and Hutchinson, 976). Again, Meno tells Socrates that 'a man's virtue consists of being able to manage public affairs and in so doing to benefit his friends and harm his enemies and to be careful that no harm comes to himself' (*Meno* 71e Cooper and Hutchinson 872). (The popular conception which Meno represents is that men and women have their own virtues: a woman's virtue, he immediately adds, is to 'manage the home well, preserve its possessions, and be submissive to her husband'.)
24. For this line of argument, see Nill, *Morality and Self-Interest in Protagoras, Antiphon, and Democritus*.
25. I am grateful to David Boucher, Susan Mendus, and Fred Rosen for their very helpful comments.

# 3 Socrates

Fred Rosen

### Contents



## Chapter guide

Socrates, who claimed to know nothing and probably wrote nothing, is nonetheless the first to see the connections and the potential opposition between the philosopher's search for truth and the world of politics. His conception of virtue, the so-called Socratic paradoxes, the method of question and answer (the *elenchus*), and the use of the craft analogies are among the ideas explored here in connection with his attempts to define the unique role of the philosopher in relation to 'the many' in society. Socrates' way of life and his philosophy leads almost inevitably to his trial and death, which is examined through Plato's dialogues the *Apology* and *Crito*. Socrates shows here how the quest for wisdom challenges the acknowledged experts and leaders in society, but at the same time looks for points of reconciliation so that politics will not be wholly devoid of contact with truth and justice. Attention is also paid in this chapter to the sources of information for Socrates' life and ideas, and the way different interpretations of the evidence affect the meaning and significance of his philosophy.

## Biography

Socrates was born in 470 or 469 BC and was executed, following his trial, in 399 at the age of 70. His parents were called Sophroniscus and Phaenarete of the deme Alopeke. His father, a respected citizen, was a stonemason or possibly a sculptor, and his mother was said to have been a midwife. He was married to Xanthippe, whose name became a byword for bad temper and shrewishness. They had three sons, the eldest of whom was Lamprocles, still a youth at the time of Socrates' death.

Socrates probably followed in his father's footsteps as a stonemason before he abandoned it for his unique pursuit of wisdom as a philosopher and for a life of self-imposed poverty. As an Athenian he performed his civic and military duties and was known for his courage in at least three campaigns during the Peloponnesian War. Although he shunned active politics, he lived in very difficult times, and was unfairly associated with the rule of the Thirty Tyrants because of his earlier association with Critias and Alcibiades. He was brought to trial by the restored democracy, accused of impiety (a capital crime) and corrupting the young. The vote against Socrates was fairly close at approximately 280 votes for conviction and 220 for acquittal.

In appearance Socrates was well known for his ugliness. His snub nose, prominent staring eyes, thick lips, and large stomach were often the subject of comment. He was known to care little about his appearance, and was usually barefoot and dressed in an old coat.

Although he probably wrote nothing and is known through the writings of others, Socrates can be credited with turning the focus of philosophy onto human activity and thus founding the Western tradition of political thought. His ideas, especially those depicted in the so-called Socratic dialogues of Plato, raise crucial questions concerning ethics and politics which have become the abiding themes of political theory for more than 2,000 years.

### Key texts

Aristophanes, *The Clouds*
Plato, *Apology, Crito, Gorgias, Protagoras*
Xenophon, *Apology of Socrates, Memorabilia*

### Main text used

Plato, *The Last Days of Socrates* (Harmondsworth: Penguin, 1993) or numerous other editions of Plato's *Apology* and *Crito*.

### Key ideas

***Elenchus***, a unique philosophical method consisting of a series of questions and answers between Socrates and an interlocutor leading to an admission of ignorance. **Virtue** (*arete*), based on knowledge, with every particular virtue (wisdom, courage, temperance, and justice) reducible to every other. ***Daimonion***, Socrates' inner voice, which opposed his involvement in active politics. ***Techne***, the arts and crafts, frequently used as analogies in the *elenchus*. The laws (*hoi nomoi*), declared the basis of civil obedience. ***Hoi polloi*** (literally, 'the many'), who are the opposing force to Socratic political theory.

## Who is Socrates?

While Socrates may stand in the company of the Sophists in having to be studied mainly through the surviving writings of others, and particularly Plato, he is unique among major figures in the history of political thought in probably having written nothing and, additionally, in claiming to know nothing. Besides the usual problems of interpreting texts in terms of various contexts, there are additional difficulties when one comes to determine what Socrates thought. At one level there are problems concerning what are to count as Socratic texts, and the solution to these problems is linked to the authority to be given to the evidence provided by various contemporaries of Socrates.

At another level the problem of evidence is compounded by highly developed and refined traditions of interpretation concerning what should count as evidence and in what measures. Among current scholars two traditions have tended to predominate, the first in the writings of Leo Strauss and the second in those of Gregory Vlastos.[1] Their approaches by no means exhaust the range of interpretations that has developed over the last 200 years. Nevertheless, their writings provide important markers for the assumptions and debates found in the secondary literature concerning how the evidence for Socrates' thought should be understood.

There are several main contemporary sources for our knowledge of Socrates. In Aristophanes' comedy *The Clouds* he features as a Sophist, a student of nature, and is ridiculed as a dubious teacher and an atheist. From the perspective of traditional Athenian values, Socrates is portrayed as a poor, needy person lacking in prudence. At the time of his trial Socrates was well aware of the importance of Aristophanes' work. In Plato's *Apology of Socrates* he refers to Aristophanes as the old accuser (18c–d, 19b–c) who had poisoned the atmosphere and turned Athenian opinion against him over several decades.

According to Strauss, *The Clouds* and other comedies by Aristophanes form the starting point for the attempt to understand the ideas of Socrates, and he interprets both Plato and Xenophon, two other important sources for our knowledge of Socrates, as writing works in defence of Socrates against Aristophanes.[2] Xenophon replies to the criticisms that Socrates lacked prudence and taught injustice by portraying him in a number of works, such as the *Oeconomicus*, *Apology of Socrates*, *Symposium*, and *Memorabilia*, as the ideal citizen and statesman, and a political educator of the highest rank. Although he is also portrayed by Xenophon as a critic of Athenian democracy, he is represented as a good and just person in his dealings with Athens generally. Plato also develops a defence of Socrates, but he emphasizes Socrates the philosopher, the lover of wisdom, as opposed to the Sophist, or the more political figure as found in Xenophon.

The Platonic dialogues, for Strauss, are to be read not as philosophical texts but as works of art: dramas in which the author hides himself, in which Socrates is not necessarily Plato's spokesman and in which he cannot be said necessarily to speak for himself.[3] Thus, the *Apology*, often presumed to be an accurate report of Socrates' trial, is treated like any other Platonic dialogue, with the whole of the Platonic corpus to be approached as highly complex dramas which, sphinx-like, do not easily divulge the deepest thoughts of the author. Strauss rejects the commonplace distinction of Plato's works as consisting of early Socratic dialogues, middle dialogues in which Plato often uses Socrates as a spokesman but develops doctrines foreign to Socrates such as the theory of Forms in the *Republic*, and later dialogues where a number of the themes of the middle period are revised and examined from different perspectives.[4] He accepts the dialogues and their arrangements as roughly set forth by Thrasyllus, who classifies them according to theme and makes no distinction between an early, middle, and late Plato, and between those in which Socrates speaks for himself and those where he speaks for Plato.

A very different approach to the identification of authentic Socratic texts may be found in Vlastos's highly influential writings. For Vlastos, *The Clouds*, however important for the actual trial of Socrates, is of no significance in revealing his philosophy. Xenophon, however, presents a different problem, as Vlastos is concerned with the way Xenophon wrongly (in his view) interprets Socrates as a political figure and one who is hostile to Athenian democracy. Here too one does not find the authentic Socratic doctrine, for which we must turn to Plato's dialogues. Drawing on stylometric analysis, mainly carried out in the late nineteenth and twentieth centuries, which examines the language and terminology used in the various dialogues, and using a certain amount of biographical evidence, as well as evidence supplied by Aristotle (such as that Socrates does not advance the metaphysical theory of the Forms), Vlastos holds that one can identify a number of Socratic dialogues (fourteen, including the first book of the *Republic* as a separate dialogue) in which Plato places an authentic philosophical doctrine in the mouth of Socrates (see the 'early' dialogues listed in note 4).

Unlike Strauss, for whom the dialogues are dramas and the message emerges from the action of the play and the interaction of the characters, Vlastos believes that one can extract a coherent and consistent Socratic moral philosophy from the utterances of Socrates himself in these dialogues, and, furthermore, that this doctrine can be defended as the philosophy of the historical Socrates. One particular difficulty is posed by the first book of the *Republic*, which stylometric evidence has linked with the rest of the *Republic*, but which is characterized by numerous features, such as the method of question and answer (the *elenchus*), the absence of a positive doctrine, and the absence of a metaphysical dimension in the discussion of justice. This has led Vlastos to insist that it was originally a separate Socratic dialogue, later combined with books 2–10, where Socrates sets forth the doctrine of the Forms, a doctrine supposedly never held by the historical Socrates. For Strauss, however, the whole of the *Republic* is as Socratic (or Platonic) as any other dialogue, in so far as Plato uses the character of Socrates in his dramas. For example, Strauss makes a clear link between the *Republic* and the *Apology*, as both dialogues are presented using the dramatic device of compulsion (Socrates compelled to stand trial in the *Apology* and compelled to remain in Piraeus in *Republic* 1). For Vlastos, there is no connection between the Socratic doctrine of the *Apology* and *Republic* 1 on the one hand and the rest of the *Republic* on the other, even though Socrates is a key figure in these texts.

It is important to appreciate how textual considerations affect, if not determine, the philosophical and political doctrines which are nowadays ascribed to Socrates. The numerous scholars who accept the approach of Vlastos simply assume that whatever speeches Plato puts into the mouth of Socrates in certain dialogues is an authentic Socratic doctrine. The main problem then is showing that there is a consistent doctrine in all of these dialogues. For example, in the *Apology* Socrates is far less reverential towards Athens than he is in the *Crito*. For earlier scholars this difference posed no special problem and could be explained by the differing circumstances and objects of the two dialogues. More recently, however, much scholarly debate has been devoted to showing their consistency. In *Socrates and the State* Richard Kraut argues that Plato's Socrates allows for civil disobedience in the *Crito*, as well as in the *Apology*, while Brickhouse and Smith in *Plato's Socrates* and *Socrates on Trial* argue against Kraut that the *Apology* as well as the *Crito* contain a doctrine that requires obedience to the law.[5] The stark difference between these scholars, however, is more apparent than real, as they are attempting to realize the same object, that is, to establish a wholly consistent doctrine in the fourteen 'early' dialogues of Plato. The student will notice that, unlike the followers of the approach of Strauss, there is no great concern with the structure and drama of the dialogues themselves. Plato might have spared these scholars considerable effort by writing treatises rather than dialogues, since all that counts in their interpretations is what Plato makes Socrates say. The other elements of the drama are rarely considered. The success of this approach depends in part on whether or not this consistent moral and political theory can be found in the dialogues. This is no easy task for a thinker who claims to know nothing, presents some of his most important ideas as apparent paradoxes, and is well known for his irony.

## Socratic paradoxes and the *elenchus*

What distinguishes Socrates from earlier philosophers is that he was the first to turn away from the study of nature to an almost exclusive concern with human affairs, and began what has become a long tradition of reflection on the encounter between the philosopher's love of wisdom and the established conventions and beliefs of political society which may threaten this love. The political outcome of this first encounter between philosophy and political society in the history of political thought is the trial and death of Socrates. If we attempt to follow the Vlastos school, we must also say that the philosophical outcome is a rational theory of morality which can be identified through the *elenchus*, the method of question and answer, and which unites knowledge with virtue.

Socrates is well known for setting forth in his various conversations a series of related paradoxes: (*a*) virtue is knowledge, that is to say, if we know what is right we shall perform right actions; (*b*) no one does wrong voluntarily, that is, if our right actions are based on our knowledge, wrong acts must spring from ignorance rather than from a will which intends evil; and (*c*) the unity of virtue, that is, if the various virtues are, in effect, knowledge, then any virtue, say courage, is equivalent to any other, e.g. moderation. The wise person is necessarily courageous and it follows that he or she is also necessarily moderate and just. The three paradoxes are related in that they follow from the doctrine that virtue is knowledge. They are paradoxes because we (and, it seems, a number of Socrates' interlocutors) intuitively believe that it is one thing to know what is courageous, for example, but another to act courageously. That virtue is knowledge seems too intellectualist for many, and hence a first reason for the ascription of paradox to these doctrines. In addition, Socrates' use of various analogies with the arts (*technai*) in support of the doctrine that knowledge of virtue is sufficient to make one virtuous has been questioned in its extension to morals and politics. Whoever knows the art (*techne*) of medicine is a doctor and heals sick patients, and whoever possesses the art of making shoes is a shoemaker and makes shoes. But does the person who knows what is right and good necessarily act virtuously and can the person who possesses the political art prescribe, like a doctor, medicine for the ills of a whole society? One difficulty with the analogy with the arts is that implicit in the craftsman's knowledge is a moral neutrality which does not make much sense in the spheres of morality and politics. The doctor's art does not discriminate between healing a saint and healing a criminal, and the cobbler's shoes may be used equally to help a senior citizen across the street or to kick the neighbour's cat. It is difficult to conceive of a political art which is morally neutral.

One approach to these problems is to consider them in relation to the *elenchus*, which, for Vlastos at least, is less a contribution to an epistemological method and more a substantive moral theory. The *elenchus* is a way of searching for the truth in which the genuine moral beliefs of one's interlocutors are tested and, if necessary, refuted. It is meant to engage in the search for truth and is unlike the debates employed by the Sophists (*eristic*), which are designed to achieve victory, whether or not the arguments are true or false. The *elenchus* is also not appropriate for obtaining knowledge of a particular craft, like medicine, shipbuilding, shoemaking, or of fields such as mathematics and logic. Its main object, as I have noted, is to obtain knowledge about morality and politics, and within this sphere it is used by Socrates for discovery and proof and not simply to correct mistakes. Socrates never questions his method and does not reflect on its utility for the tasks he sets it. Furthermore, the object of the *elenchus* is to combine philosophical understanding with a therapeutic reformation of one's life. Not only is one searching for the truth about the good life through the *elenchus* but one is also being directed to living it (based on the doctrine that virtue is knowledge).

Let us look more closely at how the *elenchus* works. Socrates characteristically asks his interlocutor to provide a definition of a key moral term, like justice, or to assert a related thesis, as when Polus in the *Gorgias* states that it is better to commit injustice than to receive it (*Gorgias* 474b–c). Socrates insists that the thesis should be one in which Polus believes and one that he is not setting forth simply for the sake of argument. Believing the thesis to be false, Socrates obtains agreement from the interlocutor to related premisses. In the case of Polus, the main admission is to the thesis that it is more shameful to commit injustice than to suffer it (474c). Socrates then argues on the basis of this admission that Polus must accept the thesis that it is worse to commit injustice than to suffer it (on the basis that shamefulness entails badness). The reason for Polus' admission, which leads to his refutation, is not entirely clear and is not logically entailed by any preceding argument. All that is important for Socrates is that Polus is willing to regard his admission as his belief. It may have become his belief owing to social conventions regarding shamefulness which Polus holds in an unthinking manner, or Polus' supposed profession of an art, in this case of rhetoric, may have led him to hold this belief. But, whatever the reason, Polus' admission forms the basis on which Plato constructs the argument.

The *elenchus* is often considered a negative doctrine, leading only to the refutation of the interlocutor, and one feature that is used to distinguish a Socratic dialogue from later Platonic dialogues, in which Socrates also participates, is that they end without an apparently positive outcome. But Socrates never intends his conversations to be wholly negative, and he often asserts principles and reaches conclusions that not only are positive in character but are regarded by him to be truths achieved through the *elenchus*. Furthermore, when one sees other aspects of his thought, such as the craft analogies or the assertion that virtue is knowledge, as part of the *elenchus*, then it is clear that the *elenchus* itself is both positive and negative in character. It should be capable of generating doctrines that are true and that are consistent.

The problem then arises as to the relevance of Socrates' frequent disavowal of knowledge, supported by the oracle at Delphi, to these positive assertions of knowledge, which are the outcome of the *elenchus*, even where the dialogue itself reaches no positive conclusion. There have been numerous attempts to square the circle, including distinctions between a form of knowledge Socrates would not disavow, i.e. that compatible with the *elenchus*, and an absolute and certain form of knowledge that he would disavow. Nevertheless, one is left with two distinct Socratic positions: one that claims that Socrates is wise because he knows nothing and one that refers to knowledge attained through the *elenchus*. Reflection on Socrates' unique mission to submit all moral and political ideas to a rigorous questioning, nevertheless, leads to the conclusion that there must be a kind of knowledge, held however tentatively, that has survived the *elenchus* and has not yet been refuted. Any greater scepticism may threaten the whole Socratic enterprise with absurdity and any less scepticism would call into question the whole point of the *elenchus*. Even where the dialogues end in *aporia* (without answering the question initially posed), there may be some knowledge (however incomplete) achieved by the *elenchus*.

## The trial of Socrates

In the speeches that constitute Plato's *Apology* the reader is continually reminded of the power and authority of political rhetoric, which Socrates claims is foreign to his own method and which threatens even his own identity ('I almost forgot myself', 17a). Even his *daimonion*, the divine voice which he claims has a negative role in turning him away from a certain course of action (see 31d) and preventing him from playing an active role in politics, cannot prevent (though it might delay) the powerful opinions generated by the older accusers, like Aristophanes, leading eventually to his trial. Nor can his proverbial wisdom, confirmed by the oracle at Delphi (20e–21a) and based on the fact that he alone is aware of his own ignorance, provide more than temporary shelter from political storms. Testing his wisdom against others who claim to be wise leads Socrates and his youthful followers to challenge and embarrass his fellow citizens, as he attempts to persuade the politicians, poets, and craftsmen that their claims to wisdom are unfounded without the probing scalpel of the *elenchus* as part of a life of self-examination. Here is one basis for political opposition to Socratic philosophy and not a prudent way of avoiding such opposition. The reader senses the gulf between Socratic philosophy and political society, here and also in Socrates' ironic tone, which, contrary to some recent scholarship,[6] seems apparent from the first lines of the *Apology* and seems to measure the distance between the freedom of the philosopher who neither fears nor pleases the *hoi polloi* (literally, 'the many', or the people) and the necessity that governs their thoughts and actions.

Socrates has been brought to trial to reply to two specific accusations: (*a*) impiety (believing not in the gods in whom the *polis* believes but in other divine things, *daimonia kaina*), an offence punishable by death; and (*b*) the corruption of the young. He knows that these charges and similar accusations, brought by Meletus, Anytus, and Lycon, who represent poets, craftsmen, public figures, and orators, have been in the air for many years. Socrates distinguishes between his present accusers, whom he treats with contempt, and the older ones, whom he links directly with *The Clouds* of Aristophanes (19b–c). The older accusers charge him with being an unjust busybody, investigating things beneath the earth and in the heavens and making the weaker argument the stronger. The great danger in these accusations is the link with impiety towards the gods, if not atheism, a link which Aristophanes reinforced by associating Socrates with the natural philosophers and the Sophists. Nevertheless, the problem for Socrates is not the specific legacy of Aristophanes, but the fact that these prejudices against him, whatever their source, have become embedded in society, and are believed by 'the many' (see 19d, 20c). Socrates believes that this hostility from 'the many', and not the particular accusation of Meletus, is the actual source of his condemnation (28a).

It is tempting to regard this aspect of Socrates' defence, that is to say, his belief in the role of 'the many' in his condemnation, as one that reveals a hostility to democracy, but Socrates is developing a more sociological point concerning the transmission of ideas and values in society rather than expressing ideological opposition to democratic rule. As Socrates makes clear in the discussion of his *daimonion*, his indifference to politics is an indifference to both the democracy and the earlier oligarchy (the rule of the Thirty) (32b–d). Socrates' position is reminiscent of that of Protagoras, who explains in the 'Great Speech' of Plato's *Protagoras* how morality is passed on by parents, teachers, and friends from one generation to another (320c–328d). This speech, often taken for an early statement of the virtues of democracy, is more an account of the transmission of values in any society.

In the *Apology* Socrates is ostensibly being accused by experts or representatives of experts in various fields, but the real source of his condemnation is a pattern deeply embedded in the beliefs of 'the many'. Against this force he juxtaposes only himself. Although he recognizes that he has many friends in the court (and the vote is a close one), his emphasis is placed on the opposition of himself, as a philosopher who actively pursues the truth wherever it leads, to the confused opinions held by 'the many' and reflected in different respects by their representatives. In the *Apology* itself Socrates chooses Meletus to represent 'the many'. To the accusation that Socrates corrupts the young, Socrates 'refutes' Meletus by forcing him to adopt the Protagorean argument that everyone in society, and especially the laws, teaches virtue, while Socrates argues that, as with horses where the trainer makes the horses better, so it is the one person or a few who make people better. It is as though Meletus cannot see himself as distinct from 'the many' to whom Socrates ascribes the source of his present predicament. While he goes on to deal with other aspects of the indictment with great effect, especially the self-contradictory nature of Meletus' position in holding that Socrates is an atheist but he believes in divine beings, the problem of the opinions of 'the many' and the legacy of the old accusers give an air of inevitability to the outcome of the trial.

What prevents the *Apology* from being read as a tragedy, in which Socrates' fate is determined from the outset, is his attitude towards death. Socrates' belief that he knows nothing of death and hence cannot fear it makes him remarkably fearless in the face of death and beyond the reach of the opinions and accusations of 'the many'. His attitude towards death, indifferent at the outset but which at the end of the dialogue becomes almost a positive enthusiasm (under the influence of his *daimonion*, 40b ff.), rescues the dialogue from the realm of tragedy, and under the guidance of Socratic irony turns it towards comedy. 'The many' apparently do not share his serenity in the face of death.

The account of Socrates' trial in the *Apology* is both an attempt to defend Socrates against the specific charges against him and an opportunity to explain the political significance of his unique way of life. In this respect Socrates' discussion of his *daimonion* is especially relevant. It has already featured in the trial as part of the accusation of Meletus, who referred to Socrates as believing not in the gods of the *polis* but in other divine things (24b–c). Socrates himself refers to the *daimonion* as having prevented him from taking an active role in politics, and he makes the remarkable statement in the face of the anger of the court that it has been this that has kept him alive to the ripe old age of 70 years when an active political life in the service of justice would have led to a certain death at the hands of 'the many' (31c–32a).

He presents two examples of how the *daimonion* helped to preserve his life (32b–d). In the first when he was a member of the Council of Five Hundred, as one of the prytanes, he alone opposed a move to try ten generals who had failed to rescue survivors from a naval battle, because he believed that such a trial would be illegal. At the time, he notes, the orators were prepared to lead the action to arrest and try him. In the second example he was summoned by the Thirty and ordered with four others to arrest Leon of Salamis. While the others did as they were ordered, Socrates refused to carry out the unjust order and went home. He notes here that had the Thirty not fallen from power shortly afterwards he would probably have been put to death.

Scholars have found it difficult to determine what political role Socrates claims for himself, when he states that to survive one should live 'a private but not a public life' (32a). The two examples reveal Socrates performing his duties as a citizen but refusing to commit injustice or any illegal act. They show him as an active participant in politics, as far as his role as a citizen requires, though he obviously makes no attempt to become a political leader in Athens or to bring his ideas before the community as a whole. His depiction of himself prior to the discussion of his *daimonion* as being attached to the *polis* as a stinging gadfly to a horse (30e) is hardly one that is compatible with a wholly passive private life apart from politics. Yet the image of the gadfly is particularly apt in depicting both the power and the vulnerability (a painful sting but easily destroyed) of Socrates and his peculiar standing in the *polis*. In conjunction with this account one might see Socrates' poverty (31b–c) as a badge of his involvement in public life; he has not devoted himself to his family or to money-making in place of a devotion to public affairs.

At the beginning of his defence Socrates provides an important account of his wisdom which may have a bearing on this attempt to explain what he means by living a private life. He insists that his reputation in Athens and the long-standing prejudice against him are due to a sort of wisdom (20d–21a). This was confirmed by his late friend Chaerephon, who, when asking the oracle at Delphi about Socrates' wisdom, was told that there was no one wiser than Socrates. Socrates then set out to test this statement and began to question those with a reputation for wisdom: the politicians, poets, craftsmen, and orators. He found that these people had a reputation for wisdom but in his view were not wise at all. One assumes that he questioned these various experts by means of the *elenchus*, and no other test is suggested. The *elenchus* probably enables Socrates to reach the conclusion that they are not wise and that he is wiser in knowing nothing about these matters. Such a conclusion could not be reached by self-examination in private, as it requires others for the *elenchus* to take place. Where Socrates states that the 'unexamined life is not worth living' (38a), he clearly does not mean only self-examination. The use of the *elenchus* to determine whether others are wise makes it a public method for assessing wisdom, and when one recalls that reputations for wisdom are generated not only by the experts but by 'the many' who accord the experts their reputations, it is clear that the *elenchus* takes Socrates to direct opposition to the opinions of 'the many'.

Although Socrates never wavers in his commitment to knowledge and virtue, his attempts to avoid public condemnation with the assistance of his *daimonion* actually leads to public condemnation, in so far as his *daimonion* is believed to challenge the gods of the *polis*. His use of the *elenchus* also brings him into conflict with those who without wisdom consider others to be wise and give them an undeserved reputation. Socrates has lived a private life only in so far as he has not sought to become a political leader and has not been willing to compromise his search for wisdom and virtue. But he has also lived a public life and like the gadfly will be slapped down by 'the many'. The *Apology* ends with Socrates content to face death. His *daimonion* has not opposed this end to his life. Paradoxically, he turns his sons over to 'the many', whom he charges with the task of rebuking them if they neglect virtue as Socrates has rebuked them (41e). At the end of his defence Socrates thus begins a kind of reconciliation with the *polis* which is continued in the related dialogue, the *Crito*.

## Reconciliation and political philosophy

For so brief a dialogue, the *Crito* has been the subject of considerable debate. At least since David Hume, scholars have seen in Socrates' conversation with the laws (*hoi nomoi*) an early statement of the doctrine of the social contract, albeit one that seems to enjoin passive obedience to the law. More recently, the dialogue has featured in a debate over whether or not Socrates advocates strict obedience to law as a matter of justice or allows for a measure of disobedience to unjust laws. The *Crito* has also contributed to another debate as to whether or not Socrates' preference for Athens over other states (51c ff.) establishes him as a proponent rather than an opponent of democracy. Despite this interest in the dialogue, its most important point of continuity with the *Apology* has tended to be overlooked. For in the dialogue both Socrates and Crito, his interlocutor, acknowledge the power and danger, but ultimate irrelevance, of 'the many' to Socrates' way of life. The dialogue is prompted by Crito's fear that 'the many' will think it odd that he and Socrates' other friends have not rescued him from imprisonment (44b–c). Socrates responds with an expression of indifference to the opinions of 'the many', even though he fully acknowledges that 'the many' possess the power to put them to death (44c, 48a). Crito is also afraid that Socrates fears that, if he escapes, Crito and his friends will suffer at the hands of 'the many' by the confiscation of their property and other penalties. But Socrates dismisses this and related fears with the remark that 'the many' have the power neither to do good nor to do evil; they cannot make a person wise or foolish; they only do whatever occurs to them (44d). It is as though 'the many' are driven by chance alone, and Socrates (47b) contrasts 'the many' with the one person who knows (a reference perhaps to the horse-trainer analogy which Socrates used when he challenged Meletus to explain how Socrates alone corrupted the young).

Having identified 'the many' as the force in society which not only can put Socrates (and Crito) to death but also prompts Crito's fears for reputation, money, Socrates' children, etc. (48c, 49b), Socrates draws a line between his own beliefs on the one hand and those of 'the many' on the other with his assertion that one should never commit evil or return evil with evil (49c–d). As 'the many' commit good or evil acts at random, they can never subscribe to this truth, which seems to have been established through much exercise of the *elenchus*. Socrates' principle clearly establishes him in direct opposition to 'the many'. Although Crito himself agrees with Socrates, it is clear from his concerns for friendship and his reputation that he is more strongly influenced by 'the many' than Socrates himself. At this point Socrates turns away from his trusted friend to speak to himself, as he creates a peculiar abstraction, 'the laws and community of the *polis*' (*hoi nomoi kai to koinon tes poleos*, 50a), with whom he carries on his discussion without any intrusion from 'the many' or, for that matter, from Crito.

This curious invention sets forth the case for remaining in Athens. 'The laws' first pose the problem that they and the whole *polis* might well be destroyed if Socrates flees Athens, because public decisions will then be seen to be undermined. The statement is on the surface extraordinary, as one can easily argue that the departure of one person would have little impact on the *polis*. But Socrates' point may well be more subtle and not a matter of numbers. His departure would mean that his commitment to justice, which finds its reflection in 'the laws' though not in 'the many', who do good or evil indifferently, would also disappear. In Socrates' speech, therefore, Socratic justice and political justice join together to create a force that might counter the force of 'the many'—just as it has in Athens for the seventy years during which Socrates has lived there.

In the next speeches 'the laws' accuse Socrates of acting unjustly in proposing to leave Athens. They stress the fact that Socrates was born, raised, and chose to remain in Athens all of his life. He might have taken his goods and gone to live elsewhere, but he did not do so. He might even have chosen exile as his penalty. 'The laws' emphasize the nurturing aspect of the *polis* in caring for him as well as an implied agreement with him to obey the laws. Socrates must do what the *polis* commands or try to persuade it to take the right path, that is to say, the path of justice (51c). If such persuasion fails, one must still obey the law, as 'the laws' offer no clear option for civil disobedience. Nevertheless, even the unjust commands of 'the laws' are different from those of 'the many'. The actions of 'the many' are guided by chance, while the commands of 'the laws' are known and settled. 'The laws' do not command in a rough way and always provide the option to be persuaded of their injustice (52a). 'The many' do not appear to be open to such persuasion, except perhaps as individuals via the *elenchus*.

Socrates' personification of 'the laws' concludes by rescuing his children and even Crito himself from the clutches of 'the many'. If at the end of the *Apology* Socrates was content to leave the care of his children in the hands of 'the many', at the end of the *Crito* 'the laws' assure him that they will be better off in Athens than if he takes them into exile and that they will be cared for by friends. 'The laws' seem at this point the main civilizing force and opposition to the power of 'the many', and Socrates, speaking through his creation, insists that he has been treated unjustly not by the laws but only by men (54c).

One of Socrates' contributions to political philosophy is to raise the political horizon above the actual state of day-to-day politics in Athens. At this level of Athenian politics there seems to be an unbridgeable gulf between the philosopher who will never act unjustly and who believes that it is better to receive injustice than to commit it on the one hand, and, on the other hand, 'the many', who act by chance (they do whatever occurs to them) and commit unjust acts as readily as they commit just ones. But Socrates looks beyond day-to-day politics and sees that there are important points of contact between philosophical understanding and politics, in this case via his conception of 'the laws'. In one sense this is merely Socrates' invention designed to persuade Crito, if he can, that it is right to remain and die, and not a violation of friendship. In another sense this is a profound idea linking philosophical wisdom with the real needs of political society, and has echoes in our day whenever one asserts the importance of the rule of law over the more arbitrary rule of men. So general an idea is given concrete expression in the decision of Socrates to remain in Athens and drink the juice of the hemlock.

## Socrates and Athenian democracy

In raising the question of Socrates' attachment to Athenian democracy or to democracy generally, it is important not to confuse Socratic philosophy with any ideological commitment one might ascribe to him. A number of scholars have argued that Socrates' conception of the *elenchus* alone reveals a deep democratic faith. Its use is open to all and discriminates against no one, rich or poor, intellectually strong or weak. It eschews technical language and leads to no philosophical system that might be accessible only to a few. But one might equally argue that Socrates calls into question and challenges the conventional bases of morality and, indeed, religion on which the security of many people depends. It is no accident that a sufficient number of ordinary citizens in a democracy felt that Socrates had so undermined their way of life that his conviction was secured. The Socratic paradoxes which seem to make virtue depend on knowledge might also be seen not only as challenging common understanding but also as devaluing a simple virtue that is based more on habit than on knowledge. Though the *elenchus* is open to all, Socrates is no egalitarian, and only a few, if any, would seem to seek wisdom. To believe that the Socratic *elenchus* is somehow democratic or demophilic is to politicize the *elenchus*.

The Socratic *elenchus* was established within a framework of what can be described as philosophical politics and represents Socrates' legacy to Western political thought. He not only urges each person to care for his or her soul, but also suggests on numerous occasions the political implications of doing so. His commitment to rational argument leads him to challenge established morality and to suggest a raising of the political horizon beyond ideology to grasp certain truths, for example, as we have seen, the importance of the rule of law in any political society.

Another element in Socratic philosophy that has recently been politicized, and for the same reasons as the *elenchus*, is his use of the analogies with the various arts and crafts. Given Socrates' claims in the *Gorgias* (521d) for the existence of a true political art and his numerous arguments concerning moral expertise, one might conclude that he favoured rule by moral and political experts and is hostile to democracy. It has been suggested that this emphasis on moral and political experts was passed on from Socrates to Plato, where it reappears in the guise of the ultimate political expert, the philosopher–king. Others argue that because Socrates takes the position (following the oracle at Delphi) that he is wise precisely because he knows nothing and thereby rejects expert knowledge, Socrates (but not Plato) is therefore favourable to democracy. Still others argue that Socrates does not in fact reject the ruling expertise of the possessor of craft-knowledge but only believes that he himself has not yet discovered such expertise. On these grounds Socrates is not considered pro-democratic.

I have argued that Socrates employs various analogies with the arts and crafts as part of the *elenchus* in order to develop and elucidate points. Such use does not necessarily commit one to political rule by experts even though the suggestion of a true political art in the *Gorgias* might lead to that conclusion. But this suggestion should be seen in the context of the overall argument in the *Gorgias* in which a contrast is being developed to undermine the claims of rhetoric to be the true political art. Socrates' use of the craft analogy is thus politicized, when aspects of analogies used in the *elenchus* are taken from the context of particular dialogues and revealed to have special political significance. But when he speaks of the importance of craft knowledge or when he denies all knowledge, the implications for democracy are actually minimal.

One reason for the belief that the craft analogy is pregnant with political significance has evolved from a political undercurrent that has emerged to distinguish the views of Socrates from those of Plato. It is commonly asserted that Plato's *Republic*, for example, represents a betrayal of Socratic philosophy. According to this view, Plato's belief that only the wise, a tiny elite, should rule constitutes a rejection of Socrates' doctrine, which is individualistic, liberal, and open to everyone.

The complex and highly stipulative arguments that distinguish Plato's Socrates from Plato himself using Socrates as an interlocutor in the end are combined with the use of the craft analogy to make political points about democratic and authoritarian tendencies in both Socrates and Plato. This political dimension then obscures the rich philosophical understanding in both Socrates and Plato, and their numerous discoveries, which form the foundation of Western political thought. The starting point for these discoveries is the recognition of the gulf between Socratic philosophy on the one hand and the power and authority of 'the many' on the other. The foundation of Western political thought is that every political society needs to have the truth or, at the minimum, to allow the quest for truth. Socrates establishes this point in numerous ways (see the example of his being the gadfly in Athens), but fundamental to his understanding is that the very existence of the quest for truth is opposed by 'the many', and unless some accommodation is made between the philosopher and *polis*, there can be no true understanding, no virtue, and especially no justice. Compared with this enterprise, that Socrates admired or disliked Athenian democracy is of little account, as is his apparent admiration of the laws of Sparta.

But 'the many' and their views exist everywhere, and in Athens are addressed by Socrates in particular ways. Socrates refers to 'the many' on numerous occasions, but there is no way to speak to this body directly. He is content to speak to their representatives, like Meletus in the *Apology*, or to the Sophists in various dialogues, where he reveals their confusions and their lack of concern for the truth. They merely reflect 'the many' and administer to this 'Great Beast' (see Plato, *Republic* 493a–c).

The political thought of Socrates begins a tradition in Western thought of searching for the truth about humanity and society apart from the opinions of 'the many', and then bringing these truths to 'the many' to attempt to restore moral sanity and establish intelligibility in a world often, but never wholly, indifferent to the search for truth on which that sanity and intelligibility rest. The trial and death of Socrates is a powerful symbol of this quest and its potential consequences.

---

## FURTHER READING

Brickhouse, Thomas C., and Smith, Nicholas D., *Plato's Socrates* (New York: Oxford University Press, 1994).

Brickhouse, Thomas C., and Smith, Nicholas D., *Socrates on Trial* (Princeton: Princeton University Press, 1989).

Guthrie, W. K. C., *Socrates* (Cambridge: Cambridge University Press, 1971).

Kahn, Charles H., *Plato and the Socratic Dialogue: The Philosophical Use of a Literary Form* (Cambridge: Cambridge University Press, 1996).

Kraut, Richard, *Socrates and the State* (Princeton: Princeton University Press, 1984).

Reeve, C. D. C., *Socrates in the 'Apology': An Essay on Plato's Apology of Socrates* (Indianapolis: Hackett, 1989).

Strauss, Leo, *The City and Man* (Chicago: Rand McNally, 1964).

Strauss, Leo, *The Rebirth of Classical Political Rationalism: An Introduction to the Thought of Leo Strauss* (Chicago: University of Chicago Press, 1989).

Strauss, Leo, *Socrates and Aristophanes* (New York: Basic Books, 1966).

Vlastos, Gregory, *Socrates: Ironist and Moral Philosopher* (Cambridge: Cambridge University Press, 1991).

Vlastos, Gregory, *Socratic Studies* (Cambridge: Cambridge University Press, 1994).

## NOTES

1. Leo Strauss, *The City and Man* (Chicago: Rand McNally, 1964); id., *The Rebirth of Classical Political Rationalism: An Introduction to the Thought of Leo Strauss* (Chicago: University of Chicago Press, 1989); id., *Socrates and Aristophanes* (New York: Basic Books, 1966); Gregory Vlastos, *Socrates: Ironist and Moral Philosopher* (Cambridge: Cambridge University Press, 1991); id., *Socratic Studies* (Cambridge: Cambridge University Press, 1994).
2. Strauss, *Socrates and Aristophanes.*
3. Strauss, *The City and Man* and *The Rebirth of Classical Political Rationalism.*
4. According to Vlastos (*Socrates: Ironist and Moral Philosopher*, 46–7, and *Socratic Studies*, 135), the early Platonic, i.e. Socratic, dialogues are (in alphabetical order): *Apology, Charmides, Crito, Euthydemus, Euthyphro, Gorgias, Hippias Major, Hippias Minor, Ion, Laches, Lysis, Menexemus, Protagoras*, and *Republic* 1. The dialogues of the middle period are (in probable chronological order): *Cratylus, Phaedo, Symposium, Republic* 2–10, *Phaedrus, Parmenides*, and *Theaetetus*. The later dialogues are (in probable chronological order): *Timaeus, Critias, Sophist, Politicus, Philebus*, and *Laws*. A modified arrangement has recently been proposed by Charles H. Kahn, *Plato and the Socratic Dialogue: The Philosophical Use of a Literary Form* (Cambridge: Cambridge University Press, 1996), who has set forth a more sophisticated version of the development of Plato's dialogues (including those traditionally regarded as Socratic).
5. Richard Kraut, *Socrates and the State* (Princeton: Princeton University Press, 1984); Thomas C. Brickhouse and Nicholas D. Smith, *Plato's Socrates* (New York: Oxford University Press, 1994). id., *Socrates on Trial* (Princeton: Princeton University Press, 1989).
6. Vlastos, *Socrates: Ironist and Moral Philosopher*, 21–44; C. D. C. Reeve, *Socrates in the 'Apology': An Essay on Plato's 'Apology' of Socrates* (Indianapolis: Hackett, 1989), 184–5.

# 4 Plato

C.D.C. Reeve

## Contents



## Chapter guide

The chapter begins with a sketch of the overall argument of the *Republic* and a characterization of the philosopher–kings who are its centrepiece. The second section deals with the Form of the good, knowledge of which is exclusive and essential to these kings, since it is in the light of it that they design the ideal city in which they rule. The third and fourth sections describe the structure of this city and its central operating principle. The remaining sections evaluate this city from a variety of politically significant perspectives: Is the city based on false ideology? Does it involve a totalitarian intrusion of the political into the private sphere? Does it treat its least powerful members in an unjust way? Does it limit freedom of speech or of artistic expression? Does it limit personal freedom and autonomy?

## Biography

Plato was born in 429 BC and died in 347/8. His father, Ariston, was descended—or so legend has it—from Codrus, the last king of Athens; his mother, Perictione, was related to Solon, architect of the Athenian constitution. His family was aristocratic and well off. He had two brothers, Glaucon and Adeimantus, both of whom appear in the *Republic*, as well as a sister, Potone, whose son, Speusippus, also a philosopher, later became head of Plato's school, the Academy. While Plato was still a boy, his father died and his mother married Pyrilampes, a friend of the great Athenian statesman Pericles. Thus Plato was no stranger to Athenian politics even from childhood and was expected to enter it himself. Horrified by actual political events, however, especially the execution of Socrates in 399 BC (*Apology*), he turned instead to philosophy, thinking that only it could rescue human beings from civil war and political upheaval and provide a sound foundation for ethics and politics (*Seventh Letter* 324b–326b).

Plato's dialogues make fundamental contributions to almost every area of philosophy from ethics, politics, and aesthetics to metaphysics, epistemology, cosmology, the philosophy of science, the philosophy of language, and the philosophy of mind. In addition to composing them, he also founded and directed the Academy, arguably the first university (385 BC). This was a centre of research and teaching both in theoretical subjects, such as philosophy and mathematics, but also in more practical ones. For example, various cities invited its members to help them in the practical task of developing new political constitutions. One might see the *Republic*, therefore, with its curious mix of philosophy, mathematics, and politics, as a synthesis of all that the Academy represented.

## Key texts

Plato's works are customarily divided into four chronological groups, though the precise ordering (especially within groups) is controversial. The following are the best known in each group:

EARLY (alphabetical): *Apology, Crito, Euthyphro, Laches*

TRANSITIONAL (alphabetical): *Gorgias, Meno, Protagoras*

MIDDLE (chronological?): *Phaedo, Symposium, Republic, Phaedrus, Parmenides, Theaetetus*

LATE (chronological?): *Timaeus, Sophist, Statesman, Philebus, Laws, Seventh Letter*

## Main text used

Plato, *Republic*, trans. G. M. A. Grube and C. D. C. Reeve (Indianapolis: Hackett, 1992).

## Key ideas

**Forms** are intelligible, unchanging objects, accessible to the mind but not the senses, which provide the only reliable standards for knowledge and good judgement. The chief of these, on which the others depend both for their being and their knowability, is the **Form of the good.** Collectively, Forms constitute the realm of **Being.** In the perceptible world around us, images of the Forms are interrelated and in continual change or flux. This is the realm of **Becoming.** By looking to the Form of the good, of which he alone has knowledge, the philosopher discovers the true blueprint for the best human world. The **Republic** is the story of what sort of society such a philosopher would produce if he were to acquire political power and become a **philosopher–king.** Central to that story is an attempt to establish that **justice pays**—the we cannot achieve **happiness** except in a just city, so that the best city must be just. Central to that justification, in turn, is a **theory about the human soul or mind**. Each of us has three primary kinds of desires—**appetitive, spirited**, and **rational.** These result in a division of us into three different natural classes: **appetitive** ones, who take happiness to consist in the long-term satisfaction of their appetites; **spirited** ones, who take it to consist in the satisfaction of desires for honour and approval; and **rational** ones, who take it to consist in satisfaction of desires for truth and the overall good. In the just city, each of these classes will have a distinct social role: the appetitive will be **producers** or workers; the spirited will be **guardians** or soldier-police; and the rational will be **rulers.** In fact, justice for a city, it is argued, consists precisely in the enforcement of a **principle of specialization**, which restricts each class to the one social role for which it is naturally best fitted. Political rule or authority depends, therefore, on knowledge, not simply on power or consent of the governed. To ensure the continued identity of the three classes, the rulers tell a 'noble lie': producers have bronze in them, guardians silver, rulers gold. To ensure an adequate supply of guardians and rulers, a **eugenics policy** is instituted, in which a rigged lottery ensures that best will breed more often with best. To prevent the guardians from competing with the producers, 'private property' is outlawed for them. To prevent them from competing with each other, a form of 'communism' is mandated for them, requiring them to hold their property, spouses, and children in common. To prevent them from being corrupted, strict **censorship** of art is imposed by the rulers on the entire community.

## An overview of the *Republic*

In book 1, Thrasymachus argues that those who are stronger in any society—the rulers—control education and socialization through legislation and enforcement. But, like everyone else, they are self-interested. Hence they make laws and adopt conventions—including linguistic conventions—that are in their own best interests, not those of their weaker subjects. It is these conventions that largely determine their subjects' conceptions of justice and the other virtues. By being trained to follow or obey them, therefore, subjects are unwittingly adopting an ideology, a code of values and behaviour, that serves not their own but their ruler's interests. That is why Thrasymachus defines justice, not as what socialized subjects—like Socrates—think it is (something genuinely noble and valuable that promotes their own happiness), but as what it really is in all cities: *the interest of the stronger*.

In book 1, Socrates tries to refute Thrasymachus using his familiar *elenchus*. But his attempts are not adequate (357a–b, 358b–c). That is why Plato abandons the *elenchus* in subsequent books, and tries to answer Thrasymachus (whose views are taken over by Glaucon and Adeimantus) by developing a positive defence of justice of his own. At the centre of his defence is the concept of the philosopher–kings, who unite political power and authority with philosophical knowledge (based on mathematics and dialectic) of the transcendent, unchanging Form of the good—knowledge that is unmediated by conventionally controlled concepts, and so is free from the distorting influence of power or ideology.

The philosopher–kings are clearly intended to be very intelligent, then, capable of mastering a lot of mathematics and other abstract subjects. But it would be a mistake to consider intelligence alone to be their distinguishing trait. For if they were intelligent, but vicious or immoral, they would simply be Thrasymachus' exploitative tyrants in disguise. To be entitled to rule not only must they know how to do so well, but they must rule in a just and virtuous way. Political authority for Plato is based not on force or on the consent of the ruled alone, therefore, but on knowledge and virtue both. Hence the education Plato designs for the philosopher–kings, as we are about to see, aims as much to make them virtuous—to shape their desires, so that they will want and enjoy only what is really good—as to make them knowledgeable. But it would also be a mistake to separate these factors: knowing the Form of the good is an ethical achievement as well as a cognitive one. For the philosopher–kings would not recognize the right thing as the good if they did not also love and take pleasure in it above all else (580a–592b).

What the philosopher–kings do, once in office, so to speak, is to construct a political system—including primarily a system of socialization and education—that will distribute the benefits of this specialized knowledge among the citizens at large. There is no question of the knowledge itself being so disseminated; like much expert knowledge in our own society, it is far too complex and difficult for that. As a result, the examined life, which Socrates thought best for all human beings (*Apology* 38a), is now led only by mature adults who have had very extensive scientific and dialectical training (531d ff.).

The nature of the system the philosopher–kings design is based on Plato's psychology, or theory of the soul (*psyche*). According to it, there are three fundamentally different kinds of desire: *appetitive* ones for food, drink, sex, and the money with which to acquire them; *spirited* ones for honour, victory, and good reputation; and *rational* ones for knowledge and truth (437b ff., 580d ff.). Each of these types of desire 'rules' in the soul of a different type of person, determining his values. For people most value what they most desire, and so people ruled by different desires have very different conceptions of what is valuable, of their good or happiness. But just which desire 'rules' an individual's soul depends on the relative strengths of his desires and the kind of education and socialization he receives. It is scarcely surprising, in light of these views, that Plato believes that the fundamental goal of ethical or political education isn't to put knowledge into people's souls but to train or socialize their desires, turning them around (to the degree possible) from the pursuit of what they falsely believe to be happiness to the pursuit of true happiness (518b–519d).

The famous allegory of the Cave illustrates the effects of such education (514a). Uneducated people, tethered (or ruled) by their untrained or unsocialized appetites, see only images of models of the good (shadows cast by puppets on the walls of the cave). They are not virtuous to any degree, since they act simply on their whims. When their appetites are trained through physical education and that mix of reading and writing, dance and song, that the Greeks call *mousike* (music), they are released from these bonds and are now ruled by their trained or socialized appetites. They have at least that level of virtue required to act prudently and postpone gratification. Plato refers to them as *money-lovers*, since they pursue money as the best means of reliably satisfying their appetitive desires for food, drink, and sex in the long term (580d–581a). They see models of the good (the puppets that cast the shadows). For stable satisfaction of appetitive desires *is* a sort of good.

Further education, now in mathematical science, leaves these people ruled by their spirited desires. They are *honour-lovers*, who seek success in difficult endeavours and the honour and approval it brings. They have true beliefs about virtue and hence that greater level of it that Plato calls 'civic' virtue (430c).

Finally, yet further education in dialectic and practical city management results in people who are bound only by their rational desires. They are free from illusion, and see not mere images of the good, but the good-itself. They are *wisdom-lovers*, or philosophers, who have knowledge rather than mere true belief about virtue and so are fully virtuous.

Not everyone is able to benefit, however, from all these types of education; there are some at each stage whose desires are too strong for education to break. That is why there are producers, guardians, and philosopher–kings in the ideal city. That is why, too, as the citizens of the ideal city, or *kallipolis*, they can cooperate with one another in a just system, where the money-loving producers trade their products for the protection provided by the honour-loving guardians and the knowledge provided by the wisdom-loving kings, rather than competing with one another for the very same goods. Nonetheless, everyone in this ideal system is enabled to travel as far out of the cave of unsocialized desires as education can take him given the innate strength of those desires. Thus everyone comes as close to being fully virtuous and to pursuing and achieving genuine happiness as he can. It is this that makes Plato's city both an ethical and a prudential ideal, both maximally just and maximally happy. Hence it constitutes a response to the Trasymachean challenged raised anew by Glaucon and Adeimantus in book 2. For if maximal justice and maximal happiness go together, then it pays in terms of happiness to be just rather than unjust.

## Forms and the good-itself

In the discussion of music and poetry in book 2 Socrates says: 'You and I, Adeimantus, aren't poets, but we *are* founding a city. And it's appropriate for the founders to know the patterns (*tupoi*) on which poets must base their stories and from which they mustn't deviate. But we aren't actually going to compose their poems for them' (378e–379a). Adeimantus responds by asking what these patterns for stories about the gods actually are. Socrates' lengthy answer, extending over many pages, may be summed up without much loss as follows: No 'bad images of what the gods and heroes are like' (377e); only stories that will make the guardians 'least afraid of death' (386a); no 'frightening and dreadful names for the underworld' (387b); no 'lamentations of famous men' (387e); no representation of 'worthwhile people as overcome by laughter' (388e–389a); no representation of gods or heroes as failing 'to rule the pleasures of drink, sex, and food for themselves' (389d–e); no 'headstrong words spoken in prose or poetry by private citizens against their rulers' (390a); no imitators except 'the pure imitator of a decent person' (397d); no modes except the Dorian and Phrygian (399a); no music played on flutes, triangular lutes, harps, or 'other multistringed and polyharmonic instruments' (399c); no rhythms except those appropriate to 'someone who leads an ordered and courageous life' (399d).

The way the philosopher reaches these patterns, moreover, is readily intelligible. He looks at the effects that various kinds of poetry have on a guardian's soul. He determines what kind of soul the guardians should have by looking to the role of guardians in the good city (500b–501c, 618b–e), and he determines what that role should be by looking to the good-itself, since it is only through knowing it that he knows any other kind of good at all (534b–c).

The patterns the philosopher reaches in this way are Forms. But they are, as we have seen, quite unspecific: they are not detailed blueprints for actual poems. All they determine are the features that a *good* poem must have. The same, presumably, is true of beds and the rest. Thus the philosopher's pattern of an *F* simply specifies the features an *F* must have, or must lack, *if it is to be good*. It isn't a blueprint for an actual *F*, and it certainly isn't an *F* of any kind (paradigm or otherwise).

To see more clearly what such a Form or pattern is, we turn to the difficult Sun analogy. This has both an epistemological side, dealing with knowledge and its objects, and a metaphysical or ontological side, dealing with being or reality. We shall begin with the former:

> [1] [*a*] What gives truth to the things known, and the power to know to the knower is the form of the good. And [*b*] though it is the cause of knowledge and truth, it is also an object of knowledge. [*c*] Both knowledge and truth are beautiful things but the good is other and more beautiful than they. In the visible realm, [*d*] light and sight are rightly considered sunlike, but it is wrong to think that

> they are the sun, so here it is right to think of knowledge and truth as goodlike, but wrong to think that either of them is the good—for the good is yet more prized. (508e–509a)

The good, then, is (1*d*) something like a self-illuminating object that can shed the intelligible analogue of light on other objects of knowledge—other paradigms—in such a way as to render them intelligible: it is an intelligible object that is somehow a condition of the intelligibility of other things. This suggests that the 'light' the good itself gives off is something like rational or logical order, and that it itself is a paradigm of such order or structure.

To make all this a little less metaphorical, suppose we have a correct account or definition of a Form, *F*. Since the account is correct, it must exhibit whatever level of rational or logical order is required for truth—at a minimum, it must be consistent. And because the account is made true by *F*, that Form itself must, at a minimum, possess the level of rational order that is an ontological correlate of consistency. Without rational order, then, there would be no truth, and so no knowledge. If the good-itself were indeed the Form or paradigm of rational order, therefore, (1*a*) would be readily intelligible. But so, too, would (1*b*–*c*). For since the good is itself a Form, it would be an object of knowledge just like all the others. But as the cause of their intelligibility or knowability, it would be 'other than they'.

The metaphysical side of the Sun analogy is next:

> [2] You'll be willing to say, I think, that the sun not only provides visible things with the power to be seen but also with coming to be, growth, and nourishment, although it is not itself coming to be . . . Therefore, you should also say that the objects of knowledge not only owe their being known to the good but their being is also due to it, although the good is not being, but superior to it in rank and power. (509b)

Visible things—including the sun—are components of the visible realm. But the sun has a very special role therein: without it there would be no such realm. The same holds of the good considered as a paradigm of rational order. Like the other Forms, it is a component of the intelligible realm. But it has a special place therein: without it, there would be no such realm. That would explain why the good is characterized as 'not being, but superior to it in rank and power'.

The relationship between the good-itself and the other Forms, to which I now turn, is best revealed by a particularly problematic case, namely, that presented by 'bad' Forms, such as the Form of the ugly or shameful, the Form of injustice, and the Form of the bad (402b–c, 475e–476a). For it is particularly hard to see how these can owe their being and their knowability to the good-itself. We are helped, however, by the discussion of good and bad in book 10. There Plato writes that 'The bad is what in every case destroys and corrupts and the good is what preserves and benefits' (608e). But goodness and badness are not generic; rather, they are so indexed to kinds of things that only a kind's *natural* goodness or badness preserves or destroys it: thus rot, not rust, destroys wood, and rust, not rot, destroys iron (608e–609b). Relative to each kind of thing, then, we have a pair of opposed items, the (natural) good and the (natural) bad, each with a distinct function: the function of the good is to preserve or benefit the kind; the function of the bad is to destroy or corrupt it. On the (simplifying) assumption that preserving is low-level benefiting and that destruction is high-level corruption, I shall call these three related items *kinds*, *benefiters*, and *corrupters*.

If the good is a paradigm of rational order, all three of these items, as members of the intelligible realm, must be instances of rational order. Yet they differ significantly from one another. Perhaps the easiest way to capture these differences is as follows: A kind is an instance of rational order which *as such* is neither good nor bad. To be good it needs to have its level of rational order enhanced by the appropriate benefiter; to be bad it needs to have its level of rational order reduced by the appropriate corrupter. For example, a body, as such, is neither bad nor good—it exhibits only a moderate level of rational order: 'I believe that there are, as it were, three kinds—the good, the bad, and the neither good nor bad . . . Disease is a bad thing, and medicine is beneficial and good . . . But a body, of course, taken to be just a body, is neither good nor bad' (*Lysis* 216d5–217b3). Add health (the appropriate benefiter) to a body, then, and it has sufficient rational order to be a good body; add sickness (the corresponding corrupter) and it is sufficiently deficient in rational order to be a bad one. But despite the fact that a body as such is neither good nor bad, it yet owes a debt to the good. If there were no such thing as rational order, even the level of rational order exhibited by the Form of a body as such—the level needed for it to be a truth-maker for the account of a body—would be impossible, and the Form would not be an intelligible, knowable entity.

Now consider a corrupter, such as the Form of injustice. It is a pattern of rational order—a knowable, intelligible thing, 'a kind of civil war between the three parts [of the soul], a meddling and doing of another's work, a rebellion of some part against the whole soul in order to rule it inappropriately' (444b). Hence it owes its knowability or intelligibility—indeed its very being—to the existence of rational order, to the existence of the good-itself. But the fact that it is a pattern of rational order does not make it a good thing—it could be neither good nor bad (like a body as such) or it could be good (like health or virtue), or it could be bad (like ophthalmia, rot, or disease). What makes it in fact bad is that it is a pattern of rational order that is opposed to the rational order of a kind, which will corrupt instances of it by causing their natural level of rational order to degrade to such an extent that they no longer fit the kind at all (609c). Contrariwise, what would make injustice a *benefiter*, if it were one, would be that it enhances the rational order of some kind.

The good preserves and benefits. Benefiters are indexed to kinds. It would seem to follow that the good must also be indexed to a kind. But which one? The answer suggested by the Sun analogy is this: the kind to which the good is indexed is itself. In other words, the good-itself is a self-benefiter (more accurately, a self-preserver, since it does not increase the level of its own rational order) that depends epistemically and metaphysically on itself. Perhaps this seems mysterious, but if the good just is the Form of rational order, it is actually quite natural. To think otherwise would be to think that the sun could not be the source of the very light that makes it itself visible. What about the bad-itself? Well, as a Form, as a pattern of rational order, it owes its being and its being knowable to the good. So the bad is dependent on the good. But since—like the Form of injustice discussed earlier—it is a destroyer, it is not itself good but bad.

The good-itself is not specifically political goodness, then, but it is a standard or paradigm that enables the philosopher to determine what political goodness is, just as it enables him to determine this about poetic goodness or scientific goodness or any other kind of goodness. It is for this reason that the crafts as a whole need philosophy. Consider shoemaking, for example. The shoemaker knows how to make a shoe—he has access to the Form of a shoe (596b). But he does not, *qua* shoemaker, know how to make a good shoe—one that reliably contributes to human happiness. For that he must turn to the philosopher. For only the philosopher knows the good-itself, and so can judge the goodness of the cities of which shoemakers, and all other craftsmen, must form a part if human happiness is to be reliably achieved. That, and the philosopher's rather differently based need of them, is what makes the good city possible in Plato's view (369b ff.).

## The structure of the *kallipolis*

Owing to divine inspiration, Socrates already knows the good-itself at the outset of the *Republic*, and so is in a position to act as a pretend philosopher–king (496a–e, 506d–e)—'pretend' because he isn't a king, only a philosopher. We might expect that his first step in this role will be to draft a constitution and a set of laws for the *kallipolis*. Instead, he focuses almost exclusively on designing a social structure that will dispose all the citizens to virtue. The reason for this is ultimately psychological. Plato believes two things: first, that unless socialization (including education) makes our appetites and emotions as responsive as possible to reason, so that we acquire civic virtue, no system of laws will be effective; secondly, that once we acquire civic virtue, legislation is a routine matter (422e–427d). Put the other way round, he believes that the threat posed to political good order by 'anarchic' appetites is the greatest political evil of all. It is this belief that explains so much that we are likely to find most abhorrent in the *Republic*, such as the lies of the rulers, the critique of the family and private property, and the censorship of art. Of more immediate relevance, it is also what explains the way in which Plato structures his account of the *kallipolis*—the good or maximally happy human community that is the centrepiece of Plato's political theory and of the *Republic* itself.

This account is laid out in three stages, each of which describes an apparently different city (472d–e): city-1 (369a–372d), city-2 (372e–471c), and city-3 (473b–544b). In reality, however, each of these apparently autonomous cities is a part of the *kallipolis*, not an autonomous city at all. In book 5, for example, Socrates undertakes to show that the city-2 is a real possibility—that it could really exist (473a–b). What he actually does, however, is to show that city-3 has this feature (473b–544b). And city-3 is not the same as the city-2. For though city-2 is 'good', city-3 is 'still finer' (543c–544b). The question is, why does Plato proceed in this way?

A natural line of thought is this: city-2 is not *by itself* a real possibility. That is why no attempt is made to show that it is one. But when modified in some respects it is a part of a city—namely city-3—which is a real possibility. Hence if Plato can show that city-3 is a real possibility, he will have shown that the same holds of city-2. If city-2 stands in this relation to city-3, however, the thought suggests itself that the three cities might constitute an ordered series of city-parts each of which, when modified, is a component of its successor, with only city-3 being a complete, actually realizable city. This, in turn, suggests that this ordered series is Plato's way of explaining why the *kallipolis* must have the elaborate structure it does, replete with philosopher–kings, guardians, and producers.

City-1, for example, seems to be the part of the *kallipolis* inhabited by the money-lovers or producers. It is not a real possibility, however, because it includes nothing to counteract the destabilizing effects of unnecessary appetites, and the *pleonexia* (the desire to have more and more without limit) to which they inevitably give rise (372e–374a). For this guardians (soldier–police) are required. When these are added, the result is city-2, which contains the political and educational institutions necessary to produce such guardians. City-2 contains both the part of the *kallipolis* inhabited by honour-lovers, or guardians, and also city-1. But city-2 is not a real possibility either, because it includes nothing to counteract the destabilizing effects of an untrammelled love of honour. For this philosopher–kings are required. When these are added, the result is city-3, which contains the political and educational institutions necessary to produce philosopher–kings. City-3, which Plato thinks *is* a real possibility, is the *kallipolis* for money-lovers, honour-lovers, *and* philosophers. To use a convenient Hegelianism, city-1 is 'overcome but preserved' in city-2, and city-2 in city-3.

On this view, Plato is at work on the *kallipolis* from the moment he begins the account of city-1 at 369b5. His method is more nearly one of slowly drawing back the veil to uncover more and more of what he has in mind than of introducing and discarding first one city then another.

## Specialization

In books 2–5 Plato seems to accept the *unique aptitude doctrine*, according to which each person is born with a natural aptitude for a unique craft or type of work—a unique way of life or social role: 'A physician has a different nature than a carpenter' (454d), 'one woman is a physician by nature, another not, one is by nature musical, another non-musical' (455e). On the basis of this doctrine, moreover, Plato seems to accept a prescriptive principle: each member of the *kallipolis must* practise exclusively throughout life the unique craft for which he has a natural aptitude (370a–b, 374a–c, 394e, 423c–d, 433a, 443b–c, 453b). This is *the principle of specialization*. It invariably rubs up readers of the *Republic* the wrong way, since it is so counterintuitive and restrictive. Yet despite all the apparent evidence to the contrary, Plato accepts neither the unique aptitude doctrine nor the principle of specialization.

If Plato did accept the unique aptitude doctrine, his psychological theory would presumably have to have room for it; but it doesn't. Indeed, it absolutely excludes the possibility of one person having a natural aptitude for carpentry and another for pottery. For, according to it, all 'lovers of crafts' have the same cognitive abilities—they have belief rather than knowledge (475d–480a)—and all of them are money-lovers, with the same ruling desires, the same conception of the good (580d ff.). Something similar is true of rulers (wisdom-lovers) and guardians (honour-lovers). That is why, while we hear of the children of producers being taken off to be trained as guardians because of their natural aptitudes (415b–c), and of guardians being demoted to the ranks of producers for failing to live up to expectations (468a), we never hear of a carpenter's child being removed to a potter's house for upbringing because he has no aptitude for his father's craft. Indeed, Plato seems simply to assume that the normal thing is for a child to follow in the craft of his parents (456d, 467a).

Plato does not hold the unique aptitude doctrine, then, and so he cannot hold the principle of specialization either, since the latter presupposes the former. What he does accept, however, is *the unique upper-bound doctrine*, according to which a person's ruling desires set a distinct upper limit to his cognitive development. Indeed, this doctrine, as we saw, is the cornerstone of his psychological theory. Moreover, because he accepts the unique upper-bound doctrine, he also accepts *the principle of quasi-specialization*, which states that each person in the *kallipolis must* practise exclusively throughout life whichever of producing, guardianship, or ruling demands of him the highest level of cognitive development of which he is capable: money-lovers must be producers of some kind; honour-lovers must be guardians; philosophers must be kings (434a–b).

It should come as no surprise, then, that in book 4 the principle of specialization is identified as a merely provisional first stab at the principle of quasi-specialization, and is explicitly replaced by it. If *all* the practitioners of the various ordinary crafts 'exchange their tools and honours', so that the principle of specialization is thoroughly violated, that does 'no great harm to the city' (434a). Violations of the principle of quasi-specialization, on the other hand, are a political disaster, the 'ruin of the city' (434a–b). For the principle of specialization was never anything more than 'a sort of image of justice' (443c), whereas the principle of quasi-specialization is the very essence of both individual and political justice (434c, 443c–d): a soul is just if its three constituent parts—reason, spirit, appetite—obey this new principle, as is a city when its parts—rulers, guardians, producers—do the same. Not only does the principle of specialization have no place in Plato's psychological theory, therefore; it has no place in his politics, in his theory of justice, either.

## The lies of the rulers

On a number of occasions we are told that the philosopher–kings will often find it necessary or useful to lie to the guardians and producers. The spectre of false ideology and exploitation is immediately raised. At the end of book 2, however, a distinction between two types of lie or falsehood (*pseudos*) is introduced. The first type, referred to as 'the genuine lie' or 'what is really a lie' (382a, 382c), is a 'lie about the governing things [told] to the governing parts of the soul' (382a–b). The second type of lie, referred to as 'the verbal lie' or 'the lie in words', is a 'sort of imitation' of a genuine lie (382b–c), which is useful 'against enemies and those of one's so-called friends who, through madness or ignorance, are attempting to do some wrong, in order to turn them away from it' (382c–d).

To be a genuine lie, or the content of one, then, a proposition must be held or believed by the governing part of the soul, i.e. reason—the part that is concerned about the good of the soul as a whole. In essence, then, a genuine lie is one that misleads reason, and so prevents the soul itself from achieving the good. The account of verbal lies now seems straightforward. *B* is attempting to do *x*, falsely believing—'through madness or ignorance'—that it is good to do it. *A* knows that it is not good for *B* to do *x*. Hence *A* tells *B* something he knows to be false in order to prevent *B* from doing *x*. *A* has lied to *B*. But *B* does not come to have a false belief about the good in the rational part of his soul as a result. Indeed, he is steered towards the good, not away from it. A genuine lie misleads the governing part of the soul about the good. A verbal lie may seem to do the same—especially to the person (*B* in our example) who discovers he has been lied to. For *B*, of course, believes that doing *x* *is* a good thing to do. That is why a verbal lie is 'a sort of imitation' of a genuine lie. But it is not 'an altogether pure lie' because it does not in fact mislead reason about the good. The verbal lie 'comes into being after' the genuine lie (382b–c), because *A* cannot reliably lie in words until he knows the good-itself and is in a position to tell genuine lies that mislead reason about it. That is why everyone, except the philosopher–kings, who alone know the good-itself, must avoid lies altogether (389b–c).

That the lies of the rulers are all intended to be verbal rather than genuine is made clear by Plato's examples. One of these is the well-known myth of the Metals (414b–415d). Since it is referred to as 'one of those lies that are sometimes necessary, of which we were just now speaking, one noble lie' (414b–c), it is clearly intended to be verbal. Its function is to tie the members of the *kallipolis* to each other by bonds of love or friendship (415d). But their friendship is in fact well founded in mutual self-interest. So this lie fits our account. Those who believe it do not come to believe a genuine lie. For the belief benefits them, and leads them towards the good-itself, not away from it.

We last hear about the lies of the rulers in book 5 in connection with the lottery secretly rigged by the rulers to ensure that the best men 'have sex with the best women as frequently as possible' (459c–460a). Here again the lie that luck not planning controls the sexual lottery is intended to be verbal, since it is supposed to benefit the city as a whole by preserving the quality of the guardian class. One cannot help feeling, however, that Plato's intentions are less than well realized here. For sex is something even honour-loving guardians enjoy—that is why getting to have it often is a reward for them (460b, 468b–c). Consequently, the loss of it, which inferior guardians suffer in the *kallipolis*, is a real loss—one, moreover, for which they are not compensated. If this is a defect in the *kallipolis*, however, it is surely a minor one. Plato has, for contingent historical reasons, simply chosen a less than optimum solution to the problem at hand. For he has no objection to sex per se—when guardians are beyond the age of reproduction they are allowed to have sex with anyone they want, provided they avoid incest (461b–c). Hence contraception would provide a better solution to the eugenics problem than rigged lotteries.

To grasp the philosophical significance of all this, we need to draw a few distinctions. If the citizens in a city falsely believe that they are happier there than elsewhere, in part because the world-view they have been taught is false, and known to be false by the rulers, they are the victims of *false ideology*. If, on the other hand, the citizens have a true belief that they are happier, but have it because they have been taught to accept a world-view that is false (or contains some beliefs that are false), and known to be false by their rulers, their ideology is *falsely sustained*. Finally, if the citizens in a city believe that they are happier there and their belief is both true and sustained by a true world-view, they and their city are *ideology-free*. Because the lies of the rulers are verbal lies it is clear that the producers and guardians who believe them are not the victims of false ideology. But because what they believe is false, and known by the philosopher–kings to be false, their ideology is falsely sustained.

However, the world-views available to the producers and guardians in the *kallipolis* are intended to be as close to the truth as their natural abilities and ruling desires allow. For it is only when guided by the knowledge of the philosopher–kings that the producers' and guardians' (imperfect) access to the good-itself is as reliable as possible. So although the producers and guardians do not see their values or their place in the *kallipolis* with complete clarity, their vision is as undistorted as their natures, fully developed by education, allow.

It is obvious that everyone has a self-interested reason to avoid a city in which he is the victim of false ideology. But it is not so clear that everyone has a reason to avoid one in which his ideology is falsely sustained, especially if the degree of falsehood involved is minimal. Indeed, it may be rational for him to prefer such a city to one that is altogether ideology-free. It all depends on what his natural abilities are, and on what he most wants in life. If, for example, he most enjoys a life devoted to the pleasure of knowing the truth, he will be maximally happy only in a city in which he is ideology-free. But if what he most wants is the pleasure of making money or the pleasure of being honoured, he has every reason to trade some truth in his world-view for more of his own favourite pleasure. Indeed, if he lacks the natural ability to escape ideology altogether, he may have no choice in the matter. So the fact that the ideologies of the guardians and producers are falsely sustained, while the philosopher–kings are ideology-free, seems to be a strength in the *kallipolis* rather than a weakness. There, and only there, do honour-lovers and money-lovers get the benefits of the freedom from ideology of which they are themselves incapable. There and only there do philosophers get to see the world as it is.

## Private life and private property

Upon returning to the topic of the way of life appropriate to the guardians in book 5, Socrates raises the question of how female guardians should be trained and educated. Should they reduce the amount of work required of the males by sharing their duties, or 'be kept indoors on the grounds that because they must bear and rear offspring they are unable to do so' (451d)? It is argued by Socrates' imaginary critic, as it has been throughout the ages, that difference in reproductive roles does indeed entail difference in social ones. Socrates sees through this, however, pointing out that it is not clear that one's role in reproduction has anything to do with one's aptitude for a craft or way of life (454d–e). Individual women, he holds, are either money-lovers or honour-lovers or philosophers, just like individual men. Hence in the *kallipolis* women will not be confined to the home, but will be trained in the craft, whether it is producing or guarding or ruling (456a, 540c), for which their natural aptitude is highest.

While these provisions are certainly enlightened, even by our own standards, it may seem that they are intended to apply only to female guardians, not to female producers. Stray remarks which have clear application to female producers, however, suggest that this may not be the case. The principle of specialization (or of quasi-specialization, as it finally becomes), for example, is said to apply to 'children and women, slaves and freemen, producers, rulers, and ruled' (433d1–5). The implication is that female producers, being as subject to the principle of specialization as any other member of the *kallipolis*, will be trained in the craft or way of life for which they are naturally best suited. Since Socrates implies that there are women with a natural aptitude for carpentry (454d), explicitly mentions female physicians, and claims that natural aptitudes for each craft are to be found in both sexes (455d–e), it is difficult to avoid the conclusion that female producers are intended to be apprenticed in an appropriate craft in precisely the same way as the males.

It must be conceded, however, that Plato is not a feminist. He shows no interest in liberating women as such, and implies that they are generally inferior to men (455c–d). Moreover, his casual remarks reveal a streak of unregenerate sexism and misogyny (431b–c, 469d, 557c, 563b). But these are relatively small matters, and do not affect the general point that in the *kallipolis* men and women with the same natural assets receive the same education and have access to the same careers. Still Plato is regrettably vague about the producers, whether male or female, and has left us somewhat in the dark on the important question of who will do the housework, and rear the children, if both parents are employed full-time outside the household.

In the case of the guardians, to be sure, he is more forthcoming—though what he describes may not appeal to us. If the guardians and producers were in competition for the same social goods, producers would fare very badly, since the guardians are armed and trained for warfare in a way that they are not (419a). But because the guardians are honour-lovers and the producers money-lovers, this problem can be solved. Education is, once again, a large part of the solution, though it needs to be reinforced by the structure of the *kallipolis*. Hence the guardians are segregated from the producers, and denied both private property and private family life, on the grounds that 'if they acquire private lands, houses, and currency themselves, they'll be household managers and farmers instead of guardians—hostile masters of the other citizens instead of their allies' (417a–b). The result is coupling by lottery as part of a state-sponsored eugenics programme, state-run 'rearing pens' for guardian offspring (451c–461e), and the totalitarian domination of the private sphere by the public. Scarcely anything in the *Republic* estranges our sympathies so thoroughly.

Rather than indulging in moral outrage, however, we do better to attempt diagnosis: what has led Plato in this unprepossessing direction? Part of the answer, no doubt, is his profound suspicion of the appetites, and the politically destructive potential, of greed and self-interest. Removing the things that stimulate them therefore becomes appealing. But another part of the answer is more interesting.

Men traditionally value honour and the competitive activities (including warfare) in which it is won, whereas women traditionally value domestic life, the having and rearing of children, and the emotional closeness and intimacy it makes possible. Consequently, if men and women were treated equally in the *kallipolis*, honour, on the one hand, and emotional closeness, on the other, would have to be taken equally seriously as genuine human goods. But they aren't. Instead, Plato just assumes that honour is valuable, and that anyone, male or female, will want to win it if possible, while emotional closeness is implicitly treated as valueless (465b–c), and so is made wholly unavailable to the guardians. The result, it seems, is that Plato has not treated women justly at all, and has not advocated their claims and rights in the way that he does those of men. What he has done instead is, first, to make an entirely 'masculinized' world and then given women the freedom to be 'men' in it. The hegemony of males in the *kallipolis* is, therefore, more subtle and insidious than it first seems. And the awful result is the totalitarianism—the evisceration of the private sphere—that rightly disquiets the *Republic*'s contemporary readers.

## Invalids, infants, slaves

One rough-and-ready measure of the justice of a political community is its treatment of its least well-off or least fortunate members—those who are most at its mercy. In this section I shall consider how three such groups are treated in the *kallipolis*.

On the basis of the brief remarks in book 3 (405a1–410b9) about the kind of medicine available in the *kallipolis*, Plato has been taken to advocate the view that medical treatment should be distributed solely on the basis of social productivity. If this is what he had in mind, we would all agree that the *kallipolis* could not be the happiest or most just human community. So it is important to our assessment of the *Republic* to see whether this is indeed what Plato intends.

If one has been properly trained and educated, one will have little need for constant medical attention. Indeed, it is shameful 'to need medical help, not because one has been wounded or because of some of the seasonal diseases, but because of idleness and a [self-indulgent] way of life' (405c–d). The purpose of medical treatment is to restore people who already possess good habits to a life worth living, not to prolong lives which can be a benefit neither to those who live them nor to anyone else (408b).

In the case of producers, Plato thinks, this view is uncontroversial: 'If someone prescribes a lengthy regimen for [a carpenter] . . . he would soon say that he has no leisure to be ill, nor is such a life—paying attention to a disease while neglecting the work at hand—of any profit to him . . . Because if he could not perform his own work, it would not profit him to go on living' (406d–407a). Notice that there is no question of coercion here, or of the carpenter's being denied medical treatment by someone else. If he cannot carry on with his craft, and get the pleasure of making a profit which alone makes his life worth living, Plato thinks that *he himself* would refuse medical treatment. The point is not, then, that the interests of the city must override the individual's interests, or that if people are of no further use to the city they should be left to die. Indeed, Plato thinks that what holds of the craftsman is equally applicable to rich people who have no assigned craft, and who can afford to be ill and under treatment throughout their lives. His reasoning is that giving one's life over to cosseting an illness prevents one from practising virtue, just as surely as it prevents one from working, and that without virtue life is not worth living even if one has money (407a–c). Whether someone is rich or poor, therefore, the goal of medical treatment must be to restore him to a life worth living, not simply to keep him biologically ticking over. If this goal is not achievable, he 'will be allowed to die' (410a2–3). Clearly, nothing in this account entails that those with an illness that prevents them from ever being socially useful, or from returning to their craft, will be left without any medical treatment whatsoever, or that nothing will be done to ease their suffering. They simply will not be kept alive if their lives are not worthwhile to them.

In the case of incurable psychopaths, however, whose unnecessary appetites cannot be moderated through training and education, this picture of Platonic medicine may seem hard to sustain. 'The ones whose souls are naturally bad and are incurable', he says, 'they will kill' (410a). But, as before, Plato's thought is focused as much on the individual as on the *kallipolis*. For, on his view, life is not worth living when our soul, the 'very thing by which we live, is confused and corrupted' (445a–b). Psychopaths are put to death, in other words, as much because their lives are not worth living as because they are not socially productive.

There is plenty of room for debating the merits of this view of medicine, of course, and whether doctors should keep their patients alive at all costs, regardless of the quality of the lives they will lead. Indeed, these are currently among the most controversial topics in medical ethics. But it could hardly be claimed that the view is notably anti-philanthropic or inhumane, or that no rationally prudent person would choose to live in a society that institutionalized it. Indeed, one might well consider positively enlightened its commitment to providing medical care to those who will benefit from it, rather than to those who can simply afford to foot the bill.

Deformed guardian infants, infants born to inferior guardians, and infants born to guardians who are beyond the optimum ages for childbearing (50 in a man, 40 in a woman), Plato claims, should be allowed to die of exposure (460c–461c). This is very harsh doctrine. It is worth noting, therefore, that it does not follow from the application of Plato's general theory to infants. No doubt part of what he has in mind is covered by his views on medicine.

Sufficiently deformed infants may have minimal prospects of living a worthwhile life. By being allowed to die they may well be benefited. But it is difficult to see how the offspring of inferior or older guardians are benefited by being exposed. For they are likely to be no more inferior than their parents (415a). There is no doubt, then, that it can be a misfortune to be an infant in the *kallipolis*, and that this is so in large part because Plato refuses to extend the humane protections of his general theory, which are intended to safeguard the happiness of the individual, to infants.

The question is, why does he do this? In the absence of direct evidence, the most plausible answer seems to be this. The Athenians practised infant exposure as a method of family planning. Their attitude to it was perhaps akin to the attitude many in our own culture take to abortion or contraception—there was no law against it, for example. So Plato was culturally primed to refuse full ethical standing to infants. Whether he was justified in adopting the views of his fellows on this matter, rather than, as in so many other cases, rejecting them out of hand, remains a controversial question.

Slavery is too obviously bad to be controversial. Few in the ancient world, however, thought that there was anything wrong with it, and Plato was not among them: the *Laws* gives what can only be described as ruthless advice about how slaves should be treated (776b–778a). But there is a difference between condoning slavery and thinking—as Aristotle, for example, does—that the best human community must contain slaves.

In book 4, to be sure, Plato includes slaves in a catalogue of the members of the *kallipolis*, saying that the principle of specialization applies as much to them as to anyone else (433d). Elsewhere, he writes that, while the *kallipolis* must never enslave fellow Greeks, it 'must behave toward barbarian enemies as the Greeks now do toward each other' (471b). This seems to imply that the *kallipolis* will enslave its barbarian captives. The most we can infer from these passages, then, is that, *if* there are slaves in the *kallipolis*, they are barbarians, who are as subject to the principle of specialization as everyone else. For the only provision the constitution of the *kallipolis* makes for the acquisition of slaves is precisely the capture of barbarians in defensive war. Consequently, the presence of slaves in the *kallipolis* is by no means a sure thing.

There is no question, therefore, of the *kallipolis* being based on slavery, as Athens was, or of slaves being essential to its functioning. And even that conditional conclusion is problematic. For if slaves really are subject to the principle of specialization, it seems that a slave will be legally and constitutionally on a par with every other member of the *kallipolis*. The craft he practises and the social role he occupies will be determined by his natural talents only, not by his status as a slave. All of which raises the obvious question of just what it could mean to be a slave in the *kallipolis*. But it is a question which, in the absence of further textual evidence, there is simply no profitable way to pursue. This much, however, does seem certain. Plato did not think that the *kallipolis*, the best of all possible cities, had to contain slaves. Considering the views of his age, that seems to be a step in the right direction.

## Censorship of the arts

Even a cursory reading of the *Republic* leaves one in no doubt that Plato thinks that the most important political institutions in the *kallipolis*, or in any other society, are educational. The 'one great thing', he says, is 'education and upbringing'. Hence the philosopher–kings must 'guard *above all else* that there should be no change in music and gymnastics . . . For poetry and music are not changed anywhere without change in the most important laws of the city' (423d–424c). Apprenticeship in a craft, education in music and poetry, in mathematical science, dialectic, and practical city management—these, and not Marx's relations of production, are the base. Everything else, and that includes everything we think of as quintessentially political, is superstructure (425b–e).

It is not surprising, then, that, having completed the account of his own revolutionary educational proposals, and having justified them by showing that they promote both maximal justice and maximal happiness of those who receive them, Plato should turn in book 10 to attack his competition—the poets and playwrights who were the purveyors of traditional Greek ethical education. The philosophers, not the poets, he argues, are the true teachers of virtue. For, first of all, being able to imitate virtue or virtuous people in rhythms and rhymes that please and entertain most people does not qualify one to teach human beings how to live. The poet or dramatist writes for a non-specialist audience. Hence he must employ a conceptual framework similar to theirs. Character, motive, plot—all must be drawn from folk psychology, not, say, from cognitive science, or neurophysiology, or whatever the true theory of the soul turns out to be. This means that art represents people and their motives and actions not necessarily as they really are, but only as they seem to people without specialist training. The languages of art are not, then, the technical mathematics-like language of Platonic truth. The scientist, or philosopher–king, by contrast, is free of this constraint, since his is primarily an audience of fellow specialists (601a–b, 603b–605c).

Secondly, poetry and drama, like all art, aim to provide a certain characteristic pleasure or satisfaction (606b), which on Plato's view, as on Freud's, is related to repression. Art enables us to satisfy without reproach or shame the very desires we must repress in real life. These are characteristically appetitive desires, especially sexual ones. This might plausibly be taken to entail that the representation of ethically good people, like the representation of happy families, does not provide the kind of satisfaction art typically provides. So it is not knowledge of what good people are like that the poet needs (604e–605a). If we suppose, as Plato does (485d), that even artistic indulgence of repressed desires strengthens them and weakens the repressive mechanisms, we will see reason here to mistrust art in general (605b, 606b).

Finally, we must look at the poet himself, and why he writes. Plato is confident that no one would be satisfied merely to represent life if he knew how to live it well, or could teach others how to do so (599b–601a). If we think again of the characteristic pleasure art provides, his view becomes intelligible, and again rather like a view of Freud's. A life devoted to making things that provide a fantasy satisfaction for unnecessary appetites could not rank very highly among lives.

These arguments may not command our assent, but there is much to admire in them. They make the philosophy of art continuous with ethics, politics, and the philosophy of mind, and that seems right. Moreover, the deep differences they identify between art and philosophy (at least as Plato conceives of it and its relations to science) are arguably there. Art is, and must be, bound up with ordinary life and thought in a way that philosophy need not be. Art is related to pleasure, and to sex, in a way that philosophy, perhaps, is not. Most important of all, even if they are inconclusive, Plato's arguments extend the right invitation to philosophers who think that art has something to teach us about how to live: develop a metaphysics, epistemology, psychology, and politics on the basis of which it will be clear that the knowledge a good poet or dramatist needs is relevant to ethics. It is precisely as an invitation, indeed, and not as what Berkeley calls 'the killing blow', that Plato himself seems to understand those arguments (607d–e).

## Freedom and autonomy

A person's needs, wants, and interests are in part determined by the natural lottery, in part by his education and upbringing, and in part by his actual circumstances. They also depend on his beliefs, which in turn depend to some extent on the same factors as his needs, wants, and interests themselves. His *real interests* are those he would form under optimal conditions—those in which his needs are satisfied, he is neither maltreated nor coerced nor the victim of false ideology, and he is as fully aware as possible of his actual circumstances, and the real alternatives to them. Happiness is optimal satisfaction of real interests in the long term.

The relevance of this picture to the *Republic* should now be clear. For the *kallipolis* has emerged as a community intended by Plato to provide optimal conditions of the type in question. Each of its members has his needs satisfied, and is neither maltreated nor coerced nor the victim of false ideology. Each is educated and trained so as to develop a conception of the world, and his place in it, which is as close to the truth as his nature, fully developed with an eye to his maximal happiness, permits. Each has his ruling desires satisfied throughout life. Thus each develops his real interests, and is made really happy.

It sounds wonderful put like that. But that is not, surely, how the *Republic* feels to us when we read it. It feels authoritarian and repressive. I think our reaction is partly justified. But part of it is due as much to controversial beliefs we bring to the *Republic* as to what we find there. For example, because of where and when we live, we are inclined to presuppose that no amount of knowledge of the way the world is validates or underwrites a unique conception of the good. Different conceptions are determined by what different individuals happen to want or prefer. The state exists not to judge between these conceptions, but to allow each individual to realize his own conception as far as is compatible with others' realizing theirs to the same extent. In this way, the state at once respects the individuality of its members and treats them equally. An activity, institution, or issue is paradigmatically political for us if it pertains to disputes between people who may have different conceptions of the good, yet must coexist and have dealings with one another in the same community, or, more generally, in the same world. Individual freedom, on this broadly liberal conception, which we find in Locke and Hume, is freedom to do what one wants, or—to bring in the good—freedom to live in accordance with a conception of the good that is rooted in one's own desires, preferences, or choices. And a state is free to the extent that it limits individual freedom only to guarantee equal freedom to all its members. It is not surprising, then, that, when in imagination we project ourselves into the *kallipolis*, we feel repressed and unfree. For, given our actual desires and interests, and presupposing the liberal conception of freedom, we would be repressed and unfree there.

This conception of political freedom is not the only one, however, and even if we leave aside worries about its metaphysical commitment to the distinction between facts and values, it is not clear that it is the best or most defensible conception. It may even fail in its own terms. For, by seeking neutrality above all, the state may undermine certain conceptions of the good which, even though they do not illegitimately limit the freedom of others, cannot easily survive in a neutral state. Because of the extensive labour mobility necessitated by a free-market economy, for instance, those who want stable neighbourhoods, extended families, close ties between the generations, or collective living are likely to find it very difficult to achieve their goals within the state. From their perspective, the supposedly neutral state is biased against their conception of the good. But even if the liberal conception does not fail in its own terms, the foundations of the freedom it supposes might be questioned.

Freedom to do what we want, or instrumental freedom, is certainly important. Its importance can be undermined, however, by the desires on which it depends. For if the desires we are free to satisfy are ones we would not have if we had engaged in a process of ideal rational deliberation, being free to satisfy them is scarcely something worth caring about. If our desires themselves, like those of a drug addict, can enmire us in unfreedom, instrumental freedom cannot be sufficient for real freedom or autonomy. Perhaps, then, we should move away from instrumental freedom towards deliberative freedom. Perhaps the freedom we should be concerned about is the freedom to have and to satisfy only the desires we would choose to have if we were aware of the relevant facts, were thinking clearly, and were free from distorting influences.

If we are persuaded to move in this direction, we can see at once that a state which guaranteed deliberative freedom might look and feel very repressive to someone solely concerned about instrumental freedom. It would very much depend on what his desires happened to be. Since the costs of repression, in both psychological and political terms, are high, however, we can well imagine that an enlightened state, committed to deliberative freedom, would want to devote much of its resources to education and training, so as to ensure that its members are as close to being deliberatively rational as possible. Such a state would already begin to look a little like the *kallipolis*, and to share some of its priorities.

Even a state whose citizens enjoy complete deliberative and instrumental freedom can seem to be defective from the point of view of what we might call critical freedom. For desires that are deliberatively rational may not be rational in general. Brought up in a capitalist democracy, which arguably does not provide optimal conditions for developing one's needs, wants, and interests, a person desires profit above everything else. And the more he deliberates under the aegis of that desire, the clearer it may become that his desire is perfectly rational. Yet it may not be in his real interest to make profit his goal. But to discover this he would have to begin deliberating already possessed of desires other than those he actually has. If, for these sorts of reasons, deliberatively rational desires can fail to be the best ones for a person to have, then the same considerations that caused us to favour deliberatively free states over instrumentally free ones might cause us to favour critically free ones over those that are only deliberatively free. And this would certainly bring us closer still to the *kallipolis*. For, like the *kallipolis*, any critically free state would have to devote much of its resources to ensuring that the actual interests of its citizens coincide as far as possible with their real interests. And that would require, not just extensive commitment to education and training, but extensive commitment to all branches of knowledge relevant to human beings and their interests. More than that, it would require political institutions that guarantee that knowledge thus gained would serve human good. If one cannot quite see producers, guardians, and philosopher–kings in all of that, one can at least see their outlines.

In any case, it seems clear that the *kallipolis* is intended to provide its members with as much critical freedom as their natures, fully developed in optimal conditions, permit:

It is better for everyone to be ruled by divine reason, preferably within himself and his own, otherwise imposed from without, so that as far as possible all will be alike and friends, governed by the same thing . . . This is clearly the aim of the law, which is the ally of everyone. But it's also our aim in ruling our children, we don't allow them to be free until we establish a constitution in them, just as in a city, and—by fostering their best part with our own—equip them with a guardian and ruler similar to our own to take our place. Then, and only then, we set them free. (590d–591a; also 395b–c)

Thus even if we retain our liberal suspicion about the possibility of a science of values, we might still, by coming to see merit in the idea of critical freedom, also come to see the *Republic* in a new light—not as predominantly a totalitarian hymn to the benefits of repression and unfreedom, but as an attempt to design a city whose members enjoy as much real happiness, and as much real freedom, as possible.

## FURTHER READING

Annas, Julia, *An Introduction to Plato's 'Republic'* (Oxford: Clarendon Press, 1981).

Kraut, Richard, *Plato's 'Republic': Critical Essays* (Lanham, Md.: Rowman & Littlefield, 1997).

Popper, Karl, *The Open Society and its Enemies*, vol. i (Princeton: Princeton University Press, 1971).

Reeve, C. D. C., *Philosopher-Kings: The Argument of Plato's 'Republic'* (Princeton: Princeton University Press, 1988).

# 5 Aristotle

Tony Burns

## Contents



## Chapter guide

This chapter assumes that one cannot understand Aristotle's political thought, and specifically the argument of Aristotle's *Politics*, unless one relates it to the theory of justice which Aristotle develops in his *Nicomachean Ethics* and to the metaphysical beliefs which he expounds in his *Metaphysics*. The chapter is divided into four main sections. The first deals with Aristotle's view of human nature, which is the starting point for understanding his views on both ethics and politics. It seeks to explain what Aristotle means when he describes man as a 'social and political animal' (*zoon politikon*). The second section discusses the theory of justice developed in Aristotle's *Ethics* and focuses on Aristotle's elucidation of the concept of justice by reference to the notions of proportional and arithmetical equality. It also says something about the two main areas of social life in which the concept of justice has a practical application, the spheres of rectificatory and distributive justice. The third section considers how Aristotle applies his theory of justice in his *Politics*, especially to the problem of the just distribution of political power. It discusses Aristotle's classification of the different types of political constitution in this connection. The final section considers the continuing relevance of Aristotle for political philosophy today, especially for the debate between John Rawls and his communitarian critics.

As in the case of any other major thinker, interpretations of Aristotle's thought vary. There are, however, four interpretations in the current literature which are especially significant. The first interpretation is to be found in the work of Fred D. Miller Jr., who maintains that Aristotle is a natural law theorist, or ethical deontologist, who recognizes the existence of a universally valid standard of justice which might be used to critically evaluate positive law.[1] The second interpretation is advanced by the neo-Kantian legal philosopher Hans Kelsen. It is that Aristotle is an ethical and constitutional relativist whose views resemble closely the doctrine of legal positivism.[2] The third interpretation, that of John Rawls, maintains that Aristotle's ethical thought represents a form of ethical consequentialism. The fourth interpretation presents Aristotle as an exponent of 'virtue ethics' and is associated above all with the communitarian political thought of Alasdair MacIntyre.[3] I argue that although the interpretations of Miller and Kelsen are open to criticism for being only partially correct, nevertheless they might be fruitfully synthesized into a third doctrine which captures very well Aristotle's approach to ethics and politics as a whole. I go on to argue that there are also difficulties with the interpretations offered by Rawls and MacIntyre, each of whom presents a highly selective reading of Aristotle's political thought so as to make it in some way support their own theoretical position. My conclusion is that for this reason, like Miller and Kelsen, neither Rawls nor MacIntyre does justice to Aristotle.

## Biography

Aristotle (384–322 BC) was born in Stageira in Macedonia (now northern Greece), the son of the court physician to the King of Macedonia. At the age of 17 he went to Athens to study at the Academy under Plato. When Plato died, in 347 BC, Aristotle left Athens. Between 342 and 336 BC he was tutor to the teenage son of the King of Macedonia, the future Alexander the Great. He returned to Athens in 335 BC to set up his own school, the Lyceum, as a competitor to the Academy. Aristotle spent much of his life attempting to establish a critical distance between his own philosophy and that of Plato. The popular understanding of the intellectual relationship between Plato and Aristotle is best symbolized by the Raphael's painting *The School of Athens*, in which an 'otherworldly' Plato is depicted gesturing towards the heavens, while his rebellious pupil Aristotle is seen insistently pointing towards the ground. In the sphere of metaphysics the suggestion in Raphael's painting is that Plato is a rationalist and an idealist, concerned only with universals, the ideas and concepts that constitute the world of the Forms, whereas Aristotle is an empiricist and a materialist who is interested exclusively in particulars, or the individual things that are observable in the world around him. So far as ethics and politics are concerned, this conventional view sees Plato as a utopian dreamer who in his *Republic* outlines a blueprint for a rationally organized society which provides an objectively valid and universally applicable transcendent ethical ideal which might be used to criticize all existing societies. Aristotle, on the other hand, is depicted as an ethical relativist or conventionalist who denies the existence of such a transcendent ethical ideal and who insists in his *Politics* that we should concentrate, rather, on carrying out a 'scientific' study of the particular, the local, and the historically specific, that is to say, the multifarious ethical ideals and values which are empirically observable in a variety of different societies. It is evident to anyone who has paid close attention to Aristotle's writings, especially the *Metaphysics* and the *Nicomachean Ethics*, that this popular view of the relationship between Plato and Aristotle is based on a misunderstanding of Aristotle which exaggerates the differences between his philosophy and that of Plato. It does, however, capture very well the basic cast of Aristotle's approach to philosophy, which is simply to understand the world around him rather than attempt to radically change it. After the death of Alexander the Great in 323 BC, Aristotle fled Athens to avoid anti-Macedonian feeling. He died in 322 BC aged 62.

Aristotle has a strong claim to being regarded as the greatest philosopher who ever lived, and certainly the most influential. He has had a tremendous influence on the history of political thought. His ideas dominated European political thought in the later Middle Ages, largely because of his influence on St Thomas Aquinas' *Summa theologiae* in the thirteenth century. His classification of constitutions in the *Politics* was still being seriously discussed 2,000 years later by Hobbes in his *Leviathan* (1651) and Montesquieu in his *The Spirit of the Laws* (1748). Aristotle's influence on the central texts in the history of conservatism, such as Burke's *Reflections on the Revolution in France* (1790) and Hegel's *Philosophy of Right* (1821) is readily apparent. His contribution to our understanding of the concept of justice in the *Nicomachean Ethics* is the greatest in the history of Western philosophy and has never been bettered. Almost all those who have discussed the subject owe an acknowledged or unacknowledged debt to Aristotle and often simply repeat wittingly or unwittingly what Aristotle has already said long ago. Even now there are communitarian critics of liberalism, like Alasdair MacIntyre, Michael Sandel, and Hans-Georg Gadamer, who think that Aristotle still has something important to teach us about politics. Deploring the alienation and atomistic individualism of contemporary society, and being critical of liberal political philosophers like John Rawls who appear to provide a theoretical justification for the principles upon which this society is based, communitarian thinkers have sought recently to develop an alternative approach to politics based on a return to the writings of Aristotle, focusing especially on the ancient ideal of civic virtue which is central to Aristotle's ethical and political thought. It is this attempt, in so far as it is theoretically and practically possible, to revive the republican ideals of classical Greece in current political conditions that more than anything else explains the continued relevance of Aristotle's political thought today.

## Key texts

*Eudemian Ethics*
*Metaphysics*
*Nicomachean Ethics*
*Politics*

## Main texts used

*Eudemian Ethics*, trans. J. Solomon, in Jonathan Barnes (ed.), *The Complete Works of Aristotle*, 2 vols. (Princeton: Princeton University Press, 1991).

*Metaphysics*, trans. Hugh Lawson-Tancred (Harmondsworth: Penguin, 1998).

*Nicomachean Ethics*, ed. and trans. Roger Crisp, Cambridge Texts in the History of Philosophy (Cambridge: Cambridge University Press, 2000).

*The Politics and the Constitution of Athens*, ed. Stephen Everson, trans. Benjamin Jowett and Jonathan Barnes, Cambridge Texts in the History of Political Thought (Cambridge: Cambridge University Press, 1996).

## Key ideas

**Human nature**: for Aristotle man is by nature a social and political animal (***zoon politikon***). A fully human life is one of harmonious fellowship with others, living together in a particular community or ***polis***. A *polis* is not only a political but also an ethical community based on a commitment to shared values. Because human beings are by nature unequal, **slavery** in such a community is justified. **Ethics**: the ultimate goal and the best life for human beings, ***eudaimonia***, is a life of virtue. There are many virtues, but the most important of all is **justice**. A just person is in the habit of doing the right thing for the right reason. Leaving questions of motivation aside, just actions are actions that conform to the requirements of the principle of **equity** or **proportional equality**, which is the most fundamental principle of **natural justice**. This principle has two main areas of application, that of **distributive justice** and that of **rectificatory justice**. In the sphere of rectificatory justice, because all concerned are considered to be strictly equal, the principle of equity is reduced to that of **arithmetical equality**. The principles of natural justice are instantiated in the principles of political justice, the laws or the constitution of a particular *polis*, which therefore constitute the standard of right and wrong for all of its inhabitants including its citizens. **Politics**: Aristotle is best known for his commitment to **constitutionalism** and the idea of the rule of law, and for his classification of the different types of political constitution. He thinks of a constitution as being the framework of customary laws associated with a particular *polis* and its way of life. **Values**: Aristotle's ethical and political values are usually considered to be typically pre-modern. The most important value for Aristotle is justice, but this in turn is associated with the values of community, hierarchy, order, inequality, and duty. These values are often contrasted with what are alleged to be the peculiarly modern principles of individualism, equality, freedom, and rights, including natural rights.

---

## Aristotle's view of human nature

The starting point for understanding Aristotle's views on ethics and politics is his theory of human nature and his well-known assertion that man is 'by nature' a social or a 'political animal' (*Politics* 1253$^{a}$13). In the first instance this suggests nothing more than that individual human beings are sociable or gregarious because they are always to be found living together with others in society or in a *polis*. Additionally, however, Aristotle considers it to be a 'characteristic of man that he alone has any sense of good and evil, of just and unjust' (*Politics* 1253$^{a}$). According to Aristotle, then, man is by nature a moral or an ethical being. In his view, for all human beings a natural life is a life of justice. It is this characteristic above all which differentiates the human species from other species of animals (*Politics* 1332$^{b}$). If it is true, as Aristotle says at the very beginning of the *Nicomachean Ethics*, that 'the good has been aptly described as that at which everything aims' (*Ethics* 1094$^{a}$), then a life of justice represents the 'good' for man. This is the ultimate end towards which all human beings do strive and to which they ought to strive (*Politics* 1334$^{a}$; also 1333$^{a}$). This is the very essence of what it is to be human. Only if they live a life of justice do they satisfy the requirements of their own nature and thereby become human beings properly so called. For Aristotle the ultimate aim of politics is to enable such a process of personal development to take place. It is political society which makes it possible for individual human beings to live a 'good life' in this sense of the term (*Politics* 1278[b], 1280[a]; 1281[a], 1282[b], 1325[a]). To fulfil one's potential as a human being in this way is to achieve a condition which in the *Nicomachean Ethics* Aristotle refers to by the Greek word 'eudaimonia' (*Nicomachean Ethics* 1095[a]). This term is often misleadingly translated as 'happiness', and sometimes as 'flourishing', 'fulfilment' or 'excellence', but is probably best rendered into English by the notion of moral 'self-perfection'. In Aristotle's view, the achievement of *eudaimonia* necessarily requires that there be moral rules or laws which serve as a standard of right and wrong for particular moral agents. For Aristotle, in the final analysis (though only then), these moral rules are the principles of 'political justice' of the *polis* in which they happen to live.

Precisely because an ethical life is only possible in political society, it is inevitable that Aristotle's views on ethics and politics are closely related to one another. It is for this reason that in the *Ethics* Aristotle maintains that for human beings the study of politics (in the broadest possible sense of the term) is the 'highest master science' because it incorporates within itself the study of ethics. As such it is necessarily concerned with 'what is noble and what is just' and 'lays down laws' about what we ought to do and what we ought not to do (*Ethics* 1094[b], 1102[a], 1180[b]). Fred D. Miller Jr. has rightly argued that the views expressed in Aristotle's *Ethics*, especially the 'treatise on justice' in book 5, are presupposed throughout the argument of his *Politics* (1261[a], 1280[a], 1282[b], 1295[a], 1332[a]).[4] In what follows, therefore, I shall concentrate mainly on Aristotle's theory of justice, first as it is outlined in book 5 of the *Ethics* and then as it is applied in the *Politics*.

## The *Nicomachean Ethics*

### Virtue ethics

By focusing on Aristotle's theory of justice I shall be ignoring a great deal of what Aristotle has to say about other things in the *Ethics*. In particular, I will not be discussing what Aristotle has to say about moral virtue in general or moral virtues such as honesty and courage in particular. Nor will I be discussing Aristotle's famous theory of 'the mean' (*Ethics* 1106[a]–1107[a]). I will consider justice, not as a moral virtue, but only in so far as it is something which Aristotle associates with a definite framework of moral rules or laws. This brings me into conflict with a number of recent commentators, who consider Aristotle to be an exponent of 'virtue ethics'.[5] According to Alasdair MacIntyre, the difference between Aristotelian virtue ethics and modern ethical doctrines is that virtue ethics attaches little or no importance to moral rules, as opposed to psychological motivation or moral character, as a determinant of what is just and unjust. The (allegedly) modern 'preoccupation with rules', MacIntyre insists, is an indication of the fact that philosophers today tend to adopt a decidedly '*un*-Aristotelian' approach to ethics.[6] MacIntyre claims that for Aristotle it is not moral rules but the moral virtues which 'have the central place'.[7] For an exponent of virtue ethics, then, what makes actions just or unjust is solely the motivation which lies behind them.[8] Largely because of MacIntyre's influence, the view that Aristotle subscribes not to an ethics of moral rules or laws but to an ethics of virtue has become increasingly prominent recently, although this view has been rightly challenged by at least some commentators.[9]

In my view, however, Aristotle is not an exponent of virtue ethics in this sense of the term. In the *Nicomachean Ethics* he insists that 'some people who do just actions' are nevertheless 'not yet just', and hence also not yet virtuous, if they do these actions 'involuntarily or through ignorance or for some other reason, and not for the sake of the actions themselves' (*Ethics* 1144[a]). When he makes this remark Aristotle is using the word 'just' in two different, though related, ways. He presupposes that one could meaningfully describe an action as just simply because it is a right action, even though one could also say that the person who performs it is not acting justly if they do so for the wrong reason. According to Aristotle, then, we can logically separate the question of the justice or injustice of actions from that of the presence or absence of moral virtue in the persons who perform them. It follows from this, however, that for Aristotle whether or not an action is indeed just or unjust in at least one sense of the term, in other words whether it is right or wrong, has nothing to do with the motive that lies behind it. On this reading, Aristotle is of the opinion that even a virtuous motive could not transform an action that is intrinsically unjust into one that is just and therefore morally permissible (*Ethics* 1107[a]). It also follows that in Aristotle's view for an action to be a just action, in the strictest possible sense of the term 'just', it has to be not only appropriately motivated but also objectively right. It must satisfy the requirements of an independent standard of right and wrong that is external to the individual moral agent. In short, it must conform to some rule or law.

Those who interpret Aristotle as an exponent of virtue ethics in the extreme sense referred to above offer a one-sided account of his views on ethics in general and especially of his views on justice. They focus exclusively on what Aristotle says about the role of psychological motivation and moral character in the *Nicomachean Ethics* and ignore completely what he says about the role of moral rules or laws in the determination of what is just and unjust. They misunderstand Aristotle's view of what it is that makes actions right or wrong and, as a result, offer a partial and incomplete account of his view of what it is that makes actions just or unjust. In my view, Aristotle adopts what is usually referred to as a 'deontological' approach to questions of right and wrong and of justice and injustice. In other words, he thinks that certain actions, such as murder, lying, theft, and adultery, are wrong, and hence also unjust, not because of their motivation but intrinsically, in and of themselves (*Ethics* 1107[a]). The fact that Aristotle says relatively little about moral rules or laws in the *Ethics* as a whole (outside book 5) should not be taken as implying that he considers them to be unimportant for our understanding of ethical conduct, especially where questions of justice and injustice are concerned.

## Theory of justice

Aristotle outlines his theory of justice in book 5 of the *Nicomachean Ethics*. The discussion begins by pointing out that justice is not simply a state of mind, or a moral virtue in MacIntyre's sense of the term, but also has to do with the rightness and wrongness of our actions (*Ethics* 1129[a]). If we focus on this aspect of justice, Aristotle argues, it is clear that we commonly think about justice in two ways (*Ethics* 1130[a]–[b]). Speaking generally, we associate justice with righteousness, or with doing the right thing, that is to say with lawfulness and with obedience to law. From this point of view, to act unjustly is simply to do that which 'is contrary to law' (*Ethics* 1130[a], 1130[b]), or that which conflicts with the requirements of what Aristotle refers to as the principles of 'political justice' (*Ethics* 1134$^{b}$) of one's own *polis*. By law here Aristotle means moral law. However, consistent with his view that the spheres of the ethical and the political are identical, he does not distinguish between this moral law and what today we would refer to as the positive law of a *polis*. In Aristotle's view, therefore, the principles of political justice of a *polis* might correctly be said to constitute the standard of justice or of right and wrong for its citizens.[10] This conclusion is a logical implication of Aristotle's understanding of the relationship between ethics and politics, although this is sometimes not recognized. Because the positive laws of a *polis* are also its moral rules, Aristotle cannot (or should not if he is consistent) allow that there is any independent standard of justice by means of which positive law might be critically evaluated. As Aristotle himself puts it, the aim of the true politician is to produce good citizens who are 'obedient to the laws' (*Ethics* 1102$^{a}$20)—no matter what the specific character of these laws happens to be. For 'whatever is lawful is in some way just' (*Ethics* 1129$^{b}$).

Aristotle goes on to point out that, more particularly, we associate the concept of justice with that of 'fairness' (*Ethics* 1129$^{b}$)—a concept which, in turn, is connected to that of 'equality' (*Ethics* 1131$^{a}$–$^{b}$, 1131$^{b}$–1132$^{a}$, 1132$^{b}$, 1133$^{b}$; *Politics* 1282$^{b}$, 1301$^{a}$–$^{b}$). Justice in this second or 'particular' sense has to do with those actions that affect other people, many of which are also regulated by law. The actions which are just or unjust in this second sense therefore constitute only a 'part' of the class of just and unjust actions as a whole (*Ethics* 1130$^{a}$). They represent a subclass of those actions that are regulated by law and therefore just or unjust more generally. Most of book 5 of the *Ethics* concentrates on developing a theory of justice in this sense and with a consideration of its application to various areas of social and political life (*Ethics* 1130$^{b}$).

Aristotle's understanding of 'particular' justice is expressed most clearly in the *Politics*, although he makes it plain that the understanding which he has of justice there is the same as the one outlined in the *Ethics*. Aristotle points out that although the concept of justice has to do with that of equality (*Politics* 1282$^{b}$), nevertheless the concept of equality itself requires further clarification. We must, he says, distinguish between two types of equality. He refers to these as 'proportional' equality, on the one hand, and 'arithmetical' equality on the other (*Politics* 1301$^{b}$). The first of these is more important than the second, which Aristotle considers to be a special application or a limiting case of the first. The principle of proportional equality, or fairness, requires that those who are equal ought to be treated equally if their circumstances are similar in some relevant respect. It also requires that those who are not equal in a relevant respect ought *not* to be treated equally. Unequals ought to be treated differently provided the difference in treatment is proportional to the inequality that exists between them. If this condition is satisfied, then according to Aristotle we may legitimately claim that they have been treated justly even though they have been treated differently. The principle of arithmetical equality has an application in those situations where we may safely assume that the persons involved are as a matter of fact equals and that their circumstances are as a matter of fact relevantly similar. In such situations justice requires not proportional but strictly equal treatment. Here the principle of equity reduces itself in effect to that of pure reciprocity. It is an alternative formulation of the 'golden rule' of 'doing as one would be done by'.

For Aristotle, the principle of equity constitutes the supreme principle of justice, in so far as justice has to do with moral rules or law. In the *Ethics* he states that there are two areas of human activity, in particular, where this principle of justice has a practical application. These are the spheres of rectificatory and distributive justice. The sphere of rectificatory justice (*diorthotikon dikaion*) (*Ethics* 1131$^{b}$–1132$^{b}$) has to do with regulating the social or ethical relationships between the citizens of a particular *polis*. Here, Aristotle concedes, we may assume that the persons involved are as matter of fact equals in all relevant respects. Consequently, in this area, all of these persons should be treated in accordance with the principle of strict arithmetical equality. Citizens should treat one another as equals and they should all be treated 'as equals' by the laws of the *polis* (*Ethics* 1132$^{a}$). When this does not happen, it is the function of law to correct any imbalance that arises as a result. In the *Ethics* Aristotle states that the principles of justice which forbid those actions such as murder, theft, and adultery which are intrinsically wrong fall within this sphere of rectificatory justice (*Ethics* 1107$^{a}$, 1130$^{b}$–1131$^{a}$). In my view, Peter Simpson's claim that Aristotle 'never bothers to give us any reason why adultery or murder is wrong' is incorrect.[11] It is clear from what he says about rectificatory justice in the *Ethics* that the reason why such actions are wrong or unjust is because those who commit them have done something which they would not have wished to have been done to themselves and consequently have not respected their fellow citizens as their own equals. They have not acted in accordance with the requirements of the principle of equity, interpreted in this particular context as simple reciprocity. Aristotle seems to think that the moral rules forbidding these actions can be logically inferred from the more general principle of equity or reciprocity combined with certain obvious facts about human nature. We may observe in passing that, despite this, one thing that Aristotle does *not* do is extend this principle of rectificatory justice to all human beings. Aristotle does not think that all human beings are by nature equal or that they have a natural right to be treated as such. As is well known, in the *Politics* Aristotle defends the institution of slavery. He criticizes the view that slavery is necessarily unjust because it involves treating equals as if they were unequals and he refuses to accept that slavery is, for this reason, 'contrary to nature' (*Politics* 1253$^{b}$–1255$^{b}$). Aristotle does not, therefore, subscribe to a doctrine of natural law in anything like the sense of the later Stoic philosophy. Although it is clear from what he says about slavery in the *Politics* and in the *Rhetoric* that he was familiar with natural law arguments of this sort, nevertheless he emphatically rejects them.

According to Aristotle problems of distributive justice (*dianemetikon dikaion*) (*Ethics* 1131$^{a}$–$^{b}$) always possess three elements. There is some good to be distributed; there is a body of persons among whom this good is to be distributed; and there is some standard of distribution which indicates an attribute the degree of possession or non-possession of which is considered to be relevant for determining the extent to which some persons are entitled to receive more and others less of the good in question (*Politics* 1282$^{b}$). Again Aristotle usually, but not always, assumes that these persons are the citizens of a particular *polis*. Sometimes, however, he discusses the situation in which citizenship itself is the good to be distributed. In this case it is the male adult inhabitants of a *polis* who constitute the relevant population. Problems of distributive justice, for Aristotle, have to do with the relationship that exists between individual citizens and the *polis* as a whole. This theory of distributive justice is central to the argument of Aristotle's *Politics*.

For Aristotle the principle of equity is a purely *formal* principle. It states simply that both justice and logic require that equals ought to be treated equally in relevantly similar circumstances or that 'like cases be treated alike'. It does not, however, stipulate who are to be considered equal, how they are to be treated, or when their circumstances are to be considered as relevantly similar. It amounts in effect, therefore, to no more than a commitment to the principle of impartiality or the 'rule of law' in both ethics and politics. This formal principle must be given a particular concrete realization within the principles of political justice of a particular *polis*. An important issue for Aristotle is how this substantive content is to be derived. Here, as Kelsen rightly observes, at least in the final analysis this content is provided by positive law.[12] Consequently, substantive justice must always be mediated by the customs and traditions or the ethical conventions of a particular *polis*. It is for this reason that, in Aristotle's view, it is necessary for us to make the transition from the study of ethics, which deals with abstract or formal principles of justice, to the study of politics (in the narrow sense of the term), which deals with the concrete realization of these principles in the historical circumstances of particular *poleis* and with the differences which exist between *poleis* in this respect.

## The *Politics*

### Natural law and the classification of constitutions

Central to Aristotle's political thought is his classification of the various different types of political constitution in the *Politics*. Here Aristotle applies the theory of justice which he develops in the *Ethics*. He starts with Plato's question 'Who should rule?' or Who *would* rule in an ideal society?' In his view, this is a problem of distributive justice. Aristotle's treatment of this subject is based on two separate arguments. The first focuses on who does the ruling and on the issue of whose interests are promoted by a particular system of government. In all societies, he says, government is 'in the hands of one, or of a few, or of the many' (*Politics* 1279$^a$; also 1278$^b$). Moreover, government can be either in the 'common interest' or in the 'private interest' of those who rule (*Politics* 1279$^a$). If we place these two principles together, then it is clear, Aristotle argues, that there are just six *pure* types of constitution possible—although in practice these might be combined in different ways, thereby generating various types of 'mixed constitution'. The first three pure types are constitutions in which the one, the few, or the many rule in the interests of all (or the common interest) and hence justly. Aristotle labels these types as 'kingship', 'aristocracy', and 'polity' respectively. The other three pure types, which Aristotle calls 'tyranny', 'oligarchy', and 'democracy', are constitutions in which the one, the few, or the many rule in their own private interests and hence unjustly (*Politics* 1279$^a$–$^b$). Aristotle describes these as corrupt or perverted constitutions (*Ethics* 1160$^a$–$^b$; *Politics* 1275$^b$, 1279$^a$, 1282$^b$, 1283$^a$). Aristotle's classification of constitutions may be presented in the form of a matrix. See Fig. 5.1.

Aristotle's second argument takes a slightly different tack. It focuses on the issue of what *standard* should be used when distributing political power among either the citizens or the inhabitants of a *polis*. There are, he suggests, three possible standards of distribution which might be used here, namely wealth, citizenship, and moral virtue or goodness (*Politics* 1282$^b$–1283$^a$, 1294$^a$). In all six types of constitution some people have more political power and others less, but in each case the justification offered for this is different. For example, in an oligarchy the standard of distribution is wealth. The wealthy have more power than the less wealthy. Moreover, this is considered to be just because the unequal distribution of power is

| | | Rule by | | |
|---|---|---|---|---|
| | | one | few | many |
| Rule in the interests of | the whole community (just constitutions) | kingship | aristocracy | polity |
| | the ruler(s) (unjust constitutions) | tyranny | oligarchy | democracy |

**FIG. 5.1**

exactly proportional to the unequal distribution of wealth. In a democracy the standard of distribution is citizenship. Here Aristotle assumes that power is distributed between the adult male inhabitants of a *polis* and not just its citizens, and that those inhabitants who are citizens will receive more of this good than those who are not. In this case, however, because all citizens possess the attribute of citizenship to the same degree, justice demands that political power be distributed between them in accordance with the principle of strict arithmetical equality (*Politics* 1317$^{b}$, 1318$^{a}$). Once again, Aristotle notes that in a democracy this pattern of distribution is considered to be just because it accords with the requirements of the principle of equity (*Politics* 1280$^{a}$, 1301$^{a}$).

Given that he concedes that in both an oligarchy and a democracy the principle of equity *is* in fact respected, it might well be asked why Aristotle nevertheless occasionally insists that these two types of government are unjust? Why does he think that oligarchy and democracy are corrupt or perverted constitutions? The reason for this is that he does not consider the standards of wealth or citizenship to be relevant standards for the purposes of this particular problem of distributive justice. Hence, he argues, although these constitutions may be said to be associated with 'a kind of justice', when evaluated by an absolute standard of justice they are faulty (*Politics* 1301$^{a}$). The advocates of oligarchy and democracy are speaking of 'a part of justice only' (*Politics* 1281$^{a}$). According to Aristotle, to distribute political power in the way that they do is just as arbitrary as giving more power to some people on the grounds that they are taller than others (*Politics* 1282$^{b}$). Aristotle agrees with Plato that ruling is a job like any other and that those who are best fitted to the job should be the ones to do it (*Politics* 1283$^{a}$). For Aristotle, the appropriate standard here is nobility, merit, or excellence, that is to say moral goodness or virtue, an attribute which is distributed unequally and is possessed to the necessary degree by only a few people, who are therefore 'the best' (aristoi) at ruling (*Politics* 1279$^{a}$, 1280$^{b}$–1281$^{a}$, 1286$^{b}$, 1293$^{b}$, 1294$^{a}$). In Aristotle's opinion, the good life for anyone is only possible if they are brought up in a *polis* which is ruled by such people. On this view, the reason why there is a wide variety of different constitutions is because although in *every* society there has 'always been an acknowledgement of justice and proportionate equality', nevertheless mankind has 'failed' to create a truly just *polis* in practice because it has invariably employed the wrong standard when distributing political power (*Politics* 1301$^{a}$).

For Aristotle as for Plato the people who should rule (and who would rule in an ideal society) are those who know about politics. They are the minority who are educated, virtuous and wise. Aristotle concedes that, as a matter of fact, such people will come from the wealthy, propertied stratum of a *polis*. They possess what he considers to be moderate wealth. He has in mind those who have enough property to be released from the need to work daily for a living (perhaps because they own slaves) and who as a result have sufficient leisure to engage in the pursuits of the mind and to cultivate their higher faculties (*Politics* 1323$^{b}$, 1328$^{b}$–1329$^{a}$). Aristotle calls these people the 'middle class' of a *polis* (*Politics* 1295$^{b}$–1296$^{a}$). From this standpoint Aristotle's ideal constitution is really a form of aristocracy. However, if this should turn out not to be possible in practice, he allows that a suitable alternative is *polity*. In its pure form polity is an ideal type of democracy in which all citizens are assumed to be virtuous and good. It is therefore, Aristotle concedes, as much an ideal as a pure aristocracy is. Aristotle argues, however, that polity may also be thought of as a type of 'mixed' constitution (*Politics* 1265$^{b}$, 1293$^{b}$, 1294$^{b}$). In his opinion, polity in this second sense is a realistic and hence practically attainable form of democracy in which rule by 'the people' (*demos*), who are assumed by Aristotle *not* to be virtuous and good, is balanced in some way by the influence of the minority who are wealthy and educated.

When arguing in this vein, then, Aristotle is of the opinion that the best or ideal constitution is one in which political power is distributed, not simply in accordance with the principle of equity or proportional equality but *also* in accordance with the correct standard of virtue or goodness. Only in such circumstances could the distribution of political power be said to be absolutely just. It is clear that this vision of an ideally just constitution might be used as a critical standard for assessing the justice or injustice of existing constitutions. This is, presumably, what Aristotle has in mind when he says in the *Ethics* that there is only one constitution which is 'naturally the best everywhere' (*Ethics* 1135$^{a}$) and in the *Politics* 'that the unequal should be given to equals, and the unlike to those who are like, is contrary to nature' (*Politics* 1325$^{b}$). In an important recent work Fred D. Miller Jr. has appealed to statements like this in the *Politics* in order to support his claim that Aristotle is best interpreted as a natural law theorist.[13] Miller argues that in these passages Aristotle is committed to the idea that there is a universally valid critical 'standard of justice by which inferior constitutions can be evaluated'.[14] On these grounds he maintains that Aristotle's argument 'supports a theory of natural justice'.[15] In the great debate which dominated Athenian politics in the fifth and fourth centuries BC between at least some of the Sophists and their critics over the issue of whether justice exists by convention only or by nature, Miller claims that Aristotle clearly takes the latter side against the former. He 'appeals to an objective normative principle' of natural justice and 'not merely to convention or opinion'.[16]

## Ethical relativism and the classification of constitutions

It cannot be denied that there is much evidence to support Miller's interpretation of Aristotle. On the other hand, however, there is also at least some significant evidence that counts against it and which supports the opposite view that Aristotle is an ethical or constitutional relativist. This interpretation of Aristotle is best represented in the work of Hans Kelsen.[17] Although Kelsen himself does not refer to them all, there are four good reasons why one might take this view. The first of these is that Aristotle says things in the *Politics* that directly contradict a natural law reading of his thought. For example, he says that in every *polis* 'the citizen should be moulded to suit the form of government under which he lives' (*Politics* 1337$^{a}$195). Elsewhere he states that in every *polis* the young must be 'trained by habit and education in the spirit of the constitution, if the laws are democratic, democratically, or oligarchically, if the laws are oligarchical' (*Politics* 1310$^{a}$; also 1276$^{b}$, 1308$^{b}$, 1309$^{b}$). Here Aristotle makes no judgement about the ethical merits or demerits of the different types of constitution under discussion. Given these remarks, it is not too surprising that Kelsen has argued that Aristotle is a constitutional or ethical relativist who agrees with those Sophists who argued that all justice is a matter of convention. In Kelsen's opinion, it is Aristotle's view that 'every positive law must be just' because 'positive law and justice coincide'.[18] In the *Politics* Aristotle excludes 'in advance any justice distinct from positive law, which might possibly conflict therewith'.[19]

When arguing in this vein, Aristotle has the greatest respect for the ideal of constitutional government generally (*Politics* 1289$^{a}$). Here the hallmark of constitutional government is simply that the rule of law is indeed respected and that like cases (as defined by the ethical values of the constitution in question) are indeed treated alike. The phrase 'the rule of law' in this context refers to existing law or to the principles of political justice associated with the customs and traditions of a particular constitution as it currently stands. A constitution is simply a coherent framework of laws, or of principles of political justice, which is impartially applied. As Aristotle himself puts it, 'where the laws have no authority' or where the laws do not rule 'there is no constitution' (*Politics* 1292$^{a}$; also 1282$^{b}$). There is considerable truth in the claim that 'constitutionalism' in this sense is Aristotle's enduring legacy to the later history of political thought. From this point of view, as Aristotle points out in his *Eudemian Ethics*, constitutions 'are all of them particular forms of justice' (*Eudemian Ethics* 1241$^{b}$). It follows from this that for Aristotle a constitution is by definition a system of justice and that strictly speaking no constitution could possibly be unjust. On this reading, it is Aristotle's view that the idea of an unjust constitution is a contradiction in terms.

The second reason for thinking that Aristotle is or should be an ethical and constitutional relativist is that such an interpretation of Aristotle's politics is consistent with and arguably required by the basic principles of Aristotelian metaphysics. According to Aristotle the world generally is composed of a multiplicity of individual things or substances. Each of these is a composite entity associated with a certain matter, on the one hand, and a certain form on the other (*Metaphysics* 1029$^{a}$, 1033$^{a}$, 1033$^{b}$, 1034$^{b}$, 1035$^{a}$, 1038$^{b}$). The form of a substance is encapsulated within the definition of its concept (*Metaphysics* 1026$^{b}$, 1028$^{a}$, 1032$^{b}$, 1042$^{a}$, 1043$^{a}$). This lists the characteristic features that are necessarily associated with this concept—features that are to be found universally in all examples of this type of substance everywhere (*Metaphysics* 1015$^{a}$–$^{b}$). According to Aristotle, these necessary features constitute the essence of a substance (*Metaphysics* 1030$^{a}$, 1031$^{a}$). They may be contrasted with other features which Aristotle considers to be accidental, which are not to be found in all examples of the type of substance in question (*Metaphysics* 1006$^{b}$, 1017$^{a}$, 1025$^{a}$). Now, considered from the standpoint of Aristotelian metaphysics, a particular constitution is an individual substance in the sense just indicated. As such it contains both essential features and accidental ones. For Aristotle, the form or essence with which it is associated is an idea or concept. Given that all constitutions are by definition systems of justice, not surprisingly Aristotle maintains that the concept in question is the concept of justice. In his opinion, therefore, justice is the very essence of any constitution. It is the essential nature of *all* constitutions to be just. Aristotle considers all particular constitutions to be concrete instantiations of the essence of justice. It follows from this, however, that if his ethical and political thought is to be consistent with his metaphysical beliefs, Aristotle cannot or *should* not acknowledge the existence of any independent standard of justice by means of which the constitution of a particular *polis* might be evaluated and declared to be unjust. According to this interpretation of Aristotle, if the views on justice expressed in the *Politics* are to be made consistent with Aristotle's metaphysical beliefs, then Aristotle ought consistently to adopt the relativist position attributed to him by Kelsen.

Considered from this point of view, the only way in which, for example, democracy and oligarchy might be criticized for being unjust is by saying, not that they are perverted forms of constitution, but rather that they are not constitutions at all, properly so called, because the rule of law is not respected within them. There are occasions when Aristotle *does* suggest this (*Politics* 1292$^{a}$, 1293$^{b}$, 1308$^{b}$), despite the fact that such remarks evidently undermine the sixfold classification of constitutions for which the *Politics* is famous. More usually, however, he is willing to allow that democracy and oligarchy are indeed constitutions in the strict sense of the term (*Politics* 1279$^{a}$, 1292$^{b}$, 1301$^{a}$). For example, at one point he says that in all constitutions, whether these are aristocracies, democracies, or oligarchies, we find the same 'notion of justice'. For these constitutions 'all recognize the claims of superiority', though not of course 'the *same* superiority' (*Politics* 1288$^{a}$). And elsewhere he concedes that we must 'assume as our starting point that in the many forms of government which have sprung up there has *always* been an acknowledgment of justice and proportionate equality' (*Politics* 1301$^{a}$). On these occasions, then, Aristotle concedes that democracy and oligarchy are correctly said to be types of constitution and that within them there is therefore respect for equity and the rule of law. Even in a democracy and an oligarchy those who are considered to be equals *are* treated equally and like cases are treated alike. It follows from this, however, that such constitutions could not possibly be unjust in the sense in which Aristotle defines this concept in his *Nicomachean Ethics*.

The third reason for thinking that Aristotle is a constitutional relativist is his claim that man is by nature a political animal, which is also logically inconsistent with his remarks about corrupt and perverted constitutions. As again Kelsen has noted, this claim implies that all positive law must 'be regarded as natural law' and hence that '*every* state' is a 'product of nature'.[20] Kelsen rightly observes that if this is the case, then even those constitutions which Aristotle considers to be perverted, precisely because they might properly be described as being constitutions or states in the strict sense of the term, must *also* be products of nature. Hence, for Aristotle, nature can provide no criterion for the negative evaluation of these constitutions. Any argument criticizing these constitutions could not possibly rest on the claim that their existence is contrary to nature.[21] Kelsen maintains that, when Aristotle makes this claim, what he says stands in 'open contradiction' to one of the main theses of his political theory, namely 'the natural givenneness of *all* states'. Kelsen asserts that this claim is clearly 'at variance with the intellectual scheme of the whole Aristotelian theory' and that it contradicts 'everything that Aristotle otherwise says about the nature of the state'.[22] He also claims, on these grounds, that it is 'more than doubtful' that Aristotle's remarks about perverted constitutions being contrary to nature are authentic and that it is difficult to avoid supposing that the text of the *Politics* at these points, which is 'so crucial' to the 'alleged natural law theory of Aristotle', is 'not corrupt'.[23] This explanation for the logical inconsistency in Aristotle's remarks about the justice or injustice of democracy and oligarchy seems to me to be untenable. It is equally possible, and just as plausible, to suggest that Aristotle's views on this subject are logically inconsistent, or alternatively that they simply altered over time. Nevertheless, adherents of the relativist interpretation of Aristotle would agree with the main thrust of Kelsen's argument here. From their standpoint, Kelsen is right to suggest that in the passages upon which Miller rests his case the views which Aristotle expresses are inconsistent with his claim that man is by nature a social and political animal. According to the relativist reading of Aristotle, then, it makes no sense to say that one type of constitution is better than another, or that there is one constitution which is the best, or that some constitutions must be unjust because they are contrary to nature. Rather, constitutions are simply different from one another, although of course only with respect to their accidental and not their essential features. The reason why there is a variety of different constitutions here is not because in some societies the *wrong* standard of distribution is used, but simply because *different* standards of distribution are used.

The fourth reason for thinking that Aristotle is a constitutional relativist has to do with what he says about the relationship that exists between natural justice (*phusikon dikaion*), legal or conventional justice (*nomikon dikaion*), and political justice (*politikon dikaion*) in an important passage in book 5 of the *Ethics* (*Ethics* 1134$^{b}$–1135$^{a}$). By 'natural' in this context Aristotle means that which is ethically necessary and which applies universally in every case. By 'conventional' he means that which relates to a matter of moral indifference and is, therefore, merely accidental, a product of the customs and traditions of a *polis*, varying legitimately from *polis* to *polis*. Aristotle states here that natural justice and conventional justice are both a 'part' of political justice. What he means by this is that every principle of political justice is composed of a principle of natural justice combined with a principle of legal or conventional justice. From this point of view, natural justice is something which is immanent within the principles of political justice of a *polis*. To serve as a guide to action natural justice must be applied to the specific circumstances of a *polis* and given a determinate existence within its principles of political justice. We saw earlier that according to Aristotle the essence of justice is the principle of equity, which demands that equals be treated equally in relevantly similar circumstances. We also saw that this is a formal principle that cannot be applied in practice unless it is given a content that determines which persons are equal, how they should be treated, and so on. We can now say that for Aristotle the principle of equity is the most fundamental principle of *natural* justice and that the principles that provide it with a definite substantive content are the principles of legal or conventional justice of a particular *polis*. It follows from this, however, that for Aristotle the latter principles must relate to matters that are indifferent from the moral point of view. In other words, if Aristotle's beliefs are to be made logically consistent, it ought to be of no importance to him how these things are actually determined in the case of any particular constitution. As Kelsen points out, generally speaking Aristotle is happy to leave this determination to positive law and he acknowledges that the constitutions of different *poleis*, for example oligarchic and democratic ones, will therefore inevitably differ from one another in these morally irrelevant respects.[24] But again this clearly implies that for Aristotle whether a constitution is an oligarchy or a democracy ought to be a matter of indifference so far as our assessment of its justice or injustice is concerned. In so far as oligarchy and democracy are indeed types of constitutional government which respect the rule of law, Aristotle's theory of justice requires that they each be regarded as both natural and just.

According to the relativist interpretation, then, Aristotle's claim in the *Politics* that there are corrupt or perverted constitutions which are unjust because they are contrary to nature is contradicted by what he says elsewhere in the same text. It is inconsistent with his own metaphysical beliefs. It runs counter to his doctrine that man is by nature a social and political animal. And it conflicts with what he says about the relationship between natural, legal, and political justice in the *Ethics*. From this point of view, although it seems implausible to deny that Aristotle actually made this claim, nevertheless it would be unwise to base one's interpretation of his political thought as a whole entirely upon the fact that he did so. There is, therefore, good reason to question the validity of Miller's natural law interpretation of Aristotle precisely because of its undue reliance on this evidence.

## Synthesis of natural law and ethical relativism

It could be argued that neither Miller's natural law interpretation of Aristotle nor the ethical and constitutional relativist interpretation of Kelsen and others is entirely correct, although each of them has something to be said for it, and that there is a third possible interpretation which removes at least some of the inconsistencies in Aristotle's thinking, though not all of them. Despite the relativist critique of it, there is definitely something in Miller's interpretation. Aristotle certainly does attach importance to the concept of natural justice or natural law, and no assessment of his ethical and political thought is acceptable which does not appreciate this fact. What is alien to the spirit of Aristotle's thinking, however, is the Platonic idea that there is an independent or transcendent standard of substantive justice which individuals might employ to critically evaluate the positive law or the constitution of the *polis* in which they live and declare it to be unjust. With respect to this issue I agree with the relativist interpretation of Aristotle, for all four of the reasons suggested above. In my view, Aristotle's remarks about unjust or corrupt constitutions being contrary to nature are indeed inconsistent with the central thrust of his general approach to ethics and politics. Kelsen has argued on these grounds that we should set these remarks aside and that if we do the only appropriate conclusion is that Aristotle is not a natural law theorist at all but an ethical and constitutional relativist whose views are very close to what today is referred to as legal positivism.[25] But this is going much too far. Kelsen is right to argue that we should set these remarks aside; however, if we do, we are not then compelled to abandon the view that Aristotle is a natural law theorist, albeit in a different sense from that suggested by Miller.

It is fruitful to place Aristotle's thought within the context of the debate between some of the Sophists and their opponents in ancient Athens in the fifth century BC. As we have seen, the traditional understanding of the Sophists is that they maintained that all justice is conventional. From this point of view, the existing social and political order in ancient Athens and the rule of law associated with it did not have the divine or religious sanction which it had traditionally been thought to possess, for example by writers such as Sophocles. In the context of fifth-century Athenian politics, therefore, the views of these Sophists were perceived to have radical political implications. They were considered to be subversive of the existing social and political order. Aristotle is best seen as an opponent of this doctrine. He should not, therefore, be interpreted as an ethical relativist. On the contrary, one of his aims in the *Ethics* is to provide a refutation of this Sophist claim that there is no such thing as natural justice and that all justice is merely conventional. On the other hand, however, Aristotle does not go to the opposite extreme and advocate that justice is in its entirety something that is either natural or rational. He does not suggest that the principles of natural justice can provide a rational or ahistorical standard by means of which the positive law or the constitution of any society might be criticized. For in the context of Athenian politics, such a doctrine would have been just as radical as that of his Sophist opponents. It could, for example, have been used (and arguably *was* used by some) to condemn the institution of slavery. Rather, Aristotle seeks to combine the ethical and legal conventionalism of this group of Sophists with the idea of a universally valid natural justice or law into a third doctrine which, in his view, possesses the strengths of each and the weaknesses of neither of these two alternatives.

One could think of Aristotle's theory of justice as a whole along the same lines as Aristotle himself thinks of the principles of political justice and the political constitutions with which they are associated, as having two separate though related parts. Just as each of these things contain a part that is natural and a part that is conventional, so also, in a manner of speaking, does Aristotle's theory of justice. The first of these is to be found in book 5 of the *Ethics*. The principles of justice which Aristotle considers to be natural and hence universally valid are presented there in an outline sketch. In his *Politics* he goes on to discuss the circumstances within which these principles are concretely realized in some of the constitutions of the many different *poleis* in fourth-century Greece. This second part of Aristotle's theory is, therefore, concerned not with the similarities that exist between the constitutions of these *poleis*, but with the differences in their history, customs, traditions, and conventions. Each of these two elements is vital for understanding Aristotle's thought as a whole and neither is on its own sufficient. If we focus exclusively on the former, then (like Miller) we present Aristotle as a natural law theorist in an excessively rationalistic sense and we lose sight of the historical and relativistic dimension of his views on ethics and politics. If we focus exclusively on the latter, then (like Kelsen) we transform Aristotle into an ethical relativist and lose sight of the fact that he wishes to defend the existing social order in any society (especially in Athens) by means of reasoned argument and philosophy rather than an appeal to religion, on the one hand, or mere custom and tradition, on the other. What this third doctrine amounts to in the end, therefore, is a sophisticated philosophical justification of the customs and traditions associated with the constitution of any *polis*, no matter what they might be. Aristotle's reply to the Sophists is that there is a reason or justice which lies behind and supports these different customs and conventions and that, consequently, in any given case the existing social and political order is not as arbitrary as the Sophists think. For Aristotle as for Hegel it might be said that reason is 'the rose in the cross of the present'. In my view, the best way to characterize such a doctrine, as again in the case of Hegel, is as a form of philosophical conservatism.

## Aristotle and contemporary political theory

What is the contemporary relevance of Aristotle's ethical and political thought, and especially his views on justice? John Rawls's *A Theory of Justice*[26] is the most important and most influential contribution to discussion of the subject of justice in recent times, and the debate between Rawls and his 'communitarian' critics has set the agenda for many of those who are interested in questions of political philosophy today.[27] It is both interesting and enlightening to see how Aristotle has been taken up and appropriated by the protagonists in this debate.

Rawls never directly engages with Aristotle's theory of justice. Yet it is plain that Rawls's theory resembles Aristotle's in a number of significant respects. For example, Rawls's account of 'justice as fairness', his treatment of the concept of justice, and his understanding of 'formal justice' in sections 1 and 10 of *A Theory of Justice*, together with his emphasis on the importance of the principle of reciprocity for any adequate theory of justice, are all Aristotelian in spirit.[28] Like Aristotle, Rawls suggests that we need to distinguish between formal and substantive justice and that formally speaking justice is simply a matter of 'treating like cases alike'.[29] He also observes, referring to Aristotle explicitly by name in this particular context, that if it is to be of any practical value, the purely formal principle of justice needs to be provided with a definite substantive content.[30] Unlike Aristotle, however, Rawls maintains that this content might be discerned solely from our knowledge of human nature, which remains the same always and everywhere. Given these similarities, the fact that Rawls refers to Aristotle on only a very few occasions in his book, and hardly ever to Aristotle's views on justice, is very surprising.[31] One possible reason for this is that Rawls wrongly assumes throughout that Aristotle is an ethical consequentialist and that Aristotle's 'eudaimonism' is a consequentialist doctrine.[32] Thus Rawls attributes to Aristotle the view that there are no actions which are intrinsically right or wrong and that whether any particular action is right or wrong depends solely on the consequences of performing it, which is the very opposite of what Aristotle actually thinks. Rawls himself, of course, is extremely critical of ethical consequentialism. His own theory of justice is a deontological theory. It states that whether an action is right or wrong, just or unjust, has nothing to do with consequences. According to Rawls, his theory of justice is for this reason much closer to the moral philosophy of Immanuel Kant than it is to that of any other philosopher.[33] Rawls does not recognize the striking similarity that exists between Kant and Aristotle, and hence also between himself and Aristotle, with respect to this particular issue. This is not, of course, to say that there are no significant differences between Aristotle's theory of justice and that of Rawls. As Rawls's critics have rightly observed, the most important of these is that Rawls's theory, associated as it is with the idea of the 'unencumbered self' and the principles of abstract individualism, is excessively universalistic and rationalistic and lacks Aristotle's sense of community and of the historical rootedness of the ethical conduct of individual moral agents. As we have seen, for Aristotle, formal justice is always given a substantive content by the customs and traditions of a particular *polis*. There is therefore a strong communitarian dimension to Aristotle's thinking about justice which is absent from the work of Rawls.

Nevertheless, it could be argued that communitarian critics of Rawls like Alasdair MacIntyre also offer a highly selective reading of Aristotle. For despite the fact that he acknowledges Aristotle's employment of the concept of natural justice,[34] MacIntyre tends to share Hans Kelsen's inclination to interpret Aristotle as an ethical or constitutional relativist who attaches little or no significance to the idea that there are universally valid objective standards in ethics. When presenting his own views on justice, MacIntyre is so keen to get away from the rationalism and the universalism of the unhistorical approach to justice adopted by figures such as Plato, Kant, and Rawls[35] that he sometimes overemphasizes the importance of the values, customs, and traditions of particular communities and the idea that it is solely the 'common good' with which the laws of these communities are associated that determines what is just and what is unjust for their members.[36] At the same time however, as we know, MacIntyre also appeals throughout to Aristotle's ethical and political thought in his own support. Not surprisingly therefore, given his own antipathy towards moral rules, MacIntyre severely downplays the significance of that part of Aristotle's theory of justice which is premissed upon the belief that there are indeed certain universally valid, and rationally apprehensible, principles of natural justice or law. As a result, he does not appreciate the specific character of Aristotle's critique of ethical relativism. Hence MacIntyre, also, offers us a highly selective interpretation of Aristotle which does not sufficiently recognize the importance of certain key aspects of Aristotle's ethical and political thought as a whole. His communitarian reading of Aristotle appears to be driven more by a desire to criticize the views of Rawls and Kant than by a desire to do justice to Aristotle.

## FURTHER READING

Kelsen, Hans, *Essays in Legal and Moral Philosophy*, ed. O. Weinberger (Dordrecht: Reidel, 1973).
Kymlicka, Will, *Contemporary Political Philosophy: An Introduction*, 2nd edn. (Oxford: Oxford University Press, 2000).
MacIntyre, Alasdair, *After Virtue: A Study in Moral Theory* (1981; 2nd edn. London: Duckworth, 2000).
MacIntyre, Alasdair, *Whose Justice? Which Rationality?* (London: Duckworth, 1988).
Miller, Fred D., Jr., *Nature, Justice and Rights in Aristotle's Politics* (Oxford: Clarendon Press, 1997).
Rawls, John, *A Theory of Justice* (1972; rev. edn. Oxford: Oxford University Press, 1999).
Statman, Daniel (ed.), *Virtue Ethics: A Critical Reader* (Edinburgh: Edinburgh University Press, 1997).

## NOTES

1. Fred D. Miller Jr., *Nature, Justice and Rights in Aristotle's Politics* (Oxford: Clarendon Press, 1997).
2. Hans Kelsen, *Essays in Legal and Moral Philosophy*, ed. O. Weinberger (Dordrecht: Reidel, 1973).
3. Alasdair MacIntyre, *Whose Justice? Which Rationality?* (London: Duckworth, 1988).
4. Miller, *Nature, Justice and Rights in Aristotle's Politics*, 67.
5. Alisdair MacIntyre, *After Virtue: A Study in Moral Theory*, 2nd edn. (London: Duckworth, 2000); and Daniel Statman (ed.), *Virtue Ethics: A Critical Reader* (Edinburgh: Edinburgh University Press, 1997).
6. Ibid. 153.
7. Ibid. 257.
8. Statman, *Virtue Ethics*, 21–2, 26–8, 189–90.
9. Ibid. 10, 19–21, 26–8, 30, 245–59, 260–85.
10. Kelsen, *Essays in Legal and Moral Philosophy*, 127–9.
11. Ibid. 249.
12. Kelsen, *Essays in Legal and Moral Philosophy*, 127.
13. Miller, *Nature, Justice and Rights in Aristotle's Politics*, pp. vii, 67, 74–5, 191.
14. Ibid., pp. vii, 187–8.
15. Ibid. 16.
16. Ibid. 14–15.
17. Kelsen, *Essays in Legal and Moral Philosophy*.
18. Ibid. 127.
19. Ibid. 124.
20. Ibid. 132.
21. Ibid. 133.
22. Ibid. 147.
23. Ibid. 134–5.
24. Ibid. 126–7.
25. Ibid. 129–32, 147.
26. John Rawls, *A Theory of Justice*, rev. edn. (Oxford: Oxford University Press, 1999).
27. Will Kymlicka, *Contemporary Political Philosophy: An Introduction*, 2nd edn. (Oxford: Oxford University Press, 2000).

28. Rawls, *A Theory of Justice*, 5–6, 10–13, 26–8.
29. Ibid. 5, 47–52, 444–5.
30. Ibid. 45, 50–2, 444–5.
31. Ibid. 10, 22, 45, 79, 214, 286, 351, 374, 466, 468, 481, 488.
32. Ibid. 22.
33. Ibid. 28, 38, 129–30, 156–7, 221–7, 233, 513.
34. MacIntyre, *After Virtue*, 150–1; MacIntyre, *Whose Justice?*, 120–1.
35. MacIntyre, *After Virtue*, 9, 11, 22, 68–70, 113, 220–1, 265–6.
36. Ibid. 151–2; MacIntyre, *Whose Justice?*, 121–2.

# PART II

# The two kingdoms

# 6 St Augustine

Jean Bethke Elshtain

## Contents



## Chapter guide

The chapter begins by examining the fate of St Augustine's texts within the world of academic political theory and the general suspicion of 'religious' thinkers within that world. The problem with managing a thinker whose works are so extensive, cover nearly every possible topic, and take the form of complex narratives are also noted. The first major section explores Augustine's understanding of the human person as a bundle of complex desires and emotions that, in the process of growing up, are formed within the framework of family, Church, school, and the wider cultural surround. This makes their formation an ethical task of premier importance. Augustine's view of the person and his or her complexity also enters into his description of the human mind and our ability to take account epistemologically of what we learn through experience. A theory of language that was later to influence the philosopher Ludwig Wittgenstein also flows from his fertile pen. The second section takes up the implications of Augustine's insistence that human sociality is a given and goes all the way down. There are temporal goods that human beings rightly cherish and ought to strive to achieve, among them civic peace, order, and a measure of justice. In discussing the moral orientations of persons and of cultures, Augustine looks at the interplay of *caritas* and *cupiditas*. Finally, Augustine's well-known reflections on the themes of war and peace, locating him as the father of the tradition of 'just war' thinking, is taken up.

## Biography

Augustine of Hippo was born in Roman North Africa in 354. He died as Bishop of Hippo, a seaport city on the Mediterranean coast. Augustine's formidable mother, Monnica, was Catholic. His father, Patricius, was a town councillor in Thagaste, his birthplace. Well educated in provincial Roman schools, Augustine embarked upon a career as a rhetorician and teacher of rhetoric. A precocious student with a wide-ranging intellect, he was tormented by the question of good and evil and, for a time, became a disciple of

Manichaean teaching. His years as a student stretch from 371 to 385 and he describes these years as somewhat dissolute although intellectual development had converted him to the study of philosophy. After a period of teaching in his home town and in Carthage, he headed, first, to Rome and then to Milan. It was in Milan, in 384–6, that Augustine encountered the great St Ambrose, Bishop of Milan, and his teaching and preaching. Augustine's mother had followed him to Milan. Although he had been baptized, he was not a Catholic Christian until his dramatic conversion, recounted in some of the most famous passages in Western literature in his *Confessions*. Following his conversion, Augustine withdrew from his life as a rising rhetorician and joined a small group of companions in Cassiciacum, in 386–7, where they pursued contemplation and philosophic discussion. It was in this period that Augustine embarked on his prodigious writing career. In 387 he journeyed with his compatriots and his mother to Ostia, where Monnica died and was buried. In 388 Augustine returned to Africa and took up his ministry in Hippo. He was quickly immersed in some of the most dramatic and even violent quarrels of the age, including the Donatist controversy. He was named Bishop of Hippo in 395, against his will, but he went on to serve in that capacity until his death in 430, when the Vandals were laying siege to the city. His greatest work, *The City of God*, composed over a twenty-seven-year period, was occasioned by the fall of Rome to the Visigoths in 410. When he died in 430, he left behind a body of work that stunned subsequent generations even as it amazed a contemporary, who noted that Augustine had written so much it was impossible for one person to read it all. His books number some ninety-three; over 400 sermons and 300 letters are extant. The estimate is that he preached 8,000 sermons. Augustine bequeathed to the Western tradition a restless, dynamic quality of intellect but always with an eye towards coming to know and to claim the truth that belief makes possible: the famous *credo ut intelligam*.

## Key texts

*Letters* (386–430)
*The Confessions* (397–401)
*The Trinity* (397–426)
*The City of God* (413–27)
*Retractiones* (426–7)

## Main text used

*The City of God*, trans. Henry Bettenson (Baltimore: Penguin, 1972) (*DCD*).

## Key ideas

**The human person** is a complex bundle of emotions and desires, torn by conflict, wanting to do good but faltering given a divided and weak will. **Language** is a constitutive part of human nature that expresses our humanity but also divides us one from the other. Language separates us but also associates us to one another. **Belief** is a route to understanding rather than in conflict with warranted claims. **Human life** is intrinsically social and this is the source of complex human friendships and loves but also a cauldron of hostility, suspicion, and enmity. **Peace** is the foremost yearning of the human heart. A lust to dominate threatens earthly peace and divides the soul as well as creating rifts in human societies. **The heavenly city** stands in contrast to the earthly city of division, imperfection, and violence but a city in which peace and justice can nonetheless be attained if imperfectly. **Evil** is a falling away from the good as human beings fall into the sin of pride. **War** flows from the lust to dominate and its ravages are, in part, a punishment for sin. The just wage wars only from stark necessity and in order to protect those who cannot defend themselves.

## Introduction: Augustine and political theory

The fate of St Augustine in the world of academic political theory has been, at best, mixed. He is, first of all, enveloped in that blanket of suspicion cast over all 'religious' or 'theological' thinkers: do they *really* belong with the likes of Plato and Aristotle, Machiavelli and Hobbes, Marx and Mill? Weren't their eyes cast heavenward rather than fixed resolutely on human political and social affairs? There are, as well, particular features to St Augustine's work that make him a tough nut to crack. He is an ambitiously discursive and narrative thinker. From the time of his conversion to Catholic Christianity in 386 to his death as Bishop of Hippo in 430, he wrote some 117 books. He touches on all the central themes of Christian theology and Christian life: the nature of God and human persons, the problem of evil, free will, and determinism, war and human aggression, the bases of social life and political order, Church doctrine, Christian vocations: the list is nigh endless.

Although a number of his works follow an argumentative line in the manner most often favoured by political theorists, especially given the distinctly juridical or legalistic cast of so much modern political theory, most often he paints bold strokes on an expansive canvas. His enterprise is at once theological, philosophical, historical, cultural, and rhetorical. His works are characterized by an extraordinarily rich surface as well as vast depth, making it difficult to get a handle on if one's own purposes are not so ambitious. He traffics in what we generally call 'universals', but he is also a nuanced 'particularist' and historicist.

Given this towering enterprise it is, perhaps, unsurprising that attempts have been made to reduce Augustine to manageable size. To that end he has been tagged a political realist and canonized, if you will, as the theological grandfather of a tradition that includes Machiavelli and Hobbes. Then, too, Augustine, if he is read at all, is read primarily in and through excerpts from his great works that most favourably comport with this 'political realism'. To this end, his *Confessions* are ignored and book XIX of his 1,091-page masterwork *The City of God* (in the Penguin Classics unabridged version[1]) is reproduced with certain parts highlighted, perhaps along with a chunk from book I, chapter 1, on 'the city of this world, a city which aims at dominion, which holds nations in enslavement, but is itself dominated by that very lust of domination' (*DCD* I. I, p. 5). Book II, chapter 21, is helpful on Augustine's alternative to Cicero's judgement (according to Scipio) on the Roman commonwealth. Book XV, chapter l, traces lines of descent of the 'two cities, speaking allegorically'; book XIX, chapter 14, as already noted, is mined for a few precepts about the interests government should serve; chapter 15 makes an argument against slavery 'by nature'; and chapter 21, in which Scipio's definition of a commonwealth as advanced by Cicero makes a second appearance, also seems pertinent. Chapter 7 of book XIX is culled as the justification of war argument. Perhaps—just perhaps—excerpts are drawn from chapters 14 to 16 in order to demonstrate Augustine's insistence that there is a connection between the peace and good of the household in relation to the city. That, plus his scathing comment that what pirates do with one boat Romans do with a navy, but the one is called brigandage while the other is named empire, and the student has her quick intake of what I have called 'Augustine Lite'. The upshot is a shriven Augustine, numbered among the pessimists and charged with being among those who stress human cruelty and violence with a concomitant need for order, coercion, punishment, and occasional war as the upshot.

Recognizing the inadequacy of this 'normalized' Augustine doesn't mean one has an easy task if one's purpose is to be fair to his complexity with the enterprise of political theory in mind, in part for the reasons noted above concerning his way of writing and arguing. But even more pertinent is the theorist's sense of the task of political theory. If one construes that task as a way of putting together anthropological presuppositions (what we used to call 'theories of human nature'), claims about the political and social order in light of those presuppositions, the role of political theory in relation to these interrelated tasks, and the perils and possibilities inherent to any political activity or order, then Augustine's expansiveness is a welcome thing indeed. If one's aims are narrower or more modest, his expansiveness is a frustration. I begin from the point of view that his expansiveness is welcome. What follows is a way of highlighting key points of theoretical demarcation in Augustine's work that are rich with implications for political theory.

## The self

In his wonderful biography of St Augustine the noted historian of the late antique world Peter Brown claims that Augustine has 'come as near to us . . . as the vast gulf that separates a modern man from the culture and religion of the later empire can allow.'[2] How so? One reason, surely, lies in Augustine's complex ruminations on the nature of selfhood. This is a theme close to our own preoccupations. Augustine, in fact, anticipates postmodern strategies in dethroning the Cartesian subject even before that subject was erected. For Augustine, the mind can never be transparent to itself; we are never wholly in control of our thoughts; our bodies are essential, not contingent, to who we are and how we think; and we know that we exist not because 'I think, therefore I am' but, rather, 'I doubt, therefore I know I exist'. Only a subject who is a self that can reflect on its self can doubt. His *Confessions* is a story of a human being who has become a question to himself.

The story begins with an infant—here, too, Augustine is radical within the context of political theory, which often seems to assume that human beings spring full-blown from the head of John Locke. Augustine starts with natality and intimates a developmental account featuring a fragile, dependent creature who is by no means a tabula rasa, but, rather, a being at once social and 'quarrelsome'. The human being is driven by hunger, desire, and frustration at his or her inability to express himself or herself and to get others to respond. Growing up is not about getting rid of these childish emotions—these are key ingredients of our natures and our ability to understand—but, rather, about forming and shaping our passions in light of certain presuppositions about human beings, human willing, and our faltering attempts to will and to act rightly. Augustine's awareness of the sheer messiness of human existence lies at the heart of his withering fire directed at Stoic *apatheia*. For the mind to be in a state 'in which the mind cannot be touched by any emotion whatsoever, who would not judge this insensitivity to be the worst of all moral defects?' (*DCD* XIV. 9, p. 56).[3] We begin as, and we remain, beings who love, who yearn, who grieve, who experience frustration. The most important point here is Augustine's insistence that thought can never be purged of the emotions and that the thinking self expresses complex emotion through thought and in a language that is, hopefully, up to the task.

Epistemologically, thinking, including that mode of thinking called philosophic, should not pretend to a clean separation between emotion and reason; rather, these are interlaced and mutually constitute one another. Augustine argues that certain philosophies abstract from, or offer unreal assessments of, our human condition by taking insufficient account of embodiment and should be rejected for that reason. The body is epistemologically significant, a source of delight, of travail, of knowledge of good and evil. The body is the mode through which we connect to the world and through which the world discloses itself. Mind is embodied; body is thought. The heart of Augustine's case against the Pelagians also lies here given their overestimation of human control of the will, of *voluntas*. In the words of the philosopher James Wetzel, 'Pelagius seemed in the end to deny that there were ever significant obstacles to living the good life, once reason had illuminated its nature, [thus] he stood in more obvious continuity with the philosophical tradition than Augustine, who came to disparage the worldly wisdom of pagan philosophy for its overconfidence.'[4] Augustine is an epistemological sceptic who believes, nonetheless, that we can come to know certain truths. There are warranted beliefs but we can approach these only through complex indirection and through love (*caritas*), a formed desire and the name given to a 'good' of a sort that spills over the boundaries of the self and reaches out to others and to the source of love, God. We may not be able to verify most of what we believe—as we cannot be everywhere, see everything, experience everything—but our believing isn't a flying leap into the darkness.

Given the fact that all human beings are creatures attempting to express desire (whether disordered or ordered), and that they must do so though language, our words are open to misunderstanding and to multiple, ambiguous interpretation by other similarly desiring creatures. This suggests a theory of language, and Augustine offers one that influenced the work of Ludwig Wittgenstein, among others. (I will say more on this below.) What captures the interest of such desiring creatures? Our selves, for one thing. Because we are driven by *delectio*, by desire and yearning, we search for enjoyment, including pleasures of the intellect. Indeed, we acquire self-knowledge by trying our 'strength in answering, not in word but in deed, what may be called the interrogation of temptation' (*DCD* XVI. 32, pp. 693–4). We come to self-knowledge through our interaction with the world. We make mistakes—proving that we exist—and we carry on having learned something from the very clumsiness of our deed-doing.

But it is never easy for the mind to unlock things. As beings circumscribed by the boundaries of time and space, we require certain fundamental categories in order to *see* the world at all. Otherwise all would be flux. In addition to time and space, we require a form that incorporates reason and the will—that is, so to speak, up to our complexity. Augustine finds this form in the Trinity, a principle that works through complex relational analogies involving similarities and dissimilarities, things seen and unseen, at one and the same time.[5] We are capable of forming concepts about things we have seen and things we have not seen. We imagine many things to be, in part because we know what it means to have, or to bear, the 'trace' of an image. We believe many things exist—rightly so—that are not personally known to us. Augustine writes:

> And in fact when I wish to speak of Carthage, I seek for what to say within myself, and find an image of Carthage within myself; but I received this through the body, that is, through the sense of the body, since I was present there in the body, and have seen and perceived it with my senses, and have retained it in my memory, that I might find the word about it within myself whenever I might wish to utter it. For its image in my mind is its word, not the sound of the three syllables when Carthage [Car-tha-go in Latin] is named, or even when that name is silently thought of during some period of time, but the word that I see in my mind when I utter this word of three syllables with my voice, or even before I utter it. . . . So too, when I wish to speak of Alexandria which I have never seen, an image of it is also present within me. (*DCD* VIII. 6, p. 257)

Augustine uses the metaphor of fabrication—of making things—in order to drive home this point. 'A worker makes a chest. At first he has the chest in his skill-knowledge: For if he did not have it in his skill-knowledge, how could it be brought forth by making? But the chest as it is in his skill-knowledge is not the chest as it appears to our eyes. In skill-knowledge it exists invisibly, in the work it will exist visibly.'[6] When we gaze upon things in the mind, through a complex word–name–image nexus, we are not untrammelled in this imagining. There is an available repertoire. It is linguistic, historic, contingent, time-bound. It is caught within the confines and limits of our embodiment. So although naming and imagining is 'wonderful', it is also constrained. We cannot imagine just anything. If, as Wittgenstein says, a lion could speak and we could not understand him, so we can say that if a giraffe could imagine, we could not recognize the imagining. We are not nibbling off treetops and gazing across the savannah from a great height. (This and more, but I assume the point is taken.)

This leads directly to Augustine on language and the constraints imposed on us by language. As *par excellence* the language-users among God's creatures, we bump up all the time against opacity and constraint. In book XIX, chapter 7, Augustine muses about the ways in which all humans are divided by linguistic differences. These differences make it very hard for us to understand one another.

> The diversity of languages separates man from man. For if two men meet and are forced by some compelling reason not to pass on but to stay in company, then if neither knows the other's language, it is easier for dumb animals, even of different kinds, to associate together than these men, although both are human beings. For when men cannot communicate their thoughts to each other, simply because of difference of language, all the similarity of their common human nature is of no avail to unite them in fellowship. So true is this that a man would be more cheerful with his dog for company than with a foreigner. I shall be told that the Imperial City has been at pains to impose on conquered peoples not only her yoke but her language also, as a bond of peace and fellowship, so that there should be no lack of interpreters but even a profusion of them. True; but think of the cost of this achievement! Consider the scale of those wars, with all the slaughter of human beings, all the human blood that was shed! (*DCD* XIX. 7, p. 861)

Here Augustine moves from the murkiness of language, how it divides us despite our common human nature, to the imposition of a language on diverse peoples but at a truly terrible price. We find, then, a drawing together of notions of human nature, language, and its centrality in constituting us as living creatures; the complexity of a search for fellowship; and a pithy critique of the enforced homogeneity of empire.

The upshot of the force of linguistic convention, finally, is that human beings can only achieve what Augustine calls 'creature's knowledge'. Full knowledge is not available to human knowers, no matter how brilliant and learned that knower. We are both limited and enabled by the conventions of language. No one can jump out of his or her linguistic skin. We are obliged to bow to 'normal usage' if we hope to communicate at all, and we are driven to communicate by our sociality, a sociality that goes all the way down. This sociality lies at the basis of Augustine on the nature of human societies.

## Social life

Human beings are, I noted above, social through and through. Created in the image of God, human relationality defines us. The self is not and cannot be free-standing. Social life is full of ills and yet to be cherished. Thus, civic life, among those social forms, is not simply what sin has brought into the world but what emerges, in part, given our capacity for love, our use of reason, as well (alas) as a pervasive lust for domination attendant upon human affairs. 'The philosophers hold the view that the life of the wise man should be social, and in this we support them heartily.' Indeed the city of God—Augustine's way of characterizing that pilgrim band of Christians during their earthly sojourn in and through a community of reconciliation and fellowship that presages the heavenly kingdom—could never have had 'its first start . . . if the life of the saints were not social' (*DCD* XIX. 6, p. 860). All human beings, without exception, are citizens of the earthly kingdom—the city of man—and even in this fallen condition there is a kind of 'natural likeness' that forges bonds between us. These 'bonds of peace' do not suffice to prevent wars, dissensions, cruelty, and misery of all kinds, but we are nonetheless called to membership based on a naturalistic sociality and basic morality available to all rational creatures. A kind of unity in plurality pushes towards harmony; but the sin of division—with its origins in pride and wilfulness—drives us apart.

Yet it is love of friendship that lies at the root of what might be called Augustine's 'practical philosophy', his history, ethics, and social and political philosophy.[7] Pinioned between alienation and affection, human beings—those 'cracked pots'—are caught in the tragedy of alienation but glued by love. Our sociality is given, so for Augustine the question is not 'Should we be social or should we trust enough to love?' but rather 'What shall I love and how shall I love it?'[8] His complex ethical theory follows and can only be touched on here, but it must be noted that political life is one form that human social and ethical life assumes. We are always in society and we always seek the consolation of others. Society, for Augustine is a species of friendship, and friendship is a moral union in and through which human beings strive for a shared good. All of Augustine's central categories, including war and peace, are in the form of a relation of one sort or another. And the more we are united at all levels in a bond of peace, the closer we come to achieving that good at which we aim and which God intends.

For Augustine, neighbourliness and reciprocity emerge from ties that bind, beginning with familial bonds and extending from these particular relations outward: the filaments of affection must not stop at the portal to the *domus.* Augustine writes: 'The aim was that one man should not combine many relationships in his one self, but that those connections should be separated and spread among individuals, and that in this way they should help to bind social life more effectively by involving in their plurality a plurality of persons' (*DCD* xv. 16, p. 623). The social tie is 'not confined to a small group' but extends 'more widely to a large number with the multiplying links of kinship' (*DCD* xv. 16, p. 624). The importance of plurality, of the many emerging from a unique one—for God began with the singular—cannot be underestimated in Augustine's work. It is his way of putting into a single frame human uniqueness and individuality with sociality and plurality. Bonds of affection tied human beings from the start. Bonds of kinship and affection bound them further. These relationships became dispersed, finally encompassing the entire globe.

In light of the confusion and confounding of human languages, it is sometimes difficult to repair to this fundamental sociality, but we yearn for it and seek it in and through the social forms we create: thus civic order, a primary requisite for human existence. This civic order is a normative good although, *pace* Aristotle, civic order, or what we routinely call 'the state', does not fulfil or complete our natures; rather, it expresses them and may do so in ways deadly or ways less cruel. Here it is important to note that, for Augustine, no human being has natural dominion over any other. There is no slavery by nature. We are by nature social, but that doesn't dictate any particular form of social order. Nor does Augustine analogize from the authority of fathers in households to political rule. Classical patriarchal theory holds that rule by fathers is at once natural and political; that a natural right translates into political authority and legitimation. But for Augustine, political authority is different from familial authority. To the extent that one is subject to a ruler, one is subject to him in status only and not by nature.

There are temporal goods that are worthy, peace first and foremost. So human civic life is not simply a remedy for sin—with order and coercion needed to constrain our wickedness—but an expression of our sociality; our desire for fellowship; our capacity for a diffuse *caritas.* It follows that Cicero's definition of a *respublica*, as refracted through the writings of Scipio, is wanting. For Cicero civic order is an association based on common agreement concerning right and on shared interests. Insufficient, argues Augustine; rather, a people gathered together in a civic order is a gathering or multitude of rational beings united in fellowship by sharing a common love of the same things. Using this definition, we not only define what a society is, but we can also assess what it is people hold dear—what *sort* of society is *this*? It is worth noting at this juncture that a debate in current Augustinian scholarship concerns precisely how one should rank the good of political society for Augustine. The traditional, and overly simple, claim that civic order is simply a remedy for sin for Augustine has been effectively challenged. Now the question seems to be just how important to Augustine's thought overall is the good at which civic life tends and how much this derives from and can be achieved through the exercise of human voluntary activity. The dangers inherent within earthly political life are manifest, the fruits of pride that seeks domination over others and glories only in the self or the 'empire'. The goods to be attained through civic life are sketchier but begin with Augustine's basic rule of thumb for human earthly life, namely, that we should do no harm and help whenever we can (a requisite of love of one's neighbour).

It is the interplay of *caritas* and *cupiditas* that is critical, and whether one or the other prevails at a given point in time, whether within the very being of a single person or within the life of a civic order. Augustine would tame the occasions for the reign of *cupiditas* and the activation of the *libido dominandi*, or lust to dominate, and maximize the space within which *caritas* operates. For a lust to dominate taints and perverts all human relations, from family to city. Similarly, a decent love, a concern for the well-being of all in the household or in the city, strengthens the delicate filaments of peace. The sin that mars the earthly city is the story of arbitrary power or the ever present possibility of such. By contrast, the basis for a more just order is fuelled by love. The theme of the two cities is the metaphor that enables Augustine to trace the choreography of human relations. Every human community is plagued by a 'poverty stricken kind of power . . . a kind of scramble . . . for lost dominions and . . . honors', but there is simultaneously present the life-forgiving and gentler aspects of loving concern, mutuality, and domestic and civic peace (*DCD* XI. 1, p. 429). There are two fundamentally different attitudes evinced within human social life and enacted by human beings. One attitude is a powerful feeling of the fullness of life. A human being will not be denuded if he or she gives, or makes a gift of, the self to others. One's dependence on others is not a diminution but an enrichment of the self. The other attitude springs from cramped and cribbed selfishness, resentment, a penury of spirit. The way one reaches out or down to others from these different attitudes is strikingly distinct. From a spirit of resentment and contempt, one condescends towards the other; one is hostile to life itself. But from that fellow feeling in our hearts for the misery of others, we come to their help by coming together with them. Authentic compassion (the working-out of *caritas*) eradicates contempt and distance. But this working-out can never achieve anything like perfection in the realm of earthly time and history (the *saeculum*).

In Robert Markus's book *Saeculum*, widely acknowledged as one of the most important attempts to unpack and to situate Augustine as civic and political theorist, he argues that Augustine aimed for a number of complex things with his characterization of the two cities. One was to sort out the story of all earthly cities. Augustine, he argues, provides an account of the earthly city (*civitas terrena*) from Assyria to Rome, and shows the ways in which even the cherished goal of peace all too often ends in conquest and domination, hence no real peace at all. The fullness of peace is reserved for the heavenly city (*civitas dei*) and its eternal peace. In this way Augustine creates barriers to the absolutizing of any political arrangement. His repudiation of the theology underwriting the notion of an *imperium Christianum* lies in part in his worry that any identification of the city of God with an earthly order invites sacralization of human arrangements and a dangerous idolatry. At the same time, earthly institutions have a real claim on us, and our membership in a polity is not reducible to misery and punishment. Augustine begins with a presumption of the priority of peace over war and he repudiates all stories of mythical human beginnings that presume disorder and war as our primordial condition. The earthly city derives from our turning away from love and its source (God) towards wilfulness and a 'poverty stricken kind of power'. The upshot is division—within the self, between self and other, between nations and cultures: this is a destructive division by contrast to the plurality and contrast Augustine cherished.

So temporal peace is a good. Amid the shadows that hover over and among us, there are, as I already noted, two rules within our reach and that we should follow: 'first, to do no harm to anyone, and, secondly, to help everyone whenever possible' (*DCD* XIX. 14, p. 873). The most just human civic arrangements are those that afford the widest scope to non-harm doing and to fellowship and mutuality. If mutuality, even of the earthly, imperfect sort, is to be attained, there must be a compromise between human wills, and the earthly city must find a way to forge bonds of peace. This she finds very difficult by definition given the distortions of the lust to dominate.

By contrast, the heavenly city on earthly pilgrimage is better able to forge peace by calling out 'citizens from all nations and so collects a society of aliens, speaking all languages'. She—the *civitas dei*—does this not by annulling or abolishing earthly differences but even through maintaining them so 'long as God can be worshipped' (*DCD* XIX. 18, p. 878). Here it is important to note that whatever Augustine's acquiescence in the received social arrangements of his time, he left as a permanent legacy a condemnation of that lust for dominion that distorts the human personality, marriage, the family, and all other human social relations, including civic life and membership. Augustine is scathing in his denunciation of arrogant pridefulness; unstinting in his praise of the works of service, neighbourliness, and a love that simultaneously judges and succours (judges because we must distinguish good from evil, selfishness from kindness, and so on). Love and justice are intertwined, on earth and in heaven. Yet the world is filled with horrors, including war. How does Augustine square his regretful justification of a certain sort of war with his call to love and peace? It is to this theme that I now turn.

## War and peace

A full treatment of this theme—indeed of all the issues taken up to this point—would require an assessment of Augustine's complex theodicy. That is beyond the scope of this chapter. But a brief discussion is needed in order to grasp Augustine's theology of war and peace. Augustine acknowledges the seductive allure of evil. He famously tells the story of a youthful prank—stealing pears—that was done not from hunger but from pleasure in the deed itself and in the fellowship with others who took part in the deed. It took Augustine many years, including a sustained detour through Manichaeism, before he rejected decisively metaphysical dualism and repudiated any claim that evil is a self-sustaining, generative principle of opposition to good. The Manichaeans had located evil in creation itself as the work of a demonic demiurge; thus, the body was tainted by definition. But, for Augustine, creation is good. The body is good, not polluted. It is what we do with the body, what we do to creation, that either marks our bodies with the stain of sin, wickedness, and cruelty or does not at any given point in time. Augustine's famous articulation of human free will enters at this juncture—a concept Hannah Arendt credits with being an original contribution by Augustine. We can choose to do wrong and we often do, for we are marked from the beginning with the trace of originary disobedience. The choice of evil is in and of itself 'an impressive proof that the *nature* is good' (*DCD* XI. 17, p. 448).

Evil is a falling away from the good and we are the agents of this falling away, not because the body is corrupt, but because we can defile it. There is no such thing as evil 'by nature'. Evil is the turning of a limited creature from God to himself and, hence, to an absolutizing of his own flawed will. This turning may become habitual, a kind of second nature. In this way, Augustine gives evil its due without giving it the day. Evil is the name we give to a class of acts and putative motives. The fruits of this turning away include a hatred of finitude and a fateful thirst for what might be called a kind of anti-creation: a lust to destroy. War is a species of that destruction; hence, war is always a tragedy even 'when just'. But if war is *primus inter pares* an example of human sinfulness and a turning from the good, how can it possibly be justified under any circumstances?

It works like this. Augustine begins by deconstructing the Roman peace as a false claim to peace. Instead, Rome conquered and was herself conquered by her own lust to dominate over others. 'Think of all the battles fought, all the blood that was poured out, so that almost all the nations of Italy, by whose help the Roman Empire wielded that overwhelming power, should be subjugated as if they were barbarous savages.'[9] Rome was driven by a lust for vengeance and cruelty, and these triumphed under the cherished name of peace. The empire became a kingdom without justice, and this is little more than a criminal gang on a grand scale. Here Augustine famously repeats the story of the rejoinder given by a captured pirate to Alexander the Great when Alexander queried him about his idea in infesting the sea. 'And the pirate answered, with uninhibited insolence, "The same as yours, in infesting the earth! But because I do it with a tiny craft, I'm called a pirate: because you have a mighty navy, you're called an emperor." '[10] Augustine even suggests that the Romans should have erected a monument to the foreign 'other' and called her 'Aliena' because they made such good use of her by proclaiming that all their wars were defensive; it was, therefore, necessary to conjure up an implacable foreign foe in order to justify these ravages. For Rome, peace became just another name for *dominium*. If war's ravages are, in part, a punishment for sin, human beings sin, often savagely, in enacting that punishment. Primarily, however, Augustine emphasizes the freely chosen nature of war and assigns responsibility to those who engage in it.

If you reflect on the terrible slaughter of war carried out for wicked motives and to unworthy ends, you will determine to wage only limited, justifiable wars even as you lament the fact that they must sometimes be waged given injustice: so Augustine argues. There are occasional real wars of defence. The wise ruler and polity takes up arms only with great reluctance and penitence. Given Augustine's account of limited justifiability for wars fought only for certain motives, he is frequently lodged as the grandfather of just war thinking. (Others, of course, rank him as a forebear of political realism. There is no reason he cannot be both, depending on what one understands by realism and just war respectively.) Augustine appreciates what modern international relations theorists call the 'security dilemma'. People never possess a kingdom

> so securely as not to fear subjugation by their enemies; in fact, such is the instability of human affairs that no people has ever been allowed such a degree of tranquillity as to remove all dread of hostile attacks on their life in this world. That place which is promised as a dwelling of such peace and security is eternal, and is reserved for eternal beings, in 'the mother, the Jerusalem which is free'. (*DCD* XVII. 13, pp. 743–4)

One must simply live with this shadow, a penumbra of fear and worry on this earth. But one must not give oneself over to it, not without overweening justification. When one capitulates to this fear, one gets horrible wars of destruction, including social and civic wars. And each war invites another given the mimetic quality of instantiations of destruction. Each war breeds discontents and resentments that invite a tendency to even the score.

By contrast, the just ruler wages a justifiable war of necessity whether against unwarranted aggression and attack or to rescue the innocent from certain destruction. The motivation must be love of one's neighbour and a desire for a more authentic peace. This is a grudging endorsement of a lesser evil, and war is never named as a normative good—only as a tragic necessity. It must be noted that rescuing the self alone is not a justification for violence: better to suffer wrong than to commit it. But our sociality embeds certain requirements of love of one's neighbour, most powerfully and poignantly so in the case of the ruler who bears the responsibility for the well-being of a people. It is, then, our intrinsic sociality, and under the requirement to do no harm and help whenever one can, that war is occasionally justifiable. Augustine's reasoning here falls within the domain of accounts of comparative justice, and his argument, which is not a fully fleshed-out systematic theory of war so much as a theological account of war, involves the occasional violation of a fundamental principle—do not kill unjustly, or murder—in the name of an overriding good. It is important to observe that a close reading of Augustine's account shows that one must lament even justifiable wars and reflect on them, not with vainglory, but with great sorrow. Not to look back with grief marks one as pitiable and contemptible. There are no victory parades in Augustine's world, for, however just the cause, war stirs up temptations to ravish and to devour, often in order to ensure peace. Just war, for Augustine, is a cautionary tale, not an incautious and reckless call to arms. For peace is a great good, so good that 'no word ever falls more gratefully upon the ear, nothing is desired with greater longing, in fact, nothing better can be found'. Peace is 'delightful' and 'dear to the heart of all mankind' (*DCD* xx. 11, p. 866).

## Conclusion

The vast mountain of Augustinian scholarship keeps growing. It long ago surpassed a book version of Mt Everest, so much so that no single scholar or group of scholars could master it all. This is true of Augustine's work alone. Peter Brown claims that Isidore of Seville once 'wrote that if anyone told you he had read all the works of Augustine, he was a liar'.[11] One always has the sense with Augustine that one has but scratched the surface. Indeed, his works have not yet been translated entirely into English. That project is now under way and there are some seventeen volumes of his homilies alone that have made their way into translation. Much of the new scholarship on Augustine remarks, often with a sense of critical wonderment, on just how 'contemporary' he is given the collapse of political utopianism, by which I mean attempts to order political and social life under an overarching *Weltanschauung* that begins, as any such attempt must, with a flawed anthropology about human malleability and even perfectibility. We recognize, looking back, the mounds of bodies on which so many political projects rest, including the creation of the nation-state system we took for granted for over three centuries and now observe to be fraying around the edges.

The teleology of historical progress is no longer believable, although a version of it is still touted by voluptuaries of techno-progress or genetic engineering that may yet 'perfect' the human race. The presumably solid underpinnings of the self gave way in the twentieth century under the onslaught of Nietzsche and Freud. Cultural anthropology taught lessons of cultural contingencies. Contemporary students of rhetoric have rediscovered the importance and vitality of rhetoric and the ways in which all of our political and social life and thought must be cast in available rhetorical forms.

None of this would have surprised Augustine. What would sadden him is the human propensity to substitute one extreme for another, for example, a too thoroughgoing account of disembodied reason gives way to a too thoroughgoing account of reason's demise. Importantly, one must rescue Augustine from those who would appropriate him to a version of political limits or 'realism' that downplays his insistence on the great virtue of hope and the call to enact projects of *caritas*. That does not mean he should be called to service in behalf of 'markets and democracy'. It does mean he can never be enlisted in behalf of the depredators of humankind.

## FURTHER READING

Brown, Peter, *Augustine of Hippo* (Berkeley: University of California Press, 1967).

Brown, Peter, *Body and Society* (London: Faber, 1989).

Burt, Donald X., *Friendship and Society: An Introduction to Augustine's Practical Philosophy* (Grand Rapids, Mich.: Eerdmans, 1999).

Markus, Richard, *Saeculum* (London: Cambridge University Press, 1970).

Wetzel, James, *Augustine and the Limits of Virtue* (Cambridge: Cambridge University Press, 1992).

## NOTES

1. Trans. Henry Bettenson (Baltimore: Penguin, 1972) (hereafter *DCD*). References are to book, chapter, and page number.
2. Peter Brown, *Augustine of Hippo* (Berkeley: University of California Press, 1967), 181.
3. Whether Augustine offers an adequate account of Stoic philosophy is, of course, a separate question. Whatever one's position on that issue, the most important point here is Augustine's insistence that thought can never be purged of the emotions.
4. James Wetzel, *Augustine and the Limits of Virtue* (Cambridge: Cambridge University Press, 1992), 15.
5. I cannot unpack the complexities of Augustine's analogical reasoning here. The interested reader is advised to turn to the key text itself, *The Trinity* (Washington: Catholic University of America Press, 1992).
6. Augustine, *Select Writings (from Homilies on the Gospel of St. John. First Homily)* (New York: Paulist Press, 1984), 278.
7. A recent, interesting entry on the nigh infinite secondary works on Augustine on this theme is Donald X. Burt, *Friendship and Society: An Introduction to Augustine's Practical Philosophy* (Grand Rapids, Mich.: Eerdmans, 1999).
8. Ibid. 5.
9. The key Augustinian discussion of war is, of course, *DCD* XIX. But his deconstruction of the Roman Pax takes place throughout all of part I, books I–X. See e.g. *DCD* IV. 15. Citations in this section are internal to my discussion of Augustine in *Women and War* (New York: Basic Books, 1987), here p. 130.
10. Elshtain, *Women and War*, 130.
11. P. R. L. Brown, 'Political Society', in Richard Markus (ed.), *Augustine: A Collection of Critical Essays* (Garden City, NJ: Doubleday Anchor Books, 1972), 311.

# 7 Aquinas

Joseph Canning

Contents



## Chapter guide

Aquinas was primarily a theologian rather than a political thinker. He combined Aristotelian ideas with Christian concepts, distinguishing between the natural and supernatural orders, and attributing inherent validity to the natural order, including political life. His theory of law linked, through reason, the eternal law of God, natural law, human positive law, and divine law. For Aquinas, government's justification was its purpose—securing the common good. He favoured limited monarchy in a mixed constitution. Government by the many was valid but had advantages and disadvantages. Tyranny involved infringing the common good. Aquinas had little to contribute on the topic of Church–State relations, and was concerned with city-states and monarchies, not the Roman Empire. His enunciation of just war theory was highly influential. His main contribution to political thought was that government and human law must have a moral purpose. He was a prime exponent of the natural law tradition.

## Biography

Thomas Aquinas was a university professor and teacher. Born in 1224/5 at Roccasecca in southern Italy, from 1239 to 1244 he was a student at the University of Naples. In 1244 he joined the Dominican order. From 1245 to 1248 he studied at Paris, and from 1248 to 1252 at Cologne under Albert the Great. From 1252 to 1259 Aquinas taught at Paris, as regent master in theology from 1256. He was in Italy from 1259 to 1269, teaching at Orvieto,

Rome, and Viterbo; in 1269–72 he lectured at Paris. In 1272 he went to Naples to organize the Dominican house of theological studies. In 1273 Aquinas ceased to write, and he died in 1274 on his way to the Second Council of Lyons. He was canonized in 1323.

During Aquinas' lifetime he and Albert the Great were the pre-eminent theologians of the Dominican order. Aquinas' system of thought, which developed into the school of Thomism, had to compete with other theological and philosophical schools, and encountered much opposition in the late Middle Ages (indeed, the condemnations of 1277, of Averroist and Aristotelian propositions, at Paris and Oxford included some of Aquinas'). It was only from the time of the Counter-Reformation (or Catholic Reformation) of the sixteenth century that Aquinas acquired his canonic status as the leading theologian of the Catholic Church. His influence within Catholic theology has lasted until the present day.

## Key texts

*Writings on the Sentences* (1252–6)
*Summa contra Gentiles* (1259–64)
*On Kingship to the King of Cyprus* (between *c.*1265 and *c.*1273)
*Summa theologiae* (1266–73) (*ST*)
*Exposition on the Books of the Politics* (1269?–72?)

## Main texts used

I have produced my own translations from Latin.

For the Latin text of Aquinas, see:

*Aquinas: Selected Political Writings*, ed. with introd. by A. P. D'Entrèves, trans. J. G. Dawson (Oxford: Basil Blackwell, 1970) (contains Latin text and Eng. trans. of *On Kingship*, *On the Government of Jews*, *Summa contra Gentiles*, *Summa theologiae*, *Writings on the Sentences*, *Exposition on the Ethics*, and *Exposition on the Politics*).

*De regimine principum ad regem Cypri [De Regno]*, ed. R. M. Spiazzi (Turin: Marietti, 1954).

*In octo libros politicorum Aristotelis expositio*, ed. R. M. Spiazzi (Turin: Marietti, 1966).

*Opera omnia*, ed. R. Busa (Stuttgart-Bad Cannstatt: Friedrich Frommann Verlag, Günther Holzboog KG, 1980).

*Summa contra Gentiles*, ed. C. Pera, P. Marc, and P. Caramello (Turin: Marietti, 1961–7).

*Summa theologiae*, ed. with Eng. trans. T. Gilby *et al.*, Blackfriars, 61 vols. (London: Eyre & Spottiswoode, 1964–80).

Readers could consult the following modern translations:

*Aquinas: Selected Political Writings* (see above; still the most useful selection for students).

*On the Government of Rulers. De Regimine Principum. Ptolemy of Lucca with Portions Attributed to Thomas Aquinas*, trans. James M. Blythe (Philadelphia: University of Pennsylvania Press, 1997).

*Summa theologiae* (see above).

## Key ideas

**Natural and supernatural orders**: the fundamental distinction. **Grace** does not destroy nature but perfects it. **Law**: reason links eternal, natural, human, and divine. **Immoral law**

is invalid. **Common good**: government exists for the purpose of achieving this. **Limited monarchy** within a mixed constitution is the favoured form of government. **Tyranny,** both of the many and of a monarch, infringes the common good. **War** may be just on the grounds of the authority of the ruler, just cause, and right intention.

---

## Introduction

Thomas Aquinas is rightly judged to be the pre-eminent theologian and philosopher of the Middle Ages. He was not primarily a political thinker, and his contribution to political thought forms only a very small part of his huge output as a writer. Yet his ideas have been accepted as a major contribution to medieval political thought and, indeed, no modern treatment of the subject would or could ignore his work. But important though he was recognized to be in his lifetime, his true fame and recognition emerged after his death and especially from the Counter-Reformation of the sixteenth century onwards, when his theology came to be awarded canonic status within the Catholic Church.

Aquinas wrote during a revolutionary period in the history of ideas. In the years between the 1120s and the 1270s virtually the whole corpus of Aristotle's works was rediscovered in the West. Earlier in the Middle Ages only two of Aristotle's works were known through translations in Boethius (480–525): the *Categories* and *On Interpretation* (comprising, together with Porphyry's *Isagoge*, the 'old logic'). Aristotle's political thought became known through translations into Latin from Greek manuscripts. A fragmentary version of the *Nicomachean Ethics* was produced in the twelfth and early thirteenth centuries; but the work was translated in its entirety by Robert Grosseteste by about 1246/7. The *Politics* was translated by William of Moerbeke (the most prolific and influential translator of Aristotle): he made an incomplete attempt in about 1260 and a second complete version by the first half of 1265. The process of assimilation of the new Aristotle was, however, slow, and Aristotelian studies only really flowered at the Universities of Paris and Oxford in the 1240s and 1250s. Because Muslim Spain was a prime source for the revived Western knowledge of Aristotle, Latin scholars were also influenced by Arabic interpreters of Aristotle, notably al-Farabi, Avicenna, and (above all) Averroes (Ibn-Rushd) of Cordoba (1126–98), most of whose commentaries on Aristotle were available in Latin translations by about 1250. It has to be said, however, that Latin Scholastics almost invariably used translations based on Greek texts for their commentaries.

Medieval theology and philosophy were deeply indebted to their inheritance from antiquity, and this massive influx of pre-Christian ideas both enriched the material available for investigation and posed a massive problem for traditional Christian thought, which may loosely be termed Augustinian. In general terms, Aquinas' work may be seen as setting out to accomplish an intellectual synthesis between Christian concepts and Aristotelian ideas: he used Aristotelian philosophy in the service of theology, an approach heavily influenced by his mentor, Albert the Great (*c.*1200–80). In so doing, Aquinas was a protagonist in the often bitter conflict between those scholars who utilized Aristotelian ideas and those who maintained that Aristotle's philosophy was antithetical to Christian revelation. This dispute was institutionalized through the hostility between the secular clergy and the mendicant friars—the Franciscans and Dominicans (to which order Aquinas belonged)—and between the mendicants themselves, because the Franciscans tended to be more traditionalist than the Dominicans on this matter. Aquinas during his periods at Paris also found himself in opposition to extreme Aristotelians, notably in his second sojourn, when he was faced with scholars like Siger of Brabant (*c.*1240–84) who were heavily influenced by Averroes, and who approached the position that a proposition could be true in philosophy and untrue in theology and vice versa. These battles culminated, shortly after Aquinas' death, in the condemnations of 1277 (at Paris and Oxford) of certain Averroist and Aristotelian propositions, including some of Aquinas himself. There was thus no general acceptance of Aquinas' ideas in his lifetime, or indeed in the remainder of the Middle Ages—quite the reverse.

The significance of the impact of the rediscovery of Aristotelian ideas on medieval political thought has proved contentious among modern scholars. There was an older orthodoxy which saw the influx of Aristotelian political ideas as revolutionary in permitting the development of naturalistic ideas of political man and of the state, in contrast to earlier medieval views which, lacking an avowedly political dimension, saw government and rulership within the overarching context of the Christian community—the Church in its wider sense.[1] The other pole of interpretation downgrades the revolutionary aspect of the recovery of Aristotle and stresses the continuities with the immediately preceding philosophy and theology, and places Aristotelian language side by side in importance with others derived from antiquity, notably Ciceronian and that of Roman law.[2] Clearly, the overall assessment of Aquinas' political thought in part depends upon the position adopted as regards the impact of Aristotle. The view taken in this chapter is that the recovery of the works of Aristotle permitted a systematic treatment of the natural order, including the state and political life. The way for this approach was prepared by the previous emergence of a somewhat inchoate and unworked-out naturalistic and this-worldly direction in twelfth- and thirteenth-century philosophy, theology, literature, and jurisprudence. Political science emerged as an autonomous scholastic discipline with its own authoritative texts, the *Ethics* and the *Politics*. This is not to deny that the vast treasury of Aristotle's works was also raided by those seeking eclectically to incorporate Aristotelian elements into structures of thought which owed little or nothing to the philosopher.

The works of Aquinas that are relevant to political thought are his *Writings on the Sentences* of Peter Lombard (not strictly speaking a commentary and composed in Paris in 1252–6); his two systematic works of theology, the *Summa contra Gentiles* (Paris, Naples, and Orvieto, 1259–64) and his masterpiece, the *Summa theologiae* (Rome, Viterbo, Paris, and Naples, 1266–73); his *Exposition on the Books of the Politics* (probably Paris, 1269–72), which broke off at 3. 6[3] and, it is generally accepted, was completed by Peter of Auvergne (d. 1303); and his *Exposition on the Books of the Ethics* (Paris, 1271). There is also the tract *On Kingship to the King of Cyprus* (or *On the Government of Princes*). The overwhelming majority of scholars have accepted that this is the work of Aquinas up to the middle of 2. 4;[4] all are agreed that the rest of the book is by Ptolemy of Lucca (*c.*1236–1327). The manuscript evidence is, on the whole, in favour of Thomas' authorship up to 2. 4; the strongest arguments against relate to content and style[5]—a less safe approach since he wrote nothing else in this mirror-of-princes genre.[6] What is possible is that there was some posthumous interference with his text.[7] The date is also uncertain: sometime between *c.*1265 and *c.*1273; it could have been dedicated to either Hugh II or Hugh III of Cyprus.[8]

On the whole Aquinas' political thought is highly theoretical and only to a limited extent a response to thirteenth-century political reality. His early writings on the *Sentences* were composed in fulfilment of the normal requirement that a theologian beginning his career should prove his competence by producing such a work. The profoundest expression of his thought is contained in his two *Summae* (Summaries). There is a problem of interpretation with his commentary on Aristotle's *Politics*: it is a close exposition of the text rather than an elaboration of Aquinas' own views. The part of *On Kingship* attributed to him is written within the conventions of the mirror-of-princes genre.

## The natural and supernatural orders

The fundamental distinction underlying Aquinas' political thought was the one he made between the natural and the supernatural orders. Unaided human reason could perceive the principles of nature, but there was a point beyond which reason could not go—that was, into the realm of divine revelation contained in the Scriptures and accessible through faith. There was a hierarchy of human ends culminating in the enjoyment of God in heaven. In this way, Aquinas was able to combine Aristotelian philosophy with what he perceived to be the truths of Christianity. His approach was summed up in what may well be the most famous statement in his works: 'Grace does not do away with nature but perfects it' (*ST* 1a. 8. 2[9]).

The significance of Aquinas' approach was that it accepted the inherent validity of the natural order within which the state and political life existed. For him the state was a natural, organic entity identified with its members rather than being distinct from them. As such it was a unity of order for the common good, a congregation distinguished by its purpose from a mere aggregation of individuals. But, because, as a Christian, Aquinas accepted a hierarchy of ends for human beings, he parted company with Aristotle in a profound sense. Aristotle held that 'man is a political animal', meaning that the fulfilment of human nature, as the realization of its potentialities, could be achieved only within the perfect community, the Greek *polis* (city-state). The political aspect of man's life was the defining one and included all others within it. For Aquinas, the state was not enough—it could never be the perfect community. The purpose of human life transcended this world:

> Because man living according to virtue is ordained to a higher end, which consists in the enjoyment of God . . . there should be the same end for a multitude of men as for one man. The final end of a congregated multitude, therefore, is not to live according to virtue, but through a virtuous life to arrive at the enjoyment of God. (*On Kingship*, 1. 15)

Thus, although Aquinas accepted the intrinsic validity of the 'political virtues' (prudence, justice, fortitude, and temperance), faith, hope, and charity were also required for the Christian life with its other-worldly goal. Furthermore, even at a natural level, Aquinas was unwilling to identify society totally with the state. He placed his own gloss on Aristotle, saying, 'Man is by nature a political and social animal, as is proved in book One of the *Politics*' (*ST* 1a2ae. 72. 4). This addition of 'and social' meant that Aquinas saw the human need for association as going beyond any particular state organization. Man's use of language showed at a basic level that he was a social animal, because, being unable to survive and develop on his own, he needed to communicate with others.

Aquinas' acceptance of the naturalness of political and social life meant that he parted company radically from the traditional medieval patristic view, which held that man's true nature existed only before the Fall, after which rulership, like property, became necessary as a remedy for sin, a view fundamentally different from any conception of human nature as it existed in the here-and-now. In contrast, Aquinas maintained that, because there was a continuity between man's nature before and after the Fall, politically ordered society had existed before that catastrophic event, although, in the state of innocence, dominion would have been directive rather than coercive in kind—it would have directed free men to the common good:

> One man can rule another who remains free, when he directs him to the latter's own good, or to the common good. And such dominion of man over man would have existed in the state of innocence . . . because man is naturally a social animal. As a result, in the state of innocence men would have lived in society. But there could be no social life for a multitude of people, unless someone were in charge to look after the common good. (*ST* 1a. 96. 4)

Aquinas agreed that human nature had been damaged by the Fall—that we are all damaged goods, as it were—but he also considered that postlapsarian man could perfectly well know the principles of nature through the unaided use of his reason: it was man's will to fulfil the precepts and requirements of natural law that had been damaged.

## Theory of law

The concept of natural law, indeed, lay at the centre of Aquinas' political thought. He produced a classic treatment of the hierarchical interrelation of the different forms of law within the overall structure of the natural and supernatural orders. The link between these forms of law was reason. The guarantee that there was such a link was this: because man was made in God's image and likeness, human reason could, to some degree, participate in the divine reason. Respect for the rational capacity of human beings was a pre-eminent characteristic of Aquinas' thought.

Aquinas considered that there were four types of law: the eternal law, natural law, human law, and divine law. He gave his systematic treatment of them in *ST* 1a2ae, 90–7. The eternal law was the plan of divine providence for governing the universe: 'the eternal law is nothing other than the plan of divine wisdom considered as directing all actions and motion [of creatures]' (*ST* 1a2ae. 93. 1). It directed all created things to the attainment of their ends. Ultimately all laws, of whatever kind, in so far as they accorded with right reason, derived from this eternal law. Because human beings were rational creatures they could perceive the principles of the eternal law that applied specifically to them, that is, the principles that constituted the natural law. Through the exercise of their reason, they were thus participators in the eternal law: 'It is clear that the natural law is nothing other than the participation of the eternal law in a rational creature' (*ST* 1a2ae. 91. 2). Human beings were distinguished from other creatures because they actively participated in divine providence through having responsibility for themselves and others. Natural law was the product of human reason in that human beings perceived it through the exercise of their reason. It was not, however, simply a construction of human reason, with its validity depending on that reason alone, because its validity derived from God's providence. In perceiving the principles of natural law humans discovered what was the case. Natural law had an objective existence. Aquinas treated its precepts under three headings, which reflected humans' inclination towards good according to their nature: first, the preservation of life; secondly, more specific ends, shared with the animals, such as sexual relations and the rearing of offspring; and thirdly, actions proper to man alone as a rational creature, reflecting his inclination to know God and live in society. For Aquinas the common principles of natural law were universal and the product of speculative reason. But he recognized that, when one applied the principles of natural law to specific cases, through the exercise of practical reason, there was more and more room for exceptions to the conclusions drawn, the further one departed from common principles. Aquinas tried to explain what he meant. He argued that it would, for instance, be injurious and irrational to repay a debt if the money would be used to attack one's country. He recognized also that people could come to differing conclusions through defective knowledge of the common principles of natural law or a lack of desire to apply them:

> Natural law, as far as its common first principles are concerned, is the same for all, requiring both a right attitude to it and knowledge of it. But as for certain particular points, which are like conclusions drawn from common principles, it is the same for all people in most cases, as regards their right attitude to and knowledge of it, but in a fewer cases both the right attitude . . . and the knowledge can be lacking. (*ST* 1a2ae. 94. 4)

The first principles of natural law did not change, and its secondary precepts, when drawn as immediate conclusions from these, remained generally valid for most cases. There were, however, two senses in which natural law could be understood to change. Both human and divine law could add to it if that was useful for human life. The most glaring cases in point were those of private property and servitude. The patristic view was that human beings had originally enjoyed the common possession of all things and the equal liberty of all. Aquinas agreed that neither private property nor servitude were introduced by nature: rather, they were the product of human reason for the good of human life, and as such an addition to natural law, not an alteration of it. Secondly, circumstance might dictate that subtractions from natural law were necessary if its observation became impossible in particular cases.

Aquinas held that human law in turn is derived by reason from natural law. Human law had two forms: the law of peoples (*ius gentium*) and the civil law (*ius civile*). The law of peoples consisted of the immediate conclusions of natural law and had general application (such as the norms governing buying and selling). The civil law contained particular applications of natural law for particular states. Thinking in terms of civil law, Aquinas defined law as 'an ordinance of reason for the common good and promulgated by him who has care of the community' (*ST* 1a2ae. 90. 4). Law had to be promulgated by the ruler, who could be one, few, or many, depending on the form of constitution. In any treatment of ideas concerning the nature of law the relationship between reason and the lawmaker's will is crucial. Aquinas considered that will put reason into action: 'All law proceeds from the reason and will of a legislator: divine and natural law from the rational will of God; human law from man's will, regulated by reason' (*ST* 1a2ae. 97. 3). It was a characteristic of human law that it had coercive force as regards those subject to it; but such command, to be valid, had to be in accordance with reason.

Aquinas therefore maintained that human law was invalid, if it went against natural law: 'Every human law has the character of law in so far as it is derived from the law of nature. If in any case it is incompatible with the natural law, it will not be law, but a corruption of law' (*ST* 1a2ae. 95. 2). As regards the prince, whose command gave law its force, Aquinas understood the Roman law tag 'what has pleased the prince has the force of law' (*Digest* 1. 4. 1) to mean that the prince's law must be in accordance with reason for it to be valid. The prince was, however, above the coercive force of the law, because one cannot coerce oneself. Nevertheless, Aquinas considered that the prince should voluntarily subject himself to the directive power of his law, expressly quoting the *locus classicus* in Roman law on this point (*Codex* 1. 14. 4).[10] The ruler was, therefore, above the law in that he could change it or dispense from it, but limited by the rational precepts of natural law and not free from the unenforceable requirement that he should obey his own laws. Aquinas therefore produced a classic statement of natural law theory and one opposed to any purely positivist notion of law. The overall purpose of human law was to serve the common good.

But because man had a supernatural destiny, and because law directed him to his end, Aquinas held that man required more than just natural law and human law as his guides: 'Because man is ordained to the end of eternal blessedness which exceeds what is proportionate to natural human faculties . . . it was necessary that, over and beyond natural and human law, he should be directed to his end by a divinely given law' (*ST* 1a2ae. 91. 4). This law was divine positive law: it both commanded what reason had discovered to be naturally and thus objectively right, and steered man towards his supernatural goal. In the *Summa theologiae* Aquinas exemplified divine law as that of the Old and New Testaments. In the *Summa contra Gentiles* he said, 'the divine law is divine providential reason for governing human beings' (3. 115). Divine law instructed man in what he should do and what avoid. Aquinas accepted that human law could only be concerned with man's exterior actions, but that, for perfect virtue, man should also be upright as regards his interior thoughts, decisions, and intentions as well. Divine law is the law of this interior realm: 'It belongs to God alone, the maker of the divine law, to judge concerning the interior motions of the will according to Psalm VII, "The searcher of hearts and minds is God"' (*ST* 1a2ae. 100. 9). Not everything that was sin was punished by human law, but it was important that sin should be recognized and not go unforbidden or unpunished (in the next life), 'For human law does not punish him who intends to kill and does not—divine law does however punish him according to Matthew 5: 22, "Whoever is angry with his brother shall be in danger of the judgment"'(*ST* 1a2ae. 100. 9).

## Theory of government

### The purpose of government

For Aquinas, government, like law, existed for a purpose: the ordering of the common good. This concentration on the primacy of purpose was a fundamental direction in his thought, a teleological approach which he shared with Aristotle. Aquinas was, in comparison, less concerned with the forms of government or its origins. Following Aristotle, he was willing to accept as valid government by the one, the few, or the many: monarchy, aristocracy, or rule by the people. This has led to widely differing assessments of his views by modern scholars. He has been seen as an advocate of absolute monarchy, limited monarchy, mixed constitution, and government by the people, or, indeed, as being rather inconsistent in his approach.[11] It is rather that Aquinas did not advocate any one form of government to the exclusion of any other—his political theory could support any form that sought to serve the common good.

His treatment of the common good was highly sophisticated and complex and included metaphysical, ethical, and political dimensions. As far as his political ideas were concerned, there were certain fundamental considerations. He held that the common good was greater than that of the individual: 'the good of the multitude is greater and more divine than that of one person' (*On Kingship*, 1. 9), that is, a judgement of quantity. But he also said that they were different in quality:

> The common good of the city and the individual good of one person do not differ only according to whether one is greater or less, but according to difference in kind: the nature of the common good differs from that of the individual good, as does the nature of the part from that of the whole. And thus the Philosopher in the first book of the *Politics*, chapter 1, says, "they do not say well that a city and a house and other things of this kind differ only in size, and not in kind." (*ST* 2a2ae. 58. 7)

There was thus a hierarchy of goods or ends at the level of man's natural life but, on the higher plane of his supernatural destiny, the final end of both a multitude and one man was, as we have seen, the same: the enjoyment of God.[12] As regards this life, however, the crucial question was whether the good of the individual was subsumed into that of the whole. Aquinas distinguished, in this respect, between intrinsic and extrinsic goods. The individual parts of a whole participated in an intrinsic good of order in their relations with one another. Thus the virtuous co-operation of individual members of a city resulted in the common benefit of peace and security—the common good in the sense of public utility (*utilitas publica*). But individuals, in addition to being ordered towards one another, were also ordered to the extrinsic common good (*bonum commune*) of the ruler and of the community as a whole. Thus the common good of the political community (the moral good of the common life of virtue and happiness) was superior to and included the individual good of virtue of the citizen or subject, which itself was superior to the common benefit of peaceful self-sufficiency which it brought about. The result, in Aquinas' thought, was a tendency to subsume the individual into the community: the individual good was contained within the common good, but it remained different in kind. The common good was more than the sum of individual goods, which it comprised. The emphasis varied in different parts of Aquinas' work, but overall he was not willing to make the individual totally subordinate to the community as a whole.[13]

## The forms of government

Aquinas devoted a considerable amount of attention to the subordinate question of the forms government took. His approach was predominantly theoretical and only in part reflected the variety of kinds of political regime that existed in the thirteenth century. His treatment was heavily influenced by Aristotelian categories and was mainly focused on monarchy—to a lesser extent on aristocracy and rule by the people. He was concerned with city-states and kingdoms but had no contribution to make as regards the Roman empire of his day. Why was this? Only partially satisfying and tentative answers can be suggested. The Aristotelian model for the political community which Aquinas was applying, namely the city-state (in Latin, the *civitas*), could relatively easily be extended to include kingdoms, as also being single political entities. Aristotle did not supply an exemplar for the concept of empire as such, although of course his ideas concerning rulership could be applied to any rulers, the Roman emperor included. The main source for notions of emperorship remained, of course, the Roman law, of which Aquinas had a very limited knowledge, restricting himself to using certain well-known passages from it, examples of which we have seen. Aquinas did, indeed, on occasion refer to the political history of Rome under both the republic and the empire, but his treatment was designed to use historical examples illustrating what he considered to be generally valid points about government and politics, not to produce arguments specifically relevant to the Roman emperorship of the thirteenth century. It might be thought that Aquinas was also making a judgement that the Roman emperorship had become an outdated and moribund institution in his day. This would, however, be applying historical hindsight on our part, especially given his own family's involvement in imperial politics. The idea of empire remained a viable political thesis in the next century, as the works of, for instance, Dante Alighieri (1265–1321) and Marsilio of Padua (1275/80–1342/43) would attest.

Aquinas was an advocate of monarchy, but it is difficult to see that his views were, to any great extent, the result of reflection on experience. His justifications of monarchy were mostly theoretical and above all traditional—he was not original in this area of his thought. Indeed, the ideas which he expressed in his most extended treatment of the topic, the tract *On Kingship*, were largely determined by the requirements of the genre of mirror-of-princes writing. He used the metaphysical argument that monarchy, in that it expressed the principle of unity, was best suited to bringing about peace and thus securing the common good. He combined this with the long-established organic analogy 'Every natural government is by one; for in the multitude of the body's members there is one which moves all, namely the heart', and continued his argument with time-worn images: 'There is one king amongst the bees, and in the whole universe one God, maker and lord of all' (*On Kingship*, 1. 3). He also used the argument of the relationship between the soul and the body and the macrocosm and the microcosm: 'A king should understand that he has undertaken the duty to be in his kingdom like the soul in the body and God in the universe' (ibid., 1. 13).

Monarchy, being a form of rule for the common good and voluntarily subject to the directive force of law, existed in two forms: 'political rule'—that is, rulership limited by the laws of the state—and 'regal rule'—that is, 'full power' unlimited by human laws (*Exposition on the Politics*, 1. 1. 13). Aquinas favoured the more limited form, but he did accept as valid, kingship unrestricted by human laws but exercised for the common good. His preferred form of government, however, was that of a limited monarchy in the form of a mixed constitution. He approached this position from the principle that all should participate in the government of the state, which was the way to preserve peace in the community. Adopting Aristotle's division of the forms of government he said, 'This is the best form of constitution which is a good mixture, of the kingdom, in that there is one person at the head of it; of aristocracy, in that many participate in government according to virtue; and of democracy, that is the power of the people, in that rulers can be elected from members of the people, and the election of rulers belongs to the people' (*ST* 1a2ae. 105. 1). In reaching this conclusion, he had made clear that, in the case of the monarchical and aristocratic parts of the state, virtue was the justification for their participation in government. However, because Aquinas shared Aristotle's reservations about the bulk of the populace's capacity for political virtue, he was willing to accord, to all the members of the people, participation not in a direct but in an ultimate sense: 'Such a government concerns all, both because all are eligible for election, and because election is also by all' (*ST* 1a2ae. 105. 1). Clearly, the actual exercise of government was to be limited to a very small part of the theoretically eligible population.

The historical example which Aquinas then gave for the mixed constitution was drawn from the Old Testament: the divinely sanctioned form of government of the Jews under Moses and his successors (Deut. 1: 13 and 15; Exod. 18: 21). Clearly the regime at this period was not kingship as such—this was established later with Saul: Aquinas meant that a monarchical element was included, in the sense of the headship of one man. His use of this biblical example also shows that his general statement, mentioned above, concerning the mixed constitution could be applied to forms of rulership that were not described as kingship in the strict sense. In the medieval context, however, monarchy in the form of limited kingship would be what Aquinas had in mind. For him, 'rule by a king is the best government of a people, so long as it is not corrupted' (*ST* 1a2ae. 105. 2). But the problem was that candidates of sufficient virtue to be kings were hard to find and tended to deteriorate once in office. The Old Testament tradition about kingship was, furthermore, ambivalent: the prophet Samuel anointed Saul as king in the name of Yahweh, but only with reluctance, pointing out the disadvantages of having a king and that Israel was wicked in desiring one, because its only true king was Yahweh. As Aquinas went on to say, 'From the beginning the Lord did not institute for them a king with full power, but a judge and governor to watch over them. But afterwards, as if in anger, he let the people have a king at their request, as is clear from what he said to Samuel' (1 Kgs. 8: 7 (=1 Sam. 8: 7)[14]). 'They have not rejected you, but me, in order that I should not reign over them.' Aquinas then reiterated, from 1 Samuel, the divine moral injunctions about how a king should act towards God and his subjects; and that God had instituted election by the people as the means of setting up a king.

There was, therefore, an element of popular involvement in Aquinas' theory of monarchy in terms of both his model of the mixed constitution and the biblical support he adduced for this. But he went further. In his theory of legislation he was willing to accept a form of ultimate authority of the people: 'Making law belongs either to the whole multitude or to the public person who has care of the whole multitude,' as also did the power of legal coercion (*ST* 1a2ae. 90. 3). He was, therefore, willing to accept both popular and monarchical governmental regimes, so long as the latter served the good of the whole community. The people's law-making capacity was also revealed in custom, which Aquinas saw as expressing its law-creating will and reason through actions: 'Through repeated exterior acts, the interior motions of the will and the exercise of reason are most effectively revealed. For when something is done many times, it seems to derive from a deliberate judgment of the reason. And in accordance with this, custom has the force of law, abolishes law, and is the interpreter of law' (*ST* 1a2ae. 97. 3).

In the case of an independent political community, because ultimate authority lay with the multitude of the people, the ruler was its representative (in the sense of standing for it), whose laws had therefore less authority than popular custom: 'If it is a free multitude, which could make law for itself, the multitude's consent, manifested by custom, has more weight in observing something than the authority of the prince, who only has the power to make law, in so far as he bears the person of the multitude' (*ST* 1a2ae. 97. 3.) Aquinas could also see advantages in government by the citizen body—the common good might be better served. He argued first of all from experience:

> When they see that the common good is not in the power of one, each person attends to it as if it were his own, not as if it were something pertaining to someone else. For this reason it seems by experience that one city administered by annual rulers can achieve more sometimes than a king, if he were to have three or four cities, and small services that kings exact weigh more heavily than great weights imposed by the community of citizens. (*On Kingship*, 1. 5)

Popular government could, in short, produce a greater readiness to co-operate for the good of the whole multitude. He then went on to support this argument with the authority of history by referring to the example of republican Rome.

Although Aquinas' predilection was undoubtedly for limited monarchy with an attenuated popular involvement, it is clear that he did nonetheless accept the validity of overt government by the people. His view should be seen against the background of the self-governing city-republics that existed in north and central Italy in his lifetime and which were characterized by a rapid turnover of personnel in government. It would be a mistake, however, to overstress Aquinas' support for a thesis of government by the people:[15] he was no advocate of republicanism.

## The case of tyranny

Indeed, Aquinas also stressed the disadvantages of government by the many: because of the internal dissensions that tended to arise under such a regime, he considered it more likely than monarchy to lead to the worst of evils—tyranny. He drew this conclusion both from the history of the last days of the Roman republic and observation of contemporary political life. He would have had in mind the growing number of city-communes that had come to be ruled by lords (*signori*)—'tyrants' to their opponents—in north and north-central Italy during his adult lifetime, a development largely and notoriously caused by faction-fighting within these republics. On balance, given this problem of internal conflict, Aquinas considered that, 'it is more expedient to live under one king, than under the rule of many' (*On Kingship*, 1. 6) in the first place. If, however, a popular regime were in existence, he believed that democracy (the tyranny of the majority) was preferable to the tyranny of one person, to which it could lead. He had to admit that rule by one man was potentially both the best and the worst form of government.

Aquinas treated tyranny extensively in *On Kingship*, because it was an established topos in mirror-of-princes writing, and also addressed it occasionally elsewhere in his writings. The figure of the tyrant, the shadow side of the monarch ruling for the common benefit, clarified, through antithesis, how a good ruler should act. Aquinas followed Aristotle's fundamental distinction between regimes that operated for the good of all and those deviations (including tyranny) that acted solely for the good of the rulers. The concept of the common good was the touchstone for the acceptability of regimes, not the form of government in terms of the one, the few, or the many. The basic question that Aquinas' discussion of tyranny addressed was this: 'Could the moral and normative content and limits of government be enforced? What, in short, could be done about a tyrant?'

Aquinas presented a range of solutions to this question. In his early *Writings on the*

*Sentences* of Peter Lombard (2. 44. 2. 2),[16] he discussed political obedience: the Christian's duty of obedience to authority rested on the derivation of that authority from God and ceased when this was lacking, 'but authority can fail to derive from God in two ways: as regards the mode of acquiring it, and its use'. Tyranny could result both from defect of title and from the ruler's abusive mode of action, a distinction to be developed by the jurist Bartolus of Sassoferrato (1314/15–57). Commenting on Cicero's discussion of the murder of Julius Caesar in *On Duties* 1. 26, Aquinas reached the conclusion that in the case of a person who had gained power by violence, and where there could be no appeal to higher authority, then, 'someone who kills a tyrant to free his country is praised and accepts his reward.' This could well be an observation of what happened rather than any support for tyrannicide. In his later work, Aquinas appeared very circumspect as regards dealing with tyrants. In *On Kingship* 1. 7 he rejected the argument that a tyrant could be killed, saying that this went against New Testament teaching (1 Pet. 2: 19). He went on to argue that the multitude, but no private person, could depose a tyrant and was freed from any pact it might have made with him, because he had not faithfully fulfilled the office of king. But Aquinas was concerned lest the successful or unsuccessful attempt to remove a tyrant result in greater evil. He therefore recommended acquiescence in a slack tyranny. This was a common good argument, as he made clear elsewhere:

> Tyrannical government is not just, because it is not directed to the common good, but to the private good of the ruler . . . and thus the overthrow of this government does not have the character of sedition, unless perhaps when the tyrant's government is overthrown with such excess that the subject multitude suffers greater loss from the consequent disruption, than from the tyrant's government. (*ST* 2a2ae. 42. 2)

Indeed, not all laws of tyrants were necessarily invalid. In *On Kingship* 1. 11, Aquinas gave a message of reassurance about tyranny. Fear was not a firm foundation for rulership. The teaching of history was that the rule of tyrants could not last long. He preached a doctrine of biblical quietism against tyrants, leaving them to the judgement of God, who would in the end cast them down, having first permitted them to rule for the punishment of the people's sins. Aquinas' overall message was not that of the justice of tyrannicide but a recommendation to Christian acquiescence.

## Temporal and spiritual power

One of the central concerns of medieval political thought had been the relationship between temporal and spiritual power. This area was, however, one of the least satisfying parts of Aquinas' thought. He had little of note to say about Church and State as power structures: the question did not seem to have interested him greatly.

In his early work on the *Sentences* he expressed ideas which were entirely conventional: the temporal and the spiritual powers were distinct and were both derived from God in such a way that the spiritual was to be obeyed before the temporal in matters affecting salvation, and the temporal before the spiritual in those concerning civil welfare. This division applied 'Unless perchance the secular power is also joined to the spiritual as in the case of the pope, who occupies the summit of both powers, spiritual and secular, through the dispensation of

Him who is priest and king, priest for ever according to the order of Melchisedech, King of kings, and Lord of lords' (2. 44. 3. 4). It was not, however, at all clear what precisely Aquinas meant by this. Elsewhere in this work he also expressed the view that the pope had both the temporal and the spiritual sword, interpreting a statement by Bernard of Clairvaux (1090–1153) to mean that the Church also possessed the temporal, because it commanded the lay power to use it. The significance of the medieval usage of the two-swords analogy has been hotly debated by modern scholars; indeed, there has been no agreement over Bernard's own meaning. Aquinas was merely giving a conventional reiteration of Bernard's words, which had themselves become the common coin of Scholastic debate.

In *On Kingship* Aquinas emphasized the role of guidance which priests exercised to lead men to their higher end, the enjoyment of God; the role of kings was the lower one of governing temporal affairs. Because of the hierarchy of the ends of human life, no secular government could be totally autonomous. The ministry of Christ's kingdom was committed to priests,

> And in particular to the High Priest, the successor of St Peter, the Vicar of Christ, the Roman Pontiff to whom all kings of the Christian people should be subject, just as to the Lord Jesus Christ himself. For thus those who care for antecedent ends should be subject to him who cares for the ultimate end, and be directed by his command. (1. 15)

Indeed, he went on to say, 'under Christ's law kings should be subject to priests'. That kings were in some sense subject to priests, and to the pope in particular, was clearly Aquinas' meaning. But he did not give further information about the relationship between the two powers and, above all, gave no attention to the question of conflicts between them, nor did he discuss whether the Church instituted kings or whether the pope could depose them. For him, priests had a higher mission than kings, who were to that extent subject to them, but there is no sign that Aquinas attributed to priests the power to enforce control over secular rulers.

Outside the Christian community Aquinas accepted the validity of infidel governments on the basis of the *jus gentium*, but he did in certain circumstances admit the power of the Church over non-believers. He maintained that the Church had the right to abrogate infidel rule over Christians, and that it could not allow the new establishment of any such regimes over the faithful. But the enemy within was the worst: heretics merited death, and the subjects of any apostate ruler were automatically freed from his rule and their oaths of allegiance to him rendered null and void (*ST* 2a2ae. 10–12).

## Just war theory

There remained one further area in which Aquinas did make an important contribution to political thought—just war theory. In doing so, he formed part of a long medieval tradition of theological and juristic writing on this topic. It was significant that it was thought necessary to justify war. For medieval writers, Augustine of Hippo's theory of the just war was fundamental: their theories were mostly developments of and dialogues with his definitions—for them reference back to Augustine on this topic was the norm.

Aquinas' own treatment of the just war was also primarily Augustinian. He did not innovate, but produced an easily memorable formula for the assessment of whether a war was just:

> For some war to be just three things are required. Firstly, the *authority of the ruler* at whose command the war is to be waged . . . Secondly, there is required a *just cause*: that is that those who are attacked for some offence should merit the attack . . . Thirdly, there is required, on the part of the belligerents, a *right intention*, by which it is intended that good may be accomplished or evil avoided. (*ST* 2a2ae. 40. 1)

A just war was to be waged by public authority, that is by rulers who had responsibility for the affairs of the state; no private wars were licit. According to Aquinas, there was no place for war where recourse could be had to a superior authority for resolution of disputes. Just cause included defence and the Augustinian notion of avenging injuries done. (Aquinas also noted in *On Kingship* 1. 16 that 'the king is responsible for ensuring that the multitude subject to him remains safe against its enemies'.) Right intention was also defined by reference to Augustine: the aim of war was peace, and a war that was called by legitimate authority and for a just cause could be made illicit by vices such as cruelty and the desire for domination.

Aquinas' just war theory articulated a common good argument, with the Augustinian element of the punishment of sin added. A just war was the means of procuring the common good of preserving the state in the area where law could not be enforced—that is, in its external relations with other rulers and states.

## Conclusion

As a theologian and philosopher Aquinas remained highly influential, through the Thomist School named after him, well into the twentieth century. For anyone studying the history of political thought, he merits attention as a pre-eminent example of Scholastic method. His main contribution to political thought, his characteristic message, was that government and human law must have a moral purpose to be valid: that immoral law is no law at all, and that rulers must act for the common good of those they rule—that the exercise of power is not its own justification. He provided classic arguments that could later be employed against absolutism and totalitarianism, and, indeed, against any illegitimate use of state power. A prime exponent of the natural law tradition, Aquinas was the apostle of reason in political thought.

---

### FURTHER READING


Copleston, F. C., *Aquinas* (Harmondsworth: Penguin, 1991).

Finnis, John, *Aquinas: Moral, Political and Legal Theory* (Oxford: Clarendon Press, 1998).

Gilby, Thomas, *Principality and Polity: Aquinas and the Rise of State Theory in the West* (London: Longmans, 1958).

Gilson, E., *The Christian Philosophy of St Thomas Aquinas* (London: Victor Gollancz, 1957).

Kenny, A., *Aquinas* (Oxford: Oxford University Press, 1980).

Weisheipl, James A., *Friar Thomas d'Aquino: His Life, Thought and Works* (Oxford: Basil Blackwell, 1975).

## NOTES

1. Walter Ullmann, *Principles of Government and Politics in the Middle Ages* (London: Methuen, 1961), 231–7.
2. Antony Black, *Political Thought in Europe, 1250–1450* (Cambridge: Cambridge University Press, 1992), 11–12; Cary J. Nederman, *Medieval Aristotelianism and its Limits: Classical Traditions in Moral and Political Philosophy, 12th–15th Centuries* (Aldershot: Variorum, 1997), pp. ix–xii.
3. References to the *Exposition on the Books of the Politics* are to book, part, and lecture (here book 3, lecture 6).
4. References to *On Kingship* are to book and chapter (here book 2, ch. 4).
5. Walter Mohr, 'Bemerkungen zur Verfasserschaft von De regimine principum', in *Virtus Politica. Festgabe zum 75. Geburtstag von Alfons Hufnagel*, ed. Joseph Möller and Helmut Kohlenburger (Stuttgart: Friedrich Frommann Verlag, Günther Holzboog KG).
6. But see *On the Government of Rulers. De Regimine Principum. Ptolemy of Lucca with Portions Attributed to Thomas Aquinas*, trans. James M. Blythe (Philadelphia: University of Pennsylvania Press, 1997), 3–5.
7. I. T. Eschmann, 'A Catalogue of St. Thomas's Works', in E. Gilson, *The Christian Philosophy of St Thomas Aquinas* (London: Victor Gollancz, 1957), 412–15.
8. Christoph Flüeler, *Rezeption und Interpretation der Aristotelischen Politica im späten Mittelalter*, vol. i (Amsterdam: B. R. Grüner, 1992), 28.
9. *ST* refers to *Summa theologiae*. This is divided into three books, the second of which is subdivided into two parts. The first book is conventionally referred to as 'Prima' (1a), the first part of the second as 'Prima secundae' (1a2ae), the second part of the second as 'Secunda secundae' (2a2ae), and the third as 'Tertia' (3a). References to *ST* are in this order: book, question, article (thus *ST* 1a. 8. 2 = book 1, question 8, article 2).
10. 'It is a saying worthy of reigning majesty for the prince to profess himself bound by the laws, for our authority derives from the authority of the laws' (*lex 'Digna vox'*).
11. For a useful account of modern interpretations, see James M. Blythe, *Ideal Government and the Mixed Constitution in the Middle Ages* (Princeton: Princeton University Press, 1992), 40.
12. See above, p. 112.
13. M. S. Kempshall, *The Common Good in Late Medieval Political Thought* (Oxford: Clarendon Press, 1999), 100 and 128–9.
14. In the Vulgate, which Aquinas used, 1 Kings corresponds with 1 Samuel, in modern editions.
15. As in Ullmann, *Principles of Government and Politics in the Middle Ages*, 255.
16. References to his *Writings on the Sentences* are to book, distinction, question, article (here book 2, distinction 44, question 2, article 2).

# 8 Marsiglio of Padua

Cary J. Nederman

## Contents



## Chapter guide

Marsiglio of Padua's political theory stems from his opposition to the pope's control of secular political affairs. Marsiglio formulates theoretical principles to explain the origins and nature of the political community that depend upon a strict distinction between the temporal and spiritual realms. According to him, government and law exist in order to support the civil peace. Peace is construed as the material sufficiency of the lives of every citizen, including artisans and farmers as well as the wealthy and privileged. In order to ensure that the interests of all citizens are advanced by the political community, Marsiglio insists upon the necessity of broad consent to prospective statutes and rulers. Moreover, Marsiglio regards the Church as subject to the decisions of the entire community. Ecclesiastical officials enjoy no independent powers, but are subject to the regulation of the faithful, whose interests are represented by the General Council of the Church.

## Biography

Marsiglio (often known as Marsilius, the Latinized version of his name) was born in Padua in 1275/1280. Probably educated in medicine at the University of Padua, he moved to

Paris, where he became Rector of the University in 1313. Marsiglio also involved himself in the political intrigues of northern Italy. Following completion of the *Defender of Peace* in 1324, he moved to the court of the German king (and would-be emperor) Ludwig of Bavaria. Marsiglio is sometimes identified as the architect of Ludwig's expedition to Rome in 1327–8. Ludwig arranged for his own imperial election and coronation by the people of Rome, then deposed Pope John XXII and named an anti-pope. After the collapse of the expedition Marsiglio retired from public view, re-emerging only near the end of his life to write the *Defender Minor*. He probably died in late 1342. The *Defender of Peace* afforded a model of secular government and ecclesiology imitated by many later medieval authors, including Dietrich of Niem and Nicholas of Cusa. The *Defender of Peace* was first printed in 1522; translations into several vernacular languages became available between the fourteenth and sixteenth centuries. During the Reformation many eminent Catholics accused Luther of subscribing to Marsiglian doctrines. Later the *Defender of Peace* served as a source for Richard Hooker, Johannes Althusius, and George Lawson.

## Key texts

*Defender of Peace* (c.1324)
*On the Transfer of the Empire* (c.1326)
*Defender [of Peace] Minor* (c.1340)

## Main texts used

*The Defender of Peace*, trans. Alan Gewirth (New York: Columbia University Press, 1956).

*Marsiglio of Padua. Writings on the Empire: Defensor Minor and De Translatione Imperii*, trans. Cary J. Nederman (Cambridge: Cambridge University Press, 1993).

## Key ideas

**Peace** is threatened by popes and the Church hierarchy. All secular governments should oppose the ecclesiastical hierarchy. Political society arises from infirmities of human nature. **Citizenship** derives from all vital functions in society. **Consent** forms the basis of **law** and **government.** The **pope** is subject to the community **of the faithful. The Church** is governed by the **General Council. Roman Empire** is legitimate as a result of popular consent.

# Introduction

Few political theorists have generated more controversy during their own times, as well as among succeeding generations, than Marsiglio of Padua. Reviled by defenders of Christian religious and institutional orthodoxy during the later Middle Ages, Marsiglio's teachings were nonetheless disseminated even by those who besmirched his name. More recently, his writings have been read as foreshadowing various main currents of modern political thought, ranging from Marxism and participatory democracy to republicanism and liberalism. In his major work, the *Defender of Peace* (1324), Marsiglio upheld a strict separation between the temporal and the spiritual ends of human existence, and constructed conceptions of the secular community as well as the Church accordingly. He taught that natural inclination and reason stood behind the creation of human society, but that volition and consent formed the basis of government and law—both earthly and religious. Marsiglio's originality and sophistication must be balanced against the political and intellectual context in which he wrote. His work was profoundly stimulated by his desire to oppose the temporal pretensions of late medieval popes, who had advanced quite extensive claims regarding their secular powers on the basis of their ecclesiastical office. Moreover, Marsiglio's thought is framed in the conventional political languages of the fourteenth century. In addition, many of his doctrines (especially his conception of human nature) suggest the influence of his scientific and medical training. Yet Marsiglio is also an innovative thinker in many significant ways, departing from his sources in order to construct unique and dramatic accounts of human political and religious life. His thought is far more eclectic and less tightly bound to Aristotle and other classical and Christian authorities than most of his contemporaries.

## The *Defender of Peace*

### Friends and enemies of peace

At the centre of Marsiglio's political project is his stalwart opposition to the earthly pretensions of the priesthood and especially the papacy. This theme, more than any positive dedication to a particular set of constitutional arrangements, shapes his theory. The character of this opposition is not, however, always immediately evident, in part because of the organization of the *Defender of Peace* into three distinct discourses. Discourse I discusses the origins and nature of earthly political authority; the second discourse severely criticizes claims made on behalf of the rights of the Church and, particularly, the papacy, to exercise temporal power, and defends an alternative, conciliar ecclesiology; a brief third section summarizes those conclusions derived from the preceding discussions that Marsiglio regards to be especially useful or worthy of emphasis. The structural division between the substance of Discourse I and of Discourse II was unusual for its time, inasmuch as it implies a distinction between the treatment of temporal government and of ecclesiastical affairs.

Yet the *Defender of Peace* is by no means formed of two separate, self-subsistent, and internally coherent treatises. Rather, it is possible to identify a single central theme that binds together the tract as a whole: the danger posed to human happiness (as experienced in the peaceful and self-sufficient community) by the interference of papal government in secular life. The entire force of the argument in the *Defender of Peace* is directed towards demonstrating the disruptive effects of the papacy's attempts to regulate temporal affairs. Approached from this perspective, Discourse I stipulates the arrangements necessary to bolster the stability and unity of secular communities so as to repulse papal interference, while Discourse II substitutes the principles of papal monarchy with those of a conciliar ecclesiology.

The ultimate lessons of the *Defender of Peace* cannot be learned in isolation from its primarily polemical goal. Marsiglio hopes that all temporal authorities who are fit to act will halt and reverse the spread of the papacy's earthly powers before the papal plan of global dominion is realized. By rolling back the pope's secular influence, in turn, Marsiglio presumes that those territories already damaged by the papacy may begin to repair their internal disorder and disunity. He resolves to demonstrate why rulers and communities—especially in locales where the papacy's threat had not yet penetrated—ought to wager their salvation and temporal safety against the renunciation of the pope's right to intercede in earthly affairs. Marsiglio argues that opposition to the papacy is obligatory for both spiritual and temporal reasons. On the one hand, he appeals to the Christian duty to bear witness to the divinely ordained truth. Christian love for one's fellows dictates an obligation to correct them whenever they stray by showing them the error of their ways and the path to their deliverance. Among the dangers to Christian believers, according to Marsiglio, may be counted the papal 'pestilence' which threatens the 'civil life', which may be regarded a 'the best object of desire available to mortal man', and thus interferes with the divine design (*Defender of Peace*, I. 1. 8[1]). A Christian who knows his fellows to be in need, and yet who turns his back, does not possess the central religious virtue of charity.

Marsiglio reinforces the Christian duty to reject papal infringement upon earthly jurisdiction with a parallel obligation arising from the sociable nature of human beings. The *Defender of Peace* quotes at length from Cicero's *On Duties* to the effect that human beings exist, according to their natures, in order to serve their fellows. Nature instils in humanity the duty to act for the public benefit above all else. Human sociability forms a universal bond, not confined to one's own community but extending beyond fixed political units to all civilized peoples. The doctrine generates the naturalistic foundations of a generalized human responsibility to discover and to stamp out anti-social beliefs and practices wherever they occur. The resistance advocated by the *Defender of Peace* is of two sorts. First, one must repel enemies of earthly tranquillity by revealing their identities to all who will listen. Instruction can be a powerful tool in the war against those who seek to disturb the social order. Secondly, one must move beyond education to direct action: whoever takes up the banner of discord and temporal misery must be halted by any means available to knowledgeable antagonists. In defence of his view, Marsiglio cites Cicero's claim that justice entails not only that one refrain from doing injury, but also that one protect others from imminent harm. Tranquil social relations are impossible without the acknowledgement of this obligation.

## Generic political theory

By the very nature of Marsiglio's polemical intentions, the success of his argument depends upon the breadth and viability of its appeal to all forms of political organization. To the extent that he was able to create a framework equally relevant to the experiences of urban communities, national monarchies, and more amorphous territorial units such as the German Empire, he could propose concerted and unified temporal opposition to papal interference in secular affairs. This plan informs the 'generic' character of his political thought. Marsiglio's political theory is 'generic' in so far as he attempts to frame a set of criteria for the good social and political life in general, without reference to constitutional, institutional, or territorial considerations. The generic quality of Marsiglian theory profoundly demarcates it from predecessors and contemporaries. Where ancient and medieval political theory had traditionally sought to specify a single mode of political life which best suited or realized the ends of political association, Marsiglio adopted the more encompassing view that diverse forms (although *not just any* form) of political arrangement may equally promote the purposes implicit in social intercourse.

The generic character of the *Defender of Peace* is explicitly woven into Marsiglio's argument. This is evident from the outset of Discourse I, where the very first substantive issue he addresses is the nature of the *regnum* ('kingdom,' although sometimes anachronistically translated 'state'). There are, Marsiglio observes, four ways in which *regnum* may be defined (*Defender of Peace*, I. 2. 1). The first three are reasonably conventional. A *regnum* may be conceived geographically, as a collection of cities or provinces ruled by a single government; or constitutionally, as a form of government in which one virtuous man rules over the citizens (the concept that Marsiglio attributes to Aristotle); or in a compound sense, which combines the first two meanings and which is, he says, 'the most familiar sense of this term'. But Marsiglio explains that 'the sense in which we shall use this term in our determination of questions' differs from common definitions: in the fourth, distinctively Marsiglian, sense, *regnum* denotes 'something common to every species of temperate government, whether in a single city or in many'. In other words, *regnum* is used in a wholly generic fashion to indicate those properties that render a government well ordered or 'healthy' regardless of either the size of the territory it rules or the specifics of its institutional arrangement. All properly organized communities have shared features; *regnum* (along with *civitas* ('city' or 'civic community'), which he often uses as a rough equivalent) is the word Marsiglio employs when he wishes to speak generally about such communities. In line with his polemical aim of directing his argument to a broad audience, he professes indifference to geographic or constitutional distinctions so long as a community is governed in a 'temperate' manner, that is, according to principles befitting a *regnum*. Marsiglio reinforces this generic approach at crucial moments throughout Discourse I. He makes the typical Aristotelian distinction between the three modes of healthy constitution (kingship, aristocracy, and polity) and the three types of diseased regime (tyranny, oligarchy, and democracy). But given the opportunity to express a preference for government by the one, the few, or the many, he declines the invitation entirely: 'As to which of the temperate governments is best or which of the diseased governments is worst, and the relative goodness or badness of the other species, the discussion of these points is not part of our present concern' (ibid. I. 8. 4). This is a remarkable deviation from medieval convention; political authors of the Latin Middle Ages normally either assumed or expressly defended the superiority of one form of government over others.

Similar care to include diverse modes of political life is evident in the seventeenth chapter of Discourse I, where Marsiglio discusses the numerical unity of government. He argues that one characteristic of a well-ordered *regnum* is that all its sections must ultimately be governed by a single, supreme ruler. Any other arrangement will produce chaos and confusion. But while Marsiglio claims that 'in a single city or kingdom there must be only a single government', he does not make this statement in an unqualified fashion. Rather, he adds: 'If there is more than one government in number and species, as seems expedient in larger cities and especially in a kingdom taken in its first sense, then there must be among them one in number which is supreme, to which all the others are reduced, and which corrects any errors arising in them' (ibid. I. 17. 1). To specify the absolute unity of government as a precondition of good order, Marsiglio realizes, would have the consequence of eliminating a portion of the political spectrum from his prospective audience, namely, those communities in which exigencies of territorial or population size, or tradition and custom, had resulted in multiple layers of rule. Marsiglio's self-consciously generic design reveals itself in the extent of his tolerance for political diversity and his attention to theoretical inclusiveness. Not even the imperial system of rule is accorded priority by Marsiglio. In spite of the fact that the *Defender of Peace* is addressed to the aspiring emperor, Ludwig of Bavaria, Marsiglio's indifference to constitutional and geographical variation is extended to world dominion: 'The question of whether it is advantageous to have one supreme government in number for all those throughout the world who exist in a civil life . . . merits reasoned study, but it is distinct from our present concern' (ibid. I. 17. 10). Marsiglio's refusal to take a stand on the question reinforces the impression that his political tenets are intended to apply equally and without exception to all manner of governments.

## Principles of secular theory

### Demarcating the temporal realm

Marsiglio's ability to pursue his anti-papal line of 'generic' political reasoning depends heavily upon his postulation of a sharp distinction between temporal and spiritual realms in the *Defender of Peace*. In typical Christian Aristotelian fashion, Marsiglio acknowledges that human ends 'fall into two kinds, of which one is temporal or earthly, while the other is usually called eternal or heavenly' (*Defender of Peace*, I. 4. 3). But the resemblance between his view and more conventional medieval thought is largely superficial. According to the *Defender of Peace*, temporal ends are for the most part indifferent to spiritual goals. The term 'spiritual', Marsiglio says, 'refers to every immanent action or passion of human cognitive or appetitive power' (ibid. II. 2. 5), where 'immanent' acts are understood as 'actions or passions' that 'do not pass over into a subject other than the doer, nor are they exercised through any external organs or locomotive members; of this kind are human thoughts and desires or affections' (ibid. I. 5. 4). Because they are wholly internal and self-regarding, immanent acts are not susceptible to public inspection and control; they are spiritual in the sense that they do not transgress the boundaries of the soul, hence are invisible to human observation and are known only to God. By contrast, Marsiglio identifies three possible meanings of the temporal realm: first, in connection with the physical world other than humankind, the objects of which 'are ordered toward [human] use, needs, and pleasures in and for the status of worldly life'; secondly, as connoting 'every human habit, action, or passion, whether in oneself or directed toward another for a purpose in this world or the present life'; and thirdly, and most narrowly, as stemming from 'those human actions and passions which are voluntary and transient, resulting in advantage or disadvantage to someone other than the agent' (ibid. II. 2. 4). The temporal activities of a human being, Marsiglio believes, are only of concern to someone else to the extent that they are 'transient', that is, have an impact on others. Consequently, 'transient' acts—'other-regarding' may be the modern equivalent—are the proper object of regulation by the laws and rulers of the political community (ibid. I. 5. 7). When transient behaviour is performed 'in due proportion', it results in benefits to others as well as to oneself. When transient action is 'excessive', however, it disadvantages another person. Marsiglio therefore enshrines temporal advantage as a fundamental and entirely legitimate goal of human conduct. Indeed, he establishes 'as the starting-point of everything to be demonstrated' 'that all human beings not deformed or otherwise impeded naturally desire a sufficient life, and avoid or flee what is harmful thereto' (ibid. I. 4. 2). Marsiglio then quotes Cicero's proclamation in *On Duties* that the basic purpose of all living creatures is self-preservation. The advantage of human beings is achieved by gaining those conditions of existence that confer upon them a physically adequate life. Although Marsiglio makes passing mention of the Aristotelian conception of a higher 'good life', constituted by the exercise of the practical and theoretical virtues, the material sufficiency of human life receives the overwhelming measure of his attention.

## Functional foundations

Consistent with his emphasis upon temporal existence, Marsiglio formulates a philosophical reconstruction of the origins of human association and of government which serves as an explanation of both the purpose of civil life and its relation to human nature. The secular advantage of individuals is achieved most fully and 'naturally' under conditions of human cooperation in the context of an ordered and organized community. Marsiglio holds that 'human beings came together in the civil community in order to pursue advantage and a sufficient life and to avoid the opposite' (*Defender of Peace*, I. 12. 7).

The claim that human beings associate primarily on account of self-interest indeed grounds the account of the origins of communal life in the *Defender of Peace*. The 'perfected community' emerges along with the differentiation of the functions necessary for a materially sufficient existence, these tasks being defined by the various arts created by humankind in order to redress their physical infirmities (ibid. I. 3. 2–5). Marsiglio thus posits that the commission of 'transient' acts is absolutely necessary for human beings to attain a sufficient life. Successful self-preservation demands perpetual interaction between human beings, each of whom makes a particular contribution through his specialized occupation (ibid. I. 4. 5). Marsiglio postulates a permanent social division of labour, arising from the possession in all human beings of fixed, quasi-natural inclinations towards particular tasks. Marsiglio expressly specifies these functions in terms of the occupations necessary to maintain the physical well-being of the community: farmers, merchants, craftsmen, and warriors (ibid. I. 5. 6–9). All of these occupations are necessary for achieving a sufficient temporal life, and none are to be denigrated. Many earlier theorists had employed such division of function as a justification for the exclusion of entire classes of human beings from political identity or involvement. By contrast, Marsiglio insists that the intercommunication of functions required for the public welfare necessitates a politics of inclusion, and he thus construes citizenship in a remarkably extensive fashion. Citizenship in the community is consequently conferred on a strictly functional basis, judged according to the usefulness of various human activities for the meeting of material human needs.

## Communal consent

Marsiglio intends citizens within the community to take an active role in their own governance, locating popular consent at the centre of his theoretical framework. Such consent arises directly from the functional character of the community. First, all whose interests are served or affected by a community must be conceded full membership in it and must agree to the conditions of association (i.e. law and rulership). Secondly, having so consented, all such citizens are absolutely bound to obey the law and the determinations made by rulers in accordance with it. In other words, people must individually as well as collectively submit to the terms of their cooperation, after which they can be held strictly accountable for 'transient' actions detrimental to the advantage of fellow citizens. As a consequence, the *Defender of Peace* holds that the legitimacy of both laws and rulers depends wholly upon their 'voluntary' character, that is, the extent to which those subject to their jurisdiction have publicly and overtly consented to their authority (*Defender of Peace*, I. 9. 5, 12. 3). What Marsiglio in fact regards to be distinctive of citizenship is the ability to express one's will in the political venue, by judging for oneself the validity of prospective rulers and laws. All matters 'whose proper institution is of the greatest importance for the communal sufficiency of citizens in this life, and whose depraved institution impends communal detriment, must be instituted only by the whole body of citizens' (ibid. I. 12. 7). This implies for Marsiglio not merely formal, corporative assent, but an extensive privilege on the part of each individual citizen to examine prospective laws and rulers (ibid. I. 13. 8). Each and every member of the community reserves to himself final judgement about all matters of public regulation. This is required, Marsiglio contends, because a government's very legitimacy depends upon its congruence with the voluntary acquiescence of those over whom it rules. And the only way to assure such congruence is by a prior act of explicit consent on the part of citizens. Hence, Marsiglio asserts that no one can protest against the enforcement of a law to which that person has already assented (ibid. I. 12. 6). The peace is best upheld when it is regarded as an expression not of the power of the government but of the will of the civil body.

## Legislative principles

Marsiglio must be absolved of the charge sometimes levelled by commentators that his conception of active citizenship leads to a tyrannical or totalitarian popular will whose declaration is sufficient to command obedience. It is true that Marsiglio regards citizen assent to be necessary for the authorization of communal laws. But the *Defender of Peace* does not regard public volition or command to be sufficient for the legitimacy of any public act. Rather, the traditional standard of natural law, which grounds the validity of statutes upon their conformity with justice, is upheld by Marsiglio. His contention is simply that widespread consent affords the most reliable guarantee that such conformity will occur, because a greater degree of consent reflects a greater application of reason. At the same time, however, Marsiglio advocates an unusual procedure for arriving at the criteria by means of which citizens discern the worthiness of legislative measures. Most medieval thinkers, to the extent that they considered popular consent a necessary component of the political system, would probably have responded that members of the community must consult some abstract principle of natural justice in reaching their determination. In striking contrast, Marsiglio answers that every person correctly and adequately evaluates laws and rulers when he measures them against the yardstick of his own self-interest. Marsiglio asserts, 'Those matters, therefore, that can touch upon the advantage and disadvantage of everyone ought to be known and heard by everyone, so that they can obtain advantage and repel its opposite' (*Defender of Peace*, I. 12. 7). Simply stated, the common good for Marsiglio is coextensive with the aggregate advantage of the individuals within the community. No power may legitimately be imposed upon the polity that is inconsistent with the materially sufficient life of citizens. Therefore, by consulting one's own direct benefit in the evaluation of public affairs, one simultaneously discovers the communal benefit (ibid. I. 12. 5). Marsiglio's concern is that, unchecked by the consent of the body of citizens, people in power will quite naturally and unavoidably create laws and make decisions that will favour themselves. But if every citizen considers a proposed statute, and none finds it detrimental to his own interests, then it must meet the test of reason and hence merit promulgation.

## Secular government

It might be tempting to look to the *Defender of Peace* for an early defence of limited or constitutional government in a modern sense. Yet the activities that Marsiglio ascribes to the ruling part of the community (regardless of its composition) are not exceptional according to the standards of his own time. He was at one with his contemporaries in viewing the ruler as the leading segment within an organic whole, charged with a special responsibility for coordinating the smooth and peaceful operation of the other parts of the body in conducting those functions which touch upon the public good. The appropriate tools of government are laws and the moral characters of the officials themselves. What makes Marsiglio's conception of rulership exceptional is his further claim—parallel to his notion of legislation—that the true source of good government lies with the exercise of the consent of the members of the civic body. Without stipulating any preferred constitutional regime, Marsiglio draws a line between legitimate ('healthy') and illegitimate ('diseased') forms of rule according to the criterion of 'volition'. But why is government necessary at all, if citizens are reasonable beings interested in pursuing their mutual advantage? Marsiglio acknowledges that it is entirely possible that people, by seeking their own benefit, may harm others, whether intentionally or not. 'Transient acts', he observes, 'can be done for the advantage or for the disadvantage or injury of a person other than the agent for the sake of one's condition in the present life' (*Defender of Peace*, I. 5. 7). The problem, of course, is that, should human beings seek their own interests at the expense of their fellows, conflicts would readily emerge within the community (ibid. I. 4. 4, 5. 7). Here we encounter Marsiglio's central preoccupation in the *Defender of Peace*: the maintenance of civil peace. He closely identifies his main objective—peace—with the very reason for which society and government exist. In his opening sentence of the *Defender of Peace* he lauds 'the advantages and fruits of the tranquillity or peace of civil regimes', chief among which is 'the sufficient life, which no one can obtain without peace and tranquillity' (ibid. I. 1. 1). At the close of the first discourse he returns to the same theme. His purpose, he says, is to identify the causal factor—the papacy—that, in his own day, 'has deprived and is still depriving the community of peace or tranquillity and of the above mentioned advantages that follow therefrom, and has vexed it and still vexes it with every kind of disadvantage' (ibid. I. 19. 4). Peace for Marsiglio is not an end in itself, but a requirement for the realization of stable intercourse within the community towards the end of a materially sufficient life. Whatever threatens the peace is necessarily inconsistent with the natural and proper goal of human society.

## Ecclesiology

### Origins and nature of the church

The larger part of the *Defender of Peace*, comprising the second discourse, consists of a direct examination and critique of papalist theories of ecclesiastical government, along with the defence of a conciliar ecclesiology. The views expressed in Discourse II were especially notorious in Marsiglio's own age, earning him and his writing condemnation by successive popes and their apologists. The foundation for much of this theory of the Church was laid already in the first discourse, however. Marsiglio stipulates there that the priesthood must be counted as simply one of the functions necessary for a perfected community (*Defender of Peace*, I. 5. 10–14). Therefore, priests are exempt neither from the secular laws nor from the public burdens required for the maintenance of civil order. Furthermore, the activities of priests, just as of other offices within the social body, must be strictly regulated according to the principles of temporal welfare. In short, Marsiglio denies to the clergy any autonomy in the exercise of their appointed tasks, at least when these touch upon the realm of 'transient' action. Marsiglio's refusal to permit the priesthood any earthly independence from the community derives primarily from his conception of law. Prescriptions for human activity that have a coercive force, and hence can be forcibly imposed upon individuals, are by definition temporal in nature. But the proper function of the priesthood is the education and preparation of souls for eternal life, a task that is of a wholly spiritual character. Consequently, Marsiglio reasons, the clergy (including the papacy) lacks the authority to require or prohibit any action of a temporal sort, unless that deed has already been licensed or outlawed by the consent of the entire community. For priests to have such legislative power would amount to one 'part' of the civil body dictating its will to the remaining segments, a situation the validity of which Marsiglio had already discounted in Discourse I. Marsiglio's argument amounts to a denial of the status of 'law' to the 'canons' of the Christian Church. Canon law provides at best 'counsels' to the faithful about deeds they may wish to perform or refrain from for the sake of their souls. But no priest, purely on the basis of ecclesiastical canons, may licitly command his fellow citizens to behave in any fixed way with regard to temporal affairs. Only the law of the community, approved by all, may rightfully do that. The ecclesiology of the *Defender of Peace* likewise draws upon the first discourse when offering a conception of the Church. Marsiglio defines the Church as 'the whole body of the faithful who believe in and invoke the body of Christ' (*Defender of Peace*, II. 2. 3). While such a definition would have been unexceptional in Marsiglio's time, the conclusions he draws from it are entirely novel. In his view, the 'whole body of the faithful' is equivalent to the 'perfected community' when regarded in its spiritual, rather than temporal, aspect. Hence, the citizen body forms the supreme authority in the ecclesiastical realm as well as the secular sphere. The community alone enjoys the authority to appoint and remove priests, to legislate regarding spiritual affairs, to punish members of the faithful, and to impose interdiction and excommunication. Marsiglio hence undermines not merely priestly power, but the entire edifice of the ecclesiastical hierarchy, with the papacy at its apex. Neither the pope nor any of the bishops may properly claim for their office a divine origin or basis; their powers are conferred entirely by the 'whole body of the faithful', who always retain the right to suspend, limit, or eliminate any position or its incumbent. There is quite literally nothing sacred about the exalted structure of papal government.

## Conciliarism

Marsiglio recognizes, of course, that the body of the faithful is far too vast and unwieldy to exercise its rightful powers directly. As a consequence, the community of believers selects representatives to meet as a General Council of the Church in order to establish Christian doctrine in all matters pertaining to religion. The Council appoints and removes ecclesiastical officials, proclaims and interprets canon law, and gives final authority to every action undertaken by the temporal institutions of the Church. The Council becomes on Marsiglio's view the effective governing body of the Church, while the pope and other clerical officials serve simply as executors of the conciliar will.

Yet the Council does not act or determine anything on its own authority in isolation from an external source of legitimation. On the one hand, the members of the Council should be seen as 'representing the whole body of the faithful by virtue of the authority which these [their electors] have granted them' (*Defender of Peace*, II. 20. 2). But since, according to Marsiglio, the central purpose of the Council is the canonical interpretation of Holy Scripture, the members of the Council cannot be understood as mere delegates of their constituents. Marsiglio adopts the standard medieval position that the truths of Scripture are fixed for all time. It is up to the Council, the *Defender of Peace* contends, to discover and articulate these eternal truths when issues of doubtful understanding arise. Hence, the representative quality of the Council stems from the fact that it ultimately represents the inspiration of the Holy Spirit as manifested through successive generations of members of the body of the faithful. Marsiglio explains that since the Council represents by succession the congregation of the apostles and elders and other believers (of the early Church), it is likely (if not certain) that in the definition of doubtful meanings of Scripture, especially those where error would involve the threat of eternal damnation, the virtue of the Holy Spirit is present to the General Council, guiding its deliberations and revealing the truth (ibid. II. 19. 2). This claim is reinforced by Marsiglio's later remark that the General Council 'alone represents Christ, the maker of the eternal law, or the congregation of the apostles and their church' (ibid. II. 28. 21). In these passages, we encounter the theological premisses of Marsiglio's conception of the General Council. The Council simply codifies the truth of Scripture which is known to all believers—past, present, and future. Marsiglio's theory of the General Council thus derives very novel conclusions from quite conventional Christian teachings.

# Later writings on empire and church

As a result of the overwhelming attention devoted to the *Defender of Peace*, Marsiglio's other writings have been overshadowed. In addition to several works on metaphysical topics, written early in his career, Marsiglio also wrote two further political tracts, the *Defender [of Peace] Minor* (c.1340) and *On the Transfer of the Empire* (c.1326). The *Defender Minor*, so called because it purports to be a recapitulation and synopsis of the main points of the *Defender of Peace*, is itself made up of several component treatises. Appended to the first twelve chapters of the *Defender Minor* are slightly revised versions of two independent writings by Marsiglio, *On Marriage* and *The Form of a Dispensation with Respect to the Relation of Consanguinity*, both written explicitly as works of advice for King Ludwig.

## Legitimizing the Roman Empire

One of the polemical weapons in the arsenal of the papacy against independently minded emperors such as Ludwig of Bavaria was a document known as the 'Donation of Constantine'. The 'Donation' purports to be a fourth-century grant of lordship over all the lands within the Roman Empire to the Bishop of Rome by the first Christian emperor, Constantine I. This document, in turn, became the basis for medieval explanations of how the seat of the empire was transferred first to the Franks and later to the Germans: it fell to the authority of the papacy, as warranted by the 'Donation', to assign imperial rights to one particular dynasty or people. Although the 'Donation of Constantine' was shown at the beginning of the Renaissance to be a medieval forgery, it nevertheless proved to afford powerful ammunition for late medieval popes and the writers who served their cause. In the *Defender of Peace* Marsiglio had attempted to refute the consequences which papal proponents derived from the 'Donation'. In particular, he argued that since the exercise of rulership in any temporal society can only stem from the community itself, or its greater part, no pope or other priest could rightfully invoke his own authority to transfer political power from one person to another or the seat of the empire from one place to another (*Defender of Peace*, II. 22. 19–20). Such a position depends directly upon his teachings about the nature of secular politics in Discourse I. Two conclusions might be drawn from this argument: first, that the papacy had on its own initiative directed the transfer of the empire among individuals or nations, and hence that all such transfers were illegitimate; or secondly, that whatever the role the papacy played in successive transfers of the empire, its contribution was not decisive, so that such transfers in fact occurred in accordance with the principles outlined in the *Defender of Peace* and were therefore de jure as well as de facto. Marsiglio says in Discourse II that, while he will assume the latter conclusion to be valid, the legitimacy of the successive imperial transfers needs to be demonstrated, a task which he proposes to undertake in another work, by which he clearly means the text we know as *On the Transfer of the Empire.*

The purpose of *On the Transfer of the Empire* is twofold. First, it seeks to establish that the modern incumbent of the office of the Roman emperor holds his position as the result of a series of rightful transfers of power and in accordance with the correct procedure for his selection. Secondly, it aims to show that no matter how central a role the papacy played in encouraging the transfer of the imperial seat, its function was purely honorific and incidental, inasmuch as the rights to the empire were acquired by the Franks and then the Germans on the basis of wholly secular events. From the latter it may be concluded that, even if custom has permitted popes to crown new emperors, the source of imperial authority is not vested in the papacy but in an earthly historical process external to papal control. The philosophical and legal premiss supporting Marsiglio's view may be characterized as follows: if a ruler (or indeed any person) is in possession of a set of rights as a result of an earlier series of just transfers (inheritance, gift, and so on), then no extraneous grounds may be invoked to override or deny those rights. In the body of *On the Transfer of the Empire* Marsiglio collects and adduces the historical evidence that such a series of just transfers in fact occurred.

## Imperial government and conciliar authority

The most important contribution of Marsiglio's later career, the *Defender Minor*, is a more conventional work than the *Defender of Peace*, structurally speaking. The *Defender Minor* does not divide its discussion of temporal government from the analysis of ecclesiology, and, by inference, distinguish rigidly between the natural and supernatural realms or between reason and revelation. Rather, the *Defender Minor* concentrates directly upon the relationship between earthly jurisdiction and spiritual authority. This feature places the *Defender Minor* squarely within the standard genre of 'emperor and pope' treatises typical of the later Middle Ages. Marsiglio's focus in the *Defender Minor* specifically upon the empire does not signal a departure from the *Defender of Peace*. Rather, adapting the 'generic' approach pioneered in the *Defender of Peace*, the *Defender Minor* applies Marsiglio's general principles of temporal government to the concrete terms of one type of political arrangement. The *Defender Minor* demonstrates, in a sense, how the political theory of the *Defender of Peace* applies in the case of an imperial regime, as opposed to a city or kingdom. Marsiglio contends that the Roman Empire, no less than any other earthly polity, has an independent foundation stemming from the consent of its own citizen body, and hence its own functions and responsibilities as assigned to it by citizens. The papacy enjoys no greater right to interfere in the affairs of the empire than it does to intervene in any other form of political association. The *Defender Minor* thus renders the doctrines of the *Defender of Peace* specifically relevant to the unique circumstances of imperial government. Consequently, the characteristic doctrines of the *Defender of Peace* are re-encountered in the *Defender Minor*. Marsiglio's conceptions of the well-ordered political community and of the General Council, as well as his critique of papal power, all play a central role in the *Defender Minor*.

If only because the *Defender Minor* operates at a greater level of specificity than the *Defender of Peace*, it erases some of the ambiguities present in the earlier work and affords us greater insight into Marsiglio's fundamental intellectual and political commitments. For example, the *Defender Minor* explicates with greater precision the foundations of law for Marsiglio. As in the *Defender of Peace*, the *Defender Minor* argues that there are two basic kinds of law: divine law, ordained by God who, along with his son, judges in accordance with it; and human law, established by the citizen body and imposed by those people to whom the community assigns the judicial role (*Defender Minor*, I. 2–6[2]). Because Marsiglio insists so adamantly in the *Defender of Peace* that no human law merits obedience which has not first been expressly authorized by citizens, he has sometimes been understood to advocate the idea of 'legal positivism', that is, the notion that the essential ingredient in the legitimacy of a statute is its de facto enactment by the state. Marsiglio explicitly denies this implication in the *Defender Minor*, however. Instead, he proclaims that human and divine laws should be consistent and mutually reinforcing: God-given law decrees obedience to all human legislation which is not incompatible within divine dictates (*Defender Minor*, 8. 3–5); human law must promulgate nothing which conflicts with God's will. He adds that, should a case arise in which some human statute commands what is opposed to divine law, the latter takes absolute precedence over the former (ibid. 13. 3–9). Marsiglio thus embraces a version of the traditional

Christian doctrine of passive resistance: all duly ordained human power must be obeyed unless its commands conflict with God's law, at which time the Christian must refuse to submit. But he revises one prominent feature of this doctrine: it pertains not to priests or prelates to decree such resistance—inasmuch as they may only advise but never command—but the individual believer is to decide for himself. In turn, since human law is an emanation of the whole civic community itself, it seems unlikely that such conflicts of divine with temporal law will emerge in the first place, since the citizen body is coextensive with the body of the faithful.

The *Defender Minor* also permits us to appreciate more thoroughly the nature and operation of the General Council of the Church. According to the *Defender of Peace*, the declarations of doctrine proclaimed by the General Council are effectively infallible in a way that the statements of individual priests or prelates, or various groupings thereof, cannot be; the Council alone has access to eternal truth. During the 1330s the Franciscan philosopher William of Ockham had launched a stinging attack on this doctrine of conciliar infallibility by claiming that, since individual members of the Council were not capable of unerring insight into God's wisdom, the Council as a whole could not know unequivocally what is true. Marsiglio's response is instructive philosophically as well as theologically (ibid. 12. 1–5). He points out that what cannot be accomplished by one person may often be achieved by the cooperation of many. In the case of a General Council, this cooperation occurs as the result of discussion and mutual education, by means of which a consensus about the truth is eventually attained. What individual members of the Council may have been incapable of discovering for themselves, they realize through communal intercourse; the Holy Spirit is infused in them exactly as a result of their reciprocal interaction.

Marsiglio sketches in the *Defender Minor* a fully integrated conception of the temporal realm of politics, and of the place of religion and the clergy within it, which, if somewhat less detailed than the *Defender of Peace*, achieves a level of precision and clarity lacking in the earlier work. The *Defender Minor* thus constitutes a mature and advanced statement of the leading principles of Marsiglian political theory.

## FURTHER READING


De Lagarde, Georges, *La Naissance de l'esprit laïque au declin du moyen age*, iii: *Le Defensor Pacis* (Louvain: Nauwelaerts, 1970).

Di Vona, Piero, *I principi del 'Defensor Pacis'* (Naples: Moreno Editore, 1974).

Gewirth, Alan, *Marsilius of Padua and Medieval Political Philosophy* (New York: Columbia University Press, 1951).

Nederman, Cary J., *Community and Consent: The Secular Political Theory of Marsiglio of Padua's 'Defensor Pacis'* (Lanham, Md.: Rowman & Littlefield, 1995).

Quillet, Jeannine, *La Philosophie politique de Marsile de Padoue* (Paris: J. Vrin, 1970).

## NOTES

1. *The Defender of Peace*, trans. Alan Gewirth (New York: Columbia University Press, 1956); references are to discourse, chapter, and section.
2. *Marsiglio of Padua. Writings on the Empire: Defensor Minor and De Translatione Imperii*, trans. Cary J. Nederman (Cambridge: Cambridge University Press, 1993); references are to chapter and section.

# 9 Machiavelli

Joseph V. Femia

## Contents



## Chapter guide

There is remarkably little consensus about what Machiavelli actually believed. Guiding readers through the maze of often contradictory interpretations, and identifying his contribution to political thought, are the chief concerns of the chapter. The first section outlines the main perspectives on Machiavelli and speculates about the reasons for their divergence. The next section briefly examines the historical and intellectual context that helped to shape his thinking. How did the Renaissance differ from the Middle Ages? To what extent was Machiavelli a man of the Renaissance? Why did the Italian scene stimulate creative thought about politics? The remainder of the chapter explores what I take to be Machiavelli's most innovative ideas: his rejection of metaphysics and teleology, whether of the Christian or Aristotelian variety; his empirical and historical approach to the study of political affairs; and his anti-utopianism and belief in 'reason of state'. Along the way, some interpretations of Machiavelli are challenged; others are modified.

## Biography

Niccolò Machiavelli was a Florentine civil servant and political thinker whose name epitomizes all the hypocrisy, intrigue, treacheries, and plain gangsterism that were supposedly typical of the Italian Renaissance. Born in 1469, he was not yet 30 when he became Secretary, or roving ambassador, of the Florentine republic. His duties included numerous diplomatic missions to France, Germany, and the papal court—experience later to be distilled in his political writings. In 1512 the republic collapsed after its French allies were swept aside by Spain, which established effective control over an Italian peninsula that had become a battleground for warring foreigners. The Medici family, who had long dominated Florentine politics, were returned to power, and Machiavelli was not only removed from office but soon imprisoned and tortured for allegedly participating in an anti-Medici conspiracy. Released (and exonerated) following an amnesty, he retreated to his country home seven miles south of the city and struggled to come to terms with his enforced retirement.

Diplomacy's loss was posterity's gain. A miserable soul, who continued to follow political affairs with the painful longing of a spurned lover, Machiavelli produced two classics of political thought: *The Prince*, completed in 1513, and the *Discourses on Livy*, composed from 1513 to 1517. His republican sympathies were more evident in the latter than in the former, a handbook for autocrats dedicated to Lorenzo de' Medici. But both works advocate the ruthless pragmatism for which Machiavelli became notorious. His reputation as a political theorist depends primarily on his refusal to portray an ideal world or genuflect before conventional pieties. He wanted to draw rules for successful political behaviour from history and experience, not from the realm of imagination or from the demands of Christian ethics.

Although widely circulated beforehand, Machiavelli's main works were not published until 1531, four years after his death. In 1552 the Catholic Church published its first *Index* of prohibited books, which placed Machiavelli's entire *œuvre* on its list. The legend of 'murderous Machiavel' (Shakespeare's words) had begun.

## Key texts

*The Prince* (1513; first pub. 1531)
*Discourses on Livy* (1513–17; first pub. 1531)
*The Art of War* (1521)
*The History of Florence* (1527)

## Main texts used

*Discourses on Livy*, trans. Harvey C. Mansfield and Nathan Tarcov (Chicago: University of Chicago Press, 1996).
*The History of Florence*, ed. Henry Morley (London: Routledge & Sons, 1891).
*The Prince*, trans. George Bull (Harmondsworth: Penguin, 1975).

## Key ideas

**Virtue** is to be understood in a morally neutral sense, incorporating courage, steadfastness, cunning, ability. **Fortune**: objective events and circumstances to be exploited or overcome by virtuoso action. **Empirical method**: examination of past and present events to derive general rules of political behaviour; rejection of a priori principles. **Reason of state**: the end (political stability) justifies and even dictates the means (cruelty and deception, if necessary). **Republicanism**: preference for individual liberty and a mixed constitution with popular institutions tempered by aristocratic leadership.

## The many faces of Machiavelli

'Machiavelli's theory was a sword which was plunged into the flank of the body politic of Western humanity . . .'. With this striking image, Friedrich Meinecke summed up the devastating effect of the Florentine's writings on a world where all political action was supposed to serve the highest religious aims.[1] That politics could escape from the superintendence of Christianity, the strongest bond uniting men and nations, was (officially) unthinkable. Skulduggery and pagan debauchery were common enough in practice; and Catholic doctrine, as well as the new Protestant religion, allowed rulers to overstep the bounds of biblical morality in extreme situations. But Machiavelli was the first thinker to discuss political affairs without even paying ritual obeisance to the just, the noble, and the sacred; the first thinker to elevate amoral pragmatism into a desirable principle. *The Prince*, in particular, incurred the heartfelt wrath of the righteous, not to mention the simulated wrath of the hypocritical. It was denounced, in tones of horror, as the Devil's catechism or the Ten Commandments reversed. Not everyone, however, dismissed Machiavelli as an agent of the Evil One, and by the late eighteenth century a more favourable judgement had become popular. He came to be seen as a misunderstood lover of liberty and peace, whose *Prince* was designed to expose the wicked duplicity of tyrants. 'He professed to teach kings,' Rousseau declared, 'but it was the people he really taught.'[2] Machiavelli, that is to say, was an unqualified republican who, under the guise of advising princes, tried to warn all free men of the dangers of despotism.

The growth of romantic nationalism added a new dimension to this interpretation. Herder, the early prophet of German unity, claimed that *The Prince*, far from being an iniquitous guide for political criminals, was an objective study of sixteenth-century Italian politics by a patriot hoping to rescue his beleaguered country from an unholy alliance of foreign occupiers and indigenous collaborators. This view is not without plausibility. In an age of emerging nation-states, Machiavelli's Italy was not only subject to the whims of alien rulers, it was also divided into a number of mutually antagonistic jurisdictions. Moreover, the final chapter of *The Prince*, conveniently overlooked by those who stress the author's cynicism, urges Lorenzo, the Medici prince, to expel the 'barbarians' from Italian soil and 'lead Italy to her salvation'. Using passionate language similar to that of later Italian patriots, Machiavelli laments the desolate state of the country—'lawless, crushed, despoiled, torn, overrun'—and demands a revival of the ancient Roman spirit (*The Prince*, XXVI, pp. 134–5[3]). These sentiments helped to inspire the nationalist movement known as the Risorgimento as Italy moved towards the liberation and unification of 1870. Machiavelli became a hero of Italian nationalism—an idealistic spokesman for the freedom of his country and the exemplar of all political virtues. The satanic villain was now a paragon of righteousness.

By the twentieth century both the notion that Machiavelli was inspired by the Devil and the counter-notion that he was an idealistic republican patriot began to be questioned by those who saw him as a detached, dispassionate scientist, describing political behaviour as it actually was. Ernst Cassirer, for example, hailed him as the 'Galileo of politics', applying inductive methods to social and historical material.[4] An influential variation of this interpretation was put forward by Benedetto Croce, who argued that Machiavelli understood politics as pure power and technique—a utilitarian form of activity autonomous from conventional moral norms and governed by its own distinctive laws. The task of the political analyst, as the

Florentine secretary saw it, was to discover these laws, not to exorcise them or banish them from the world with 'holy water'.[5]

The view of Machiavelli as a pure scientist was never universally shared. For Gramsci, the eminent Italian Marxist, he was the archetypal *politico in atto*, the active man of politics, embodying the unity of thought and action. Politics was, to him, a transforming, creative activity whose purpose was to mobilize the Italian 'nation' against the feudal aristocracy and papacy and their mercenaries. His 'prince' is therefore an anthropomorphic 'symbol' of a new and progressive 'collective will'.[6] For other twentieth-century commentators, such as Herbert Butterfield, Machiavelli, while purporting to erect a science of statecraft, suffered from an equal lack of historical sense and empirical discipline. Obsessed by the heritage of ancient Rome, he deduced his political maxims in an a priori manner from classical theses concerning human nature or the historical process.[7] In a recent study Maurizio Viroli portrays Machiavelli as 'a rhetorician', whose 'method of studying political reality was interpretative and historical rather than scientific', and who 'wrote to persuade, to delight, to move, to impel to act—hardly the goals of the scientist'.[8]

Meanwhile, the older interpretations of Machiavelli refused to fade away. Viroli himself, following in the footsteps of Quentin Skinner and John Pocock, has vigorously defended the idea of Machiavelli as a freedom-loving republican, who saw politics not as a game of power and self-interest but as 'the preservation of a community of men grounded upon justice and the common good'.[9] Or, as Skinner puts it, Machiavelli 'presents a wholehearted defence of traditional republican values'.[10] Harvey Mansfield, however, has criticized this interpretation for its suggestion that 'Machiavelli was not "Machiavellian"'. Mansfield's Machiavelli was a bold innovator, a purveyor of 'immoralities and blasphemies', who did not see republicanism and tyranny as antonyms. Politics, as he understood it, was a struggle for domination, the purpose of which was 'to secure order rather than justice'. The Christians who denounced Machiavelli understood him only too well.[11]

This violent disparity of judgements about Machiavelli's aims and achievements is superficially baffling and requires explanation. It should be noted, first of all, that Machiavelli was not a rigorous philosopher in the mould of, say, Hobbes or Locke. He did not develop a systematic or sophisticated account of political authority and obligation, nor did he show much interest in the analysis of political concepts. His concerns were more with the practical principles of statecraft. Viroli is right to say that Machiavelli's writings display the rhetorician's desire to persuade and arouse his audience. Like other Florentines of his social standing, Machiavelli was steeped in the rules of Roman rhetoric; vivid imagery and an insincere (sometimes ironic) invocation of values or prejudices dear to the listeners' or readers' hearts were familiar and accepted techniques. No one expected every statement to be a literal expression of the author's beliefs. Of course, there will always be a degree of doubt about the true intentions or opinions of a thinker who indulges in rhetorical ploys and flourishes. This may help to explain why Machiavelli presents so many faces to students of his ideas. Was he a malevolent counsellor of tyrants? Or a freedom-loving republican idealist? Was he an objective scientist? Or a passionate advocate of Italian unity? Was he a prophet of modernity? Or an antiquarian obsessed by ancient Rome? The relevant texts, however, hardly justify such simplistic dichotomies.

These contrasting images of Machiavelli correspond, in part, to the apparently incompatible messages of his two major works. In *The Prince* he advises rulers, good or bad, on how to 'seize absolute authority' and hold their fellow countrymen in thrall. The world of politics is depicted as a jungle in which there is no reality but power, and power is the reward of ruthlessness, ferocity, and cunning. In such a jungle the tyrant is king, and republican ideals—justice, liberty, equality—count for little. At best, they are pleasing fictions which can be used to disguise the exercise of naked power. As for the people, they are gullible and passive, though Machiavelli warns of the necessity to win their support and use them as a counterweight to the scheming and treacherous nobility (*The Prince*, IX, pp. 69–70). The *Discourses*, on the other hand, is the work of a staunch republican and reminds us of Machiavelli's selfless devotion to the service of the Florentine republic. In this work he advises both citizens and leaders of republics on how to preserve their liberty and avoid corruption. Self-government, he proclaims, is the surest guarantor of security and prosperity, since the interests of the many and those of a ruling prince are usually antithetical (*Discourses*, II. ii, p. 130[12]). He adds that the people, as a collectivity, are more stable and exhibit better judgement than most princes, and even likens 'the voice of a people' to 'that of God' (ibid. I. lviii, p. 117).

At the very least, Machiavelli was sending confusing signals to this readers. Historians have long discussed the relationship between his two main works, their apparent inconsistency, and the extent to which each represents his true thought. What is especially intriguing is that the books were written at more or less the same time, making it unlikely that their author simply changed his mind. Exhaustive scholarship has established that the first part of the *Discourses* was composed in 1513. Machiavelli then interrupted this work to write *The Prince* between July and December 1513. In 1515 he returned to the *Discourses*, finishing it in 1517. Some critics, recalling Machiavelli's flawless republican credentials, have attributed *The Prince* to crass opportunism. To be sure, in a famous letter of December 1513 to his friend Francesco Vettori, Machiavelli revealed a wretched and abject state of mind. Not only did he fear that the poverty caused by his involuntary exile would reduce him to an object of contempt, he also complained that his talents were going to waste. He made plain his intention to dedicate *The Prince* to the Medici lords so that they might employ him, 'even if they start by setting me to roll stones'.[13] This does suggest that Machiavelli, like a good rhetorician (and a job-seeking one at that), tailored his 'oration' to appeal to his audience—in this case an authoritarian ruler. But it would be an oversimplification to dismiss the work as an exercise in servile flattery. If we assume that Machiavelli chose to play the Devil's advocate merely to gain employment, we will miss the powerful combination of logic and indignation that generations of readers have found so compelling. He really did believe that desperate times called for desperate measures. Outraged by the foreign occupiers who threatened Florence and humiliated the whole of Italy, he was willing to support *any* government that might defend Florentine independence, get rid of the 'barbarians', and perhaps take the first steps towards the unification of Italy. The prospects for a republican revival were, he realized, nil in the existing circumstances; it was therefore necessary to make the best of a bad situation. Moreover, Machiavelli was committed—as we shall see—to a cyclical theory of history, according to which a principate was a recurrent and necessary phase in the life of states. All republics, he informs us in the *Discourses*, are founded by a single lawgiver, and all republics eventually sink into corruption. When they do, only tyrannical means can restore them to past glories (*Discourses*, I. ix, p. 29; I. xvi–xviii, xxxiv). While republics are to be preferred where possible, princely or despotic rule may be necessary when degeneracy and vice prevail. Let us also remember that Machiavelli's model for an ideal republic was ancient Rome, an expansionist and predatory state. The *Discourses* may be a republican text, but it does not equate republicanism with the reign of sweetness and light. Near the end of the work, for example, Machiavelli maintains that *any* action, however cruel or unjust, is legitimate if it helps to preserve the safety and independence of the country (ibid. III. xli, p. 301). The 'contradictions' between *The Prince* and the *Discourses* are more apparent than real. The mood and focus vary between one work and another, but both show equally the basic values for which Machiavelli is notorious, such as the use of conventionally immoral means for political purposes and the belief that government depends on force and guile rather than universal standards of truth or goodness.

Bearing these considerations in mind, we can avoid the reductive interpretations that bedevil the secondary literature on Machiavelli. It is, after all, possible to be a republican without elevating republicanism into an absolute ideal. Likewise, passionate conviction is perfectly compatible with attachment to the empirical method. Machiavelli's thought, as I hope to demonstrate in what follows, was too complex to be encapsulated in a tidy formula.

## Setting the context

Machiavelli is often seen as a typical man of the Renaissance—secular, sceptical, a worshipper of antiquity. He was born in a time and in a place that had witnessed the emergence of a new spirit—a new appreciation of political liberty and civic virtue, a new attitude towards the role of man in society. It was this outlook, known as 'humanism', that inspired the cultural and artistic achievements we associate with Renaissance Italy, and especially Florence. Michelangelo, Brunelleschi, Leonardo da Vinci, 'Old Nick' himself—this rollcall of names, which could be multiplied with scarcely any loss of quality, testifies to a remarkable flowering of human achievement. Historians, concerned with origins and remote influences, stress how deeply interlocked this age of the Renaissance was with the medieval world: how much it owed to the intellectual ferment in Flanders, in Paris. True as this may be, it distorts reality by its emphasis on continuity. While there was no rigid dividing line between the Middle Ages and the Renaissance, qualitative transformations, as Marx reminded us, can result from an accumulation of quantitative changes. Beyond a certain point, differences in degree become differences in kind.

What, then, distinguished the humanist world-view from the mental outlook it supplanted? In medieval times reality was defined theologically, as a static and ordered hierarchy reflecting God's purposes. The theoretical unity of Christendom made no allowances for particularistic loyalties to blood and soil. The Platonic opposition between the Idea (which is universal truth or reality) and the physical world (which is transient opinion and appearances) was taken by Christianity and translated into the religious and theological duality that St Augustine posited between the *civitas dei* (the city of God) and the *civitas terrena* (the earthly city). The essence of reality was divorced from material and practical life. The ancient Greeks and Romans had understood 'the political' as a creative activity which transforms reality and enables man to fulfil his 'essential' nature. For the medieval Christians, by contrast, politics was the world of superficial appearances whose function was merely to curb the appetitive nature of 'fallen' man and ensure obedience to God's will. The prevailing ethos stressed the frailty of everything worldly, encouraging believers to turn away from earthly pursuits and instead seek the rewards of heaven through prayer and contemplation. The desire for secular honours or glory, reverence for one's homeland, enjoyment of the human body or the natural world—these were frowned upon as sinful distractions from the quest for eternal salvation.

By the middle of the fourteenth century Italian scholars and literary figures began to cast doubt on this mental framework. They were called humanists because they put humane studies—history, philosophy, poetry, rhetoric—ahead of the study of nature. Renaissance means 'rebirth', an event combining both old and new. The humanists revered antiquity and hoped that a revival of ancient virtue could change the thoughts and habits of the age. Love of antiquity was not in itself a radical departure. Ever since the Roman Empire had crumbled into decay, Plato and Aristotle, for example, had been studied intensively in monastic schools and universities. Yet such knowledge rarely penetrated beyond the private world of scholars. At the time of the Renaissance, however, humanistic studies spread through the upper and middle ranks of society and became a formidable part of the education of those who were to wield power and authority. The humanists were tireless researchers, collectors, and copiers of long-forgotten texts, whose historical merit consists essentially in having enriched and restored our knowledge of the classical cultural heritage. Because humanism rested upon a profound devotion to antiquity, it is commonly assumed that the movement was anti-Christian or neo-pagan. This is untrue. While questioning the temporal aspirations of the Church, the humanists remained wedded, by and large, to Christian doctrine. Nevertheless, neither their methods nor their conclusions were congenial to the medieval order.

To begin with, they insisted on the objective nature of research: no political or religious idol should guide the scholar in his work. Knowing how to read a text now also meant being able to put it in the context of its period. The medieval practice of citing isolated passages from Aristotle or Plato as 'proof' of this or that Church dogma was ridiculed as absurdly unhistorical. The idea that texts should be set in their evolving context, that Truth is the daughter of Time, gave the humanists an empirical bent. For the medieval mind, in contrast, knowledge was a matter of deduction from first principles, a method premissed on the belief that the world of appearances was somehow 'unreal' and that logical consistency was the key to truth. Their respect for historical evidence made the humanists acutely aware of the impermanence and diversity of cultures and civilizations. A striking characteristic of Renaissance thought was the assumption that historical development proceeds through a succession of natural causes, with the implication that these may be understood by man and to some degree controlled through intelligent political action. Earthly affairs came to be seen as the outcome of *human* aims, skills, and resources. Rather than being helpless counters in God's unfolding plan, men were themselves the authors of their own fortune and misfortune. Nothing was foreordained.

Finally, in opposition to the medieval view of man as essentially a 'soul', Renaissance artists and writers celebrated the beauty of the human body and produced idealized depictions of it. This emphasis on human physicality and sensual enjoyment was combined with a reluctance to accept monastic isolation and the contemplative life as the highest Christian ideals. Man's vocation was to serve his homeland, his family, his friends. Rejecting the medieval denigration of the earthly city, the humanists urged men to cultivate parochial attachments and develop the civic virtues that brought glory to their ancient forebears. It became fashionable to express, not suppress, the natural human desires for affection, beauty, fellowship, and external recognition.

Italy was not the only country where the universal ideas of the medieval *corpus christianum* were challenged by secular values. But intellectual and political ferment was more pronounced in Italy, which is why we think of it as the 'cradle' of the Renaissance. Throughout the Middle Ages Italy never belonged wholly to Europe. Even in Roman times the land had been densely populated, creating an urban life that the 'barbarian' invaders never wholly destroyed. 'Feudalism', as J. H. Plumb puts it, 'was planted in Italy but never rooted deeply there.'[14] The presence of an urban proletariat, along with Italy's geographical position, making it the ideal trade link between northern Europe and the sophisticated societies of the eastern Mediterranean, meant that commerce and industry could thrive as nowhere else. The social ideal of feudalism—an ordered, graded society, unchanging and unchangeable—was hopelessly anachronistic in a rapidly developing capitalist environment.

Other factors combined to make the Italian situation unique. The Holy Roman Empire, whose writ theoretically extended to the city-states of northern Italy, found it impossible to control them from its seat beyond the Alps and ceased to have any real hold on Italian loyalties after the time of Dante (1265–1321). In other parts of Europe contraction of the empire's claims to sovereignty corresponded to the emergence of nation-states, impelled by the need to protect and regulate expanding markets. In Italy, however, centrifugal forces prevailed. The standard view, expressed by Machiavelli himself, is that the papacy, which administered large parts of Italy and enjoyed a level of wealth that no king or emperor could match, used every ounce of its ingenuity and power to prevent the peninsula from becoming a unified nation-state. And yet, divisions within the Church, by undermining its spiritual and political authority, prevented it from exercising much influence in the north of Italy. The papacy was transferred to Avignon in 1309, where it remained until 1378. From then until 1417, the Great Schism (between French and Italian factions) brought the ecclesiastical hierarchy into further disrepute.

With the disappearance of the papacy and the empire as effective political forces, much of Italy descended into a kind of anarchy. The power vacuum created by the decline of traditional authority allowed local powers to behave as they saw fit. In this atmosphere the strong devoured the weak. From 1350 to 1450 Italy scarcely knew a month of peace, as the larger cities seized villages and lesser towns by force and provoked one another's enmity with predictable regularity. By the end of this period, though, the great city-states—Florence, Milan, Naples, Venice—had grown weary of endless strife. None strong enough to overthrow the other, they lived in an uneasy equilibrium of power that lasted until 1494, when the French king invaded Italy and precipitated a series of armed conflicts more terrible than Italy had ever known.[15]

The Renaissance, then, was a time of pillage, rapine, and turmoil. Even nominally republican states, such as Florence, were controlled by powerful families or cliques who thought nothing of unleashing aggression against their neighbours, or of conducting vicious feuds and vendettas against their domestic enemies. This, paradoxically, was the backdrop for an unparalleled display of cultural excellence. But diplomacy as we know it also arose in Renaissance Italy. By the fifteenth century northern Italy, in particular, exhibited many of the features of a miniature international system. The balance of power created by the three great states of Milan, Venice, and Florence caused their leaders to work out the principles and the machinery of diplomatic practices which have governed international relations ever since. Diplomacy, of course, is all about forecasting the logic of events and devising effective responses. Those engaged in it become immersed in the mechanics of power and perhaps lose sight of the purposes for which power is supposedly exercised. There is a natural assumption that politics is an end-in-itself, almost like a game of chess. This assumption was reinforced by the pervasive instability of the Italian scene, the rapid changes in political fortune, brutal seizures of power, conspiracies, and aggressions. An inevitable consequence was the general abandonment of the principle that government should be subordinated to religious ends. Instead, the welfare of a particular prince or a particular state took priority. Almost a century before *The Prince* was written, a tradition of 'realism' had developed in Italian political thinking. At least on the practical level, issues of order and power were being confronted in almost strictly political terms. It was this secularization of politics that emboldened more systematic thinkers, such as Leonardo Bruni, to free themselves from the straitjacket of medieval political thought and praise the ancient republican values of liberty and civic participation. It also made possible Machiavelli's experiment in a 'pure' political theory, divested of religious imagery and religious values.

## Hostility to metaphysics

By the time Machiavelli wrote, the medieval view of the political realm as a microcosm displaying the same structural principles of order prevalent in creation as a whole had been shattered. Once seen as the embodiment of universal purposes, the political realm now stood exposed as a battlefield where antagonistic forces struggled for supremacy. Machiavelli held a mirror up to reality; he did not seek to change that reality in any fundamental way. Nor was his admiration for antiquity and worldly values anything new. He was soaked in the spirit of Florentine humanism and learned from his predecessors. These environmental influences and intellectual debts induce some commentators to interpret his texts strictly in terms of their context. Allan Gilbert, for example, has argued that *The Prince* was a fairly commonplace thing, similar in both content and style to treatises written in the familiar genre of advice books for monarchs, a literary form originating in the Middle Ages but still popular during the Renaissance.[16] In the medieval literature the prince is seen as an intermediary between God and man, applying the principles of natural justice and eschewing the earthly temptations of wealth and glory. The humanists, on the other hand, accepted that the prince must have worldly as well as religious attributes. *Majestas* involved outward expression—buildings, statuary, art, pageants—and helped to unite the city in admiration of its ruler. But the humanists who produced these tracts always assumed, unlike Machiavelli, the traditional identity between the ideal prince and the ideal human being. The *quattrocento* princeship literature remained enclosed within the Christian framework, where man's ultimate purpose is to attain a state of grace, and where the rational course of action is always the moral one, dictated by natural law. Machiavelli may have adapted the logical structure of *The Prince* to the conventional literary form of the advice book genre, but, as we shall see, he removed all traces of the idealized human personality from his portrait of the prince.

In a manner similar to Gilbert, some commentators subsume Machiavelli's thought into the tradition of Aristotelian republicanism that dominated Florentine political science during the *quattrocento*.[17] The civic humanists borrowed a teleological view of virtue from Aristotle, insisting that man is by nature a political animal, who achieves fulfilment through activity devoted to the common good. The city is founded on friendship, according to the conventions of civic humanism; on doing and sharing things in common, not upon the mere exchange of commodities or reciprocal protection. However, while Machiavelli was sympathetic to republicanism, he barely mentioned Aristotle and never defined politics in transformative or 'expressive' terms. As for a city based on friendship, Machiavelli explicitly rejected this as utopian. Those who picture a united commonwealth, without dissension or 'Unkindness betwixt Men', are 'egregiously mistaken', he tells us (*History of Florence*, VII, p. 326[18]).

The relentless quest for precedents has led some to forget that a doctrine must be judged not by the letter but by the spirit. Great thinkers will use conventional forms or conventional language to express new ideas. Machiavelli's redefinition of the pivotal concept of *virtù* is a case in point. For the civic humanists, *virtù* was understood in its Aristotelian sense, as a moral good, denoting a humane, prudent, wise form of behaviour. A virtuous deed is done for its own sake, for the sake of being virtuous. To Machiavelli, *virtù* was more like a force of nature, embracing in its meaning qualities such as ambition, drive, courage, energy, will-power, shrewdness, and self-reliance. This is Roman rather than Greek (or Christian) virtue. It does not permit us to use locutions such as 'virtue is its own reward'. For virtue, in the special Machiavellian sense, always exists for the sake of something else. It finds its classic expression in war.

Machiavelli's originality is not only signalled by his unconventional use of conventional language. It is also evident in what he does *not* say, in the vocabulary he avoids. For example, neither in *The Prince* nor in any of his other works does he even mention, let alone endorse, natural justice or natural law, concepts central to the classical and medieval tradition and commonly found in the writings of his contemporaries. Machiavelli seems to have no time for such abstract universals, for standards outside history; and history, as he treats it, is merely a series of physical events, with no transcendent meaning. What we call absolute values are relics of traditional metaphysics—an invention of man masquerading as an invention of God. Our moral strictures, in his estimation, are purely conventional and reflect the existential needs of human beings living in communities. They are the result of natural *necessity*, not natural *law*; they exist because they are necessary to human survival, not because they are an inheritance from God (as the Bible says) or inscribed in human nature (as the Aristotelians say) (*Discourses*, I. ii).

Also significant is the absence of the word 'soul' (*anima*) from *The Prince* and the *Discourses*. As conceived by Plato and Aristotle, and later in Christian theology, the soul differentiates man from the rest of nature, giving him a special dignity. Whereas *anima* never occurs in Machiavelli's two main works, *animo* ('spirit' or 'spiritedness') occurs frequently and is used in the sense of 'fighting spirit', or the will to defend one's own (body, family, homeland, etc.) against actual or potential enemies. Spirit, thus construed, depends on physicality, whereas soul (*anima*) always attempts to transcend physicality. Again, Machiavelli seems to be saying that we are primarily objects in nature, and that we are therefore governed by 'natural necessity' (*The Prince*, III, p. 35).

Notwithstanding these suggestions of heresy, and the open hostility of all those guardians of Christian morality who denounced him—posthumously—as the Antichrist, it is often assumed that Machiavelli was a devout, if somewhat unorthodox, Christian. I fail to see how this interpretation can be sustained. It is certainly true that he did not wish to separate politics from religion. Thus he advised rulers 'to maintain the ceremonies of their religion uncorrupt and hold them always in veneration', since states are 'secure and happy' only when they are 'maintained . . . by religious institutions' (*Discourses*, I, xii, p. 36; *The Prince*, XI, p. 74). Piety and fear of divine retribution are irreplaceable sources of social discipline. But what such sentiments express is an *instrumental* approach to religion; the truth-value of *any particular* religion was a matter of indifference to Machiavelli. So his hostility to the papacy was prompted by motives quite different from those that inspired, say, Martin Luther. The Church of Rome, Machiavelli thought, was to be reproached for its *practical* failings, not because it had strayed from the path of righteousness. For one thing, its transparent greed and territorial ambitions had caused Italians to lose 'all devotion and all religion—which brings with it infinite inconveniences and infinite disorders'. Furthermore, the papacy had kept Italy divided in order to maintain 'dominion over its temporal things' (*Discourses*, I. xii, p. 38). But Machiavelli did not simply attack Christian *practice*; he also denounced Christian *doctrine*—for its apotheosis of servility and weakness. Whereas pagan religion venerated 'captains of armies and princes of republics' and regarded worldly success as the supreme good, Christianity 'has glorified humble and contemplative more than active men. It has then placed the highest good in humility, abjectness, and contempt of things human'.

These principles, Machiavelli continues, undermine social cohesion and civic responsibility; they 'have rendered the world weak and given it in prey to criminal men', who can do what they please, secure in the knowledge that most men hope to reach heaven by patiently enduring injuries rather than by avenging them. Strangely, Machiavelli claims that this interpretation of Christianity is 'false' and not in keeping with Christ's message, which 'permits us the exaltation and defense of the fatherland'; though in a later chapter he acknowledges that St Francis brought Christianity back to its origins by exemplifying and preaching the ethic of meekness and submission to authority, however corrupt (ibid. II. ii, pp. 131–2; III. i, pp. 211–12).

If Machiavelli was a Christian, he was certainly a most peculiar one. The Christian psychology of sin and redemption is nowhere to be found in his two major works. For him, a 'sin' is a political error, often committed by rulers who try to obey Christian ethics when objective circumstances require cruelty or deception (*The Prince*, XII, p. 78). The idea of a tormented conscience seeking atonement or comfort has no place in his cosmology. The Christian virtues he decries—self-abnegation, humility, and other-worldliness—are precisely those virtues connected with the interior good of the soul as it struggles against our 'evil' impulses. Nor do we find in Machiavelli the usual Christian imagery of divine intervention in earthly affairs. He never invoked a supernatural will as the ultimate reason for things. A brief look at his concept of 'Fortune' should help to illustrate this point.

In medieval times Fortune was seen as an agent of Divine Providence, mocking human vanity by disposing her rewards without regard to merit or expectations, and thus reminding us that worldly riches and glory, being ephemeral, are of no account in the final scheme of things. This Christian element is missing from Machiavelli's usage. He revives the pagan notion of Fortune as an essentially uncontrollable goddess, who may nevertheless grant her favours to a man of *virtù* (*virtus* in Latin), a man of courage and audacity (*The Prince*, XXV; *Discourses*, II. XXX, pp. 199, 202). Where such *virtù* is lacking, fortune will be pitiless, making or breaking men with wilful abandon. Yet, when Machiavelli personifies Fortune as a fierce goddess, he appears to be speaking metaphorically. Fortune, in his writings, is not so much a supernatural figure as a literary or rhetorical device to describe the logic of events, the external constraints on human behaviour, the web of earthly accidents in their inexorable succession. Machiavelli liked to employ figurative language. In *The Prince* he also compares Fortune to an elemental force—a raging river, which can nevertheless be controlled by 'constructing dykes and embankments'. What he wants to hammer home is that rulers must never surrender to Fortune, which is 'the arbiter of half the things we do, leaving the other half or so to be controlled by ourselves' (*The Prince*, xxv, p. 130). Machiavelli recognizes that Fortune may succeed in overwhelming even the greatest leaders, few of whom have the capacity to transform their own characters to suit changing circumstances. He cites the example of Piero Soderini, *gonfaloniere* (Head of the Signoria) of Florence in the early 1500s, who governed his city with patience and humanity, allowing it to thrive. But in 1512, when brutal measures were required to defend the republic against its mortal enemies (foreign and domestic), he found it impossible 'to vary his procedure' (*Discourses*, III. ix, p. 240; *The Prince*, xxv). Nevertheless, Machiavelli is careful 'not to rule out our free will' in the face of 'great changes and variations, beyond human imagining' (*The Prince*, xxv, p. 130). The Christian idea that we must submit meekly to the fate God has assigned to us was anathema to him. Human beings are free, within the constraints imposed by 'natural necessity', to mould their own destiny.

While Machiavelli never professed atheism, a non-believer could read him without suffering any intellectual discomfort. There is no sense in his works of a universe governed by Mind or a Supreme Creator. He implicitly rejects the very notion of a metaphysical structure of the universe, the attempt to say that certain things have 'essences', or purposes, implanted in them by God or by nature. There is, in other words, no trace of Aristotelian or Christian teleology, no reference to any ideal order, to any doctrine of man's place in the great chain of being, to any culminating fulfilment towards which creation moves. There is no discernible assumption of the existence of divine law; the only natural laws Machiavelli mentions are laws of physical necessity. Nor does he concern himself with the salvation of souls or the contemplation of God's handiwork. His gaze was firmly fixed on terra firma.

Machiavelli, according to Francesco De Sanctis, a nineteenth-century Hegelian liberal, gave expression to the emerging antagonism between theology and science, two 'ways of thinking and acting'. The scientific perspective was founded on the revolutionary idea that human consciousness is independent of any transcendent authority and is merely the self-knowledge of human beings acting in society and history to subdue nature for their own purposes. Machiavelli, in helping to pioneer this new outlook, thus represented 'the most profound negation of the middle ages'.[19] He sought truth on earth instead of in heaven—in observation, not in deduction from axiomatic principles.

## Empirical method

Because of his hostility to metaphysics, it is commonly assumed that Machiavelli's principal contribution to intellectual history was the 'inductive method'—the idea of grounding knowledge on the collection, collation, and analysis of what we call facts. This method is contrasted to the medieval practice—not entirely abandoned by Machiavelli's contemporaries—

of seeking explanations by a long process of inference and deduction. Machiavelli is thus acclaimed as the founder of modern political science. As noted earlier, this view has not gone unchallenged. Commentators point out that he is hardly 'value-neutral' or dispassionate, that he does not systematically sift through the evidence and allow generalizations to emerge 'naturally', that his maxims are based on 'hunches' or prejudices, which are then illustrated by arbitrarily chosen examples, and that he never even suggests an equivalence between political predictions and scientific predictions. Let us explore this issue further.

Machiavelli undoubtedly saw himself as an innovator who substituted 'things as they are' for 'things as . . . they are imagined'. He wanted to examine 'what is actually done', not 'what should be done' (*The Prince*, XV, pp. 90–1). By positing a separation between analytical and normative political inquiry, he was, according to his own self-image, taking 'a path as yet untrodden by anyone' (*Discourses*, I, Preface, p. 5). For him, the vast array of facts to be analysed included the whole of history from antiquity to the present. Understanding 'things as they are' obviously requires an understanding of things as they were. History, he thought, could furnish a stable body of knowledge transcending the flux of events. Republican Rome, above all, provided later ages with a timeless model on which to base political actions and institutions. Whereas the Greek philosophers and Christian theologians sought truth in 'reason' or else 'faith', the new 'path' found its certainty in the examples of greatness or success supplied by history. Machiavelli noted a discrepancy between the present state of art, medicine, and law, on the one hand, and the poverty of political knowledge on the other. The former fields had succeeded in absorbing the experience of the past and adapting it to present circumstances. In politics, however, one finds 'neither prince nor republic' that turns to the ancients for instruction. To assume, as many do, that we can derive no practical lessons from the past is to argue that every situation in every age is essentially different, 'as if heaven, sun, elements, men had varied in motion, order, and power from what they were in antiquity' (ibid. I, Preface, p. 6). For Machiavelli's contemporaries, the variability of conditions and circumstances from one context to another made it impossible to predict the consequences of any particular type of political practice or action. It was therefore dangerous to speculate about general laws of politics or to imitate ancient models in modern contexts. Machiavelli disputed this because he thought that human psychology acted as a link or common denominator between past and present. The constancy of human nature ensures that historical incidents tend to fall into recognizable and repetitive patterns: 'whoever wishes to see what has to be considers what has been; for all worldly things in every time have their own counterpart in ancient times. That arises because these are the work of men, who have and always had the same passions, and they must of necessity result in the same effect' (ibid. III. xliii, p. 302).

It was probably unwise of Cassirer and others to compare Machiavelli to Galileo. The latter's methods of measurement and experimentation were alien to the Florentine secretary, who always retained the diplomat's fascination with the changing shapes and colours of political life, and consistently underlined the need for adaptability in the face of impermanence and uncertainty. Given the vicissitudes of Fortune, and the infinitely variable quantities of *virtù*, it is unlikely that Machiavelli thought his 'laws' of political behaviour would yield exact predictions. The balance of probabilities, not eternal and immutable truth, was what he sought to discover.

But those who dispute Machiavelli's scientific credentials often press their arguments too far. It is unfair, for example, to accuse him of deducing crude generalizations from ancient Roman precepts and practices without regard to contextual particularities.[20] *The Prince* is full of references to *recent* history and *contemporary* politics, and certainly reflects Machiavelli's experience in the chancery service. In all his works he ordinarily supports his general propositions with examples drawn from several different periods of history—thus suggesting that he appreciates the difference between a type of behaviour characteristic of some particular period and a more general historical law.

Nor—*pace* his critics—does Machiavelli systematically ignore examples that might disprove his *regole generali*; his usual procedure is to explain why they are the exceptions that prove the rule. Consider his reflections on mercenary soldiers in chapter XII of *The Prince*. He begins by denouncing such troops as 'useless and dangerous', since they are 'disunited, thirsty for power, undisciplined, and disloyal'. Yet the historical record forces him to concede that the Venetians and Florentines did extend their territories in the past through the use of mercenaries. While his explanations for this anomaly may not have been convincing ('luck' in the case of the Florentines; the modesty of their territorial ambitions in the case of the Venetians), the discussion demonstrates a willingness to confront and deal with contradictory evidence (pp. 77–81).

By no stretch of the imagination could Machiavelli be described as a 'pure' scientist. His intention was not merely to *explain* but also to *prescribe* and sometimes to *condemn*. His work abounds in precepts, warnings, criticisms, practical suggestions, prescriptions, and useful maxims. The final chapter of *The Prince*, where realistic appraisal and detached advice give way to fervent nationalism, destroys any notion that Machiavelli was merely a cold-eyed technician, devoid of ideals and utterly cynical. But a passionate commitment to certain political ideals and principles is not incompatible with an equally passionate attachment to objective methods of analysis. His new 'path' required him to maintain a rigid distinction between the object of inquiry and the inquiring mind, to prevent his value-preferences from colouring his empirical analysis. No doubt he failed on occasion, but what strikes readers of Machiavelli is his remarkable degree of objectivity, his ability to set aside his personal bias in the pursuit of knowledge. Although, for example, he wanted the foreign invaders out of Italy, this did not prevent him from devising a set of rules, based on historical observation, that might enable such invaders to succeed in their nefarious ventures (*The Prince*, III). Machiavelli could put himself into the shoes of any ruler, admirable or not, analyse the situation from his point of view, state the alternatives, and prescribe the best moves.

Those who belittle the scientific claims made on behalf of Machiavelli tend to judge him by anachronistic standards. In his day scientific method as we know it—deliberate, systematic, self-conscious—was only in its infancy. If it is accurate to describe him as a scientist, he was more like a physician than a physicist, diagnosing his patient's illness and then prescribing a remedy based on what has worked in the past. Indeed, he thought of his endeavours in precisely these terms, comparing the body politic to the human body and likening himself to a doctor called upon to cure political disorders (*The Prince*, III, pp. 39–40; *Discourses*, III. i, p. 209). Medicine, of course, is an inexact science. Symptoms can be interpreted in different ways, and remedial measures can be ineffective if the doctor has made an incorrect diagnosis or if the patient's physiological functions are in any way peculiar. What especially worries Dr Machiavelli's legion of critics is their perception that his prescribed 'cures' are far worse than any disease.

## Political realism

Machiavelli's realism, as much as his commitment to the empirical method, stemmed from his rejection of metaphysics and teleology. If the universe is not governed by Reason or Mind, then effective truth, practical reality, is all there is. There is no natural order of the soul, and therefore no natural hierarchy of values. In determining how people *ought* to live, we must be guided by how they *do* live, by their actual thoughts and behaviour. Machiavelli criticized previous writers on politics for valuing abstract speculation over practical experience, for envisaging ideal and imaginary states:

> in discussing this subject, I draw up an original set of rules. But since my intention is to say something that will prove of practical use to the inquirer, I have thought it proper to represent things as they are in real truth, rather than as they are imagined. Many have dreamed up republics and principalities which have never in truth been known to exist; the gulf between how one should live and how one does live is so wide that a man who neglects what is actually done for what should be done learns the way to self-destruction rather than self-preservation. (*The Prince*, XV, pp. 90–1)

This quotation incorporates three distinct propositions, each of which will be discussed in turn: (1) men are not what they seem; despite their professions of Christian goodness, they are generally wicked and unreliable; (2) ideal projections—depictions of perfect states, perfect rulers, perfect citizens—are both absurd and harmful; and (3) security—the precondition of all other political goods—often requires actions at variance with traditional biblical morality.

### *Proposition 1*

'One can make this generalisation about men,' asserts Machiavelli: 'they are ungrateful, fickle, liars, and deceivers, they shun danger and are greedy for profit' (*The Prince*, XVII, p. 96). Elsewhere, he declares, more succinctly, that 'all men are bad' (*Discourses*, I. iii, p. 15). Machiavelli's view of the human condition rivals that of Thomas Hobbes in its reductivism. Because of boundless desire, insatiable pride, and inevitable scarcity, men are in a constant state of competition and strife. The security and integrity of the collectivity are perpetually endangered by both internal foes, determined to destroy existing arrangements, and external foes, bent on expansion at its expense. Political life is, at bottom, a gladiatorial arena where the strong subdue the weak and obtain preferential access to the limited number of goods (ibid. I. xxxvii, p. 78). Men are reluctant, though, to accept this harsh truth, and try to soften it by creating an illusory world of ideals that give a spurious moral justification to our predatory instincts. Even if society's rulers do not themselves believe in these doctrines, they would be well advised to pretend otherwise. For it is a Machiavellian theme that a state founded on common values and cultural traditions has a greater chance of survival than one founded almost exclusively on naked force (*The Prince*, III–V). It is rarely sufficient, in Machiavelli's opinion, for political leaders to behave like lions; they must also possess the cunning of a fox, an ability to manipulate prevailing images and emotive symbols. Fraud, as well as force, is a necessary component of effective government (ibid. XVIII). Machiavelli showed great foresight in recognizing that 'the people' were an increasingly powerful factor in modern society, a constituency that had to be satisfied, even in principalities or monarchies (ibid. XIX, p. 113). But—rather like modern politicians—he had limited faith in the rational or self-governing capacities of ordinary folk, for they 'are so simple, and so much creatures of circumstance, that the deceiver will always find someone ready to be deceived'. While 'the common people' can make or break regimes, they are like a mass of malleable matter, ready to respond to the shaping hand of the ruler–artist. And since they are 'always impressed by appearances', it is necessary for a successful ruler or politician to be 'a great liar and deceiver' (*gran simulatore e dissimulatore*) (ibid. XVIII, pp. 100–1). All the deceit in the world, however, will not obviate the need for force, because men will 'use the malignity of their spirit whenever they have a free opportunity for it' (*Discourses*, I. iii, p. 15). To Machiavelli, fear rather than love or solidarity is the ultimate foundation of political authority.

### *Proposition 2*

Inherent in Machiavelli's view of the human condition is that states will always be struggling against the tendencies of dissolution. The natural selfishness of men will regularly subvert the state, reduce it to chaos, and transform it into something different. The perpetual flux of human affairs rules out the possibility of a perfect state as timeless as a geometric theorem. Neither does Machiavelli believe in the evolutionary progress of mankind. For him, human history is a ceaseless process of deterioration and renewal, a never-ending cycle of recurrent patterns:

> For Nature having fixed no sublunary Things, as soon as they arrive at their acme and perfection, being capable of no farther ascent, of necessity they decline. So, on the other side, when they are reduced to the lowest pitch of disorder, having no further to descend, they recoil again to their former perfection . . . Virtue begets Peace; Peace begets Idleness; Idleness, Mutiny; and Mutiny, Destruction: and then *vice versa*, that Ruin begets Laws; those Laws, Virtue; and Virtue begets Honour and good Success. (*History of Florence*, V, p. 227)

While human selfishness inevitably brings about political decline, human ingenuity will usually generate a revival—assuming that a dissolute state is not first devoured by a neighbouring state, which may be experiencing its 'acme and perfection'. The ascent from 'Ruin' to 'Honour and good Success' requires the intervention of a wise and dictatorial ruler, who may have to resort to brutal actions to restore political health. A people that have fallen prey to self-indulgent passions cannot spontaneously transform themselves into a body of virtuous citizens. This is a task for special men, men of *virtù* in the distinctively Machiavellian sense. Even in a well-run republic, according to Machiavelli, the vast majority of citizens will be dull-witted, passive, and self-obsessed. Even in these republics it is the talented and purposeful few who prevent society from collapsing into chaos and squalor. In his opinion, society will always be divided into those who command and those who serve, regardless of the constitutional order. 'For in all republics, ordered in whatever mode', we are told, 'never do even forty or fifty citizens reach the ranks of command' (*Discourses*, I. xvi, p. 46). Machiavelli bore no hostility to popular participation when it was mediated by representatives of superior intellect and virtue. Yet he never doubted 'the uselessness of a multitude without a head' (ibid. I. xliv, p. 92). Equality in any real sense was neither possible nor desirable.

While he attacked egalitarianism, Machiavelli was—as we have seen—partial to republics and republicanism. But this preference owed nothing to abstract idealism, to visions of human excellence or of a united community in pursuit of the 'good life'. Values must be aligned with facts. Idealism must always be tempered by the limitations of human nature and the fragility of all human constructions. Politics, for Machiavelli, is a matter of managing or reducing inconvenience and pain, not eliminating it. Political choice characteristically involves identifying the lesser of two evils (*Discourses*, I. vi, p. 21; *The Prince*, XXI, p. 123). If Machiavelli prefers republics to monarchies, it is purely for practical reasons. Where circumstances are appropriate, the former can produce the optimal combination of security and prosperity—the main goals, to him, of any political system. The common people may not be very bright, but they are generally less capricious than princes. This is not all. Popular institutions, as a rule, promote patriotism and habits of civility and thereby diminish the need for extreme acts of repression. The feeling of security created by the rule of law allows individuals to pursue their personal projects in an adventurous and innovative spirit. Republics can also adapt better to changing times, since hidebound or idiotic rulers face the prospect of dismissal at regular intervals. Finally, in monarchical systems the common good is often confused with the private good of the prince (*Discourses*, II. ii, pp. 130–3; III. ix, p. 240).

However, whereas Aristotle had assumed that the common good was qualitatively different in nature from that of the individual, Machiavelli took the notion to represent a preponderance of interests and forces within the community. In other words, he abandoned the classical and medieval idea of the community as a natural unity. Society, as he conceived it, was naturally divided into competing interests and could never be kept to a perfect unity of purpose. Unity is artificial and constantly under threat; it comes from a resolution of conflicting interests, made possible by a common devotion to the *patria*. In a striking anticipation of modern pluralist theories, Machiavelli actually welcomes the continuous conflict of political life and even identifies the glory of Rome with the perennial 'tumults between the nobles and the plebs'. He sees a balance of competitive social forces as conducive to liberty and civic responsibility. In the ancient Roman republic the people were inspired by the grandeur and heroism of the nobles, while the latter, constantly menaced by the people, channelled their ambitions into activities that furthered the good of all. Moreover, the compromises needed to resolve disputes between these 'two diverse humors' fostered an atmosphere of tolerance and mutual respect (*Discourses*, I. iv, p. 16). Machiavelli thinks it self-evident that if the constitution is so arranged to give one or other of these groups total control, the state will descend into corruption and violence. Hence his advocacy of a mixed constitution, aiming for a balanced equilibrium between opposing social forces (ibid. I. ii). Nevertheless, his willingness to support a prince with absolute authority, where necessary, indicates his deference to 'things as they are in real truth, rather than as they are imagined'. Normative preferences cannot be divorced from empirical reality. With this basic principle in mind, he challenged an assumption taken as gospel by his medieval and humanist predecessors: that political success and the happiness of the people could be guaranteed by the exercise of traditional moral virtues. This brings us to the final proposition.

### *Proposition 3*

Although Machiavelli is commonly assumed to be the inventor of *raison d'état*, the idea of political necessity and public utility overriding conventional morality was already enshrined in canon law. However, such violations were meant to be exceptional, and they were permissible only when necessitated by some religiously laudable goal. In Machiavelli actions once deemed exceptional or regrettable were now declared commonplace and even admirable. What outraged Machiavelli's readers was not so much his *description* of political life, with its crimes and treacheries, as his apparent determination to teach the *art* of political criminality and treachery, as if the usual moral rules had no relevance to politics. He was not talking about the occasional bending of the rules, nor simply about abnormal situations requiring drastic solutions. Political affairs, on Machiavelli's description, *always* entail risk and danger, because of the essential venality and depravity of mankind. Securing a good end—an island of political security in a sea of corruption—will *regularly* demand acts of violence and betrayal. Political leaders who deny this 'truth', who flaunt their 'clean hands', will condemn their citizens or subjects to untold misery.

In the popular imagination Machiavelli is an advocate of political immorality. A more refined interpretation—the one advanced by Croce—sees him as a defender of political *a*morality. Politics, that is to say, obeys its own logic, follows its own rules, and judges actions in accordance with its own standards of success or failure. It is—to borrow a phrase from Nietzsche—beyond good and evil. Croce adds that Machiavelli suffered anguish, a kind of moral nausea, over his conclusion that politicians must often do evil for the sake of a higher good. He did not, on this account, deny the absolute validity of Christian morality, still less its applicability to private relationships. He simply recognized the contradiction between politics and ethics.[21]

While Croce's thesis has become conventional wisdom, it is open to question. It requires us to accept that Machiavelli was a consequentialist with respect to political judgements, but a believer in the universal truth of Christian doctrine when it came to moral judgements. Indeed, he sometimes professes to deplore the methods he recommends. In these cases, his advice takes the form of a 'hypothetical imperative' in the Kantian sense: 'If you want to achieve *X*, it is essential that you do *Y*'. Machiavelli is therefore not to be taken as necessarily approving either the postulated end or the recommended means. If he is merely acting as a technical adviser, identifying what is useful or useless, it is logically possible for him to counsel behaviour he regards as immoral. To be sure, there are a couple of passages in *The Prince* where he seems to adopt a conventional moral stance, just before offering advice that contradicts it. He agrees that it would be 'praiseworthy' or 'laudable' for a prince to possess all those qualities normally regarded as good, but then adds that these 'good' princes would be crushed in a world full of evil men (*The Prince*, XV, p. 91; XVIII, p. 99). Such evident neutrality fits in with the idea that politics is the sphere of instrumental rationality, where moral judgements can have no practical relevance.

But other aspects of Machiavelli's thought are not so easy to square with Croce's thesis. First of all, the inner torment Croce attributes to Machiavelli is hard to detect. When deducing the necessity of unappetizing behaviour, the Florentine seems to delight in his ruthless logic. At best, his tone is clinical and detached. Secondly, we have already seen how he offers a utilitarian explanation of and justification for ordinary moral rules. Their existence and validity is determined by their usefulness, not by Scripture or God's will. Not just his political judgements but his moral preferences were consequentialist. It is doubtful, then, that Machiavelli really considered cruelty or deceit to be morally 'bad' in those circumstances where they promoted political stability and (therefore) the welfare of the community. If he occasionally implied otherwise, perhaps he was indulging in the rhetorical dissimulation he recommended to princes. There are several passages in his writings that could support such an interpretation.

In the *Discourses*, for instance, he defended Romulus over the killing of his brother Remus. This act was necessary, Machiavelli said, so that supreme authority in founding the new state of Rome should be in one person's hands, as was essential for the success of such a venture and thus for the 'common good'. No wise person, he insisted, would ever condemn a ruler for such extraordinary actions where they were beneficial to the public. Quite the reverse, for 'when the deed accuses him, the effect excuses him; and when the effect is good . . . it will always excuse the deed; for he who is violent to spoil, not he who is violent to mend, should be reproved' (*Discourses*, I. ix, p. 29). Machiavelli wanted to highlight the irony of the political condition. Where the well-being of society is at stake, conventional vice might become political virtue, and conventional virtue might result in political ruin. In politics, it follows, we cannot draw a sharp line between moral virtue and moral vice: the two things often change place.

The prime example of this paradox—adduced by Machiavelli—is Cesare Borgia, whose brutal methods were necessary to rid the Romagna of the plague of petty tyrants that had reduced the population to abject servitude. Borgia 'was accounted cruel; nevertheless, this cruelty of his reformed the Romagna, brought it unity, and restored order'. He must therefore be judged kinder than the Florentines, who, to avoid resorting to violent and oppressive measures, allowed the warring factions in Pistoia to destroy the city's peace and prosperity. Tough-minded princes, prepared to take harsh action to keep their people loyal and united, are infinitely more merciful (and, by implication, moral) than princes who, 'being too compassionate, allow disorders which lead to murder and rapine'. Disorders, Machiavelli continues, 'always harm the whole community, whereas executions ordered by a prince only affect individuals' (*The Prince*, XVII, p. 95). Consider, too, the following statement: 'In the actions of all men, and especially of princes, where there is no court of appeal, one judges by the result.' By ignoring the exigencies of statecraft, the ruler who 'never preaches anything except peace and good faith' turns out to be 'an enemy of both' (ibid. XVIII, pp. 101–2).

What Machiavelli is saying is that so-called 'dirty hands', in some circumstances, are actually clean. The realm of politics is indeed special, but it is not beyond morality. Since private relationships rely on trust and familiarity, Machiavelli acknowledges that they should be governed by tried and tested moral rules. But politics inhabits a world of dark suspicion and hidden dangers, where the only reality is power. Here a fetishistic attachment to traditional morality will deliver the very opposite of happiness. Machiavelli's approach to morality is consistently consequentialist, but in politics conventional guidelines are often inappropriate, which means that a direct calculation of benefits and disadvantages is required in each case.

## Conclusion

The key to understanding Machiavelli is to avoid false standards of comparison. True, he was not a scientist in the way that Galileo was a scientist, but his application of the empirical method to human affairs does mark an important stage in the evolution of political science. By distinguishing between man as he ought to be and man as he is—between the ideal form of institutions and the pragmatic conditions under which they operate—he planted the seeds of the modern behavioural approach.

It is also misleading to interpret Machiavelli as a classical republican, inspired by ideals of justice and human excellence. He *was* a republican, but one who had few illusions about man's political condition. Again, he was an innovator, inaugurating a tradition carried on by Hobbes and sceptical liberals ever since. To Machiavelli, the eternal 'malignity' of the human spirit meant that men never do good unless through necessity. He had little faith in the potential of human beings, in our power to learn from experience, in our capacity for spiritual growth. But are we really the perfidious and unruly creatures depicted by Machiavelli? And does our nature never change? Is there no historical development? He thought history *always* repeats itself; modern historians and social theorists are inclined to think it *never* repeats itself. Living as we do in an age of optimism, most of us instinctively recoil from Machiavelli's pessimism. But let us not lose sight of the valuable lessons we have learned from his disdainful dismissal of idealists and tender-minded reformists. Our modern definition of politics as the pragmatic interplay of conflicting values and interests, as a sphere of activity unconcerned with the cultivation of man's interior life, owes much to Machiavelli's reformulation of political theory. Of equal significance was his emphasis on the paradox of politics: that good often results in evil and vice versa. History has confirmed his belief that regimes and statesmen must be judged not by their intentions but by the fruits of their policies. After all, noble intentions, when aligned with power, brought us the Inquisition, the Jacobin Terror in France, and the Soviet gulags. On the other hand, no one, apart from pacifists, would now deny that deviations from strict moral standards are sometimes necessary to achieve a higher political good. Still, the Machiavellian conviction that 'reason of state' is the only measure of political wisdom will never satisfy the elemental human urge to believe that established arrangements are, or should be, determined by universal principles of morality rather than force and fraud.

## FURTHER READING

Berlin, Isaiah, 'The Originality of Machiavelli', in his *Against the Current: Essays in the History of Ideas*, ed. H. Hardy (London: Hogarth Press, 1979).

Butterfield, Herbert, *The Statecraft of Machiavelli* (London: G. Bell & Sons, 1940).

Mansfield, Harvey C., *Machiavelli's Virtue* (Chicago: University of Chicago Press, 1998).

Skinner, Quentin, *Machiavelli* (Oxford: Oxford University Press, 1981).

Viroli, Maurizio, *Machiavelli* (Oxford: Oxford University Press, 1998).

## NOTES

1. Friedrich Meinecke, *Machiavellism* (New Brunswick, NJ: Transaction Publishers, 1998), 49.
2. Jean-Jacques Rousseau, *The Social Contract and Discourses*, trans. G. D. H. Cole (London: J. M. Dent & Sons, 1966), 59.
3. Machiavelli, *The Prince*, trans. George Bull (Harmondsworth: Penguin, 1975); references are to chapter and page numbers.
4. Ernst Cassirer, *The Myth of the State* (New Haven: Yale University Press, 1946), 153–6.
5. Benedetto Croce, *Elementi di politica* (Bari: Laterza, 1925), 59–67.
6. Antonio Gramsci, *Quaderni del carcere*, 4 vols., ed. Valentino Gerratana (Turin: Einaudi, 1975), iii. 1555, 1572.
7. Herbert Butterfield, *The Statecraft of Machiavelli* (London: G. Bell & Sons, 1940), 57.
8. Maurizio Viroli, *Machiavelli* (Oxford: Oxford University Press, 1998), 3.
9. Maurizio Viroli, 'Machiavelli and the Republican Idea of Politics', in Gisela Bok, Quentin Skinner, and Maurizio Viroli (eds.), *Machiavelli and Republicanism* (Cambridge: Cambridge University Press, 1990), 144.
10. Quentin Skinner, 'Machiavelli's *Discorsi* and the Pre-Humanist Origins of Republican Ideas', in Bok *et al.* (eds.), *Machiavelli and Republicanism*, 141.
11. Harvey C. Mansfield, *Machiavelli's Virtue* (Chicago: University of Chicago Press, 1998), pp. 177, ix, 257.

12. Machiavelli, *Discourses on Livy*, trans. Harvey C. Mansfield and Nathan Tarcov (Chicago: University of Chicago Press, 1996); references are to book, chapter, and page numbers.
13. *The Literary Works of Machiavelli*, ed. and trans. J. R. Hale (Oxford: Oxford University Press, 1961), 140.
14. J. H. Plumb, *The Italian Renaissance* (New York: American Heritage Library, 1989), 9.
15. Ibid. 21–2.
16. Allan H. Gilbert, *Machiavelli's 'Prince' and its Forerunners* (Durham, NC: Duke University Press, 1938).
17. J. G. A. Pocock, *The Machiavellian Moment: Florentine Political Thought and the Atlantic Republican Tradition* (Princeton: Princeton University Press, 1975), chs. VI–VII; Viroli, *Machiavelli*, ch. 4.
18. Machiavelli, *The History of Florence*, ed. Henry Morley (London: Routledge & Sons, 1891); references are to book and page numbers.
19. Francesco De Sanctis, *Storia della letteratura italiana*, vol. 1, ed. Benedetto Croce (Bari: Laterza, 1965), 420–1.
20. Butterfield, *The Statecraft of Machiavelli*, 57.
21. Croce, *Elementi di politica*, 59–67.

PART III

# The rationalist Enlightenment

# 10 Hobbes

Deborah Baumgold

## Contents



## Chapter guide

Thomas Hobbes's *Leviathan* (1651) is the third version of a political theory that was composed over the course of the English Civil War. By tracing the theory's history and examining in detail the first version (titled *The Elements of Law*), this chapter provides a fresh look at two basic questions. Does Hobbism rest on the assumption of egoism? Does the theory depend on the idea of a social contract? The chapter surveys the treatment of these questions in modern interpretative literature; then outlines the sequential composition of the three versions of the theory. Taking up the question of egoism, the next section shows that Hobbes's basic assumption about human nature is a form of solipsism. He holds that our thinking is necessarily self-referential, which need not be equivalent to holding that we are necessarily self-interested (egoistic). The last section separates three veins of contractarian reasoning to show the importance of the idea of consent in his political arguments.

## Biography

Thomas Hobbes was born in April 1588, at the time of the Spanish Armada. The son of a ne'er-do-well minister, an uncle sponsored his education at Oxford. After university he was hired as a tutor for the son of the Earl of Devonshire and remained in the household for most of his life. In the 1630s the patronage of the Earl of Newcastle, a Devonshire cousin, aided the development of his philosophical and scientific ideas. He fled into exile to Paris in 1640 and spent the Civil War years in the company of leading French thinkers and the English court in exile. *Leviathan* was published in spring 1651; the following winter Hobbes returned to England and made peace with Cromwell's regime. Despite this, he enjoyed the patronage of Charles II after the Restoration. He died in 1679 at the age of 91.

In the seventeenth century Hobbism was known as an atheistic doctrine that presented a bleak portrait of human nature. His theory is read today for its accounts of human nature and the logic of the social contract rather than its defence of absolute government.

## Key texts

*The Elements of Law, Natural and Politic* (MS 1640)
*De Cive* (1642; enlarged edn. 1647)
*Leviathan* (1651)

## Main texts used

*The Correspondence of Thomas Hobbes*, ed. Noel Malcolm (Oxford: Clarendon Press, 1994).
*De Cive: The English Version entitled in the first edition Philosophicall Rudiments Concerning Government and Society*, ed. Howard Warrender (Oxford: Clarendon Press, 1983).
*The Elements of Law, Natural and Politic*, ed. J. C. A. Gaskin (Oxford: Oxford University Press, 1994).
*Leviathan*, ed. C. B. Macpherson (Harmondsworth: Penguin, 1968).

## Key ideas

**Absolutism**: unconditional and unified sovereign authority; no collective right of resistance. **Egoism**: individuals motivated by self-interest. **Political obligation**: individuals relinquish natural rights with the exception of the right of self-preservation. **Law** equated with the will of the sovereign. **The social contract**: a contract between subjects establishing absolute government. **Sovereignty**: absolute, with a preference for monarchy. **The state of nature**: war of all against all in which life would be 'solitary, poore, nasty, brutish, and short'.

---

# Introduction

Thomas Hobbes's *Leviathan* (1651) is commonly described as one of the greatest masterpieces of political theory in the English language and the first of the great social contract treatises. In simple outline the main steps in Hobbes's logic are clear and widely known: because a state of nature would be a state of war, individuals in such a condition would choose to enter into a social contract creating absolute government, preferably taking the form of a monarchy. Hobbes's reputation attaches to his accounts of human nature and the logic of the social contract rather than his constitutional doctrine. His preference for unadulterated absolutism was a minority position even in the seventeenth century and long since ceased to be at all persuasive. The interest of Hobbes's theory lies, instead, in his effort to show how cooperative civil society can develop and exist among human beings if we are assumed to be antisocial by nature.

Although the main lines of Hobbes's theory are well known, its component arguments are notoriously slippery. Considerably more than is the case, say, with Locke's political theory,

Hobbes's positions are open to a variety of interpretations, many times contradictory ones. Consider, for example, his psychological premisses, which are telegraphed in the famous statement that life in a hypothetical state of nature would be 'solitary, poore, nasty, brutish, and short' (*Leviathan*, I. xiii, p. 186[1]). Many readers have taken this to imply that Hobbes holds us to be naturally self-interested. Others argue, however, that he is an egoist only in the formal sense that he makes it true by definition that whatever an individual wants is in her interest. A third camp entirely rejects the egoist characterization, arguing, instead, that Hobbes's political theory presupposes us to be moral agents who acknowledge and obey a natural moral law.

Disputes over Hobbes's view of human nature spill over into contradictory characterizations of his political reasoning. Although commonly said to be the first of the trio of great contract theorists, it has not seemed plain to all readers that Hobbes is a contract thinker at all. Consonant with the view that he starts with self-interested individuals, some think the contract metaphor obfuscates an otherwise straightforward discussion of the political arrangements and obligations which selfish individuals would accept. 'Perhaps Hobbes would have done better', John Plamenatz suggested in this vein, 'had he explained political obedience entirely as an effect of self-interest and fear, [and] had he spoken only of maxims of prudence in the state of nature and never of divine laws' such as promise-keeping.[2] More in keeping with his traditional classification as the first of the great contract philosophers, others think his account of political obligation hinges on making and keeping promises. But human nature and motivation remain issues for this view, too, since the question immediately arises why individuals should keep promises when it is not in their interest to do so. Some think Hobbes explains in terms of self-interest;[3] some think his explanation entails an independent account of moral agency;[4] others think he does not satisfactorily answer this key query.[5]

In one variant or another, the twin questions of whether or not Hobbes is an egoist and/or a contractarian have dominated the modern interpretative literature on his political theory. In the nineteenth century his reputation was revived by Utilitarians, starting with James Mill, who thought highly of his unsentimental account of human nature and realistic discussions of sovereignty and law. In Mill's view, Hobbes was correct in thinking that human nature inclines men to war and we therefore require a powerful sovereign to maintain peace. John Austin ensured that generations of law students would come to know Hobbes as the originator of the 'command' theory that law is simply what the sovereign says it is.[6] Later Utilitarians did Hobbes's reputation a lasting service by organizing the production of his collected English and Latin works; these editions remain the only available source for many of his writings.[7]

The next wave of interpretation made Hobbes over from a proto-Utilitarian into a natural law thinker, arguably a forerunner of Kant. In 1938 A. E. Taylor brought out an article on Hobbes's ethical doctrine that was sharply critical of the prevailing egoistic interpretation.[8] While granting that the theory includes an egoistic psychology, Taylor uncovered a Hobbesian deontological moral theory—that is, an account of our duties, most especially our duty to keep promises, as contrasted to his egoistic description of our motivations. Although this theory could be described in Kantian terms as consisting in an account of moral imperatives, Taylor thought it finally required a theological foundation, which was problematic since Hobbes held God to be incomprehensible. In effect, Taylor depicted Hobbes's political theory as a modern, contractarian variant of traditional natural law philosophy.

Twenty years later Howard Warrender elaborated Taylor's thesis in a natural law interpretation of Hobbes's account of political obligation.[9] Basic to Hobbes's moral theory, he argues in *The Political Philosophy of Hobbes*, is a distinction between the moral obligation to keep promises, which applies universally, and 'validating conditions', which make the obligation operative by eliminating fear as an excuse for non-performance. According to Warrender, there would be a prima facie obligation to keep promises even in a state of nature, but performance of the obligation would be 'suspended' until, with the political covenant and institution of sovereignty, the causes of insecurity are removed. Thus political authority is the 'validating condition' for the performance of moral duty. While agreeing with Taylor that the idea of universal natural law requires a theological foundation, Warrender rejects Taylor's Kantian spin on the argument. Taylor opposed moral duty to egoistic psychology, whereas Warrender thinks duty and interest cohere at the theological level: fear of divine punishment furnishes a self-interested motivation for performance of these duties.

Much of the subsequent interpretative literature has been devoted to rebutting the Taylor–Warrender thesis and elaborating one version or another of the older, egoistic understanding. The first attacks on their deontological view were historical; then, in the 1970s and 1980s, rational choice thinkers incorporated debate over the nature of Hobbesian self-interested individualism into their own theoretical arguments.

A wave of historical work began with C. B. Macpherson's *Political Theory of Possessive Individualism*,[10] which presents a Marxist version of the egoistic interpretation. Claiming that Hobbes's dark picture of the state of nature and brief for a strong state require the assumption of self-interested, competitive individualism, Macpherson argues that the assumption reflects the emergence of a bourgeois market society in seventeenth-century England. Although Hobbes may have thought he was giving an account of human nature everywhere and always, he unconsciously built the class relations of the coming age into his theory.

Shortly thereafter Quentin Skinner launched an entirely dissimilar historical attack on Warrender's thesis. Whereas Macpherson claims to reveal Hobbes's unconscious presuppositions, Skinner focuses on seventeenth-century readings of the theory. The Taylor–Warrender thesis, he argues, is historically incredible. Seventeenth-century readers associated Hobbes with a group of early Interregnum apologists for de facto authority, who defended the Commonwealth using the principle of a 'mutuall Relation between Protection and Obedience' (*Leviathan*, 'A Review and Conclusion', p. 728).[11] In other words, contemporaries did not take Hobbes to be a natural law thinker at all, but thought his theory grounded political obligation in self-interest. Nor did they take the theory to be essentially contractarian, since the de facto argument derives subjects' duty to obey from government's power to protect rather than their consent.

Whether or not Hobbes's theory is contractarian becomes a central issue in rational choice reconstructions of Hobbes's logic. As game-theoretical analyses proliferated in philosophy and the social sciences, many harked back to Hobbes's account of the state of nature as an exemplary description of collective goods dilemmas, including the prisoner's dilemma. This approach assumes self-interested individualism and uses Hobbes's theory to address the game-theoretical question 'How can self-interested individuals be brought to cooperate when they would be better off free-riding on the contributions of others?' Jean Hampton's *Hobbes and the Social Contract Tradition*[12] argues that Hobbes's description of the state of nature is not a genuine prisoner's dilemma, but rather a situation in which self-interest inclines individuals to cooperate. Creating civil society therefore requires merely the coordination of individuals' interests rather than a fully fledged social contract. In reply, David Gauthier has defended the contractarian position that cooperation requires a contract in order to override individuals' selfish interest in non-compliance.[13]

One can sum up the range of mainstream interpretations of Hobbism over the past 150 years in a list of the disparate thinkers to whom he's been linked; these range from Bentham to Kant, Thucydides to Buchanan. If this interpretative history brings to mind the proverbial story of the blind men examining the elephant, this is partly due to the differing interests of various interpreters. For instance, the current opposition of historical versus rational choice schools of interpretation reflects sharply different interpretative interests: the one concerned with what Hobbes meant, or could have meant, by his arguments; the other unconcerned with intentions and contextual meaning, and interested, instead, in reconstructing and improving the logic of his theory. But it is also something of a peculiarity of Hobbism that it lends itself to so wide a variety of interpretations. None of the disparate and contradictory interpretations can readily be dismissed as incorrect because all have supporting evidence in *Leviathan* and other writings. The Taylor–Warrender thesis builds, for example, on a passage in which Hobbes says of the laws of nature that they 'oblige in Conscience alwayes, but in Effect then onely when there is Security' (*Leviathan*, I. xv, p. 215; emphasis omitted). In attacking that thesis, Skinner highlights *Leviathan*'s 'Review and Conclusion', which was written after the regicide and fall of the Stuarts, and explicitly justifies submission to a conqueror's regime. The rational choice approach invokes yet other passages, such as Hobbes's reply to the 'fool' who questions why promises should be kept when they cross self-interest.

It is curious that a theory should support such inconsistent interpretations. In another case this might evidence simply a confused or self-contradictory author, but here it reflects a complex composition process. *Leviathan* is the third and last version of a treatise that Hobbes wrote and rewrote over the span of more than a decade, with different audiences in view, and in continually changing political circumstances. The first version, titled *The Elements of Law, Natural and Politic*, circulated in manuscript form in 1640, prior to the Civil War. Following Hobbes's flight to Paris in the same year, he reframed the work's political chapters in Latin and published this version as *De Cive* in 1642 and, in a larger edition, 1647. *Leviathan* was published four years later, in the spring of 1651, shortly before Hobbes returned to England and made peace with the new regime. His friend and first biographer, John Aubrey, put the relationship between the three works succinctly: 'This little MS treatise [*The Elements of Law*] grew to be his book *De Cive*, and at last grew there to be the so formidable LEVIATHAN'.[14] The several versions are sufficiently parallel in structure that one can trace the evolution of Hobbes's arguments paragraph by paragraph through them. A process of composition by revision was not unusual in sixteenth- and seventeenth-century literature. Philip Sidney wrote 'old' and 'new' versions of *Arcadia* in the 1580s, and in the same period there were three successive editions of Montaigne's *Essais*. In Hobbes's own time, Milton published several versions of *Paradise Lost* after the Restoration.[15]

## Three treatises

In Hobbes's case there is little extant evidence regarding his purposes in revising the treatise several times. Unfortunately, he burned many personal papers in the 1660s out of fear of persecution by Parliament. But it is likely that the several versions were written, at least partly, to serve his changing personal circumstances during the Civil War period. In the latter half of the 1630s, when he began writing *The Elements of Law*, he was closely associated with the Earl of Newcastle, who was governor to the Prince of Wales and would become a prominent royalist general in the Civil War. Although employed as a tutor in the household of Newcastle's cousin the Earl of Devonshire, Hobbes found an intellectual home in a circle of scientifically minded intellectuals surrounding Newcastle. We do not know precisely when or why he started working on the *Elements*, although the dedication to Newcastle records that it was written at the earl's command. It may have been as early as 1635, when a letter to the earl mentions another protégé's work on 'y^e^ facultyes & passions of y^e^ soule', which would be the subject of the first part of the *Elements*. If he can give a good account of this in plain English, Hobbes writes, 'he is the first (that I euer heard of) could speake sense in that subiect. if he can not I hope to be y^e^ first' (Hobbes to William Cavendish, Earl of Newcastle, from Paris, 15/25 August 1635, *Correspondence*, 29[16]). Most scholars, however, date the work's composition to the period of the Short Parliament, based on Hobbes's recollection at the end of his life. According to a 1679 autobiography, 'When the Parliament sat, that began in April 1640, and was dissolved in May following . . . Mr. Hobbes wrote a little treatise in English, wherein he did set forth and demonstrate, that the said power and rights were inseparably annexed to the sovereignty' ('Considerations', 414[17]). While the work was left in manuscript and not published, Hobbes hoped that Newcastle's favour would help 'insinuate' it 'with those whom the matter it containeth most nearly concerneth' ('The Epistle Dedicatory', in *Elements*, p. 20). It circulated sufficiently widely that he became afraid for his safety later in the year with the seating of the Long Parliament, which was soon attacking similar defences of absolute monarchy.

Hobbes hurriedly fled into exile in Paris, where he joined a scientific circle led by Marin Mersenne, a Minim friar, whom he had met during a tour of the Continent in the mid-1630s. Within a year he completed a Latin version of his political theory, titled *De Cive*, and published it pseudo-anonymously in a limited edition, signed only with his initials, and dedicated to the Earl of Devonshire, in April 1642. The first section of the *Elements*, thirteen chapters on epistemology and psychology, are dropped from *De Cive*, which covers only the political portion of a planned tripartite work on 'body', 'man', and 'civill government and the duties of Subjects' ('The Authors Preface to the Reader', in *De Cive*, p. 35;[18] emphasis omitted). In working up *De Cive*, Hobbes revised and expanded some arguments, and added a section on religion, but otherwise the work's chapter and internal paragraph organization largely parallel the earlier treatise. The introduction to the second edition of 1647 gives a political rationale for the separate publication of this section of the larger theory: 'My Country some few yeares before the civill Warres did rage, was boyling hot with questions concerning the rights of Dominion, and the obedience due from Subjects . . . And was the cause which . . . ripen'd, and pluckt from me this third part' (ibid. pp. 35–6; emphasis omitted). Yet the circumstances and character of the project suggest it may also have served the more immediate and personal purpose of establishing Hobbes's credentials with Mersenne and his friends. Hobbes depended on patronage all his life, but lived in greater insecurity in these early years before his reputation was established. Taking an existing work, translating it into Latin, and making piecemeal revisions and additions would have been an attractive route for swiftly proving his intellectual stature to this European audience. We know the book circulated among the Mersenne circle, although there was some speculation even within the circle that Descartes was the author. By the spring 1646 Hobbes had prepared a second edition with a new preface and notes answering critics. Published the following year, this second edition of *De Cive* marked the first appearance of Hobbes's political theory in a sizeable and signed edition, and the work made his reputation as a political philosopher.

Why, then, did Hobbes continue to revise the treatise, put it back into English, and ultimately publish *Leviathan* in 1651? The royalist court in exile was in residence in Paris starting in the summer 1646, and Hobbes was mathematics tutor to the Prince of Wales at court. He probably started working on *Leviathan* at this time, although serious illness interrupted the work in the autumn of 1647.[19] Just as, some five years previously, *De Cive* had likely been framed as a ticket to the Mersenne circle, Hobbes may well have conceived the new work as a way of establishing his position at the exile court. Given the declining Stuart fortunes, however, he was also taking care not to become overly identified with the prince. A March 1647 letter requests the removal of a portrait noting his position as the prince's tutor from the new edition of *De Cive*: 'This title will prevent me from returning to my own country . . . and I do not see why I should not wish to return, if it is permitted, when England has somehow or other been pacified' (Hobbes to Samuel Sorbière, from Paris, 12/22 March 1647, trans. Noel Malcolm *Correspondence*, 157–8).

Thirty-seven of a projected fifty chapters were completed by May 1650, and *Leviathan* was published in London the following spring.[20] The changing political circumstances of the last years of the Civil War and early Interregnum, and Hobbes's efforts to protect himself from political danger, are reflected in the text. Some material clearly dates to the late Civil War period, such as chapter xviii on sovereign right, which makes reference to the 'subjects to a Monarch' and 'the next return of Peace' (II. xviii, pp. 229, 237). Similarly, the next chapter includes the observation that 'in a Monarchy, he that had the Soveraignty from a descent of 600 years, was alone called Soveraign' (p. 241). Later chapters incorporate arguments from the Engagement Controversy of 1650–1 over the new Commonwealth's demand for an oath of allegiance from all adult Englishmen. For instance, chapter xxix notes a distinction between sovereign right and subjects' obligation, which was a theme of an influential 1649 tract titled *The Lawfulness of Obeying the Present Government*: 'though the Right of a Soveraign Monarch cannot be extinguished by the act of another; yet the Obligation of the members may. For he that wants protection, may seek it anywhere; and . . . is obliged . . . to protect his Protection' (p. 375). By the time Hobbes wrote the 'Review and Conclusion', however, he had shifted to the different and contradictory Engagement position that might can generate right: '*Conquest* (to define it) is the Acquiring of the Right of Soveraignty by Victory' through 'the peoples Submission, by which they contract with the Victor, promising Obedience, for Life and Liberty' (p. 721). Whether haste, confusion in his reactions to the new regime, opportunism, or some combination of these is responsible for the contradiction, it would serve Hobbes's interest during the political changes of the next decade. Cromwell's regime left him in peace after he returned home in the autumn of 1651. Then, following the Restoration, he would play up the description of Cromwell as an *unjust* conqueror and claim that *Leviathan*'s defence of submission was meant narrowly to apply to royalists who otherwise would have lost their fortunes ('Considerations', 420–4).

We think of *Leviathan* as a unified treatise, comparable as an artistic creation to Plato's *Republic* or Locke's *Second Treatise of Government*, but the impression is false. Its lengthy and peculiar process of composition results in its being a pastiche of arguments that evidence the changing times and Hobbes's changing interests and preoccupations. In composing the masterpiece, he restored the first section, 'Of Man', which had been cut from *De Cive*, added chapters on political topics, and effectively doubled the work in length by including two long parts on religion. But the process of revising arguments and reframing the whole in English was carried out unevenly. In Part I, chapters on human faculties and passions (vi to xii) are extensively revised, whereas the first five chapters on epistemology and speech largely follow *The Elements of Law*. The core chapters of the political theory (xiii to xviii)—on the state and laws of nature, the political covenant, and sovereign right—are less revised, although a chapter is added explaining the concept of authorization. Aubrey's description of Hobbes's manner of working suggests that he approached *Leviathan*'s composition in an unsystematic fashion. Apparently he worked on ideas piecemeal, then fitted them into a prior chapter structure: 'He walked much and contemplated . . . and as soon as a thought darted, he presently entered it into his book . . . He had drawn the design of the book into chapters, etc. so he knew whereabouts it would come in'.[21] When adding arguments to existing material, Hobbes typically failed to go back through the rest of the work to bring it into line with the new formulation, thus producing contradictions of the sort noted in the previous paragraph.

Given *Leviathan*'s history and method of composition, it makes sense to drop the assumption of coherence, which is appropriately applied to more systematic and unified writings, and instead focus on tracing the foundation and development of specific arguments through the several versions. Since the work is a more or less heavily revised and expanded version of *The Elements of Law*, particular attention deserves to be paid to Hobbes's initial formulations in that first version. With the exception of the treatment of religion, the *Elements* largely sets out the framework within which Hobbes would locate his evolving ideas over the next decade. With this in mind, let us turn back to the core issues of the interpretative literature: egoism and contractarianism.

## Solipsism and egoism

> His doctrine is that each man is unavoidably shut up within the world of his own sensations; and there is no more meaning in speaking of him as 'selfish' than there is in speaking of anything else that is monadically conceived as selfish—the universe as a whole, or an electron.
>
> (Michael Oakeshott, 'Thomas Hobbes', 1935)

Following his return from Europe in 1636, Hobbes was preoccupied with the basic epistemological question of how we come to have knowledge of the world. *The Elements of Law* opens with a chapter laying out the idea that 'image or colour is but an apparition unto us of that motion . . . which the object worketh in the brain' (ii. 4, p. 23). In other words, the qualities that our senses perceive are not inherent to external objects (as Aristotelians held) but are caused by motion from the external object upon the brain. Such sense-perceptions are the building blocks of all knowledge and work in concert with language, which allows us to record and manipulate our perceptions. The 'motion thesis' extends into an explanation of the passions: 'conceptions . . . are . . . motion in some internal substance of the head; which motion not stopping there, but proceeding to the heart, of necessity must there either help or hinder that motion which is called vital'; and this is the source of our appetites, passions, and, by extension, moral judgements. 'Every man . . . calleth that which . . . is delightful to himself, GOOD; and that EVIL which displeaseth him' (vii. 1–3, pp. 43–4).

By nature, then, our method of knowing the world is solipsistic: the only way we know, feel, or judge anything is according to how it strikes us. At an extreme, solipsism takes the form of denying the existence of the outside world, which is not a step taken by Hobbes since he holds that our perceptions are caused by motion from external objects. His solipsism consists in the weaker proposition that 'each man is unavoidably shut up within the world of his own sensations'.[22] Our knowledge of the 'world', and attitudes towards it and towards other people, consist entirely in the internal processing of 'apparitions' from those external motions.

Solipsism can extend into egoism, but need not do so. To hold that our ideas, feelings, and judgements are necessarily self-referential does not need to imply that we are narrowly self-interested. In other words, Hobbes is committed to a particular causal account of the generation of our feelings and judgements rather than an account of their specific content. Solipsism can readily underwrite altruism via the argument that we come to have altruistic feelings, such as compassion for others, by imagining that their misfortunes could befall us.

Interpreters are generally in agreement that Hobbism became less egoistic over time. *The Elements of Law* tends to give solipsism an egoistic coloration, as in this comparison of life to a race: 'This race we must suppose to have no other goal, nor no other garland, but being foremost'. In the competition, 'To see another fall, [is] disposition to laugh'; 'Continually to be out-gone is misery'; and 'Continually to out-go the next before is felicity' (ix. 21, pp. 59–60). Yet the passage is far from thoroughly egoist. It also includes neutral definitions of love and charity that imply neither egoism nor altruism: 'To hold fast by another is to love'; 'To carry him on that so holdeth, is charity'.

This muddled egoism is further diluted in *Leviathan*. The work's psychology qualifies as egoist only in the formal sense that voluntary acts are said to aim, by definition, at the agent's good. In a classic discussion of the contrast between Hobbes's early 'psychological' egoism and mature 'tautological' egoism, Bernard Gert cites the example of parallel definitions of pity in the *Elements* and *Leviathan*.[23] According to the former, 'PITY is imagination or fiction of future calamity to ourselves, proceeding from the sense of another man's present calamity' (ix. 10, p. 53), which appears to dissolve pity for another into anxiety for oneself. By a simple reversal of clauses, *Leviathan*'s definition becomes other-regarding and demonstrates the compatibility of solipsism with altruism: '*Griefe*, for the Calamity of another, is PITTY; and ariseth from the imagination that the like calamity may befall himselfe' (I. vi, p. 126).

Hobbes's several discussions of the state of nature show a similar movement away from an initial egoism. One of the classic problems of social contract theory is explaining why a state of nature would be a state of conflict. According to the *Elements*, there are three reasons for war in the state of nature. The first is structural rather than psychological: in the absence of coercive authority, so long as some are naturally aggressive, all must behave in an aggressive manner in order to defend themselves. Another cause of conflict, also circumstantial, is competition for the same goods. Thirdly, however, war is directly traced to ubiquitous egoism: 'every man thinking well of himself, and hating to see the same in others, they must needs provoke one another' (xiv. 3–5, p. 78). The last proposition disappears from *Leviathan*, where the accent is rather on 'Competition' over goods; 'Diffidence' or fear of one another; and the desire for 'Glory' on the part of the ambitious, which sets in motion a dynamic of universal aggression (I. xiii, p. 185).

If *Leviathan* is the least egoistic of the works, it is also the version that most clearly frames egoism as a problematic issue. In the earlier works Hobbes was preoccupied with a different set of problems—namely, the nexus of solipsism and relativism, and the social conflict generated by these epistemological facts. As we have seen, it follows from the 'motion thesis' that judgements of good and evil (etc.) are self-referential and will therefore vary inasmuch as individuals differ from one another. This natural condition, Hobbes explains in *De Cive*, produces 'discord, and strife': 'They are therefore so long in the state of War, as by reason of the diversity of the present appetites, they mete Good and Evill by diverse measures' (iii. 31, p. 74). The early versions of the theory canvass two solutions, two ways of generating moral consensus. One looks to the notion of a universal interest in self-preservation as the basis for 'rational'—as opposed to relativist—moral judgement (*Elements*, xviii. 14, p. 98, and *De Cive*, ii. 1, p. 52). A second solution is to seek a common standard in the collective good: 'we call "good" that which pleases the commonalty, such as obeying the laws or fighting for one's country' (Hobbes, *White's 'De Mundo' Examined*, 379[24]; cf. *De Cive*, ii, 1 (annotation), p. 52).

*Leviathan* takes up egoism as a problem with the introduction of the figure of the 'fool' who thinks it rational to keep or break promises depending on self-interest. In reply, Hobbes argues that social life is an 'iterated game' (to use the language of twentieth-century game theory), so that keeping promises always serves our interest in self-preservation. He 'that breaketh his Covenant . . . cannot be received into any Society . . . and [this is] consequently against the reason of his preservation' (I. xv, p. 205). The upshot is to collapse any distinction between egoistic and moral behaviour by redescribing morality as prudential behaviour and ignoring situations in which duty might diverge from interest.

Looking back over the development of Hobbesian psychology from the *Elements* through *Leviathan*, one can see why the question of egoism is perplexing. The question is a modern one, which takes its force from the Kantian—but un-Hobbesian—view that morality is completely different from self-interest. Hobbes assumed that we are self-interested creatures, and, added to the assumption that we know the world in a solipsistic manner, this gives his theory the appearance of being egoistic. The appearance was more pronounced at the outset in the stark comments on our selfish motives to be found in the *Elements*. Even there, however, Hobbes muddled egoistic with non-egoistic formulations. Then, focusing on the issue in *Leviathan*, he developed an argument for the compatibility of self-interest with the duty of promise-keeping. However famous he has become for defending egoism, Hobbes seems never to have imagined that selfishness is at odds with altruism and other moral sentiments.

## Contractarianism

> Civil society is a complex of authority and power in which each element creates its own appropriate obligation.
>
> (Michael Oakeshott, 'Introduction', in *Leviathan*, 1946)

The question of whether or not Hobbes is a contractarian is similarly complex. *Leviathan* amalgamates contractarian with non-contractarian principles for understanding the relationship between ruler and ruled. Hobbes presents three distinct lines of argument: an 'agency' or 'authorization' version of the social contract; a 'non-resistance' version; and the non-contractarian principle of a 'mutuall Relation between Protection and Obedience'. According to the first, subjects authorize the ruler's acts and it would therefore be self-accusation to charge a ruler with misconduct. The second denies accountability on the different, but still contractarian, ground that there is not, and cannot be, a contract between ruler and ruled on which to base accountability. The last is a defence of de facto authority, albeit with a thin contractarian veneer in the form of the proposition that living under the protection of a conqueror constitutes a form of tacit consent.

Criticizing Hobbesian contractarianism, commentators have accented the seeming discrepancy between the authorization formulation, which implicates subjects in their government's actions, and the non-resistance version, which removes any tie between ruler and ruled. Yet this seems not to have concerned Hobbes as he worked out the germs of both lines of argument for the *Elements*. As we will see, it reduces the discrepancy to proper measure to think of the several accounts of the political covenant not as statements of some broad view of the relationship between government and the people, but much more narrowly as separate arguments in support of different aspects of personal rule.

## Agency and authorization

Consider, first, the core concept of consent, which is introduced as a vehicle for coordinating individuals' wills: 'When the wills of many concur to some one and the same action, or effect, this concourse of their wills is called CONSENT' (*Elements*, xii. 7, p. 72). It follows, then, that the purpose of consent in a *political* context is to institute an agent for the whole: 'every man by covenant oblige[s] himself to some one and the same man, or to some one and the same council . . . to do those actions, which the said man or council shall command them to do; and to do no action which he or they shall forbid' (xix. 7, p. 106). This idea of political agency harks back to the solipsistic 'motion thesis' with its implication that disagreement is inherent to the human condition. Hobbes seems to have arrived at the contract idea by interpreting political conflict through a solipsist lens, so to speak, as simply another manifestation of the strife caused by conflicting individual judgements. His inspiration lay in identifying consent, and the idea of the political covenant, as an alternative to consensus: agreement on a collective agent can substitute for that substantive consensus which is a human impossibility.

The 'agency' covenant extends, next, into a defence of absolutism via the added propositions that political authority must and should be unified. In a striking departure from his usual practice of ignoring thinkers with whom he agreed, Hobbes invoked the authority of Bodin in support of unified sovereignty: 'If there were a commonwealth, wherein the rights of sovereignty were divided, we must confess with Bodin, Lib. II. chap. I. *De Republica*, that they are not rightly to be called commonwealths, but the corruption of commonwealths' (xxvii. 7, pp. 166–7). Furthermore, he agreed with Bodin that the purpose of government requires unified sovereignty. Hobbes was intent, in particular, on rebutting doctrines of limited monarchy and, especially, parliamentary authority over taxation. These are erroneous views, he argues, because a single body must control taxation and the military for government to be sufficiently strong to maintain peace. 'The division therefore of the sovereignty, either worketh no effect, to the taking away of simple subjection, or introduceth war; wherein the private sword hath place again' (xx. 16, p. 116).

The latter point made transparent reference to the controversy over Ship Money of 1635–8. In the famous *Hampden's Case*, Charles I justified the tax by claiming authority to provide for national defence in an emergency without need of parliamentary approval. The *Elements*—with its definition of government as the corporate agent and explanation of the necessity for unified control of major state powers—in effect provided a set of supporting reasons for the king's position. Recall that Hobbes described the work as an effort to 'demonstrate, that the said power and rights were inseparably annexed to the sovereignty'.

The idea of political agency is later taken in an individualistic direction in the 'authorization' version of the political covenant in *Leviathan*. Now, subjects are told to regard the sovereign as their personal agent: 'every one [is] to owne, and acknowledge himselfe to be Author of whatsoever he that so beareth their Person, shall Act . . . and therein to submit their Wills, every one to his Will, and their Judgements, to his Judgment' (II. xvii, p. 227). Here, the salient principle is unconditional rather than unified sovereignty. There is an important, intervening discussion in *De Cive* in which Hobbes reflects on the erroneous opinion that a parliamentary majority could hold a ruler accountable. In rebuttal, he writes that 'government is upheld by a double obligation from the Citizens, first that which is due to their fellow citizens, next that which they owe to their Prince' (vi. 20, p. 105). This idea of a direct tie between sovereign and subject becomes the authorization covenant in which each subject swears, 'I Authorise and give up my Right of Governing my selfe, to this Man, or to this Assembly of men' (*Leviathan*, II. xvii, p. 227; emphasis omitted). As a consequence, political accountability is as nonsensical as self-accusation: 'he that complaineth of injury from his Soveraigne, complaineth of that whereof he himselfe is Author; and . . . to do injury to ones selfe, is impossible' (II. xviii, p. 232).

## The non-resistance compact between subjects

Let us turn, now, to the second line of Hobbesian contract argument: the non-resistance covenant. Here, the accent is on a promise by incipient subjects not to resist the ruler: 'This *submission* . . . is then made, when each one of them obligeth himself by contract to every one of the rest, not to resist the *will* of that *one man*, or *counsell*, to which he hath submitted himselfe' (*De Cive*, v. 7, p. 88). The formulation makes two key points in support of the principle of unconditional sovereignty: the parties to the contract are only the incipient subjects; and what they promise is non-resistance. Since rulers do not participate in the contract, they do not stand in a contractual relationship with their people and, therefore, there is no basis for governmental accountability. 'Because the Right' of ruling, Hobbes explains in *Leviathan*, 'is given to him they make Soveraigne, by Covenant onely of one to another, and not of him to any of them; there can happen no breach of Covenant on the part of the Soveraigne; and consequently none of his Subjects, by any pretence of forfeiture, can be freed from his Subjection' (II. xviii, p. 230). A further dimension of unconditional sovereignty is the age-old issue of whether tyrants may be resisted. For Hobbes, the issue is complicated because it seems to pit his belief in absolutism against his equally strong belief in individuals' right of self-preservation. Through the several versions of the theory, we will see, he manages to work out how the two can be made compatible.

The claim that there cannot be a contractual relationship between ruler and ruled originates in a curious proposition in the *Elements* that all governments are initially democracies (xxi. 1, p. 118). Ill suited though the proposition was to defending absolute monarchy, Hobbes had hit on it as a way of proving that sovereignty must be unconditional. The absence of a contractual relationship was self-evident, he thought, in the specific case of democracy: 'In the making of a democracy, there passeth no covenant, between the sovereign and any subject. . . . For it cannot be imagined, that the multitude should contract with itself . . . to make itself sovereign'; therefore, 'whatsoever the people doth to any one particular member . . . of the commonwealth, the same by him ought not to be styled injury' (xxi. 2–3, p. 119). Later, when aristocracy or monarchy evolve out of democracy, the absence of a constitutional compact between ruler and ruled carries over to the new form of government (xxi. 7, p. 121). The point, then, of stipulating that democracy is foundational is to extend the same logic to all forms of government. Still, the argument better suited the parliamentary cause than the royalist, which is presumably why Hobbes watered it down in *De Cive* by inserting the crucial modifier that the step 'almost' constitutes a democracy (vii. 5, p. 109). By the time he wrote *Leviathan*, he had realized that the argument could be eliminated altogether. Here he simply observes that the absence of a contractual relationship between ruler and ruled in democracies is exemplary of a universal fact about all forms of government: 'no man is so dull as to say, for example, the People of *Rome*, made a Covenant with the Romans, to hold the Soveraignty on such or such conditions . . . . That men see not the reason to be alike in a Monarchy . . . proceedeth from the ambition of some', who hope to establish parliamentary government (II. xviii, p. 231).

Hobbes turned these observations into a logical proposition about the necessary structure of the political covenant. The early versions of the theory progressively refine the description of the political covenant so as to formalize and universalize the absence of a contractual relationship between ruler and ruled. The key issue is who is party to the covenant. In the *Elements* this is left vague: 'every man by covenant oblige[s] himself to some one and the same man, or to some one and the same council . . . to do those actions' which government shall command (xix. 7, p. 106). By *De Cive* he had worked out the specification that the parties are only the incipient subjects and in *Leviathan* explains why this must be so. On the one hand, there cannot be a contract between the ruler and the people as a whole, since there is no such thing as a corporate 'people' in existence before the covenant. It might be possible to conceive, on the other hand, of a contract between the ruler and each incipient subject separately, but an image of multiple contracts between ruler and ruled runs up against the logic of authorization. Even if such contracts were made, they would subsequently be void because it is the nature of sovereignty that rulers are authorized by and are the agents of their subjects (II. xviii, p. 230). This adds up to a logical proof of the principle of unconditional sovereignty: the political covenant can only be a pact among subjects; so rulers cannot break promises they haven't made (or which are void); and therefore their subjects lack grounds for holding them accountable.

In addition to the question of who is party to the covenant, there is an additional, relevant question about its parameters: namely, 'What kind of promises can and would rational individuals make?' This was a particularly difficult question for Hobbes because, like Grotius before him, he wanted to endorse seemingly contradictory propositions. On the one hand, typical of absolutist thinkers generally, he denies that subjects have a right to resist tyrannous rulers and makes renunciation of the right of resistance the very definition of political subjection. On the other hand, his account of human nature, with its accent on the universal drive for self-preservation, makes it inconceivable that rational individuals would renounce the right to defend themselves. The dilemma is apparent in the discussion of non-resistance in the *Elements*: 'No man in any commonwealth whatsoever hath right to resist him, or them, on whom they have conferred this power coercive . . . supposing the not-resistance possible. For . . . covenants bind but to the utmost of our endeavour' (xx. 7, p. 112). In laying out the laws of nature, which amount to principles of rational action, he elaborates on what is possible in this regard and what subjects cannot promise: 'As it was necessary that a man should not retain his right to every thing, so also was it, that he should retain his right to some things: to his own body (for example) the right of defending, whereof he could not transfer' (xvii. 2, p. 93).

Hobbes resolves the apparent paradox, in *De Cive*, by carefully distinguishing a permissible right of self-defence from impermissible collective resistance. The revision comes as part of his clarification of the terms of the political covenant. In the same contract passage in which he specifies that only incipient subjects are party to the covenant, Hobbes adds the important stipulation that self-defence is an inalienable right: 'he is supposed still to retain a Right of defending himselfe against violence' (v. 7, pp. 88–9). The supporting discussion of possible contracts acknowledges that his view of human nature makes renunciation of the right inconceivable. 'Since therefore no man is tyed to *impossibilities*, they who are threatned either with *death*, (which is the greatest evill to nature) or wounds . . . and are not stout enough to bear them, are not obliged to endure them.' What he had come to realize is that individuals' right to defend themselves against violence does not undermine peaceful society. Social peace requires simply 'that no man offer to defend others' from the sovereign or, in other words, a ban on collective resistance (ii. 18, pp. 58–9).

## De facto authority

Hobbes seems to abandon contractarian thinking altogether in the concluding paragraph of *Leviathan*: 'I have brought to an end my Discourse of Civill and Ecclesiasticall Government, occasioned by the disorders of the present time . . . without other designe, than to set before mens eyes the mutuall Relation between Protection and Obedience' ('A Review and Conclusion', p. 728). Does this signify, as some readers have thought, an admission that the contract is epiphenomenal in Hobbism and the theory better fits the tradition of utilitarian, interest-based political philosophy?

Once again, tracing the history of the idea within Hobbes's theory yields a different view. It makes its first appearance, in *The Elements of Law*, in opposition not to consent but to patriarchy. Subsequent to treating sovereign right and forms of government, the *Elements* takes up the traditional Aristotelian comparison of various authority relationships: family, household, and political. A key purpose of the chapter titled 'Of the Power of Fathers, and of Patrimonial Kingdom' is to deny the patriarchal paradigm that dominated much early modern thinking about politics and all authority. How more emphatically to do this than to claim that paternity is irrelevant even to familial authority? This is just what Hobbes does: 'The title to dominion over a child, proceedeth not from the generation, but from the preservation of it' (xxiii. 3, p. 130). Subsequent explanation shows, first, that he has in mind a mutual relationship between preservation and obedience and, secondly, that he conceives this as a form of tacit consent rather than an alternative to consent. 'It is to be presumed', he writes, 'that he which giveth sustenance to another, whereby to strengthen him, hath received a promise of obedience in consideration thereof' (xxiii. 3, p. 131).

When events made conquest a pressing issue, Hobbes imported this concept of tacit consent to explain the relevance of contract reasoning. Consistent with his accounts of familial and household authority, he had always maintained the general proposition that consent is necessary to legitimize a conqueror's authority (*Elements*, xxii. 2, pp. 127–9). But specifics did not particularly concern him until the period of the Engagement Controversy, when he framed *Leviathan*'s 'Review and Conclusion' explicitly to address the question '. . . what point of time it is, that a Subject becomes obliged to the Conquerour' (p. 719). The principle of tacit consent, as he had defined it in the context of familial authority, provided a ready explanation: 'a man that hath not been called to make such an expresse Promise' of allegiance to a conqueror 'if he live under their Protection openly, hee is understood to submit himselfe to the Government' (pp. 720–1). The equation of enjoying protection with giving consent no doubt strains the idea of consent, as critics commonly observe about the parallel Lockean concept of tacit consent. But this makes it a poor argument rather than a proto-utilitarian one, and the equation indicates that Hobbes saw the 'mutual relationship between protection and obedience' as simply another in a series of contract arguments.

The appropriation of the conquest argument by supporters of the Commonwealth has become a familiar story, yet the origin of the argument is of more significance for understanding the intentions informing Hobbes's political theory. The audacious claim that patriarchy is irrelevant even to familial authority distanced him from what was, in the period, establishment royalism. Modern readers rightly class Hobbes among the great conservative thinkers by virtue of his defence of absolutism. But he seems to have seen himself differently—as, instead, a moderate arguing against the excesses of traditional royalism, on the one hand, as well as the claims of the parliamentarians, on the other. Of *Leviathan*, he wrote in its dedication to a friend killed in the Civil War, 'I know not how the world will receive it . . . For in a way beset with those that contend on one side for too great Liberty, and on the other side for too much Authority, 'tis hard to passe between the points of both unwounded' (p. 75). This statement deserves to be taken seriously. Within the *ancien régime*, monarchic horizon of conventional political thinking in his day, he was as much an enemy of traditional legitimations of authority as he was an opponent of popular government.

There is one final, and important, piece of contract logic laid out in the *Elements*, which is the qualification that consent is a necessary but not sufficient condition of social order. 'It remaineth therefore still that consent . . . is not sufficient security for their common peace, without the erection of some common power' (xix. 6, p. 106). The explanation recurs to the familiar themes of diversity and conflict: 'by the diversity of judgments and passions in so many men contending naturally for honour and advantage one above another: it is impossible . . . that the peace should last between themselves, without some mutual and common fear to rule them' (xix. 4, p. 105). The qualification can be taken as yet another instance of a tendency to blur the distinction between consensual and de facto authority, since it implies that one ought to obey any government with the power to protect its citizenry. Indeed, passages stating that security is the purpose for which subjects enter political society and this purpose determines the extent of submission were excerpted from the *Elements* in publications by a Commonwealth supporter, Marchamont Nedham.[25]

From a different angle, though, the qualification is the bridge that allows us to map the relationship among the major, philosophical and political, components of Hobbes's original vision—namely, solipsism, relativism, consent, and the constitutional principles of unified and unconditional sovereignty. As we have seen, contractarianism solves the root problem of conflict, born of our solipsistic grasp on the world and the relativism this generates, by instituting a collective agent. It matters, though, how this collective agent is constituted since the purpose requires government to have adequate power to suppress conflict. Those who think, for instance, that conditional sovereignty can constitute a secure commonwealth deceive themselves (*Elements*, xx. 13, p. 114). The upshot is the Bodinian proposition that either sovereignty is absolute or there is no state in existence (ibid. xx. 14, p. 115). Thus, social order requires a covenant, but not just any covenant will do; it must establish a sovereign with sufficient power, which can only be an absolute sovereign.

The epigraphs to the several sections of this chapter are intended to acknowledge its debt to Michael Oakeshott's classic writings on Hobbes. Oakeshott rejected the prevailing egoistic interpretation, arguing, more carefully, that solipsism is Hobbes's core premiss. He is also known for describing the Hobbesian concept of obligation as a combination of moral, physical, and rational elements—i.e. consent, might, and self-interest. This corresponds to the recognition that consent and power are dual components of Hobbes's account of political authority; or, as Oakeshott put the point, 'civil society is a complex of authority and power'.[26]

But Oakeshott misconceived Hobbes's achievement. 'Hobbes stands out', he thought, 'as the creator of a system'.[27] This confuses Hobbes's intentions and cast of mind with his achievement. He undoubtedly possessed an unusually logical mind, and he hoped to create a deductive system uniting physics, psychology, and political science. But, as we have seen, the process of creation leading up to *Leviathan* was at odds with the intention: writing and rewriting the text three times produced a multi-layered, complex, and sometimes internally contradictory masterpiece. *The Elements of Law* is the most systematic of the three texts but has attracted the least attention from readers over the years, whereas the richer and sloppier *Leviathan* is the masterpiece. It seems that Hobbes was fortunate to have political and personal circumstances interfere with his system-building ambitions.

## FURTHER READING

Hampton, Jean, *Hobbes and the Social Contract Tradition* (Cambridge: Cambridge University Press, 1986).

Macpherson, C.B., *The Political Theory of Possessive Individualism: Hobbes to Locke* (Oxford: Oxford University Press, 1962).

Malcolm, Noel, 'A Summary Biography of Hobbes', in Tom Sorell (ed.), *The Cambridge Companion to Hobbes* (Cambridge: Cambridge University Press, 1996).

Oakeshott, Michael, 'Introduction', in Thomas Hobbes, *Leviathan* (Oxford: Basil Blackwell, 1946).

Skinner, Quentin, 'The Ideological Context of Hobbes's Political Thought', *Historical Journal*, 9 (1966), 286–317.

Sommerville, Johann P., *Thomas Hobbes: Political Ideas in Historical Context* (New York: St. Martin's Press, 1992).

Taylor, A. E., 'The Ethical Doctrine of Hobbes', *Philosophy*, 13 (1938), 406–24.

Tuck, Richard, *Hobbes.* (Oxford: Oxford University Press, 1989).

Warrender, Howard, *The Political Philosophy of Hobbes: His Theory of Obligation* (Oxford: Clarendon Press, 1957).

## NOTES

1. Ed. C. B. Macpherson (Harmondsworth: Penguin, 1968); references are to part, chapter, and page number.
2. John Plamenatz, *Man and Society: Political and Social Theory: Machiavelli through Rousseau*, vol. i (New York: McGraw-Hill, 1963), 147.
3. Brian Barry, 'Warrender and his Critics', in Maurice Cranston and Richard S. Peters (eds.), *Hobbes and Rousseau: A Collection of Critical Essays* (Garden City, NY: Anchor-Doubleday, 1972); Thomas Nagel, 'Hobbes's Concept of Obligation', *Philosophical Review*, 68 (1959), 68–83.
4. A. E. Taylor, 'The Ethical Doctrine of Hobbes', *Philosophy*, 13 (1938), 406–24.
5. Richard Peters, *Hobbes* (Harmondsworth: Penguin, 1956), ch. 7.
6. Leslie Stephen, *The English Utilitarians*, 3 vols. (New York: G. P. Putnam's Sons, 1900).
7. George Croom Robertson, *Hobbes* (Philadelphia: J. B. Lippincott, n.d.), 233.
8. Taylor, 'The Ethical Doctrine of Hobbes'.
9. Howard Warrender, *The Political Philosophy of Hobbes: His Theory of Obligation* (Oxford: Clarendon Press, 1957).
10. (Oxford: Oxford University Press, 1962).
11. Quentin Skinner, 'The Ideological Context of Hobbes's Political Thought', *Historical Journal*, 9 (1966), 286–317.
12. (Cambridge: Cambridge University Press, 1986).
13. David Gauthier, 'Hobbes's Social Contract', in G. A. J. Rogers and Alan Ryan (eds.), *Perspectives on Thomas Hobbes* (Oxford: Clarendon Press, 1988).
14. John Aubrey, 'The Brief Life', in Thomas Hobbes, *The Elements of Law, Natural and Politic*, ed. J. C. A. Gaskin (Oxford: Oxford University Press, 1994), 236; references to *The Elements of Law* are to chapter, section, and page number.
15. I am grateful to Roland Greene for this information. My thanks, too, to William Davie for his advice on a draft of this chapter.
16. *The Correspondence of Thomas Hobbes*, ed. Noel Malcolm (Oxford: Clarendon Press, 1994).
17. 'Considerations upon the Reputation, Loyalty, Manners, and Religion of Thomas Hobbes', in *The English Works of Thomas Hobbes*, ed. William Molesworth, vol. iv (London: John Bohn, 1840).
18. Hobbes, *De Cive: The English Version entitled in the first edition Philosophicall Rudiments Concerning Government and Society*, ed. Howard Warrender (Oxford: Clarendon Press, 1983); references are to chapter, section, and page number.
19. This is indicated in Thomas Hobbes, 'The Verse Life', in his *Elements of Law*, 259, which records that he 'finish'd' *Leviathan* after recovering from the serious illness.
20. Noel Malcolm, 'A Summary Biography of Hobbes', in Tom Sorell (ed.), *The Cambridge Companion to Hobbes* (Cambridge: Cambridge University Press, 1996), 31.
21. Aubrey, 'Brief Life', 236.
22. Michael Oakeshott, 'Thomas Hobbes', *Scrutiny*, 4 (1935), 275.

23. Bernard Gert, 'Hobbes and Psychological Egoism', *Journal of the History of Ideas*, 28 (1967), 509. See also F. S. McNeilly, 'Egoism in Hobbes', *Philosophical Quarterly*, 16 (1966), 193–206.
24. Hobbes, *Thomas White's 'De Mundo' Examined*, trans. Harold Whitmore Jones (London: Bradford University Press, 1976).
25. See Marchamont Nedham, *The Case of the Commonwealth of England, Stated*, ed. Philip A. Knachel (Charlottesville: University Press of Virginia, 1969), 129–30, 135–9.
26. Michael Oakeshott, 'Introduction', in Thomas Hobbes, *Leviathan* (Oxford: Basil Blackwell, 1946), lx–lxi.
27. Ibid., p. xv.

# 11 John Locke

Jeremy Waldron

**Contents**



## Chapter guide

This chapter discusses and defends the relevance of John Locke's writings *as political philosophy*. Because historical research by Peter Laslett, John Dunn, and others into the circumstances of the composition of Locke's major political writings has been so productive, it has become fashionable to play down the philosophical aspect of these writings and emphasize their function as pieces written for particular political occasions. I believe this is a mistake, and in the chapter that follows, I associate myself with those (like A. John Simmons, for example) who see the historical dimension more as a complement to, than as a substitute for, serious philosophical analysis. Locke's political philosophy continues to have an immense impact on the framing and the pursuit of liberal ideas in modern political thought—ideas about social contract, government by consent, natural law, equality, individual rights, civil disobedience, and private property. The discussion and application of Locke's arguments is thus an indispensable feature of political philosophy as it is practised today.

## Biography

The most important works of John Locke (1632–1704) were published in the decade following the Glorious Revolution of 1688. Before that, Locke's career had taken him from an established and respectable country family in Somerset, to a studentship in medicine at Christ Church, Oxford, to the household of the Whig politician and Exclusionist agitator Anthony Ashley Cooper, first Earl of Shaftesbury, and eventually into subversive intrigue and hasty exile in Holland during the reign of James II. Though a couple of early works are known from his Oxford days—*Essays on the Law of Nature* (1660) and *An Essay on Toleration* (1667)—Locke's mature political theory was developed during his time with Shaftesbury. Historical research has indicated that his most influential work, the *Two Treatises of Government*, may have been written as early as ten years before Locke deemed it safe to publish it and that therefore the position he adopts in this work is not, as it appears to be, an apology for a revolution that has succeeded but a call for a revolution to take place—a call that might easily have cost the author his life had it been published in the 1680s.

The year 1688 was a turning point for Locke: though some of his works were published anonymously, they soon acquired for him a very considerable reputation, and he enjoyed both political influence and minor political and administrative office (membership of the Board of Trade and Commission of Appeals) in the last fifteen years of his life. His *Essay Concerning Human Understanding* established him as perhaps the greatest philosopher of the age, and embroiled him in scientific disputes with Isaac Newton, and others, as well as providing a basis for his work on education. Locke's *Two Treatises of Government* were published anonymously in 1689, but their authorship soon became well known. His religious views—never orthodox—also embroiled him in dispute, both as a result of his work on toleration and in regard to his late work *On the Reasonableness of Christianity*, which defended a rather minimalistic characterization of Christian belief.

Locke's health was always delicate, and the strains of office and controversy, and the London climate, drove him to make a home in his final years with Sir Francis and Lady Masham (with the latter of whom he had some mild romantic as well as intellectual association) in Oates, Essex. He died there in 1704.

## Key texts

*A Letter Concerning Toleration* (1689)
*Two Treatises of Government* (1689)
*An Essay Concerning Human Understanding* (1690)
*Thoughts on Education* (1693)
*On the Reasonableness of Christianity* (1695)

## Main text used

*A Letter Concerning Toleration*, ed. J. H. Tuky (Indianapolis: Hackett, 1983).
*Two Treatises of Government*, ed. P. Laslett (Cambridge: Cambridge University Press, 1988).

## Key ideas

**Equality**: everyone in the state of nature is born equal, although there is some dispute over whether women were included in this conception. **Executive power of the law of nature**: no one has any right to exercise power over another and hence everyone has executive power in the state of nature. **Express and tacit consent**: the exercise of authority over one person by another can only be effected by consent, which may be explicit and overt, as in swearing an oath of allegiance, or it may be indicated by the mere fact that a person enjoys the protection of the laws of a country. **Liberty versus licence**: liberty is to act within the constraints of the natural law, whereas licence is to be motivated by passions and may be inimical to social life. **Mixing one's labour**: this is at the heart of

Locke's theory of property and differentiates him from the many theories that ground it in consent or first sighting. Mixing one's labour with something is a sign of appropriation and gives one title to the object, e.g. picking an apple. **Private property**: with the invention of money and the setting up of political society people are permitted unlimited accumulation of private property. **Natural rights**: we all possess natural rights in the state of nature, and they are independent of government. The aim of government is to protect our natural rights, including our natural right to property. **Political versus patriarchal power**: the purpose of the distinction is to undermine Sir Robert Filmer's derivation of political power from God's granting of patriarchal authority to Adam and his heirs. **Religious toleration**: Locke was quite radical in his views on toleration, but he did not extend it to Catholics or atheists because Catholics have a primary obligation to Rome, and atheists have no foundations for their promises and thus constitute a danger to the state. **Right to revolution**: Locke is an advocate of constitutional government, and if governments act outside the constitutional constraints imposed upon them, he advocates a right of resistance, the famous 'appeal to heaven'. **The social contract**: the social contract in Locke establishes political society (the state of nature is already social), and a second stage establishes the government. If the government falls, political or civil society remains, and by consent a new government can be instituted.

## Introduction: Locke as a liberal theorist

The political writings of John Locke offer the earliest example we have of a well-worked-out *liberal* political theory; and it is still one of the most influential. The stand that Locke took against political absolutism is the definitive starting point of modern liberal constitutionalism; and the positions he outlines on natural rights, limited government, religious toleration, executive accountability, and the rule of law are essential elements of modern liberal politics. Also his theory of private property rights has been very influential: although it inclines perhaps to one wing of the liberal tradition, it remains an indispensable point of reference in modern discussions of the topic.

Important as they are, however, it would be a mistake to identify the modern relevance of Locke's political theory with the mere fact that these Lockean positions are politically congenial to modern liberals. Nor is the importance of his work simply a matter of the historical interest of Locke's positions in relation to the politics of his time. Some historians have suggested that Locke's political theory is most interesting to us as the expression of a particular kind of late seventeenth-century sensibility, evoked primarily by political events in the 1670s and 1680s; and that it is of limited interest to us now apart from that. I believe they are wrong: the main interest of Locke's political writings for us, now, more than 300 years after their publication, is normative and theoretical, not just historical.

Locke constructed an elaborate and powerful body of argument, connecting a whole array of (what are now) familiar liberal positions with profound and difficult claims about human equality and natural law. His political and institutional arguments are predicated on the proposition that humans are really one another's equals so far as jurisdiction and authority are concerned; and that they are bound by principles of natural law to respect one another as right-bearers. In turn, these claims about natural rights and equality are defended on the basis of a deep and comprehensive conception of the human position in the world, its relation to God, and our capacity for reason and understanding. Since we today continue to accept the claim about equality and at least some version of the natural rights idea, but are unsure about both their grounds and their implications, we have every reason to pay attention to the analytic structure and direction of Locke's political arguments. In many respects Locke's way of doing political philosophy may be unfamiliar and disconcerting to our twenty-first-century ears—indeed, he acknowledged that some of his positions might seem 'very Strange' even to his seventeenth-century contemporaries (e.g. *Second Treatise*, para. 9[1])—but they are familiar enough in the problems they address and the premisses they elaborate to be read also as moves in current conversations about how best to ground a robust liberal politics.

## Locke's use of the social contract idea

Of Locke's *Two Treatises of Government*, the second has been the more important and influential. The first, which is incomplete, attempts a detailed refutation of the political theory of Sir Robert Filmer (1588–1653), which purported to vindicate monarchy as a patriarchal institution founded by God in an original donation to Adam.

Much of Locke's response in the *First Treatise* aims to show that the Old Testament does not in fact establish Adam and his heirs as the God-given rulers of the whole world. More generally—though this is something one has to pick out from his over-elaborate study of the biblical texts—Locke uses the *First Treatise* to dissociate Judaeo-Christian premisses from contemporary views about natural hierarchy. He rejects Filmer's position that 'there cannot be any Multitude of Men whatsoever, either great or small . . . but that in the same Multitude . . . there is one man amongst them, that in Nature hath a Right to be King of all the rest' (*First Treatise*, para. 104). And his arguments are particularly interesting in their critique of Filmer's view about the basis of sexual inequality. In general Locke was far from consistent on this issue: compare *Second Treatise*, para. 82). But in the *First Treatise*, at any rate, he is adamant that man and woman were both created in God's image, with Godlike intellectual powers (ibid., para. 30), and that neither Adam nor men generally have been singled out by God with any mark of natural authority over the rest of humanity.

The *Second Treatise* is more constructive in character, though Locke develops his argument with opposing political and theoretical conceptions clearly in view. His most consistent target is *political absolutism*, understood as the exercise of power unconstrained by law or by any procedures for settling disputes between rulers and ruled. Some, like Thomas Hobbes, have argued that, humans being what they are, absolute power is necessary to keep the peace between them. But Locke insists that the point of political institutions is 'to avoid, and remedy those inconveniences of the State of Nature, which necessarily follow from every Man's being Judge in his own case' (*Second Treatise*, para. 90). These 'inconveniences'—which include attempts at enslavement, unpredictable aggression, and a social atmosphere of miserable uncertainty—are not solved, he says, by subjecting *all but one person* in society to the rule of law. If the person exempted is the most powerful force in the society, then the rest will be worse off under his absolute power than they would be if they were left to the uncertain mercy of each other's judgement in a situation without government at all: 'he being in a much worse condition, who is exposed to the arbitrary power of one man, who has the command of 100,000, than he that is exposed to the arbitrary power of 100,000 single men' (ibid., para. 137).

In order to make this argument, Locke proceeds on the basis of a 'contractarian' approach to politics: he develops normative arguments about human law and political institutions based on an account of what the point of government is; and that functional account is based in turn on an ideal representation of government as an invention set up to ameliorate certain conditions that would obtain among human beings in its absence. Thus government in its ideal form is represented as performing certain functions; and this then provides a basis on which various actually existing forms of government may be rejected as dysfunctional. However, it is important to understand that liberal contractarianism is not the same as functionalism: it is a particular species of functionalism. The image of the social contract makes it particularly apparent that we are looking for the functionality of government in the benefits it confers *on individuals*: it is an individualized functionalism, not a functionalism of irreducible social value, for example. The prospect of benefit is represented as the motivation that individuals might perceive for agreeing to submit themselves to government, and to give up powers they would otherwise have (to decide for themselves how to cooperate with and respond to others in society). So an institution or practice that is detrimental to individual men and women (relative to what they might secure on their own without government) is illegitimate, 'for no rational creature can be supposed to change his condition with an intention to be worse' (ibid., para. 131).

This individualized functionalism does not require us to accept the story of the social contract as literally true: that is, we don't have to believe that once upon a time people lived in the state of nature and then, because of its difficulties, they got together and agreed in a social contract to set up institutions of government. Hypothetical contractarianism is enough to do a lot of the normative work of Locke's theory, particularly the negative normative work: he condemns absolutism and arbitrary discretion in government on the grounds that nobody in his right mind would agree to these things. Hypothetical contractarianism also provides a helpful model of Locke's argument about religion in *A Letter Concerning Toleration*. In that work Locke argues that the state has no business meddling in religious affairs or concerning itself with issues about worship or salvation. Part of his argument is that the means available to the state are incapable of producing the inner conviction without which religious practice is meaningless. This is pure negative functionalism, based on lack of means; it doesn't even require the individualism of the social contract. Part of his argument, though, is more individualized than this: no rational person, Locke says, would trust the salvation of his soul to a secular ruler, given how high the stakes are.

But Locke is not content to confine the social contract to this hypothetical role. As far as one can tell, he believes that the social contract story offers the most accurate and illuminating account of how government was actually invented. He does acknowledge that, to a superficial eye, the growth of political institutions seems to support the patriarchalism of Filmer: government, he says, seems to have grown out of the family, and 'the natural fathers of families, by an insensible change, became the politic monarchs of them too' (*Second Treatise*, para. 76).

But he believes that this gradualist political anthropology is best interpreted using the template of contractarianism. (The idea is that the social contract provides a useful set of categories for understanding what actually happened, not just a moral perspective for evaluating it.) Locke argues that, although in early times grown men and women may have submitted without fuss to the authority of a father or patriarch, they did so by implicit agreement rather than by recognizing an inherent patriarchal right, and they trusted the patriarch–monarch to rule them wisely and in the interests of them all. The difference between those early ages of mankind and the period in which the *Two Treatises of Government* were written is marked, he says, by a decline in political virtue (which Locke associates with the growth in material greed and ambition) and thus in the conditions that would enable people to proceed with a patriarchal monarchy founded in tacit agreement and implicit trust. Now everything had to be made explicit. People found they needed an articulate political theory which would emphasize the conditional and contractual basis of government. They needed a theory (like Locke's) that they could use as a public basis for figuring out new institutional arrangements and articulating express limitations and restraints on their rulers to 'prevent the abuses of that power, which they having intrusted in another's hands only for their own good, they found was made use of to hurt them' (*Second Treatise*, para. 111).

Two other aspects of Locke's political philosophy support the view that he believed in the literal not just the hypothetical application of the social contract idea. The first has to do with his theory of property. As we will see, Locke believes that property rights do not depend upon positive law for their existence, although positive law may be necessary for their effective protection. So, he thinks that there could be rights of private property in existence prior to the institution of government, and that if there were, the government would be morally constrained to respect them. Some political philosophers—again Thomas Hobbes is the best-known example—have denied this, even as a theoretical possibility. John Locke seems to believe, however, that it is not just a theoretical possibility, but a reality. There are natural property rights, and what they are and who has them depend on the literal occurrence of certain events and the time and the circumstances in which those events took place: at time *t*, person *X* mixed his labour with a piece of land, *L*, in circumstances *C*; therefore *X* is the owner of *L* beginning at *t*, and other people, including any government instituted to rule over *X* at a time subsequent to *t*, have an obligation to respect these rights. This argument will not work unless the property right is grounded in a literal occurrence. (It is not enough to say that a property right for *X* in *L might have been* created in this way.) And the argument will not work either unless the institution of the government supposedly constrained by this right is an actual event subsequent to the right's coming into existence. Otherwise it might reasonably be said, from the perspective of purely hypothetical contractarianism, that regulating the basis on which property rights come into existence is a task for government, and that government should not be thought of as constrained in that task by property rights whose institution has escaped its supervision.

The second reason for thinking that Locke's contractarianism is literal, not just hypothetical, has to do with its application to individuals. Locke believes that every human being is *born free*, subject only to natural law, absolved from the obligations of any social contract supposedly entered into by his parents or ancestors or fellow members of society. His account of each individual's political obligation (i.e. his obligation to obey human laws, to accept direction from the state, and to refrain from exercising what would otherwise be his own natural right to punish natural law offences) is based on that individual's agreement, 'nothing being able to put him into subjection to any earthly power, but only his own consent' (*Second Treatise*, para. 119). So even if one rejects the argument that governments were set up pursuant to an agreement among the people (albeit an implicit and inarticulate agreement) as a literal historical account, one still has to reckon with the 'born free' idea as a characterization of the initial position of each person. Of course it is also a moral characterization: to say that *X* is born free is to say that it is wrong for a ruler to treat *X* in certain ways without *X*'s consent and that *X* himself does no wrong in ignoring a ruler's commands until such time as he consents to that ruler's authority. But the fact that 'born free' is a *moral* characterization doesn't take it out of the realm of literal contract theory. The moral content is simply what flows from the literal facts about *X*, given the best moral theory that we have (natural law). And any change in what a given ruler is entitled to do to *X* or demand from *X* requires a very literal and quite specific change in *X*'s situation—namely, *X* giving his actual consent to *Y*'s rule.

It is sometimes thought that Locke waters down this literal contractarianism by acknowledging tacit consent rather than express consent as a basis for political obligation. (We have already seen the role that tacit consent plays in his political anthropology, i.e. in his explanation of why early forms of government were not, despite appearances, patriarchal.) He argues that the enjoyment of one's property under the state's protection may amount to tacit consent to the state's authority, and he suggests too that even the mere use of the highways or simply lodging at an inn might commit a person to political obedience. Locke's critics argue that this completely undermines his basic contention that political obligation is incurred voluntarily, for it seems there is virtually nothing that an inhabitant of a country can do without giving his allegiance to the rulers of that country. Such criticisms may be reasonable: but it is important to see that the idea of tacit consent does not affect the moral conclusions that Locke infers from the underlying contractarianism. A person who consents—or who is deemed to have consented—to the authority of some set of political institutions thereby acquires a reasonable expectation that those institutions will protect and promote his life, liberty, and property. Thus by his consent (whether it is tacit consent or express consent), he acquires not a blind obligation to obey, but standing in the community to evaluate and if need be criticize and resist the laws laid down in civil society. Consent brings one within the community that is entitled to scrutinize laws on this basis and hold lawmakers accountable; indeed, to take it one step further, consent brings one within the community that might lawfully raise a revolution against a corrupt, unjust, or incompetent ruler. Without consent, one would be entitled to resist such a ruler merely as a bandit might be resisted; with consent, however, one's resistance takes on the character of legitimate civic grievance, for one is now a member of 'the people' to whom Locke's theory accords a right *in extremis* to overthrow this particular ruler.

We need to remember also that the consent requirement doesn't settle anything about the legitimacy of any given law: consent doesn't make an unjust law right, nor does it preclude resistance or disobedience if the law is unjust. Here the importance of the inalienability of many Lockean natural rights becomes evident: an imputation of consent cannot excuse their violation. I want to go into more detail at the end of this chapter on Locke's theory of revolution and its relation to his views about constitutionalism and the rule of law. But before I do,

I want to indicate how what I have said so far is related to the philosophical and religious foundations of Locke's comprehensive liberal theory.

## Foundations: equality and natural law

The starting point of Locke's political philosophy is the claim that human beings are, by nature, one another's equals, so far as authority and rule are concerned. Because we are naturally one another's equals, no one may be put under the political authority of another except by his own consent (*Second Treatise*, para. 95). The premiss of equality, therefore, is key to the social contract theory and to everything which is built on it.

At the beginning of the *Second Treatise* Locke puts forward negative and affirmative versions of the claim about natural equality. On the one hand, he says God has not endowed anyone with any evident mark of natural superiority; and on the other hand, there seems to be a rough equality among us so far as our natural capacities are concerned. So far as the affirmative version of the claim is concerned, Locke gives the impression that natural equality is founded on humans' common membership of a single species—'there being nothing more evident, than that creatures of the same species . . . promiscuously born to all the same advantages of nature, and the use of the same faculties, should also be equal one amongst another without subordination or subjection'. But a *species*-based account of equality cannot be sustained for two reasons: first, it fails to explain why the equality of humans matters much more in Locke's scheme of things than the equality of co-members of other species; and secondly, it runs into immediate difficulties posed by Locke's own scepticism about species distinctions developed in book III of *An Essay Concerning Human Understanding*. Locke's discussion there makes it apparent that the basis of equality must be some capacity that we all share, rather than our alleged species membership itself.

The capacity that he emphasizes in the *Essay* as distinctive—and *importantly* distinctive—of the persons who engage in politics (as either putative subjects or would-be rulers) is the 'power of abstracting', the capacity to reason on the basis of general ideas. It is 'the having of general ideas', says Locke in book II of the *Essay*, that puts 'a perfect distinction betwixt man and brutes'. The argument for the significance of this capacity appears to be its connection to (what Locke thought of as) the human ability to reason to the existence of God. The understanding of ordinary men and women is far from perfect, but yet 'they have light enough to lead them to the knowledge of their Maker, and the sight of their own duties'. And Locke thinks that the fact that a being has this capacity shows that it is a creature with a special *moral* relation to God. As someone who knows or can find out about the existence of God and who is therefore in a position to answer responsibly to his commandments, this is someone whose existence has a special significance. Now, that specialness is a matter of intense interest, first and foremost of course to the person who has the relevant property. Knowing that he has been sent into the world by God, 'by his order, and about his business', the individual person has an interest in finding out pretty damned quick what he is supposed to do. But Locke believes this also affects the way we ought to deal with one another. When I catch a rabbit, I know that I am *not* dealing with a creature that has the capacity to abstract, and so I know that there is no question of this being one of God's special servants, sent into the world about his business, etc. But if I catch a human in full possession of his faculties, I know I should be careful how I deal with him. Because creatures capable of abstraction can be conceived as 'all the servants of one sovereign master, sent into the world by his order, and about his business', we must treat them as 'his property, whose workmanship they are, made to last during his, not one another's pleasure' (*Second Treatise*, para. 6), and refrain from destroying or harming or exploiting them.

What about intellectual differences above this threshold? Locke has been read by some commentators as arguing that differential rationality (among humans) entitles some to vastly different political power. This is thought to be the basis of his views about the natural subordination of women (though in fact, as we have already seen, Locke rejects any such basis for subordination in the *First Treatise*). And it is also thought to be the basis of his subordination of the labouring classes—'men who drudge all their lives in laborious trade . . . enslaved to the necessity of their mean condition, whose lives are worn out only in the provisions for living'. But even with regard to day-labourers, Locke denies that there is anyone who lacks the opportunity 'to think of his soul, and inform himself in matters of religion'. Thus even the meanest man can establish his status as someone with a special relation to God. (The Christian religion, he said in his late work *The Reasonableness of Christianity*, is 'a religion suited to vulgar capacities', and men can learn about equality and the ground of one another's preciousness on the same basis as the 'ignorant, but inspired fisherman' to whom the gospel was originally preached.) Moreover, Locke's political and epistemological writings are suffused with suspicion of the political pretensions that tend to be associated with intellectual abilities that rise above this threshold: the *Treatises* talk of the dangers attending the virtuoso exercise of intellectual powers, whereby 'the busy mind of man can carry him to a brutality below the level of the beasts' (*First Treatise*, para. 58), and book III of the *Essay* contrasts 'learned disputants' and 'all-knowing doctors' unfavourably with 'the unscholastic statesman' and 'the illiterate and contemned mechanic' to whom most improvements in human affairs can be attributed.

It is true that Locke's account of natural law is rationalistic. He rejects any innatist account of moral knowledge. Natural law is the law of reason, and it is reason that teaches us the basis of our duties to one another. Specifically, Locke believes that reason teaches us to have special respect for one another, not just as creatures of God—after all, rabbits are creatures of God too—but as creatures of God of whom it may plausibly be said (in virtue of their potential knowledge of God's existence) that they have been 'sent into the world by his order, and about his business . . . made to last during his, not one another's pleasure' (*Second Treatise*, para. 6). It is on this basis, Locke reckons, that we can figure out that 'Every one . . . is bound to preserve himself, and . . . by the like reason, when his own preservation comes not in competition, to preserve the rest of mankind, and may not . . . take away, or impair the life, or what tends to the preservation of the life, the liberty, health, limb, or goods of another' (ibid.).

Thus Locke's natural law commands certain duties to others. It commands negative duties not to attack or injure one another, and even positive duties—duties to preserve others (not leaving them for example to starve, if one has the resources to help them) so long as this does not prejudice one's own self-preservation. Even the priority of self-preservation has a moral edge for Locke. We tend to read it as a right. But it also has the character of a duty owed to God; it's a matter of stewardship. And so, considered as a right, it is *inalienable*: no one may give up his right to preserve his own life or subject himself to the arbitrary power of another. And so no theory of government may be predicated on the hypothesis that people have consented—again, expressly or tacitly—to their own enslavement or transferred their lives to a sovereign. The inalienability of certain natural rights is one of the crucial premisses of Locke's approach to politics.

## Property, economy, and disagreement

Modern commentators often say that Locke failed to elaborate his theory of natural law in any detail. I believe that is falsified by the presence in his *Second Treatise* of a sustained natural law argument about property.

Locke's views about private property are well known and controversial; in recent years they have attracted considerable discussion by virtue of their association with arguments set out in Robert Nozick's book *Anarchy, State and Utopia.*[2] Briefly, Locke believed that private property rights could be established unilaterally, by the initiative of hunters, gathers, or farmers, quite independently of positive law or social convention. Someone who transforms an object by labour acquires a right to it, Locke believed, and he may then transfer that right to another person by gift or sale, thus initiating a complex economy of natural property rights. The acquisition of such rights is governed by one or two conditions, or 'provisos' as they are sometimes called: the amount initially acquired must be related closely to the labour performed, the acquisition must not lead to waste, and my appropriation of resources must not drastically worsen the position of others. (Thus I cannot appropriate a whole territory, simply by turning a sod, in order to deny resources to everyone else.) Within these constraints, Locke believed that natural property rights form part of the natural law endowment which people bring to the state, or with which they confront the demands of positive law. And though it is entitled to regulate property, even naturally acquired property, the state is not entitled to confiscate it or redistribute it, unless that is necessary to ensure that the natural law constraints are respected.

From the point of view of Locke's theory of natural law, the important thing about these positions is that they are argued for, not just announced, in chapter v of the *Second Treatise.* The chapter, therefore, furnishes a fine example of Lockean natural law argumentation in a most difficult and important area. It shows us how Locke thought one might reason about natural law. And it also shows how he proposes to use and deploy the initial premiss of natural law equality with which the *Second Treatise* begins. For although his ostensible aim in the chapter is to justify 'disproportionate and unequal possession of the earth' (*Second Treatise,* para. 50), he does so in a way that claims to respect our status as equals. This makes his argument extremely interesting to us, because one of the features of our modern debates about property and social justice is that we too are interested in showing how something like a market order, with considerable disparities in people's access to and control of resources, nevertheless treats us as equals even if it does not command equal treatment or equal outcomes in any literal sense.

It follows from Locke's premiss of equality that the earth's bounty is initially made available by God for everyone's use (*Second Treatise*, paras. 25–6). No one has any original title in any resource, apart from his own body, that would exclude the right of other men: this is established in the *First Treatise* (paras. 29–30), where Locke rejects the idea of an original donation to Adam and his heirs exclusive of any other human. This is a view that Locke shared with his predecessors in the natural law tradition Grotius and Pufendorf. He rejected, however, their inference that the allocation of the benefit of this common heritage to individuals must be understood as a matter of convention. So far as individual use is concerned, it is evident that every man has a peremptory right 'to the use of those things, which were serviceable for his subsistence'. Indeed, in this regard, reason reinforces man's natural inclination:

> God having made Man . . . and furnished the world with things fit for food and raiment and other necessaries of life, subservient to his design, that man should live and abide for some time upon the face of the earth, and not that so curious and wonderful a piece of workmanship by its own negligence, or want of necessaries, should perish again, presently after a few moments continuance. (*First Treatise*, para. 86)

The right Locke talks about here is peremptory in the sense that it does not depend on anyone's consent—'If such a consent as that was necessary, man had starved, notwithstanding the plenty God had given him' (*Second Treatise*, para. 28)—and it remains in the background of Lockean political economy, always available (by virtue of its proximity to the foundations of Locke's natural law theory) to trump both naturally acquired private property rights and property rights established by positive law (*First Treatise*, para. 42).

Arguably the right to use resources is not itself a private property right, though Locke argues that it already involves a prototype of proprietary exclusion (*Second Treatise*, para. 28). Full private property is established in the first instance by labour, that is by productive actions that instil something of oneself in the animal, object, or piece of land that one has laboured upon. What I labour on, what I cultivate, 'hath by this labor, something annexed to it, that excludes the common right of other men' (ibid., para. 27). He supports this in a number of ways against those who might complain of an acquisition: sometimes he uses a version of the labour theory of value to show that the labour which generates entitlements (on his theory) creates almost all the value which property has, and sometimes he relies on the point that others have their own opportunity to create private property by labour, 'at least where there is enough, and as good, left in common for others' (ibid.). Eventually, of course, that last condition will fail, and all the usable natural resources—certainly all the land—will have been taken into private ownership. In that eventuality, the theory is buttressed by a claim that even the landless will prosper in an economy in which all the resources are in private hands. Certainly they will prosper by comparison with societies that have not organized themselves around private cultivation. Locke thought the clearest demonstration of this was aboriginal America, whose inhabitants are 'rich in land, and poor in all the comforts of life'. The native Americans, for want of improving their land by labour, 'have not one hundredth part of the conveniencies we enjoy: and a king of a large and fruitful territory there, feeds, lodges, and is clad worse than a day-labourer in England' (ibid., para. 41).

This attempt to show that everyone benefits is crucial to Locke's natural law argument for private property. Without it, there would be no way of defending property rights against the charge that they are prejudicial to the survival of some of God' special servants. Given his egalitarian premisses, Locke is in no position to be nonchalant about the possibility that property for some might mean deprivation for others. Indeed, as I said a moment ago, he is committed to the view that *in extremis* desperate poverty has a foundational, trumping right against property: charity, as he puts it, gives 'every man a title to so much out of another's plenty, as will keep him from extreme want, where he has no means to subsist otherwise' (*First Treatise*, para. 42). Commentators sometimes treat this as an anomalous insertion in the *First Treatise*, with little relevant to the argument about property in the *Second*. But it is unavoidable for Locke, given the basis on which his overall theory of natural law is established.

Though it claims, as we have seen, a rationalist natural law foundation, Locke's theory of property is quite controversial. Modern socialists deny his assumption that cultivation or other productive uses of God's bounty require private property. And the argument based on 'mixing one's labor' has seemed puzzling to many. In Locke's day the most controversial feature of his account—apart from his rejection of consent as a basis of property—was his argument against first occupancy theory. Both with regard to aboriginal modes of subsistence in America, and with regard to things like common grazing rights in England, this was seen (quite accurately) as Locke's taking the side of the colonist and the encloser, treating them as entitled unilaterally to brush aside immemorial practices of occupancy and common use simply because they did not answer to a particular intensive, individualistic, agricultural understanding of labour. Now, to say this is not necessarily to refute Locke's theory of property: he *was* taking sides for what he thought were perfectly good reasons on an issue that had to be resolved in any inquiry into the legitimacy of contemporary property. Nor is Locke necessarily wrong to think that this is something that should be raised and dealt with in natural law theory, for the considerations that he brings up—the importance of labour both to individuals and to the modern economy (*Second Treatise*, paras. 27 and 40–4), the improvement that it promises for everyone, even the worst off (ibid., para. 41), and the divine injunction to labour and be fruitful (ibid., para. 35)—are paradigmatic natural law considerations.

Still, the controversial nature of Locke's argument about property means that any realistic theory of politics must expect disagreement on this issue. Locke no doubt believes that he has figured out the truth of the matter, so far as natural law is concerned. But he acknowledges that in this respect, as in many others, his natural law conclusions will seem 'strange' to many (ibid., paras. 9, 40, and 180). The implication of this, of course, is that others will have reached opposite or contrary conclusions. And even though it is part of the logic of natural law reasoning that only one of these competing accounts can be true, still the political reality that a Lockean polity has to face is that there will in fact be rival theories held in good faith among the members of such a polity as to what the basis of property is, and therefore (on Locke's account) about how property-based constraints on government are to be conceived.

## Limited government, toleration, and the rule of law

This brings us back, finally, to the theory of limited government. I said earlier that Locke's political theory may be interpreted partly in terms of hypothetical contractarianism and partly in terms of a literal, historical social contract argument. Thus some of what he says against absolutism has the character of 'No individual would have agreed to that', and some of what he says has the character of 'Individuals actually entered into political society to protect particular property rights which they actually held'. He relies on both strategies to establish that the supreme power in a political society cannot be regarded as absolute—that it must be understood as subject to certain limits or constraints based on natural law and the natural rights of individuals.

So far as the latter kind of argument is concerned, the argument is deceptively simple:

> The supreme power cannot take from any man any part of his property without his own consent: for the preservation of property being the end of government, and that for which men enter into society, it necessarily supposes and requires, that the people should have property, without which they must be supposed to lose that, by entering into society, which was the end for which they entered into it; too gross an absurdity for any man to own. (*Second Treatise*, para. 138)

The difficulty arises, as we have seen, because the members of a society are likely to disagree about the natural law basis of property (assuming they even accept the idea that actual property rights can be based on natural law); or if they accept the broad outlines of a particular theory of property like Locke's, they may well disagree about its application, particularly so far as the conditions or provisos are concerned.

How are we to think, then, about the proposition that the legislature is bound to respect natural property rights in the light of this disagreement? One point can be established immediately. When the legislature makes law on any issue affecting property, it must do so with an awareness that property is an area in which there are pre-existing rights—an awareness that it would be wrong to legislate without paying attention to the question of what those pre-existing rights are (lest the legislation that is enacted encroach on them). So much follows from the form of the Lockean approach. Then the question is whether we are to think of this issue—of what the natural rights of property are—as something on which it is appropriate for the *legislature* to arrive at a common view. I think it is undeniable that the Lockean legislature has this responsibility. People are tempted to deny it, because they know Locke thought the legislature should be constrained by natural property rights, and they ask, 'How could the legislature be constrained, if the legislature itself is determining what the natural rights are?' But the legislature may have this responsibility without thinking that its determinations are, by definition, correct; it may shoulder this responsibility in an objectivist and thus fallibilist sprit. And we must ask what the alternatives are. One alternative is that the issue is entrusted to a non-legislative body—a supreme court, for example. But this alternative would merely reproduce the difficulty—for natural law must surely be supposed to bind such a non-legislative institution as well. Anyway Locke, we know, insisted on the supremacy of the legislature in civil society (*Second Treatise*, para. 149), in large part because he believed that the most fundamental issues that a society had to address should be addressed in a large representative body, rather than a small oligarchy or junta (ibid., para. 94).

The other alternative is for this to remain a matter of individual determination, with each person figuring as best he can what the natural rights of property are and thus what constraints the legislature should be held to. In the end, I guess, it comes down to that, for, as Locke acknowledges (ibid., paras. 222ff.), if the people (or any segment of them) believe sincerely that the legislature has betrayed its trust in this regard and the legislators sincerely deny this, there is no judge on earth who can determine the issue between them. But if it were purely a matter of individual reasoning, the result would be that almost every legislative initiative would be vulnerable to the idiosyncrasies (not to mention biases and misapplications) of the natural law reasoning of each person. We must remember here that natural law is not given or innate, according to Locke; it appears on earth only as a result of people's reasoning, and that reasoning must take place in real time and it is vulnerable like all reasoning to various vicissitudes.

> For the law of nature being unwritten, and so no where to be found but in the minds of men, they who through passion or interest shall miscite, or misapply it, cannot so easily be convinced of their mistake where there is no established judge: and so it serves not, as it ought, to determine the rights, and fence the properties of those that live under it. (ibid., para. 136)

The move from the state of nature to civil society is supposed to ameliorate this predicament at least to some extent. For that reason, then, I don't think Locke can plausibly be read as denying that, once we set up a legislature, we should treat it as a place in which we do natural law reasoning together. One of the things that Lockean legislators are supposed to do is attempt as honestly as they can (by reasoning together) to work out whether various proposals before them are in line with what natural law requires. To the extent that members of the society disagree about this—to the extent that natural law is controversial—legislation just *is* the adjudication of those controversies.

Now of course the legislature may get it wrong: that's the upshot of the objectivity of natural law. But what we must not say—what Locke is not entitled to say—is that the legislature can be actually constrained by the truth about natural law rights of property. Of course, it *ought to be* constrained by the truth. But it will only (and at most) ever in fact be constrained by somebody's determination of what the truth is: either the legislator's collective determination, or the determination of some other institution or official, or the determination of individuals either singly or en masse acting to criticize or resist its impositions. No amount of solemn invocation of *the idea* of natural law constraints can ever obviate the fact that natural law truths only ever appear on earth and in politically effective terms as fallible human opinions.

The difficulty about property points up a more general limit on the effectiveness of Locke's constitutionalism and his commitment to the rule of law. Locke insists that the prerogative authority must be exercised by executive officials in accordance with law or, in emergencies, 'for the public good' (ibid., paras. 160 ff.). But he acknowledges that if there is disagreement between the executive and the legislature or between the government and the people as to whether this criterion is satisfied, the issue cannot be settled by any institutional means, and if the parties persevere in the disagreement and it matters enough to them, the issue can only be resolved by fighting:

> though the people cannot be judge, so as to have, by the constitution of that society, any superior power, to determine and give effective sentence in the case; yet they have, by a law antecedent and paramount to all positive laws of men, reserved that ultimate determination to themselves which belongs to all mankind, where there lies no appeal on earth, viz. to judge, whether they have just cause to make their appeal to heaven. (ibid., para. 168)

The same is true of cases where it is alleged that the supreme power—the prince, say, or the legislature—has broken the law, or violated the terms of the political society's constitution. Locke is a great theorist of the rule of law, and what I have called his hypothetical contractarianism involves an insistence on the need for 'settled, standing laws', without which people are no better off under government than they would be without it (ibid., paras. 136–7). Indeed if they were ruled by a prince's 'extemporary arbitrary decrees', they would be in effect 'in a far worse condition than in the state of nature'; it would be like being in the state of nature having 'armed one, or a few men with the joint power of a multitude, to force them to obey at pleasure the exorbitant and unlimited decrees of their sudden thoughts, or unrestrained, and till that moment unknown wills, without having any measures set down which may guide and justify their actions' (ibid., para. 137). But Locke also wants to go further than this. It is not enough that the people be ruled by settled, standing laws; he thinks it is also important that their rulers be subject to those laws as well. Otherwise, as he puts it, the peace and predictability for civil society is just like the peace and predictability of the farmyard, where the farmer keeps the animals from harming each other, but provides them with no assurance against his own depredations (ibid., para. 93).

Now Thomas Hobbes, notoriously, had argued in *Leviathan* that it is impossible to hold the supreme power (or sovereign) of any political society to obedience to its laws, because *ex hypothesi* there is no greater power in the society to adjudicate disputes that may break out between sovereign and subject as to whether the law has actually been broken. Locke's argument about the rule of law is commonly taken as an answer to or a refutation of Hobbes's position. (Whether it was actually intended as such, or whether it was directed instead at views of Robert Filmer, which in this regard were remarkably similar to Hobbes's, is something we can leave for the historians to decide.) *But it is not an answer at all.* Hobbes said that if there is disagreement between sovereign and subject or between subject and subject as to whether the sovereign has broken the law, the matter will have to be settled by fighting. And Locke did not deny that. He was unable to come up with any institutional solution to the dilemma Hobbes had posed: either the matter is settled by an earthly institution, in which case the problem is reproduced when someone accuses *that* institution of breaking the law; or it is settled outside the political framework, by 'an appeal to heaven', i.e. by fighting. The only differences in this regard between Locke and Hobbes have to do with the value of preserving the practice of accusing the sovereign of breaking the laws, and the estimation of social dangers associated with it. According to Locke, the practice is an important one and a society is better off if its members regard it as legitimate (on natural law grounds), even though it leads ultimately to an 'appeal to heaven'. Hobbes denies his: he thinks a society can function only if this sort of accusation is widely regarded as inappropriate. Hobbes believes that the opinion 'that he that hath the sovereign power, is subject to the civil laws' will lead to the dissolution of the commonwealth: for it will expose it to the constant threat of civil war. Locke, by contrast, argues that we should not be panicked out of this opinion. Certainly the risk of violence is real, and Locke has no way of denying it. Instead he insists that sometimes, certainly in extreme cases, resistance, even revolution, with all the disruption that it brings, is the lesser evil: 'Which is best for mankind, that the people should be always exposed to the boundless will of tyranny, or that the rulers should be sometimes liable to be opposed, when they grow exorbitant in the use of their power . . . '.

In addition, he develops a complex (and often misunderstood) argument to the effect that the risk of violence—from the practice of accusing the ruler of breaking the laws—is not at all proportional to the good that the practice may do in a well-ordered society. The presence of this practice in a political culture will itself have a restraining effect. But the practice will lead to fighting in far fewer cases than a literal application of it might lead one to believe. The natural caution and conservatism of most people will mean that these issues will usually be settled without fighting. Either the ruler will find it prudent to pull back from the brink of a confrontation of this kind, accepting *pro tanto* the normative force of the rule of law; or the sense of grievance will die down among the people, when the ruler's wrongdoing has impacted only a few. Some commentators have tried to read that latter point as a normative condition, as though Locke thought it would wrong to resist an unlawful exercise of authority 'if it reach no farther than some private men's cases' (*Second Treatise*, para. 208). But that's not what Locke says at all. His argument at this point is about social contingency, not normative principle. He is trying to show—as against a fearful view like Hobbes's—that the risks implicit in holding rulers accountable for breaches of law are risks worth running. He has not solved the Hobbesian conundrum, but he has made perhaps the best response to it, on contingent grounds of social realism, that one could reasonably expect.

In the *Letter Concerning Toleration* Locke makes a similar argument about the possibility of disagreement between the people and their government about the latter's encroachment on religious matters. Locke's basic position in the *Letter* is that the state has no business in the realm of religious belief, in part because the tools of government are ineffective in this matter (belief cannot be coerced), in part because no one consenting to government would possibly think it safe to trust the magistrate with the salvation of his soul, and in part because people are not harmed by one another's religious beliefs and practices. But this last position admits of a number of exceptions. First, the fact that the basic premisses of Locke's account are organized around a religiously defended conception of natural law and human equality means that atheism cannot be tolerated. Secondly, aspects of religious practice may become legitimate targets for state action if the latter is undertaken for secular reasons: animal sacrifice may not be prohibited, but animal slaughter (for both religious or non-religious reasons) may be prohibited on economic or public health grounds. Now Locke acknowledges that there is room for disagreement here: 'what if the magistrate believe that he has a right to make such laws and that they are for the public good, and his subjects believe the contrary?'[3] Once again, there is no choice but passive submission or 'an appeal to heaven'. This may seem unsatisfactory, and Locke acknowledges that his theory has no capacity to ensure a proper solution: 'I only know what usually happens where controversies arise without a judge to determine them. You will say, then, the magistrate being the stronger will have his will and carry his point. Without doubt; but the question is not here concerning the doubtfulness of the event, but the rule of right.' This, I think, is a startlingly honest conclusion, the more so because it is not coupled with any assurance that the aggrieved subject actually is in the right. He may be wrong or the magistrate may be more powerful. There is an objective truth, but no guarantee that either side has hold of it, or that it will necessarily prevail even if they do.

## Conclusion: Locke's legacy

For many people Locke's legacy consists in the array of Lockean positions that we modern liberals are also inclined to: the rule of law, religious toleration, government by consent, and a moderate commitment to markets and private property. And for some his legacy consists in certain commitments which we have read back into his work, but which in reality Locke did not really develop at all. For example, he motioned towards the constitutional principle of the separation of powers, but he did not develop it in anything like the detail that we find in Montesquieu, for example, or *The Federalist Papers*. And though his political theory is democratic in spirit, Locke was by no means committed to political democracy as a matter of principle: his views on the franchise are the subject of continuing controversy, and the only clear position he held was that it would be prudent for a society to establish an assembly of part-time representatives as its supreme legislature (*Second Treatise*, para. 94). In the end his real contribution to these issues and to the ones we have discussed is his clear perception of what was at stake in the political and philosophical arguments surrounding them. Locke did not develop a complete or watertight theory of politics; but he developed a profound and convincing political philosophy—by which I mean a foundation in thought for approaching and reflecting upon the real problems of right, equality, objectivity, and power in politics.

## FURTHER READING


Ashcraft, Richard, *Revolutionary Politics and Locke's 'Two Treatises of Government'* (Princeton: Princeton University Press, 1986).

Dunn, John, *The Political Thought of John Locke: An Historical Account of the Argument of the 'Two Treatises of Government'* (Cambridge: Cambridge University Press, 1969).

Marshall, John, *John Locke: Resistance, Religion and Responsibility* (Cambridge: Cambridge University Press, 1994).

Simmons, A. John, *The Lockean Theory of Rights* (Princeton: Princeton University Press, 1992).

Simmons, A. John, *On the Edge of Anarchy: Locke, Consent, and the Limits of Society* (Princeton: Princeton University Press, 1993).

Tully, James, *A Discourse on Property: John Locke and his Adversaries* (Cambridge: Cambridge University Press, 1980).

Waldron, Jeremy, *God, Locke, and Equality: Christian Foundations of John Locke's Political Thought* (Cambridge: Cambridge University Press, 2002).


## NOTES

1. Locke, *Two Treatises of Government*, ed. P. Laslett (Cambridge: Cambridge University Press, 1988); 17th-century spelling and capitalization has been modernized.
2. (New York: Basic Books, 1974).
3. Locke, *A Letter Concerning Toleration*, ed. J. H. Tully (Indianapolis: Hackett, 1983), 49.

# 12 Hume

Paul Kelly

## Contents



## Chapter guide

Although his contemporary reputation was based on his six-volume *History of England*, Hume's subsequent reputation has grown into that of one of the most important political thinkers of the eighteenth century and certainly one of the greatest philosophers of the European Enlightenment. He is credited as a major influence on the development of conservative ideology and a significant precursor of utilitarianism. His influence can be seen in the ideas of Burke. Jeremy Bentham saw his own utilitarianism as a development of Hume's philosophical enterprise and Immanuel Kant famously credits Hume with rousing him from his own 'dogmatic slumbers'. Hume's great philosophical achievement is as a relentless and unforgiving critic. Unlike Kant or Hegel he is not a great systematizer. However, his negative critical thinking was acutely important for his whole project. He is both a sceptical philosopher and a common-sense moralist and political theorist. In drawing sceptical conclusions from the prevailing empiricist theory of knowledge associated with his English predecessor John Locke, he was not merely trying to point out logical problems with the theory to replace it with his own preferred metaphysics. Instead he is concerned to point out the limits of reason. By doing so he wished to undermine the claims of the natural law, natural rights, and contract theories, and their possible use as an ideology of radical reform. In place of reason he offers an account of morality 'naturalized', that is rooted in the passions. Our moral motivation and the explanation of the origin of political institutions are based on an account of human interest rather than human reason. This new 'naturalistic' approach to the explanation and justification marks the final rupture with traditional natural law theory and paved the way for the utilitarianism of Bentham and Mill. At the same time it provided for the conservative emphasis on the legitimacy of received traditions and practices because they have evolved to serve human purposes.

This chapter will commence with an account of Hume's theory of knowledge and associationist psychology. It will trace the implications of this approach for the account of moral judgement and motivation, especially focusing on the distinction between natural and artificial virtue. This will lead on to a discussion of the rise of the conventions of justice, property, and promise-keeping and Hume's account of government. There will follow a short discussion of Hume's relationship with utilitarianism. The chapter will conclude with an assessment of his significant and often contradictory legacy.

## Biography

The Scottish philosopher, historian, and essayist David Hume was born into a strict Presbyterian family in 1711. After an early education at Edinburgh University and an attempt to study for a legal career Hume retreated to La Flèche in France to devote himself to carving out a literary reputation. The result was *A Treatise of Human Nature*, composed when he was only 26. Despite its subsequent significance the book fell 'still born from the press'. Following this initial failure and his subsequent failure to obtain university professorships at either Edinburgh or Glasgow University on grounds of (rightly) suspected atheism, Hume rewrote the argument of the *Treatise* in two works subsequently published as *An Enquiry Concerning Human Understanding* and *An Enquiry Concerning the Principles of Morals*. His subsequent philosophical reputation was built on these works although they also were not initially a great success. Having failed to establish his reputation with his philosophical works, Hume turned to writing short essays. These essays include some devastating critical works on natural religion. He then turned his attention to the writing of history. His six-volume *History of England* was written while librarian to the Faculty of Advocates in Edinburgh. It was a huge success and finally made his reputation and secured his financial position. After this success Hume lived shortly in Paris and became a darling of the salons. It was here that he met and commenced his stormy and thankless relationship with Rousseau. Towards the end of his life he filled a minor government position in London. His early death as a result of bowel disease was faced with stoic resignation and cheerfulness, giving rise to his reputation as a secular saint. He died as he had lived, convinced in his atheism and cheerfully without the comforts of religion.

## Key texts

*Enquiries Concerning Human Understanding and Concerning the Principles of Morals*, 3rd edn. rev. P. H. Nidditch (Oxford: Clarendon Press, 1979).

*A History of England*, 6 vols. (Indianapolis: Liberty Fund, 1983).

*A Treatise of Human Nature*, 2nd edn. rev. P. H. Nidditch (Oxford: Clarendon Press, 1978).

## Key ideas

**Impressions**: these are the immediate consequences of perception; they are the experiences we have when we see, hear, touch, or taste objects and their properties in the material world. **Ideas** are the 'imprints' that impressions leave on the human mind. Our ideas are the result of impressions and are used in all cognitive processes. **Passions**: if our cognitive and intellectual processes are confined to ideas and their relations, the source of all our actions and motivations are the passions. The passions include all those natural, non-intellectual sources of motivation such as fear, shame, love, sympathy, and anger. **Conventions**: those informal rules that emerge through the recognition of common interests and mutual advantage. **Artificial virtues** such as justice and promise-keeping depend for their existence on institutions that are created to meet human purposes such as the system of private property. In the absence of these institutions we would have no reasons to act in accordance with the dictates of justice or in accordance with promises.

## Introduction

Although born in Scotland, Hume was a 'British' political theorist who identified very much with the Union of 1707. The temper of his writings reflect a commitment to the stability and security that the Union was supposed to provide. Hume's philosophy and political theory is best characterized as an anti-enthusiastic, tolerant, and humane conservatism. The object of conservation is the new social and political arrangements made possible by the Union. Not prone to elevate the genius of received traditions of behaviour or beliefs, Hume was a sceptic and an atheist when it came to religion, but he was equally critical of the aspirations of many radical Enlightenment thinkers who wished to sweep away all that had gone before. Hume's modest and cautious conservatism is directed at both the religious and political enthusiast and the arch-traditionalist. He was both an Enlightenment thinker and a critic of Enlightenment hubris; that is, the idea that power of human reason can reconstruct the world in a more rational, benign, and perfect fashion. The problem with such views is that they tend to mask sectional political interests in the guise of the onward march of reason and truth.

The key to understanding both Hume's critical and constructive philosophy is to see it as an attempt to rein in the pretensions of reason and philosophy. Hume begins by following John Locke in trying to construct certain knowledge on the basis of experience alone. But when this is shown to lead to sceptical conclusions, Hume draws the important implication that this indicates not merely a limitation of a philosophical theory, but rather a limitation of reason itself. It is on the basis of this limited view of the role of reason that he is able to seek an account of moral and political concepts, motives, and practices in the non-rational aspects of the human psyche. The philosophical naturalism made possible by the assault on reason transforms the terms of political theory, but at the same time—and this was Hume's intention—it left everything unchanged. It is this view that a radical philosophy could give rise to a conservative 'common-sense' moral and political theory that makes Hume so interesting to those who reject many of his philosophical beliefs and positions. To understand Hume's moral and political theory we have to start with his assault on reason and in particular his account of knowledge and experience.

## Experience and knowledge

Historians of philosophy tend to place Hume alongside John Locke as one of the three great British Empiricists (the other being Bishop Berkeley). Historians of political thought emphasize the difference between Hume's naturalistic conventionalism and Locke's contractarianism and theory of original natural rights. In terms of philosophical psychology, Hume is a disciple of Locke, but in terms of political theory he could scarcely be more different. John Locke had hoped to provide a secure epistemological foundation for his natural rights theory on the basis of his empiricist 'way of ideas'. He proposed to show that all our ideas and all the contents of consciousness are derived from experience. From this he hoped to build up a picture of human knowledge that would lead from simple sense-experience to complex moral ideas such as the law of nature.

Hume also starts with empiricist psychology, but he drew the opposite conclusions from Locke. Empiricists believe that all our ideas are based in sense-experience, and Hume is an empiricist. He begins his *Treatise of Human Nature* by claiming that the contents of the mind resolve themselves into either ideas or impressions. Impressions are the direct deliverance of the senses—experiences such as hot, cold, red, yellow, loud, remote, sticky, etc. Hume's choice of name for these perceptions emphasizes the decidedly physical way in which the world impacts upon the human mind. Mind is clearly an organ that can be pressed upon rather like a ball of soft wax. These direct deliverances or impressions leave marks on the mind, and it is these that Hume terms 'ideas'. Ideas are the faint traces left by direct impressions. We can have no idea of red without some impression or perception of a red thing, an apple or tomato or sunset. All the ideas that form the content of human consciousness are derived in this way. In contrast to philosophical rationalism, Hume's empiricism leaves no room for a priori knowledge; that is, ideas that precede experience. Even the abstract ideas of mathematics ultimately have their origin in experience. Ideas are the stuff of thought and reasoning, whereas impressions are the direct deliverance of experience either of the external world or of the imagination and passions. Both ideas and impressions can be distinguished as simple or complex. A simple idea cannot be resolved into a more basic idea or impression. The idea of red is simple, as is the impression of red. However, the idea of a golden mountain or a red apple is complex in that it can be broken down into simpler ideas, such as large, rock, gold, mountain, etc.

The crucial lesson that Hume wishes to draw out from his adoption of the empiricist 'way of ideas' is where it leaves the role of reason. Reason is clearly a second-order capacity that depends upon the prior capacity of sensation, emotion, and passion. Reasoning does not generate ideas and therefore knowledge; it merely establishes relations between ideas that have their origins in experience. The clear implication of this position is that we cannot have knowledge of that which cannot be found in human experience. This is a dramatic enough conclusion in that it already calls into question some of the claims on which traditional natural law theories of morality depend, as Locke himself found in attempting to ground his natural law theory in the 'way of ideas'. But Hume draws particularly sceptical conclusions from this argument, which undermine the very possibility of an empiricist metaphysics.

All claims to knowledge about the world involve the justification and combination of beliefs that are in turn composed of complexes of ideas derived from experience. But not all our claims to knowledge are mere reports about experience such as 'That cat is on that mat'.

Instead in the process of reasoning we attempt to construct beliefs about things which we are not currently experiencing. If we see a film of a forest fire, we infer that the flames we see signify great heat, although we cannot feel the heat. The connection between the flames we see on the film and the heat we infer is provided by the idea of causation. We reason that the fire (shown by the presence of the flames) causes heat and therefore reason to the belief that the forest fire was hot even though we do not experience the heat. The belief depends upon the causal connection between flames and heat. But where does the idea of causation come from? Reason uses the idea of causation; it does not create it, as reason is not a source of ideas. But if reason does not create the idea of cause, where does it come from? Experience only delivers the idea of the constant conjunction of events, not an experience of cause. We cannot infer from the constant conjunction of events that flames always signify heat as our experience, however broad, will always be limited—it is not logically impossible that there could be cool flames. To infer that flames always signify heat we would need to presuppose the uniformity of nature, but our experience cannot warrant that inference. We cannot deduce the idea of the uniformity of nature because we can always envisage experiences that do not support the connection. Probabilistic reasoning also cannot support a claim to knowledge, as it too must rely on the uniformity of experience, and no matter what we have experienced in the past we cannot rule out the possibility of contrary experiences in the future.

Hume's scepticism about causation has complex and far-reaching consequences, not least of which is that it undermines one of the major arguments for the existence of God and therefore the natural theology which is a key premiss of rationalistic natural law theories. We cannot infer from the order we currently experience in the universe anything about its law-governed status or the origins of those laws. If we cannot claim certainty for the idea of a law-governed universe in the natural sciences, how much more difficult will it be to claim that the universe is regulated by moral laws?

How far are we expected to take Hume's scepticism? Common sense tells us we cannot do without causal reasoning. If we take Hume's conclusions too seriously, we would be unable to go about our daily business. But Hume does not intend that we live his scepticism. Indeed, if we look at his account of the grounds for our beliefs about causation, we can see that we cannot live this scepticism. Hume argues that the basis for our beliefs about the causal association of fire and heat is not an inference of reason but an association of ideas in the imagination. Habit will establish that this connection is simply a fact about how the human mind works. Whatever our doubts about reason, we just cannot help making this connection—it is a fact about human psychology rather than of logic or reason. What Hume does in effect is to use the empiricist 'way of ideas' against itself and against philosophical rationalism to deflate the pretensions of philosophy and claims for human reason that are based on such philosophical theories. The world does not change as a result of Hume's conclusions: fires still burn, apples drop from trees, and humans cannot help thinking that what goes up must come down! The only thing that has changed is the pretensions of philosophy to provide us with new knowledge beyond the bounds of experience, habit, and common sense. Deflating philosophy leaves the way open to a naturalistic or experience-based science of man, one that explains moral and political values and principles in terms of human psychology and interest rather than in terms of some external and abstract conceptions of human nature based on 'philosophy' as opposed to experience. In the remainder of this chapter we shall see how

Hume builds a naturalistic theory of morality on the ground now clear of philosophical rationalism.

## Facts and values

Before turning to the details of Hume's moral and political theory there remains one further implication of his assault on philosophical rationalism and the empiricist 'way of ideas' which has direct bearing on his moral and political theory. One of the central claims of Hume's epistemology is that all our ideas are derived from sense-experience and we can only know what can be experienced—and even *that* with only limited certainty or probability. Furthermore, the power of reason is restricted to matters of the relation between ideas, matters of fact, and number. It is not a source of ideas, for, as we have seen, ideas are based on experience or sensation. Either moral beliefs must be based on experience of external moral properties or they must be derived from some other source. Are moral distinctions and properties like matters of fact about the world? Hume suggests that, if moral distinctions were derived from experience of the external world, they would be like other ideas derived from experience. But moral distinctions are not like other ideas or impressions in that they do not have the same relation to action. Judgements about the redness of an apple leave one wholly indifferent to judgements about its value, goodness, or desirability. The concept of truth, Hume argues, applies only to the relations between ideas or between ideas and real existence; it does not move us to judgements of praise or blame in the way that moral distinctions do. So moral distinctions, judgements, and values are not like judgements of matters of fact or the relations between ideas. Whatever underpins moral distinctions is not merely matters of fact. This brings us back to the question of the origin of moral distinctions. Hume's argument thus far has been about the limitation of reason. Reason does not generate ideas or original impressions. But in making this case Hume is opening up the terrain for the introduction of one of the most original features of his argument, namely the significance of the non-rational parts of the human psyche. The second book of the *Treatise* is devoted to a discussion of the passions, and it is these non-rational original sources of action and belief that Hume relies on to build his account of moral distinctions and ultimately his political theory.

This reliance on the passions transforms Hume's account of moral distinctions from things that are the deliverance of reason to things that are more properly felt; they are original sensations complete in themselves and are prior to reason. Their completeness derives from the fact that they are feelings or original sensations that do not refer to or reflect objects beyond themselves, in the way that judgements about redness or heat do. The core moral distinctions for Hume are praise and blame; these are clearly sentiments or feelings. The long, detailed analysis of the passions in book II of the *Treatise* is a seminal contribution to the history of moral philosophy, as it marks one of the most dramatic attempts to provide a purely naturalistic account of moral distinctions and sentiments. From this part of Hume's theory originates much of the subsequent development of moral philosophy in the English-speaking world, with its focus on the analysis of moral terms, and the explanation of moral motivation in terms of desire, interest, or the sensation of pleasure or pain. Much subsequent moral philosophy or meta-ethics either has proceeded on the basis of the truth of Hume's categorical distinction between matters of fact and value, or has been concerned with undermining that distinction. Whatever view one takes of Hume's distinction, it has transformed subsequent thinking about moral and political theory.

## Moral judgement

As we have seen, Hume's assault on moral reason does not leave us with nihilism—a cold Godless and valueless world in which anything goes. For Hume, this does not follow. Although reason might leave me indifferent to the plight of a suffering child experienced on the wayside, sympathy and the passions do not. For Hume, non-rational nature provides for values and saves the day. It is precisely in this way that his assault on reason leaves everything as it is. We can give an account of the origin and normative force (that which makes us act or feel obligated) of our moral judgements without recourse to elaborate theories of moral sense, rational intuition, or the existence of natural normative laws.

Hume's follows the example of his near contemporary Francis Hutcheson (1694–1746) in drawing a close connection between morality and aesthetics. Morality is concerned with judgements of pleasure and pain. When we judge a work of art beautiful, we derive a certain sort of pleasure from it. The task of aesthetics or criticism is to explain the complex of ideas associated with that feeling, but it is the feeling that gives rise to the judgement. Similarly, in morality we are concerned primarily with judgements of praise or blame (*Treatise*, III. i. 1[1]). When we experience an example of suffering, we feel the pain of sympathy for that person in our non-rational nature, and it is this that leads to the judgement of blame. When we see actions derived from the good character of a person, we experience pleasure, and again it is this that explains the judgement of praise. Crucial to Hume's account of moral judgement are the concepts of pleasure and pain. This has often lead to simplistic accounts of Hume as a utilitarian. This is misleading. Whatever relationship Hume has to the subsequent development of utilitarianism, he is not using pleasure and pain to give meaning to moral concepts as Jeremy Bentham does; rather he uses these concepts to *explain* moral judgements. For this reason Hume is called a non-cognitivist, in that moral judgements and values originate not in reason or our cognitive capacity but in the passions. Passions may be judged wise or foolish, praise-worthy of blameworthy, but not true or false. A sentiment, however blameworthy, is always true. Consequently, the man who fails to judge the suffering of the innocent child at the wayside as blameworthy does not fail in the exercise of reason; his defect is not in the capacity to reason but in the capacity to feel sympathy for another's suffering.

One further feature of Hume's account of moral judgement that should be noted is that the object of judgement is not states of affairs but virtues of character. If we look at the above example of the suffering child, Hume's focus is on the character of the observer who shows a lack of sympathy at human suffering, and not the state of affairs itself. After all, the child's suffering might well be the result of blameworthy actions of others, but equally it might be the result of some natural tragedy. Hume wishes to reserve the concepts of moral approbation or praise for virtues of character rather than states of affairs. One explanation of this is that we ordinarily distinguish between the suffering caused by a bad man and that caused by a bad storm, although in terms of suffering caused the latter might outweigh the former. Similarly, if we focus merely on outcomes or states of affairs, we will fail to be able to distinguish between the person who acts from good intentions but whose acts accidentally give rise to suffering and the person who deliberately sets out to do bad acts but unintentionally reduces suffering. This is a further important difference from utilitarianism, which traditionally judges states of affairs and not merely virtues of character.

## Natural and artificial virtues

The significance of Hume's distinction between facts and values provides the basis for a naturalistic theory of morality that accounts for moral judgements in terms of feelings of pleasure and pain rooted in the passions. Alongside the distinction between facts and values Hume draws another distinction within his theory of morality, which is equally famous and which is essential to understanding his political theory. That is the distinction between natural and artificial virtues. This distinction opens the way for his discussion of justice, property, and the origin and nature of government, and obligation to it.

The key to understanding this distinction between natural and artificial virtues is the idea of the *public interest*. Hume explores the distinction by explaining what artificial virtues are and then turning to those remaining virtues which he describes as natural because they are not dependent on conventions of public interest. Although the natural virtues are important for his account of moral psychology, the place of the artificial virtues in his argument and their significance for his political theory make their discussion by far the more significant. The most important example of an artificial virtue for Hume is provided by the concept of justice, by which Hume means (crudely) the idea of giving someone his due. Justice is intimately connected with property, and this gives a clue to what he means by describing justice as an artificial virtue.

The account of artificial virtue begins with the question where the idea of justice comes from. Hume has already ruled out the idea that it is a representation of some matter of fact about the universe. Instead we are offered an account of virtues as aspects of character that elicit pleasurable feelings and the consequent judgement of approval. Vices elicit painful feelings and consequently judgements of disapproval. But the question that Hume has to answer has to do with the cause of these sentiments. Why do we feel a sense of approval or pleasure when we see someone act justly in respecting the property of another? And, more to the point, how does this judgement on the part of others transform itself into an account of our own obligation to repay our debts and respect the property of others? Hume asks us to think of an obligation of justice such as repaying a debt. Wherein does the feeling of approval reside? It cannot be in the natural 'fittingness' of the act, as there is no idea of justice that reflects a property of justice in the world (*Treatise*, III. ii. 1). Virtue and moral approbation, as we have seen, relate to human character not objects in themselves. But what is it about repaying debts that elicits our approval and praise? Do we only have a natural sympathy for just acts? Hume clearly thinks not. If we look at our natural motivations, they are of a broadly self-regarding kind. He does not claim that humans are naturally egoists, only concerned with maximizing their own advantage irrespective of the consequences to others—that would be one further error of rationalism. But equally he does not want to claim that individuals are natural altruists, with a natural motivation to pursue the interests of others impartially. People tend to be partial to their own interest and judge the propriety of acts of justice in relation to that interest. Thus while individuals might not simply deny the possibility of any obligation that conflicted with the advancement of their own interests, Hume argues that human partiality is such that they will not naturally tend to the burdens of impartiality that the idea of justice elicits. For Hume, property is supposed to be protected from the illicit encroachment of all men. Private benevolence, or the feeling of sympathy towards those we care about or approve of, will take us as far as feeling an obligation towards some people's property. But what about those with whom we have no natural ties of benevolence or care, or those we do not particularly like or approve of? Take the case of foreigners. Hume claims that our obligations to respect the property of foreigners in our own county—traders or visitors alike—do not lapse because we have no natural attachments or ties to them.

If obligations of justice cannot be found in the simple natural motive of private benevolence because of the fact of human partiality, then we must conclude that justice is not a natural virtue. But Hume claims that, because it is not natural, one should not assume it is any less important. In describing justice as an artificial virtue, he simply means that it is one that depends on the human artifices of education and convention. That is, the artificial virtues are praiseworthy motives and character traits that are inculcated by education in order to sustain institutions from which all benefit but from which not all benefit equally and all of the time. In the absence of those institutions, these artificial virtues would be irrelevant. Furthermore, as they are inculcated to sustain institutions from which people do not benefit equally and all of the time, these virtues cannot be reduced to some private or personal interest even if that concept is stretched to include the interests of some others. Instead the idea of the public interest is used to extend our concern beyond those to whom we are naturally tied by feelings of sympathy.

The contrast between natural and artificial virtues reveals the character of Hume's naturalization of moral and political philosophy. Virtue concepts are not derived from the fabric of the universe; either they are rooted in the natural sentiments of sympathy and benevolence, or they are derived from the artifices of convention and education to sustain some institution that serves a public rather than a private and partial interest. Having shown that the virtue of justice is not like a simple natural motive such as benevolence, Hume turns to the question of the origin of the institutions and conventions upon which the artificial virtues depend. This leads to his discussion of the origins of the institution of property and ultimately to the sustaining institutions of government. Along the way he addresses the convention of promise-keeping. Out of his account of the artificial virtues comes his assault on all of the key features of Lockean (and not just Lockean) contractarianism.

## Justice and conventions

As we have seen, the idea of justice is based on the idea of a convention. But what is a convention? Conventions are rules that regulate conduct. Conventions of property regulate the way in which each one of us reacts to the possessions of others. The key to conventions is the source of their authority, or that in virtue of which they become rules. They are unlike municipal laws that regulate conduct because they impose sanctions or because they emerge from a recognized authority such as the sovereign, or parliament. Instead conventions are less formal, but they are no less obligation-creating. Hume uses the famous example of two men rowing a boat to illustrate what he means by conventions (*Treatise*, I. ii. 2). The two rowers have a common purpose, or interest, in propelling the boat, and this commonality of interest is enough to create conformity of behaviour. Their shared common interest gives them a reason to act in a particular way. They do not need a further reason to give that common reason an authoritative status. Conventions bind because they embody a common interest and purpose; that is sufficient to give them an obligation-creating or normative force. When Hume turns his attention back to the idea of property on which the virtue of justice depends, he identifies the key convention in the idea of reciprocity. Each person recognizes that he has an interest in respecting the property of others provided that others recognize a similar interest. This recognition of a common interest gives rise to the conventions on which stability of possession and ownership depends. It is important to note that Hume does not introduce the idea of contract or promise here. His point is that the recognition of a common interest is enough to provide the authority of a convention. The introduction of a promise only introduces a further tier of redundant reasoning. If we have a common reason to recognize each other's property, then we might have a common reason to promise each other to recognize each other's property. But we rely on the same basic common interest and purpose to sustain the convention as we do to sustain the promise to maintain the conventions, so what additional work is being done by the idea of a promise? Hume's naturalism provides an account of the obligation of justice and of promise-keeping in the idea of conventions and the convergences of reason that they imply. Promises in themselves have no magic quality to conjure up a feeling of obligation independently of the conventions on which they rely.

In challenging the idea of the promises as the basis of obligations, Hume undermines the basic claim of contractarian theories of obligation, which claim that obligations can only emerge from contractual agreements. Hume not only wants to undermine the role of promise-keeping in such reasoning on the grounds that they are redundant in the face of common interests; he also wants to argue that contractarians introduce them in the wrong place, because promise-keeping itself depends upon prior conventions. Promises therefore cannot be an original source of obligation either to respect property or to create society. This argument is central to Hume's critique of contract-based political theories in his essays. Political legitimacy cannot be based on a contract or promise because the 'practice' of promise-keeping itself depends upon a widely accepted convergence of interest that undermines the basic premiss of social contract arguments, namely that the natural condition is one of conflict. Whatever convergence of interest is necessary to legitimize a promise is sufficient to legitimize government.

## Property and justice

We now have the key elements of both Hume's critique of the epistemology that sustains natural law and natural right arguments and a critique of contractarianism on the grounds that promises do not create obligations but depend upon pre-existing conventions and rules. But one important element remains, and that is to explain how conventions arise. Hume has argued that conventions provide the basis of obligation by establishing a commonality of interest as the basis of our sense of obligation and consequently of our judgements of right and justice. But he has also noted that our natural interests are always limited and partial and that we need education and convention to extend them; otherwise we would have Hobbesian men each narrowly pursuing his own self-interest with no possibility of a natural convergence on a common purpose. Again Hume's interest is in challenging the tyranny of a theory. A Hobbesian theory of motivation denies us the possibility of reasons and motives that we quite clearly have. Certainly we have a natural partiality, but Hume's point is that experience shows that we are not simple egoists. What an adequate theory must do is explain how we have the motives we actually have and feel obligated by. It is for this reason that Hume turns to the institution of property to explain the emergence of our conventions of justice.

Hume's account of the origin of property is rooted in the hostility of man's outward natural condition. He acknowledges man's natural sociability as evidenced in the natural desire for sexual union and the tendency to take responsibility for offspring. However, while in his internal state man might be secure, his external condition is far from it. Our natural concern is limited, so our generosity is confined. Worse still, our natural condition is one of scarcity: the world will not provide all of the things we want all of the time, and this creates competition. In order to provide for our needs and the needs of those for whom we care, we acquire possession of things, whether previously unowned objects or land or the produce of our labour. But the need to overcome competition leads us to translate possession into ownership. This transformation arises out of a mutual recognition of the benefits of allowing each to enjoy the benefits of their possessions in return for a reciprocal recognition of others' similar possession. This recognition of reciprocal secure enjoyment is the basis of property rights. These are based not on some primordial notion of self-ownership or the mixing of labour, but rather on the growth of a convention of recognition based on common needs in the face of the hostility of the natural condition. This convention gives rise to the artificial notion of a public interest. We have a public interest in the enjoyment of a stable system of property, from which we all benefit, even though as individuals we might have a private interest in having more than we currently enjoy under the existing distribution.

Property evolves as a response to the inconveniences of our external natural condition. The burdens of competition and conflict and the recognition of mutual benefit from stable possession give rise to the idea of a system of property rights. These property rights are, however, conventional, being based on a public convergence of interest. But this convergence of interest is never perfect, so conventions of justice develop to reinforce the convergence of interest and support the public interest when it conflicts with our private interest. This further illustrates the conventional nature of the three rules of justice: these are, first, stability of possession; secondly, the transference of property by consent; and, finally, that promises must be performed. Beyond these three basic considerations Hume's discussion of property rights is conventional. The rules of justice grow out of the practice of property and reinforce it; they have no role prior to the practice of private property. Stability of possession is only a good because of the expectations that arise from ownership. It is to protect these expectations that we refer to justice. Hence such rules are artificial in being dependent on a human practice. The motive to act justly is based on our public interest in the benefits that result from secure systems of private property. This public interest is not simply reducible to the private interest in secure possession as our private interest might give us reasons to maximize our advantage in some case by violating a rule of property. However, our public interest is based on the long-term convergence of private interests in stability and security of possession, not our short-term particular interest in maximizing our advantage. As it is not our natural inclination to take the long view or adopt the impartial perspective, the priority that we attach to the public interest and justice over our private interest is something that depends for its enduring force on education and socialization. We have to learn to act justly; hence it cannot be a natural virtue. That said, once we have a system of property, we have the grounds for restricting our own present interests in accordance with the public interest, which we would not have had in the absence of the artificial practice and rules of private property and justice.

Having defended the origin of the practice of private property and its connection with the conventions of justice, the rest of Hume's theory of property is both conventional and familiar. He devotes much space to explaining the rules governing ownership. These are occupation, prescription, accession, and succession. The first is equivalent to first occupancy. Someone acquires ownership when they are the first occupiers of what was previously unowned. Prescription modifies the idea of first ownership. One acquires rights through prescription when one has long-standing possession of property even though this may not be first occupancy. Prescription is the basis of most claims to title in land. Accession is what we call title, which arises out of something else that was already owned. This might be title to the crops which grow on one's land. Finally, succession involves the basis of title as a result of transfer through inheritance, bequest, or contract. All of these bases of title are analysed in great detail. However, it is important to note that Hume's concern is solely with the origin of the rules that give rise to a distribution of property titles, rather than with the distribution itself. Political theory does not give Hume any reason to prefer any particular distribution over any other. If the distribution is grossly unequal, that is irrelevant to the question of the legitimacy of the distribution or more importantly to the question of justice. Rules of justice are always internal to a system of property and not external criteria that can be applied to judge whether a distribution of property rights is itself legitimate. Justice rules out theft, fraud, and illegitimate ownership, but it does not rule out inequality or poverty.

## Government

### Why we need government

Hume's account of property and justice leads to his account of government. Again, as with property, his concern is not with the form or constitution of government but rather with its function or utility. Thus, much of his discussion of government comprises a challenge to contractarian accounts of the origin of political authority or patriarchalist accounts of natural authority. Contrary to such views Hume argues that the authority and legitimacy of political rule is derived not from the origin of government but from its utility. Hume's view is that the form of constitution is purely a conventional matter and what really matters is the utility of any constitution in maintaining the utilitarian good of stability and secure expectations. This utilitarian good will rule out certain forms of government, such as arbitrary absolutism, on the grounds that it fails to secure expectation. However, it is a utilitarian criterion that is being used and not one that bases legitimacy on consent or contract. Again consent is only forthcoming in either its express or tacit forms, as a result of the utilitarian benefits of government. That said, Hume is not wholly indifferent to the character of rule. The fundamental responsibility of government is to secure and maintain property. In this way his views converge with those of fellow Scottish advocates, such as his friend Adam Smith, of the growth and development of commercial society as a condition of peace and freedom.

The rationale of government is fundamentally utilitarian. However, Hume is not simply providing an account of the 'good' of government, in order to challenge prevailing ideologies of 'original' contract or consent; he also needs to provide an alternative account of its origin. This is provided in two ways, the first in terms of a speculative history about the emergence of leadership and rule as a consequence of the exigencies of war. The more substantive strand of Hume's argument turns away from speculative history and focuses on the function of political rule in relation to his previous account of private property and the conventions of justice.

As we have seen, the existence of private property grows up to compensate for the inadequacies of man's natural condition, and the convention of justice regulates that institution. However, thus far Hume's argument is incomplete because each man's motivation is partial and limited. The weakness in human nature is not that man is irredeemably egoistic, but rather that he lacks imagination. The passions dictate our actions, and in their untutored state these passions are self-reflective, applying egoistically or at best taking account of the interests of those near to us. They also have a tendency to confine our attention to the immediate consequences of our actions. Thus there is a tendency for our judgements of public and private interest to come apart and for us to neglect the public interest or our long-term interest in security of property and justice. In small-scale societies the external reinforcement of conventions of justice is relatively easy, because those failing to comply with their obligations of justice will come face to face with those who are affected by such departures from convention. The natural sanctions of non-cooperation with defectors will give people a general reason for complying with the rules of justice. Hume uses this kind of argument to reinforce the obligations of promises. An interest in reputation and the need for reciprocity is enough to give the normative force of promises even without the existence of an external lawgiver threatening physical punishment. The informal reinforcements of small and proximate social relations provide the extension of our identification to others with whom we interact and cooperate with. However, in larger societies the opportunities to defect from the obligations of justice are greater without being noticed. Furthermore, our imaginative identification is weakened because we will not necessarily, indeed in most cases we will never, meet all who are members of such communities. If we are unlikely to meet such people, we are unlikely to establish the imaginative bonds with them with the same force that we do with those more closely related to us; consequently, we are more likely to prefer our partial interest to the public interest. It is to bridge this gap of imaginative identification that we need government.

It is important to note that Hume's argument is not simply that government provides the material sanctions—threats of force etc.—that cause us to subordinate present partial interests to the long-term public interest. This does form part of the argument, but Hume also looks at government as an educative institution which extends our identification and sympathy to those with whom we are not in direct relationships of mutual cooperation. Unless we are to remain in small-scale, relatively face-to-face social relationships, we need government to reinforce conventions but also to extend the scope of our conception of the public interest.

## Against consent theory

Hume's account of government and its connection with the good of private property and the associated conventions of justice challenges the prevailing ideology of government being based on consent. This argument is most closely associated with John Locke, but it was by no means exclusive to Locke. The consent argument used by Locke combines an account of the origin of government in a primordial contract with an argument for the basis of legitimacy being located in some subsequent act of consent whether express or tacit. As with his assault on the empiricist 'way of ideas', Hume's political theory is developed in the shadow of Locke's consent theory. Why is he so keen to challenge this Lockean theory when in substance there is much that unites the two, not least their emphasis on the primacy of security of property and soft government in the public interest? The reason is connected to Hume's assault on the 'way of ideas'. Hume does not claim that there is a straightforward logic that takes one from an empiricist psychology to constitutional 'liberalism', as Locke hoped to show, nor does he claim that there is a straightforward implication from his philosophical scepticism to his own political conclusions. However, it would be a mistake to suggest, as some commentators such as Duncan Forbes do,[2] that there is no connection between the philosophical project and Hume's politics.

Hume's assault on consent theory is part of his general assault on the tyranny of a certain kind of political rationalism. His argument is that we don't need consent theory to support soft government and the protection of private property. The trappings of consent theory are redundant and dangerous: redundant because we don't need contracts, promises, and consent to explain either the origin of government or allegiance to it, and dangerous because the logic of consent can serve to undermine the genuine bases of legitimacy.

Hume's critique of consent theory detaches the account of the origin of government from an account of its legitimacy and utility. As we have seen, he explains the legitimacy of government in its utility in sustaining property and the conventions of justice in large societies. Government is far from natural, and in very small societies, where the conventions of justice and property can be sanctioned informally, it is not necessary. Thus Hume challenges both those who argue that government is natural and those who argue, like Hobbes, that sovereign political power is a condition of society. But the crucial difference between Hume and the consent theorist is that Hume's utilitarian argument makes the idea of consent and original promises redundant. The idea of basing the origin of government on a promise or consent is misconceived because it presupposes the existence of binding promises prior to the existence of society. But, as we have seen in the account of justice and property, it is the mysteriousness of the reason to obey promises that needs explanation in terms of the sanctions and educative function of government. Our motive to obey a promise to establish government is just the same as our motive to set up government, so it is not clear what work the idea of the promise is doing. When it comes to the issue of extending the sense of obligation to those beyond one's immediate circle, it is not clear that the idea of a promise can have any role at all, for it is the problem of compliance that needs to be explained, and that is merely presupposed by explaining it in terms of another obligation.

If government is not based on a promise or contract, why is it legitimate? Here the answer is simply that it is legitimate as long as it serves a particular purpose, namely securing peace and the enjoyment of property. Unlike the contract theorists, Hume does not provide a general speculative history of the origin of government. Instead he suggests how the idea of a magistrate might arise; that is, a person whose job it is to act as the arbiter and enforcer of the public interest (*Treatise*, III. ii. 8). He argues that the first rudiments of government may well have arisen out of the problem of dealing with external threats to a society. It is in these circumstances that the need for a centralizing force becomes most pressing, and it is out of this sort of circumstance that the roles of leadership and military organization arise. However, Hume is insistent on separating the historical origin of government from its legitimacy. And it is this fundamental mistake that the consent theorists make, for it is because of this that they get caught up in trying to ground a right of resistance or rebellion in the face of their accounts of promise or consent-based legitimacy. The historical origin of government is irrelevant to legitimacy, so Hume does not have to introduce spurious quasi-acts of 'tacit' consent, nor does he have to specify the terms under which consent lapses. For Hume our obligation simply ceases when the magistrate acts against the public interest by failing to secure property and order and takes no account of consent. Political obligation is based on habits of obedience that are rooted in a recognition of the public interest. The danger with consent theories is that, by over-rationalizing political obligation, they have the tendency to undermine the forms of habitual behaviour on which political stability ends. Hume's concern here is twofold: to show that the absence of consent does not throw individuals into a state of subservience without any recourse against tyrants, and to support the habits of behaviour on which political obligation depends against rationalists.

Hume's willingness to separate the account of the 'basis of allegiance' from its historical origins does not, however, mean that he was indifferent to history. Given that he went on to write a six-volume history of England, this would be absurd. History is certainly important in determining the legitimacy of rule and the form of government, but not in the ways suggested by contract and consent theory. Instead of looking for a specific historical act of contract or consent creating and legitimizing government, we should look to history for a different kind of support for specific regime types and rulers. History provides us with a reason to prefer one form of government or set of rulers in the same way in which it endorses particular regimes of private property. In order to assess the legitimacy of a particular monarch we only need to take account of succession, prescription, present occupancy, or conquest. All of these considerations are similar to the grounds for legitimate ownership. But, as with property, these grounds of legitimate rule are all conditional on the basic utilitarian argument about the legitimacy of government as a guarantor of security and peace.

Hume undermines the reasons behind Lockean consent theory by showing that recourse to consent introduces an unnecessary epicycle into arguments for the legitimacy of government and that the straightforward appeal to reciprocity and mutuality is sufficient. Instead Hume draws out the implicit utilitarian argument in Locke's account of tacit consent and uses this as a free-standing justification. This raises the fundamental question of the extent to which Hume really was a utilitarian, to which I will now turn.

## Was Hume a utilitarian?

Hume's work is replete with arguments that suggest an implicit utilitarianism. His account of the moral judgements in terms of feelings of pleasure at the manifestation of virtue and good character in following conventions or exhibiting certain natural virtues suggests a utilitarian argument. Furthermore, as we have seen, his account of the origin of government and of political obligation in terms of the benefits they provide reinforces that perception. Hume occupies a position in British philosophy between the natural law empiricism of Locke and the overt utilitarianism of Bentham, J. S. Mill, and Sidgwick. Indeed Bentham even acknowledges that Hume drew his attention to the importance of utility. So it must be the case that Hume was a utilitarian or at least a proto-utilitarian. Most standard histories of thought link Hume with the Utilitarians. However, a recent strand of scholarship has also attempted to weaken that connection by linking Hume more closely to a distinct Scottish Enlightenment, or to deny that he fits neatly into the categories of utilitarian arguments. Bentham may well have thought he was following Hume, but Bentham may have just been confused.

Making any kind of clear assessment of the extent to which Hume was a utilitarian depends (as it always does in the history of thought) upon what one means by a utilitarian. Mainstream classical Utilitarians such as Bentham and Mill are generally agreed to be psychological hedonists and direct or act utilitarians. That is, they both argue that individuals are motivated by the desire for pleasure over pain and that the right action to do in any case is that which results in the most pleasure, however that is distributed. The principle of utility, or the injunction to act in a way that maximizes pleasure over pain, is the sole ethical obligation and is used not simply to explain morality and politics but also to offer a critique of political institutions and practices.

In light of this (admittedly controversial account of classical utilitarianism—see the chapters on Bentham and J. S. Mill), Hume's argument is clearly different in a number of key respects. First, Hume does use the concept of utility and pleasure, but he is not a psychological hedonist. Pleasure is not reducible to utility, as utility in Hume's hands means something much less precise, such as usefulness. Utility, for Hume, is important, but it is only one of the ultimate ends of actions. Similarly, the concept of pleasure is used by Hume to account for our judgements of right and wrong, good and bad, but he does not reduce these concepts to questions of the quantity of pleasure. He also attaches such judgements to character and motive and not consequences or states of affairs as such. A good act manifesting benevolent motives may result in less overall utility in terms of its external consequences, just as an act derived from malicious motives may well result in more overall welfare because of the incompetence or ignorance of the agent. Hume is not a straightforward consequentialist in his use of these two concepts as he uses these two key utilitarian concepts in a different way from the classical Utilitarians.

A second substantive difference between Hume and the classical Utilitarians is that for Hume the quasi-utilitarian components of his theory of justice, property, and government have an explanatory rather than a prescriptive function. Hume uses these ideas to explain the origins of these practices and institutions, but he does not apply them to assess *critically* these institutions and practices. It is crucial that for Hume these philosophical categories have an explanatory but not a critical role. Classical utilitarianism, on the other hand, is famously seen as a reforming theory. It is concerned not simply with the benefits of private property as such, but with which distribution is the most beneficial. It is important to note that this is not simply to argue that Hume has a rule or indirect utilitarian strategy as opposed to Mill's act utilitarianism, where rule utilitarianism focuses on the general benefits of systems of rules and practices as opposed to individual acts. This sort of indirect version of utilitarianism can be attributed to Hume, but it does not affect the crucial difference that Hume rejects the critical role of utility, using the concept solely to explain and describe.

So Hume is not a straightforward consequentialist. He does not use the concept of utility in the narrow classical utilitarian sense. Neither is he a psychological hedonist. Furthermore, his moral theory is explanatory and descriptive rather than prescriptive and critical. At best Hume can only be an interesting contributor to a tradition or theory that develops in a radically different direction in the hands of Bentham and Mill.

However, before totally dismissing the attempt to link Hume to his later utilitarian successors we might consider the important ways in which he does contribute to that tradition. Hume was not in any straightforward sense a utilitarian. But he does contribute to the character of that theory. He poses challenges that are taken up by the likes of Bentham and Mill in constructing a critical utilitarian theory, challenges that are posed by the underlying conservatism of Hume's moral and political theory. But most importantly, Hume contributes a theory of sceptical naturalism, which underpins and makes possible utilitarianism. This is the idea that morality and politics is a purely human artifice that emerges to compensate for the shortcomings of our natural motives. This view rejects any appeal to external or transcendental moral norms or principles. Crucially it explains how we can go on without recourse to God or natural law, the two concepts upon which Locke relied so heavily. However, Hume's sceptical naturalism is much more limited than that of Aristotle. Hume's account of human nature is much less narrow and eschews any account of human excellences or perfectionism as we find in Aristotle, where human nature is usually capitalized and is intended as something that one achieves, rather than as something that is given. This sceptical naturalism sets out the intellectual terrain in which utilitarianism becomes possible. The pared-down or sceptical account of human nature coupled with the emphasis on the way in which institutions shape our interests all form part of the peculiarly British mentality that gives rise to utilitarianism. So while Hume may not have been a utilitarian in any illuminating sense of that deeply contested label, he is clearly essential in providing the intellectual terrain in which Bentham and Mill could construct their own theories. Perhaps this is what Bentham intended in his acknowledgement of Hume: without Hume there would have been no Bentham.

## Hume's enduring legacy

Hume's legacy is considerable but also complex. As we have seen with his relationship to utilitarianism, giving a simple yes or no answer is misleading. He is a utilitarian, but he is not a utilitarian like Bentham. But even this conclusion is contestable, as some contemporary political philosophers find traces of contractarianism in his thought.[3] Clearly Hume is not a contractarian if that implies the idea that obligations depend upon promises or that political obligation is based on expressions of consent. Promises are of secondary importance for

Hume. They require explanation as much as any other social artefact; they are not the basis of such a explanation. Yet does this mean that Hume is not a contractarian? If by that we mean the idea that obligations and norms can be explained in terms of what could be the basis of a reasonable agreement, it is certainly possible. Many contemporary theorists of justice who think of contractarianism in this way as a hypothetical thought experiment certainly draw on Hume's legacy. This is certainly true of some of the most significant contemporary theorists of justice. Our understanding of contractarianism has certainly changed since Hume's attack on Lockean consent theory and the political radicalism that followed from it.

However, if we think of Hume's legacy in light of contemporary debates about social and distributive justice, we can see just how hotly contested it is. Utilitarians of a Benthamite or Millian cast of mind can accept much of Hume's account of the origin and justification of regimes of property, without concluding that any particular conventional account of property rights is beyond philosophical criticism. Utilitarians tend to think that cautious revision of existing distributions of private property are not only justifiable on broadly Humean grounds, but are actually required. This view is taken up by contemporary contractarian theorists of justice such as Rawls and Barry, who see the task of social justice as one of transforming existing distributions of property (among other things). Other significant contributors to debates about social justice use Humean arguments to mount radical challenges to 'redistribution'. Among the most famous such *anti* social justice theorists is F. A. Hayek.[4] For Hayek, regimes of property are part of the spontaneous order of market societies. They grow up as a result of the myriad micro-decisions of individual agents, and therefore represent a convergence of individual wisdom and reason that cannot be fully comprehended by any single mind. Hayek follows Hume both in his conventionalism and in his rejection of rationalism, which Hayek claims re-emerges with the desire for justice as redistribution.

No single authoritative interpretation of Hume will settle debates between advocates of redistribution or respect for private property, because his legacy pulls in both directions. He is both a conservative and a liberal: conservative in that he rejects the hubris of human reason with its attempts to build rational utopias of whatever kind. This caste of mind is as hostile to the utopianism of the left as it is to the libertarian fantasies of many on the right who wish to dispense with government except as an enforcer of natural rights. However, as we have seen, Hume's conservatism is also liberal in that he does not retreat into the worship of received practices and traditions. Tradition and convention might well have sound political and sociological value, but that is the limit of Hume's endorsement. His sceptical cast of mind constantly runs up against religious and political enthusiasm and orthodoxy. Government should therefore be light in its touch, allowing people to go about their business with security but without delving too deeply into their private beliefs. Hume's argument ends up endorsing the ideal of toleration that is implicit in Locke's political philosophy. But he does so without the appeal to contract theory and natural law, precisely the ideas which in the wrong hands were used to endorse the French Revolution.

Perhaps Hume's most significant and lasting legacy is to attempt to provide a 'foundationless' political theory, one which is sensitive to the lessons of history, psychology, and anthropology without being in thrall to any particular philosophy of historical change. This hybrid of history, psychology, anthropology, and sociology is at the heart of the modern study of political science. Hume's greatest legacy is to have transformed the way in which we understand political practice and political principle.

## FURTHER READING

Barry, Brian, *Justice as Impartiality* (Oxford: Clarendon Press, 1995).
Barry, Brian, *Theories of Justice* (Berkeley: University of California Press, 1989).
Forbes, Duncan, *Hume's Philosophical Politics* (Cambridge: Cambridge University Press, 1975).
Gauthier, David, 'David Hume, Contractarian', in David Boucher and Paul Kelly (eds.), *Social Justice: From Hume to Walzer* (London: Routledge, 1998).
Hayek, F. A., *The Constitution of Liberty* (London: Routledge & Kegan Paul, 1960).
Hayek, F. A., *The Road to Serfdom* (London: Routledge & Kegan Paul, 1944).
Miller, D., *Philosophy and Ideology in Hume's Political Thought* (Oxford: Clarendon Press, 1981).
Norton, D. F., *David Hume: Common-Sense Moralist, Sceptical Metaphysician* (Princeton: Princeton University Press, 1982).
Plamenatz, J. P., *The English Utilitarians* (Oxford: Basil Blackwell, 1958).
Rawls, John, *A Theory of Justice* (Cambridge, Mass.: Harvard University Press, 1971).
Whelan, F. G., *Order and Artifice in Hume's Political Philosophy* (Princeton: Princeton University Press, 1985).

## NOTES

1. Hume, *A Treatise of Human Nature*, 2nd edn. rev. P. H. Nidditch (Oxford: Clarendon Press, 1978); references are to book, part, and section.
2. Duncan Forbes, *Hume's Philosophical Politics* (Cambridge: Cambridge University Press, 1975).
3. Brian Barry, *Theories of Justice* (Berkeley: University of California Press, 1989), and David Gauthier, 'David Hume, Contractarian', in David Boucher and Paul Kelly (eds.), *Social Justice: From Hume to Walzer* (London: Routledge, 1998).
4. F. A. Hayek, *The Road to Serfdom* (London: Routledge & Kegan Paul, 1944), and *The Constitution of Liberty* (London: Routledge & Kegan Paul, 1960).

# 13 Montesquieu

Yoshie Kawade

## Contents



## Chapter guide

Montesquieu's political theory, and his *Spirit of the Laws* in particular, has been read as a complex mosaic of varied and sometimes disparate intellectual traditions. Despite the forbidding structure of his works, we can find important and impressive discussions of issues such as the justification of universal justice, a scientific approach to the law, a new typology of governments, a materialistic theory of climate, and the idea of a free state based on separate and balanced powers. In its interweaving of issues of philosophical and normative justification and issues of historical and sociological explanation, Montesquieu's political theory is both immensely rich and suggestive as well as being extremely difficult to reduce to any of the received categories of political theory that he inherited from either the ancient or the early modern world. Yet in his discussion of justice and law, and of the material and geographical conditions of types of association and government, Montesquieu still provides a sophisticated and subtle defence of the conditions of modern liberal political institutions. Despite these intimations of contemporary political sociology and normative political theory, commentators have still asked whether Montesquieu had a synthetic principle that organized these discrete considerations, and, if there was one, how we can relate it to the normative implications of his political writings. This chapter will try to answer this questions and to clarify the multiple but not necessarily unsystematic structure of Montesquieu's arguments. The chapter begins with a discussion of Montesquieu as a critic of despotism. This is followed by a discussion of his early writings, such as the *Persian Letters*, after which the chapter turns to a discussion of the key themes of his mature political theory; the separation of powers, the three forms of government, the lessons of history, and finally the conditions of political liberty.

## Biography

Charles Louis de Secondat was born in 1689 at La Brède near Bordeaux. His family was one of provincial nobility, derived from both the legal nobility of the robe and the military nobility of the sword. He was sent to the famous Collège de Juilly near Paris, maintained by the Congregation of the Oratory, where he studied ancient and modern history. On graduating from the Collège he left Paris and enrolled at the University of Bordeaux, becoming a licentiate in law in three years. From Bordeaux he returned to Paris and continued his studies in the law courts. In his twenties, after the death of his father and uncle, he inherited the barony of La Brède and that of Montesquieu, as well as the office of the President in the Parliament of Bordeaux. Montesquieu was not prepared to be a passive landowner enjoying the fruits of others' labours; instead he became involved in the farming of his estates, the quality of his vines, and the international wine trade. However, the quiet life of a magistrate and a landowner did not fully satisfy the intellectual ambition of the young Montesquieu. In 1721 he anonymously published his first book, *Persian Letters*. The success of this romance gave him an entrée to intellectual society in Paris and made him decide to give up the legal office of magistrate. From 1728 to 1731 he travelled, visiting Italy, Germany, and other European countries. It was during this time that he spent one-and-a half years in the England of George II. While there he became familiar with the works of Bolingbroke and Pope, and especially with the workings of the English Parliament, which was to so influence his views on the separation of powers. On his return to France he settled down in his estate and dedicated himself to producing his two major political works, *Considerations on the Causes of the Greatness of the Romans and their Decline* and *The Spirit of the Laws*. In later life he enjoyed the reputation of being among the first generation of Enlightenment thinkers. He died in Paris in 1755. *The Spirit of the Laws* was to influence thinkers as diverse as David Hume, Adam Smith and Adam Ferguson, all key figures in the Scottish Enlightenment, as well as James Madison, one of the authors of *The Federalist Papers* and an architect of the American Constitution.

## Key texts

*Considerations on the Causes of the Greatness of the Romans and their Decline*, trans. D. Lowenthal (Indianapolis: Hackett, 1999).

*Pensées*, ed. L. Desgraves (Paris: Robert Laffont, 1991).

*Persian Letters*, trans. C. J. Betts (Harmondsworth: Penguin, 1973).

*The Spirit of the Laws*, ed. and trans. A. M. Cohler, B. C. Miller, and H. S. Stone (Cambridge: Cambridge University Press, 1989).

## Main texts used

*Persian Letters* (1721)

*Considerations on the Causes of the Greatness of the Romans and their Decline* (1734)

*The Spirit of the Laws* (1748)

## Key ideas

**Law**: Montesquieu defines law as 'the necessary relations deriving from the nature of things'. As such he means to give the broadest possible definition, to include natural physical laws, fundamental moral norms, and the civil and criminal norms of a municipal legal code. Thus *The Spirit of the Laws* is concerned with the fundamental moral norms behind positive laws as well as with the character of different positive legal codes. **Spirit**: this idea reflects the complex ordering principle behind different forms of government and society. Each form of government has a principle determining the number of rulers, but also an animating principle specifying the type of society it reflects and the virtues appropriate to that form of society and government. Thus each form of government has both a fundamental constitutional norm and a *spirit*. **Separation of powers**: this is the idea that a regime of liberty requires the separation and balance of powers. This is often taken to mean a strict functional separation between the legislative, executive, and judicial branches of the state. While Montesquieu sees the idea of separation of powers as a constitutional principle, he also links it to the balance of interests in a constitution. In the case of the English parliamentary system the separation of powers is achieved by the balance between the monarch, the aristocratic class, and the commons as a commercial class. **Despotism** refers to political corruption or the subordination of the public interest to the private interest of the ruler or rulers. It is not strictly a form of government but a corruption of any type of government. **Political liberty** is contrasted with the idea of philosophical liberty. This latter refers to freedom of the will, whereas the former refers to the feeling of security. Political liberty is thus inextricably connected to the ideas of justice and property.

# Introduction: Montesquieu as a critic of despotism

Most commentators agree that Montesquieu's political theory belongs within the liberal tradition, but opinions vary over the precise sense in which it can be regarded as liberal. An obvious focus for many commentators is his analysis of the English constitution, an analysis that is said to have contributed to formulating his theory of the separation of powers, one of the principal foundations of modern liberal constitutionalism.[1] Other commentators attach more significance to his commitment to a form of government which allows its citizens a free pursuit of self-interest and which combines the demands of political liberty and a negative conception of personal freedom as non-interference.[2]

It is also sometimes pointed out that Montesquieu was a moderate reformer who assumed, before moderate anti-rationalist liberals such as David Hume and Edmund Burke, that civil and political society was too complex to be artificially redesigned.[3] There are of course objections to these mainstream interpretations. Some more historically minded interpreters place Montesquieu whithin the tradition of early modern French constitutionalism,[4] or regard him as an ideologue of the French Parliament, whereas others who are more sympathetic to Montesquieu emphasize his latent commitment to the republican virtue.[5] Alongside these interpretations of his substantive political ideas there are differing conceptions of his methodology and approach to political theory as challenging the terms of the natural law tradition. His last major work, *The Spirit of the Laws*, has been considered a pioneering work that led to the establishment of the empirically oriented 'value-free' social sciences and a forerunner of modern positivist sociology. It has even been assumed that his theory of climate, an analysis of the influence of physical environment on social institutions, was an embryonic form of the economic determinism of the Marxists.[6] These interpretations focus on the 'scientific' elements of Montesquieu's theory, though they are based on different views of what constitutes a science. In recent years some of these interpretations of Montesquieu's methodological position have given way to a renewed interest in his substantive political theory. Arbitration between these complex and sometimes conflicting interpretations is complicated by the fact that Montesquieu did not aim to construct a rigorous and formal philosophical system such as we find (at least in part) in Hobbes or Locke. The object and style of theory of Montesquieu's approach often varied from work to work, sometimes even from chapter to chapter. Many commentators therefore focus on aspects of Montesquieu's writings as if they are a vast encyclopedia of matters political, but without a single organizing narrative. Despite this, Montesquieu thought his works had coherence and expected them to be read as complete texts and not simply as collections of loosely organized but profound insights. In the face of overwhelming complexities of social phenomena, Montesquieu frequently digressed from the main topic, thereby giving rise to ambiguities and contradictions, and often obscuring his main point. Thus he can be read as providing insights into concepts and institutions while leaving the reader uncertain whether he is actually endorsing or merely analysing these things. Nevertheless, he maintained that there is in his work a continuous and profound organizing concern which he sustained and elaborated all through his life. Tracing the development of this chief organizing concern will perhaps help us to acquire an understanding of his political thought as a coherent whole.

What then was his chief concern? In brief, it was to criticize the pathological phenomena in politics which Montesquieu called 'despotism'. By 'despotism' he implied not only a particular type of government as we find in both Plato and Aristotle. Instead despotism was seen above all as a symbol of political corruption which threatened every type of government. The problem, however, is that his criticism of despotism is not based on a single straightforward logic. There are at least three distinct levels of criticism in his major works, and this multi-layered criticism may be one of the sources of complexity in his arguments and the confusion surrounding the coherence of his political theory. It is helpful to begin by presenting a brief account of these three levels of criticism. The first criticism of despotism revolves around the idea that despotism is contrary to justice. The issue of justice was discussed mainly in his first work, *Persian Letters* (1721). The second level of criticism is concerned with the tendency of the modern state to centralize its political powers. Montesquieu confronted the 'despotic' power of absolute sovereignty as found in modern theorists such as Hobbes and Jean Bodin with a pluralistic vision of political power. This was a central thesis of the *Considerations on the Causes of the Greatness of the Romans and their Decline* (1734), which was subsequently developed and applied to his famous analysis of the English constitution. The third level of criticism is a central feature of the main parts of *The Spirit of the Laws* (1748) and can be called a sociological criticism as it contends that despotism is unacceptable because it undermines 'the general spirit' of a political society. While Montesquieu's focus shifted from one level to another at different times and within the same work, he never abandoned any of them. As we shall see, they are all integrated into his final masterpiece, *The Spirit of the Laws*, in which he achieved one of the most profound understandings of liberal politics.

## Early writings

Montesquieu made a successful public debut with the *Persian Letters*, a work which clearly illustrates his commitment to the ideal of justice. This curious romance takes the form of a series of letters exchanged between two Persian princes visiting Paris and their friends, servants, and wives at home. The two primary characters and their servants and wives allow Montesquieu to adopt many different personae in order to explore a variety of social, political, and moral questions. The work is not simply about political matters; indeed it raises profound questions about the social and political causes of dehumanization. That said, it allows Montesquieu to engage a variety of critical engagements with both contemporary philosophy and politics. This criticism of contemporary philosophy and Montequieu's assertion of his fundamental commitment to justice is most clearly illustrated in the episode of the Troglodytes, which he wrote as a satire on the logic of Thomas Hobbes's *Leviathan.* The Troglodytes were a 'mythical' people who did not have any ideas of justice. They could not endure any sort of political authority, neither a foreign king nor a leader of their own choice; as a result, they agreed that everyone would confine himself to the pursuit of his own self-interest. The consequence of this was a fatal antagonism, or war of all against all, which ended not only in death, but in the total extinction of this egoistic people. It is evident that in this episode Montesquieu reverses the Hobbesian process of reasoning, which begins with the 'state of nature' and ends in the formation of an absolute sovereign. The logic of Hobbes's state of nature simply leads to annihilation and ultimate extinction. Without any principles of equity or justice, suggests Montesquieu, men can neither form nor sustain any political society, falling into the eternal struggles of every man against every man, ending only in death.

According to Montesquieu, justice signifies a relation of equity which exists prior to any positive laws: 'Justice is a relation of suitability, which actually exists between two things' (*PL* 83, p. 162[7]). This relation does not depend on any human conventions but must be presupposed by such conventions, and even God cannot arbitrarily change it. Such a notion of justice or natural right does not necessarily originate with Montesquieu. His approach bears the influence of early modern theorists of natural law such as the German philosopher Leibniz. But above all, Montesquieu was influenced by the writings of Cicero, who became a rich source of inspiration for many of those who argued against Hobbes in the eighteenth century.

Following the success of the *Persian Letters*, Montesquieu set out on a long journey travelling through Europe and visiting England. Upon his return to France he published his second major work, *Considerations.* The central topic of this historical inquiry is concerned with the cause of the decline of the Roman republic. According to the standard explanations, for example that of the authoritative work of J.-B. Bossuet (1627–1704), the Roman republic declined because of its internal divisions. As Rome became large and strong, the spirit of freedom became excessive, and this provoked endless and disastrous conflicts between fellow citizens. To overcome this fatal anarchy, Bossuet concluded, the ideal of the republic needed to be replaced by a more stable, one-man rule such as an absolute monarchy.[8] Thus absolute monarchy becomes a superior political form to republicanism because of its ability to overcome the inherent instability of the latter polity.

Contrary to these conventional views, Montesquieu contended that the internal divisions in the last period of the Roman republic were not the cause of its decline, for these divisions were 'necessary to it, that they had always been there and always had to be' (*Considerations*, 93[9]). Montesquieu maintained, as Machiavelli had before him,[10] that a republic needs some conflicts and even factional strife if it is to sustain its vigour and fend off decadence and decline. If total tranquillity is achieved in a state that calls itself a republic, it will cease to be free. This observation led him to come up with a remarkable insight on politics in general: 'What is called union in a body politic is a very equivocal thing. The true kind is a union of harmony, whereby all the parts, however opposed they may appear, cooperate for the general good of society—as dissonances in music cooperate in producing overall concord' (*Considerations*, 93–4). While true unity within a state is achieved through the interaction of conflicting powers, or through what we might call 'dissonant harmony', the unity of a despotic state is based on uniformity and homogeneity. Underlying this unanimity of despotism, there is always a 'real' latent division within society. Under despotism the citizens become so deeply isolated from political power that the one (or absolute ruler) can oppress the others (subjects or citizens) without meeting any resistance. Thus the unity of a despotism is a unity of dead bodies buried one after another. Following the above analysis, Montesquieu presented his second and perhaps the sharpest criticism of despotism. What distinguishes a 'moderate' government from despotism is that the former is based on the plurality of powers; the citizens are integrated only through mutual conflicts. Such a dynamic and heterogeneous power structure is, in Montesquieu's judgement, a fundamental precondition for a state to be free and stable over time.

## The separation of powers

This analysis of a heterogeneous power structure as a condition of political liberty takes us to Montesquieu's most important single work, *The Spirit of the Laws*, a work to which he dedicated twenty years of his life. We shall begin by inquiring how his vision of 'dissonant harmony' developed into his celebrated analysis of the English constitution. This analysis can be found in *The Spirit of the Laws*, book XI, the title of which is highly indicative: 'On the Laws that Form Political Liberty in its Relation to the Constitution'. Political liberty is seen as a function of constitutional form.

Before Montesquieu a number of Continental writers saw in the constitutional structure of Hanoverian England a model for political liberty. Pierre Jurieu (1637–1713), a Huguenot in exile, admired England for its institution of a constitutional monarchy controlled by Parliament. While, for Voltaire, England was a country where the people enjoyed both freedom of speech and religious toleration. These arguments reflect to a certain degree the justification of the post-revolutionary regime made by the Whig ideologues. However, Montesquieu's viewpoint differs from all of these arguments. He attempted to demonstrate in his own way in what sense the English political system was free. In the first place, he raised objections to the established notions of political liberty. For Montesquieu, political liberty does not simply entail the ability to elect one's own rulers, nor does it signify the right to resist a tyrannical leader. Furthermore, it by no means consists in simply doing what the people want. To be more precise, one cannot say that a state is free simply because each or all of these powers is attributed to a part or even the whole of its citizens. 'It has eternally been observed', argued Montesquieu, 'that any man who has power is led to abuse it' (*Spirit*, 155[11]). What then does political liberty mean for Montesquieu? His answer is that it consists in imposing limits on political power. Accordingly, the most effective and desirable way to limit power is to establish some form of institutional mechanism that allows power to be restrained by another power. Equilibrium is achieved by a balance of equal and opposite forces, and this precludes any single power acting as an obstacle to liberty. The constitution of England is for Montesquieu, a brilliant example of such a device for constraint, and is the ground on which he calls his neighbouring country a 'free state'.

These arguments led Montesquieu to make a clear contrast between a moderate government in which powers are limited and a despotic government in which all the powers are concentrated in one place or person. This typology is an improved version of the approach he discussed in the *Considerations*. One might, however, be left with the impression that the arguments in *The Spirit of the Laws* have lost the positive nature which the vision of 'dissonant harmony' held. In the latter work Montesquieu's chief focus seems to be on the prevention of the abuse of power, rather than on the dynamic interaction between powers. Pluralism in *The Spirit of the Laws* has a negative 'checking' function rather than a positive endorsement of the good of a plurality of forces and functions within a dynamic political society. Nevertheless, both of these aspects are ultimately connected. To limit power, it is necessary to maintain the plurality of powers in a political society. Conversely, to maintain such a plural power structure it is necessary to limit power. The positive and negative aspects of Montesquieu's pluralism are mutually reinforcing.

What Montesquieu discovered in his interpretation of the English constitution is a system of checks and balances among the three functional branches of government: making laws or legislation; implementing them in particular circumstances, the executive branch; and punishing those who violate them, the judicial branch. Yet Montesquieu's famous theory of the separation of powers has a certain ambiguity that has led many commentators to differing conclusions. Many scholars had once believed that Montesquieu formulated in *The Spirit of the Laws* the principle of the modern constitution, which demands the strict separation among the three independent sectors, the legislative, the executive, and the judicial. Yet such a strictly legalistic interpretation shaped by reading Montesquieu in the light of the subsequent founding of the American Constitution is not acceptable without considerable modifications.

Montesquieu's concern is not only with the functional differentiation of government and the mutual checks of the three divisions unlike the American Constitution and the writings of the founding fathers. He is also concerned with the mechanism in which these three represent the interests of different social classes, by which he means mainly the traditional three estates: the king, the lords, and commons. Checks and balances operate on the level of social structure as much as on the level of the institutional relations of government. This may explain why Montesquieu emphasized the significance of the English two-chamber system, in addition to the well-known separation of the three branches (*Spirit*, 160). In this respect, he was influenced by the English advocates of the balanced constitution. He pays homage to the English constitution just *because* it is an amalgam of the two principles: the functional separation of government *and* the substantial division of social powers. Both are closely connected and mutually supported. One without the other will not, for Montesquieu, guarantee political liberty, and this is the mistake of subsequent constitutional theorists who simply focus on the functional separation of government powers.

While Montesquieu provides a fascinating analysis of the English constitution from the perspective of a foreign observer, one should not take his account as a straightforward description of English constitutional practice, for he misunderstood at least in one crucial point the spirit of this system. The actual constitution of England did not claim complete equality for its three divisions, because it was a consensus of the Glorious Revolution to assign higher priority to the legislative body over the executive. The supremacy of Parliament had been established at least in theory. Montesquieu almost neglects this decisive aspect of the new regime.

## Law and the concept of general spirits

When Montesquieu undertook his ambitious enterprise, in *The Spirit of the Laws*, to search for the true basis of laws, or what he called 'spirit of the laws', he encountered the problem of legislation, and especially that of legislative supremacy. The notion of legislative supremacy forms an essential part of the classic theory of sovereignty, established by writers such as Jean Bodin (1529/30–96) in the late sixteenth century. The right to make laws is a distinctive and exclusive attribute of sovereignty, according to Bodin.[12] In other words, a law is nothing more than a commanding 'will' of the sovereign body, which is in principle exempt from any further binding principle except the direct intervention of God himself. Bodin's idea had a powerful influence on the reconstruction of the French monarchy, but such an extreme voluntaristic notion of law necessarily met with various kinds of criticisms. Orthodox theorists of French constitutionalism continued to claim that the true basis of laws is the authority of custom, and thus a product of a long and complex process of history. Many natural law theorists made an effort to ground positive laws on the rationality of nature as the only source of universal justice. These arguments did not always result in an attack on the absolute claims of government, as some natural law theorists were absolutists, but in general the natural law tradition shared the deep suspicion of unlimited legislative sovereignty. Montesquieu's theory of law inherited many elements of these criticisms. His point of departure was early-modern natural law theory, especially that of Hugo Grotius (1583–1645) and Samuel Pufendorf (1632–94). For Montesquieu, just like his predecessors, nature is not only subject to the physical laws, but also includes the invariable and necessary relations of fairness (equity) (*Spirit*, 4). Positive laws must therefore be derived from the 'nature of things', not from the arbitrary command of the legislator, as Hobbes and Bodin claimed. Montesquieu did not think, however, that the 'nature of things' could be identified simply through the deductive methods which his precursors had employed. His main concern shifted from the a priori reasoning of justice to the analysis of the diversity of laws observed in different times and places. Understanding the rationality of laws, or the 'spirit of the laws' to use his term, requires empirical methods, because it enormously varies with the geographical, historical, economic, and cultural conditions of each country.

Montesquieu could bring himself to regard law neither as the sacred but unknowable principle underlying the custom of each community, nor as an irrational product of their contingency, as the early modern sceptics had often claimed.[13] To uncover the rationality of 'spirit of the laws' he assiduously collected numerous facts, classified them into several categories, and compared them. By these 'sociological' methods, he believed he could explain the phenomenal diversity of the positive laws of different states. It is certain that these attempts led Montesquieu to develop his 'notorious' theory of climates, according to which the climates, hot, temperate, and cold, have definitive effects on human mind and behaviour and consequently the principles underlying the different forms of society in which men are found. Yet despite the apparent reductionist materialism of this approach he never actually yielded to the idea of a single causal explanation of societal and legal differences. Instead, he introduced a more comprehensive and flexible idea, which he called 'general spirit'. This idea later inspired Hegel to formulate his conception of the *Volksgeist*, yet the former contained none of the latter's metaphysical elements. According to the idea of 'general spirits', each political society, according to Montesquieu, acquired the general spirit through its long history, as a characteristic pattern of mind shared by its members. This collective character of mind is formed not only by the physical causes such as territory and climate, but also by the moral causes such as 'religion, laws, the maxims of the government, examples of past things, mores, and manners' (*Spirit*, 310). All these factors are mutually influential, determining and determined. The general spirit is shaped as a result of this complex process.

What constitutes an essential part of the 'spirit of the laws' in any given society or state is, after all, this 'general spirit'. By this quasi-scientific approach to the laws, Montesquieu expanded upon the traditional doctrine of the rule of law. As the 'spirit of the laws' is so closely connected with each society and its particular circumstances one can conclude that those that are effective for one nation may be harmful to another. A legislator must therefore base his laws on the 'general spirit' of his own country and people. This is all the more necessary when he attempts to change a given society, because the 'general spirit' is fragile and susceptible to injury. In this new approach to the rule of law the profound and accurate knowledge of the social and political structure imposes a limit on the arbitrary legislative will of Bodin or Hobbes's absolute sovereign, who is supposed to be bound by no other principle.

To put this new rule of law into practice, Montesquieu relied on nothing except the mechanism of the balance of powers. Legislative power must be checked, not by appeal to a higher 'natural' law but rather by appeal to some independent institutions, which have better knowledge of the 'spirit of the laws' of their country. Examples of such institutions are the 'faculty of vetoing', exercised by the executive power and the House of Lords in England (*Spirit*, 161), the 'depository of laws' (ibid. 19), such as the Parliament in France, which has a right to accept and refuse the registration of laws, and the authority of the senate and the system of a dictator of the Roman republic, both of which limit the overwhelming legislative power of the people (ibid. 177). These institutions do not, however, hold any privileged positions: they themselves are counterbalanced by the other institutions, notably by the legislature. The rule of law is realized in the institutional framework of the separation of powers. In this way Montesquieu combined two of the three dimensions of his critique of despotism and consolidated the foundation of the moderate government in which the 'spirit of the laws' is manifested.

## The theory of the three forms of government

By classifying governments into moderate and despotic, Montesquieu's inquiries were guided by the conditions of political liberty. Yet he also provides another typology, which is better known and more explicitly demonstrated; that is, the typology of the three forms of government. The complex relation between these two classifications has puzzled many interpreters of his work, but before turning to this question, we must first clarify the implications of his particular typology of the three forms of government. Montesquieu followed Aristotle and divided governments into three types according to their 'nature': republican, monarchical, and despotic. A republic, which can be further subdivided into either democracy or aristocracy, is a government in which the people as a whole or a part of the people have sovereign power; a monarchy is a state in which a single person governs by fixed and established laws; a despotic government is that in which one man rules without law, guided solely by his will and caprices (*Spirit*, 10). He develops this Aristotelian perspective by the addition of what he calls the 'principle' of each constitutional form, thus rearranging this received classification. Each form of government has its distinct 'principle', disposition, or 'passion' of the people which activates it: in the case of a republic the principle is 'virtue', in a monarchy it is 'honour', and in a despotic regime it is 'fear'. Clearly Montesquieu did not simply mean by 'principle' the virtue appropriate to each form, as 'fear' does not count as a virtue in the relevant sense. Instead he means the principle that animates the people and makes them act in each regime, and this principle can either be moral in a conventional sense or, as with fear, a more basic passion.

The important category of despotic government becomes a repository of all the evils and corruptions that Montesquieu associated with politics from his earliest writings. These include such things as violent domination without law, the simple and uniform structure of powers, the use of cruel and unusual punishments, and corruption that spreads from the ruler to the subjects. Many of these corruptions were illustrated with supposed examples from Asian countries. In this Montesquieu was, no doubt, caught up in the stereotyped discourse of oriental despotism. Yet it mattered less for Montesquieu where or even whether such grotesque regimes existed in the world, indeed he clearly states that the *perfect* despotism has never existed and will never exist (*Considerations*, 210). Despotic government remains a paradoxical category in Montesquieu's works, because, however much it appears to enjoy its enormous political power, ultimately it reveals itself to be both unstable and self-defeating. Fear is the principle of despotism; that is to say, a people's naked fear of dying and of being deprived of its property is what maintains a despotic regime. In so far as the violence of the ruler and the threat of violence work on the people's instinct for self-preservation, a certain order may be maintained. It is, however, temporary and unstable, because once the real present threat is removed, political union cannot be sustained. Once people can see beyond the immediate presence of fear their compliance with the regime starts to dissipate. As Montesquieu eloquently put it, despotic power is like a flood, which, 'destroying everything on one bank, leaves stretches of land on the other where meadows can be seen in the distance' (*Spirit*, 29).

Montesquieu's model of a democratic republic is the ancient Greek *polis* and republican Rome. By 'virtue', or, more properly, 'political virtue', as the 'principle' of a popular state, he meant the love of country and its laws or patriotism. By entrusting government to all its citizens, a republic demands 'a continuous preference of the public interest over one's own' (ibid. 36), or the opposite of despotism, which is the complete subordination of the public interest to the private interest of the ruler. In order to sustain this republican regime, it becomes necessary to establish frugality and goodness in mores, by using the full power of public education. It is also necessary to divide both land and fortunes equally among the citizens, since political equality is only sustained by economic and social equality. Without this egalitatian ethos personal pride and envy undermines the patriotic subordination of private interest to the public good.

The principle underlying the third regime type is not virtue but honour. This Montesquieu defines as the 'prejudice of each person and each condition' (*Spirit*, 26), and its ultimate essence is to prefer oneself to others, so that the quest for honour continually encourages men to distinguish themselves among their fellows. Consequently, monarchy as a form of government signifies an unequal society where men and women compete with each other for higher positions and reputations. Luxury, fashion, and vanity prevail in monarchical polities, but the result of this dynamic principle is also the steady development of industry and commerce. Owing to this mechanism, monarchy becomes a rich and sophisticated society. As Montesquieu argued, it has a particular structure of unity, wherein it happens that 'each person works for the common good, believing he works for his individual interests' (ibid. 27).

By ironically suggesting that virtue (in the republican sense) is useless and even pernicious in a monarchy, Montesquieu challenges the conventional argument that has its root in Aristotle's *Politics* that, if a virtuous king rules, a monarchy is the best government possible. On the other hand, he contrasts monarchy, and no doubt he had the case of France in mind, with the ancient republic. The contrast between these two governments corresponds to the contrast between the two distinct modes of social integration: in the former, the pursuit of private interest is paradoxically in harmony with the public interest, whereas in the latter the two are in acute tension.

In analysing the paradoxical character of monarchy, Montesquieu draws on Bernard Mandeville's *The Fable of the Bees* (1723) and was probably also influenced by the moral theories of the French Jansenist writers such as Pierre Nicole (1625–95) and La Rochefoucauld (1613–80). Yet unlike these thinkers Montesquieu was less concerned with the psychological analysis of a corrupted human nature and more with the consequences and social conditions that arise from this nature. In particular Montesquieu demonstrates a close relation between the character of a society that allows enough space for the pursuit of private interest and the development of 'commerce'. In part IV of *The Spirit of the Laws* he describes how commerce had steadily developed over a long period of time and on a worldwide scale. This remarkable expansion was favourable to monarchy as a form of government. Montesquieu also assumed that a monarchy could not sustain itself over time unless the excessive consumption of wealthy men redistributed wealth to the poor (*Spirit*, 99). Furthermore, Luxury is not only a result of the structure of this unequal society, but its very *basis*. The global expansion of commerce, which provides one luxurious and novel commodity after another, contributes to strengthening this basis. However naive as an economic analysis of the growth of commercial society, these arguments inspired many Scottish Enlightenment thinkers, most notably David Hume and subsequently Adam Smith, who went on to provide more sophisticated analyses of modern commercial societies.

## Politics and history

Having outlined Montesquieu's views on the types of government and the 'principles' underlying them, we can now turn to the normative implications of his analysis. Two major issues are relevant here. The first concerns his position regarding the desirability of a republic or a monarchy. On this issue, most commentators conclude that, for Montesquieu, only monarchy could qualify as a viable option, at least for the France of his day. On the face of it this seems a difficult position to contest given what he says about the connection between form of government and size of territory. One of the conclusive statements of the theory of three forms of government is that a despotic government is best suited to large empires, a monarchy to 'medium-sized states', and a republic to small states, especially city-states (*Spirit*, 124–6). By a medium-size state he means what we now call a nation-state. He was acutely aware of the rise of the nation-states system in modern Europe, so he had no illusions about the possibility of restoring the ancient-type small republic.

Nevertheless, this does not necessarily imply that Montesquieu regarded republicanism merely as a thing of the past, or as an unattainable ideal based on anachronistic notion of civic virtue. Among various examples of the republican forms of governments, he clearly favoured ancient Rome over the modern aristocratic republics. The Roman republic was highly regarded for its elaborate system of the balance of powers (ibid. 170–86), whereas the modern Italian aristocratic republics, notably Venice, where the nobility held exclusive sovereign power, was seen in a much less favourable light (ibid. 15). Furthermore, Montesquieu contrasted Athens, a commercial republic, with Sparta, a military republic, and opposed the conventional opinion that the mores of rich Athenians were more corrupt than those of the more frugal Spartans. In his judgement, great wealth did not corrupt the mores of the Athenians in so far as the 'spirit of commerce' brought with it 'the spirit of frugality, economy, moderation, work, wisdom, tranquillity, order and rule', whereas in Sparta, 'one wanted the citizens to be idle' (ibid. 48). These formulations suggest that, upon closer examination, a certain type of republic never lost its attractiveness or feasibility for Montesquieu. Thus it was not a gross misunderstanding for the American founding fathers to regard *The Spirit of the Laws* as an important source of ideas for founding their new republic.

The second issue that follows from his analysis of the three types of government relates to the question of whether or not Montesquieu viewed the English constitution as a model that the French monarchy ought to follow. This issue raises the problem that in *The Spirit of the Laws* there are, as we have seen, two distinct theories of government, the theory of two governments—moderate and despotic—and the theory of three types of government—republican, monarchical, and despotic. Although the term 'moderate government' is used in some cases merely as a general term that includes both monarchy and republics, in other instances the meaning of this term is more strictly defined: a moderate government is a state in which 'a power is limited by another power' (*Pensées*, 369[14]) and, in order to form a moderate government, 'one must combine powers, regulate them, temper them, make them act' (*Spirit*, 63). Without a constitution that achieves the balance of powers, neither a monarchy nor a republic can be regarded as a moderate government in the strict sense of the term, as we see from Montesquieu's equivocal attitude towards the Venetian aristocratic republic. As a consequence, neither type of government can secure political liberty, and this explains why Montesquieu was obliged to introduce some additional qualifications to his analysis of the three forms of government, such as 'moderate monarchy' and 'regulated democracy'. It must also be noted that Montesquieu's notion of 'moderate government' in *The Spirit of the Laws* differs from the form of mixed government idealized by the Roman writer Polybius; that is a mixture of all three forms of government, monarchy, aristocracy, and democracy. He also differs from the post-revolutionary English proponents of the mixed government such as the country ideologue Viscount Bolingbroke (1678–1751), whose works were also an important influence on his understanding of English government. In Montesquieu's judgement, the existence of the mechanism of the balance of powers was crucial for political liberty, but whether this balance was achieved by combining all three forms of governments was a secondary question.

These two assumptions concerning the desirability and feasibility of republicanism as opposed to monarchy, as well as the need for a balance of powers to secure political liberty, provides us with an insight into the normative implications that Montesquieu drew from his analysis, especially as this applied to the circumstances of the French state. First we see Montesquieu's strong commitment to the role of the nobility. In *The Spirit of the Laws* he identifies the importance of what he describes as the 'gothic government', which was seen as the common origin for both English and French government. The Germanic peoples who conquered the Roman Empire established a gothic government in both parts of Europe. In France it took a mixed form, combining aristocracy and monarchy, and it lacked from the beginning a democratic element. Despite the absence of a democratic element, Montesquieu believed that the French monarchy remained sufficiently 'moderate' and 'tempered', as long as the powers of the nobility and of the clergy were in concert with those of the king. In this way the French government could be a mixed and balanced government without its having to combine monarchical, aristocratic, and democratic forms as the Polybian model suggests it should. It is precisely the spirit of nobility, with its sense of honour and dignity, that contributed to preserving political liberty in the French regime. Montesquieu demonstrates the significance of this spirit of nobility by alluding to the examples of French nobles during the civil war period, such as Crillon and the vicomte d'Orte: both of whom refused the despotic commands of the kings in the name of their honour (*Spirit*, 33). Although their courageous actions did not derive from the principle of *virtue*, because they were only eager to be distinguished from their fellow citizens with their fine and extraordinary actions, their sense of *honour* contributed to limit the absolute power of the monarch.[15] Thus Montesquieu concluded that it was unnecessary for the French monarchy to imitate the English constitution and institute a parliamentary system in order to secure political liberty and moderate government. To establish and secure a moderate monarchy in France, it is necessary and sufficient to maintain intermediate powers, especially those of the nobility.

The other implication that Montesquieu draws from his analysis of the 'principles' underlying republicanism and monarchy concerns the development of commercial society. Despite his sympathy for republican virtue and his understanding of the threat of despotism that arises from subordinating the public to the private interest of rulers, he was not unsympathetic to the claims of an emerging commercial society in France. In spite of his unconcealed commitment to his social class (the nobility), Montesquieu accepted the gradual change of power structure in his country, where the spirit of commerce was gradually prevailing. A typical example is his attitude towards the new class of nobility, formed through the expansion of government posts and political offices. He claimed that venality is good in the monarchy, on the grounds that it inspires the industry of people who want to reach higher social positions (*Spirit*, 70–1). This unconventional attitude reveals that Montesquieu was not simply nostalgic for the original gothic feudal order nor interested in the ideological defence of the nobility in terms of ancient lineage. This flexible attitude to the demands and benefits of commercial society led him to a new type of balance of powers which he found emerging in England. While he described England in *The Spirit of the Laws*, book XI, as a country that had a power structure inherited from its ancient constitution, he took a rather pessimistic view of the future of the ancient balance of powers in other chapters (see especially book XIX, chapter xxvii). In his judgement, the traditional intermediate powers—especially the English nobility—were on the verge of disintegration, and he pointed out that England was a monarchy under which a republic hides (*Spirit*, 70). In addition, England was also an advanced commercial state where even the nobility engaged in commerce (ibid. 350). Yet, with all these conditions, the political liberty of England was not necessarily in crisis, for instead of the traditional balance of powers between the conventional estates, a new balance between political parties was being formed.[16] These were made up of free men, so that 'if one party gained too much, the effect of liberty would be to lower it' (ibid. 326).

As for political liberty in the French monarchy, Montesquieu recommended in a very modest way sustaining the intermediate powers such as the nobility and promoting the spirit of commerce. While this might seem to suggest that he was simply too cautious in matters of reform, it should not imply that he simply accepted the status quo in his country. Reform must certainly be carried out, but it must also be in harmony with a gradual change in the general spirit of the nation. If he was reluctant simply to introduce the English system into France, it was not because he thought that it contained any serious defects. It was merely because he regarded an artificial imposition of one country's system on another country as a form of despotism.

## Political liberty: 'the liberty of the citizen'

While Montesquieu was resistant to changing radically the form of government in his country, there is one important area in which he can be described as an uncompromising or radical reformer: this is the important issue of justice and political liberty. As we have seen, Montesquieu begins *The Spirit of the Laws* in a way which bears close resemblance to the tradition of natural law. He assumes that justice as 'relations of fairness' exists prior to the creation of positive laws, just as the idea of equal radii exists prior to a circle being drawn (*Spirit*, 4). Although the main parts of *The Spirit of the Laws* were primarily concerned with the diversity of laws and governments, the idea of justice is not abandoned. It appears once again in book XII, which deals with 'the laws that form political liberty in relation to the citizen'. The concept of political liberty in *The Spirit of the Laws* contains two subcategories: political liberty in relation to the constitution, which we have already examined, and political liberty in relation to citizen, or, more simply, the 'liberty of the citizen'. According to Montesquieu, the liberty of the citizen 'consists in security or, at least, in the opinion one has of one's security' (ibid. 188). As we shall see, principles of justice have a close relation with this conception of liberty.

Montesquieu believed that certain civil laws, and especially the criminal laws, are central to securing the liberty of citizens. Such laws, for example, define and secure the property rights of a citizen. And property rights are an essential part of the liberty of the citizen, so the state cannot deprive one of one's property without sufficient compensation, even if it does so in the name of the public good (ibid. 510). Indeed Montesquieu argues that it is a fallacy to say that the property and goods of an individual should yield to the public good, because the latter actually requires that each and every one can best preserve his or her own property. Part of the meaning of the public good is that each person should be left secure in the enjoyment of his own property. In this case, the public authority should obey the principle of equity and be 'like an individual who deals with another individual' (ibid. 510). Although Montesquieu does not explicitly describe it as such, we might safely describe security of property as one of his cardinal principles of justice.

His position in relation to the criminal laws was more definite. In criticizing the defects of the criminal justice system in despotic countries, and sometimes even alluding to the experience of his own country, he proposed radical reform of the criminal law to assure the safety of the citizen. The principle of criminal justice is simple: to maintain the proportional relation between the penalty and the crime. 'It is the triumph of liberty', says Montesquieu, 'when criminal laws draw each penalty from the particular nature of the crime' (ibid. 189). The essence of punishment is 'a kind of retaliation'. Society can refuse to give security to a citizen who deprives another of it, but the degree of the punishment must always be proportional to the harm of the original crime. Although penal codes may vary to a certain degree in accordance with the different structure of each government and society, their primary foundation should be the same and it must be derived from the universal principles of justice.[17]

The role of this universal conception of justice is even more clearly demonstrated in his discussion of slavery. Montesquieu condemned all kinds of slavery, from natural slavery to slavery established as a result of conquest or consent. No one should be so much in servitude to another man that he or she becomes the private property of that person. The ideal of personal security, although not couched in terms of rights, reveals a fundamental commitment to equality that rules out slavery in all its forms. Slavery is not good 'by its nature' (ibid. 246) and in an argument reminiscent of Kant's universalizability test Montesquieu points out that no one who defends slavery because of its utility would 'want to draw lots to know who was to form the part of the nation that would be free and the one that would be enslaved' (ibid. 253). Here, again, the principle of equity and fairness underpins his arguments.

When dealing with questions concerning the life and property of citizens, Montesquieu appeals to universal principles, which he derives directly from nature, rather than appealing to the historical conditions inherent in each form of government. He acknowledges that the ancient republics encouraged slavery, a fact that may be explained and even justified from a political and historical viewpoint. But Montesquieu never accepts it as anything more than a historical fact, because it violates the principles of justice. The gothic government in feudal France could have established political liberty *in relation to the constitution* without providing any political rights to the third estate. However, this would still be against the demands of justice as long as the common people were treated as slaves (ibid. 167). It was only after having established the civil liberty of the people that a regime could become 'the best kind of government men have been able to devise' (ibid. 168). In connecting the liberty of the citizen with the principle of justice, he placed the liberty of the citizen, as it were, above the sphere of politics. As we have seen, Montesquieu did not hesitate to acknowledge the diversity of laws, forms of government, and general spirits, yet he set a limit on how far this diversity has a normative significance: diversity is ultimately acceptable only when civil liberty is guaranteed.

There remains one more further dimension to his account of the liberty of the citizen. At the beginning of *The Spirit of the Laws*, book XII, Montesquieu argues that, while the constitution is free, it remains possible that the citizen is not, and vice versa (ibid. 187). This is because, as far as political liberty in relation to the constitution has its ultimate basis in the dynamic conflicts between the separate powers, there remains a potential danger that this 'dissonant harmony' might entail serious antagonism and violate the security of citizens.[18] To avoid this danger, political liberty at the constitutional level should be accompanied by liberty of the citizen. Only when both the constitution and the citizen are free is perfect political liberty achieved. Thus, unlike the contemporary accounts of republican liberty offered by Philip Pettit and Quentin Skinner,[19] Montesquieu's does not contrast the ideal of political liberty with liberty as the absence of constraint. For Montesquieu, political liberty requires both the dynamic balance of powers within a constitution and the absence of interference with an individual's person and property: neither part above provides a sufficient account of freedom.

## Conclusion

Each of Montesquieu's three criticisms of despotism with which this chapter began can now be seen to permeate his main political work, *The Spirit of the Laws*. We are now in a position to assess his contribution to the development of modern political liberalism. In the first instance Montesquieu's contribution to the development of liberalism is through his formulation of some of the essential principles and commitments of liberal politics such as the idea of justice as fairness, a pluralist vision of political power, and a modernized doctrine of the rule of law. What is more, he also reflects the complexity of liberal politics in the real world, in that these principles and the actual conditions that support them are sometimes in tension, if not in contradiction. While some thinkers emphasize the inconsistency between legislation and the rule of law, between national diversity and the possibility of universal principles of justice, and above all between liberty in the sense of republican self-rule and liberty in the sense of enjoying personal security, Montesquieu prefers to reconcile these tensions rather than to pursue the ultimate grounds of their inconsistency. This is perhaps the main reason why there remains ambiguity about how best to read and interpret his theory. Yet it is his fundamental belief that each of these features is an integral part of free government, and this belief has fascinated those who care about the character of liberal politics.

### FURTHER REFERENCES

Althusser, L., *Politics and History* (London: NLB, 1972).

Bodin, J., *On Sovereignty*, ed. and trans. Julian Franklin (Cambridge: Cambridge University Press, 1992).

Bossuet, J. B., *Discours sur l'histoire universelle* (Paris: Mabre-Cramoisy, 1681).

Carcassone, E., *Montesquieu et le problème de la constitution française au XVIIIe siècle* (Geneva: Slatkine, 1978).

Carrithers, D. W., 'Montesquieu's Philosophy of Punishment', *History of Political Thought*, 19/2 (1998), 213–40.

Cohler, A. M., *Montesquieu's Comparative Politics and the Spirit of American Constitutionalism* (Lawrence: University Press of Kansas, 1988).

Kawade, Y., *Kizoku no toku, Shogyo no seishin: Montesquieu to sensei hihan no keifu* (Tokyo: University of Tokyo Press, 1996).

Keohane, N. O., *Philosophy and the State in France* (Princeton: Princeton University Press, 1980).

Kingston, R., *Montesquieu and the Parlement of Bordeaux* (Geneva: Droz, 1996).

Krause, S. R., *Liberalism with Honor* (Cambridge, Mass.: Harvard University Press, 2002).

Machiavelli, *Discourses on Livy*, trans. H. C. Mansfield and N. Tarcov (Chicago: Chicago University Press, 1996).

Oakeshott, M., *On Human Conduct* (Oxford: Clarendon Press, 1975).

Pangle, T. L., *Montesquieu's Philosophy of Liberalism* (Chicago: University of Chicago Press, 1973).

Pettit, P., *Republicanism* (Oxford: Clarendon Press, 1997).

Shackleton, R., *Montesquieu* (Oxford: Oxford University Press, 1961).

Shklar, J. N., *Montesquieu* (Oxford: Oxford University Press, 1987).

Skinner, Q., *Liberty before Liberalism* (Cambridge: Cambridge University Press, 1998).

## NOTES

1. R. Shackleton, *Montesquieu* (Oxford: Oxford University Press, 1961).
2. T. L. Pangle, *Montesquieu's Philosophy of Liberalism* (Chicago: University of Chicago Press, 1973).
3. Michael Oakeshott finds his model of *societas*, contrasted with that of *universitas*, in Montesquieu's formulation of the monarchy. *On Human Conduct* (Oxford: Clarendon Press, 1975), 245–51.
4. Although many detailed studies have been made on this issue, the classic study of Carcassonne remains reliable and influential (E. Carcassone, *Montesquieu et le problème de la constitution française au XVIIIe siècle* (Geneva: Slatkine, 1978) ).
5. Keohane argues, for example, that Montesquieu criticizes some corrupted aspects of modern 'liberal' monarchies from the standpoint of the classical republican ideal. See N. O. Keohane, *Philosophy and the State in France* (Princeton: Princeton University Press, 1980), 415–19.
6. L. Althusser, *Politics and History* (London: NLB, 1972).
7. *Persian Letters*, trans. C. J. Betts (Harmondsworth: Penguin, 1973) (hereafter *PL*).
8. J.-B. Bossuet, *Discours sur l'histoire universelle* (Paris: Mabre-Cramoisy, 1681), 1021–2. The source of Bossuet's historical perspective is the thesis of historians of the early Roman Empire, such as Florus and Appian.
9. Montesquieu, *Considerations on the Causes of the Greatness of the Romans and their Decline*, trans. D. Lowenthal (Indianapolis: Hackett, 1999).
10. Machiavelli, *Discourses on Livy*, trans. H. C. Mansfield and N. Tarcov (Chicago: University of Chicago Press, 1996), 16.
11. Montesquieu, *The Spirit of the Laws*, ed. and trans. A. M. Cohler, B. C. Miller, and H. S. Stone (Cambridge: Cambridge University Press, 1989).
12. Jean Bodin, *On Sovereignty*, ed. and trans. Julian Franklin (Cambridge: Cambridge University Press, 1992), 56.
13. The emphasis on the irrationality of the laws spreads from Montaigne and theorists of the reason of the state such as Gabriel Naudé (1600–53), to Jansenist thinkers, notably Pascal.
14. Montesquieu, *Pensées*, ed. L. Desgraves (Paris: Robert Laffont, 1991).
15. Krause finds in this episode a kind of liberalism

that the idea of honour generates (S. R. Krause, *Liberalism with Honor* (Cambridge, Mass.: Harvard University Press, 2002) ). See also my study, written in Japanese (Y. Kawade, *Kizoku no toku, Shogyo no seishin: Montesquieu to sensei hihan no keifu* (Tokyo: University of Tokyo Press, 1996)).

16. Shackleton thinks that for Montesquieu this denotes mainly a court–country conflict, not a Tory–Whig conflict (*Montesquieu*, 295–8).
17. For further and different discussion of Montesquieu's idea of criminal justice, see e.g. R. Kingston, *Montesquieu and the Parlement of Bordeaux* (Geneva: Droz, 1996), and D. W. Carrithers, 'Montesquieu's Philosophy of Punishment', *History of Political Thought*, 19/2 (1998), 213–40.
18. He once made critical remarks on England and ancient Greek republics, because they fail to secure the property of citizens. The political liberty at the constitutional level of these countries 'often yields two factions in a state'. 'The superior faction enjoys its advantages over the inferior without mercy. A faction which dominates is less terrible than a prince in anger' (*Pensées*, 195).
19. Philip Pettit, *Republicanism: A Theory of Freedom and Government* (Oxford: Clarendon Press, 1997), and Quentin Skinner, *Liberty before Liberalism* (Cambridge: Cambridge University Press, 1998).

# 14 Rousseau

David Boucher

## Contents



## Chapter guide

The chapter begins by demonstrating the diversity of interpretation of Rousseau's political ideas, and suggests that, because of his emphasis upon civic virtues and freedom as lack of an insidious form of dependence, the republican tradition best reflects his concerns. The chapter then examines Rousseau's distinctive contribution to the idea of the state of nature, which is self-consciously critical of that of Hobbes. The springs of action in Rousseau's state of nature are not reason, because this will be at a rudimentary level, which differentiates him from many natural law and natural rights thinkers, but self-preservation and sympathy. He identifies the source of modern evils in the invention of private property and the social contract as the device by which the consequent inequalities arose as the means to consolidate them. His book *The Social Contract* is a redemptive tract in that it seeks to rectify the contingent evils of the original contract with a new theory of freedom conceived in terms of obedience to the general will. A number of aspects of the theory are examined in the light of severe criticisms of their potential totalitarian consequences. It is suggested that such an interpretation is less than generous. The chapter concludes with a discussion of Rousseau's concern with freedom and dependence.

## Biography

Jean-Jacques Rousseau was born in Geneva in 1712 to a family of middle-class connections. His father had married a woman of higher social status, but his pretensions to social grandeur soon evaporated as his liking for hunting, dancing, and duelling took priority over his watchmaking. Although Isaac Rousseau's circumstances rapidly changed from residing in the more sought-after region of Geneva to the working-class area of St Gervais, he thought of himself as naturally aristocratic, and cheated of his rights. Isaac Rousseau, whose wife died shortly after giving birth to Jean-Jacques, was exiled from Geneva when his son was 10 years old for challenging a gentleman above his rank to a duel. On being accused of being no gentleman, he brandished a sword.

On a personal level Rousseau often appears unattractive. He thought himself like no other person, and exhibited tendencies towards hypochondria and paranoia, compounded by the fact that he was often ill and had many enemies. Rousseau's was a demonic mind. David Hume at first quite liked him, but soon became distraught after becoming the victim of one of Rousseau's character assassinations. Hume described him as a 'pernicious and dangerous' man who 'lies like the devil'.[1] Diderot, the French *philosophe*, similarly came to feel uneasy in Rousseau's company because he felt as if a soul condemned to damnation stood before him, capable of persuading Diderot of the existence of devils and hell. Casanova met Rousseau in the summer of 1759 in Montmorency, where Rousseau was earning a living as a copyist of music. While Casanova appreciated his powers of reasoning, in other respects he found Rousseau impolite and unpleasant.[2]

Rousseau was a true Renaissance man in that he put his talents to a variety of quite different activities. He was a novelist whose *Émile*, a treatise on the education of a child, and *Nouvelle Héloïse*, complement and cast light on his political writings. He was also a composer of some note. Although Rousseau is most famous for his political philosophy, he was also a well-respected composer of operas, and compiled a scholarly and authoritative dictionary of music, something that occupied him more than anything else throughout his life. During his time in Turin as a youth and later as secretary to the French Ambassador in Venice, he developed a passion for Italian music, which he publicly defended against the claims to superiority of French music. Rousseau's opera *The Village Soothsayer* was Italian in style, and much admired and imitated.

Rousseau converted to Catholicism in 1728 and found refuge with a fellow convert, a Swiss baroness by the name of Madame de Warens, twelve years his senior. It was she who ignited his passion for learning. He lived with Madame de Warens between 1729 and 1742, first as guest and then as lover. He called her Mamam and she him Petit. When she invited Rousseau into her bed, she was already intimate with her amanuensis, six years older than Rousseau and someone he greatly admired. To sleep with his protector, and the lover of a friend, engendered feelings of guilt. He was a party to a *ménage à trois* and at the same time felt that he was committing incest. Rousseau escaped the situation by moving to Paris in 1842, where he met some of the leading *philosophes*, such Denis Diderot and Jean Le Rond d'Alembert, who jointly edited the *Encyclopédie*. He fathered five children in rapid succession by the same woman, Thérèse Le Vasseur, a maid he met while staying in a Paris hotel, and whom he married late in life at the age of 56. He committed all of the children to the foundling home shortly after birth, which he justified by exclaiming that he was not financially fit to be a father, and that they would have a much better upbringing there. This added to an already troubled conscience. Rousseau's personal life, more so than that of most philosophers, is closely related to his philosophy, which is an attempt to recapture lost innocence and a blueprint for moral redemption.

Having indulged himself to excess in the sensuous pleasures, Rousseau experienced remorse and at the age of 37 he renounced his former life. The occasion for his new illumination was an advertisement for a prize essay the subject of which was the question of whether the revival of arts and sciences had led to an improvement in people's morals. He realized in a flash of inspiration that such progress had the opposite effect. In the essay which he wrote for the Dijon prize, which he won with his *Discourse on the Sciences and the Arts*, Rousseau argued that progress is illusory and that the so-called sciences were causing the ruin of mankind. Furthermore, the developments in modern culture had done nothing to make men more happy or virtuous. Only in simple societies, he argued, where people lived a Spartan existence, could virtue flourish. The more sophisticated a culture, the more corrupt it is likely to be. Rousseau uses Plato as evidence in support of his ideas. Plato had seen the danger of allowing poets and artists to live uncensored in the *Republic*. He recommended that they be exiled from the ideal *polis*. By the early 1750s Rousseau had moved away from Catholicism and proudly adopted the title of citizen of Geneva. In his *Letter to D'Alembert* (1758) Rousseau denounces a plan to introduce and establish a theatre in Calvinist Geneva. It was a dangerous invitation to immorality and an affront to Genevan republican virtue. He argued that, while theatres may be appropriate for monarchies, free entertainments such as games, athletics, dances, and concerts were much more in keeping with the idea of a republic. With the publication of *Émile* and *The Social Contract* Rousseau was denounced both in France and Geneva in 1762 for his unorthodox and heretical views on religion, despite describing himself as the only man in France who believed in God. From then on he lived a somewhat nomadic existence. He died unexpectedly on 2 July 1778 at Ermenonville. His body was exhumed and transferred to the Panthéon during the French Revolution.

## Key texts

*Discourse on the Sciences and the Arts* (1750)
*Discourse on the Origin of Inequality* (1754)
*Discourse on Political Economy* (1755)
*The Social Contract* (1762)
*Émile* (1762), trans. Allan Bloom (New York: Basic Books, 1979).
*Constitutional Project for Corsica* (1765), trans. Frederick Watkins, in *Rousseau's Political Writings* (Edinburgh: Thomas Nelson, 1953).
*The Government of Poland* (1772), trans. Willmoore Kendall (Indianapolis: Hackett, 1985).
*The Confessions of Jean-Jacques Rousseau* (1782), trans. J. M. Cohen (London: Penguin, 1953).

## Main texts used

Jean-Jacques Rousseau, *The Basic Political Writings*, ed. Donald A. Cress, introd. Peter Gay (Indianapolis: Hackett, 1987) (includes *Discourse on the Sciences and Arts*; *Discourse on the Origin of Inequality*; *Discourse on Political Economy*; *On the Social Contract*).

*Rousseau on International Relations*, ed. Stanley Hoffmann and David P. Fidler (Oxford: Clarendon Press, 1991) (includes the Geneva Manuscript of *The Social Contract*; *Constitutional Project for Corsica*; *Considerations on the Government of Poland*; *The State of War*).

## Key ideas

**Dependence** could take a benign form or one that leads to domination and servitude. Much of Rousseau's theory is concerned with avoiding the latter type. **The state of nature**: used as a theoretical device to show the contingency of human development. The prominent motivating factors in the state of nature are self-preservation and pity. **The social contract**: a hypothetical device in the early writings to show that character traits evident in society need not be viewed as universal and inevitable features of human nature. In the book of the same name it is the means by which individuals, already having rights and property, constitute themselves into the sovereign body of citizens in which their rights and property are secured on a different and firmer foundation. **The general will**: an ambiguous concept meant to capture what is the real will of the citizen, free of selfish interests. It is not discovered by acclamation, nor majority rule, and may indeed be the will of one enlightened person. **The lawgiver** assumes the persona of a semi-divine leader whose charismatic personality enables him to persuade the sovereign body, without force, that those thing necessary for redeeming a corrupt people have behind them the authority of God. **Civil religion**: a civic profession of faith. It is taken by critics to be a clear sign of Rousseau's totalitarian tendencies, along with his **censorial tribunal** meant to shape the public morals of the people.

# Introduction

Like Giambattista Vico, the Italian historicist, Rousseau saw the human world as a product of human intelligence. The evils that he saw around him—the power politics, insecurity, and immorality—were all of human creation, and far from being structurally inherent and deterministic, could be overcome by human will. Thus, far from being the extreme pessimist that he is often portrayed to be, Rousseau had faith in the human capacity for self-redemption, starting with the reconstitution of the state on ethical principles. It is the details of his argument that have given rise to a considerable diversity of interpretation.

Rousseau is notorious for the ambiguity that surrounds many of his most important doctrines. Despite the diversity of the subjects on which he wrote, he claimed always to employ the same principles, beliefs, and maxims. He almost invited wildly divergent interpretations because of his alacrity of style and talent for coining epigrams so striking that they have been abstracted from their contexts and used against him. He did not attempt to be a systematic philosopher, and largely reacted against the formalized rules of clear, witty exposition practised by the Enlightenment *philosophes*.[3] Since Rousseau's death in 1778 interpreters of his thought have taken very different views on his intended meaning. His political philosophy has at once been condemned as proto-totalitarian and praised for its liberal democratic sympathies. If one gives prominence to Rousseau's preoccupation with moral creativity and redemption, he exudes the character of a liberal, but if one gives priority to the tendency towards enforcing conformity and the imposition of social and civic values, he begins to look much more like a totalitarian. It may, however, be more appropriate to see him as a republican firmly rooted in the republican traditions of virtue, patriotism, and citizenship.

## Totalitarian, liberal, or republican?

Rousseau, like Hegel, has had a considerable degree of responsibility placed on his shoulders for the ills of the twentieth century. He is said to have given rise to the Hitler phenomenon in European history. L. G. Crocker, adopting a psycho-historical approach to interpretation, labels Rousseau an authoritarian and equates his political writings with this character trait. Robespierre is accused of implementing the 'total collectivist state of *The Social Contract* in which "virtue patriotism" would rule'.[4] J. L. Talmon, among Rousseau's detractors, has articulated the most persuasive case for totalitarianism. He claims that Rousseau, tormented by paranoia, personally a mass of conflicting emotions and psychological undercurrents, wanted to impose an inflexible pattern of behaviour and prescriptive range of feelings on society, in order to eradicate contradictions and anti-societal urges. The aim was to create citizens who could will only what the general will dictated in order to subdue the possibility of enslavement to egoistic tendencies. Rousseau is, for Talmon, a typical case of 'the strange combination of psychological ill-adjustment and totalitarian ideology'.[5] It is Rousseau's conflation of a natural harmonious order with the idea of popular sovereignty that gives rise to totalitarian democracy.

On the other hand, commentators have noticed Rousseau's emphasis upon freedom and the importance of autonomy to be indicative of his liberal credentials. C. W. Hendel, for example, takes Rousseau to be engaged in exploring what constitutes the good life. The problem that he sets himself, Hendel claims, is to set men free of tyranny, both from within and from without.[6] One of the most notable exponents of this view was Ernst Cassirer. He saw Rousseau as the philosopher of liberty, both spiritual and ethical. Ethical liberty complements the spiritual, but 'could not be achieved without a radical transformation of the social order, a transformation that will wipe out all arbitrariness and that alone can help the inner necessity of law to victory'.[7] Cassirer was nevertheless cognizant of the fact that, unlike French *philosophes* such as Diderot, and for that matter English liberals, Rousseau did not subscribe to the Whig view of history that posited a certain inevitability to progress. His guiding principle was that man is basically good, and that society has corrupted him, but paradoxically it is only society that can redeem him. A society that produces only corrupt fools does not deserve to exist.

With renewed contemporary interest in the republican tradition in political thought, primarily stimulated by J. G. A. Pocock's *The Machiavellian Moment*,[8] Rousseau is seen in a light that more adequately becomes him. Maurizio Viroli, a leading advocate of modern republicanism, contends that Rousseau fully comprehended the immense importance of the unity of a people, both culturally and spiritually. This unity is achieved through the conscious promotion of civic virtues. Rousseau thought of the *patrie* in terms of ancient republicanism and its modern exemplars, and not as a nationalist. Like the *philosophes*, whose cosmopolitanism he despised, Rousseau equated *patrie* with 'republic' and subscribed to the general view that political virtue is synonymous with love of the fatherland, an ancient legacy that modern politics was intent to destroy. In both his *Discourse on the Sciences and the Arts* and *Discourse on Political Economy* Rousseau maintains that in order to make citizens virtuous you must first instil in them the love of one's country (*Basic Political Writings*, 4–5 and 121[9]). Rousseau to some extent appropriates the language of Montesquieu in lamenting the decline of political virtue among his contemporaries. Montesquieu praised the ancients for their political virtue, and the moderns for their civility. Rousseau, while agreeing with the former judgement, was vehemently critical of the corruption of civility among the moderns, against which he contrasts the virtue of rustic peasants, the demi-god citizens of Sparta, and the Roman republic. Rousseau is a passionate promoter of civic virtue, by which he means the strength of moral character to fight against corruption and oppression.[10] It is a passion for virtue born of the love of one's country, an erotic love, an ardour far more intense than that for a mistress, akin to that which Pericles extols in the funeral oration in Thucydides, that he wants to instil in modern citizens. It is a love of one's own people, institutions, and collective memory, manifest in a love of liberty, for ourselves and our compatriots. Consistent with republican ideals Rousseau believed that liberty and law were correlative and consistent as long as those who fall within their jurisdiction are also those who prescribe the law, and sovereignty as a consequence resides in the people and not above them.[11] In republican theory the liberty of the individual is not constrained by obedience to the state. Just laws are far from being a constraint upon liberty, but, on the contrary, an essential element of it. There is a great difference between obedience to the law and being enslaved by it. Rousseau contended that 'a free people obeys, but it does not serve, it has leaders but no masters; it obeys the laws, but it obeys only the laws, and it is due to the strength of laws that it is not forced to obey men'.[12]

## Rousseau's state of nature

Rousseau almost seems to take a perverse pleasure in rejecting the conventional wisdom of the day and presenting ideas that were both novel and shocking. He rejected the view of Samuel von Pufendorf that men are naturally social, as well as Hobbes's contention that men are self-seeking and competitive by nature. Furthermore, he denies that history has brought progress in the condition of mankind. Rousseau begins his exploration into the human condition with the isolated individual in a state of nature. The difficulty of using the idea of a state of nature, Rousseau acknowledges, is that those who employ it project characteristics found only in society upon men in their original condition. The state of nature for him was simply a useful hypothesis. We should therefore disregard recourse to the 'facts' when employing the concept in argument and rely instead upon 'right and reason' (Geneva Manuscript, 114[13]). The purpose of positing basic postulates about human beings is in order to conjecture and reason conditionally, not about the factual origin of the present condition of society, but upon its contingency and how it may have been other than it is. In effect, what he is saying is that we should not infer from the current condition of society and the human characteristics indicative of it that there is anything inevitable or necessary in how it came to be as it is. The state of nature in Rousseau is an idea against which the present condition of society and international relations may be judged.[14]

## Rousseau's criticisms of Hobbes

Rousseau's characterization of the state of nature, although different in detail, has similarities with that of Hobbes. For Rousseau, in contrast with thinkers such as Pufendorf and Locke, the state of nature is neither a social nor a moral condition. Nature gives us no sanction for legitimate authority or rule. It is a condition in which no one has the right to rule over another. There is no justice nor injustice, and men are portrayed as solitary and self-sufficient.

## Self-preservation and sympathy

According to Rousseau there are two principles that humans exhibit prior to developing reason, self-preservation and sympathy or pity. The first principle is shared with Hobbes. The state of nature is an asocial condition. Humans pursue their own interests, and have a capacity for self-preservation, but there is no natural right to everything merely because we have certain needs.[15] It is Hobbes's propensity to project human characteristics found only in society back into the state of nature that leads him to conclude that the savage man's concern for self-preservation is prejudicial to the survival of others. It is self-respect that disposes people to their own preservation, and this should not be confused with egoism, which is something that emerges in society and is a relative and adversarial feeling unknown in the state of nature. While acknowledging Hobbes's undoubted genius, Rousseau thinks him perverse for imagining a race of people who imagine that its welfare depends on the destruction of its fellow human beings. It was Hobbes's passionate desire to established absolute rule and the demand for absolute obedience to it that lead him to characterize man in a perpetual state of war with his fellow men (*The State of War*, 45).

Rousseau maintained that Hobbes was wrong to suggest that in the absence of goodness in the state of nature man is naturally evil, or that there is nothing to inspire a person to help another to whom he has no obligation. Rousseau's portrayal of natural man was quite shocking for his contemporaries and drew the condemnation of leading churchmen. Effectively in emphasizing the natural goodness of natural man Rousseau rejected the fundamental Christian notion of original sin. Hobbes had failed, in Rousseau's view, to identify the second principal characteristic in humans prior to reason, the natural virtue of, or capacity for, pity or sympathy. It is pity, prior to all reflection, that mitigates the excesses of self-preservation. Suffering in other human beings is something to which we have a natural aversion. Pity is the source from which all the rest of human virtue flows. Rousseau argued that 'Pity is what takes us without reflection to the aid of those we see suffering. Pity is what, in the state of nature, takes the place of laws, mores, and virtue, with the advantage that no one is tempted to disobey its sweet voice' (*Discourse on the Origin of Inequality*, 55[16]). The implication is that while there is no transcendental natural law discoverable through reason, there are natural sentiments which make us averse to certain kinds of action.

Egoism, not sociality, then, are characteristics of Rousseau's pre-social humans. Despite the fact that they have not yet developed reason, they understand the principles of self-preservation and pity. They are compassionate, but not naturally social.[17] Human beings have little need of each other's company or support in Rousseau's state of nature. There is little inclination or need to associate other than to procreate. Peace and tranquillity are what the savage man desires. Men are relatively equal in the state of nature, and their early actions are characterized by innocence and goodness. The inequalities that exist among men are due to their natural limitations (*The State of War*, 37).

Humans are distinguished from animals in the state of nature in possessing two potentialities. Because humans are not completely governed by impulse they have the potential to be free. Animals are incapable of anything other than succumbing to the impulse of nature, but humans are conscious of alternatives and in varying degrees free to choose between them. This potential for self-determination remains nascent outside society, and is manifest only in immediate self-survival. So why would this 'noble savage', content with his or her surroundings, and in relative harmony with a nature that satisfies physical needs, want to escape from the solitary existence that appears to be conducive to an existence for the most part free of conflict and competition? In this condition the potential for moral and psychological growth lies untapped because there is no incentive to change. It is the necessity to adapt to changing conditions that generates or impels the natural man towards society or social relations. Increased population, climate change, and a less plentiful food supply alters the harmony in which individuals found themselves with nature. As the satisfaction of desires become more difficult in time of relative scarcity, humans are faced with having to think and deliberate, even intermittently cooperate with others in order to achieve what they want. This is a process that allows no return to the natural condition because the stimulation of intelligence by the desires leads to the formulation of more and sophisticated wants.

The potential for perfectibility entails possessing a nature that is capable of being developed. Rousseau indicates that this development is self-directional unless our choices divert or pervert its course. As humans acquire reason, they begin to discern an idea of what this potential perfectibility intimates, and what obligations and values are implied by it. Individuals may choose to follow this course, or deviate from it. The facility we possess for self-improvement when acted upon by circumstances precipitates the development of the rest of our faculties. Fully developed human potential entails finding the greatest contentment in values and courses of action deemed right by conscience and reason.

In being forced to associate through scarcity and in formulating new wants through the stimulation of the intelligence, the potential for perversion becomes actual. In society humans become self-seeking and egoistic, desiring things not because of their intrinsic worth but because they want to excite the admiration of others. In comparing ourselves with others the self is never satisfied because in valuing ourselves above others we vainly demand that others value us above themselves. At this point the capacity for both freedom and self-perfection are undermined. A person is not free in pursuing goals that are expected of him or her, or merely because that person wants to better the attainments of others. It is a form of dependence inimical to freedom and perfectibility. Dependence can be benign in that we rely upon other people for all sorts of things, security, commodities, emotional support, and for personal development. There is a danger, however, that these benign forms of dependence offer opportunities for a perverse type that leads to exploitation and servitude.

In Rousseau's theory, then, evil is not attributed to original sin, nor is it generated by something endemic in human nature. The noble savage as an isolated, relatively content, innocent, and sympathetic being is characterized by *amour de soi*, or self-love, and it is not until he enters into society that he exhibits *amour propre*, vanity or selfish love. It is selfish love, argues Ernst Cassirer, the famous interpreter of Rousseau, that 'contains the cause of all future depravity and fosters man's vanity and thirst for power'.[18] In characterizing the non-social condition of humanity devoid of *amour propre*, or vanity, Rousseau distanced himself from the dominant tradition of ascribing to the pre-eminence of the selfish passions in the state of nature our propensity to set up society.[19]

## The source of inequality

The invention of property is, for Rousseau, the source of inequality and of most of the depravities that are manifest in the human race. Property gives rise to the inequalities of power and reputation. The only conceivable source of a claim on property is the mixing of one's labour with the land, which in turn suggests an entitlement to the produce. The wheat I cultivate in the field is mine. Cultivation of the field over successive years must have given rise to the claim that it is one's own. However, the powerful among the inhabitants of the state of nature realized their strength and described their own needs as 'a sort of right' to the property of others, which gave rise to a vicious conflict between 'the right of the strongest and the right of the first occupant'. Thus, Rousseau argued: 'Emerging society gave way to the most horrible state of war . . . [and] brought itself to the brink of ruin' (*Discourse on the Origin of Inequality*, 68). Man's self-interestedness (*amour propre*), or pride, is the wrong foundation for society and can lead only to disputes. Egoistic individualism led to the breakdown of emerging society into a Hobbesian war of all against all. To resolve the conflict by basing the social contract on similar principles, as Hobbes does, is extreme folly.

Those accustomed to society are not content with living within themselves and live only for the attention and recognition of others. It is in the judgement of others that they are aware of their own existence. The disputes which arose as a consequence of property led those advantaged by them to propose the establishment of society in order to protect themselves and their property. In the state of nature there are, of course, natural inequalities of age, strength, ability, and health. People are unsuspectingly duped into consenting to those very institutions, based on egoistic individualism or self-love, that compound artificial inequalities that are social in origin: honour, prestige, power, and privilege. The establishment of society immediately destroyed natural liberty and legitimized the acts of usurpation by which property had been acquired and inequality instituted, condemning the whole of the human race to 'labour, servitude and misery' (*Discourse on the Origin of Inequality*, 70). What Rousseau wanted to emphasize was that the passions that incline us to violence, aggression, and war are not pre-societal, but actually acquired in society itself. In this context men and women, motivated by pride, acquire their characteristics and values from their co-associates, and are unable to acknowledge their propensity for virtue and morality. Reason and conscience is unable to influence the formation of their characters because they have fallen victim to reciprocal egoism.[20]

It is important to emphasize that Rousseau's *Social Contract* is an attempt to overcome the immorality and degradation consequent upon establishing a society based on a multiplicity of particular wills. A society based on the principle of the general will, at the heart of which is the idea of the common good, would eradicate the ills of modern society. He is committed to civil equality and the full responsibility of all citizens to participate in the legislative process.

The state of war is for Hobbes a consequence of human nature. Without a Leviathan to keep states in awe they will always adopt the posture of war in relation to each other. States sustain a way of life and make life more commodious for their citizens, so that the posture of war against other states is never so unmitigated as it is in the state of nature. For Rousseau, war is the result of a corruption of human nature. It is a condition that prevails among states and not among individuals, and its consequences are far more destructive. Instead of alleviating violence, states accentuate it. Rousseau maintains that the weak consider themselves bound to the strong by informal agreements, alliances, and treaties. The strong, on the other hand, feel no similar obligation to the weak. There is no claim here that the strong have a right in nature to dominate the weak.

## Natural law and natural rights

Rousseau was familiar with the writings of Grotius, Pufendorf, and Burlamaqui, and himself uses the vocabulary of the Natural Law School. He nevertheless transforms the doctrine. He does not deny that God is the source of all justice. Indeed, he suggests that independently of conventions that which conforms with order is good. Rousseau qualifies his position, however, by suggesting that we are unable to receive justice from such an abstract source. It is therefore necessary for us to establish governments (*Social Contract*, 160). Natural law in the state of nature is related to natural sentiments which make us turn away from acts of cruelty. It is not a law of nature discoverable by, nor consistent with, reason. Natural man has not yet developed rational capacities that would enable him to know this law. This must await the institution of civil society.

Rousseau argued that modern exponents of natural law restrict its scope to moral relations among rational men, whose reason enables them to apprehend it. They are all agreed, despite variety in definition, that it is impossible to come to know the precepts of natural law and to obey them without being a 'great reasoner and profound metaphysician' (*Discourse on the Origin of Inequality*, 34). Paradoxically, in order to establish society men must already require what only a select few acquire within it: a highly developed rational faculty. In order to make just laws, men should already be what they will become as a result of the laws (*Social Contract*, 164).

Rousseau denied one of the most typical claims of natural law theorists and contended that it is fallacious to assume a general society of mankind united under a universal moral law. The common feeling necessary to constitute humanity as one is not evident, nor is there any sense that in acting as an individual an end relative and general to the whole is being pursued. Ideas of God and natural law could not, in Rousseau's view, be innate in men's hearts. If they were, it would not be necessary to teach them. Far from the moral community of humanity being manifest in society—the universal giving rise to the particular—it is actually constituted societies that engender ideas of an imagined universal society on humankind. In order to conceive ourselves as men, we must first become citizens. The facts confirm what reason teaches. The laudable ideas of natural right and the brotherhood of man emerge relatively late in human development, and they do not become widely accepted until the advent of Christianity, and even then such beliefs are unsettled and intermittently held. Even under the laws of Justinian the humanity of the Romans extended only as far as the boundaries of the empire (Geneva Manuscript, 104–9). Rousseau denied, then, that men in a state of nature have natural rights that they carry over into political society, and hold against the state. The only sense in which he has a conception of natural rights is in maintaining a general right, or perhaps potential would be a better word, to self-realization.

Whatever other qualities men in the state of nature may have possessed when looked at retrospectively, they were nevertheless still brutes and savages. They were not self-conscious of being free and knew nothing of human relationships. Within the state of nature principles of natural law would simply be inapplicable because its inhabitants have no recognizable moral relations with, nor obligations to, each other. They simply lack the capacity of following its precepts. The inequalities found among men in society are not sanctioned by the moral natural law in a state of nature; they are in Rousseau's view most certainly the consequence of human law.

Exponents of natural law begin by identifying rules that it would be appropriate for men to agree upon as socially useful and give to them the name of natural law on no other grounds than the supposed good that would result from their universal observance. Such explanations of the nature of things are based on more or less arbitrary notions of what seems right. Rousseau's main contention against natural law jurists was that they assume what they seek to prove. They consistently fail to strip away those characteristics of man acquired in society. They take what men have socially acquired and project it back into a state of nature. In other words, natural law jurists fail to go back far enough or deep enough into the origins of man.

## Plastic man

Despite the fact that Rousseau used the fashionable vocabulary of natural rights, his ideas were a considerable departure from what was conventionally associated with the doctrine. Primarily, he denied that humanity has an immutable moral nature, or that society is created to protect pre-existing and inalienable natural rights. His state of nature is not a moral condition, and its inhabitants are so deficient in reason that, even if there were a moral law under which natural rights were subsumed, they would not be capable of coming to know it. Human nature is not immutable. Rousseau maintains that the human race differs in character from age to age. The soul and passions of human beings, along with needs and pleasures, change. What was the ultimate happiness for the savage would reduce the civilized man to despair. Robert Wokler has pointed out that more than any modern thinker Rousseau believed that human nature is shaped by politics.[21] Leo Strauss has gone as far as to suggest that for Rousseau man is infinitely malleable.[22] We should not, however, overstate this aspect of his thought. While there is considerable scope for moulding human nature, it is not limitless. The historical process works on material that is restricted in its potential. Natural man is motivated by the sentiments of self-love and pity, but he also possesses a free will and the capacity for perfectibility, or self-improvement. Rousseau was certainly of the opinion that man's plasticity was amenable to both exalted and depraved influences. A good society provides the environment for the development of virtuous citizens whose interests are in harmony with the common good. Rousseau did believe that there is a moral self to be realized and that its realization is consistent with man's nature. A corrupt society produces citizens motivated by their particular selfish wills.

Decline is not inevitable on emerging from the state of nature. Potentially all that is greatest in humanity can be nurtured and flourish. Alternatively, man's nature may be stained with the vilest depravity. The route taken is determined by humans themselves. The state of nature is barely a human condition, and is neither sociable nor moral. It is in society that people acquire what is distinctly human. The individual becomes transformed 'from a stupid, limited animal into an intelligent being and a man' (*Social Contract*, 151). Justice is substituted for instinct, duty for physical impulse, and right for appetite. Only then can the souls of men become elevated, their minds develop, their intellectual horizons become more expansive, and feelings take on new depths. Rousseau's theory is constitutive in that the nature of man is related to the social relationships into which he is interwoven and which extend over long periods of time. Human nature and human community are inextricable, the latter being constitutive of the former.

The purpose of his *Discourse on the Origin of Inequality* is to demonstrate not only the social and historical origins of human wickedness, but also the social origins of morality.[23] Humans could be the most elevated of creatures if it were not for the abuse of their new social condition, which often degenerated lower than the one that they left. In looking at the corruption and immorality around him, Rousseau charted the path to degradation that men have trodden because of their estrangement from conscience. Conscience harnessed to reason is the internal source of moral teaching.

In sum, then, Rousseau objected to government premissed on self-interest and the inequalities consequent upon it. The purpose of *The Social Contract* is to bring about a transformation in this condition and bring conscience back in line with reason.

In *The Social Contract* Rousseau outlines the arrangements for the sort of political association that would precipitate moral progress and virtuous conduct, something that the advances in arts and letters had failed to achieve. In this book Rousseau attempted to formulate a criterion of conduct that would overcome the difficulties associated with the abstractness of the Natural Law School and the narrow self-interestedness of doctrines such as that of Hobbes.

The criterion of ethical conduct is to be, not an abstract natural law divorced from the experience of human beings, nor principles based upon self-interest and capable of justifying any capricious act, but instead a criterion that is immanent in the real will of individuals, a criterion based upon the principle of a common good rather than self-interest, the idea of the general will rather than a particular will. This is what he means at the beginning of *The Social Contract* when he says, 'I will always try in this inquiry to bring together what right permits with what interest prescribes, so that justice and utility do not find themselves at odds with one another' (*Social Contract*, 141). He goes on to say that the rights of a social order are the most sacred of all and are the foundation of all others. The rights are not natural, but instead 'founded upon conventions'. Unlike the human constitution, which is a work of nature, the constitution of the state is a work of art (ibid. 1994).

## The problem of freedom

The problem that Rousseau sees human beings confronting is that they want to be free, but they also want the advantages of living in society, because it is only as a citizen that man can fulfil himself and become virtuous: 'Man was born free, and he is everywhere in chains' (*Social Contract*, 141). It is necessary, then, to devise a political and social order in which this contradiction can be resolved. *The Social Contract* is meant to answer this question: 'How to find a form of association that defends and protects with all common forces the person and goods of each associate, and by means of uniting with all, nevertheless obeys only himself and remains as free as before?' (ibid. 148). The way that this can be achieved, Rousseau believed, is by means of the social contract. Everyone in entering into civil association must give up his rights to the whole community. Rousseau argued that 'This passage from the state of nature to the civil state produces quite a remarkable change in man, for it substitutes justice for instinct in his behaviour and gives his actions a moral quality they previously lacked' (ibid. 150). The whole citizen body is the sovereign, thus it cannot have interests contrary to the individuals who comprise it. The sovereign need give no guarantees to the citizens: 'The sovereign, by the mere fact it exists, is always all that it should be (ibid.).

## The general will and democracy

Rousseau makes a distinction between two types of will relating to reason on the one hand and passion on the other. When a man's will is dominated by passion and caprice this is what Rousseau calls his particular will. When it is ruled by reason Rousseau calls it his real will. When the real will is understood in the social context it is, for Rousseau, the general will. The general will is more than the sum of individual wills because it is a reflection of the common good and not of the interests of particular groups. To go against the general will is to be in conflict with your real will. Thus: 'whoever refuses to obey the general will will be forced to do so by the entire body. This means merely that he will be forced to be free' (*Social Contract*, 150). Associations smaller than the state, such as trade unions, or guilds, necessarily, in Rousseau's view, reflect their own self-interest and not the common good of the whole. These associations must therefore be discouraged, and individuals make up their minds for themselves, unconstrained by interest groups, what the general will is. If partial societies cannot be prevented, then their number should be multiplied and inequalities among them reduced to a minimum (ibid. 156).

The problem is, of course, how do we know what the general will is? Rousseau's remarks on this subject are not very helpful. The general will is not necessarily the will of all. There may be a difference between the general will and the collective wills of the citizens. He also suggests that the general will is the residue left after the pluses and minuses have cancelled themselves out. Unanimity is not a condition of the general will, nor indeed will a majority necessarily reflect the general will. Where most people are dominated by their passions and thus follow their particular wills, a minority, or even one person, could reflect the real, or general, will. In Rousseau's view, 'The general will is always right, but the judgement that guides it is not always enlightened. It must be made to see objects as they are, and sometimes as they ought to appear to it' (ibid. 162).

There is much in Rousseau to indicate that he advocated a pure democracy. Right, he argued in an allusion to Hobbes, cannot be based on force. Force is not able to give rise to morality. All that can result is at most an act of prudence (ibid. 143). No one has a natural authority over other men, and since force is not the basis of right, it is conventions that are the foundation of 'all legitimate authority among men' (ibid. 144). No one can be placed under the subjection of another without consent (ibid. 205). He argued against the principle of deputies, or representatives, ridiculing the British system in being free only at the time of elections. He argued that sovereignty cannot be represented, nor alienated: 'any law which the people has not ratified in person is void; it is not law at all'. When the sovereign body of citizens assembles, all government jurisdiction and executive power are suspended because 'the person of the humblest citizen is as sacred and inviolable as that of the first magistrate' (ibid. 197).

## The lawgiver, religion, and censorship

However, there are aspects of his theory, such as the lawgiver, or legislator, the civil religion, and the office of the censor which detract from a democratic interpretation of *The Social Contract*.

The difficulty is that people are currently so dominated by their passions and guided by their particular wills that they would have extreme difficulty in knowing what the general will is. This situation has be transformed. Here the role of the lawgiver, or legislator, is of particular significance. It is his job to frame the basic constitutional laws. The lawgiver is in the odd position of having a superhuman task and yet possessing no authority for its execution: the people are in the paradoxical position of not being able to recognize and acknowledge wise political principles until they enter into a society which is governed by these principles: 'The social spirit which ought to be the work of that institution, would have to preside over the institution itself. And man would be, prior to the advent of laws, what they ought to become by means of laws' (*Social Contract*, 164). The lawgiver thus formulates the fundamental laws, and by obeying these the people will be acting in accord with the general will; he is a type of benevolent father forcing people to be free. He does not rule over the people because the people is sovereign. He must therefore have 'recourse to an authority of a different order, which can compel without violence and persuade without convincing' (ibid.). The lawgiver or legislator must appear to be directed by God. Thus the people will feel when they are subject to the state that they are really subject to God's law. The distinguishing feature of the lawgiver in contrast with a tyrant is the timing. It is almost impossible for a lawgiver to be successful during periods of social and political turmoil such as famine, war, and sedition.

The appearance of Rousseau's *Social Contract* in 1762 gave rise to a considerable outcry, not because of his elevation of the people to the status of sovereign, nor because of his ideas on liberty, but because of his views on religion. The book was prohibited in France, and Rousseau escaped almost certain imprisonment by fleeing, and the same reaction in Geneva prevented him from settling there. Religion was one of the principal instruments through which the lawgiver could exercise influence. The lawgiver must use religion as an instrument in order to impose the laws upon the people. The people, because the state and religion are divided, have a dual allegiance. Rousseau distinguished three principal forms of religious belief: the religions of man, the citizen, and the priest. The first is characterized by the simple faith of the Gospels and undermines allegiance to the state. The second conjoins the love of law and divine worship, resulting in credulity and intolerance. The third creates a dual obligation to the priest and to the civil government, generating conflicts among individuals and their neighbours. All three forms of religious belief are subversive to good government, but none more so than the first. The Christianity of the gospel, Rousseau believed, produced a people of slaves amenable to being oppressed by tyranny rather than to enjoy the liberty of a republic. 'Christianity', he asserted, 'preaches only servitude and dependence' (*Social Contract*, 225).

Following Hobbes, Rousseau maintained that the state and religion should be closely allied. The state should take the responsibility for prescribing the religious code to be adhered to by its citizens: 'There is, therefore a purely civil profession of faith, the articles of which it belongs to the sovereign to establish, not exactly as dogmas of religion, but as sentiments of sociability, without which it is impossible to be a good citizen or a faithful subject' (ibid. 226). Anyone who refused to believe in the articles of the civil religion would be banished from the state.

Another office which the legislator can use to facilitate the general will is that of the censorial tribunal. The general will is declared in the laws of the state, and the censorial tribunal declares public judgement. Censorship is meant to regulate the judgement of the people and educate it towards choosing what is moral and good. Its role is to promote and preserve morality and to prevent the morals of the people from becoming corrupted.

These are the aspects of Rousseau's thought that have led many commentators to criticize him for being a totalitarian thinker. However, some of these institutions and pronouncements can be interpreted more generously. On the question of forcing people to be free if they fail to obey the general will, this may not be as sinister as it at first sounds. We need to remind ourselves that for Rousseau the general will finds expression in the laws of the land. Failing to obey the general will effectively means that you would be a lawbreaker. In this context forcing someone to be free would be to punish him or her for a crime, and try to get that person to repent and see the error of his or her ways: the same, in other words, that happens in every state. Furthermore, there is no evidence that Rousseau envisaged that the legislator would be a permanent feature of the state. His role appears to be a temporary one in that he has to guide a corrupted population to accept some fundamental constitutional laws which are meant to be for the common good, but which the people in their corrupt condition, dominated by their particular will, may not see. The civic religion is not meant to force everyone to hold the same theological beliefs. Instead it is meant to support a set of rules which contribute to the sociability of members of society. In other words, it is a moral code for practical purposes. In addition, given that Rousseau believed that people had become so depraved and corrupt censorship was meant to put them back on a moral path, it could not be so at variance with public morality that its 'decisions are vain and futile' (*Social Contract*, 219).

## Freedom and dependence

What is most striking about Rousseau, despite his many ambiguities, is the extent to which the theme of dependence unifies his thought. It is the failure to break free of insidious dependence, the type that leads to exploitation and servitude, and achieve autonomy that for him explains moral decay and personal discontent. It is his emphasis on freedom from dependence that distinguishes him from liberalism and places him squarely in the republican tradition. For the classical liberal we are free in so far as we are liberated from interference, whereas for republicanism we are free when we are free of dependence.[24] This view of freedom is best articulated by the Italian republican Francesco Mario Pagona, a martyr for the Napoleon republic of 1799. Pagona contends: 'The mere belief that one *might be oppressed with impunity* strips us of the free faculty to avail ourselves of our rights. Fear attacks liberty at its very source.'[25]

Rousseau's preoccupation with freedom and independence find political expression in numerous tracts, including *Constitutional Project for Corsica*, *The Discourse on Political Economy*, and *The Social Contract*. Independence is action unconstrained by external social or moral laws, not being dependent upon the arbitrary will of another, and freedom is acting in conformity with the moral law, free of other constraints. Both independence and freedom meet two negative criteria. Both require the absence of subjection to another person and to one's own lower nature. Man in the state of nature is capable of being independent because he is solitary and the qualitative distinction between higher and lower nature does not apply. His freedom in the civil condition is more difficult to attain. To avoid personal servitude Rousseau proposes to make individuals dependent, not on other individuals or institutions, but upon the whole community, which protects the goods and person of every citizen with the united force of all. He is liberated from subjection to his lower nature in uniting with others, and in doing so the individual obeys only himself as the author of the laws to which he subscribes. Freedom is equated with obedience to law, and law is equated with the expression of the general will of the whole community. Freedom, or liberty, can only be maintained by full and enthusiastic participation of the citizenry in the legislative process and activity of governance of the *patrie*. To remain silent and passive while corruption and the abuse of power become endemic is to put the personal liberty of citizens at risk because the public interest and common liberty are synonymous with their personal interest and liberty.

Inequalities are in fact forms of dominance and dependence, and, as we have seen, they are artificially instituted to the detriment of the whole society. He is not suggesting that there should be no inequalities, only that there should be none based on birth. He argued that 'the state should grant no distinction save for merit, virtue, and patriotic service; and these distinctions should be no more hereditary than are the qualities on which they are based' (*Corsica*, 148[26]). In order to avoid dependency by one region upon another within the state Rousseau would, as far as possible, reduce the gross inequalities that currently exist to a minimum.

The virtuous person is the person whose will is in conformity with the general will. Patriotism, or love of one's country, is what most effectively promotes this identity because when we love a people we more readily want what they want. The sympathy, sentiment, and obligations we feel towards our fellow citizens are all the more powerful in being circumscribed by community. The moral rights we acquire as citizens arise out of conventions. Conceptions of a universal moral order of humanity arise out of our circumscribed communities, and do not exist prior to them. Like Pericles, Rousseau extols the virtue of a passionate love of one's country which is 'a hundred times more ardent and delightful than that of a mistress' (*Discourse on Political Economy*, 121),[27] The community of the whole world dilutes the sentiment of humanity and provides little or no foundation for obligations to each other as fellow human beings rather than citizens. The most virtuous acts, Rousseau contended, arise out of the sentiment of patriotism (ibid. 121). Each people has, or ought to have, a national character. If it did not, it would have to be given one. It is national traditions and institutions that shape the character of a people and give rise to its genius. Education 'must give souls a national formation' by instilling in the young the whole cultural heritage of its people. A people whose love of liberty and country has been brought to the 'highest pitch' will not easily be conquered (*Government of Poland*, 190). A free nation, in Rousseau's view, is not dependent upon any other nation for anything. Contrary to Kant's belief that progress in international relations will develop out of greater interdependence, Rousseau believed that interdependence creates the conditions for international conflict.

If a state maintains its independence, it will neither need to conquer nor will it be vulnerable to conquest. He advised both the Corsicans and Poles that if they wish to be self-sustaining, happy, free, and peaceful nations, they must revive the laudable and wholesome aspects of their customs. Money should be replaced if possible by stronger and more patriotic motives for performing 'great deeds' (*Government of Poland*, 177; cf. *Corsica*, 143).They should foster a healthy and courageous warrior spirit without allying it with ambition. This can be accomplished by the establishment of a citizen's militia requiring the whole nation to undergo military training. Traditional trades should be encouraged and agriculture developed. In the *Constitutional Project for Corsica* Rousseau argued that the development of agriculture is the only sound means of making a state independent in external affairs. No amount of wealth is a substitute for self-sufficiency in the production of food. To be dependent upon another state for imports of food is to be at its mercy. Commerce, while it produces wealth, leads at the same time to dependency. Rousseau equates agriculture, however, with freedom (*Corsica*, 145). He is also aware that the temptations of the city draw young men away from agricultural life. His remedy is to make land the basis of the rights and status of citizens, and to encourage close family ties by making paternity conditional upon land (ibid. 155). Furthermore, he would not leave the depletion of resources to the discretion of the individual. He advocated the intelligent, planned, and sustainable exploitation of such resources as the forest.

When men enter into society, they cannot be free of all dependence, but they can substitute one form of dependence for another. Personal dependence on others is to be avoided by the dependence of all upon the law or the general will. Each citizen in pledging himself to the whole safeguards himself against personal dependence (*Social Contract*, 150). This, Rousseau believed, is a condition of the successful operation of the institutions of government. Governments, however, are inclined to undermine the general will because of the personal biases of their officers, reducing the people to personal dependence. This is circumvented in Rousseau, however, by popular assemblies to which the government whose authority is in suspension for so long as the populace meets is accountable. The people is the sovereign, and the government is accountable to it. At each assembly a vote of confidence is moved, and it takes the form of two questions. The first relates to the desirability of continuing the present form of government, and the second to the suitability of the current personnel (ibid. 203).[28]

## FURTHER READING

Chapman, John W., *Rousseau—Totalitarian or Liberal?* (New York: Columbia University Press, 1956).

Cranston, Maurice, *Jean-Jacques: The Early Life and Work of Jean-Jacques Rousseau 1712–1754* (Harmondsworth: Peregrine, 1987).

Dent, N. J. H., *A Rousseau Dictionary* (Oxford: Blackwell, 1992).

O'Hagen, Timothy, *Rousseau* (London: Routledge, 1999).

Riley, Patrick, *The General Will before Rousseau* (Princeton: Princeton University Press, 1986), ch. 5.

Strong, Tracy B., *Jean-Jacques Rousseau: The Politics of the Ordinary* (London: Sage, 1994).

Wokler, Robert, *Rousseau: A Very Short Introduction* (Oxford: Oxford University Press, 2001).

## NOTES

1. Letters from David Hume to Richard Davenport, 8 and 15 July 1766, in *Rousseau's Political Writings*, ed. Alan Ritter and Julia Conway Bondanella (New York: Norton, 1988), 198.
2. Giacomo Casanova, *History of my Life*, trans. W. R. Trask (New York: Brace & World, 1968), 223–4.
3. Maurice Cranston, 'Remembering Rousseau', *Encounter*, 51 (1978), 38.
4. L. G. Crocker, *Rousseau's Social Contract: An Interpretive Essay* (Cleveland, Ohio: Press of Case Western Reserve University, 1968), 120.
5. J. L. Talmon, *The Rise of Totalitarian Democracy* (London: Mercury, 1961), 39.
6. C. W. Hendel, *Jean-Jacques Rousseau, Moralist* (London: Oxford University Press, 1934), ii. 323.
7. Ernst Cassirer, *The Question of Jean-Jacques Rousseau*, 2nd edn. trans. Peter Gay (New Haven: Yale University Press, 1989), 58.
8. J. G. A. Pocock, *The Machiavellian Moment: Florentine Political Thought and the Atlantic Republican Tradition* (Princeton: Princeton University Press, 1975).
9. Rousseau, *The Basic Political Writings*, ed. Donald A. Cress, introd. Peter Gay (Indianapolis: Hackett, 1987).
10. Maurizio Viroli, *For Love of One's Country: An Essay on Patriotism and Nationalism* (Oxford: Clarendon Press, 1997), 79–80.
11. Robert Wokler, *Rousseau: A Very Short Introduction* (Oxford: Oxford University Press, 2001), 79.
12. Rousseau, cited in Maurizio Viroli, *Republicanism* (New York: Hill & Wang, 2002), 9.
13. Rousseau, *First Version of the Social Contract* (the Geneva Manuscript), in *Rousseau on International Relations*, ed. Stanley Hoffmann and David P. Fidler (Oxford: Clarendon Press, 1991), 114. Elsewhere Rousseau contends that 'it is here less a question of history and facts than of right and justice, and that I wish to examine things according to their nature rather than according to our prejudices' (*The State of War*, in *Rousseau on International Relations*, 36).
14. Michael C. Williams, 'Rousseau, Realism and *Realpolitik*', *Millennium*, 18 (1989), 190.
15. In *The Social Contract* (Indianapolis: Hackett, 1987), 151, Rousseau does claim that man in the state of nature has 'an unlimited right to everything that tempts him and that he can acquire'.
16. In *Basic Political Writings*.
17. John W. Chapman, *Rousseau—Totalitarian or Liberal?* (New York: Columbia University Press, 1956), 3–4.
18. Cassirer, *The Question of Jean-Jacques Rousseau*, 75.
19. Wokler, *Rousseau*, 55.
20. Chapman, *Rousseau—Totalitarian or Liberal?*, 9.
21. Robert Wokler, 'Rousseau's Pufendorf: Natural Law and the Foundations of Commercial Society', *History of Political Thought*, 15 (1994), 373.
22. Leo Strauss, *Natural Right and History* (Chicago: University of Chicago Press, 1953), 271.
23. Arthur M. Melzer, 'Rousseau's Moral Realism: Replacing Natural Law with the General Will', *American Political Science Review*, 77 (1983), 640.
24. Viroli, *Republicanism*, 10.
25. Cited ibid. 37.
26. In *Rousseau on International Relations*.
27. Cf. Rousseau, *Considerations on the Government of Poland*, in *Rousseau on International Relations*, 168.
28. This last section draws upon my discussion of Rousseau and international relations in *Political Theories of International Relations from Thucydides to the Present* (Oxford: Oxford University Press, 1998).

# 15 The Federalist Papers

Terence Ball

**Contents**



## Chapter guide

My aim in this chapter is to exhibit *The Federalist Papers* in its decidedly *political* context—the defence of the newly drafted US Constitution of 1787. This defence was necessary because the Constitution was highly controversial. Delegates had been sent to the Philadelphia convention to revise the Articles of Confederation (1783). In the event they scrapped the Articles and drafted an entirely new frame of government, leaving to the citizens of the thirteen states the decision whether to ratify or reject the new Constitution. This set the stage for the heated and hard-fought Ratification Debate of 1787–8, pitting Federalist defenders of the Constitution against its Antifederalist foes. *The Federalist Papers* is a political intervention in and contribution to this debate. It consists of eighty-five newspaper columns—leaders, or 'op ed' pieces, as Americans say—in defence of the new design. These articles are wide-ranging, covering everything from public finance to trial court procedures. To make the chapter manageable I focus on a key theme to which Federalists and Antifederalists returned repeatedly: whether the system of government constituted by the new Constitution was 'republican' or not. Federalists contended that it was, and Antifederalists that it was not. By tracing disputes over a number of key issues—the meaning of the term 'republic', its optimal size and extent, its system of representation, the sources of civic corruption and virtue, whether a standing army is preferable to a citizen militia, whether a republic requires a bill of rights to protect its citizens' liberties—we find a unifying thread tying together the disparate strands of this heated and complex debate.

## Biography

Publius, the pseudonymous author of *The Federalist Papers*, was actually three men: Alexander Hamilton, John Jay, and James Madison.

Alexander Hamilton was born in the West Indies in 1755, 'the bastard son of a Scots peddlar', as John Adams derisively described him. Having emigrated as a teenager to the British colony of New York, he studied at King's College (later Columbia University) and subsequently served with distinction as a gunnery officer and aide-de-camp to General George Washington during the American Revolution. He was among the most ardent supporters of the new Constitution, even though he thought it gave too little power to the federal (central) government. The original design of *The Federalist Papers* was his, and it was he who enlisted the help of his fellow New Yorker John Jay and the Virginian James Madison as co-authors of that series. As first Secretary of the Treasury under President Washington, he proposed a plan for a National Bank and had the federal government assume and pay the Revolutionary War debts of the several states. He was killed in a duel with Aaron Burr, Jefferson's Vice-President, in 1804.

John Jay, born in 1745, played a prominent role in the political life of the new nation. He served New York as a delegate to the Second Continental Congress, signed the Declaration of Independence, and presided over Congress until being named American Ambassador to Spain. In 1787 his fellow New Yorker Alexander Hamilton enlisted Jay's help in the Ratification Debate in New York state. In the event he wrote only five of *The Federalist Papers*, having fallen seriously ill shortly after the series began. He served as first Chief Justice of the Supreme Court under the new Constitution. He died in 1829.

James Madison was born in Virginia in 1751, was trained in the law, and was soon involved in the politics of pre-revolutionary Virginia, serving as a member of that colony's House of Delegates and of the Continental Congress. Deeply dissatisfied with the Articles of Confederation, he led the fight for their revision and ultimately their replacement with an entirely new Constitution. His efforts on behalf of the new design—as leading member of the Constitutional Convention of 1787, co-author of *The Federalist Papers*, and ardent advocate of the Bill of Rights (1791)—earned for him the title Father of the Constitution. Although allied with Hamilton during the Constitutional Convention and Ratification Debate, he soon broke with Hamilton and took the side of his friend and fellow Virginian Thomas Jefferson. He subsequently served as President Jefferson's Secretary of State (1801–9) and as fourth President of the United States (1809–17). He died in 1836.

Brutus—Publius' Antifederalist arch-foe in the New York debate over ratification—cannot be identified. It is likely (though far from certain) that he was Robert Yates, a prominent New York lawyer and legislator. He had been sent, with Alexander Hamilton and John Lansing Jr., as a delegate to the 1787 Philadelphia convention to revise the Articles of Confederation. Yates and Lansing favoured revision, Hamilton outright replacement. When it became clear that the Articles were to be abandoned and an entirely new Constitution drafted, Yates returned to New York and began to prepare for his part in the Antifederalist assault on the proposed Constitution.

## Key texts

*The Federalist*, ed. Terence Ball (Cambridge: Cambridge University Press, 2003) (*FP*).

*The Complete Anti-Federalist*, ed. Herbert J. Storing, 7 vols. (Chicago: University of Chicago Press, 1981) (*CAF*).

*The Anti-Federalist*, abridged edn. of *The Complete Anti-Federalist*, ed. Murray Dry, 1 vol. (Chicago: University of Chicago Press, 1985) (*AF*).

Constitution of the United States (written 1787; ratified 1789) (*CUS*).

## Key ideas

**Antifederalists**: opponents of the newly drafted US Constitution. **Bill of rights**: an enumeration of constitutionally guaranteed rights; in the US Constitution the first ten amendments, adopted in 1791. **Citizen militia**: an army comprising civilian volunteers; the kind of armed force favoured by classical republicans. **Corruption**: in classical republican discourse 'corruption' refers to a lack of concern about and attention to public matters; it is the absence of (civic) virtue. **Federalists**: supporters of proposed constitution. **Republic**: a state ruled by its citizens. **Representation**: the delegation of political authority to an elected or appointed representative. **Standing army**: a professional army comprised of full-time soldiers—anathema to classical republicans, who favoured a citizen militia.

# Introduction: context and background

The first thing one notices when one first picks up *The Federalist Papers* is its bulk. At nearly 500 closely printed pages it is as long as Hobbes's *Leviathan* or Machiavelli's *Discourses*. But the appearance is deceptive, for *The Federalist Papers* is not a systematic treatise on political theory. It is instead a collection of eighty-five newspaper columns—what the Americans now call 'op ed' pieces, and the British 'leaders'—written at white-hot speed over a seven-month period (October 1787–May 1788), in support of the newly drafted United States Constitution. Its three authors—Alexander Hamilton, James Madison, and John Jay[1]—wrote under the pseudonym Publius. And Publius' aim was to persuade the citizens of New York state to ratify, that is, approve and adopt, the new Constitution.

That, Publius knew, would be an uphill battle. Many, perhaps most, Americans were suspicious of the document drafted in Philadelphia in the hot, sticky summer of 1787. The delegates had been sent there to revise the Articles of Confederation (1781), which had bound the thirteen former colonies into a loose confederation of sovereign states. But instead of revising the Articles, the delegates drafted an entirely new Constitution. Some delegates went home in a huff, warning that treachery and treason were afoot in Philadelphia ('I smell a rat,' sneered Patrick Henry, who had refused to attend the Philadelphia convention). The newly drafted Constitution, critics claimed, would turn sovereign states into subservient pawns of an all-powerful federal government. Tariffs and other sources of state revenue were viewed as barriers to inter-state commerce and would be dismantled; there would be a single currency; and all member states would be answerable to the authority of the central government. So claimed the Antifederalist foes of the new Constitution.[2]

To read *The Federalist Papers* is to be privy to only one side of the first of the two most momentous debates ever conducted in America. (The second—over slavery and secession—ended in civil war.) Truly to understand that debate, and indeed *The Federalist Papers*, requires that we also attend to Antifederalist arguments against the proposed Constitution. My aim here is to restate important parts of the Antifederalist case against, and *The Federalist Papers*' case for, the new Constitution.

Because Antifederalist sentiment was widespread, in New York as elsewhere, Publius had his work cut out for him. The debate over the ratification of the newly drafted Constitution produced an enormous outpouring of newspaper articles, pamphlets, sermons, and tracts, both for and against the new design. Of the former *The Federalist Papers* is by far the most famous and certainly the most widely read in our day.[3] The Antifederalist case against the Constitution, by contrast, is today rarely read or even remembered. Yet had there been no reasonable or plausible arguments against the Constitution, there would have been no need for the concentrated firepower of *The Federalist Papers*. And had there been no *Federalist Papers*, our understanding of the Constitution would today be greatly diminished. For the Constitution is a terse document, devoid of all argument and explanation. *The Federalist Papers* gives us a window into the minds of the founders. It explains why they found the Articles of Confederation unsatisfactory; why they sought to separate the powers of the several branches of the government; why they subdivided the national legislature into two houses; why they thought that a federal court of last resort was both desirable and necessary; why they outlawed titles of nobility; why (initially at least) they believed a bill of rights an unnecessary addition—and why many other prescriptions and proscriptions were written into the Constitution or omitted entirely.

The series of articles that we now know as *The Federalist Papers* was the brainchild of Alexander Hamilton. He had been one of three New York delegates to the 1787 Philadelphia convention. His fellow delegates, John Lansing and Robert Yates, left Philadelphia in a fury when it became clear that Hamilton and most other delegates were bent on scrapping the Articles of Confederation and drafting an entirely new document. It is probable (though we do not know for certain) that Robert Yates became the feared Brutus—the most ardent and articulate Antifederalist pamphleteer in New York, as we shall see shortly.

Why did Hamilton and most of his fellow delegates feel it necessary to replace the Articles of Confederation with an entirely new Constitution? There are several answers, all given (or alluded to) in *The Federalist Papers*. The first is that a loose confederation of thirteen sovereign states could not adequately defend itself against foreign assault or invasion (*FP* 3–8, 22–9).[4] Another answer is that the confederation created by the Articles allowed states to erect tariffs and other barriers to trade and commerce, thereby endangering the prosperity of the parts and the whole (*FP* 11–13). Moreover, the Articles allowed for multiple sovereigns—thirteen squabbling and quarrelsome states without a strong national government to adjust and adjudicate their differences (*FP* 15–17) or to tax them for the good of the whole (*FP* 21). The Articles had worked well enough in the heady days following the defeat of the British in the American Revolution. But by the mid-1770s the political climate had begun to alter appreciably. The fabric of civility and cooperation had begun to fray. Shays's Rebellion in western Massachusetts and other local protest movements were seen by some as a series of interconnected conspiracies being hatched by democrats and debtors (see *FP* 6). It was in this climate of crisis that the Philadelphia meeting was called, the Articles scrapped, and a new Constitution drafted. That done, the task facing Publius and his fellow Federalists was to have this new document ratified by the citizens of the thirteen states. *The Federalist Papers* is an extended exercise in political persuasion. As a piece of political theory, then, *The Federalist Papers* flies fairly close to the ground, rarely soaring into the stratosphere of philosophical abstraction.

Despite their differences, Federalist friends and Antifederalist foes of the new Constitution were agreed that the Articles of Confederation were unsatisfactory and needed changing. They differed, however, over the newly drafted alternative to the Articles. They agreed that the new Constitution would, if adopted, reconstitute the American body politic in a radically new way. Specifically, it would take some important powers away from the thirteen states and give them to the federal (or central) government. Antifederalist critics contended that the federal government would be too powerful and that states would be stripped of powers that were rightfully theirs. The ratification debate of 1787–8 opened a veritable hornet's nest of questions: What is a republic? What is its optimal size and extent? What are republican liberties? How are they best protected, and how can they be lost? What system of representation best suits a republic? How can the corruption of the government and the citizenry be slowed or stopped altogether? By what constitutional means and mechanisms might a republic be maintained over many generations? Is a republic best protected by a standing army or by a citizen militia? Does government by and for the people require a bill of rights to protect the people from themselves and/or their own elected representatives?

And so began the greatest non-violent verbal battle ever waged in America. To revisit that debate is to enter a world both different from and yet formative of that in which Americans now live. The late Herbert Storing was surely correct in claiming that the new American republic was the joint creation of Federalists and Antifederalists alike. It was a new political system, created not by the dictates of a lone legislator, but argued into existence and quite literally constituted out of an intense debate between partisans of different political persuasions and theoretical convictions (*CAF* i. 3[5]). During this debate Antifederalist criticism brought forth Federalist defences that not only clarified but helped to establish the meaning of, and theoretical justification for, the new Constitution. Much of that debate revolved around the meanings of the concepts constitutive of republican discourse—liberty, tyranny, virtue, corruption, representation, even 'republic' itself.

## Arguments about 'republican' government

In the late eighteenth century the term 'democracy' did not have the favourable connotation that it has for us today. Democracy was widely viewed as class rule—specifically, rule by the lower or working class in their own class's political and economic interest. In Aristotle's sixfold classification of regimes democracy was the 'bad' or 'perverted' form of rule by the many (see Chapter 5 in this volume). Its virtuous counterpart was the *politeia* ('polity'), which the Romans later rendered as *respublica* ('republic'). Republican political thought, revived during the Renaissance by Machiavelli and others (see Chapter 9 in this volume), was later adapted by James Harrington in the mid-seventeenth century and by Bolingbroke, Trenchard, and Gordon, and other English republican theorists (the so-called 'Commonwealthmen') in the early eighteenth century. Among the main features of 'republican' theory and practice were the following: rule by (or on behalf of) the people, whose rulers' or representatives' powers are restricted by law so as to protect the rights and liberties of the people. If this form of government was to survive, the people and their governors must be 'virtuous', that is, they must exhibit the qualities of public-spiritedness and concern for the common good. For a people to lack or to lose these qualities is to become 'corrupt' and therefore in immediate and grave danger of losing their 'liberty'—that is, their freedom to govern themselves—to princes or petty tyrants. Among the means of maintaining liberty and civic virtue was the formation and training of a 'militia' of armed citizens, and a corresponding prohibition on 'standing armies' of paid professional soldiers whose very presence posed a grave danger to republican liberty. These are among the defining features of what has come to be known as 'the Atlantic republican tradition' of political thought.[6]

During and after the American Revolution (1776–83) 'republic' was the watchword on every patriot's lips. When Patrick Henry proclaimed 'Give me liberty or give me death', he was speaking specifically of the republican (or 'public') liberty of a people to govern themselves. It is therefore scarcely surprising that when the proposed Constitution was published on 17 September 1787, the first question to be asked—and asked repeatedly—was whether the form of government it created was in fact truly 'republican'.

Its Federalist defenders claimed that the proposed Constitution would create a republican government; Antifederalists denied it. As one Antifederalist writer, the pseudonymous Federal Farmer, put it, the issue was not so much between 'federalist' and 'antifederalist' as between 'real republicans' like himself and 'pretended' ones like Publius: 'if any names are applicable to the parties, on account of their general politics, they are those of republicans and anti-republicans. The opposers are generally men who support the rights of the body of the people, and are properly republicans. The advocates are generally men not very friendly to those rights, and properly anti republicans' (*AF* 67–87). Publius, by contrast, defended the new design as being fully in 'conformity . . . to the true principles of republican government' (*FP* 1) and as being 'wholly and purely republican' (*FP* 73) and 'republican in spirit' as well as in letter (*FP* 39).

But here was the rub: Publius and his fellow Federalists were defending a design not only for a republic, but for a new *kind* of republic, the likes of which had never been seen before—an 'enlarged' or 'extended republic'. And this was an entirely new wrinkle in the annals of republican political theory and practice.

## Arguments about size and extent

The American republic created by the Constitution was to be an extended republic, taking in a large, indeed empire-sized, territory and an ever-increasing population, with the prospect of further extension to the south and west (still under increasingly shaky Spanish and French control). Antifederalists were quick to seize upon what they regarded as a rank contradiction. An 'extended republic', they argued, is an oxymoron and not really a *republic* at all. One of the ablest Antifederalists, New York's Brutus (probably Robert Yates), held that if we consult 'the greatest and wisest men who have ever thought or wrote on the science of government' we shall have to conclude that 'a free republic cannot succeed over a country of such immense extent, containing such a number of inhabitants, and these encreasing in such rapid progression as that of the whole United States'. If you doubt it, you need only turn to the past 'History', he says, 'furnishes no example of a free republic, anything like the extent of the United States. The Grecian republics were of small extent; so also was that of the Romans.' And when they 'extended their conquests over large territories of country', they ceased to be republics, 'their governments [having] changed from that of free governments to those of the most tyrannical that ever existed in the world' (*AF* 113).

The most revered of 'the many illustrious authorities' cited by Brutus is Montesquieu, who had observed that 'It is natural to a republic to have only a small territory, otherwise it cannot long subsist.' Large territories, having heterogeneous populations, widely differing interests, and immoderate men of large fortunes, are by their very nature incapable of self-government. They are, therefore, more naturally governed either by monarchs or despots (*AF* 113). 'I have attempted to shew', says Brutus, 'that a consolidation of this extensive continent, under one government, for internal, as well as external purposes . . . cannot succeed without a sacrifice of your liberties.' Hence, he concludes, 'the attempt [to create an extended republic] is not only preposterous, but extremely dangerous' (*AF* 122–3). These were powerful—and recognizably 'republican'—objections that Publius had to counter immediately and decisively.

Publius quickly countered in *Federalist* nos. 9 and 10. Not to be outdone by Brutus' reference to the supposedly authoritative 'science of government', Publius (Hamilton) in no. 9 contends that Brutus' so-called science is woefully out of date. It relies on the experience and the authority of the ancients. But since the glory days of Greece and Rome, Hamilton says,

> the science of politics, like most other sciences, has received great improvement. The efficacy of various principles is now well understood, which were either not known at all, or imperfectly known to the ancients. The regular distribution of power into distinct departments—the introduction of legislative ballances [*sic*] and checks—the institution of courts composed of judges, holding their offices during good behaviour—the representation of the people in the legislature by deputies of their own election—these are either wholly new discoveries or have made their principal progress toward perfection in modern times. They are . . . powerful means, by which the excellencies of republican government may be retained and its imperfections lessened or avoided. (*FP* 9)

Hamilton then confronts Brutus' criticism head on by 'ventur[ing], however novel it may appear to some, to add one more' truth to an ever-expanding body of scientific knowledge. Employing the language of astronomy, Hamilton explains: 'I mean the ENLARGEMENT of the ORBIT within which such systems are to revolve . . .' (*FP* 38). Taking a larger and less localized view of the American political universe, Publius tries to undercut the force of any appeal to antiquity or to arguments from authority, including that of the illustrious (and decidedly modern) Montesquieu. 'The opponents of the PLAN proposed have with great assiduity cited and circulated the observations of Montesquieu on the necessity of a contracted territory for a republican government,' Hamilton says. But the Antifederalists cannot legitimately employ Montesquieu's arguments about the restricted size of republics because Montesquieu's very scale or standard of measurement is, in America, already outdated. 'When Montesquieu recommends a small extent for republics, the standards he had in view were of dimensions, far short of the limits of almost every one of these States. Neither Virginia, Massachusetts, Pennsylvania, New York, North Carolina, nor Georgia, can by any means be compared with the models, from which he reasoned and to which the terms of his description apply' (*FP* 39). Thus the size and scale that Montesquieu recommends for republics is inapplicable in America, not only under the new Constitution as regards the federal government but even under the Articles of Confederation as regards the thirteen American states. A new standard and a new scale are therefore required for the modern republic envisioned in the proposed Constitution.

Publius goes on to suggest that this new standard or scale is to be found in Montesquieu's notion of a 'confederate republic'. The Antifederalists' own most respected and illustrious authority 'explicitly treats of a CONFEDERATE REPUBLIC as the expedient for extending the sphere of popular government and reconciling the advantages of monarchy with those of republicanism'. By quoting extensively from Montesquieu, Publius shows that the famous French sage offers 'a luminous abridgement of the principal arguments in favour of the Union'. Thus does Publius adroitly turn the Antifederalists' chief authority against them.

## 'Republic' redefined

Hamilton's rebuttal of the restricted-size argument in *Federalist* no. 9 prepares the way for Madison's redefinition of 'republic' in no. 10—arguably the most famous of all the *Federalist Papers*. Madison begins by decrying the evils of 'faction' which can be avoided in either of two ways. The first is to eliminate their causes, the second, to control their effects. The first would require the equal division of property—since envy is a primary source of faction—and the elimination of 'liberty, [which] is to faction what air is to fire, an aliment without which it instantly expires'. But this, says Madison, would be 'folly', for the 'remedy [would be] worse than the disease' (*FP* 10). The only reliable cure is to control the effects of faction. This is a remedy that only a republic—or rather, an *extended* republic—affords.

Madison draws a sharp distinction between a 'democracy' and a 'republic'. By 'democracy' Madison means what we would today call direct democracy—that is, rule by an assembly of citizens who inhabit a relatively restricted territory. A democracy is simply a system in which the numerically largest group rules. To term this ruling part 'the majority' does not sanctify it—nor does it alter the fact that it is (or can quite easily degenerate into) a 'faction' ruling unchecked and in its own interest. A 'pure Democracy', therefore, 'can admit of no cure for the mischiefs of faction'. An altogether different form—a republic—'opens a different prospect, and promises the cure for which we are seeking' (*FP* 10).

A republic, as Madison (re)defines it, is characterized by two key features. The first is its system of delegation or representation; the second is its enlarged extent (or 'orbit' in no. 9). As we shall see in the section following, representatives chosen from a much larger pool of possible candidates are able to 'refine' and adjudicate between competing interests, and thus to control the otherwise baleful effects of faction.

## Competing conceptions of representation

Antifederalist arguments about the evils of a large or extended republic size are, *pace* Madison, hardly a defence of direct 'democracy'. They are actually about the conditions under which representative government can be said to be truly representative. Federalist and Antifederalist disagreements about the kind and quality of representation afforded by the new constitution stem from the two sides' subscribing to two quite different theories of representation—the so-called 'mandate' and 'independence' theories.[8] According to the mandate theory, the task of a representative is to 'mirror' or 'reflect' the views of those he represents; he thinks and acts as they would, were they in his place. His role is not merely to represent his constituents' interests but to share their attitudes and feelings as well. He is to be their 'actual' representative. The independence view, by contrast, holds that the representative is a trustee who must make his own judgements concerning his constituents' interests and how they might be best served. He is to be their 'virtual', not their 'actual', representative. His constituents' feelings and attitudes are, from this perspective, largely irrelevant.[9]

Generally speaking, Antifederalists subscribed to the mandate view, and Federalists to the independence view. To be sure, Antifederalists did not all speak with a single voice on this, or any other, matter. But most Antifederalist writers agreed on at least three points regarding representation. The first was that the House of Representatives, if not the Senate, should be a representative cross-section or microcosm of the larger society. Secondly, members of the House should be guided by the actual or 'mandate' theory of representation, even if Senators did not do so. Thirdly, most Antifederalists agreed that the House did not in fact meet the first two requirements and was therefore not a genuinely representative body. Like many of his fellow Antifederalists Brutus believed that the new Constitution created two representative bodies that were so in name only. His harshest words were reserved for the House of Representatives, which he thought misnamed. 'The more I reflect on this subject, the more firmly am I persuaded, that the representation is merely nominal—a mere burlesque . . .' (*AF* 126). And, given the master metaphors and controlling imagery of Antifederalist discourse, and their mandate theory of representation in particular, this charge is quite predictable. In picturing the relationship between a constituent and his 'actual' representative, mandate theorists, including Brutus, invoke the pictorial imagery of 'resemblance', 'reflection', and 'mirroring':

> The very term representative implies, that the person or body chosen for this purpose, should *resemble* those who appoint them—a representation of the people of America, if it be a true one, must be *like* the people. It ought to be so constituted, that a person, who is a stranger to the country, might be able to form a just idea of their character, by knowing that of their representatives. They are the *sign*—the people are the thing signified. It is absurd to speak of one thing being the *representative* of another, upon any other principle. . . . those who are placed instead of the people, should possess their sentiments and feelings, and be governed by their interests, or, in other words, should bear the strongest *resemblance* of those in whose room they are substituted (*AF* 123–5; my emphasis).

From this 'mirroring' or mandate view of representation Brutus derives what he takes to be the mathematically warranted conclusion that a mere sixty-five representatives[10] are too few to really represent a large and still-growing number of citizens; and as the population increases, the representativeness of this relatively small body can only decrease: 'It is obvious, that for an assembly to be a true likeness of the people of any country, they must be considerably numerous.—One man, or a few men, cannot possibly represent the feelings, opinions, and characters of a great multitude. In this respect, the new constitution is radically defective' (*AF* 125).

Of course Brutus is *not* suggesting that representatives should, or even can, represent each of their individual constituents in their uniqueness. Clearly that would be impossible, for the number of representatives would then equal the number of people represented. The result would then be, not representative government, but direct democracy. And that assuredly is not the system that Brutus and most of his fellow Antifederalists were defending. Theirs was, rather, a system of representation resting upon the mandate theory of 'actual' representation, to which is added yet another earlier republican conception, namely representation not of individuals but of 'orders' or 'ranks' or 'classes' (though not in our modern socio-economic sense). As Brutus puts it: 'This extensive continent is made up of a number of different classes of people; and to have a proper representation of them, each class ought to have an opportunity of choosing their best informed men for the purpose.' If there is to be a 'just resemblance' between 'the several classes of people' in the society and those whom they elect to speak on their behalf in the representative assemblies—and the House of Representatives in particular—it then follows that 'the farmer, merchant, mechanick, and other various orders of people, ought to be represented according to their respective weight and numbers; and the representatives ought to be intimately acquainted with the wants, understand the interests of the several orders . . . and feel a proper sense and becoming zeal to promote their prosperity' (*AF* 125).

But, Brutus charges, the mode of election and system of representation prescribed by the new Constitution are designed not only to thwart the representation of the various orders or ranks, but to exclude them entirely:

> The great body of the yeomen of the country cannot expect any of their order in this assembly [namely, the House of Representatives]—the station will be too elevated for them to aspire to—the distance between the people and their representatives, will be so very great, that there is no probability that a farmer, however respectable, will be chosen—the mechanicks of every branch, must expect to be excluded from a seat in this Body. (*AF* 126)

Thus 'in reality there will be no part of the people represented, but the rich, even in that branch of the legislature, which is called democratic.' The Federalists' claim that those elected will disinterestedly serve all the people, including the 'democratical part', is little better than a bald-faced lie. 'The well born, and highest orders in life, as they term themselves,' warns Brutus, 'will be ignorant of the sentiments of the middling class of citizens, strangers to their abilities, wants, and difficulties, and void of sympathy, and fellow feeling.' Theirs 'will literally be a government in the hands of the few to oppress and plunder the many' (*AF* 126).

Brutus' and other Antifederalists' charges that the new Constitution was a design for disfranchisement, oppression, and tyranny struck deeply resonant republican chords. They therefore had to be met and countered as quickly as possible. Brutus' paper of 15 November was met one week later by Madison's most powerful broadside, the justly famed *Tenth Federalist*. After attempting to tar the Antifederalists with the brush of direct democracy, the real choice, as Madison finally acknowledges, is not really between democratic and republican forms, but between two types of republic and the kinds of representatives likely to be chosen in them. Is a small classical republic to be preferred to a large modern one? The answer depends less upon *whom* is to be represented than upon *what* is to be represented. The real choice comes down to this: should the legislature represent the private interests of the various orders—which Madison pejoratively terms 'factions'—or the public good? If Americans subscribe to the mandate theory of representation, he warns, their legislation will consist of an impure amalgam of narrow factional interests, not a duly filtered distillation of pure public interestedness. Since real republicans will want the latter rather than the former, the only 'question resulting', says Madison, 'is, whether small or extensive republics are most favorable to the election of proper guardians of the public weale'. The issue is 'clearly decided in favor of the latter' by 'two considerations', both of which he believes to be 'obvious'. The first is that the pool of worthy candidates or 'fit characters' is likely to be larger in a large republic than in a small one. The second consideration is that the greater the number of voters in any given election, the more difficult it is for 'unworthy candidates to practice with success the vicious arts, by which elections are too often carried' (*FP* 10).

Madison's argument is designed to counter Brutus' charge that the wealthy would acquire undue influence under the new Constitution. But if wealth brings one kind of corruption, a 'numerous representation' would result in corruption of another, and much worse, variety. Where Brutus had decried the actions of unrepresentative representatives, Madison decries the stratagems of 'unworthy candidates' who were likely to triumph in a popular free-for-all. Bribery, bombast, demagoguery, and the various 'vicious arts' would be their stock-in-trade. In other words, while Brutus and the Antifederalists focused on what representatives are likely to do after they are elected, Madison and his fellow Federalists focused initially on what candidates might do in order to be elected in the first place, and secondarily upon what 'wicked or improper project[s]' they might pursue after their election (*FP* 10).

But, brilliant as Madison's argument was, it did not settle the issue of 'actual' versus 'virtual' representation, and Hamilton returned to face it again in no. 35. The Antifederalist argument in favour of actual representation he portrays as 'specious and seductive' and 'altogether visionary', consisting only of 'fair sounding words' which are 'well calculated to lay hold of the prejudices of those to whom [they are] addressed'. Hamilton counters with two arguments. The first is simply a reminder that a greatly enlarged representative body would be unwieldy and unworkable. If the Constitution were to require 'an actual representation of all classes of the people by persons of each class', then 'each different occupation [would have to] send one or more members' to the Congress. This would require a representative body so large and unwieldy that 'the thing would never take place in practice'. Besides being 'impracticable', such a system is also 'unnecessary', since there is a natural tendency for those of lower social standing to defer to their social superiors: Mechanics and manufacturers will always be inclined

> to give their votes to merchants in preference to persons of their own professions or trades. Those discerning citizens . . . know that the merchant is their natural patron and friend; and they are aware that however great the confidence they may justly feel in their own good sense, their interests can be more effectually promoted by the merchant than by themselves . . . We must therefore consider merchants as the natural representatives of all these classes of the community.

The Antifederalists, Hamilton adds, believe it 'necessary that all classes of citizens should have some of their own number in the representative body, in order that their *feelings* and interests may be the better understood and attended to'. But this is to overlook the likelihood that their 'feelings' are apt to be of inadequacy, inferiority, and incompetence. The lower orders would therefore be understandably reluctant to send people like themselves to Congress to represent their 'feelings and interests'! The 'altogether visionary' hope of creating a system of actual representation 'will never happen under any arrangement that leaves the votes of the people free' (*FP* 35).

Hamilton fails to address, much less to answer, the recurrent Antifederalist charge that the new Constitution would exacerbate and intensify these feelings of civic incompetence, leading inevitably to popular apathy, political corruption, and the loss of civic virtue.

## Virtue versus corruption

The concepts of corruption and virtue, as used by many Antifederalist writers, have deep republican roots. In classical republican discourse, 'corruption' referred to a condition in which rulers and citizens have ceased to know or care about the common good, preferring instead to seek their own private (and especially economic) interests. Just as the human body becomes 'corrupt' with age, so likewise must the body politic sooner or later lose its unity and organic integrity, its 'parts' becoming partisan 'factions' and ceasing to work together for some greater shared purpose. To have lost interest in the common good is to have ceased to be a citizen, or at any rate a virtuous one. Corruption is, in short, the loss or absence of virtue in the larger civic body and in the smaller body (or bodies) that represent them.

The Antifederalist critique of the Constitution echoes many of the themes to be found in the earlier republican and radical Whig warnings of the dangers of corruption, especially those sounded by eighteenth-century English 'country' party ideologists against the 'court' ideology of Walpole and the new Whigs.[11] Thus, for example, the Real Whig warnings about the dangers of political appointees or 'placemen' is repeated by Brutus when he decries 'that kind of corruption, and undue influence, which will arise from the gift of places of honor and emolument'. This, combined with other forms of 'influence', is certain to corrupt the executive and the legislature:

> when it is considered what a number of places of honor and emolument will be the gift of the executive, the powerful influence that great and designing men have over the honest and unsuspecting, by their art and address, their soothing manners and civilities, and their cringing flattery, joined with their affected patriotism: when these different species of influence are combined, it is scarcely to be hoped that a legislature, composed of so small a number, as the one proposed by the new constitution, will long resist their force. (*AF* 128–9)

Without 'an equal and full representation in the legislature' there could be 'no security against bribery and corruption' (*AF* 128).

The corruption of officials or representatives was one thing, but the corruption of the citizenry another, and even more serious, matter. In the Antifederalist view, these were linked in either of two ways. On the one hand, if the members of the various orders should agree that 'fit characters' not of their order were by nature or disposition better able to represent their interests, they might then be willing to consign their liberties to the doubtful safekeeping of their social superiors. On the other hand, should the citizens feel themselves to be powerless and voiceless, they will lose interest in public affairs. In either event they will concentrate on their own purely personal or private affairs and grow lazy or lax as regards the good of their own order and, by implication, the common good. Either would result inevitably in the corruption of the citizenry and, ultimately, in the loss of liberty.

The new Constitution, as depicted by Antifederalist critics, embodied both defects. Suspecting a massive Federalist conspiracy against republican ideals and institutions, many

Antifederalists felt that the new Constitution was designed precisely for the dual purpose of making citizens trust their social superiors even as they themselves forgot the revolutionary Spirit of '76 and became inward-looking and inattentive to matters of common concern. The new Constitution could therefore be viewed, in the parlance of classical republicanism, as a medium or instrument of civic corruption and an enemy of liberty.

From the republican perspective of the Antifederalists, a properly constructed Constitution is more than a codification of laws. It should also be a source of inspiration and an instrument educating the citizenry about their rights and duties. However hastily drafted and ill written the various state constitutions may have been, they supposedly fulfilled that educative function. They admonished governors and representatives even as they reminded the citizens that republican liberties are too easily lost when the public is inattentive.[12] From this perspective one can more readily appreciate the Antifederalists' complaint that the new Constitution sent the wrong sort of message to the citizenry. Not only did its 'independence' or 'virtual' theory of representation imply that their views did not much matter and that the protection of their and the public's interest is best left to an elite; it also failed to inculcate the all-important sense of civic virtue that would result from participation of several sorts, including that of military service.

## Standing army versus citizen militia

One of the staples of classical republican discourse is a deep distrust of 'standing armies'. And it is easy to see why. Professional soldiers are accustomed to unquestioning obedience ('Theirs not to reason why . . .'); their allegiance is to their commander; and military commanders from Julius Caesar through Cromwell and Napoleon and down to the present day have had their political ambitions backed by armed force. If republican liberties are to be safeguarded, standing armies must be outlawed and the republic protected by a 'militia' made up of citizen–soldiers.

One oft-repeated Antifederalist criticism of the new Constitution concerned its provision for a professional army and navy (CUS, Art. I, sect. 8[13]) in addition to state-controlled citizen militias (the forerunner of today's National Guard). Brutus and his fellow Antifederalists believed that a full-time 'standing army' was one of the greatest dangers to liberty (*AF* 115–16, 151–62, 284–5).

Antifederalists agreed that since the proposed Constitution provided for a standing army and navy, the regime it created could not really be 'republican' in letter, and still less in spirit.

Once again Publius had to exhibit the Constitution's republican bona fides to a sceptical public. And again his argument is ingenious. In no. 24 Hamilton observes that while almost all state constitutions contain a warning about the danger of standing armies, only two—Pennsylvania and North Carolina—go so far as to say that 'they ought not to be kept up' in peacetime. But this, says Hamilton, 'is in truth rather a *caution* than a *prohibition*'. And, he adds, the New York constitution 'says not a word about the matter' (*FP* 24). Nor, significantly, do the Articles of Confederation contain any warning about, much less prohibition of, standing armies. Turning the tables on Antifederalist critics, Hamilton proceeds to note that the new Constitution—unlike the Articles of Confederation and the several state constitutions—

actually erects a safeguard against a standing army's potential threat to liberty. That safeguard is that the legislature is to authorize, arm—and pay—the soldiery:

> the whole power of raising armies [is] lodged in the *legislature*, not in the *executive*; [and] this legislature [is] to be a popular body, consisting of the representatives of the people, periodically elected; and [Art. I, sect. 8] forbids the appropriation of money for the support of an army for any longer than two years: a precaution which . . . will appear to be a great and real security against the keeping up of troops without evident necessity. (*FP* 24)

In short, the armed forces will 'stand' only as long as the legislature allows them to do so.

Not content with this seemingly decisive allaying of Antifederalist fears, Hamilton offers a second set of arguments about the desirability of maintaining a paid professional army and navy. The first is concerned with technology; the second, with training. The security of the thirteen American states has heretofore been helped by geography. But no longer. America's distance from Europe is decreasing with the increasing sophistication of ship design and navigational aids. Travel time between Europe and North America continues to be reduced, thereby making the prospect of surprise attack and invasion ever more likely. For reasons of national security and international commerce America therefore needs a professional navy comprising full-time sailors, well trained and fully equipped, to patrol and protect its eastern coast. And on its western, southern, and northern frontiers it needs a full-time army of professional soldiers. Important though the several states' citizen militias are, they have neither the training nor the resources to resist the military and maritime forces that the European powers can throw against them. Hamilton is prepared to admit that a 'permanent corps in the pay of government amounts to a standing army'; but how large it is to be, and how long it is to stand, is best left 'to the discretion and prudence of the legislature' (*FP* 24). And what do the people have to fear from their own elected representatives?

## Missing: a bill of rights

Most Antifederalists—and many strong supporters of the Constitution, such as Thomas Jefferson—decried the absence of a bill of rights in the document drawn up at Philadelphia.[14] Such an addition would serve as a reminder to all—rulers and citizens alike—that the government's authority was limited by its citizens' inviolable liberties. Did not England's Glorious Revolution result in a bill of rights agreed to by King William? Did not the still more glorious American Revolution of 1776 deserve no less a guarantee? For what was the revolution fought, if not to preserve American rights and liberties? If they are to be properly protected, the nature and extent of those liberties must be fixed from the outset. The good will or solicitude of rulers or representatives was not to be relied upon for very long, if at all (*AF* 126). Unless checked by the law and an active and alert citizenry, those to whom power is entrusted will sooner or later abuse it.

In any society, even in the best-ordered republic, there exists an inevitable tendency towards corruption. And in the view of the Antifederalists the new American republic created by the Constitution seemed to be singularly ill ordered, its tendency towards corruption hastened at its birth by a Constitution that encouraged corruption by empowering rulers and representatives at the national or federal level even as it disempowered the citizenry at a more local level. This emasculation was effected in part by making the individual citizen and his order smaller by enlarging the scale on which national action was to be taken by an unrepresentative elite (see the section on representation, above). Hence a 'declaration of rights' must be included in the new plan, lest the people be deceived and led into a trap from which there would be no escape (*AF* 122). Without such a declaration to protect the rights of 'the democratical part', says Brutus, 'the plan is radically defective in a fundamental principle, which ought to be found in every free government; to wit, a declaration of rights' (*AF* 122–3). Since the arguments in favour of such a declaration are so clear and compelling, its omission is an ominous portent, revealing the true colours of Publius and his fellow Federalists: 'so clear a point is this, that I cannot help suspecting, that persons who attempt to persuade people, that such reservations were less necessary under this constitution, than under those of the states, are willfully endeavouring to deceive, and to lead you into an absolute state of vassalage' (*AF* 122). Again and again the Antifederalists hammered the point home: without a bill of rights the new Constitution created a system that is republican in name only.

The charge that the main shortcoming of the new Constitution was the absence of a bill of rights would not go away and, indeed, intensified during the course of the Ratification Debate. Finally, in no. 84 Publius felt himself compelled to answer, although he did so reluctantly and under the heading of 'miscellaneous points' to be dealt with as though they were mere afterthoughts and scarcely on a par with the truly important issues discussed earlier. 'The most considerable of these remaining objections', writes Hamilton, 'is, that the plan of the convention contains no bill of rights.' By way of reply he notes that several state constitutions, including New York's, are also without bills of rights. Acknowledging the force of the Antifederalists' answer to this objection—namely, that no separate bill of rights is needed because provisions for protecting those rights are incorporated into the texts of the state constitutions—Hamilton asserts that the same is true of the new federal constitution as well. 'The truth is, after all the declamation we have heard, that the constitution is itself in every rational sense, and to every useful purpose, A BILL OF RIGHTS' (*FP* 84). Yet the bill of rights that Hamilton teases out of the text is a motley assortment of legal guarantees, prohibitions, and definitions. The 'privileges' of habeas corpus and jury trials are affirmed (although there is no requirement that the jury be composed of one's peers); 'treason' is defined; and the prohibition of titles of nobility (CUS, Art. I, sect. 9) is offered as proof positive of the republican character of the new Constitution. Hamilton then plays his ace. The Antifederalists had often charged their opponents with attempting to alter the meanings of key concepts, including 'republic' itself. Now Hamilton turns the tables by charging the Antifederalists with having attempted to alter the very meaning of the concept of a bill of rights—a concept as old as the Magna Carta and as recent as the bill of rights to which William of Orange had agreed. Because 'bills of rights are in their origin, stipulations between kings and their subjects', says Hamilton, they have no place in a truly republican constitution. QED.

## Conclusion

In the end Publius and other Federalist friends of the new Constitution triumphed over its Antifederalist critics. The proposed Constitution was ratified by all thirteen states, although several did so on the condition that a bill of rights be added as soon as possible. The Bill of

Rights—the first ten amendments to the new Constitution—was adopted in 1791, explicitly enumerating the rights to freedom of speech, press, assembly, and other protections. But many other issues remained unresolved. Foremost among these were the questions of slavery and secession.

The Constitution recognized the legality and legitimacy of slavery. For purposes of apportioning representatives in the House, each black slave in the southern states was to count for three-fifths of a person, but was to be without the rights of a citizen (CUS, Art. I, sect. 2). The Constitution also required that escaped slaves be returned to their masters (CUS, Art. IV, sect. 2). Although many northern supporters of the proposed Constitution abhorred the institution of slavery and looked forward to its abolition, they knew that the slave-holding southern states would never go along with the new plan of union unless the latter retained their rights as owners of human 'property'. The recognition of slavery in the document drafted at the Philadelphia convention was seen as an unfortunate political necessity. The new Constitution also forbade Congress to prohibit the importation of slaves until 1808 (CUS, Art. I, sect. 9). Even if Congress did so, that would not end slavery and the domestic slave trade. About that possibility the Constitution remained ominously silent.

The new Constitution was also silent on the question of whether any state might at its discretion 'nullify' national legislation that adversely affected it, or even secede from the Union. The founders hoped that the advantages of belonging to the United States would suffice to keep the states united. They were wrong. The first half of the nineteenth century saw an increasing division between the agrarian and slave-holding South and the increasingly urban and industrial North. Matters came to a head in 1861, when the southern states seceded from the United States. The Confederate States of America drafted their own Confederate Constitution, which they deemed more truly 'republican' than its earlier counterpart. Their citizen militias became the backbone and basis of the Confederate Army that confronted Federal forces for five long years. Thus the questions that remained unresolved by force of argument in 1787 were resolved by force of arms some seventy years later, in the Civil War of 1860–5. Ironically, the bloodiest and costliest war ever waged by the United States was fought by Americans, on American soil, and against other Americans. This dire possibility neither Publius nor Brutus foresaw.

The American founding, and *The Federalist Papers* in particular, has left a rich but ambiguous legacy. It raised, but never did resolve, a question that has of late been raised anew: what is 'republican' governance? Ought modern-day republicans to emphasize civic 'duties' and de-emphasize individual 'rights'?[15] Or might modern rights-based liberalism be combined with classical duty-based republicanism to form a more communally minded 'republican liberalism'?[16] A rereading of *The Federalist Papers* and its Antifederalist critics might yet shed some light on these and other questions.

---

## FURTHER READING

Cornell, Saul, *The Other Founders: Anti-Federalism and the Dissenting Tradition in America* (Chapel Hill: University of North Carolina Press, 1999).

Dahl, Robert A., *How Democratic is the American Constitution?* (New Haven: Yale University Press, 2002).

Jefferson, Thomas, *Political Writings*, ed. Joyce Appleby and Terence Ball (Cambridge: Cambridge University Press, 1999).

Pitkin, Hanna Fenichel, *The Concept of Representation* (Berkeley and Los Angeles: University of California Press, 1967).

Pocock, J. G. A., *The Machiavellian Moment: Florentine Political Thought and the Atlantic Republican Tradition* (Princeton: Princeton University Press, 1975).

Sheehan, Colleen A., and McDowell, Gary L. (eds.), *Friends of the Constitution: Writings of the 'Other' Federalists, 1787–1788* (Indianapolis: Liberty Fund, 1998).

Wood, Gordon S., *The Creation of the American Republic, 1776–1787* (Chapel Hill: University of North Carolina Press, 1969).

## NOTES

1. Jay, whose forte was foreign policy, contributed only four papers (nos. 2–5) before becoming seriously ill, leaving to Hamilton and Madison the Herculean task of completing the series. Jay returned towards the end to contribute one more paper (no. 64).
2. One might, with perhaps pardonable exaggeration, think of the American Antifederalists as the Euro-sceptics of their day: Philadelphia was their Maastricht; the Constitution their Maastricht Treaty; the US dollar their euro; and the US Capitol (later located in Washington, DC) their Brussels.
3. See the other Federalist, i.e. pro-Constitution, papers by other authors in Colleen A. Sheehan and Gary L. McDowell (eds.), *Friends of the Constitution: Writings of the 'Other' Federalists, 1787–1788* (Indianapolis: Liberty Fund, 1998).
4. *The Federalist*, ed. Terence Ball (Cambridge: Cambridge University Press, 2003) (hereafter *FP*); references are to paper numbers.
5. *The Complete Anti-Federalist*, ed. Herbert J. Storing, 7 vols. (Chicago: University of Chicago Press, 1981) (hereafter *CAF*).
6. J. G. A. Pocock, *The Machiavellian Moment: Florentine Political Thought and the Atlantic Republican Tradition* (Princeton: Princeton University Press, 1975).
7. *The Anti-Federalist*, abridged edn. of *CAF*, ed. Murray Dry, 1 vol. (Chicago: University of Chicago Press, 1985) (hereafter *AF*).
8. See Hanna Fenichel Pitkin, *The Concept of Representation* (Berkeley and Los Angeles: University of California Press, 1967).
9. The most famous defence of the 'independence' view is Burke's 1774 'Speech to the Electors of Bristol' and 'Letter to the Sheriffs of Bristol' (Edmund Burke, *Burke's Politics: Selected Writings and Speeches of Edmund Burke* (New York: Knopf, 1970), 114–17, and Pitkin, *The Concept of Representation*, ch. 8).
10. Although there are now 435 seats in the House of Representatives, there were originally sixty-five, as stipulated by CUS, Art. I, sect. 2, pending a census; 'and until such enumeration shall be made, the State of New Hampshire shall be entitled to chuse three, Massachusetts eight, Rhode-Island and Providence Plantations one, Connecticut five, New-York six, Virginia ten, North Carolina five, South Carolina five, and Georgia three'.
11. Pocock, *The Machiavellian Moment*, 509.
12. See Gordon S. Wood, *The Creation of the American Republic, 1776–1787* (Chapel Hill: University of North Carolina Press, 1969), chs. 4–6.
13. Constitution of the United States (written 1787; ratified 1789) (hereafter *CUS*).
14. For Jefferson's reservations about the absence of a bill of rights, see his letters to Madison, written during the debate over ratification (Thomas Jefferson, *Political Writings*, ed. Joyce Appleby and Terence Ball (Cambridge: Cambridge University Press, 1999), 360–1, 365–9).
15. See Philip Pettit, *Republicanism: A Theory of Freedom and Government* (Oxford: Oxford University Press, 1997); Quentin Skinner, *Liberty before Liberalism* (Cambridge: Cambridge University Press, 1998).
16. See Richard Dagger, *Civic Virtues: Rights, Citizenship, and Republican Liberalism* (Oxford: Oxford University Press, 1997).

# 16 Wollstonecraft

Carole Pateman

Contents



## Chapter guide

Wollstonecraft assumes that the private and public are interrelated, and that God has given reason to both sexes. 'Natural' qualities, including masculinity and femininity, are socially constructed; an artefact of hierarchical institutions and the system of manners they foster. Reason and virtue require cultivation. Private and public virtue demands freedom, non-sexually differentiated principles and standards, and equal rights for women and men. The dimension of rights that gives men power over women must be eliminated. Tyranny in private, especially in marriage, undermines political virtue and active citizenship. Education must be reformed, marriage transformed into an equal relationship between loving friends, and wives must have economic independence. Conceptions and practices of sexuality must be remade if women are to have dignity, and men and women are to be good parents and citizens. Motherhood, fatherhood, and managing a family, as well as rights, are an integral part of citizenship. Wollstonecraft's insights challenge standard conceptions of democracy.

## Biography

Wollstonecraft was born in April 1759 in London. She left her violent and downwardly mobile family aged 19 to earn her living (and support her siblings) as a companion, by running a school, and as a governess in Ireland. She was in Lisbon in 1785 when her close friend Fanny Blood died. In 1787 she began working as a reviewer and translator for Joseph Johnson's *Analytical Review*. She became part of a prominent circle of radical intellectuals, artists, and Dissenters. Her first book was published in 1786, and her two *Vindications* in 1790 and 1792. Her writings were widely read and admired and ranged over political theory, education, fiction, history, and travel writing. She went to revolutionary Paris at the end of 1792, and had a child, Fanny, in France by Gilbert Imlay in 1794. Deserted by him, she made two attempts at suicide. In 1795 she travelled through Norway and Sweden on business for Imlay. Wollstonecraft and William Godwin met again in 1796, and married in 1797 when she became pregnant. She died in September 1797 after the birth of Mary. Her life became a scandal following Godwin's candid memoir.

## Key texts

*A Vindication of the Rights of Men, in a Letter to the Right Honorable Edmund Burke* (1790)

*A Vindication of the Rights of Woman with Strictures on Moral and Political Subjects* (1792)

*An Historical and Moral View of Origin and Progress of the French Revolution; and the Effect it has Produced in Europe* (1794)

*Maria; or, The Wrongs of Woman* (1798)

## Main texts used

*Political Writings*, ed. Janet Todd (Toronto: University of Toronto Press, 1993).

*Maria; or, The Wrongs of Woman*, ed. Anne K. Mellor (New York: Norton, 1994).

## Key ideas

**Virtue**: cultivated in a context of freedom, rights, and non-sexually differentiated moral principles in private and public life. **Rights**: a birthright of both sexes; two-dimensional, men's rights over women must be eliminated. **Reason**: God-given to both sexes, developed within non-tyrannous, free institutions; necessary to inform an educated sensibility. **Sensibility** in both sexes requires cultivation and constraint by reason; may become vicious when seen purely as natural feeling or instinct. **Independence** needs strength of body and mind and absence of economic dependence of wives. **Marriage** embodying the divine right of husbands undermines political virtue; must be transformed into a relation of mutual respect between equal, loving friends. **Citizens**: women and men who enjoy equal rights in private and public; active participants in political life and the duties of parents.

# Introduction

Mary Wollstonecraft's writings began to be accepted as part of the history of political thought only during the 1990s. Yet Wollstonecraft was very well known in her own time—her romantic *Letters Written during a Short Residence in Sweden, Norway, and Denmark* (1796) was admired by Coleridge, Wordsworth, and Hazlitt—and she was part of a prominent circle of radical intellectuals, artists, Dissenters, and familiar figures in political theory, including Thomas Paine, William Godwin, John Horne Tooke, William Blake, and Richard Price. For a very long time Wollstonecraft's work was overshadowed by the scandal provoked by Godwin's (1798) memoir of her life.[1] That her intellectual achievements are finally being acknowledged owes a good deal to Virginia Sapiro's fine study *A Vindication of Political Virtue*,[2] the first to treat Wollstonecraft as a political theorist.

The neglect of Wollstonecraft by political theorists (including feminists) means that, unlike other figures in the history of political thought, there are no established interpretations of her political arguments, or standard assessments of her contribution. Understanding of Wollstonecraft's political theory has also been inhibited because her feminist perspective does not fit into the common classificatory schemes and assumptions of the history of political thought. She is often mentioned as the first feminist theorist, but she had been preceded by women writers in England who, for at least a century, had been concerned with issues that characterize feminism,[3] notably women's intellectual capacities, education, and marriage. Wollstonecraft is distinguished by being the first to develop a sustained theoretical argument and political theory that brings together these questions with women's rights and standing as citizens.

Wollstonecraft's writings have often been characterized in a very narrow and misleading fashion. She has been seen as a writer on education, said to be interested only in the middle classes (she is still sometimes called a 'bourgeois individualist'),[4] claimed to adhere to an 'absurd', rationalist ideal,[5] thought merely to apply familiar liberal tenets to, or to extend the rights of man to, women, and seen as an essentialist. Some of this misunderstanding arises from a failure to look beyond certain aspects of Wollstonecraft's *A Vindication of the Rights of Woman*, the book for which she is best known. Her political theory did not appear fully fledged in 1792, but was developed over the course of her career. Some of her major political themes appear briefly, for example, in *Thoughts on the Education of Daughters* (1787), and any appreciation of her political thought must at the very least take into account *A Vindication of the Rights of Men* (1790) and the unfinished novel *Maria* (1797).

Like her radical allies, Wollstonecraft was greatly concerned with the condition of the poor, and injustices committed against them in the name of property. But she parted company with her friends, as well as her favourite author, Rousseau, and authors of works on 'the female character and education' (*Woman*, 157[6]), in her analysis and criticism of men's power over women, poor and rich. Her proposals for social and political change, and the elimination of 'the cloven foot of despotism' (*Letters*, 144[7]), thus went much further than those of her fellow radicals, reaching into private life, sexual relations, and received ideas about masculinity and femininity. One of her most important political insights was that mastery and subordination in the private sphere, especially in the institution of marriage, undermined the political virtue and active citizenship advocated by Rousseau. Wollstonecraft made a considerable, although largely unrecognized, contribution to the development of democratic theory.[8] Unlike theorists typically presented as 'fathers' of democratic theory, she is concerned with the freedom, rights, and citizenship of women as well as men. She anticipated recent feminist criticism of the appeals to 'nature' by political theorists, and was one of the earliest to question the category 'man'. Another of her major, but still unacknowledged, political insights is that natural rights, or the rights of man, were two-dimensional.

Wollstonecraft 'made many dangerous choices'.[9] She was a bold and courageous woman in her life, her political allegiances, in her writing—and in her journeys, especially to revolutionary France, and to Sweden and Norway, then 'a largely unknown region'.[10] She stepped outside the subject matter deemed suitable for women, and dared to write on the important political questions discussed by famous men and to take issue with their arguments. Perhaps not suprisingly, *A Vindication of the Rights of Men*, her reply to Burke's polemical *Reflections on the Revolution in France*, was initially published anonymously.

To be a political radical, and a supporter of the French Revolution in the 1790s, when England and France were at war and prosecutions being brought for sedition, was a perilous business. Wollstonecraft was one of the few who did not denounce the revolution despite her horror at the violence she witnessed. She wished that she 'had never heard of the cruelties that have been practised here', she wrote to her lover Imlay (letter XXXVI). She had grave doubts too on another score:

> the turn of the tide has left the dregs of the old system to corrupt the new. For the same pride of office, the same desire of power are still visible . . . fearing to return to obscurity after having but just acquired a relish for distinction, each hero, or philosopher, for all are dubbed with these new titles, endeavours to make hay while the sun shines; and every petty municipal officer, become the idol, or rather the tyrant of the day, stalks like a cock on a dunghil. (*Works*, vi. 446[11])

Nor was defending the rights of women a popular cause. On this issue revolutionaries and conservatives occupied common patriarchal ground. Such figures as Condorcet, Olympe de Gouges, and Wollstonecraft stand virtually alone. In the latter part of the eighteenth century there was a good deal of discussion and worry in England about the place of women, and renewed insistence that they should remain outside the public world. But ideal and practice were a long way apart. By the 1790s women were prominent in activities that ranged from opposition to the slave trade to numerous patriotic movements. By 1832, however, they had been excluded from the electorate in a Reform Act that is usually seen simply as a landmark of democratization.

In revolutionary France women swore oaths of allegiance, formed deputations, invaded the Convention, established political clubs, participated in demonstrations and armed marches, and demanded the rights of citizens.[12] By 1795 the male revolutionaries had consigned women to the category of 'passive citizens',[13] excluded them from the electorate, and banned their clubs. The exclusion of women from the rights of citizens was justified by revolutionary spokesmen in terms that echoed Rousseau's pronouncements. Women were declared unfit by nature for public life, and their participation a danger to political order and stability.

## Nature, sentiment, and reason

Burke's *Reflections* appeared on 1 November 1790, and Wollstonecraft's response, *A Vindication of the Rights of Men*, on 29 November; a second edition was published a month later under her own name. Although composed quickly, her first *Vindication* is very complex. Wollstonecraft raises theoretical questions that go far beyond Burke's denunciation of the rights of man and defence of an aristocratic order, and her criticisms are aimed at his earlier *Enquiry into the Origins of our Ideas of the Sublime and Beautiful* as well as the *Reflections*.[14]

Wollstonecraft's first *Vindication* was prompted in part by 'indignation' at Burke's 'sophistical arguments . . . in the questionable shape of natural feelings and common sense' (*Men*, Advertisement[15]), concepts for which he was indebted to the Scottish Enlightenment. The sentiments that Burke accepts as natural are, for Wollstonecraft, 'artificial' or 'factitious'. In her second *Vindication* she argues that the femininity deemed natural is similarly artificial, and she calls for a 'revolution in female manners' (*Woman*, 119).[16] Such a revolution would lead to the replacement of manners by morality and political virtue—but not a return to nature. A social constructionist argument is central to her political theory; like Rousseau, she emphasizes the interrelationship between the qualities and appearance of individuals and the structure of social institutions. Wollstonecraft argues that the hierarchical institutions, including the Church, lauded by Burke, and the conjugal relations advocated by Rousseau, reproduce the servility, vice, and corruption of the 'very partial' civilization of Europe (*Men*, 9).

Wollstonecraft followed Locke in the assumption that there were no innate ideas. God has given humans a range of capacities, and also the means to cultivate them. Neither manners nor morality are natural in the sense of being the unmediated outgrowth of feeling and sentiment, or merely instinctive. Wollstonecraft argues that Burke adopts the popular supposition that there is a 'kind of mysterious instinct'—often called common sense or sensibility—'that instantaneously discerns truth, without the tedious labour of ratiocination' (*Men*, 30). She quotes Burke's claim that the English 'cherish and cultivate those inbred sentiments which are . . . the true supporters of all liberal and manly morals'. She asks him where the sentiments come from, how they are bred, and what role they played when 'slavery was authorized by law to fasten her fangs on human flesh' (*Men*, 32–3). To fall back on instincts and sensibility is, for Wollstonecraft, to abandon God's gifts. The brutes are part of nature and have instincts; what they lack is the potential, and reason, that God has given to women and men. She declares that 'if virtue be an instinct, I renounce all hope of immortality' (*Men*, 34).

Wollstonecraft argues that the cultivation and use of reason is a necessary condition for the development of morality and private and public virtue. She appeals to Burke: 'Quitting now the flowers of rhetoric, let us, Sir, reason together' (*Men*, 7). But reasoning together is impossible. Burke has a 'mortal antipathy' to reason, and the *Reflections* is a work of 'pampered sensibility' (*Men*, 7), emotion, passion, and insincerity, not reason. She comments that, had Burke been French, his 'romantic enthusiasm' would have made him a revolutionary (*Men*, 46). Wollstonecraft states that she will not set out Burke's inconsistencies and contradictions sentence by sentence, since it would be 'something like cowardice to fight with a man who had never exercised the weapons with which his opponent chose to combat' (*Men*, 8). Instead of a 'fixed first principle to refute', Burke offers only 'slavish paradoxes'. If there is anything like a principle to be found in his 'endless Reflections' (*Men*, 58), it is to see 'unnatural customs', consolidated by ignorance and self-interest as the 'sage fruit of experience'. When errors are discovered, he relies on 'our feelings' to excuse 'the venerable vestiges of ancient days' (*Men*, 8).

In the letter to Talleyrand that opens her second *Vindication* Wollstonecraft throws down a challenge: 'if women are to be excluded, without having a voice, from a participation of the natural rights of mankind, prove first, to ward off the charge of injustice and inconsistency, that they want reason' (*Woman*, 71). To claim that both sexes were endowed with the same rationality was extremely controversial. In popular opinion, religious doctrine, and political philosophy women were held to be creatures of feeling, naturally wanting in reason; or, at best, their reason was seen as sufficiently different by nature from men's to warrant their exclusion from many areas of human endeavour. Wollstonecraft's feminist predecessors had been vigorously combating such views for a long time, and one of their major arguments was precisely that God had not differentiated between the sexes in this respect. Astell, for example, tartly remarked that 'Sense is a Portion that GOD Himself has been pleas'd to distribute to both Sexes with an Impartial Hand, but Learning is what Men have engross'd to themselves.'[17]

This line of argument depended, in turn, on another claim; that women possessed souls. In chapter iv of *A Vindication of the Rights of Woman*, Wollstonecraft restates 'my old argument; if woman be allowed to have an immortal soul, she must have, as the employment of life, an understanding to improve' (p. 140). God has created women who are capable of seeing his wisdom, and whose souls can rise to their Creator. Thus God did not mean that a woman 'sent into the world to acquire virtue' was made only to 'submit to man, her equal'. Nor did he mean her to rely on men's reason, rather than cultivating her own. Women, too, were to climb 'the arduous steeps of knowledge' (*Woman*, 145). Wollstonecraft insisted that religion, no less than any other authoritative doctrine, must be based on reason. The 'sceptre' of her fellow men, she states, 'extends not to me, unless the reason of an individual demands my homage; and even then the submission is to reason, and not to man' (*Woman*, 109). Nor is her faith in, and submission to, God unreasoning. She fears God, but 'it is not his power that I fear—it is not to an arbitrary will, but to unerring *reason* I submit' (*Men*, 34).[18]

Wollstonecraft does not simply replace natural feeling with abstract reason. She argues that there is a close relationship between reason and sensibility.[19] 'Sacred be the feelings of the heart!' she writes; without the 'invigorating impregnation' of the heart, reason could not 'bring forth her only legitimate offspring—virtue' (*Men*, 31). Conversely, the heart goes astray without reason. Wollstonecraft argued that both feelings and reason can be educated and inform each other. 'True sensibility . . . is the auxiliary of virtue' (*Maria*, 110[20]). To act according to principles of right conduct requires reason, and feelings will respond to the same principles. Properly cultivated, sensibility provides, as it were, a short cut through long processes of reasoning.

When feeling is unconstrained by reason, sensibility can become vicious. Wollstonecraft accuses Burke of 'conspicuous' contempt for the poor (*Men*, 58). He sees poor labourers as part of nature rather than humanity, as nothing more than another form of livestock on the estates of the nobility (*Men*, 16). The poor are denied rights and 'have no asylum from oppression' (*Men*, 14), but Burke, for all his sentiment, sheds no tears for the plight of the poor man, or his family, when he is press-ganged, hanged for stealing a deer, or plunged into idleness and want through loss of employment. Wollstonecraft agrees that the condition of the poor can prompt disgust, but instead of burying 'the sympathies of humanity in the servile appellation of master' (*Men*, 61), remedies can and should be found. She mentions such measures as dividing estates and forests into small farms, and allowing cultivation of heathland. In her record of her journey through Norway she wrote that the 'distribution of landed property into small farms, produces a degree of equality which I have seldom seen elsewhere . . . the Norwegians appear to me to be the most free community I have ever observed' (*Letters*, 101–2).

Burke claims to love 'a manly, moral regulated liberty',[21] but Wollstonecraft replies that liberty is nowhere to be found in the *Reflections*; instead there is an 'unmanly servility' (*Men*, 24). Burke's 'sentimental varnish' and 'Gothic drapery' disguise the tyranny and despotism of a political system in which property is placed above everything else (*Men*, 25, 50). Burke even ignores the 'unnatural crimes' committed by parents against their children to ensure perpetuation of their property (*Men*, 21–2). How, she wonders, could Burke have defended the American Revolution when 'the whole tenor of his plausible arguments settles slavery on an everlasting foundation. Allowing his servile reverence for antiquity, and prudent attention to self-interest, to have the force which he insists on, the slave trade ought never to be abolished' (*Men*, 13; see also pp. 53–4).

Wollstonecraft was writing during a period in which rhetorical style was linked to moral improvement and the making of the English nation.[22] Sentiment, literary language, and the nation—the personal and the political—are closely interwoven. Wollstonecraft candidly states in *A Vindication of the Rights of Woman* (p. 78) that she 'shall disdain to cull my phrases or polish my style' since she wishes 'to persuade by the force of my arguments'. She is making both a literary point against theorists of nature and feelings, and a political point about reason and patriotism. Burke's essay was a response to Richard Price's sermon *Discourse on the Love of our Country* (delivered in November 1789), and, in part, Wollstonecraft took up the cudgels on behalf of Price, a mentor and friend whom she greatly admired. Burke's vitriolic *ad hominen* attack 'made Price an alien and traitor by implication',[23] but love of country was a tricky issue for Burke. By the 1790s a political culture of English nationalism was well developed,[24] and in the *Reflections* Burke makes a great deal of the sentiments of Englishmen—but he was Irish. Price linked 1789 to 1688, and, if as a Whig Burke celebrated the Glorious Revolution, as an Irishman who hated the ascendancy he could only have been reminded again of 'how anti-Catholic, and to him how alien had been the English revolution'.[25]

Towards the end of *A Vindication of the Rights of Men*, Wollstonecraft emulates Burke's flights of over-wrought prose: while 'man preys on man', Burke mourns for 'the idle tapestry that decorated a gothic pile, and the dronish bell that summoned the fat priest to prayer. You mourn for the empty pageant of a name' (*Man*, 62). The outrages that she is contemplating require more than tears—and then Wollstonecraft pauses (noted by two empty lines in the text) to recollect herself, and control the contempt she is beginning to feel for Burke's 'infantine sensibility' (*Men*, 63). Sapiro suggests that modern readers will be 'embarrassed' by this manoeuvre,[26] and Gunther-Canada argues that Wollstonecraft was 'silenced by sensibility'.[27] But Wollstonecraft can also be read as making a very good political point against the proponents of sensibility with their own literary weapons.

## Men's rights and women's freedom

Wollstonecraft argues both for and against the rights of man—and for the rights of women. One of her major contributions to political theory is to show that the rights of man are two-dimensional.[28] The first dimension encompasses familiar civil and political rights set down in documents since 1789 (now known as human rights), rights that, she insists, should be enjoyed by both sexes. The second dimension consists of rights that are exercised by all men, and that give men power over women and deny women freedom. These rights are not set out in documents but embedded, for example, in the law of coverture (highlighted in *Maria*) that sanctions a conjugal relationship of master and 'upper servant' (*Woman*, 113),[29] and in widely held social convictions about the respective characteristics, place, and duties of the sexes.

In an aristocratic political order, talk of the rights of man can be nothing more than 'grating sounds that set [the] teeth on edge' (*Men*, 55). Wollstonecraft declares, against Burke's assertion that English liberties were an 'entailed inheritance',[30] that both rights and liberty are a birthright (*Men*, 13, 54; also *Revolution*, 352[31]). In her *Vindications* she refers to the rights of man and the rights of humanity as 'sacred' (*Men*, 34; *Woman*, 163). Wollstonecraft argues that all men, whatever their station in life, must have 'such a degree of liberty, civil and religious, as is compatible with the liberty of every other individual' (*Men*, 7). However, she also asks a vital question too often ignored by historians of political thought: who is included in the category 'man'? Wollstonecraft is keenly aware that the '*rights* of humanity have been . . . confined to the male line from Adam downwards' (*Woman*, 168).

Wollstonecraft argues that all women have been denied their birthright of freedom, and wives are 'bastilled . . . for life' (*Maria*, 87). Women's subordination has spiritual as well as political consequences. 'Only a free soul can seek and know God,'[32] but women are deprived of moral freedom, and thus of the opportunity for true devotion and reward in heaven. On earth women also lack physical liberty, and are 'slaves . . . in a political and civil sense' (*Woman*, 263). The vulnerability of women, denied rights and protection by the law, is graphically set out in *Maria*, and Wollstonecraft (echoed by Virginia Woolf[33]) asks 'if women have a country' (*Maria*, 92).

It could hardly have escaped Wollstonecraft's notice that male radicals (in other respects) in her own circle, as well as famous political theorists, resisted the inclusion of women within the rights of 'man'. Rousseau and Burke, bringing together the personal and the political, denounce any change in the 'natural' order of the sexes as a threat to the order of the state. In his *Enquiry* Burke elevates 'common sense' views of masculinity and femininity into an elaboration of the sublime in terms of masculine power and awe, and the beautiful in terms of feminine weakness; a weakness which has no place in the state.[34] In the *Reflections* Burke uses fevered sexual metaphor—the abominations of harpies, furies of hell, and women lost to shame—to convey the horrors of a revolution that 'inverted order in all things'.[35] The image of unsexed women demonstrates the consequences of tearing down the draperies that must necessarily veil power.

That Rousseau, from whom Wollstonecraft learned a good deal, is her major target in *A Vindication of the Rights of Woman* is not surprising. He presents an elaborate justification of the second dimension of the rights of man. The free male citizens who inhabit Rousseau's pages rule over women in the household as well as the state. He insists that the natural characters and capacities of the sexes entail that women must be denied liberty and rights in order to safeguard political order. Women's (lack of) education must uphold and reinforce their submission; they must be taught to be creatures of feeling, and to please men. Women must learn to submit to injustice at men's hands.

Wollstonecraft's attack on such claims depends on the argument that the characteristics and appearance used to justify the denial of rights to women are artificial, the outcome of the very institutions and relationships defended by writers such as Rousseau. Burke had provided a very influential, romantic portrayal of the French queen 'glittering like the morning star', before her downfall, and had condemned the poor, uneducated women who supported the revolution as the 'vilest of women'.[36] Wollstonecraft responds that the queen deserves pity, but so do market women struggling to make a living selling vegetables and fish (*Men*, 30; also *Revolution*, 361). Social conditions and social rank, not nature, make one woman appear to Burke to glitter and another vile and gross.

Wollstonecraft argues that in societies in which 'we see only master and servant' (*Revolution*, 332), the development of reason, virtue, morality, and a cultivated sensibility is inhibited in all ranks of the social order and in both sexes. These qualities can flourish only in a context of freedom and rights for all men and women: 'Liberty is the mother of virtue' (*Woman*, 109). Wollstonecraft insists that virtue, in private or political life, has no sex. Virtue requires that 'both sexes must act from the same principle', but the conduct of men and women is regulated through arbitrary distinctions (*Woman*, 270; *Revolution*, 294). Morality is not sexually differentiated, and the same principles and standards must govern the character and rights of men and women alike.

Both sexes, that is to say, must exhibit the 'manly virtues'. Wollstonecraft's use of terms such as 'manly' and 'effeminate' refer not to the contrasting, and supposedly natural, attributes of the sexes, but to human characteristics that are associated with freedom and the development of reasoning powers. In *A Vindication of the Rights of Woman* (p. 76) she writes of 'manly virtues' as 'those talents and virtues, the exercise of which ennobles the human character'. This is why she declares, against those who decry 'masculine women', that she wishes women could grow more masculine. She notes that the popular assumption is that women 'were made to be loved, and must not aim at respect, lest they should be hunted out of society as masculine' (*Woman*, 106).

To Wollstonecraft, Burke's emotion, raw sensibility, and literary style appear to reveal an author who lacks manliness.[37] She even comments that she fears that mere mention of 'metaphysical enquiry' will 'derange [his] nervous system' (*Men*, 15).[38] Such effeminacy is endemic in a hierarchical society. The rich, sunk in luxury, idleness, sensuality, and flattery, 'have ceased to be men', and the 'profligates of rank, [are] emasculated by hereditary effeminacy' (*Men*, 8, 41). Even the military, she argues in *A Vindication of the Rights of Woman* (pp. 94–5), usually seen as the epitome of masculinity, have become effeminate in their preoccupation with dress and manners.[39]

Wollstonecraft, therefore, states that she will offer 'manly definition[s]', and speak with 'manly plainness' (*Men*, 5, 36). The boldness, and difficulty, of her strategy and argument was accentuated once her identity as the author of *A Vindication of the Rights of Men* was revealed. 'Manliness' is a human capacity, but her attack on Burke's lack of reason invokes the association of the voice of reason with the male sex.[40] For Wollstonecraft to claim manly reason for herself, to defend the rights of women, and to treat the state—seen by Burke as 'consecrated', so that any of its faults must be approached with 'pious awe and trembling'[41]—as a human contrivance, was audacious on several counts. Her boldness is frequently underestimated, as, for example, in the charge that in her second *Vindication* she is making 'an appeal to men's reason'.[42] In the existing state of society neither sex are reasonable beings. Wollstonecraft is not merely appealing to men, or claiming that women should emulate men. Both men and women have to change if the God-given reasoning capacities of humans are to be cultivated.

This means that women must enjoy the full range of natural rights—and the second dimension of the rights of man must be eliminated. Wollstonecraft also demands political representation for women, 'instead of being arbitrarily governed without having direct share allowed them in the deliberations of government'. She adds, however, that since the British political system is but 'a convenient handle for despotism', women are as well off as hard-working mechanics who pay for the upkeep of royalty when they cannot feed their children (*Woman*, 237). But rights are not sufficient to ensure women's freedom. Wollstonecraft argues that other radical social and cultural changes are required if the birthright of humanity is to be enjoyed by everyone.

## Private virtue and public order

Wollstonecraft agrees with Rousseau that marriage is 'the cement of society' (*Woman*, 260), and that the family is the foundation of the state. She is an advocate of marriage at a young age. In *A Vindication of the Rights of Men* she remarks that this is prevented by parents' desire to safeguard their property. A system of coeducation would promote early marriage and the 'salutary physical and moral effects' (*Woman*, 265) to which it gives rise. A married (male) citizen is a very different man from the single 'selfish coxcomb' (*Men*, 22). Men, like women, learn how to fulfil their public duties through the habits instilled by performing private duties—provided that the conjugal relationship is properly constituted.

Wollstonecraft argues that laws, and political theorists such as Rousseau, upholding 'the *divine right* of husbands' (*Woman*, 114) undermine public life. The rule of one man in marriage cannot form the basis for political virtue and active citizenship. Thus she rejects Rousseau's strict separation of private from public life, and his argument that the two spheres, and, hence, the sexes, must be governed by different principles. She insists that freedom and equality must obtain in both private and public, and in relations between women and men. For Wollstonecraft, the institution of marriage is central to the creation of a just public order. Marriage exemplifies the deleterious political consequences of hierarchically structured institutions that foster vices in superiors and inferiors alike.

Women's defects are the obverse of men's—Wollstonecraft presents a catalogue of their deficiencies throughout the *Vindication of the Rights of Woman*—and, like the vices of men, result from human contrivance, not nature. Neither sex can become virtuous when they live together within tyrannical institutions. Men display the typical characteristics of those who are permitted, as husbands, to exert the arbitrary power of tyrants, and women have the defects common to their underlings. Individuals in servile positions are prone, in Godwin's words, to 'slavish feelings that shrink up the soul'.[43] Women seek the favour of their masters and, at the same time, try to gain what power they can, and so become cunning, duplicitous, selfish, and mean. 'Female follies', Wollstonecraft is convinced, arise from the tyranny of men. More generally, their characters, like those of other subordinates, are 'produced by oppression' (*Woman*, 294). Wollstonecraft writes that 'the gangrene, which the vices engendered by oppression have produced . . . pervades society at large' (*Woman*, 276). Neither masters nor their subordinates can develop the (mutually reinforcing) private and public virtues necessary in a free political order.

Rousseau proclaimed that women were a danger to political order because, by nature, they lacked a sense of justice. For Wollstonecraft (anticipating J. S. Mill), women's apparent lack of a sense of justice was a consequence of their subordination. Women, 'denied all political privileges, and not allowed, as married women, excepting in criminal cases, a civil existence, have their attention naturally drawn from the interest of the whole community to that of the minute parts' (*Woman*, 283). Without civil and political rights, women are, she stresses, *forced* to 'remain immured in their families, groping in the dark' (*Woman*, 71). Women, that is, have all their attention concentrated on the narrow interests of their families, gain no understanding of the public interest, and have no opportunity to develop a public spirit or sense of justice. They must thus always appear partial, and so dangerous if they attempt to enter political life. Moreover, Wollstonecraft argues that, under such conditions, women's understanding of their private interests is distorted too; the 'private duty of any member of society must be very imperfectly performed when not connected with the general good' (*Woman*, 283).

The structure of marriage and family life means that the problem of the development of individual capacities and virtue begins very early. Parents behave like tyrants and demand the blind obedience from their children that is inimical to spiritual as well as moral development, instead of teaching them through reason. They allow children, in their turn, to tyrannize over servants. Nor are schools, presided over by 'pedantic tyrants', an improvement; boarding schools, in particular, are 'hot-beds of vice and folly' (*Woman*, 255, 252).

Wollstonecraft is very critical of the education of both boys and girls. The education of boys does nothing to prevent them from tormenting animals and developing the habit of cruelty, which, as 'domestic tyrants', they later practise over 'wives, children, and servants' (*Woman*, 269). Girls are 'educated' to please men. Wollstonecraft quotes from Burke's account of how the beautiful is exhibited by women when they totter as they walk and lisp in their speech (*Woman*, 47). How could such creatures be respected? Wollstonecraft emphasizes that strong bodies and strong minds go together. Girls must engage in plenty of physical activity. When they are kept weak as Burke prescribes, and ignorant as Rousseau advocates, no wonder that young women are looking for husbands 'to supply the place of reason'. They are fit for nothing except to marry men who want wives resembling 'gentle, domestic brutes' (*Woman*, 123, 90).

Education, Wollstonecraft declares, should be 'a grand national concern' (*Woman*, 251). She offers a scheme for reform and the establishment of a new system of national education in dayschools, which 'would be schools of morality' and 'directed to form citizens' (*Woman*, 256, 265). From the age of 5 until 9, Wollstonecraft proposed, rich and poor children and both sexes would be educated together, with the same curriculum and physical exercise, dressed alike and disciplined alike. Children of 'superior abilities or fortune' (*Woman*, 264) would then continue to be educated with no distinctions between girls and boys, but those destined for domestic work or trades would study together only in the morning, girls and boys being educated separately in the afternoons. Although the class division would be questioned today, this was a very radical proposal—but not enough to remedy the problems of a society based on hierarchy and artificial distinctions. Wollstonecraft argues that 'till society be differently constituted, much cannot be expected from education' (*Woman*, 91).

One of the most important steps towards social change and reform of marriage and conjugal relations is for women to develop what Wollstonecraft calls a 'manly spirit of independence' (*Men*, 15). Women must 'breathe the sharp invigorating air of freedom' (*Woman*, 109). 'It is vain', Wollstonecraft states, 'to expect virtue from women till they are, in some degree, independent of men' (*Woman*, 231). Strong, educated, independent women would have no incentive to marry men who did not respect them, nor to sell themselves into 'legal prostitution', i.e. marriage (*Men*, 21; see also *Woman*, 136[44]) in exchange for their subsistence.

Wollstonecraft argued two centuries ago that not only must women be 'enabled to earn their own subsistence, independent of men; in the same manner, I mean . . . as one man is independent of another' (*Woman*, 260; and p. 166), but that women should retain this independence even when they became wives. A wife should not depend on 'her husband's bounty' (*Woman*, 236), or a widow be left destitute on his death. Women of all social strata must be usefully employed. Wollstonecraft recognized that this was difficult. She noted in *Education of Daughters* (pp. 73, 69[45]) that the 'few trades which are left, are now gradually falling into the hands of the men', and that women's occupations were 'very humiliating'. Still, in her second *Vindication* she lists a range of occupations—such as physician, nurse, businesswoman, farmer, or shopkeeper—that women might pursue.[46]

Women's independence is necessary also for another social and cultural transformation. Conceptions and practices of sexuality must change, Wollstonecraft argues, if women and men are to be good parents and active citizens.

## Lovers, parents, and citizens

Wollstonecraft has been criticized by some feminists for being a prude and condemning 'physical sexuality in general'.[47] The following passage from *A Vindication of the Rights of Woman* is frequently cited:

> In order to fulfil the duties of life, and to be able to pursue with vigour the various employments which form the moral character, a master and mistress of a family ought not to continue to love each other with passion. I mean to say, that they ought not to indulge those emotions which disturb the order of society, and engross the thoughts that should be otherwise employed. The mind that has never been engrossed by one object wants vigour—if it can long be so, it is weak. (*Woman*, 102)

Wollstonecraft's formulation can no doubt appear prudish when the most intimate details of individuals' lives are paraded every day on television, but it must be read in the context of her broader political theory.

Wollstonecraft nowhere suggests that men and women should abstain from sexual relations—indeed, she comments, for example, that a woman should not have to feign coldness to excite her husband, as Rousseau recommended to Sophie. Both sexes 'ought to have the common appetites and passions of their nature' (*Woman*, 218) which God has given them. Her target in *A Vindication of the Rights of Woman* is not sexuality as such, but romantic sensibility and the political consequences of a particular conception of heterosexuality, masculinity, and femininity. Sexuality is connected to women's subordination and exclusion from rights and citizenship.

Ignorant and lacking the capacity for moral discrimination, women are vulnerable both in and out of marriage. They have no choice but to rely on their physical charms to try and captivate men. Men are thus encouraged to be libertines, and Wollstonecraft thought that sensualists were some of the most dangerous tyrants. Before marriage young girls from the lower orders all too easily met the same fates as Jemima and Peggy in *Maria*, and those from higher stations are attracted to charming and socially accomplished, but sexually unscrupulous, rakes; 'half the sex, in its present infantine state, would pine for a Lovelace' (*Woman*, 205).

Once married, a woman who relied purely on her youthful sexuality to capture a husband will surely find that he soon tires of her; 'the sprightly lover [turns] into a surly suspicious tyrant, who contemptuously insults the very weakness he fostered' (*Woman*, 205). An uneducated woman abandoned by her husband, or a widow, will quickly learn that men do not want an older woman with children to support.

Wollstonecraft wants to 'restore to [women] their lost dignity' (*Woman*, 119), so that they can enter sexual relations as equals. This is why she turns her attention to romantic love, or sexual infatuation, although she knows that to 'speak disrespectfully of love' is seen as 'treason' against fine feelings (*Woman*, 98). In the *Rights of Men* (p. 29) she defines 'romantic' as 'false, or rather artificial feelings'. The romantic 'love' that women are taught to pursue helps constitute the master–servant relations that corrode the whole of society. It is very far removed from the human love that is part of the 'glowing flame of universal love, which . . . mounts in grateful incense to God' (*Woman*, 145). Romantic love is necessarily transitory, as, she notes, Rousseau agrees (*Woman*, 170). Wollstonecraft also shrewdly observes that girls 'have such perfect power over their hearts as not to permit themselves to *fall in love* till a man with a superiour fortune offers' (*Woman*, 154).

In *A Vindication of the Rights of Woman* Wollstonecraft devotes a chapter (vii) to modesty, which she links to personal reserve. Neither characteristic is now fashionable, but Wollstonecraft treats modesty as a virtue 'not a quality' (*Woman*, 208), and as a virtue for both men and women. As the chapter title states, she is not considering modesty as a sexual virtue, nor as synonymous with chastity or 'reputation'.[48] She comments that when Richardson 'makes Clarissa tell Lovelace that he had robbed her of her honour, he must have had strange notions of honour and virtue' (*Woman*, 150). For Wollstonecraft, the development of modesty is part of a political transformation. It is an attribute of individual dignity, strength of mind, and cultivated powers of reason; 'it is vain to expect much public or private virtue, till both men and women grow more modest' (*Woman*, 213).

Modesty is also important if marriage is to be changed from an institution of master and servant into a relationship between equals, based on mutual respect. Wives and husbands, Wollstonecraft argues (again anticipating J. S. Mill), must be friends. Friendship is 'the most sublime of all affections' (*Woman*, 152), and, for Wollstonecraft, modesty is a virtue necessary if spouses are to be 'domestic friends' (*Woman*, 216). Marital friendship does not preclude continuing sexual attraction and relations, but only a weak mind remains completely engrossed by physical passion, and women and men of weak minds make very poor parents and citizens.

Motherhood and fatherhood, Wollstonecraft argues, are integral to the rights and duties of citizenship. Her view of citizenship and motherhood is easily misunderstood since it is very different from the contemporary conception of citizenship as a purely public activity. Citizenship, for Wollstonecraft, involves marriage and managing a family as well as taking part in civic affairs. Household duties as well as rights are part of citizenship.

The work of both marital partners is part of citizenship, but Wollstonecraft sees their duties diverging in certain respects—though in both cases these are '*human* duties' governed by the same principles (*Woman*, 126). She hopes that one day society will be such that a man 'must necessarily fulfil the duties of a citizen, or be despised', but she sees him as 'employed in any of the departments of civil life', while his wife, 'also an active citizen', will be engaged in household duties, and assisting her neighbours (*Woman*, 236). The 'welfare of society', she writes, 'is not built on extraordinary exertions', so the majority of women—and men—will express their citizenship, in part, through their daily familial tasks (*Woman*, 140). Wollstonecraft insists that men cannot be good citizens unless they are serious husbands and fathers. The qualities of a good 'father', as shown by her portrayal of the father and uncle in *Maria*,[49] are cultivated, not natural. Hierarchical institutions produce poor fathers as well as weak mothers.

During the course of her discussion, however, Wollstonecraft states that 'the care of children in their infancy is one of the grand duties annexed to the female character by nature' (*Woman*, 243). This exception to her general argument about nature is seen as evidence of essentialism. Contemporary feminists argue that fathers should take an equal share in child-rearing, but how likely was such an argument, especially in the case of early infancy, in the circumstances of the 1790s? Wollstonecraft agreed with Rousseau that the development of morality began from birth. Breastfeeding was the beginning of moral education, and she joined Rousseau in urging mothers to suckle their babies.[50]

Wollstonecraft's arguments about motherhood and citizenship have suggested that the 'sexual division of labor, and its corollary, the public/private split, remain structurally untouched'.[51] But it must not be assumed that it was as 'obvious' in the 1790s as it became fifty or sixty years later, in the heyday of the doctrine of 'separate spheres' in England, that women had a strictly defined place—although strenuous efforts were being made to ensure that it seemed obvious. Wollstonecraft wrote before the completion of the long process through which the home was separated from the workplace,[52] and before the ideal of the male 'breadwinner' and his economically dependent 'housewife' became the model, during the 1840s, for all respectable classes. Wollstonecraft goes quite a long way in challenging (what became) the accepted sexual division of labour.

Wollstonecraft has a very robust view of motherhood, yet it has been claimed that she 'help[ed] to define'[53] an idea, influential during the American and French Revolutions, that contemporary historians call republican motherhood. Women (wives) by virtue of their natures were allocated the political task of bearing and rearing the next generation of (male) citizens. However, their natures, it was held, necessarily excluded women from rights and citizenship. Republican motherhood was a corollary of the rights of 'man', and, therefore, exactly what Wollstonecraft was attacking. That a subordinate wife, confined to the domestic world and deprived of rights, could manage a family and perform the educative task prescribed for her was nonsensical to Wollstonecraft. Women had to be strong, educated, with a cultivated reason and sensibility, and to enjoy economic independence if they were to be good mothers—and they had to have rights and be citizens.[54]

## Wollstonecraft and democracy

Wollstonecraft offers some profound insights into the theoretical and practical requirements for a genuine democracy in which both halves of humanity have equal standing. Feminist criticism of modern political institutions as masculine preserves has a long history. The typical response of political theorists to the criticism can be summed up in J. S. Mill's words; most do not question 'practical principles in which they have been born and bred and which are the basis of much of the existing order of the world, at the first argumentative attack which they are not capable of logically resisting'.[55] Critics of the 'pestiferous purple' (*Woman*, 88), or class, rarely challenged (what later feminists called) the aristocracy of sex. The awkward questions raised by Wollstonecraft, and her feminist successors, about the connection between the 'private', masculinity, femininity, and domestic life, and the 'public', civil and political rights, were swept under the carpet.

Wollstonecraft was the first political theorist systematically to highlight and criticize the interrelationship between sexuality, marriage, the sexual division of labour, and citizenship. She refers only very occasionally to an original contract. Nevertheless, she understood the political significance of the sexual contract,[56] the dimension of the theory of an original contract that legitimized the power of men as a sex, and that has remained hidden in the history of political thought.[57] But perhaps even she might be surprised at the tenacity with which both radicals and conservatives held onto rights as a male prerogative, and clung to the ideal of the economically dependent wife, and astonished that the last legal vestiges of coverture were not abolished in England until 1992.[58]

The universal language of freedom as a birthright launched the promise of equal freedom, rights, and political standing for men and women alike—the promise of democracy. Ironically, in the 1990s, when democracy became more popular than ever before, influential theorists rejected universalism, and early modern feminists were assumed to be implicated in the so-called 'Enlightenment project', and thus to be guilty of the sins of the fathers. To be sure, universalism was never what it seemed at face value—or feminism would not have been necessary. But Wollstonecraft was one of the earliest critics of the foundationalist concept of 'man' and of essentialist claims about women's nature.[59] Moreover, the language of freedom as a birthright undercut all the established justifications for the government of one individual or group by another, save for free agreement or consent. For the first time an intellectual armoury was available to feminists to mount a general theoretical attack on masculine power, whether in the state or in the household.

These weapons still have considerable political force. Wollstonecraft's recognition of the two dimensions of the rights of man, and attack on the rights that give men power over women, anticipated recent feminist criticism of human rights.[60] In the 1990s Wollstonecraft's arguments (their source unacknowledged) were echoed in the forums of the United Nations, and in a global movement to eliminate the second dimension of the rights of man. The movement for women's human rights is still resisted in much the same terms as two centuries ago.

Wollstonecraft argued that convention and oppression, not nature, stood in the way of the cultivation of women's reason and their rights and citizenship. The paradox of women's political position is that appeals to nature have been used both to *exclude* women from citizenship and to *incorporate* them as lesser citizens. British history illustrates this very clearly. Women's political inclusion since the 1790s has been extremely complex.[61] After sixty years of campaigning, and long after being incorporated into the Tory and Liberal Parties, all women won the vote, the major emblem of citizenship, in 1928. But they exercised the franchise while still subordinate in marriage and lacking many civil rights. Women's standing and access to benefits in the post-war welfare state was primarily determined through marriage. They were not citizens in the welfare state in their own right, but included as the wives of male breadwinners and the mothers of their children.

This system of secondary citizenship has broken down since the 1970s in the face of legal and social reform, and global economic restructuring that has swept away the jobs of former male breadwinners. But the interrelationship between marriage, employment, and citizenship is only slowly being acknowledged, and the legacy of old institutions and convictions about women's proper place linger on. The conjunction of this legacy with current economic circumstances and changes to the welfare state has given new life to Wollstonecraft's argument about the political significance of household tasks, but the suggestion that motherhood and fatherhood are relevant to citizenship gets buried under controversies about 'family values'. More broadly, the important question implicitly raised by her argument is what exactly should count as a contribution to citizenship and the public good.

Two decades of feminist scholarship and intellectual upheaval, during which famous texts and central political concepts have been reinterpreted and deconstructed, have opened the way for an appreciation of Wollstonecraft's remarkable theoretical achievements. Yet the full implications of her challenge to standard conceptions of 'democracy' still remain controversial everywhere.[62]

## FURTHER READING

Falco, Maria J. (ed.), *Feminist Interpretations of Mary Wollstonecraft* (University Park: Pennsylvania State University Press, 1996).

Gunther-Canada, Wendy, *Rebel Writer: Mary Wollstonecraft and Enlightenment Politics* (DeKalb: Northern Illinois Press, 2001).

Kelly, Gary, *Revolutionary Feminism: The Mind and Career of Mary Wollstonecraft* (New York: St Martin's Press, 1992).

Sapiro, Virginia, *A Vindication of Political Virtue: The Political Theory of Mary Wollstonecraft* (Chicago: University of Chicago Press, 1992).

Todd, Janet, *Mary Wollstonecraft: A Revolutionary Life* (London: Weidenfeld & Nicolson; New York: Columbia University Press, 2000).

## NOTES

1. William Godwin, *Memoirs of the Author of 'The Rights of Woman'* (1798), in *Wollstonecraft, 'Letters Written during a Short Residence in Sweden, Norway, and Denmark', and Godwin, 'Memoirs of the Author of "The Rights of Woman"'*, ed. Richard Holmes (Harmondsworth: Penguin, 1987).
2. (Chicago: University of Chicago Press, 1992).
3. Strictly, the term 'feminism', introduced in English in the late 19th century, is an anachronism. Anachronism is warranted to ensure that the arguments and themes typical of feminism are not lost from view.
4. Moira Ferguson, 'Mary Wollstonecraft and the Problematic of Slavery', in Maria J. Falco (ed.), *Feminist Interpretations of Mary Wollstonecraft* (University Park: Pennsylvania State University Press, 1996), 143.
5. Janet Todd, 'Introduction', *Mary Wollstonecraft: Political Writings* (Toronto: University of Toronto Press, 1993), p. xxvi.
6. *A Vindication of the Rights of Woman with Strictures on Moral and Political Subjects* (1792), in Wollstonecraft, *Political Writings*, ed. Janet Todd (Toronto: University of Toronto Press, 1993).
7. *Letters Written during a Short Residence in Sweden, Norway, and Denmark* (1796), in *Wollstonecraft, 'Letters', and Godwin, 'Memoirs'*.
8. David Held, *Models of Democracy*, 2nd edn. (Cambridge: Polity Press, 1996), 63–9.
9. Sapiro, *A Vindication of Political Virtue*, p. xvii.

10. Richard Holmes, 'Introduction', in *Wollstonecraft, 'Letters', and Godwin, 'Memoirs'*.
11. *The Works of Mary Wollstonecraft*, ed. Janet Todd and Marilyn Butler, 7 vols. (New York: New York University Press, 1989).
12. On other activities, see Olwen Hufton, *Women and the Limits of Citizenship in the French Revolution* (Toronto: University of Toronto Press, 1992).
13. On this category, see William H. Sewell, 'Le Citoyen/la citoyenne: Activity, Passivity, and the Revolutionary Concept of Citizenship', in Colin Lucas (ed.), *The Political Culture of the French Revolution* (Oxford: Pergamon Press, 1988).
14. In the second sentence of *A Vindication of the Rights of Men* Wollstonecraft gives her own brief definitions of the sublime and the beautiful. She states that in morals the essence of the sublime is 'truth', and in taste the criterion of the beautiful is 'simplicity'.
15. *A Vindication of the Rights of Men, in a Letter to the Right Honorable Edmund Burke* (1790), in *Political Writings*.
16. Cf. Edmund Burke, *Reflections on the Revolution in France* (1790; Harmondsworth: Penguin, 1968), 175. See Daniel O'Neill, 'Shifting the Scottish Paradigm: The Discourse of Morals and Manners in Mary Wollstonecraft's *French Revolution*', *History of Political Thought*, xxxiii (2002), 90–116, for a path-breaking discussion of Wollstonecraft's *French Revolution* and her use of the Scottish thinkers.
17. Mary Astell, 'Reflections upon Marriage' (3rd edn. 1706), in Patricia Springborg (ed.), *Political Writings* (Cambridge: Cambridge University Press, 1996), 21.
18. For much of her life Wollstonecraft attended the Church of England, and in the mid-1780s she went to Richard Price's Unitarian chapel, but her religious views owed little to any orthodoxy. They were, Godwin wrote, 'almost entirely of her own creation' (Godwin, *Memoirs*, 215). Wollstonecraft was 'more concerned with deeply held principles and habits of mind than with institutional organization of belief' (Sapiro, *A Vindication of Political Virtue*, 45). Also see Barbara Taylor, 'For the Love of God: Religion and the Erotic Imagination in Wollstonecraft's Feminism', in Eileen Janes Yeo (ed.), *Mary Wollstonecraft and 200 Years of Feminisms* (London: Rivers Oram Press, 1997).
19. On this point, see Sapiro, *A Vindication of Political Virtue*, 63–72. Also G. J. Barker-Benfield, *The Culture of Sensibility: Sex and Society in Eighteenth Century Britain* (Chicago: University of Chicago Press, 1992).
20. *Maria; or, The Wrongs of Woman*, ed. Anne K. Mellor (New York: Norton, 1994).
21. Burke, *Reflections*, 89.
22. See Miriam Brody, 'The Vindication of the Writes of Women: Mary Wollstonecraft and Enlightenment Rhetoric', in Falco (ed.), *Feminist Interpretations of Mary Wollstonecraft*, and Gerald Newman, *The Rise of English Nationalism: A Cultural History 1740–1830* (New York: St Martin's Press, 1997).
23. Sapiro, *A Vindication of Political Virtue*, 194.
24. See Newman, *The Rise of English Nationalism*, and Linda Colley, *Britons: Forging the Nation 1707–1837* (New Haven: Yale University Press, 1992).
25. Conor Cruise O'Brien, 'Introduction', in Edmund Burke, *Reflections on the Revolution in France* (Harmondsworth: Penguin, 1968), 37.
26. Sapiro, *A Vindication of Political Virtue*, 205.
27. Wendy Gunther-Canada, 'Mary Wollstonecraft's 'Wild Wish': Confounding Sex in the Discourse on Political Rights', in Falco (ed.), *Feminist Interpretations of Mary Wollstonecraft*, 137, and Wendy Gunther-Canada, *Rebel Writer: Mary Wollstonecraft and Enlightenment Politics* (DeKalb: Northern Illinois Press, 2001), 90.
28. See Carole Pateman, 'The Rights of Man and Early Feminism', in *The Swiss Year Book of Political Science* (1994), 20–31.
29. The term 'upper servant' to characterize a wife is found in feminist argument from at least the 17th century onward.
30. Burke, *Reflections*, 199.
31. *An Historical and Moral View of Origin and Progress of the French Revolution* (1794), in *Political Writings*.
32. Taylor, 'For the Love of God', 24.
33. In *Three Guineas* (1938; London: Harcourt Brace Jovanovich, 1966), 9, 14, 109, Virginia Woolf asks what patriotism means to a 'step-daughter of England', and declares that 'as a woman, I have no country'.
34. Linda Zerilli, *Signifying Women: Culture and Chaos in Rousseau, Burke, and Mill* (Ithaca, NY: Cornell University Press, 1994), ch. 3.
35. Burke, *Reflections*, 161.
36. Ibid. 165, 169.
37. See Gunther-Canada, *Rebel Writer*, ch. 3.
38. In light of this and other sallies, it is hard to see why David Bromwich ('Wollstonecraft as a Critic of Burke', *Political Theory*, 23 (1995), 618–19)

regards Wollstonecraft as more respectful of Burke than male critics such as Paine and Priestley.

39. On the elaborate military costumes of the day, see Colley, *Britons*, 183–8.
40. In *A Vindication of the Rights of Woman*, 197, with specific reference to Burke, she defines prejudice as 'fond obstinate persuasion for which we can give no reason', and remarks that to continue to cherish prejudice in the face of reason reminds her of 'what is vulgarly termed a woman's reason'.
41. Burke, *Reflections*, 194.
42. Moira Gatens, '"The Oppressed State of my Sex": Wollstonecraft on Reason, Feeling and Equality', in Mary Lyndon Shanley and Carole Pateman (eds.), *Feminist Interpretations and Political Theory* (Cambridge: Polity Press, 1991), 116.
43. Godwin, *Enquiry Concerning Political Justice* (3rd edn. 1798; Harmondsworth: Penguin, 1976), 232.
44. Wollstonecraft was one of the earliest to use the term 'legal prostitution'; it appears in Defoe's *Conjugal Lewdness* (1727). She also argued that men should support the children they fathered out of wedlock.
45. *Thoughts on the Education of Daughters* (1787), reprinted in facsimile by Augustus M. Kelley, Clifton, NJ, 1972.
46. Jemima, in *Maria* (p. 48), disputes the widespread view that all those willing to work can find jobs, especially in the case of women. Hard, menial labour is often all that is open to poor women, and if they have lost their 'reputation' even that can be closed to them.
47. Taylor, 'For the Love of God', 27, and Cora Kaplan, 'Wild Nights: Pleasure/Sexuality/Feminism', in her *Sea Changes* (London: Verso, 1986).
48. Wollstonecraft's friend Mary Hays wrote a novel, *The Victim of Prejudice* (1799) modern edition ed. Eleanor Ty (Peterborough, Ontario: Broadview Press, 1994), about reputation. Her heroine, strongly imbued with virtue, is nonetheless undone by two men of superior station, loses her social position, and declines and dies as a result of her experiences, which include rape and imprisonment for (honourable) debt.
49. See Mary Lyndon Shanley, 'Mary Wollstonecraft on Sensibility, Women's Rights and Patriarchal Power', in Hilda L. Smith (ed.), *Women Writers and the Early Modern British Political Tradition* (Cambridge: Cambridge University Press, 1988).
50. Wet-nursing was the alternative and was widely practised—and killed many infants. Breastfeeding, as medical evidence confirms today, is basic to survival in conditions like those of two centuries ago.
51. Gatens, 'The Oppressed State of my Sex', 121.
52. Brody, 'The Vindication of the Writes of Women', 52–3.
53. Joan B. Landes, *Women and the Public Sphere in the Age of the French Revolution* (Ithaca, NY: Cornell University Press, 1988), 129.
54. Feminists continued to argue that household tasks had political significance and were a contribution to citizenship, and to argue that women's contribution as mothers entitled them to citizenship, for another 150 years. Their voices went largely unheard, defeated by the familiar construction of 'citizenship' in contrast to, and excluding, the work of the household.
55. John Stuart Mill, *The Subjection of Women* (1869), in Alice Rossi (ed.), *Essays on Sex Equality* (Chicago: University of Chicago Press, 1970), 128.
56. Carole Pateman, *The Sexual Contract* (Cambridge: Polity Press; Stanford, Calif.: Stanford University Press, 1988).
57. See Laura Brace, '"Not Empire, but Equality": Mary Wollstonecraft, the Marriage State, and the Sexual Contract', *Journal of Political Philosophy*, 8/4 (2000), 433–55.
58. Legal sanction for husbands to treat their wives' bodies as their property was finally removed when rape within marriage became a criminal offence.
59. Nor did all early feminists share in the views seen as typical of 'the Enlightenment project'. Mary Astell, for example, was an opponent of claims about natural freedom, and an absolutist, but still a brilliant critic of the philosophers and activists who adhered to the doctrine of natural rights yet denied that women were born free.
60. e.g. Hilary Charlesworth, 'What are "Women's International Human Rights"?', in R. J. Cook (ed.), *Human Rights of Women* (Philadelphia: University of Pennsylvania Press, 1994).
61. See also on 'Wollstonecraft's dilemma', Carole Pateman, 'The Patriarchal Welfare State', in *The Disorder of Women: Democracy, Feminism and Political Theory* (Cambridge: Polity Press; Stanford, Calif.: Stanford University Press, 1989).
62. I owe thanks to Dan O' Neill for advice and for sharing his insights into Wollstonecraft and Burke, to David Boucher for comments, and to Rich Moushegian for assistance.

# 17 Tocqueville

Cheryl Welch

## Contents



## Chapter guide

Tocqueville is relevant today less as a forerunner of systematic political sociology or as an example of nineteenth-century narrative history than as an idiosyncratic historian of *mentalités* with particular concerns that have paralleled those of many late twentieth-century thinkers. Those concerns—how to sustain the civic practices underpinning liberal democracy, how to create such practices in the face of hostile histories, and, finally, how to think about democracy's need for stabilizing beliefs—structure the chapter. The first issue is discussed largely through a characterization of the methods of explanation and some of the principal arguments of Tocqueville's *Democracy in America*. This second is treated through an analysis of *The Old Regime and the Revolution*. The third considers the moral substratum of Tocqueville's thought, in particular his arguments about religion and family.

## Biography

Alexis de Tocqueville was born in 1805 into a family of the old Norman nobility. Educated first by a Jansenist *abbé*, he attended *lycée* in Metz, studied law, and attended Guizot's course of historical lectures. As a young man he spent nine months in America, a journey that inspired the two volumes of his *Democracy in America* (1835, 1840). The first gained him widespread fame and election to the Académie français. A prominent man of letters and deputy in the July Monarchy, and an important participant in the Second Republic, he retired from politics after the coup of Louis Bonaparte. *The Old Regime and the Revolution* was published to great acclaim in 1856, three years before his death at the age of 54. Tocqueville's version of political liberalism deeply influenced the opposition during the empire. That influence waned with the founding of the Third Republic, since Tocqueville's work escaped both emerging disciplinary canons and the political creeds of positivism and *étatisme* that characterized that regime. He enjoyed a great revival in the second half of the twentieth century, especially following the decline of Marxism.

## Key texts

*Democracy in America* (*De la démocratie en amérique*) (vol. i 1835; vol. ii 1840)
*The Old Regime and the Revolution* (*L'Ancien régime et la révolution*) (1856)
*Recollections* (*Souvenirs*) (1893)

## Main texts used

*Democracy in America*, ed. Max Lerner and J.-P. Mayer, trans. George Lawrence (New York: Harper & Row, 1966) (*DA*).

*Œuvres, papiers, et correspondances d'Alexis de Tocqueville*, ed. J.-P. Mayer (Paris: Gallimard, 1951) (the complete edition of his works) (*OC*).

*The Old Regime and the French Revolution*, trans. Stuart Gilbert (Garden City, NY: Doubleday, 1955) (*OR*).

*Recollections*, ed. J. P. Mayer and A. P. Kerr, trans. George Lawrence (Garden City, NY: Doubleday, 1971) (*R*).

## Key ideas

**Democracy**: Tocqueville generally used 'democracy' as a social rather than a political term to refer to a society marked by **equality of social condition** (no ascriptive aristocracy, with careers open to all citizens) and by the various passions to which that condition gives rise. **Tyranny of the majority**: a danger peculiar to democracy, in which the psychological dynamics of democratic society cause the emergence of a stultifying sameness in public opinion and an unwillingness of the majority to tolerate difference. **Individualism**: the democratic proclivity to think of oneself in isolation, to believe one controls one's own destiny, and to withdraw from public life. **Aristocracy**: democracy's opposite, a caste society marked by inequality, hierarchy, and functional interdependence of classes. **Revolution**: both the inevitable historical movement from aristocracy to democracy and the violent change of regime by which that movement may be effected. **Liberty**: most broadly, the ability to exercise independent judgement, the intolerance of outside control, and the willingness to take responsibility for the fate of oneself and one's group. In democracy it means a minimum area of individual inviolability and active self-government through civil associations and representative political institutions. **Despotism**: a political condition in which the central government usurps the independent functions of citizens, asserting progressive control over the institutions of political life and civil society.

## The appeal of Tocqueville

Tocqueville's texts still exert a magnetic pull on contemporary readers across the political spectrum and across disciplinary boundaries.[1] He attracts, however, not because he delivers 'a new political science for a world quite new', as he promises in *Democracy in America* (*DA* i. 8[2]), but because he does not do so. Unlike other nineteenth-century social thinkers who strove towards systematic theory or a 'new science', Tocqueville practises an idiosyncratic version of cultural studies that is newly compelling in a world distrustful of world-theoretical dramas. Equally important, Tocqueville's overriding moral preoccupation with the need to preserve both individuality and the capacity for collective political action in a social environment increasingly subject to impersonal 'forces' has appealed powerfully to many constituencies from the mid-twentieth century to the present.

Tocqueville's texts in fact manifest a unique power to bring into sharper focus certain hopes and anxieties associated with modern democracy, hopes and anxieties stemming from efforts to sustain civic cultures that will support the practices of self-government, from attempts to create liberal democracies without violence in unpropitious historical circumstances, and, finally, from questions about the need for shared moral beliefs as the basis for democratic viability. These contemporary concerns are also Tocquevillean ones, and they structure the brief account of Tocqueville's contributions to social and political thought that I offer in this chapter.[3]

## Sustaining civic cultures: American lessons

Alexis de Tocqueville's observations in the United States and his intense intellectual engagement in writing the two volumes of *Democracy in America* in a certain sense created his social and political thought. Yet he discerned what he would call 'the shape of democracy itself' in the new world only because he had to some extent perceived its form in the old (*DA* i. 19). From the beginning, America was a stimulus for meditating on the march of equality and the retreat of liberty in Europe, twin themes that had preoccupied him for several years (*OC* xiii/1, pp. 373–4[4]). Tocqueville in fact assumed that any society in which an ascriptive aristocracy was absent must substitute equality as a regulating ideal and a motivating passion, an intuition amply confirmed by his study of America. The most important lesson, however, was not Americans' equality of social condition, but rather their achievement of a free way of life amid that condition. For the practices of democratic freedom—by which Tocqueville meant both generalized respect for basic civil rights and enough civic independence, energy, and foresight to sustain participatory institutions—were Tocqueville's principal concern. He was to struggle for the rest of his life with the question 'Under what conditions could a society of equals also be a free people?'

The new society that he saw, or thought he saw, in Jacksonian America stimulated him to develop a number of abstractions—his *idées mères*—that would henceforth guide his attempts to answer this question. Such abstractions permitted him, he thought, to explain the causes of social and political beliefs and behaviour in a democratic society and to illuminate the conditions necessary to achieve a free form of democracy. Many commentators have remarked on this use of 'ideal-typical' analysis.[5] *Democracy in America* teems with types: not just 'equality of condition', 'democracy', 'aristocracy', 'despotism', 'individualism', 'centralization', and 'revolution', but also the 'Puritan mind' or the 'Indian mentality'. Tocqueville was quite aware of constructing such notions and of manipulating them for the purposes of his own analysis. He described the practice as seeking the 'shape' or 'image' or 'model' of a phenomenon: 'Beginning from the facts furnished by American and French societies, I wished to paint the general traits of democratic societies of which no complete model yet exists' (*OC* vi/1, p. 330). Ideal-typical analysis, practised with a greater or lesser level of self-awareness, was inseparable from Tocqueville's use of the comparative method. He devised models and 'typical' trains of thought or patterns of behaviour in order to compare and contrast, in order to divine what was significant enough to be noticed, in order to identify the differences to be explained.[6] Many have also noted that Tocqueville's types—especially democracy and aristocracy—sometimes seduced him, that he spun out deductions from his *idées mères* and confused these deductions with the reality he wanted to illuminate.[7] But in moments of clarity he realized that creating a type is not explaining a social phenomenon but merely facilitating such an explanation.

Tocqueville used his 'leading ideas' to build two kinds of explanation in *Democracy in America*. The first, an account of the emergence of democracy in history, plays a limited role. Early chapters sketch the emergence of democracy in America with a few broad strokes that highlight the role of favourable geographical circumstances, political and religious institutions and practices inherited from England, and multiplier effects produced by the impact of separation from England and by changing inheritance laws. The second type of explanation, which lies at the heart of both volumes, attempts to account for the behaviours and beliefs characteristic of democracy when it has established itself as a functioning system. Among the three 'general' causes of the character of a society (circumstances, laws, and *mœurs*, or mores) Tocqueville counts a people's *mœurs* as the most important. Like Montesquieu, who categorized regimes according to their 'spirit', Tocqueville wished to identify the interconnected attitudes and motivations that underlay a regime. As he tells us in the introduction, he sought to capture nothing less than democracy's 'inclinations, character, prejudices, and passions' (*DA* i. 19).

In fashioning an account of the 'inclinations' of democracy, Tocqueville conceptualizes society into roughly delineated spheres: political, civil (including economic), and natural (familial, communal, and to some extent spiritual). The coming of democracy transforms each sphere; it also results in elective affinities and unexpected tensions among them. Jon Elster has provided a particularly useful vocabulary for describing these interconnections. He notes that Tocqueville's insights on how habits and desires are formed and how they relate to one another in a democratic society fall into three patterns: the ubiquity of a belief or activity in one sphere may cause the pattern to recur in another (the 'spillover effect'); the lack of a belief or activity in one sphere may cause a person to seek it in another (the 'compensation effect'); and, finally, the dominance of a belief or activity in one sphere may foreclose similar action in another (the 'crowding out effect').[8] Tocqueville uses these patterns of argumentation in many contexts in an effort to show how the underlying passions and behaviours induced by equality of social condition pull society into a new cultural formation.

This search for the shape of a culture has much in common with the practices of other historians of *mentalités*. Tocqueville was concerned with how people adjust their aspirations to their environment, and how they are in turn shaped by the mental patterns that come to seem natural in that environment. He takes as his special subject neither disembodied ideas nor the socio-economic foundations of societies, but rather a conceptual space somewhere between the two. This rather amorphously defined theoretical world between the history of ideas and social history resembles the territory explored in the *Annales* histories, or the narratives of Philippe Ariès and Michel Foucault. Like these twentieth-century cultural historians, Tocqueville considers collective more than individual attitudes, the thoughts of typical people rather than elites, unspoken general assumptions rather than elaborated philosophical theories, and the general structure of beliefs rather than their specific content.[9] Tocqueville's hypothetically typical Americans—their passions, interests, tastes, and desires—are shaped by the possibilities inherent in a particular mental organization of culture that Tocqueville terms democracy 'itself'.

Perhaps the most striking reason to place Tocqueville in the tradition loosely termed the study of *mentalités* is a certain ironic construction of the course of cultural history. Throughout *Democracy in America* Tocqueville explores the paradox that the democratic patterns of living and thinking that have come to structure American and French societies arise from human innovation, but also significantly constrain the human capacity to innovate in the future. Democracy 'itself' imposes new psychosocial forms of uniformity, and hence an increased threat of despotism. Thus historical change produces paradoxical outcomes and troubling antinomies.[10] Tocqueville in fact abandons the narratives of political or economic progress that to some degree characterize both idealistic and materialistic theories of civilization in the nineteenth century. In this respect, his view of the emergence and prevalence of democracy 'itself' has more in common with Foucault than with Guizot or Marx. Yet Tocqueville, unlike most twentieth-century cultural historians, imbues his work with an obvious normative agenda: a moral and civic regeneration of the French polity that will institutionalize democratic 'freedom', protect civic spaces, and foster practices of self-government in the potentially hostile world of democracy. These purposes quite deliberately influence his choice to present democracy 'itself' as containing two dichotomous patterns: one implicitly favouring despotism, the other favouring liberty.

## Democratic despotism

Tocqueville's fears about democracy stem from one 'simple fact'. At some point in the process of democratization the idea of human equality takes hold of people's souls and the desire for it becomes 'ardent, insatiable, eternal, and invincible' (*DA* ii. 506). Equality of condition generates a love of equality so tenacious, and with such close affinities to other democratic passions such as the love of material comfort, that it may precipitate a new form of despotism. Tocqueville paints several versions of this frightening future. One—stronger in the first *Democracy*—points to the power of new majorities that smother individual independence and may eventually yield to a Caesaristic tyranny; the other—stronger in the second *Democracy*—evokes a flat Orwellian landscape of servile sameness in which an equal but diminished humanity, ruled by a deceptively benevolent central state, pursues material desires in a spiritual vacuum. One might think of *Democracy in America* as a compendious catalogue of the ways in which the individual spirit might be quenched in democracies—by majority opinion, by legislatures, by the executive or a usurper, or by the bureaucratic state itself. What made these despotisms possible were the new links between a society of equals and the forces of political centralization.

Tocqueville's deepest fears centred on the potential affinities among the passion for equality, the pursuit of private interests, and psychological withdrawal from the public sphere. These inclinations, according to his account, emerge under democratic social conditions and feed on one another in ominous ways. In the second *Democracy* he introduces the term *individualisme* to help to explain these potentially devastating effects on civil and political life.[11] According to Tocqueville, individualism is the habit of thinking of oneself in isolation and imagining that one controls one's own destiny (*DA* ii. 508). It is 'a calm and considered feeling which disposes each citizen to isolate himself from the mass of his fellows and withdraw into the circle of family and friends' (*DA* ii. 506; cf. 671). While the passion for equality and the strong democratic *goût de bien-être* foster a commercial way of life that necessarily tends to crowd out public activity, individualism tends to corrode the bonds of trust and civility among citizens that are necessary for collective political action.

Unchecked by other forces, democratic individualism could drive a person to insanity or suicide, because the psychological drive inward reveals no common core of truth at the centre of collective life, and because humans cannot tolerate the resulting psychic vacuum. Tocqueville's argument here presages Durkheim on the effects of anomie in modern society and the links between normlessness and suicide. Yet he does not share Durkheim's belief that a new integrating force will arise out of the social interdependence characteristic of modern industry. The difficulty, according to Tocqueville, is that democratic conditions both unsettle current beliefs and make it particularly difficult for individuals to accept any new ones that originate outside themselves; hence, the mental vacuum is likely to be filled by new sorts of self-referential authorities. Although these authorities—public opinion or the 'will of all'—may stave off individual madness or self-destruction, they do not necessarily foster the sort of independent, yet disciplined, psychological characters who can rule themselves.

Even at the height of his admiration for America's experiment in self-government, Tocqueville thought he glimpsed a tyranny of majority opinion so strong that it crushed all independence of thought. 'I know no country in which, speaking generally, there is less independence of mind and true freedom of discussion than in America' (*DA* i. 254–5). In a society in which there is no higher appeal than majority opinion, there is a strong desire to abdicate responsibility for contributing to that opinion and simply to conform to its dictates. When the majority 'has irrevocably pronounced, everyone is silent, and friends and enemies alike seem to make for its bandwagon' (*DA* i. 254). This psychological tendency to defer to some all-powerful 'will of all' was a fault line of democratic, rather than merely American, culture.

Together, the filling up of social life with the self-interested economic activities of democratic civil society and the emptying out of psychic group life caused by individualism threaten to produce an egalitarian society that celebrates the abstract individual but undermines concrete capacities for independent judgement. Tocqueville argues that the taste for material well-being and the forces of individualism, because of a unique constellation of 'spillover', 'compensatory', and 'crowding-out' effects, make democratic peoples particularly vulnerable to the acceptance of the idea of uniform and ubiquitous state power that will relieve them of all responsibility for their collective fate. The complex interaction between growing equality of social conditions and centralization of state power emerges as Tocqueville's principal theoretical preoccupation and most powerful image, not only in the later sections of *Democracy in America*, but in the rest of his life's work. State power in democratic societies tends to expand its reach from the political to the civil spheres, and becomes at once more concentrated, more extensive, less responsible, and more dangerous to freedom.

## Freedom in democracy

Though the social-psychological tendencies operating in democratic societies may lead to an obliteration of liberty by eliminating both the opportunity and desire for it, Tocqueville also sketches a contrary version of the democratic mentality in which equality generates and sustains freedom. *Democracy in America* is filled with counter-examples of how responsible democratic citizens may avoid, reverse, check, or neutralize the insidious tendencies of democracy. Tocqueville found much to criticize in America: the potential for majority despotism and social conformity, the lack of grandeur, and the glaring injustices of race slavery and the elimination of native peoples.[12] Nevertheless, he admired the Americans for creating political freedom—however compromised and exclusive—under the challenge of democratic social conditions.

From his perceptions of this American experience Tocqueville fashioned two major lessons aimed at his European readers. First, Americans shore up native barriers and build road blocks against the forces of despotism by drawing on inherited English institutions and practices. Second, and more important, they discern stabilizing tendencies within democracy itself, and wisely allow democracy to follow its 'natural' bent in these areas. The first set of arguments employs images of the slowing down or weakening of tendencies otherwise natural to democracy, and includes much of Tocqueville's discussion of the federal constitution and American legal traditions. Of greater theoretical interest, however, is the second set of arguments, in which Tocqueville claims that the very sources of potential democratic disaster—material self-interest and the complex psychological dispositions associated with individualism—may be turned into occasions of democratic salvation.

Tocqueville in fact argues throughout *Democracy in America* that new tendencies, inherent in the democratic social condition itself, reinforce rather than destroy freedom. I will explore his treatment of two of these 'natural' tendencies—the alleged democratic affinities for religious dogma and for 'purity of morals'—in the final section of this chapter. In this section I wish to consider perhaps his most influential argument of this type: the claim that a commercial society of self-interested individuals could become a republic of public-spirited citizens through the workings of interest itself. Although Tocqueville noted the tendency of commercial life to 'crowd out' political activity, he was nevertheless sensitive to certain affinities between the commercial mentality (its energy, foresight, and capacity for delayed gratification) and the virtues needed for political independence. But, he argued, these spillover effects would manifest themselves only if the spirit of self-interest was 'properly understood' and only if this proper understanding was elicited by a certain structuring of civil and political life.

Tocqueville, then, adopts the utilitarian language of interest to describe a crucial self-equilibrating tendency observable in American democracy, labelling it first *égoisme intelligent* and then *intérêt bien entendu*. '. . . the doctrine of self-interest properly understood is not new, but it is among the Americans of our time that it has come to be universally accepted. It has become popular. One finds it at the root of all actions. It is interwoven in all they say' (*DA* ii. 526). In Tocqueville's hands, however, the idea of enlightened self-interest takes on a sociological sophistication and occasionally a detached irony that are quite foreign to its use by other utilitarian heirs of the Enlightenment. Tocqueville's fundamental innovation was to view the practical fusion of public and private interest in America as a complex social and psychological artefact, rather than as the automatic result of individual pleasure-seeking. Unlike the Utilitarians, who seldom interrogated their most basic premiss about the givenness of individual wants, he explores the conditions under which, and the mechanisms by which, individuals come to desire what is in their long-term interest.

Tocqueville claims that associations in America (including permanent local political associations such as townships, cities, and counties; as well as temporary political and civil groups formed freely by citizens) link self-interest, the only reliable individual motive in democratic societies, to the interest of the whole. Because democratic individuals focus almost exclusively on material pleasures, the desire to gain these pleasures and to prosper are natural spurs to purposeful association, which strengthens each individual's position. Associations make transparent to individuals the link between shared purposes and private well-being; once established, such associations allow for the transference of the habits of responsible action back and forth between civil and political spheres. The energy of private associations permeates the public sphere, and lively political activity in turn reinvigorates civil life. The Americans 'carry a trader's habits into the business of politics' (*DA* i. 285; cf. 215). At the same time 'That constantly renewed agitation introduced by democratic government into political life passes . . . into civil society' (*DA* i. 243). Or again 'the Americans almost always carry the habits of public life over into their private lives. With them one finds the ideas of a jury in children's games, and parliamentary formalities even in the organization of a banquet' (*DA* i. 305). Americans' success in establishing these spillovers between civil and political society, in which there is positive reinforcement between the two, is a dominant theme of *Democracy in America*.

Tocqueville's main point here is that, in the absence of a state apparatus to organize activities that require the efforts of more than one person, democratic individuals naturally form purposive associations in order to further their interests. Given a certain level of education, the freedom to form and circulate opinions, and the natural tendency of people in democracies towards independent action, voluntary association with others presents itself as an obvious and efficacious remedy to the limitations of individual action. If these associations are allowed to form freely, the patterns they promote will become instinctual and internalized; they eventually form new *mœurs*. 'At first it is of necessity that men attend to the public interest, afterward by choice. What had been calculation becomes instinct. By dint of working for the good of his fellow citizens, he in the end acquires a habit and taste for serving them' (*DA* ii. 512–13). Far from being the harbingers of social chaos that many Europeans feared, political associations would eventually stabilize democracy and reduce the need for central coordination.

There is a long history in American political science of claiming Tocqueville's discussion of decentralization, associations, and participatory democracy as the forerunner of various empirical and normative 'models' of democracy. After the Second World War, for example, many American thinkers saw in Tocqueville the proximate source of their own interest group pluralism.[13] Today a somewhat different Tocquevillean refrain has emerged in American academic and public discourse about democracy. One hears not a celebration of pluralism, but a plaintive litany of loss: the nation has lost its associational fibre; its citizens compete for the bottom line, 'bowl alone', and shirk public duties.[14] Against this frightening picture of self-absorbed narcissism, some American political scientists and political theorists hold up an idealized portrait of a vibrant civil society, filled with self-reliant individuals who practise the art of voluntary association for both private and public ends. These critics on the left and the right use *Democracy in America* to mourn the disappearance of this web of connection, of the spillover between civil and political association that is assumed to constitute the civic community.[15]

## Tocqueville's return to Europe

Tocqueville's intellectual appropriation of American experience always had more to do with his hopes for Europe than with his desire to convey an accurate picture of the United States. He looked for 'democracy itself' in the New World only because he hypothesized that the same set of dynamic tendencies was transforming the Old. But was that set of tendencies in fact the same? Throughout the two *Democracies* (and increasingly in the second volume) Tocqueville struggles to maintain this heuristic fiction and to ignore the possibility that the revolutionary manner in which democracy had appeared in France might be more influential than the generic concept of democracy 'itself'.

Tocqueville initially avoids the conclusion that the revolution unleashed creative forces of its own by arguing that it merely reinforced democracy's innate tendencies towards despotism. The spirit of revolution, on this account, intensifies the atomistic effects of self-interest and psychological individualism and accelerates the processes by which they influence each other, thus effectively stifling the benign tendencies of democratic culture. At the same time, the effects of revolution also reinforce the power of the state. '. . . among democratic nations the only form of government which comes naturally to mind is a sole and central power. This applies particularly to those democratic nations which have seen the principle of equality triumph with the help of a violent revolution' (*DA* ii. 675). The final part of the 1840 *Democracy*, 'On the Influence of Democratic Ideas and Feelings on Political Society', consists of five short chapters that sum up Tocqueville's thinking about the fatal attractions between revolutionary democracy and centralization. The underlying theme of these chapters is that all participants and all phases of the revolution in France combined, as if in some secret conspiracy, to increase the prerogatives of the state. Power seemed to rush 'spontaneously' to the centre, leaving the already weakened democratic individual defenceless and isolated (*DA* ii. 674).

Tocqueville accounts for the effects of a revolutionary legacy, then, by arguing that revolution weakens democracy's inherent immunities to despotism. The resulting afflictions are 'confusing', 'miserable', 'wretched', and 'abnormal', but will disappear when enlightened citizens learn to profit from the countervailing tendencies of democracy (*DA* i. 236; ii. 578, 606, 625). At times, however, the discrete legacies of revolution seem to merge together and to offer to the reader a powerful new ideal type: *la société révolutionnaire*. The distrust between master and servant, for example, mirrors the 'intestinal war between permanently suspicious rival powers' characteristic of the world of politics (*DA* ii. 578). Manners are unsettled, and notions of honour appeal to no common rule (*DA* ii. 606, 625). Depicted as a 'moment of hesitation' between aristocracy and democracy, revolutionary society nevertheless appears to possess distinct and internally connected mores that sharply define that moment.

As long as he envisioned the legacy of revolution as a painful but temporary period of adjustment, Tocqueville could accommodate it within the structure of his thought by assigning it transitional status. But the disturbing possibility that revolution carried its own pervasive *mentalité*, permanently embedded in French culture, suggested that his method of extracting an ideal democratic type that could serve as the principal tool for insight into both French and American society might have to be reconsidered. In his other classic work *The Old Regime and the Revolution* (1856) Tocqueville in fact shifts his focus to the unique conjoining of centralization, democracy, and revolution in France's past and present.

## Creating freedom in history's shadow: French lessons

In *The Old Regime and the Revolution* not democracy 'itself' but France emerges as Tocqueville's subject. How had France's most important national characteristics—a powerful administrative machine and a revolutionary defiance of its constraints—shaped and been shaped by the forces of democracy to create the distinctive pattern of norms and structures that formed the political culture of contemporary France? Tocqueville's study of the *ancien régime* is not a work of narrative history, but rather a philosophical and sociological essay designed to answer this question, to throw into relief both the *mentalité* of Tocqueville's time and the formation of this *mentalité* in pre-revolutionary France.

Tocqueville's first innovation was the concept of the *ancien régime* itself. Unlike most of his contemporaries, he did not use the term to refer to an undifferentiated pre-revolutionary constitution or to a nostalgically idealized time before the 'troubles'. Rather, he used it to describe a drastic transformation of feudal France that had occurred during the final 150 years of the French monarchy, a transformation in which the prejudices, habits, and passions that dominated his own time were born. A seminal period of deep disturbance and transition, this *ancien régime* was of interest not because it represented a lost past, but because it contained within it all that was most important to his own time. Tocqueville's thesis is deceptively simple: the apparent disruption of the revolutionary period masks a profound continuity in French history; the changes effected during the period of royal absolutism—changes unintended and largely unrecognized at the time—emerge after the revolution as the defining characteristics of France's political culture.

According to Tocqueville, revolutionary destruction of the monarchy revealed the foundations of an even more powerful state structure, a foundation that 'had been laid immutably in the minds of all Frenchmen, even its destroyers during the Old Regime itself' (*OR* 72[16]). Habits and customs that had originally provided the life of the feudal monarchy were in fact defunct long before the revolution. What had displaced them was a new and at first unrecognized set of *mœurs:* egalitarian and highly susceptible to despotism. Like a river, this new French *mentalité*—'the ways men thought and felt, their habits and their prejudices'—went underground in the early years of the revolution, when there was a mania to destroy everything. But the river re-emerged afterwards, 'ready to carry all before it' (*OR* 20). During the *ancien régime*, in Tocqueville's account, France had already become a democratic society fuelled by egalitarian passions, but these passions were still embedded in an anachronistic set of inegalitarian civil and political forms. To paraphrase Marx, it was inevitable that this inegalitarian integument would be burst asunder. The meaning of the revolutionary movement, then, even as it continued into Tocqueville's own time, was to excise from the body politic 'a host of ideas, sentiments, manners, and customs which, so to speak, adhered to [the old feudal institutions]' and were inconsistent with the new democratic spirit (*OR* 20).

In so far as Tocqueville identifies a particular agent of change in France's transformation into a democratic nation, he points to the policies of its Bourbon kings, who pursued a process of relentless centralization and thereby effected a secret metamorphosis in French *mœurs*. By destroying the traditional patterns of social cooperation characteristic of feudal aristocracy, royal ministers undermined the interdependence underlying the social hierarchy even as they left its outward trappings intact. They then temporarily avoided the consequences of this policy by regulating everything themselves, administering alongside, above, and beneath older aristocratic institutions in order to hold together the separate elements of a France that was increasingly fragmented in social condition. Administrative centralization during the *ancien régime*, in this account, lay at the heart of France's modern predicament: as democracy progressed and the French became more equal, they developed habits of servility and dependence on central direction.

Tocqueville had argued in *Democracy in America* that equality and indifference to the public business had a potentially fatal mutual attraction. In the introduction to the *Old Regime* he reiterated this insight: 'people are far too much disposed to think exclusively of their own interests, to become self-seekers practicing a narrow individualism and caring nothing for the public good' (*OR*, p. xiii). The policies of generations of kings, as well as fateful abdications of responsibility by nobles and bourgeois, made this connection between equality and quietism a reality in France, for monarchs and their ministers actively deprived the people of the only possible antidote to democratic individualism: self-government.

Tocqueville's portrait of civil society under the French *ancien régime*—a complicated society that was ultimately unstable because 'ill-adjusted'—is less a faithful historical reproduction than a theoretical ideal-type that forms an arresting counter-image to his portrayal of associational life in America. He reconstructs an *ancien régime* in which exemption from public responsibilities and the inclination to exclude others from one's group in order to demonstrate social worth govern social relations. Nobles, bourgeois, and peasants alike associate civil status with freedom from public demands. Paying taxes, for example, is anathema (*OR* 86). Tocqueville quotes from a letter from a noble petitioner who objects to paying a special direct tax imposed by Louis XV: 'Surely your natural good feeling will prevent you from taxing for the full vingtième a man of my position with a family to support, as you would tax a member of the lower class in such a case' (*OR* 71). Here the avoidance of public duty is fuelled less by self-interest than by a perverted sense of honour. Similarly, the tendency on the part of the bourgeoisie to form exclusive groups, to police social boundaries no matter how irrational, stems from the pursuit of interest, but even more from the desire for social recognition. Thus groups narrowly mind their 'own' business, but not the public's business. Indeed, there is a host of associations in Tocqueville's *ancien régime* but no political culture or institutional structure that facilitates a spillover of associational attachments into more extensive public sentiments. Tocqueville calls this situation 'group individualism', a phenomenon less analogous to the vibrant associational civil society that he discerned in Jacksonian America than to the incipient democratic individualism that he deplored there. In an exact inversion of Tocqueville's ideal-typical America, the French of this *ancien régime* fuse self-interest with harm to the public; they practise 'self-interest ill understood'.

*Ancien régime* society, according to Tocqueville, was held together by a shared set of dysfunctional norms that could not produce stability in the long run because they were premissed on a denial of the new realities of equality, for beneath the barriers of caste and the petty distinctions erected by middle-class groups to distinguish themselves, a new and similar type of individual was emerging. Living in the same places, educated in the same institutions, consuming the same goods, these new Frenchmen in fact thought and acted alike. 'Each set store on his status as member of a particular group because he saw others asserting their personalities in this way; yet all were quite ready to sink their differences and to be integrated into a homogeneous whole, provided no one was given a privileged position and rose above the common level' (*OR* 96). Only when the whole tissue of these rights and privileges was torn away would the sameness of social conditions be revealed, and the characteristic psychological profile of the new French citizen—unfortunately deformed by his singular historical encounter with absolutism—become obvious. Tocqueville believed such a man to be a 'familiar type . . . we have all met him!' (*OR* 92).

*The Old Regime and the Revolution* concludes with the following judgement: 'To those who study it as an isolated phenomenon the French Revolution can but seem a dark and sinister enigma; only when we view it in the light of the events preceding it can we grasp its true significance' (*OR* 210). He might well have amended his judgement to read 'in the light of the events preceding and following it', since for Tocqueville the importance of a historical narrative is measured by its ability to illuminate contemporary problems (in this case to explain the tendency of the French of his own day to acquiesce so readily in the Second Empire's destruction of their freedoms). That his account of the *ancien régime* remains compelling to other readers with different problems calls for some explanation. What is it about Tocqueville's classic interpretation of the causes of the French Revolution that continues to be significant in our time?

Part of the answer must be that Tocqueville gives a complex social and psychological account of the origins of a revolution that one can yet imagine to have turned out differently. His essay lacks any sense of moral progress or necessarily rational 'unfolding', nor does it feature any clear victors. Rather Tocqueville seems to identify with those who inherit history's 'ruins', and who strive to create new societies out of these unpromising circumstances. Thus he immediately establishes a connection with future readers struggling to weigh their own histories. Moreover, though Tocqueville offers a persuasive explanation of why things have come to be as they are, he nevertheless recognizes plural possibilities in the past. Thus he creates in his readers a sensitivity to the ways in which discrete events and choices eventually coalesce either to open up or to foreclose patterns of human action.[17] Consider, for example, his explanation of the 'inevitable' decline of the French nobility, a human drama in which a class inadvertently colludes in its own extinction. In this account, he enters deeply into the psychology of the nobility to speculate on a number of mechanisms that combined to distance the nobility from the middle classes, even though they had become 'equal' in some objective sense: the narcissism of small differences, the lack of a need to feign equal concern and respect in public settings (and thus the loss of the opportunity for psychological pretence to foster the real thing), and the phenomenon of sour grapes. By attending to the interactions between circumstances and human action at a concrete and psychological level, Tocqueville's account illuminates the changes in the class consciousness of the nobility, and enlarges our understanding of how similar changes in *mentalité* can happen in our own time.

Perhaps the best example of Tocqueville's illumination of the causes and effects of changes in collective *mentalités* is his account of the transformation of the French peasantry into a class simmering 'in a state of isolation and abjection' (*OR* 134), higher in social condition than peasants in other parts of Europe, but ignorant, exploited, and cruelly marginalized. He simultaneously pursues two explanatory strategies here. First, he uses empirical evidence to emphasize the rapidity of feudal decline and the devolution of land ownership in France in comparison to England and Germany. In support of his claim that the multiplication of peasant proprietors was accompanied by an unparalleled deterioration of social relations in the countryside, he quotes letters of intendants and discusses the cultural meaning of widespread peasant tax evasion and avoidance of conscription. In these initial efforts to establish a pattern of differences, Tocqueville uses statistical evidence, official documents, and memoirs of contemporaries. Such evidence, however, takes on meaning only when shaped into a plausible narrative. For this shaping he must imagine the motivations of the dramatis personae and their reactions to new circumstances.

Tocqueville's second strategy of explanation, then, is to ask the reader to 'picture to yourself the French peasant as he was in the eighteenth century. . . . [See] how he appears in the records from which I have been quoting.' Evoking the feelings and intentions of such a typical small proprietor, Tocqueville first surmises that the peasant's passionate devotion to the soil would have given birth to a sense of pride and independence. He then asks us to share this peasant's feelings towards faceless absentee neighbours who trample his seedlings in the hunt, who exact tolls at the river, who force him to use their mills and ovens, and who drag him away from his land to 'work elsewhere without payment'. He also re-creates this hypothetical peasant's attitude towards the official 'men in black' who come to take the rest of his harvest (*OR* 31). In this way Tocqueville historically contextualizes the allegedly instinctive secretiveness and guile of French peasants, who would naturally try to hide any wealth or good fortune to avoid being despoiled by powerful neighbours from whom they had no protection. Tocqueville further postulates that underneath the common peasant's stoicism in the face of adversity grew a hunger for social recognition based on incipient economic independence. The continued denial of such recognition would ultimately affect the peasant's disposition to rebel. Born of the discrepancy between the hopes and passions engendered by (limited) land ownership and the frustrations of having those hopes and passions blocked at every turn, the peasant's resentments constituted a revolutionary time bomb that would eventually contribute to the peculiar ferocity of the French Revolution (*OR* 134).

Tocqueville's efforts to re-create the sense of grievance and yearning experienced in the past induces a sensitivity to the possibilities of empathetic identification in the present, and an awareness of the preconditions of any collective action. Unlike accounts of the past that bring closure and a sense that an idea or purpose will be realized in the fullness of time, Tocqueville's historical writing evokes a sense of the potential for disruption and the unintended consequences that lie just beneath the surface of everyday life. Neither drowning in facts nor losing himself in abstractions, Tocqueville wished to work in 'that half-light that allows one to glimpse the country and ask the inhabitants to point out one's road'.[18] His success in achieving this controlled illumination, in creating an explanation without robbing the past of its individuality or the present of its possibilities, is what gives *The Old Regime and the Revolution* its 'classic' quality. Even in assigning a retrospective meaning to events, thus terming them 'general' or 'fated' or 'overdetermined', Tocqueville engages the reader on a ground of contingency, plurality, and choice. In unravelling a pattern of multiple causation, Tocqueville always provokes the question 'What if?' and implicitly invites his reader to answer it. It is not surprising that contemporary French intellectuals emerging from the hegemony of Hegel have discovered new affinities with Tocqueville.

It is perhaps this liberation from historical determinism, this restoration of a sense of contingency and agency in history, that has made Tocqueville so popular in a post-Marxist Europe. When the French, for example, began to confront the depressing political legacies of communism in Europe, Tocqueville's focus on a political culture alternately buffeted by revolution and authoritarianism seemed newly compelling. François Furet launched his new historiography of the French Revolution partly through an encounter with Tocqueville. Nineteenth-century French historians, and especially Tocqueville, have regained a certain relevance in an era when the agenda is not to use France to exemplify a universal history, either of bourgeois hegemony or of republican triumph, but rather to use France's 'singular' history to illuminate its current democratic malaise.[19] Similarly Tocqueville has found new readers in eastern Europe, readers who use Tocqueville to assess the possibilities of liberal recovery from the twentieth century's virulent strains of revolutionary despotism. *The Old Regime and the Revolution* is, after all, a classic study of how one political culture dies and another is born. The central preoccupation of Tocqueville's works—the difficulty of infusing liberal tolerance, restraint, and respect for rights into a majoritarian democratic political culture alternately seduced by revolutionary action and authoritarian order—has thus come to be newly persuasive at the end of the twentieth century in a Europe confronting its own patterns of ingrained illiberalism.

## Democracy's need for stabilizing beliefs

*The Old Regime and the Revolution* brings us only to the brink of revolution; Tocqueville never steps over into the abyss. Indeed, the legacy of the French Revolution, and in particular its peculiar *mentalité*, proved particularly intractable. He could not seem to achieve the kind of controlled empathy with revolutionary hopes and fears that made his re-creation of the peasant mentality so persuasive. Blocked by his own dread, Tocqueville portrayed revolutionaries as victims of a recurring disordered fever in which individuals become detached from their very humanity through an excess of hope and desire. In the introduction to the first *Democracy* Tocqueville offers this characterization of the strange confusion of French democratic practice, infected by the revolutionary 'virus':

> it would seem that we have nowadays broken the natural link between opinions and tastes, acts and beliefs; that harmony which has been observed throughout history between the feelings and the ideas of men seems to have been destroyed, and one might suppose that all the laws of moral analogy had been abolished. (*DA* i. 16)

Tocqueville sometimes feared that French democracy—unlike his exemplary American construct—had irreparably damaged its own capacity to recover a social equilibrium that incorporated freedom. The recurring revolutionary mentality had in fact produced grave disturbances in people's natural tendencies to believe in God, to limit themselves through notions of established right, and to form stable families. These diminished capacities, this complete upset in 'mental equilibrium' (*OR* 156), endangered not only liberty but, in Tocqueville's more pessimistic moments, the concept of social life itself. The revolutionary spirit both overstimulated democratic desires and prevented them from being channeled' (*OR* 161).

In *Democracy in America* Tocqueville had depicted American religious and family *mœurs*—like the theory and practice of interest properly understood—as powerful means by which Americans harnessed the 'natural' tendencies of democracy to produce a form of society at once free and disciplined. As in the case of *intérêt bien entendu* he deliberately chose to portray religion and strictly ordered family life in the United States as generically democratic, rather than peculiarly American. The disciplines of religion and family both empowered individuals to act and held them back from excesses. Unlike the 'madness' of a *société révolutionnaire* in which people 'neither know what to hold on to, nor where to stop' (*OR* 157), American democracy had managed to anchor itself in unquestioned beliefs that countered democracy's natural instabilities and created individuals capable of responsible political judgement.

Tocqueville's instinctive recoil from revolution helps to reveal the moral sentiments that inform his thinking here. Revolutionary experimentation with religion and gender relations was 'unnatural' and profoundly disturbing, he thought, because such experimentation undermined an individual's capacity to limit his or her own wants. Like Burke, Tocqueville believed that the revolution, with its attacks on religion, property, and family, had not only undermined social order, but had also shaken the moral foundations of civilization. The revolutionary spirit—the belief, according to Tocqueville, that literally anything can be willed to be other than it is—destabilizes the core of unquestioned beliefs necessary for a people to act collectively in a responsible way. He never explored the philosophical or religious foundations of these moral certainties—his 'secrets of the heart'—but he did feel himself under a spiritual compulsion to argue that the democratic social condition that represented Europe's future was not doomed to fall victim to these aberrations. In direct contrast to conservatives like Burke, he argued that democracies based on equality of social condition would be 'naturally' religious and would gravitate towards purity of morals.

## Religion

Tocqueville offered several arguments on behalf of the natural connection between religion and democratic stability, including the many spillover effects between the behaviours and psychology of American forms of Protestant Christianity and the responsible practices of political democracy.[20] Yet he was eventually drawn to emphasize a different and less obvious affinity between Christianity and democracy. On this view, religion attracts and holds democratic individuals not because it is familiar or congruent with existing patterns of social and economic life, but because it is strange and offers an arena for the satisfaction of psychological and spiritual yearnings that otherwise go unmet or find dangerous outlets. This second view—an argument for the naturally reparative function of religion—in fact favours Catholic rather than Protestant forms of Christianity. Protestantism, Tocqueville argues, does not adequately police the vulnerable borders of faith, thus encouraging unruly independent thought that is difficult to arrest before it dissolves in unbelief or pantheism.[21] Catholicism, on the other hand, serves to sustain democratic liberty because it provides a minimum of authoritative dogma that tethers the imagination and allows democratic individuals to exercise free will safely. Only a very few can 'let their minds float at random between obedience and freedom' (*DA* ii. 451). Hence Tocqueville reaches the rather strange conclusion that Americans will progressively return to Rome, which can better deliver that minimum of unquestioned authority that would provide individuals with the necessary psychological ballast to survive the instability of democratic life (*DA* ii. 450–1).

## Purity of morals

Tocqueville's deeply gendered conception of society and politics and his portrait of women in democracy also reveal his deep fears—and those of his generation—about the insanity of a society in which literally everything may be questioned. He uncompromisingly relegates women in democracy to the realm of domesticity, using a singular chain of argumentation that has the unmistakable ring of a *parti pris*.[22] As in the case of religion, particular fears cloud his arguments about women's natural place in a well-ordered democracy. The perceived nearness of a terrifying unnatural alternative—a revolutionary society in which people perceive no limits at all and women enter the public sphere as fiendish furies—strengthens his determination to work out the 'natural' democratic logic of women's separate but equal social roles. He constructs a very particular and heroic trajectory for the democratic woman's life, in a narrative that owes much less to American mores than to a particular cultural disquiet about the effects of women's participation in the public sphere.

Tocqueville's argument that democracy itself favours the cloistering of women from civil and political life proceeds in two stages. First, he shows how the coming of democracy has broken down the formal structure of the aristocratic family and hence has transformed the context in which the relationships of kinship develop. Next he demonstrates the allegedly stabilizing mechanisms that unfold along with those new relationships, the most important of which is an unexpected affinity between democracy and a consensus on 'purity of morals', a phrase that connotes complete sexual fidelity and seclusion for married women and men's avoidance of extramarital affairs with 'respectable' women.

Like his analysis of the complex affinities between Christianity and democratic stability, Tocqueville's arguments for the link between 'purity of morals' and the stabilization of a restless and potentially anarchic democratic society pursue several trains of thought at once. In democratic America, he argues, concern with the welfare of a wife and family provides a fixed goal, which fosters the acquisitive instincts but also moderates them, thus transforming potentially destructive self-interest into controlled prudence. At the same time absorption in commercial life 'crowds out' the practice of adultery and thus indirectly stabilizes political life, which is preserved from corruption and intrigue (*DA* ii. 598). When democracy comes in a revolutionary form, policing women's morality and confining them to domestic roles apparently becomes even more urgent. In such a society men are touchy and mistrustful; bitter memories, unsettled customs, and internalized instincts of disorder add to the normal causes of division. If such men also lead licentious private lives—in Tocqueville's view the inevitable result of women moving freely in the civil and political spheres—they 'come to feel scorn for natural ties and legitimate pleasures and develop a taste for disorder, restlessness of spirit, and instability of desire'. Spilling over into political society as a whole, these tastes inhibit civil and political discipline (*DA* i. 291). Finally, the seclusion of women within marriage and family life allows them to buffer the psychological shocks and reverses associated with industrial life caused by what Tocqueville calls 'the natural instability of [democratic] desires', that is, the lure of easy fortune and the chronic disposition to gamble for high economic stakes (*DA* ii. 548). 'American women', Tocqueville asserts, 'face [the gain and loss of private fortunes] with quiet, indomitable energy. Their desires seem to contract with their fortune as easily as they expand' (*DA* ii. 594).

As in the case of religion, Tocqueville argues less that a puritanical moral code is 'true' than that it is necessary to prevent the subversion of civilized life in democracies. He in fact assigns to women a complex empowering and steadying function within the psyches of democratic men that parallels the function of restraining religious beliefs. Like the dogmas of Christianity, women's adoption of a strict moral code and their retreat to the household both push forward and hold back.[23] His narrative of how and why these patterns will emerge, however, reveals more about his own moral anxieties than about democracy's natural and inevitable inclinations. Unlike his accounts of peasant psychology, or even of the attitudes of native Americans and Africans, Tocqueville's discussion of gender relations is remarkable for its failure to enter into the woman's point of view, with one important exception. He hypothesizes that women themselves voluntarily renounce the freedom of democratic girlhood at the time of marriage, and thus deliberately sacrifice the satisfaction of their own democratic passions for equality and independence by retiring from public and civic life. In a supreme moment of identification, Tocqueville portrays these decisions as heroic and 'manly' sacrifices, rather than as the result of democratic public opinion or law (*DA* ii. 601).

Tocqueville's implausible projection onto women of the self-sacrificing courage that will save democracy reveals the hidden moral anxieties that draw his arguments about gender relations and religion into the realm of rhetorical apologetic. It is not that Tocqueville does not have many complex trains of thought involving religion, family, and their roles in stabilizing democracy. But when his intellect and bent for comparison would nudge him in the direction of awkward questions—might religious doubt be a natural result of civilization? might democracy inevitably mean freedom in the public sphere for women?—he smothers these questions in an urgent train of counter-argument driven by his conviction that there are sacred moral limits beyond which no human can safely pass. Atheists, socialists, and 'scribbling women' bring too close the terrifying possibility of bursting the remaining threads that allow democratic individuals to live dignified and independent lives, threads that can be attached only to unquestioned pieties.

Tocqueville's hopes for an emerging self-discipline in democratic societies associated with 'natural' religious belief and strict assignment of gender roles continue to resonate with contemporary social conservatives. Yet the appeal of this discussion, so rooted in the particular anxieties of the early nineteenth century, when fears about social order transformed European political culture, reaches beyond those who have sympathy with its implicit disciplinary projects. Indeed because Tocqueville assumes that there is no transcendent truth that will emerge in history to guide choices in democracy, but that equal individuals cannot live together without some such consensus on truth, he poses in a particularly acute way the question of whether modern democracy can survive the erosion of old solidarities. Must democratic societies create functional substitutes for religion and traditional social ties in order to resist the atomizing effects of markets, privatization, and *individualisme*? Or can they survive fundamental contestation and permanent uncertainty about the bases of democratic legitimacy?[24]

Intellectuals at the turn of the new century continue to engage in intense scrutiny of 'post-industrial' and 'postmodern' societies, but they rarely focus on 'post-democratic' ones. Indeed democracy remains, as Sartre once said of Marxism, the 'unsurpassable horizon' of our time.[25] Tocqueville's particular preoccupations—with the texture of democratic civil society, with the historical links between equality and authoritarianism, and with democracy's need for moral ballast—have certainly not been surpassed, but rather have continued to generate spirited theoretical debate. The seemingly perennial temptation to turn to Tocqueville, however, stems not only from his subject matter, but also from the depth of his insight into the murky political psychology and the moral paradoxes of modern democracy.

## FURTHER READING

Eisenstadt, Abraham (ed), *Reconsidering Tocqueville's 'Democracy in America'* (New Brunswick, NJ: Rutgers University Press, 1988).

Lively, Jack, *The Social and Political Thought of Alexis de Tocqueville* (Oxford: Clarendon Press, 1965).

Manent, Pierre, *Tocqueville and the Nature of Democracy*, trans. John Waggoner (Lanham, Md.: Rowman & Littlefield, 1996).

Mélonio, Françoise, *Tocqueville and the French*, trans. Beth G. Raps (Charlottesville: University Press of Virginia, 1998).

Schleifer, James T., *The Making of Tocqueville's Democracy in America* (Chapel Hill: University of North Carolina Press, 1980).

## NOTES

1. For example, in January 2000 the *Journal of Democracy* chose to devote its special tenth anniversary issue, 'Democracy in the World', to commissioned articles discussing Tocqueville's *Democracy in America*. Authors as varied as Francis Fukuyama, William Galston, Philippe Schmitter, Nathan Glazer, Adam Michnik, Zbigniew Brzezinski, Terry Karl, Jean Elshtain, and Paul Cantor use Tocqueville to discuss the end of history, civil society, European federalism, race and ethnicity, the collapse of communism, war and foreign policy, international inequality, women and the family, and the democratic aesthetics of postmodernism. As the editors comment, 'as we enter the millennium one may say with little exaggeration: *We are all Tocquevilleans now*' (*Journal of Democracy*, 11/1 (2000), 9.
2. Tocqueville, Democracy in America (vol. i 1835; vol. ii 1840), ed. Max Lerner and J.-P. Mayer, trans. George Lawrence (New York: Harper & Row, 1966) (hereafter *DA*).
3. The ideas presented here appear in longer form in Cheryl Welch, *De Tocqueville* (Oxford: Oxford University Press, 2001).
4. Tocqueville *Œuvres, papiers, et correspondances d'Alexis de Tocqueville*, ed. J.-P. Mayer (Paris: Gallimard, 1951) (*OC*); references are to volume, part (where applicable), and page numbers.
5. See e.g. Raymond Aron, *Main Currents in Sociology*, trans. R. Howard and H. Weaver, vol. i (New York: Doubleday, 1968), 279; Gianfranco Poggi, *Images of Society: Essays on the Sociological Theories of Tocqueville, Marx, and Durkheim* (Stanford, Calif.: Stanford University Press, 1972), 4; Pierre Birnbaum, *Sociologie de Tocqueville* (Paris: Presses Universitaires de France, 1970), 29–39; Robert Nisbet, 'Tocqueville's Ideal Types', in Abraham Eisenstadt (ed.), *Reconsidering Tocqueville's 'Democracy in America'* (Brunswick, NJ: Rutgers University Press, 1988), 186–91, James T. Schleifer, *The Making of Tocqueville's Democracy in America* (Chapel Hill: University of North Carolina Press, 1980), 271–2; Larry Siedentop,

*Tocqueville* (Oxford: Oxford University Press, 1994), 142–3.

6. On Tocqueville's use of the comparative method, see Melvin Richter, 'Comparative Political Analysis in Montesquieu and Tocqueville', *Comparative Politics*, 1/2 (1969), 129–60.
7. Birnbaum, *Sociologie de Tocqueville*, 38–9.
8. Jon Elster, *Political Psychology* (Cambridge: Cambridge University Press, 1993), 180–91.
9. See the useful characterization of the distinctive features of the history of mentalities in Peter Burke, 'Strengths and Weaknesses of the History of Mentalities', in his *Varieties of Cultural History* (Ithaca, NY: Cornell University Press, 1997), 162. See also Roger Chartier, 'Intellectual History and the History of *Mentalités*', in his *Cultural History*, trans. Lydia B. Cochrane (Ithaca, NY: Cornell University Press, 1988).
10. For a discussion of this ironical construction as the common ground linking diverse theorists of *mentalités*, see Patrick H. Hutton, 'The History of Mentalities: The New Map of Cultural History', *History and Theory*, 20/3 (1981), 237–59.
11. The 'individualism' of the second Democracy is an evolution of the notion of 'democratic egoism' in the first. On the relationship between these two concepts, see Schleifer, *The Making of Tocqueville's Democracy in America*, 232–59.
12. Ch. 10 of the 1835 Democracy in America, entitled 'The Future of the Three Races in America', is functionally a long appendix, rather than an integral part of the whole. Tocqueville believed that issues concerning the relations between indigenous peoples, Africans, and the dominant Anglo-Americans would be crucial for Americans and the future of their democracy. Nevertheless, these issues were theoretically peripheral to his main concern, which was to separate that which was generically democratic from that which was merely American.
13. For example, see Louis Hartz, *The Liberal Tradition in America* (New York: Harcourt Brace, 1955), David Truman, *The Governmental Process* (New York: Knopf, 1951), Robert Dahl, *A Preface to Democratic Theory* (Chicago: University of Chicago Press, 1956) and id., *Who Governs*? (New Haven: Yale University Press, 1961).
14. See e.g. Robert Putnam, 'Bowling Alone: America's Declining Social Capital', *Journal of Democracy*, 6/1 (Jan. 1995), 65–78.
15. Tocqueville's famous phrase 'habits of the heart' serves as the title of Robert Bellah's nostalgic lament for the loss of 'Tocqueville's America'. See Robert N. Bellah, Richard Madsen, William M. Sullivan, Ann Swidler, and Steven M. Tipton, *Individualism and Commitment in American Life: Readings on the Themes of Habits of the Heart* (New York: Harper & Row, 1987). For more recent works on the theme of the decline of America's moral and social capital, see E. J. Dionne Jr. (ed.), *Community Works: The Revival of Civil Society in America* (Washington: Brookings Institution, 1998), Robert K. Fullinwider (ed.), *Civil Society, Democracy, and Civic Renewal* (Lanham, Md.: Rowman & Littlefield, 1999), and William Galston, 'Civil Society and the "Art of Association"', *Journal of Democracy*, 11/1 (2000), 64–70.
16. Tocqueville, *The Old Regime and the French Revolution*, trans. Stuart Gilbert (Garden City, NY: Doubleday, 1995) (hereafter *OR*).
17. Tocqueville's opposition to determinism and devotion to the importance of human choice can perhaps best be followed in his correspondence with Arthur de Gobineau. See esp. *OC* ix. 199–201.
18. Unpublished letter from *Tocqueville* to Freslon, 20 Sept. 1856, quoted in Jardin, Tocqueville, 514.
19. Françoise Mélonio, *Tocqueville et les français* (Paris: Gallimard, 1993), 7.
20. See the longer discussion in Welch, *De Tocqueville*, 95–101.
21. On this point, see Joshua Mitchell, *The Fragility of Freedom: Tocqueville on Religion, Democracy, and the American Future* (Chicago: University of Chicago Press, 1995), 194, 217.
22. Haydon White has characterized Tocqueville's style as marked by a particular turbulence that has its source in two emotions: 'an overriding capacity for sympathy for men different from himself, and a fear of the destruction of those things he valued most in both the past and the present' (*Metahistory: The Historical Imagination in Nineteenth-Century Europe* (Baltimore: Johns Hopkins University Press, 1973), 192). In the case of women in democracy, that fear almost completely inhibits his capacity for sympathetic identification and thus limits the range of his political psychologizing.
23. Tocqueville often uses the same imagery of 'loosening and tightening' in his discussions of those forces that tend 'naturally' to stabilize democracy. See e.g. *DA* ii. 58 and i. 294.
24. For a brief discussion of these 'turns' to Tocqueville in France and the United States, see Welch, *De Tocqueville*, 243–54.
25. Quoted in Mark Lilla, 'The Legitimacy of the Liberal Age', in Lilla (ed.), *New French Thought: Political Philosophy* (Princeton: Princeton University Press, 1994), 5.

# 18 Bentham

Paul Kelly

**Contents**



## Chapter guide

Reviled by those on the left as merely the political theorist of bourgeois political economy and by those on the right as the Enlightenment rationalist determined to undermine all received institutions, values, and practices, Bentham continues to evoke strong feelings. Marx saw Bentham and Benthamism as symptomatic of the modern capitalist state. More recently the conservative philosopher Michael Oakeshott has used Bentham as the epitome of the rationalist—the victim of the unbounded hubris of human reason let loose on time-honoured institutions. Among liberals Bentham's legacy is also deeply contested. The high tide of nineteenth-century laissez-faire liberalism is credited by A. V. Dicey as an age of Benthamism. Yet another important chronicler of nineteenth-century liberalism, Elie Halévy, presents a picture of Bentham as an authoritarian liberal who took traditional liberal ideas and transformed them into the tools of the modern interventionist state. In our own day post-Rawlsian liberals see Bentham's utilitarianism as a further obstacle to an enlightened and liberal political regime. Bentham is both an apostle of laissez-faire and an interventionist, a liberal rationalist and an at best equivocally liberal thinker prepared to sacrifice the rights of individuals to the well-being of the multitude. Bentham's legacy casts a long shadow over subsequent centuries, in his influence both on British politics and on the development of a British variant of political liberalism. His ideas remain contested from all quarters, yet the outline of his actual political thought remains obscure, not least because of the vast body of unpublished work he left behind. In this chapter I steer a path through these debates and defend an interpretation of Bentham as an important liberal thinker with a commitment to the role of government in defending personal security and well-being, but also with a strong scepticism about government as a vehicle for harm as well as good. The chapter begins with a discussion of Bentham's psychological theory and continues with his account of value and duty. These two sections show that Bentham did not attempt to draw a simple connection between these two pillars of his thought. The third section turns to his other great concern namely jurisprudence and the analysis of law. The fourth section shows how Bentham's concern with legal reform turned him towards democracy. The final section explores his complex relationship with subsequent liberal political theory.

## Biography

Notorious for his precocity, Jeremy Bentham was the eldest son of an ambitious father who was determined that his son would make his fortune and his mark on the world as Lord Chancellor of England. In this respect young Jeremy was clearly a disappointment. Yet he made a considerable mark on the world as the reclusive 'hermit of Queen's Square Place', from where he became the adviser and correspondent of an 'international who's who' of the Enlightenment. Jeremy Bentham was born on 15 February 1748. His education steered him towards his father's ambition. He entered Westminster School at 7 and Queen's College, Oxford, at 12. At 15 he was admitted to Lincoln's Inn to read for the Bar (a career as an advocate). Like Burke and Marx, Bentham chose against the practice of the law. During his time reading for the Bar, he began to read all the main thinkers of the European Enlightenment. This brought about a change in direction as he chose not to practice law but to become its reformer. Bentham saw himself as a contributor to the task of enlightenment, 'rearing the fabric of felicity by the hands of reason and law'. The first stage of this task was a critique of Sir William Blackstone's magisterial *Commentaries on the Laws of England*. Blackstone's was the definitive statement of the theory and practice of the English common law, precisely the system that Bentham saw as the obstacle to a reasonable, humane, and liberal political order. His critique of Blackstone was to remain a lifelong project; all his major reform projects were rooted in some aspect of Blackstone's legacy. Bentham's lasting influence was not to be the critique of Blackstone, but the tools he used to conduct that critique, the principle of utility as the ultimate foundation of morality, and a strict separation between normative criticism and logical description and analysis as the basis of his account of the nature of law. He became the founder of analytical jurisprudence and utilitarianism, and author of such works as *Of Laws in General*, *A Fragment on Government*, and *An Introduction to the Principles of Morals and Legislation*. Although a prolific published writer, Bentham was an even more prolific author. He wrote on almost every subject and left behind a huge collection of unpublished works and manuscripts. This contains plans for the reform of language and logic, prison reform and design, parliamentary procedure, and most aspects of social policy and economic policy, including schemes to frustrate counterfeiters. Some of these plans culminated in his ill-fated Panopticon scheme for prison reform. The Panopticon has since become a euphemism for the dark side of the Enlightenment, but the experience and frustration of trying to humanize the destructively cruel way in which eighteenth-century Britain treated offenders led Bentham to challenge the idea of government as a neutral vehicle for radical reform. Bentham came to see government as a vehicle for the exercise of 'sinister interests' that had to be controlled and constrained by an ever-watchful citizenry. This experience led him in his later years to an active and radical commitment to representative democracy. This resurrected and greatly expanded ideas that he had begun at the time of the French Revolution but abandoned in the face of 'the Terror'. In the last decades of his life Bentham planned and wrote complete codes of law and constitutions for emerging republics in Spanish America, Portugal, Greece, and even Tripoli. These endeavours brought him considerable fame beyond his native shores. While he developed a public persona in Britain as the leader of the 'philosophic radicals', his international reputation became immense. In all of these schemes and plans Bentham exhibits all the traits of the Enlightenment projector, the arch-rationalist spinning ever more complex implications from his simple set of principles. Yet he also had a lawyer's forensic mind of great subtlety and a keen eye for detail. Far from being the Enlightenment 'hedgehog' who knows one big thing, Bentham was acutely sensitive to the complexities of legal, political, and moral reform. Yet he was a true Enlightenment thinker in his unfailing commitment to a more humane, open, and transparent exercise of society's coercive power. By the time of his death in 1832 Bentham was an icon of radical liberal reform and the major target for all those who wished to bolster what was left of the *ancien régime*.

## Main texts used

*A Fragment on Government* (1776), ed. J. H. Burns and H. L. A. Hart, with introd. by R. Harrison (Cambridge: Cambridge University Press, 1988).

*An Introduction to the Principles of Morals and Legislation* (1789), ed. J. H. Burns, H. L. A. Hart, and F. Rosen (Oxford: Oxford University Press, 1995).

See also the *Collected Works of Jeremy Bentham*, ed. J. H. Burns, J. Dinwiddy, F. Rosen, and P. Schofield (Oxford: Clarendon Press, 1968– ).

## Key ideas

**Utility**, from which the word 'utilitarianism' is derived, means the sum of pleasures over pains, or happiness. It is the ultimate standard of value. **Sovereignty** is the power resulting from being the beneficiary of a habit of obedience by a people and not being in the habit of recognizing anyone else to whom one owes obedience. This is the core concept underlying Bentham's legal positivism. **Rights** are creatures of law, the result of duties imposed by legal norms. Bentham is the originator of a conception of rights as protected interests. Because rights are a creation of the law there cannot be any 'natural' rights. **Panopticon** means 'all-seeing' and refers to a principle of architecture developed by Bentham's brother Samuel for factory organization. It is most famously applied to Bentham's model prison in which the gaoler would be able to see all the inmates without their being certain that they were being watched. Some contemporary critics use the idea of the Panopticon as a metaphor for the darker, 'manipulative' side of the Enlightenment.

# Psychological hedonism

To contemporary moral and political philosophers utilitarianism is a very simple theory. It asserts that the good is the largest amount of utility or happiness, and that means the sum total of the happiness of all people concerned, and the right, or our fundamental duty, is to create as much of the good as is possible whenever we act. This basic theory has undergone many refinements since Bentham's time, not least in its account of the good. Most welfare economists and philosophers substitute the satisfaction of revealed preferences as a way of avoiding the difficulties of providing a measure of subjective states entailed by happiness. Nevertheless, the basic idea is the same. The good is singular; although it manifests itself in many possible actions and events, it is a single natural property such as pleasure, happiness, or utility. Our basic moral duty is also singular: we should promote or maximize the good or utility wherever we can. This view of utilitarianism is shared by commentators as diverse as John Grote in the nineteenth century and philosophers such as Michael Oakeshott, Jack Smart, Peter Singer, and John Rawls in the twentieth century.

This simple or crude theory of utilitarianism has many sources in the history of ethics, but Bentham is most famously credited with being the founder of the doctrine. Bentham was happy to call himself a utilitarian in his later life, but in doing so he was not signing up to a complete pre-existing theory, as no such theory then existed. Thus in expounding Bentham's position we should not be surprised if he departs from or bends the rules of the simple or crude theory which many contemporary philosophers take to signify the basic logic of the utilitarian position. The crude theory is at best a simplistic caricature of what utilitarianism was thought to involve by one of its greatest exponents. One needs to be as careful in applying the term 'utilitarian' to Bentham as one does in applying it to Hume.

Bentham is more properly seen as an exponent of pyschological hedonism, and it is this perspective that he sets out in the famous opening passage of *An Introduction to the Principles of Morals and Legislation* (1789). In these few lines Bentham states that 'Nature has placed man under the governance of two sovereign masters, pain and pleasure.' These two concepts provide the basis for his theory of value or account of the good, and his theory of motivation and duty, or what we *ought* to do.

The sole efficient cause of action for Bentham is the experience of pleasure and the absence of pain, hence his hedonism. Pleasure is a psychological sensation associated with many different types of experience, as indeed is pain. Thus pleasure can be associated with almost any kind of action. This leads to the possibility of speaking of types of pleasure, but here the distinction is based on the categorization of actions and occurrences with which pleasure is associated and not (as is suggested by J. S. Mill) because of any categorical distinction between distinct classes of pleasure. Pleasure is pleasure, though it may be derived from food, art, music, philosophy, sex, or splashing about in the mud! Pleasure is the only thing valuable in itself because it is that in terms of which Bentham explains desire, or the pro-attitude towards an object, which makes people choose it or be attracted towards it. What this means is that Bentham uses the idea of pleasure to explain why people choose or desire the ends that they do. He does not mean that people only consciously desire pleasure as the direct object of their action and are indifferent to the objects, characters, and events that give rise to it. The natural differences in mankind's circumstances and sensibilities explains why all do not seek the same objects and ends as giving rise to the same amounts of pleasure. It also explains why Bentham does not, contrary to the views of many subsequent commentators, think that a utilitarian legislator can bring about the maximization of utility or pleasure by imposing some single good on all people. Despite Bentham's undoubted use of phrases such as 'felicific calculus' and 'political arithmetic', he was rather cautious in drawing any simple policy prescriptions from his hedonistic theory of motivation. Certainly, human nature is sufficiently uniform for all men to find pleasure in certain goods, such as food and shelter. In acknowledging this Bentham follows not only naturalistic proto-utilitarians such as Hume, but pretty much every other political theorist. However, such judgements can only be empirical judgements and as such can be contradicted by the evidence. Variations in sensibility and natural and social circumstances severely curtail any possibility of using carefully tailored incentives to regulate behaviour precisely (the key task of the legislator). Although, Bentham identifies pleasure as the 'sovereign master' explaining all that we do, in fact he relies more often on the concept of pain in constructing his legal and political theory. For it is not only the sensation of pleasure that explains action, but the avoidance of pain—or the opposite and negation of pleasure.

In terms of his psychology, pain and pleasure are intimately connected, but in terms of his practical application of this psychology to the science of legislation and government, pain is by far the more important consideration. Whatever else it is that people want, they all want to avoid pain. The manipulation of the sensation of pleasure is an extremely complex matter, not least because it raises the problem of measuring the intensity of a sensation that must be psychologically private. (Bentham was remarkably prescient is acknowledging many of the problems that would cause later generations of thinkers to abandon psychological hedonism, despite his cavalier use of ideas such as the 'felicific calculus'.) Thankfully, given the practical task—the science of legislation and government—which prompted Bentham to turn to such foundational questions in the first instance, the concept of pain is sufficiently versatile. All manner of things can be sources of pain to some and not others, but certain things are pains whatever it is we take pleasure in. These pains include the causes of death, physical violence, and the restriction of liberty or freedom. It is precisely these things (among others) that legislators and governors need to use in order to create sanctions to back up moral and political rules or laws. Key to the science of governing is knowing when to impose sanctions in order to regulate behaviour and just how much coercive power is necessary to sanction a law. Pain is more nearly the topic of the 'two sovereigns' passage, because pain is the tool of real sovereign masters, namely legislators and magistrates.

Not only does the two sovereigns passage offer the concepts of pleasure and pain to explain our motivations to act, but also Bentham uses it to provide an account of value concepts. For Bentham, all our judgements of good or bad must ultimately be explainable in terms of the concepts of pleasure or pain. These concepts are at the heart of any account of moral evaluation because pleasure is the only thing that can be good in itself and not merely reducible to some other more fundamental good. His account of moral evaluation is intimately connected to his account of moral and psychological motivation, because, as with Hume, Bentham also thought the point of morality was to affect actions. Therefore an account of moral goodness or badness that left agents indifferent as to how to act would be very curious indeed. That said, the connection between his account of moral psychology and moral judgement is not the same as Hume's. Where Hume accepts that there can be a variety of goods, Bentham is clear that pleasure is the ultimate good. Part of Bentham's reason for preferring a monistic account of the good or value to a more pluralistic account is his claim that without a monistic theory we would be unable to make comparisons to the effect that action or object *x* is more valuable than action or object *y*, where that difference can be given a quantitative value. Another important feature of his account of the good or criterion of value is that it is naturalistic. Bentham argues that the good has to be a natural property if it provides for a public moral discourse. If there is no natural property underlying our moral concepts and judgements, then these become merely empty words and fictions. For Bentham, like logical empiricists such as Bertrand Russell and the early Ludwig Wittgenstein at the beginning of the twentieth century, words and concepts must refer to some real property in the world if they are to have any meaning. Unless there is such a referent, moral concepts become literally meaningless (this, as we shall see, is part of the problem with natural and moral rights). But this problem of meaning is not only a philosophical problem; it is a profoundly important political and moral problem as well. In the absence of some common basis of moral judgements, then, nothing is ruled out and the result is conceptual *and* moral anarchy. Bentham famously suggests that all rival moral theories must either be at root some version of utilitarianism or else they collapse into incoherence.

## Obligations and rules

Moral judgements are grounded in Bentham's psychological hedonism. To judge an action right or wrong is to offer a judgement about the quantity of pleasure it results in or the quantity of pain it prevents. As the avoidance of pain and the pursuit of pleasure are at the heart of Bentham's psychology, any judgement that an act promotes maximum pleasure will give an agent a reason (although not necessarily an overriding reason) for acting accordingly. This is taken to provide the basis for seeing Bentham as a simple or direct act-utilitarian. If the right action is always that which maximizes the greatest happiness of the greatest number, then our duty is to act in such a way as to maximize the greatest happiness of the greatest number. This simplicity is taken by some to be one of the great benefits of act-utilitarianism. Everyone has a simple and straightforward obligation: to maximize happiness or pleasure. All variants of act-utilitarianism take their cue from Bentham.

However, Bentham's argument is not actually so simple. While he does indeed appear to endorse this direct or act-utilitarian account, he also has a 'sanction-based' theory of obligation. On such a view one can only have an obligation to maximize the greatest happiness of the greatest number when it would be right to impose a sanction or punishment for failing to do so. Sanctions can take many forms, including social disapproval and pressure as well as coercive penalties imposed by the state through the legal system. Some acts which fail to maximize utility are of little consequence, especially where the issue concerns difficult judgements about how best to use one's time in private matters. But others, especially those that cause specifiable harm to assignable individuals as a means to individual advantage, are appropriately discouraged by the imposition of punishments. The most serious harms are designated crimes and offences within the criminal law. The criminal law is rarely employed to discourage acts that fail to maximize pleasure; instead it is reserved to discourage acts that cause serious pain. This sanction-based theory of obligation complicates the familiar act-utilitarian interpretation of Bentham's theory because it appears to detach his theory of the good, namely that which maximizes utility, from his account of obligation, which claims that our duties are determined by the structure of rules that impose sanctions for non-performance. Clearly, we can have obligations, such as those derived from contracts and promises that merit the sanction of the law or public opinion should we disregard them, which do not directly maximize utility. Indeed it is easy to envisage cases where one contracts to do an act but where as a result of a change of circumstances we can envisage non-compliance with the contract as delivering more utility. Not every action in accordance with a sanctionable duty will always result in the maximum utility. Bentham was not unaware of this problem, and though he retained an act-utilitarian account of moral judgement, he also recognized the significance of rules, rights, and indirect strategies for the promotion of overall utility. His moral and political theory contains an account of moral rightness in terms of the act that maximizes the greatest happiness of the greatest number, but he also recognized that an adequate moral theory cannot simply function with a single, open-ended obligation to maximize happiness without being self-defeating.

Two main reasons are offered by Bentham for not claiming that each individual is always under a direct obligation to maximize utility. The first is self-preference and the second is the concept of expectation. Both are direct implications of Bentham's psychology, but both are inadequately discussed in the literature on Bentham.

Self-preference is the empirical judgement that, on the whole, individuals are motivated to pursue their own pleasures and interests. This does not mean that individuals can only pursue their narrowly selfish interests. In so far as Bentham's psychology is essentially egoist, it is so in the weak sense that all motivations can be explained in ways that relate to the interests of individual agents even if only indirectly. Clearly, experience shows that individuals are concerned with the condition and welfare of others, but this concern in order to be motivational must tie into an individual's interest in the welfare of others. This form of psychological egoism is quite consistent with apparently altruistic and other-regarding acts. Parents clearly sacrifice their own interests to those of their children. Bentham's psychology has to explain such obvious facts. Nevertheless, Bentham also thinks that there is good empirical evidence for the simple rule of thumb that, left to themselves, most individuals will prefer their own interest to that of the greatest number. This judgement underpins his 'self-preference' principle, which becomes the first premiss of his mature constitutional theory and defence of representative democracy in his *Constitutional Code*.[1] Here Bentham's view is that the problem of self-preference is most acute because the rewards of corruption (rulers pursuing their own interests over the public interest) are greatest. But the issue is not only acute in politics and legislation. If individuals are likely to confuse their own interest with the public interest, they are unlikely to be able to take the impartial view derived from the direct pursuit of the greatest happiness of the greatest number. Consequently, Bentham relies on the institutions of law and conventional morality to bring about a convergence between interest and duty. The duties and obligations of a code of law and to a lesser extent the conventional practices of morality are necessary to coordinate individual self-regarding acts into paths that lead to the greatest happiness of the greatest number. Bentham did not think that, left to themselves, all individuals would be able to act in ways that maximize utility. Unsurprisingly, rules and laws function as a necessary instrument in delivering maximum utility. Bentham uses the same argument but applied to government functionaries in his *Securities against Misrule*.[2] In this work he discusses strategies designed to subvert the attempt by the ruling few to use their power over government against the subject many.

The idea of coordinating self-regarding acts into paths that maximize utility has suggested to some commentators an unhealthy toleration of policies of collectivist social control, with the Benthamite legislator trying to encourage and discourage individual motives in order to create the 'new men' of a utilitarian dystopia.[3] Yet despite his passion for offering projects for model prisons and Poor Law reform, Bentham retained a healthy liberal scepticism about governments' ability to bring about the greatest happiness through direct legislation and social policy. Instead he was more concerned with using the power of government to minimize pains by prohibiting actions that violate certain basic conditions of individual welfare. The chief value of law was that it enabled the legislator to protect certain basic interests through the distribution of civil and political rights, and then as far as possible to leave individuals free to pursue their own interests within this scheme of rights and obligations. The maximization of happiness would become a by-product of the direct aim of legislation, which was the minimization of pain.

Any adequate utilitarian theory is bound to acknowledge the instrumental value of rules as a means to social coordination. But this still leaves a problem if Bentham's underlying moral theory is direct act-utilitarianism, for such a theory will allow these rules to be obligation-creating when they maximize utility, and there will always be occasions when it is more beneficial to ignore such rules and principles. There remains a potential tension between utilitarianism and the requirements of law, which a simple instrumental account of the value of rules cannot overcome. However, there is more to Bentham's theory, and this brings us to the concept of expectation. Rules do not merely bring about a convergence between duty and interest, though that is important; they also have a crucial function in that they give rise to expectations and expectation utilities. The concept of expectation is central to Bentham's moral and legal theory and explains why he sees the task of utilitarian reform in terms of the science of legislation and why the reform of political institutions and the art and science of political economy are subordinate to the science of legislation. The significance of security among the four subordinate ends of legislation identified in the 'Principles of the Civil Code'[4] and the value that Bentham attached to stability of property holdings and legal rights and titles also has its basis in the significance of expectation.[5]

The concept of expectation covers all those beliefs and judgements that presuppose a degree of continuity between present and future, as it enables individuals to project themselves into the future in their plans and aspirations: 'It is by means [of expectation] that we are enabled to form a general plan of conduct; it is by means of this, that the successive moments which compose the duration of life are not like insulated and independent points, but become parts of a continuous whole.'[6] The idea of expectation forms the basis of a more complex theory of personality than is usually credited to Bentham. Expectation utilities are a special class of satisfactions which depend upon the stability of beliefs and norms. They include the pleasures of anticipation as well as pleasures that come with the fruition of plans and projects. These utilities, though not forming a distinct category from immediate satisfactions, are nevertheless considered by Bentham as an especially significant class of utilities and therefore of particular concern to legislators and rulers. This concern for security of expectation helps explain Bentham's account of obligation. While any account of the right action must ultimately be that which maximizes utility, individuals and public functionaries such as judges have a strong reason to respect rights and laws, not simply because these provide ways of coordinating action, but also because they give rise to patterns of expectation that would be undermined if individuals constantly regarded the obligation of law as purely advisory and not obligatory. Rules can only give rise to stable patterns of expectation if individual agents and public functionaries such as judges and magistrates treat them as if they have an unconditional category. It is only in this way that following such rules can maximize utility.

But if any system of rules gives rise to stable expectations, then any changes in a given system of rules in order to increase utility would seem to be trumped by the significant disutility arising from interference with expectation. This reading suggests an extremely conservative Bentham concerned that any change in the law would result in significant disutility. Bentham becomes a caricature of Burke! That said, Bentham does adopt such a cautious stance at many points in his career. Particularly when dealing with demands for the redistribution of property he was quick to argue that 'levelling' would undermine security of expectation. Yet he also remained an advocate of radical legal and social reform, so he cannot have intended his argument to preclude all change. Although he remained a cautious reformer, Bentham nevertheless believed that change could be effected within a legal system as long as adequate compensation could be given to those whose interests were affected. To this end he developed the 'disappointment-preventing principle', which was a modification of the principle of utility intended to provide compensation for changes that would otherwise upset security of expectation. In his campaign for representative democracy Bentham would not even abolish sinecures without compensating the holders. More importantly, legal reform was less of a problem when current practice created obscurity and failed to provide secure and stable expectations because of disagreements over legitimate titles and authority. Much of Bentham's advocacy of utilitarian reform was intended to take place within legal systems rather than as a form of utopian revolution of the kind employed by the French revolutionaries and criticized by Bentham so forcefully in 'Anarchical Fallacies'.[7] Even in Bentham's later years, when he became a confirmed advocate of codification and the construction of a complete 'ideal' code of laws, or 'Pannomion', he retained his concern for stability. Thus he is keen to offer his *Constitutional Code* to emerging nations such as Greece, where the issue of security of expectation under the existing system did not arise.

Given Bentham's concern with coordination, self-preference, and expectation and security, it is clear that he does not have a simple act-utilitarian theory of practical deliberation. Certainly he retains an act-utilitarian account of moral judgement, but this is distinguished from his account of decision-making. Indeed as early as the motto of the good citizen from the *Fragment on Government* (1776)—'to obey punctually, to censure freely'—it is clear that Bentham wanted to show that the connection between moral judgement and utilitarianism as a decision strategy was complex and not simple, as contemporary act-utilitarians suggest.

## Sovereignty and law

Bentham's contemporary reputation is based on his utilitarianism and his legal positivism. Indeed among his contemporary critics he is 'damned' as much for his positivism as for his utilitarianism. Legal positivism is the doctrine that 'law' is categorically distinct from morality, and that any account of the nature of a law or its obligation-creating (or normative) power must be given independently of moral reasons. What the law is can be determined by reference to a series of suitably specified authoritative sources such as a sovereign's command, or the legislation of a sovereign parliament. No further reference has to be made to the moral propriety of those rules or commands. For a legal positivist, a parliament might make a stupid or even immoral law, but it still retains its legal authority and obligation-creating power. Bentham was not the first legal positivist. Thomas Hobbes was also a positivist in this sense, as indeed were many other writers before Bentham. However, he gave the theory its classic modern impetus in a work entitled *Of Laws in General* which was completed in the 1780s but not published until the 1970s. In this work Bentham gives his clearest and most subtle defence of the distinction between 'expository' and 'censorial' jurisprudence, namely jurisdiction that explains the law, and that which declares what it should be.

In arguing for a clear distinction between law as it is and law as it ought to be, Bentham was pursuing a radical critique of the English common law and its most famous (at the time) defender, Sir William Blackstone. The assault on Blackstone became something of an obsession with Bentham. Although Blackstone's monumental *The Commentaries on the Laws of England* was published in 1769, Bentham was still wrestling with him as late as 1832, the year of Bentham's death. Blackstone's *Commentaries* is a rather uncritical compendium of common law, the law of nature, and social contract ideology, but it was not Blackstone himself who really concerned Bentham but this eclectic combination of ideas, especially the common law. To understand Bentham's obsession with the iniquities of common law adjudication and his concern with legal reform as a fundamental part of his utilitarian political theory, we have to remember the significance that he attached to stable expectations as a fundamental source of utility. Stability of expectation is for Bentham the first virtue of any legal system and indirectly the reason for having any systems of law in the first instance. Yet it is stability of expectation that is denied by the common law. To support this view Bentham appeals to the common law doctrine of *stare decisis*, or precedent, by which judges decide the law in hard cases. The problem with appeals to precedent is that the judge has to reason analogically from past precedents in order to determine issues of right, title, or responsibility in contested cases. He does not merely apply a set of pre-given rules but shows by interpretation how the law embodied in one decision should be extended to cover a later case. The problem with this paradigmatic form of common law reasoning, in Bentham's view, was that it precluded the idea of stable patterns of expectation which could grow up around clear and determinate rules. The rules that make up the law are never determinate; they may always be revised in light of a judge's 'extension' of the law. Therefore, they can never provide a secure base for practical reasoning. At its worst it could mean that a person could actually be punished for acting in a way that is prescribed by the law, but where she could never have known that and therefore acted differently. The common law is for Bentham a species of 'dog law': 'When your dog does anything you want to break him of, you wait till he does it, and then beat him for it. This is the way you make laws for your dog: and this is the way the judges make law for you and me.'[8] The common law falls foul of the utilitarian point of a legal system by failing to provide stability of expectations. To secure expectation law must have a certain character, and it is precisely this idea that leads to his positivist account of law. Once we have identified that character in terms of certain public conditions of recognition, we have a sufficient account of law. We do not need to appeal its innate moral character. Certainly, for Bentham, there will in any adequate society be a connection between law and morality, but that will be a contingent connection. It is not part of the definition of what a law is that it must have a moral character.

In contrast to the eclectic blend of English common law and natural law so characteristic of Blackstone, Bentham developed a distinctive positivist account of law. This theory identified law with authoritative sovereign commands and exception-creating permissions. Consequently, he has what legal philosophers refer to as an 'imperational' theory of law, which differs significantly from the simple command theory of Bentham's nineteenth-century follower John Austin.[9] Commands and permissions derive their validity as laws from some publicly recognized body, and this leads to the centrality of sovereignty in Bentham's theory of law.

Sovereignty is a central concept in positivist theories of law because it is the way of identifying authoritative sources of legal rules and determining the validity of a rule. Bentham uses the concept of sovereignty to explain the source and validity of law, but it also has a political dimension, which he identifies in *A Fragment on Government*. In this work he uses the idea of sovereignty to provide the criterion for distinguishing an autonomous political community such as a state. A sovereign and therefore independent political state is one in which the sovereign power enjoys the habit of obedience of a people and is not itself in the habit of obeying any other power. It will be noticed that Bentham's account relies simply on social facts about habits of obedience among peoples and states. These are things that do not have to be conjured out of moral argument, but either exist or do not exist. He does not develop this aspect of his theory to any great length as his real interest is in the jurisprudential implications of his argument.

There are three main components of his account of sovereignty in his theory of law. First, it guarantees the efficacy of law. This is the familiar positivist idea that the sovereign sanctions rules by imposing his monopoly of force or violence on those who ignore them. In this way the sovereign explains the ultimate (if not the sole) motive for obedience to law. Secondly, it provides a principle that relates systematically all the components of a legal system. This means that it provides for the relationships between legislatures and courts and between various courts in the hierarchy of a legal system. Thirdly, it defines the criteria of validity of laws so that we can distinguish between authentic and spurious claims to law. This is especially important if law is to function as a source of secure expectations. Taken together, these three components of sovereignty serve both an ontological function by telling us what things laws, principles, norms, and commands are, and an epistemological function by providing criteria by which we can distinguish real or authentic laws from spurious ones. Alongside these epistemological and ontological tasks the doctrine of sovereignty tells us something about the existence of those criteria, namely that they must be simple matters of fact and not interpretative entities, so that we can publicly identify them. This explains why Bentham uses social facts such as habits of experience that can be identified in an unambiguous way and without having recourse to the special esoteric knowledge of a particular group such as judges.

Unlike primitive positivists such as Hobbes, Bentham did not demand that the sovereign be a single person or even a single public body, though in practice this would most likely be the case. Sovereignty is constituted by a habit of recognition among a people, and as long as this occurs it does not really matter what is the object of that habitual recognition. It could be a single sovereign individual or a set of institutions under a constitution. What was essential for Bentham was that the authoritative source of law was publicly and habitually recognized as a source of valid rules that could guide actions and give rise to stable patterns of expectation.

Bentham explains sovereignty in terms of a habit of obedience among a people. This habit of obedience manifests itself not only in terms of the sovereign's commands: its explaining the efficacy of law would not explain its validity. For validity the habit of obedience must include some intentional component; that is, some beliefs to the effect that obedience is the proper response to the sovereign's commands and permissions because of expectations about what others will do. Thus, the disposition to obey is a complex idea that depends upon beliefs and expectations regarding the behaviour and attitudes of other members of the community.

Interpreted in this way Bentham's account of law and sovereignty as a series of social facts allows law to have a determinate and public content unlike the common law which he so derided in the work of Blackstone. In this way it could provide a clear focus of expectation, whatever its content, and thus secure its utilitarian function.

Of course, this will still leave open the question of whether one set of rules is a better source of utility than another, but this judgement is independent of judgements about what the law is. Bentham was cautious when it came to the law, but he remained a radical reformer despite that caution. He merely wanted to insist that the task of censorial jurisprudence under which he included his utilitarian science of legislation was to be pursued alongside the science of expository jurisprudence in the same way that he thought the good citizen should 'obey punctually, censure freely'.

## Representative democracy

Bentham's utilitarianism and legal positivism have a considerable moral and legal significance, but he is often accused of not really having a political theory. All political issues are reduced to issues of law and legislation, or else they are dealt with simply by cranking up the 'utility' calculus in order to generate some new social policy. His legacy to subsequent utilitarianism is often characterized as ending the great tradition of political thought and replacing it with modern policy science. Utilitarians have much to say about what government should do but have little of real interest to contribute to debates about the nature of government, for the simple reason that the principle of utility makes all issues of government structure merely contingent on whatever form of government best delivers the most utility. If this turned out to be democracy, then we have a justification of democracy, but if it turned out that authoritarian forms of government such as enlightened despotism delivered more utility, then we would have a utilitarian justification for that.

While Bentham's theory of government cannot overcome the idea that the connection between utility and constitutional form is a contingent one, he nevertheless comes to develop a very robust defence of representative democracy. In his early years he seems to have been indifferent to governmental forms, but in his later writings his commitment to representative democracy becomes much more important owing to his theory of 'sinister' interest, and as a result of his own experience dealing with social and political reform projects.

Much of the early part of Bentham's public career was devoted to his major works on legal theory and the principle of utility. These works, such as the *Introduction to the Principles of Morals and Legislation* and *Of Laws in General*, set out the basic conceptual structure of his peculiar science of legislation. The subsequent decades mark an important turning in the direction of Bentham's writings and reveal the character of Bentham 'the projector', which is so often associated with the nineteenth-century revolution in government, or, among his less favourable critics, Bentham the arch-'rationalist'. The 1780s also reveals a turning in his attitude towards democracy in light of the experience of the French Revolution. Until this time Bentham had taken a common stance among enlightened reformers to the effect that what was needed in order to bring about reform in government and policy was the sympathetic ear of an enlightened or benevolent despot. To this end he travelled to Russia to visit his younger brother Samuel, a naval architect, inventor, and general entrepreneur who was employed by Prince Potemkin, a favourite of Catherine II. The trip was a long and difficult one, largely overland, but Bentham put the time to good use and began work on a number of projects, including political economy, and the architectural principle of the inspection house, which was to dominate his thought on prison and Poor Law reform for the next fifteen years. When the opportunity finally came to meet Catherine, Bentham shied away.

It was the experience of the French Revolution that was to do most to transform his views on government, initially in the direction of authoritarianism. Initially, Bentham's view of the political circumstances and the absence of a potential leader led him to trust the democratic aspirations of the time. At first, he was much in favour of the reform opportunities thrown up by the revolution and even wrote a handbook (or procedure code) for the conduct of the National Assembly, which he called *Political Tactics* (1791). For this great service he, along with others such as Tom Paine—with whom he had no association—was made an honorary citizen. However, following the turn of events from 1792 onwards led Bentham radically to revise his initial optimism. This growing hostility is partly manifested in his reaction to the Declaration of the Rights of Man and of the Citizen, which Bentham appears to blame for all the defects and inadequacies of the revolution. As he turned his back on the French Revolution, he also became increasingly hostile to democracy, and for a period he even became, like Burke, a scathing critic of democracy and popular government, writing, though not publishing, a defence of rotten boroughs. As we shall see, this did not last, because he came to a significant accommodation with democratic government in a way that he was unable to do with the concept of natural rights.

Bentham's more immediate response to the situation in France and his expedition to Russia was to divert attention from legal and political reform and towards social questions instead. In particular, he became engrossed with the 'inspection principle' and its manifestation in the Panopticon Prison. This was an idea for a privately run prison that would be a factory and a school for virtue and would control prisoners through the possibility of permanent observation from a central inspection house. Bentham also used the plan for a series of poor panopticons, a kind of workhouse which again would train the indigent in the skills necessary to gain employment and the virtues of thrift and hard labour. Bentham's poorhouses were not supposed to be the grim, 'less eligible' institutions depicted in Dicken's *Oliver Twist* and partly created by Edwin Chadwick (a follower of Bentham), but they were supposed to provide a social need and to make the fortune of their proprietor—Jeremy Bentham and his shareholders.

The significance of this story for Bentham's reconversion to democracy is that it was his frustration with the obstacles put in the way of building his prison that led him to develop his account of sinister interests, and his view of government itself being a sinister interest hostile to the public interest. In 1791 Bentham put his Panopticon scheme before the prime minister, William Pitt. Pitt was initially in favour, though it took three years to bring the matter before Parliament. Eventually an Act was passed to establish a Panopticon Penitentiary at Millbank in London in 1794. Although the plan had parliamentary approval, it ran into the opposition of two powerful aristocratic families, the Spencers and the Grosvenors, who were concerned that the housing of criminals at Millbank would reduce the value of their own property development plans. Bentham badgered the Home Office for twelve years, and spent most of his inheritance before having to admit defeat in 1803 and begin the long struggle for compensation. The lesson of this experience was that it illustrated the way in which a sectional interest, such as the Spencers and Grosvenors, could use the apparatus of the state to pursue their own private pecuniary interests in opposition to the clear expression of public interest. This was a paradign (though not the only) example of a sinister interest acting against the public interest. It also illustrated how such sinister interests were able to flourish because of the lack of accountability of public institutions and the poor standards of public administration. Government lacked both accountability and a recognizably modern state and bureaucracy. The creation of a modern state and bureaucracy was to become a major concern of his writings throughout the rest of his life, especially after 1809, when Bentham began an association with James Mill (father of John Stuart) and a group that became known as the Philosophic Radicals.

Bentham's turn to democracy was not, however, a mirror image of Mill's defence of representative government. James Mill was committed to the idea of locating political power in the hands of a representative class—the emerging bourgeoisie or commercial middle classes. For Mill the suffrage needed extension, but it did not need universal extension and certainly not to women whose interests were perfectly protected by their fathers or husbands. Bentham was much more radical, and built his defence of a near-universal suffrage from his psychology of self-preference and its institutional manifestation as sinister interests. He was also much more interested in the detailed institutional structure of a modern state, and pursued this through his writing of constitutions and in legal codification.

His defence of representative democracy develops out of his account of 'sinister interests'. Sinister interests are the collective institutional manifestation of self-preference. Instead of merely an individual pursuing his own interest against the general interest, a sinister interest is when a privileged group is able to impose its own sectional or institutional interest as the public interest. For Bentham, the personnel of government is potentially a class apart from the governed, however well disposed it may feel to the governed. As a class apart, it develops an interest that is necessarily distinct from the public interest but is able to pursue this because of its control of the government or the legal system. To overcome this conflict of interest the interests of the governors have to be brought into line with the interest of the governed. This is to be achieved by the simple device of accountability and dismissal that is made possible by democratic elections. But, unlike James Mill, Bentham defends a near-universal suffrage as a means of preventing any level of government, even the representatives acting as a class apart and thus a potential sinister interest. The only restrictions Bentham was prepared to contemplate in principle were restrictions based on a minimal educational test. Potential voters would need to be able to read the ballot paper.

Yet there is more to Bentham's defence of representative democracy than a conception of the ballot as a protective device designed to 'kick out the rogues'. The ballot was one essential part of a programme that would use the power of public opinion to enlighten, inform, and reform government. As important as holding representatives accountable was shining the light of public opinion and public scrutiny into the affairs of the government. Bentham speaks of a Public Opinion Tribunal as a quasi-court in which government, legislators, and bureaucrats could be held accountable for their decisions. Representative democracy is not merely the institution of the ballot, but is rather a whole culture of government by and through public opinion. It is for this reason that freedom and expansion of the press is so important for Bentham. It is not merely a condition for representative democracy but actually a part of a representative democracy that is composed of a number of practices and institutions of government. Indeed, public opinion is even offered as the means by which the greatest happiness of the greatest number can be given voice. For it to function as the voice of the greatest happiness of the greatest number public opinion needs an institutional setting, and this is provided by the regime of constitutional rights and liberties which underpin Bentham's *Constitutional Code*, and which he refers to as 'securities against misrule' (*Securities against Misrule*). Securities against misrule also include the restrictions placed upon ministers, bureaucrats, and functionaries in Bentham's constitutional state. The provisions limit the power and money in the hands of particular individuals; they also limit the possibilities of individuals shaping their own positions to advance their prestige and therefore power. All of these concerns and more are worked out in considerable detail in the *Constitutional Code* and other associated writings of the late 1820s. Taken together, they amount to a regime of transparency and accountability all geared towards the greatest happiness of the greatest number, but where this is seen not as an external criterion, but rather something that is given voice within a liberal constitutional regime.

To return, then, to the issue with which we began, namely the connection between utilitarianism and constitutional form, it is clear that Bentham does not think that utilitarianism is indifferent to the form government takes. Although the connection between utilitarianism and the form of liberal representative democracy Bentham advocates is still a contingent matter, its contingency is weakened by the strength of the self-preference principle and the idea of sinister interests. Given what we know about human nature and its ability to exploit the institutional opportunities of government, a representative democracy with the appropriate liberal constitutional structure is the only appropriate way for the greatest happiness to emerge.

## Bentham and liberalism

One of the curious ironies of the history of philosophy is that, despite Bentham's commitment to radical reform and liberal democratic constitutionalism, his moral, legal, and political theory is taken by contemporary political philosophers to exemplify the main threats to political liberalism. The contractarian liberalism of John Rawls and his many followers is, at least in part, developed as a response to the anti-liberal inadequacies of utilitarianism.[10] Bentham's legal theory has also been criticized as a potential threat to liberalism by thinkers as diverse as Hayek and Dworkin.[11] His moral theory is either narrowly instrumentalist in that it cannot provide any person- or agent-respecting safeguards and thus potentially accommodates the sacrifice of the innocent, or of minorities to majorities. His utilitarian moral theory is criticized, alternatively, on the grounds that it provides a comprehensive theory of the good and therefore cannot accommodate reasonable disagreement about the nature of the good life. Both of these concerns are fundamental to modern contractualist liberalism. His legal positivism is also criticized on the grounds that it asserts a strong distinction between law and morality so that it can award the honour of legitimacy to evil legal regimes such as those of Nazi Germany and Stalin's USSR. It is also criticized as a threat to liberal rights and democracy by its accommodation of judicial legislation when the rules of law run out and judges are faced with deciding new cases without a pre-existing rule. This gives judges the potential to impose their will in the interstices of legislation. In these respects Bentham's moral and political theory has become a victim of the vicissitudes of philosophical fashion. For much of the nineteenth century Bentham was considered both as a founder of what we now call liberalism and as an exemplar of its two main varieties: laissez-faire and authoritarian liberalism.[12] And both of these perspectives still shape the way he is read by many subsequent commentators.

Yet the strongest, most forceful, and most troubling critique of Bentham's putative liberal credentials is mounted by Michel Foucault in his study of the modern penitentiary.[13] Admittedly, Foucault uses Bentham's Panopticon Prison as a paradigm for a much broader 'carceral' mentality found in late Enlightenment social and political ideas, as opposed to offering a historical interpretation of Bentham's thought. Nevertheless, the idea of Bentham's Panopticon Prison as an image of a utilitarian dystopia is a powerful one which has influenced Bentham scholars as well as historians of the darker side of the Enlightenment.[14] In this version of Bentham's moral universe the enlightened 'legislator of the world' (for whom we must read Bentham himself) would manipulate the character of individual minds in order to bring about social harmony and order as a condition of maximum happiness. The happiness such a regime would deliver is the 'dumb' happiness of the contented animal: precisely that which J. S. Mill tried to overcome with his distinction between higher and lower pleasures. What Bentham's moral vision lacks, according to all these critics, is a fundamental commitment to an ideal of individual liberty and agency as constitutive of well-being and happiness. Without this commitment to liberty and agency Bentham's individuals are objects for manipulation by the enlightened ruler. Thus even if Foucault is wrong about Bentham's intentions and the details of the Panopticon Prison, the idea of 'Panopticism' with its images of control and manipulation tells us something fundamental about Bentham and Enlightenment political reform.

The issue of whether Bentham is best interpreted as a liberal or not is ultimately not a historical question. Traditions of thought such as liberalism are either philosophical constructions on ideological forms which evolve in changing social and economic circumstances. Consequently, the issue is never likely to be settled by appealing to an additional piece of evidence. Bentham's complex and unique political and social theory was always likely to fit uneasily into the boundaries of any such artificial construction. Yet to concede to his contemporary philosophical and radical critics is to deny too easily the important legacy of his thought. That legacy should not be seen solely in terms of simplistic deductions from his psychological and ethical hedonism. Bentham was sensitive to the need for empirical evidence to support judgements about human motivation and reasons. His psychological pronouncements therefore have a provisional character and wherever possible are of a minimal content, as we saw with the self-preference principle. What Bentham provides is a robust and neutral naturalistic moral and political theory that eschews the legacy of religion. In this he develops and extends the legacy of David Hume. Yet this theory is not crudely deductivist in character, as many of Bentham's nineteenth-century critics thought. This fact has important implications for the claim that Bentham presages the manipulative and 'totalitarian' tendencies of modern 'enlightened' liberal states. For while Hume's naturalism has a tendency to leave social science as a tool for the manipulation of agents in ways similar to those suggested by Foucault, Bentham responds to those concerns through the way in which he develops not simply a protective conception of representative democracy. The role of public opinion as a checking and a constitutive device undermines the status of bureaucrats and government functionaries, but also all other self-appointed hierarchies of power and interest. In this way, his concern with the micro-institutional concern for dispersing power and entrenching transparency goes further in securing a regime of freedom and accountability than merely the articulation of paper declarations of rights. It even shows that the authoritative statement of the greatest happiness is something that can only be provided by the greatest number. In light of the absence of natural moral norms and rights, Bentham teaches that the only protection for liberty is the institutionalization of a culture of democracy and accountablity.

## FURTHER READING

Bahmueller, Charles F., *The National Charity Company* (Berkeley: University of California Press, 1981).

Dicey, A. V., *Lectures on the Relation between Law and Public Opinion in England during the Nineteenth-Century* (London: Macmillan, 1905).

Dworkin, R., *Taking Rights Seriously* (London: Duckworth, 1978).

Foucault, M., *Discipline and Punish* (Harmondsworth: Penguin, 1977).

Halévy, E., *The Growth of Philosophic Radicalism*, trans. M. Morris (London: Faber & Faber, 1972).

Harrison, R., *Bentham* (London: Routledge, 1983).

Hart, H. L. A., *Essays on Bentham* (Oxford: Clarendon Press, 1982).

Hayek, F. A., *Law, Legislation and Liberty* (London: Routledge, 1975).

Kelly, P. J., *Utilitarianism and Distributive Justice: Jeremy Bentham and the Civil Law* (Oxford: Clarendon Press, 1990).

Manning, David, *The Mind of Jeremy Bentham* (London: Longmans Green, 1968).

Postema, G. J., *Bentham and the Common Law Tradition* (Oxford: Clarendon Press, 1986).

Rawls, John, *A Theory of Justice* (Oxford: Oxford University Press, 1971).

Rosen, F., *Jeremy Bentham and Representative Democracy* (Oxford: Clarendon Press, 1983).

## NOTES

1. In *Collected Works of Jeremy Bentham*, ed. J. H. Burns, J. Dinwiddy, F. Rosen, and P. Schofield (Oxford: Clarendon Press, 1983).
2. Ibid. (1990).
3. See David Manning, *The Mind of Jeremy Bentham* (London: Longmans Green, 1968), *passim*, and Charles F. Bahmueller, *The National Charity Company* (Berkeley: University of California Press, 1981), 1–11 and 201–17.
4. In *The Works of Jeremy Bentham*, ed. J. Bowring, 11 vols. (Edinburgh: James Tait, 1838–43), i. 308.
5. See P. J. Kelly, *Utilitarianism and Distributive Justice: Jeremy Bentham and the Civil Law* (Oxford: Clarendon Press, 1990), 71–103.
6. *Works of Jeremy Bentham*, i. 308.
7. Ibid. ii. 496–529.
8. Ibid. v. 235.
9. H. L. A. Hart, *Essays on Bentham* (Oxford: Clarendon Press, 1983).
10. John Rawls, *A Theory of Justice* (Oxford: Oxford University Press, 1971).
11. F. A. Hayek, *Law, Legislation and Liberty* (London: Routledge, 1975), and R. Dworkin, *Taking Rights Seriously* (London: Duckworth, 1978).
12. A. V. Dicey, *Lectures on the Relation between Law and Public Opinion in England during the Nineteenth-Century* (London: Macmillan, 1905), and E. Halévy, *The Growth of Philosophic Radicalism*, trans. M. Morris (London: Faber & Faber, 1972).
13. M. Foucault, *Discipline and Punish* (Harmondsworth: Penguin, 1977).
14. Bahmueller, *The National Charity Company*.

# 19 J. S. Mill on liberty

Paul Kelly

**Contents**



## Chapter guide

John Stuart Mill is among the most significant British philosophers and political theorists, shaping both the climate of opinion in twentieth-century British politics and providing one of the most influential defences of the ideal of personal liberty. Yet he has also attracted some of the most scathing criticisms from his contemporaries and subsequent philosophical commentators. He is accused of making basic logical errors and his arguments of resting on a fundamental incoherence—namely, the attempt to derive a defence of liberty from an act-utilitarian moral theory. This chapter will attempt to explain and defend Mill's position from some of these charges as well as provide an overview of his liberalism. The chapter begins with an account of his revision of psychological hedonism in light of denunciations by Thomas Carlyle and Samuel Taylor Coleridge that Mill's hedonistic naturalism reduces humans to no better than 'swine' and convicts utilitarianism of being the philosophy of pigs in equating all pleasures with the lowest common denominator. Mill's strategy to avoid this charge was to distinguish between higher and lower pleasures, which has subsequently become a constant target of criticism. This section will assess the arguments of recent writers such as Jonathan Riley and John Gray who have tried to explain Mill's qualitative hedonism. The next section covers the equally problematic attempt to derive his liberty principle from an act-utilitarian moral philosophy. Then follows a section on Mill's doctrine of liberty and an assessment of the charge (most recently levelled by Joseph Hamburger) that Mill's religion of humanity involves a form of moral and philosophical coercion as great as anything he challenges. The final section will incorporate a discussion of *Considerations on Representative Government* and show how it reflects Mill's philosophical liberalism.

## Biography

John Stuart Mill is one of a few nineteenth-century intellectuals, Nietzsche is another, who continue to set our intellectual horizons. He was born on 20 May 1806 in London. John

Stuart was the eldest of nine children of James and Harriet Mill. His father, James, was a close disciple of Jeremy Bentham, and for a time Bentham was the mainstay of the growing family while James worked on his *History of British India* and various campaigns for radical reform that were loosely inspired by Bentham's utilitarian philosophy. For a time the Mills even lived in a house at the bottom of Bentham's garden at Queen's Square Place. John Stuart's early life, recounted in his posthumously published *Autobiography* (1873), is almost as important as many of his philosophical ideas. From a shockingly early age John Stuart was instructed in Greek and Latin literature, history, and philosophy, moving on to political economy and the sciences before he reached the age of 10. Religion formed no part of his education, and Mill famously claimed that unlike many of his Victorian contemporaries (or his father) he never underwent a crisis of faith because he had no religious beliefs. Something of a prodigy, the young John Stuart became a secretary and research assistant to his father and was inducted into an adult world of radical politics in his early teens.

John Stuart fell under the philosophical influence of Jeremy Bentham and became an apostle of Bentham's utilitarianism after reading the *Traité de Legislation* (a French redaction of some of Bentham's important early works). His father, although a close political disciple, does not really qualify as a utilitarian in any philosophical sense. John Stuart remained true to the utilitarian legacy of Bentham, despite an often uncomfortable relationship with it until the very end of his life. That said, he was an extremely critical disciple, with the ability to see both the strengths of Bentham's position and all of its many weaknesses. In addition to being a philosophical disciple of Bentham, he was a political disciple. Indeed he even spent a night in gaol with the elderly radical Francis Place for allegedly distributing contraceptive advice among the poor.

At the age of 17 he entered the employment of the East India Company, which, though technically a private trading company, was in the process of metamorphosing into the British colonial administration of India. Throughout his late teens John Stuart maintained a punishing schedule of philosophical debate with the rising stars of the British intellectual elite, public political debating, campaigning and activism, and study, including the editing of Bentham's massive *Rationale of Judicial Evidence*. All of this was combined with holding down a post in the East India Company equivalent to a senior civil servant. This no doubt contributed to the onset of a period of severe depression in the autumn of 1826 and spring of 1827, which Mill came to refer to as his 'mental crisis'. The depression itself passed, but it was to retain a great significance both for Mill and for his understanding of his own utilitarian philosophy. He characterizes the problem triggering his bout of depression as the realization that his own personal happiness would not be secured by achieving all his radical utilitarian plans for social reform. The greatest happiness of the greatest number would not make him happy! The emphasis his education and the reform policies of his father and Bentham had placed on reason and analysis had left him feeling stunted and incomplete. His recovery through the discovery of feeling and aesthetic sentiment led him to seek a more rounded ideal of personal development and happiness. His subsequent thought and writings begin from this insight as he set out to develop and expand the utilitarian legacy of Bentham and the classical liberal legacy of his father and David Ricardo. Although he sought the influence of thinkers as diverse as Coleridge, Carlyle, Saint-Simon, Auguste Comte, and Alexis de Tocqueville, his major writings retain a commitment to the utilitarian liberalism and philosophical naturalism that he found germinating in the ideas of Bentham, Ricardo, and James Mill. Thus his most important writings are *A System of Logic* (1843), *Principles of Political Economy* (1848), *An Examination of Sir William Hamilton's Philosophy* (1865), and *On Liberty* (1859). All of these works, though original and reflecting his eclecticism, remain firmly within the broad tradition of British empiricism stretching back through Hume to John Locke.

Following his 'mental crisis' and at the age of 24, Mill established one further relationship, which he described as the most important of his life. It was with Harriet Taylor, already married to John Taylor. For the next twenty-one years they were to conduct an extraordinary relationship, until they were finally married following her husband's death. This relationship, which seems to have had no physical dimension, was nevertheless one of deep and enduring love. Harriet was to exercise a complex intellectual and moral influence over Mill, and many commentators now come to accept that this was genuine and not merely the hyperbole of a besotted husband. Clearly their unconventional relationship shaped Mill's response to the tyranny of social convention and opinion. Harriet died in 1859 three months prior to the publication of *On Liberty*.

Mill retained an involvement with radical politics and was returned as a Liberal Member of Parliament for Westminster from 1865 to 1868. During that time he advocated many radical reforms, including the enfranchisement of women and proportional representation. Following Mill's failure to be returned to Parliament, he retired with his step-daughter Helen Taylor to Avignon, where Harriet was buried. Mill died in 1873 and was buried next to his wife.

## Key texts

*On Liberty* (1859)
*Utilitarianism* (1861)
*Considerations on Representative Government* (1861)

## Main texts used

*On Liberty and Other Essays*, ed. John Gray, World's Classics (Oxford: Oxford University Press, 1991) (all of the key texts are included in this edn.).

## Key ideas

**Utility** means the sum of pleasures over pains. However, Mill's account of utility is distinguished from Bentham's in that Mill allows for qualitative distinctions between pleasures. **Higher pleasures** are those pleasures which an educated and cultivated person would not sacrifice for any amount of a sensual pleasure. **Harm principle:** Mill's doctrine of liberty depends on the view that the only principle to which we should appeal when deciding to prohibit an action is whether it causes harm to another. **Self-regarding actions** are those actions protected by the realm of personal liberty and for which an individual is exempt from social and political coercion. **Individuality** is the ideal or good that is derived from a regime of liberty. **Rights** are institutionally protected interests, or, in the case of moral rights, those interests that ought to be protected by law. **Act-utilitarianism**: the idea that the right action is that which maximizes utility. **Rule-utilitarianism**: the idea that the right action is that prescribed by a rule which itself maximizes utility.

---

## The philosophy of swine

Mill's intellectual 'godfather', Jeremy Bentham, had argued that nature placed mankind under the governance of two sovereign masters: pain and pleasure. With this claim he attempted to ground all claims about human motivation and also account for how all the ends of human action can be valuable. In so arguing Bentham established the core motivational theory of subsequent utilitarianism, namely psychological hedonism. Despite an equivocal relationship with 'Benthamism' following his mental crisis, by the time John Stuart Mill came to articulate his mature philosophy, he had endorsed this basic position unequivocally. In *Utilitarianism* Mill wrote: 'that pleasure, and freedom from pain, are the only things desirable as ends; and that all desirable things (which are as numerous in the utilitarian as in any other scheme) are desirable either for the pleasure inherent in themselves, or as a means to the promotion of pleasure and the prevention of pain' (p. 137[1]). However, while Bentham was either comfortable with this view or indifferent to its consequences, Mill was more acutely aware of the consequences of adopting this monistic naturalism. Whereas Bentham was prepared to concede that, pleasure for pleasure, 'pushpin [a kind of pub game] was as good as poetry', Mill was sensitive to the charge that this kind of naturalistic reductionism reduced mankind to no better than pigs. Put simply, Bentham's point is that some kind of cardinal ranking of pleasure is possible. If we imagine a balance with any of the greatest cultural achievements of mankind on one side, then if we were to add enough of the most basic sensual pleasure on the other side, for example the scratching of an itch, eventually enough of this sensation must be more valuable than the most supreme achievements of human intellect and character. Enough piglike comforts must outweigh the pleasures of intellectual discovery, artistic creativity, or moral heroism. If humans were given enough swinish pleasures—food, warmth, sex, and sleep—this would outweigh whatever good they might forgo in terms of their liberty, creativity, and individuality. Mill wants to reject this 'Benthamite' view while accepting the basic terms of psychological hedonism and without having to concede the charge of Carlyle and others that this reduces mankind to no better than swine. He writes: 'Now, such a theory of life excites in many minds, and among them in some of the most estimable in feeling the purpose, inveterate dislike. To suppose that life has (as they express it) no higher end than pleasure—no better and nobler object of desire and pursuit—designate as utterly mean and grovelling; as a doctrine worthy only of swine . . .' (p. 137). Mill's answer to this charge requires great subtlety if he is to avoid abandoning the naturalism of Bentham's original insight while rejecting his reductionism. However, his subtlety has also created problems to the extent that he has been accused of introducing a dual standard theory of value with his distinction between higher and lower pleasures.

How can we make sense of this distinction between pleasures? Mill claims that a commitment to psychological hedonism does not open one to the charge that all human pursuits are no better than those of animals. Mill constantly refers to the higher pleasures as being those that manifest the elevated capacities of human intellect and creativity. Indeed he largely contrasts the higher pleasures with sensual pleasures. Human beings are certainly capable of desiring far more than mere sensual gratification. Even if we exclude the idea that many ascetic religions may have taught us to despise the body and its pleasures unduly, we can still see that, throughout history, accounts of human flourishing have involved more than sensuality or material gratification. Many human purposes and goals involve considerable hardship and sacrifice, yet they remain human goods. If Mill's psychology is to retain empirical plausibility, it must be able to capture all of these ends of action. That said, even Bentham would concede this. Bentham might well prefer poetry to pushpin and think others have a strong reason for doing so; what he would not claim is that there is something categorically distinct about the pleasures of poetry and the intellect. For Bentham, if poetry wins out over pushpin, it is simply because it is the source of more pleasure than pushpin. The difference is quantitative, not qualitative. There are different types of pleasure, but they can be ranked simply in terms of the amount of pleasure they give rise to. If this is what Mill thought, then his distinction between higher and lower pleasures is either spurious (he is hopelessly confused) or merely apparent (it is merely a rhetorical ploy).

Numerous subsequent commentators have argued that Mill was either confused or misleading. If he was confused, this is because he did not really mean that there is a categorical distinction between types of pleasure, but merely that there are different pleasures that differ in quantity. More recently a number of sympathetic philosophers have tried to make sense of Mill's argument in a way that does not do violence to his texts but also does not reduce Mill to making a foolish mistake. In two recent studies Roger Crisp and Jonathan Riley have offered differing interpretations of Mill's argument.[2]

For Crisp, Mill departs from the monistic utilitarianism of Bentham and is genuine in his account of a distinction between classes of pleasure which do not merely result in differences of intensity and duration of pleasurableness. How does the argument work? Crisp suggests that Mill abandons the idea of full cardinality between pleasures—this is the view that it is not merely possible to say that poetry is better than pub games, but it is also possible to give some measure of how much more valuable poetry is than pub games. Instead, Mill operates merely with an ordinal ranking of pleasures, which is to say that poetry is better than pushpin, but without being able to say by how much. What explains the difference between types of pleasure is not merely the dimensions of intensity and duration—that the intellectual pleasures are more intense and long-lasting than the intense but fleeting pleasures of the flesh—but rather the intrinsic character of the pleasures themselves. But this seems to beg the question what makes the intrinsic character of a higher pleasure superior to that of a lower pleasure. If it is not intensity and duration, then it seems that Mill is introducing a standard other than pleasure and as such he is not revising but rather abandoning hedonism. Mill's argument for the reality of the qualitative distinction between higher and lower pleasures proceeds by the introduction of moral experts or those who, having experienced both of two pleasures, one higher and one lower, would not give up the higher pleasure for any amount of the lower. Such experts raise a number of questions, not least of which is whether there are such people. What Mill's argument does illustrate is that what distinguishes the higher and lower pleasures is some experiential feature other than intensity and duration. Crisp goes on to suggest that this experienceable intrinsic nature does not need to be cashed out in terms of some quantity of value but can itself be an irreducible dimension of value. He draws a parallel with Bentham's attitude to the value of pleasure itself. For Bentham, pleasure just is the criterion of value; there is nothing further in virtue of which pleasure can be identified as valuable. In a similar way Crisp suggests that the intrinsic nature of a pleasure is also a brute fact—it is simply a fact that someone experiencing the intrinsic nature of a certain higher pleasure will value it higher than a lower pleasure. Thus within the individual life of an experienced observer the value of a higher pleasure is just recognized as being more valuable, but that difference in value cannot be reduced to some finite sum of a fungible quality.

For Mill, according to Crisp, the higher and lower pleasures are incommensurable. In this his argument is similar to that of another recent commentator on Mill, John Gray, who suggests that Mill has a neo-Aristotelian or eudaimonistic view of well-being.[3] On this view the good for man is composed of numerous constituent goods, such as pleasure, individuality, and autonomy, and these cannot be traded off against each other in terms of some simple standard such as dimension or intensity of pleasure. Crisp does not offer a fully eudaimonstic account of Mill's psychology, but his recognition of the incommensurability of higher and lower pleasures does have important consequences for ethical hedonism. The most significant of these consequences is that it rules out the possibility of constructing a general welfare function by summing the welfare of individuals. Bentham's ethical hedonism certainly acknowledged the enormous practical difficulties in constructing such a social welfare function, but his psychological hedonism did not rule it out. Mill's argument rules out this possibility altogether, according to Crisp. As Mill did not have access to a conception of preference utilitarianism (which was not developed until Edgeworth and Jevons later in the nineteenth century) Crisp's interpretation suggests that Mill was not interested in constructing an account of the general welfare by aggregating individual utilities.

Jonathan Riley offers an alternative view of Mill's distinction which tracks closely that offered by Crisp, but which avoids its counter-utilitarian consequences. Riley is more equivocal on the question of whether Mill abandoned a commitment to a cardinal ranking of pleasures. Instead of ruling this out altogether he provides an account of the distinction between higher and lower pleasures which trades on its practical difficulties. For Riley, pleasures can only be valued in terms of their intensity and duration, and the intrinsic natures of higher pleasures also have to be reducible to the dimensions of intensity and duration. This, however, seems to force Mill back into the position of merely making a rhetorical point rather than genuinely making a categorical distinction between higher and lower pleasures. Higher pleasures are simply more pleasurable in terms of intensity and duration than lower pleasures. However, Riley goes on to suggest that there is still a point in the categorical distinction, for the differences in pleasureableness are almost (or for practical purposes *are*) infinite. Thus if we go back to the experts who have experienced both higher and lower pleasures, we can make sense of their refusal to renounce the higher pleasures for the lower on the grounds that there is no finite sum of a lower pleasure that would compensate them for the loss of a higher pleasure. In terms of Mill's broader interests, there is no finite sum of sensual pleasure that would compensate for the denial of liberty and individuality.

On Riley's interpretation the near-infinite differences in pleasureableness between higher and lower pleasures makes any attempt to compensate the loss of a higher pleasure with a lower pleasure practically impossible. It does not, however, rule out the possibility or meaningfulness of aspiring to sum all individual welfare functions into a social welfare function, as does Crisp and Gray's view. As Mill retains a commitment to the idea of the greatest happiness principle, Riley's view is more fitting with this part of Mill's argument. Mill remains committed to a monistic theory of value, however much he may complicate that view, and as such he does not expressly abandon the idea of commensurability. That said, he goes much further than Bentham in recognizing the practical limitations on aggregating individual utilities, almost to the point of turning it into no more than a regulative ideal.

However, there is a further reason for retaining the Riley interpretation, and that is that it does not completely deny the possibility of trade-offs between what are taken to be higher pleasures and lower pleasures. This is important because Mill relies on putative experts to distinguish the higher from the lower pleasures. However, all putative claims that certain ends are categorically superior to others must in the end be open to the possibility of revision, no matter how unlikely it is that the revision of some judgements will ever need to be made. Thus in any particular case the judgement of an expert is always conditional on whether that person is genuinely a moral expert. What falls within the class of higher and lower pleasures will always be subject to dispute as it is a matter of judgement; consequently, whether trade-offs between higher and lower pleasures are possible must remain potentially revisable even if for all practical purposes the distinction is unlikely to be overturned.

As Mill remains wedded to the basic naturalistic structure of ethical and psychological hedonism, any revision he makes to those theories must nevertheless remain consistent with the ultimate empirical constraints of a naturalistic moral theory. In those circumstances Riley's attempt to balance the claims of utilitarianism and empiricism without at the same time reducing Mill's distinction to a mere rhetorical ploy remains among the most plausible accounts of how Mill attempted to rescue psychological hedonism from the charge that it is the philosophy of swine.

## Utilitarian liberalism

While Mill's psychological hedonism proved controversial for his contemporaries, by far the biggest concern for recent commentators has been his attempt to derive his robust defence of individual liberty from his utilitarian moral theory. This issue has become all the more acute since John Rawls's indictment of utilitarianism as an anti-liberal philosophy because of its failure to offer person-regarding constraints such as civil and political rights that are immune to judgements of social advantage.[4]

Mill clearly thought of himself as a liberal, and he remains a central character in the history of liberalism, so how does he avoid the charge that he subordinates liberal values, such as rights and freedom, to judgements of utility that are liable to undermine such values? This question is particularly acute for Mill because, unlike Bentham or later utilitarians, he attaches a great deal of weight to individual liberty. Mill writes:

> the sole end for which mankind are warranted, individually or collectively, in interfering with the liberty of action of any of their member, is self-protection. That the only purpose for which power can be rightfully exercised over any member of a civilized community, against his will, is to prevent harm to others. His own good, either physical or moral, is not a sufficient warrant. (p. 14)

This famous statement would seem to suggest that, even if the limitation of liberty would result in much greater social happiness, that is not a sufficient justification. How does this square with his statement in *Utilitarianism* that 'The creed which accepts as the foundation of morals, Utility, or the Greatest Happiness Principle, holds that actions are right in proportion as they tend to promote happiness, wrong as they produce the reverse of happiness' (p. 137)? On the one side we have a robust defence of act-utilitarianism and on the other side we have one of the most robust defences of liberalism and the priority of liberty. We cannot simply explain away this inconsistency in terms of the peculiar point of each work, because even in *On Liberty* Mill claims that he builds his account of liberty on the foundations of utility (p. 15). There is supposed to be philosophical consistency between these works, but the apparent inconsistency is glaring. Was Mill simply unaware of this? Some unsympathetic critics wish to dismiss Mill as a sloppy thinker riddled with inconsistencies and errors. But that is to trivialize Mill's achievement. Yet, if there is some possible means of reconciling these two dimensions of his thought, how is it done?

The most sophisticated recent defences of Mill have begun with a return to his utilitarianism. In a series of highly influential papers David Lyons began to set out an account of Mill as an indirect utilitarian. This approach was developed by subsequent commentators such as John Gray and more recently by Jonathan Riley and his optimal rule-utilitarian interpretation.[5] Rule-utilitarians argue that social welfare is not best maximized by individuals trying to calculate what particular action to pursue on each occasion. Instead agents should be guided by rules that indirectly result in the maximization of utility. The key question faced by rule-utilitarians is what is the status of these rules? If they are simply 'rules of thumb', or short cuts for practical deliberation, then they must themselves be justified in terms of utility. But such 'rules of thumb' are always potentially revisable in light of the additional utility derived from making exceptions. Thus, one might conceive of a rule in favour of freedom of speech as generally maximizing utility because of the expansion of knowledge, the challenging of false beliefs, and accountability of government. However, a utilitarian might accept this but say a general right of free speech is justified on utilitarian grounds, but a general right excluding offensive speech is even better at maximizing utility. So we could have a principle of free speech covering all forms of expression except 'hate speech' or pornography. The problem with the rule of thumb approach is that it seems to repeat the initial problem because it always leaves the scope of the rule subject to the constraints of utility.

In response to this argument ideal-rule-utilitarians have argued that the rules are ideal guides to what maximizes utility over classes of action and not simply time-saving short cuts for act-utilitarian deliberation. In this way they directly determine the obligations, rights, and duties of individual agents. Agents, whether individual citizens, legislators, or politicians, are guided by these rules in determining how they ought to act. The rules are the *direct* source of obligation. Calculations of utility are only *indirect* sources of obligation through their role in justifying the rules. On this indirect view, individuals are not required to make direct calculations of act utility as part of practical deliberation. This might be justified on a variety of grounds. One might argue that most individuals are never able to make accurate utility calculations because of limits of time and resources. Alternatively, one might focus on coordination conditions and the interconnectedness of acts so that no single decision can be separated from its connection with the decisions of others. For example, a judgement of utility is going to depend on judgements about the expectations of others, yet these expectations are themselves potentially vulnerable to such individual calculations or utility.

The question remains, however, that while it may be possible to defend a robust liberty principle in the way indirect utilitarians suggest, Mill does seem to endorse direct act-utilitarianism in the opening sections of *Utilitarianism* when he provides the 'proportionality' criterion of right and wrong. Lyons has, however, argued that Mill also offered a more sophisticated account of moral and legal obligation in chapter v of *Utilitarianism*, 'On the Connection between Justice and Utility'. Here Mill seems to acknowledge precisely the point raised by contemporary liberal critics. Instead of reducing questions of justice to simple calculations of utility, Mill offers what Lyons and subsequent revisionist scholars describe as a sanction-based theory of obligation. This claims that the concept of obligation or duty is analytically connected to the liability to suffer a sanction. Thus an agent is only ever under an obligation when failure to perform a certain action would justify the imposition of a sanction or punishment. This is the punishability criterion of rightness or duty that is defended by Mill in chapter v of *Utilitarianism* when he writes:

> We do not call anything wrong, unless we mean to imply that a person ought to be punished in some way or other for doing it; if not by law, by the opinion of his fellow creatures; if not by opinion, by the reproaches of his own conscience. This seems the real turning point of the distinction between morality and simple expediency. It is a part of the notion of Duty in every one of its forms, that a person may rightfully be compelled to fulfil it. Duty is a thing that may be extracted from a person, as one exacts a debt. (p. 184)

From this passage Lyons derives the conclusion that obligations, whether moral, legal, or political, are derived from the liability to suffer sanctions. The principle of utility as conveyed in the 'proportionality' criterion is not a direct source of moral obligations, as these depend upon sanctions, which in turn are related to moral rules. Rules are sanctioned by the threat of coercive punishment, as Mill suggests in conceding that 'duty can be extracted from a person'. This is most clear in the case of legal rules, where the law specifies punishments for non-compliance. Yet Mill attaches the criterion of 'punishability' to all obligations. In the moral case this means that someone is under a duty when their failure to comply with a rule should result in punishment or the imposition of a sanction. Moral obligations depend on the enforcement or sanctioning of moral rules. This does not mean that Mill is not a utilitarian or that he argues that any existing set of conventional moral rules and their respective sanctions give rise to morally justified obligations. After all, conventional morality may well include all sorts of moral strictures which a utilitarian could not justify, especially one as devoted to liberty, individuality, and self-culture as J. S. Mill. Moral obligations need to be connected to considerations of utility, and it because of this indirect connection that Lyons and others describe Mill as an indirect utilitarian.

One might conclude that this view still fits the view of Mill as a direct act-utilitarian, so that failure to comply with the principle of utility merits punishment. This, however, is an unrealistically rigorous interpretation of Mill and does not take seriously the rest of his discussion of justice. Here Mill refers the discussion of justice and the related concepts of right and duty to a subset of harms to people's most vital or weighty interests. In this way, not any action that creates disutility or pain for a person necessarily constitutes a harm, in the way in which Mill uses the term. Not getting the last slice of pie might cause me some disutility in terms of frustrated greed, but this does not mean that I have been harmed, nor does it mean that others should be punished for not giving me the last slice of pie. Mill provides an account of the language of moral right, wrong, duty, and obligation as growing up around an understanding of what our most important interests are.

Those commentators who describe Mill as a liberal utilitarian argue that the priority of liberty and individuality in his thought must entail his rejection of a direct variant of act-utilitarianism. Mill cannot have meant that all actions are to be judged in terms of the utilitarian consequences if he meant that we should accept absolute liberty in the sphere of self-regarding actions. The important works of Gray and Riley develop this general approach pioneered by Lyons. Thus actions that violate my self-regarding sphere are actions that deserve punishment, as the liberty principle connects with my most basic interests. In this way the argument of *On Liberty* connects very closely with this account of Mill's utilitarianism. Of course this still leaves open a major issue of showing why, in utilitarian terms, liberty is such a central human interest that it must result in a libertarian political order. Gray concludes that it is this issue that shows up the weaknesses of Mill's liberal utilitarianism rather than the fact that liberalism must collapse into individual judgements of utility. For Mill's defence of liberty does not merely require that liberty and individuality are central human interests but rather that they are the *overriding* human interests. For Gray, Mill's utilitarianism fails because it must assume that there is some unique form to a good or valuable life that attaches priority to the ideal of individuality when in fact there are many forms of valuable life that do not attach overriding significance to the concept of liberty. In the end, Gray argues, Mill must be committed to a giant wager that the ideal of individuality and freedom will have overriding value to people. As Mill's moral psychology is naturalistic, he cannot simply assume this as an a priori truth. History and psychology might well show (indeed probably do show) that people are happy with modest restrictions on liberty in order to secure other goods. Mill's robust defence of the ideal of individuality might just be too demanding to support even an indirect utilitarian justification of an ideal moral code based around his principle of liberty.

Yet, despite the sophistication of indirect readings of Mill's utilitarianism, they have not persuaded all recent scholars, and they have not done so for the important reason that they still need to explain the 'proportionality' criterion, rather than just abandon it in favour of the 'punishability' criterion. Focusing solely on the latter might seem a selective reading rather than a fair interpretation of Mill's real argument. The most influential recent discussion of Mill offered by the late Fred Berger provides a reconciliationist view combining a commitment to both the 'punishability' and 'proportionality' criteria. Berger's approach does not involve the straightforward denial of Lyons's thesis, but it does suggest that this was not the only standard by which to determine right and wrong. One could also refer to the 'proportionality' criterion. The 'reconciliationist' thesis suggests that the principle of utility can serve as a direct standard of moral conduct, and not simply as a principle for determining among ultimate ends. There are numerous passages through Mill's voluminous writings in which he uses either the 'proportionality' or the 'punishability' criterion. This might simply indicate a further level of inconsistency in Mill's thought. Fortunately, we can offer a general interpretation of Mill's enterprise which combines the two approaches. This reconciliationist approach is fundamentally act-utilitarian, thus abandoning the claim (most forcefully defended by Gray) that the principle of utility does not feature in moral deliberation. Conceding this role for act utility calculations in moral deliberation does not, however, entail that all practical deliberation is exhausted by direct utility calculations. Such a view would certainly undermine a liberal utilitarianism, but equally it would be unbearably demanding, so that, even if Mill thought it was what utilitarianism entailed, it would stand as a strong argument against the theory. Instead we need to distinguish between different aspects of moral deliberation. Thus we can appeal at one level to calculations of utility to determine rightness. The principle of utility as a criterion of rightness does not entail anything about what we should choose to do. This second aspect of practical deliberation might be best pursued by appeal to subordinate rules such as those of justice or the principle of liberty. The best way of achieving the goal of utilitarianism will normally involve acting in accordance with elaborate social practices such as 'common-sense' morality or the legal system suitably reformed. This might seem to collapse back into the indirect theory built around the 'punishability' criterion, but it differs in important respects. It accepts the 'indirect' theorists' view that the direct pursuit of utility can be self-defeating and have counter-utilitarian consequences, hence the role it gives to subordinate systems of rules and practices for most cases of practical deliberation. However, it differs from the 'indirect' theorists' position in that it does not make the account of rightness an indirect matter. For most indirect utilitarians the criterion of rightness is determined by subordinate rules, and not merely what one should do. The reconciliationist view allows the 'proportionality' criterion to function as the standard of rightness but allows subordinate rules, often of considerable weight, to determine how we should act.

Thus utilitarianism can accommodate liberalism at the appropriate level. For Mill the principle of liberty is not the criterion of rightness. At no stage does he suggest in *On Liberty* that his 'one very simple principle' functions in this way. Consequently, there is no need to resort to indirect theories to make sense of Mill's utilitarian liberalism. However, at the level of what we should do, Mill can quite legitimately argue that the principle of liberty is an overriding rule limiting the actions of individuals and government alike. This still leaves open the question why we should attach such significance to utility over other valuable ends of life. In the next section I will look at Mill's defence of the ideal of liberty and the charge that it is an illiberal religion of humanity. What is clear is that, despite the concerns of many contemporary anti-utilitarian liberals, there is no reason why Mill's utilitarianism in itself must expose a gaping contradiction in his thought.

## The illiberal liberal

Although Mill is undoubtedly a utilitarian, he is also a liberal utilitarian, and his commitment to liberty, particularly as it is defended in *On Liberty*, is commonly taken as the defining feature of his political thought. His account of the problem or threat to liberty and his defence of the ideal of freedom and individuality is complex, multifaceted, and controversial. Different aspects of his doctrine have been subject to criticism since the time of *On Liberty*'s publication in 1859. Some of these criticisms refer to the internal logic of his argument such as whether it is possible to define a realm of purely self-regarding action, or whether we must confer only conditional assent on all beliefs no matter how apparently certain. However, there have also been more substantive challenges to Mill's argument which do not simply turn on lacunae in his reasoning, but which challenge the whole philosophy of individuality which underpins his defence of the 'one very simple principle'. Certain critics have suggested that Mill's conception of liberty is actually based on an illiberal or perfectionist moral ideal which undermines a genuine tolerance of different choices and beliefs. In fact Mill is a highly illiberal liberal. Joseph Hamburger has defended this position most recently, but it is a persistent criticism of Mill's argument. Before turning to an assessment of this charge I will begin with an outline of Mill's defence of the ideal of liberty.

Mill's defence of liberty begins with an analysis of the main threats to freedom. Traditionally, liberals have been concerned with the way in which government as a sinister interest could tyrannize over the individual and subject her to coercive power. This was certainly a concern of thinkers such as John Milton and John Locke, as well as Bentham and James Mill. *On Liberty* opens with a history of the struggle for liberty and an account of how the threat to it has changed. Bentham thought that the problem of holding government accountable could be solved by representative democracy with an extensive franchise. James Mill's solution to the problem of government was to hold political power accountable to a 'representative class'. This class was the emerging middle class of small businessmen and owners of property. The property qualification was no longer confined to the large landed interests, but was extended to owners of movable property such as capital, thus giving considerable power to the business classes. This creation of a 'representative class' poses a new social threat to freedom which is not simply dealt with by extending the franchise, as this new form of social tyranny can be exercised through these reformed constitutional structures. John Stuart Mill saw the social changes that his father had placed such trust in as creating new threats to liberty. Thus the liberal cause needs to turn its attention to this new threat, and it is precisely this call to arms that underpins *On Liberty*. Modernity and rapid industrialization presented considerable opportunities for increasing social welfare; however, it also had its negative consequences, and it is these that animate Mill and separate his liberalism from the concerns of Bentham and his father.

Industrialization creates mass society. This can manifest itself in a number of ways: first, through the rise of the masses with their claim for levelling property distinctions. While Mill was certainly conscious of the revolutionary dangers of such claims, he was not unsympathetic to the desire for a more economically equal society. The second threat of mass society is the pressure of opinion and the imperative of conformity. Mill saw the representative class in which his father had placed such faith as posing a threat to individuality by its oppressive moral conformism. The virtues of sobriety, thrift, and industry are all essential for the progress of a commercial society. However, these virtues are also closely associated with particularly oppressive and paternalistic versions of Christian nonconformism. Non-Protestant versions of Christianity also posed a threat to liberty, although much less so in Britain after the Glorious Revolution, but the Protestant underpinnings of the virtues of commercial society and their increasing dominance posed a serious threat to the cultivation of individuality and freedom of the spirit. In this way Mill also reflects the way in which the representative class had assimilated a desiccated version of utilitarianism. This is well illustrated in terms of Charles Dickens's Mr Gradgrind from *Hard Times*. The representative class can thus pose a considerable threat to liberty by creating a culture in which informal pressures to conform are every bit as coercive as the pressures exercised through the levers of public power. Mill writes:

> when society is itself the tyrant—society collectively over the separate individuals who compose it—its means of tyrannising are not restricted to the acts which it may do by the hands of its public functionaries. Society can and does execute its own mandates: and if it issues wrong mandates instead of

right, or any mandates at all in things which it ought not to meddle, it practises a social tyranny more formidable than many kinds of political oppression, since though not usually upheld by such extreme penalties, it leaves fewer means of escape, penetrating much more deeply into the details of life, and enslaving the soul itself. (p. 8)

Consequently, the defence of liberty in *On Liberty* has two main parts. There is a defence of a constitutional norm, or the liberty principle, which rules out paternalism by restricting government interference with the individual to the prevention of harm to others. The liberty principle specifies the scope and limits of government interference. However, as we have seen, the real target of Mill's concern is not the levers of public power or the direction in which they should be exercised. Rather it is with the social threat to liberty, and in answer to this he offers a defence of an ideal of liberty and individuality as a philosophy of life. It is this latter aspect of Mill's argument that has raised the charge of Mill's fundamental illiberalism. Before turning to that issue I will provide an overview of Mill's liberty principle.

This 'one very simple principle' at the heart of Mill's essay has been the subject of considerable debate. It is in fact anything but simple. The main problem for the principle arises from its scope. Mill argues that 'the sole end for which mankind are warranted, individually or collectively, in interfering with the liberty of action of any of their number, is self-protection', or as he puts it later, 'to prevent harm to others' (p. 14). This idea is supposed to be simple, but raises many questions. The liberty principle is supposed to designate a sphere of self-regarding actions over which the individual is sovereign, and the only limits on this sphere are that actions do not harm others. Thus, if I want to use narcotic drugs, like heroin, that is my concern, unless I have to steal property or cause violence to others in order to obtain the drug. I can drink myself into a stupor unless I am a train driver or a soldier on duty. The context of whether an action is the concern of others and therefore a matter of public regulation depends on whether it is harmful to others. That it might well be harmful to the individual concerned is not the state's concern. It is no part of government's role to make men moral or even healthy if they should choose to engage in dangerous activities that are dangerous to themselves alone. This is Mill's famous critique of paternalism, or the idea that government should exercise the role of a parent, in relation to its citizens. This is but a further extension and development of Locke's rejection of patriarchalism, which also sees the role of government in paternalistic terms.

However, Mill's anti-paternalism has raised a number of problems. In the case of distinguishing exercises of self-regarding action, must we assume perfect knowledge? Can an individual experimenting with dangerous drugs, or other forms of expressive behaviour, be assumed to have a full knowledge of the risks involved? And if not, does this qualify the extent to which the person concerned is responsible for the outcomes? Or can paternalism be defended in terms of providing the conditions in which genuinely informed free choices can be made? If this view is adopted, then it would seriously qualify Mill's commitment to liberty as it would open the door to a highly active regulatory state. But if we reject that option, as Mill suggests, then we are faced with a world in which much health and safety legislation is ruled out and in which the simplest actions turn out to be potentially life-threatening. Again Mill has to square his extensive commitment to personal liberty with the apparent conflict with the general welfare.

More importantly, it is consistently argued by many anti-libertarian critics of Mill that the very idea of a realm of purely self-regarding actions is an empty set. There are no purely self-regarding actions. All our actions have an impact on others whether we like it or not. If I choose to adopt some experiment in living, that might harm my children by depriving them of care and resources; furthermore, it might harm my parent's reputation or that of my employer. Those around me might claim to be harmed by the feelings of distaste on injury to feelings that they claim follows from experiencing my actions and lifestyle. If all of these apparent harms are a justification for restricting liberty, then again we are faced with a realm of self-regarding action so small as to be non-existent. In that case Mill's defence of liberty is nothing of the sort. It merely results in a utilitarian regulative state.

Can Mill's distinction between self- and other-regarding actions be sustained? In order to make the distinction we need to provide an account of harm which limits its scope. In a recent defence of Mill's distinction Jonathan Riley has argued that

> Harm is something other than mere dislike, namely 'perceptible damage' suffered against one's wishes. (By implication, self-harm must be unintentional on this view.) It may appear in myriad forms, including physical injury (not excepting death), forcible confinement, financial loss, damage to reputation, broken promises (contractual or otherwise) and so on. Unlike self-regarding choices, other-regarding conduct directly harms others in one of these ways, or carries a reasonable probability of doing so.[6]

In order to restrict the scope of this concept of harm, Riley claims that Mill distinguished between natural penalties of actions and external or coercive penalties. Thus, according to Mill, it is perfectly legitimate for a person who is a 'born-again' Christian to express his dislike of his openly 'gay' neighbour by avoiding his company. He is not, however, entitled to impose civil disabilities on that person, or to try to campaign for that person's actions to be criminalized. Furthermore, if he is a bank manager, he cannot use his legitimate dislike of the 'gay' lifestyle to influence his commercial decisions. But it is equally illegitimate for the 'gay' man to claim that he is harmed because the 'born-again' Christian regards his lifestyle as depraved or sinful. Nobody has a right to be liked or approved of, and if individuals are allowed liberty to determine their own beliefs and lifestyles, then this is inevitably going to raise issues of dispute and disapproval. Similarly, a person cannot be harmed in the relevant sense by an action if he or she could freely avoid it. Thus one cannot be harmed by what goes on in someone else's bedroom, no matter how depraved one may regard the consensual private behaviour of others. Nor can one be harmed because other people read books or newspapers with which one disagrees and disapproves. What Mill wants to defend above all else is the view that this kind of disagreement is part of the demands of liberty and not a basis for social control and regulation. Disapproval and disagreement is a central dynamic force in a modern progressive society. Part of the confusion that persists over Mill's distinction rests on the view that the distinction between self- and other-regarding spheres should result in harmony and not dispute and disagreement, but there is no reason why this should be the case. What Mill is concerned to show is that the commitment to liberty is demanding both morally and politically, but it is not a social problem that needs to be legislated out of existence in order to create social harmony. But disagreement and dispute would seem to raise precisely the sort of issues that would lead an act-utilitarian to deny Mill's libertarianism. Mill needs to show why this demanding social ideal is in the long run also a utilitarian ideal. To make this case Mill focuses on the advantages of unrestricted liberty of thought and discussion and an ideal of personal liberty expressed through 'experiments in living'.

The commitment to freedom of speech and discussion and to 'experiments in living' underpin Mill's ideal of 'individuality', but they also raise the criticism that this ideal is simply one 'particular' moral view that is to be imposed on everyone else. As such Mill's ideal of liberty is far less libertarian than is often supposed, and, as Joseph Hamburger has recently argued, it is deliberately designed to challenge the moral authority of Christianity.

The utilitarian defence of freedom of speech and discussion turns on a concern with social and moral progress. Mill was ultimately concerned with very profound questions about what makes a life go well or have value. In response to crude psychological hedonists Mill defended the view that human nature is not simply passive and therefore a fulfilling life cannot simply be reduced to the passive sensations of pleasure. The highest pleasures are associated with the cultivation of active faculties such as the intellect, and therefore the best life will involve the cultivation and exercise of our intelligence and creativity in the arts, literature, science, philosophy, ethics, and politics. Mill was deeply influenced by the ethical and moral thought of the ancient Greeks from the time of his earliest education; consequently, it is not anachronistic to see in Mill the reflection of the Socratic ideal that the unexamined life is not worth living. Without this commitment to self-culture human societies become static and face cultural stagnation and then decline. As Mill also thought that economic growth was ultimately finite, it was likely that mankind would soon reach a stage where the only possible development of human potential was in the spheres of culture, philosophy, and morality.

It is this Socratic ideal which grounds his commitment to freedom of speech and self-culture, but it is also this ideal which puts him in conflict with the moral authority exercised by organized religion. For it denies the fact that any moral perspective can be complete and fully authoritative, and this challenges the idea of revealed religion and the authority of Churches to assert the teachings of revealed religion.

In opposition to the authoritative pronouncements of revealed religion, Mill asserts the problem of human falliblism that he inherits from Hume. For Mill the quest for knowledge requires that there is a competition between beliefs, hence his commitment to unrestricted freedom of thought and speech. It is only by allowing all views to enter into debate that we can test the truth of opinions and open up the possibility of scientific progress. And even if the balance of probability makes a certain belief apparently incontrovertible, there is still value in allowing debate as this is essential for 'truth' to retain its vitality and for people to understand the reasons for holding a belief. For Mill there is never any utility in subordinating judgement exclusively to an authority such as a Church. Without the constant test of debate and controversy, scientific progress is frustrated and social progress will wither. Furthermore, there is never a reason for censuring beliefs as such. That said, the context in which beliefs are expressed might provide a reason for restricting expression. Thus, for Mill, one has every right to hold the view that all corn dealers are thieves and to publish this in pamphlets and books. One does not, however, have the right to shout this to an angry crowd outside a corn dealer's house. Restricting the context of expression, however, can never extend to restricting the content of speech, no matter how repugnant someone's views may seem. Thus, while Mill would have no trouble with restricting incitement to racial violence, he would also have no time for the idea of 'hate speech' where the mere expression of certain views is itself a harm. Holocaust deniers, racists, homophobes, and any other category of bigots are all entitled to hold, and be protected in expressing, their beliefs, on Mill's theory. But the real challenge to revealed religion comes not simply from the contest of opinion, where religious beliefs must compete alongside atheistic views. The main challenge is the implicit denial of authority in moral and political reasoning. Authorities are to be held to account before the public tribunal of individual reason and judgement. Religion has no privileged status.

Mill makes a similar case in his defence of the ideal of individuality. Again he asserts the necessity of experiments in living (the accommodation of unconventional lifestyles and relationships) as a means to personal growth and self-culture and as a means of discovering the nature of the good life. Even though Mill had defended the idea of higher pleasures and moral experts in *Utilitarianism*, he is particularly sensitive to the claims for moral expertise. Moral expertise depends upon the challenge of experiencing alternative lifestyles and relationships. No one can claim that they have the definitive account of the good life for mankind and impose it on others. This is because from a personal perspective the good life cannot be imposed from the outside, but must be endorsed from the inside: Mill asserts the autonomy of the moral subject in the face of claims of authority. But, furthermore, Mill is concerned that the substance of the good life is not fixed and static for all time. The tyranny of mass society has the effect of turning the conventional practices into received and unquestioned truths that must be imposed on all. Yet we cannot be certain that we have acquired the truth in morality and ethics any more than we can in the natural sciences.

Mill's defence of the long-term utility of liberty rests on these two themes of falliblism and autonomy. However, it is these two themes that have also opened him to the charge of moral totalitarianism. Together they constitute a controversial conception of the moral life which is contradicted by alternative conceptions, especially those rooted in the Christian religion. However, Mill does not offer this ideal of individuality as a possible answer to the Socratic question about the nature of the good life for man. Instead it is suggested that he offers this as an account of the form of the good life. Consequently, any moral view that depends upon intellectual and practical submission to a moral or religious authority is failing to lead a good life. Mill is not impartial in this matter, but is an advocate of an irreligious moral individualism that undermines the notion of a Christian moral life. For critics such as Maurice Cowling,[7] Mill's ideal of individuality gives rise to a moral elite who, through their challenges to the conventions of common-sense morality, subvert the hold of religion on social life. Mill and his wife, Harriet, who enjoyed an 'unconventional relationship' during the lifetime of Harriet's first husband, would be examples of the liberal elite, challenging the conventions and norms of society and surreptitiously imposing their own radically individualist views on society by undermining the basis of conventional norms and practices. For Cowling, Mill is not really a liberal at all, for he does not believe in letting people alone; instead he is a moral perfectionist, trying to remake man in his own image.

A subtler and more scholarly version of the same charge has been resurrected by Joseph Hamburger.[8] For Hamburger, Mill is mounting an assault on the prevalent morality of Christianity in order to replace it with his religion of humanity. Hamburger's argument is much more subtle than Cowling's in that it does not depend solely on a tendentious reading of *On Liberty*, but is actually rooted in considerable scholarship about Mill's views on the role of religion throughout his writings. Mill was undoubtedly hostile to the way in which Christian moral precepts were used as a basis for social coercion and uniformity. Mill certainly found much of what passed for religion and popular morality as contemptible and an obstacle to social progress and reform. One must remember, in confronting Mill's robust views about religion, that, unlike many of his Victorian contemporaries, he did not go through a crisis of faith as he had never had any religious faith in the first place.

However, holding views contrary to the prevailing religious and moral views of society is not the same as imposing an irreligious religion of humanity on the wider society. Hamburger tries to bolster his claim that Mill was illiberal and intolerant of those who wished to adhere to conventional religious beliefs and norms by claiming that Mill wanted to use the sanctions of shame and humiliation to attack the selfishness of an inferior Christian and commercial class: precisely that which he identifies as posing the greatest threat to liberty at the beginning of *On Liberty*. The censorious disapproval of a liberal moral elite, made up of the Mills and those like them, is a form of moral coercion that not only is allowed by Mill's theory of liberty but is actually required by it.

Is this a fair reading of Mill? Certainly, Mill is not a straightforward libertarian in that he defends the value of liberty by means of an ideal of individuality and autonomy. At best Mill is a liberal perfectionist. The question is whether he is prepared to use this perfectionist stance as basis for coercion. Here Hamburger's thesis becomes much more problematic. Undoubtedly, Mill had negative views about revealed religion and its institutional manifestations. And, as we have seen, it was no part of the harm principle to deny individuals the ability to express disgust and disapproval. For Mill, the expression of disgust or disapproval does not undermine the self-regarding sphere of another unless it spills over into perceptible harm. So on Mill's terms the expression of a hostile attitude to religion certainly does not constitute coercion in the relevant sense. Neither religious believers nor the irreligious can expect to be free from criticism, disapproval, or even contempt in Mill's regime of liberty, but that does not mean they are subject to coercion. Thus, although Mill's liberty principle challenges the use of religious authority as a means of social coercion, he does not and cannot deny that some (perhaps many) will continue to find personal meaning and consolation in Christianity or any other religion. Furthermore, he cannot deny others the right to freely pursue Christian experiments in living. Individuals are free to establish monasteries and contemplative communities or commit themselves to living by a rule of life. The only challenge Mill explicitly makes to Christianity is to its institutional role as a source of conventional moral law. No matter how 'inferior' he might have found the religious views of the masses, even Hamburger concedes that Mill found the person and teaching of Jesus an inspiring (although ultimately human) moral ideal, and distinguished it from the institutional Christian Churches. This remains a self-regarding matter on which Mill's views are ultimately of no more authority than those of anyone else.

What is certainly disputable in both Cowling and Hamburger is the idea that Mill envisaged a superior moral elite capturing the levers of political power and exercising a tyranny over the morally inferior majority. Whatever the private views of Mill and Harriet, there is no evidence that he wanted to institutionalize the role of a moral elite. Indeed all the evidence points in the opposite direction. While Mill certainly alludes to the ideal of moral experts in order to ground his distinction between higher and lower pleasures, he remains sceptical about the claim of any particular group to possess this moral expertise. Indeed the whole thrust of *On Liberty* is concerned with undermining the authority of claims to collective moral expertise. If we turn attention to *Considerations of Representative Government*, where Mill provides a defence of the institutionalization of liberty, we can find many provisions for the role of expertise in public policy-making coupled with traditional liberal protections against such policy experts exercising a coercive role over 'inferior' subjects. Mill's constitutionalism remains distinctively liberal, unlike the views of later Fabian socialists, who were much happier with rule by a technocratic elite of socialist experts. While Mill was certainly in favour of integrating the lessons of the social sciences into enlightened public policy-making, he retained a healthy Benthamite scepticism to the governing class becoming an interest apart from that of the subject many. All his views about local government, the separation between public policy-making and legislation, plural voting, and the extension of the franchise were designed to facilitate wise policy-making at the same time as preventing any elite from permanently capturing the levers of political power. In terms of constitutionalism, Mill's concern was to educate the masses into the exercise of political power and to protect the subject many from tyranny by a ruling elite. In contrast to Hamburger and Cowling's fear of an illiberal totalitarianism, Mill remains wedded to distinctively liberal political principles and institutions, despite his reliance on fallibilism and the ideal of individuality as a means of justifying them. And all of this is perfectly compatible with whatever views he might have held about the sources of mid-Victorian conventional morality. Despite his scholarship Hamburger's critique of Mill as a moral totalitarian and illiberal liberal is deeply suspect and incompatible with important aspects of Mill's political philosophy.

## Conclusion

Although Mill's philosophy starts out as a revision of the legacy of Hume and Bentham, his concern for the ambiguous legacy of modernity with its threat to civilization and culture posed by mass society places him in the curious company of the nineteenth century's other great critics of modernity Karl Marx and Friedrich Nietzsche. All saw their times as a period in which the familiar categories of social and political theorizing would no longer have a resonance. Like Nietzsche, Mill is also drawing out the intimations of post-Christian social and political order, and how one makes sense of a disenchanted world. To this extent Mill casts a long shadow over moral and political philosophy in the succeeding century as it tried to wrestle with providing an alternative to naturalism as a basis for a liberal order. This is still the issue that is at the heart of contemporary Rawlsian liberalism. However, Mill's legacy is also interesting for another reason. Following Mill, utilitarianism appears to have relinquished the aspiration to defend a liberal constitutional order. For Mill political philosophy was at the heart of moral theory. However, by the time we get to Henry Sidgwick and the birth of modern moral philosophy at the end of the nineteenth century, we have a conception of utilitarianism as a meta-ethical doctrine about justification, and a complete rupture between utilitarianism and the defence of political and moral liberty. Following Sidgwick, utilitarianism becomes a technical academic vocabulary and political philosophy becomes a matter of technical policy-making best dealt with by the new disciplines of economics and constitutional law. It is not until the fundamental challenge posed to utilitarianism by Rawls's contractualist liberalism in the 1970s that utilitarianism begins to return to insights offered by John Stuart Mill.

---

### FURTHER READING

Berger, F., *Happiness, Justice and Freedom* (Berkeley: University of California Press, 1984).

Cowling, Maurice, *Mill and Liberalism* (Cambridge: Cambridge University Press, 1963).

Crisp, Roger, *Mill on Utilitarianism* (London: Routledge, 1997).

Gray, John, *Mill on Liberty: A Defence* (London: Routledge, 1983).
Hamburger, Joseph, *John Stuart Mill on Liberty and Control* (Princeton: Princeton University Press, 1999).
Lyons, D., *Rights, Welfare and Mill's Moral Theory* (Oxford: Oxford University Press, 1994).
Riley, Jonathan, *Mill on Liberty* (London: Routledge, 1998).
Riley, Jonathan, 'On Quantities and Qualities of Pleasure', *Utilitas*, 5/2 (1993), 291–300.
Ten, C. L., *Mill on Liberty* (Oxford: Oxford University Press, 1980).
Thomas, W., *Mill* (Oxford: Oxford University Press, 1985).

## NOTES

1. All texts used are from John Stuart Mill, *On Liberty and Other Essays*, ed. John Gray, World's Classics (Oxford: Oxford University Press, 1991).
2. Roger Crisp, *Mill on Utilitarianism* (London: Routledge, 1997), and Jonathan Riley, *Mill on Liberty* (London: Routledge, 1998).
3. John Gray, *Mill on Liberty: A Defence* (London: Routledge, 1983).
4. John Rawls, *A Theory of Justice* (Oxford: Oxford University Press, 1971).
5. Gray, *Mill on Liberty*, and more recently Riley, *Mill on Liberty*.
6. Riley, *Mill on Liberty*, 98.
7. Maurice Cowling, *Mill and Liberalism* (Cambridge: Cambridge University Press, 1963).
8. Joseph Hamburger, *John Stuart Mill on Liberty and Control* (Princeton: Princeton University Press, 1999).

# 20 J. S. Mill on the Subjection of Women

Jennifer Ring

## Contents



## Chapter guide

This chapter is a discussion of John Stuart Mill's *The Subjection of Women*, written in 1861 and published in 1869. The first section considers the context of Mill's intellectual and psychological development leading him to his lifelong commitment to the 'perfect equality' of women and men in the liberal society of his day. It focuses on his rather peculiar relationships to his father, James Mill, and his wife, Harriet Taylor, and surveys the political context in the United States and England, where the women's movement was emerging. The second section is a detailed analysis of the text of *The Subjection of Women*, both critical and appreciative. Focus in this section is upon the political import of the work, as well as its methodological perspective, characteristic of the methodology of liberal empiricist theory with all its strengths and flaws. The third section addresses the impact of Mill's *Subjection of Women* from the perspective of several major contemporary liberal feminist theorists who have written about Mill.

## Biography

John Stuart Mill, eldest child of the Scottish-born historian, philosopher, and economist James Mill, was born in London on 20 May 1806. He received an intensive and thorough classical education from his father, who raised him to be an example of the education made possible by the utilitarian teachings of Jeremy Bentham. John Stuart Mill was to demonstrate the utility of his superior education by becoming a reformer of the world. In fact he did become the most important liberal and utilitarian philosopher of the nineteenth century, whose books range from the multi-volume *A System of Logic*, to the classic treatises on liberal individualism, *Utilitarianism*, *On Liberty*, and *Representative Government*, as well as the controversial *The Subjection of Women*. *The Subjection* was a radical, indeed scandalous, document for its day, advocating as it did a condition of 'perfect equality' between the sexes. His belief in the equality of women was by no means ordinary for a man (or woman) of his day, and scholars attribute his turn to liberal feminism to his relationship with Harriet Taylor, with whom he had been deeply in love since his early twenties, but was unable to marry until some two decades later, when Taylor's husband died. Mill was elected to Parliament in 1865, and soon afterward presented a petition to the House of Commons in favour of women's suffrage, signed by nearly 1,500 women. He advocated changing the wording in Disraeli's Reform Bill of 1867 to read 'person' instead of 'man', and at his death in 1873 left half of his estate to the cause of women's education.

## Key text

*The Subjection of Women* (1869), introd. by Wendell Robert Carr (Cambridge, Mass.: MIT Press, 1982).

## Key ideas

**Subjection, subordination, oppression**: the defining of people by virtue of their membership in a group, and the limiting of their life options on the basis of group 'identity', most often stereotypical and inaccurate. These terms refer to the systematic treatment of members of a group by social, political, and economic institutions. In the case of women, for example, individual women may be wealthy, enjoy privileges, be respected by the men they know personally, and so forth, while still being oppressed *as women*, because society enforces laws limiting the educational, occupational, economic, and legal status and options of women as a group. This is antithetical to the basic tenets of liberalism, which advocates seeing people primarily as individuals. **Nature**: a complicated concept with nearly as many meanings as theorists who use it. It is most often used to imply immutability, immunity to history. When used to refer to women and racial minorities, the political implications of the term 'nature' have been conservative. When we say women are maternal, or emotional, 'by nature', or people of African descent are musical 'by nature', we are implying that no social or cultural experience will ever alter that characteristic: that it is an 'essential' quality, unamenable to the influences of history or education. Theorists such as Mill, who are progressive thinkers, often attempt to dismiss the concept of 'nature', but it is so much a part of how we think that it is very difficult. Mill uses the term 'natural' in different ways, sometimes to mean 'inevitable', either logically or as the result of education; sometimes to mean 'essential', which suffers from the problem of immutability, and tends to work against his progressive political inclinations. **Utilitarianism**: a theory articulated by English philosopher Jeremy Bentham in the late eighteenth century, denying the political significance of 'nature' and 'essences', and suggesting instead that public morality can be legislated by means of two principles: the greatest happiness of the greatest number, and the assumption that all people act so as to maximize pleasure and minimize pain. **Enfranchisement, suffrage**: the right to vote. **Women's rights movement**: a political movement, beginning in the early part of the nineteenth century in both England and the United States, advocating the equality of women in all areas of life, including the right to vote, the right to be regarded as a responsible legal individual, the right to work in the occupation of one's choice, the right to own property, the right to speak in public, and many other social and political rights that we may take for granted today; the nineteenth-century precursor of modern feminism.

---

## Introduction

He was a best-selling author, all of whose previous books had been widely acclaimed. Political and philosophical colleagues had heaped praise upon him, and the works were translated into several European languages (into German by Sigmund Freud, no less). Then, quite suddenly, John Stuart Mill fell from grace. Many of his erstwhile champions deserted him, and Freud ridiculed him in a famous letter to his fiancée. *The Subjection of Women* was turned loose on the world accompanied by a whiff of scandal, private as well as public. Was *The Subjection* that radical in its message? It is essentially a call for reform: nothing revolutionary about it. But the 'perfect equality' between the sexes that Mill advocated has still not been achieved, and the society at which the volume is aimed was so entrenched in its attitude that it seemed outrageous. 'Intimate relations' between the sexes was not regarded as a suitable subject for public discourse. Besides, the publication smacked of the intervention of his notoriously freethinking wife, Harriet Taylor.

From the perspective of today, *The Subjection of Women* seems a work at war with itself: a passion for justice no doubt animated Mill's argument, but he himself was never comfortable with passions of any sort. *The Subjection* begins in passion, then proceeds in the terms of an idealized empirical science, which gave the impression that it was not only, maybe even not primarily, women who were to be vindicated, but the methods and principles of liberal social science. Contemporary feminist theorists are respectful but critical of Mill's treatise. It was certainly one of the earliest, and at that, a powerful and highly visible manifesto of liberal feminism. It is just as certainly inadequate as a vehicle for liberating women from their traditional subjection to the institutionalized patriarchy of liberal democratic society. The majority of feminists writing on Mill find his theory lacking, to a greater or lesser degree, because of its political shortcomings and contradictions.[1] I attribute *The Subjection*'s shortcomings less to a failure of political imagination than to Mill's methodology: his attempt to adhere to his version of early social-scientific empiricism.[2] Here we shall consider the political and intellectual context in which it was written; the content of the essay itself; and finally, its significance from the standpoint of contemporary feminist theory.

## Intellectual and political context

### James Mill and philosophical radicalism

John Stuart Mill was the first-born son of his father, the historian, philosopher, and economist James Mill, and his mother, who is most commonly referred to by Mill scholars, uncharitably, as a 'mindless drudge': certainly no intellectual match for James Mill, but a beautiful woman who bore him nine children. Bruce Mazlish, author of the psychoanalytic biography of the father–son pair, goes so far as to include a blank space in the book's page of photographs with the caption 'John Stuart Mill's Mother'.[3] Whether or not the frequent references to Mrs Mill as a 'beautiful but mindless drudge for her family whose relations with James Mill were never happy'[4] are fair, or the product of scholarly sexual bias, it is evident that John Mill's early life was dominated by his father.

James Mill, the bright son of a poor Scottish cobbler, was brought to the attention of the local nobleman Sir John Stuart, who subsequently sponsored the youth's education in theology at the University of Edinburgh. James Mill never became the preacher he was licensed to be, and instead moved to London, where he was converted to the cause of Philosophic Radicalism by Jeremy Bentham. When James's first son was born, he not only named him after his benefactor, but bequeathed him an education modelled after Bentham's theory: given the right combination of rewards and punishments, even the dullest boy could receive an exemplary education and prove useful to society. John Stuart Mill's entire childhood was given over to this educational experiment, and while he was certainly not the dullest boy in England, he seems to have obliged his father's experiment by believing himself to be of profoundly ordinary intelligence. He was taught Greek at the age of 3 (so early that in his *Autobiography* John claims to have no recollection of ever having not known Greek), Latin, mathematics, grammar, history, exemplary literature, and so forth. He was also given the task of tutoring his younger siblings at the dinner table, where all the children went hungry if the youngsters did not demonstrate sufficient command of the evening's lessons.

In sum John Stuart Mill had no childhood, for his father 'was earnestly bent upon my escaping not only the ordinary corrupting influence which boys exercise over boys, but the contagion of vulgar modes of thought and feeling' (*Autobiography*, 23[5]). Of his father's influence over his early years, John Mill remarks, 'The greatest number of miscarriages in life, he considered to be attributable to the overvaluing of pleasures. . . . For passionate emotions of all sorts, and for everything which has been said or written in exaltation of them, he professed the greatest contempt. He regarded them as a form of madness. "The intense" was with him a byeword of scornful disapprobation' (ibid. 30, 31).

Given this passionless 'childhood', in the apparent absence of any female influence, how could young John possibly emerge as the principal spokesman for liberal feminism in the nineteenth century? In his autobiography he admits to a lack of independence in childhood, the result of his father's unwillingness to expose him to 'the things which boys learn from being turned out to shift for themselves' (ibid. 22). Throughout his childhood and adolescence he had been the obedient product of his father's upbringing. At the age of 15 he had been introduced to the work of his father's mentor, Jeremy Bentham, and from that time on believed he had 'what might truly be called an object in life; to be a reformer of the world' (ibid. 80). Suddenly, in the autumn of his twentieth year, he fell into a depression, a temporary loss of direction, an emotional breakdown that lasted approximately six months. Emerging from that period after reading a passage in Marmontel's *Memoirs* describing the death of Marmontel's father, 'and the sudden inspiration by which he, then a mere boy, felt and made [his mother and sisters] feel that he would be everything to them' (ibid. 85), Mill was revitalized and resumed his work of reforming the world. This episode of psychological dysfunction seems to be as close as Mill ever came to rebelling from his father. The message, if one takes seriously his psychoanalytically naive description of his escape from depression, clearly indicates a need for some independence.

## The emergence of the women's movement

The women's movement was getting started on both sides of the Atlantic in the early 1840s. In the United States the first public demands for women's rights (if one discounts Abigail Adams's ignored plea to her husband to 'remember the ladies' when he and his colleagues were contemplating independence from Britain) came from women activists in the anti-slavery movement. Sarah and Angelina Grimke were so prescient and radical that they took their cues from the French rather than the American Revolution. Maria Stewart and Frances Ellen Watkins Harper were African American women who were early advocates of both women's rights and anti-slavery. But the group that received the most public attention in the United States were New York and New England abolitionists who travelled to London with their husbands in 1840 to attend the World Anti-Slavery Convention, and, to the surprise of all the Americans, both male and female, were denied a voice at the convention hall. The Englishmen who had called the meeting insisted that the women who had come in support of the human rights of black people be seated in the balcony and not allowed to speak publicly—as was the custom of the day. The women were outraged, especially when, after a mild protest, the majority of their husbands acquiesced in the demands of the Englishmen. Arriving later than the others, William Lloyd Garrison, the most radical and celebrated American abolitionist of them all, and the one whom the English had most eagerly awaited, refused to speak, and, in solidarity with the women, seated himself in the balcony.

Recognition that they would not be able to assist effectively in the liberation of black people before they liberated themselves galvanized the women. Walking the streets of London rather than participating in the meeting, they vowed to take up the issue of women's rights upon their return to America. Eight years later the first American Women's Rights Convention was held in Seneca Falls, New York. The leaders of the new movement, Elizabeth Cady Stanton, Lucretia Mott, Susan B. Anthony, Lucy Stone, and others, were middle- and upper-class white women, many of whom had long been involved in reform politics in the United States, and who were ideological liberals. They modelled their women's rights manifesto after the Declaration of Independence, and wrote powerfully from a liberal individualist perspective.[6] The most controversial issue of the day was the demand for women's suffrage—a demand also made by Mill on behalf of English women.[7]

In Mill's England the women's movement was also under way, and quickly became so much more radical than the American women's movement that in the ensuing decades many American women activists travelled to England to learn about the political tactics of the 'suffragettes'. Women's suffrage emerged as an issue in England in the 1860s. As in the United States, it was ignored by both major political parties, which led to frustration and radicalization on the part of the women involved. The Englishwomen appear to have had shorter fuses than the Americans, taking the lead in disruptive tactics and civil disobedience. Led by the mother–daughter team of Emmeline and Christabel Pankhurst, the Englishwomen engaged in violence, civil disobedience, and street fighting, while the Americans were still holding meetings and holding their breath, at the request of American men, until the end of the Civil War. The English suffragettes interrupted meetings, provoked clashes with police, hurled stones through windows of government offices and shops, poured acid into mailboxes, heckled Members of Parliament in meetings, and attacked them outside the Houses of Parliament with umbrellas, whips, and their bare hands. They burned churches, railway stations, and other public buildings, and, when arrested, conducted highly publicized hunger strikes in gaol, demanding to be treated as political prisoners.[8] While Mill was not directly involved with these radicals, he had published an article in the *Westminster Review* in 1851 entitled 'The Enfranchisement of Women', and after having been elected to the House of Commons in 1865 (with the dubiously helpful support of a group of English women's rights advocates), Mill submitted a petition signed by over 1,500 women advocating votes for women. Mill makes no mention of the influence of the women's movement on his own thinking, but, given his personal development between the years 1840 and 1861, when *The Subjection* was written, it is difficult to imagine that he was unaware of it.

John Stuart Mill's turn to feminism was accomplished with the assistance of Harriet Taylor, the first and only female love of his life. When Mill was 25, he met Mrs Taylor, who at the time was married to a dull but respectable druggist, John Taylor. She was 23 at the time. John Mill and Harriet Taylor maintained a twenty-year friendship, which included a mutual living arrangement with the Taylors, until Mrs Taylor's husband died. Mill and Taylor married soon afterward. Their marriage was short-lived, as Harriet became ill and died seven years later. But her influence upon him was profound, and during their almost three decades of intimate friendship she seems to have provided the substitute source of strength he needed to achieve a semblance of independence from his father. His father never really accepted or approved of his relationship with Harriet Taylor (nor for that matter did his mother or sisters), accusing his son of 'living with another man's wife'. John's rebellion against his father was accomplished intellectually by means of the feminist turn of his scholarship. His intense but subordinate relationship to his father undoubtedly permitted him special access and particular insights into the perspective of intelligent women in Western society. Harriet Taylor was both the vehicle by which he achieved some degree of separation from his father, and also very likely a way to identify with his mother, or women in general. Tensions between these two conflicting forces in his life, his father and his wife, may account for the intellectual tensions that plague *The Subjection of Women*. It is to the content of that work, and the conflicts that characterize it, that we now turn.

## The Subjection of Women

*The Subjection of Women* was written nearly simultaneously with *On Liberty*, although, because of its controversial subject matter, it was not published until almost a decade later. Mill's defenders tried to dismiss the 'outrageousness' of *The Subjection* by attributing its principal ideas to Harriet Taylor. Most contemporary scholars are in agreement that it was Mill's and not Taylor's work, although his relationship with her may certainly have directed his attention more intensely to the issue of women's equality.[9] Mill himself declares in his opening sentence that he had held the opinion 'from the very earliest period when I had formed any opinions at all on social or political matters' that 'the legal subordination of one sex to the other . . . is wrong in itself, and now one of the chief hindrances to human improvement; and that it ought to be replaced by a principle of perfect equality, admitting no power or privilege on one side, nor disability on the other' (*Subjection*, 3). He proceeds, in the course of the slim volume's four chapters, to set forth the principles of liberal individualism as applied to women. The result is a work that stands today as a classic explication of the tenets of liberal feminism . . . with all its strengths and weaknesses. In terms of both its methodology and its political principles, *The Subjection of Women* is the logical extension of *On Liberty*, and thus clearly compatible with, rather than an aberration from, Mill's more conventional work.

His goal is to establish a rational basis for the equality of women, a goal thoroughly compatible with liberal utilitarian philosophy. Although he believed the subordination of women was unjust, 'wrong in itself', what animated his case was the conviction that the liberation of women, or at least some women, would be useful to society. The subordination of one sex to the other has no basis in reason, and is also at odds with the most efficient working of liberal society, since the brainpower and talents of half the human race is under-utilized. But in order to convince people, or the men who were responsible for perpetuating the inefficient state of affairs, that the goal of treating women like 'perfect equals' was feasible, Mill had to establish that the perceptions of women used to justify their inequality were grounded only in habit, and neither based upon reason nor an accurate reflection of women's 'nature'.

## Methodology: empiricism and utilitarianism

In chapter 1 Mill argues against the romanticism, or sentimentalism, of the nineteenth century, because it uncritically associated feminine nature with whatever it saw in women. His own age, he lamented, had substituted instinct for reason, and had not thought about why women had been so oppressed. He was critical of an intellectual and social milieu that institutionalized as rational, legal, and finally natural, habits based upon primitive instincts. 'Laws and systems of polity always begin by recognizing the relations they find already existing between individuals. They convert what was a mere physical fact into a legal right . . .' (*Subjection*, 7). Thus custom, sanctified by law, appears to be natural: 'Was there ever any domination which did not appear natural to those who possessed it? . . . No less an intellect, and one which contributed no less to the progress of human thought, than Aristotle, held this opinion without doubt or misgiving' (ibid. 13). There is no *reason* to assume that the way women (or men) *appear* as phenomena reflects how they actually *are* and must be by nature. Indeed, Mill suggests that the situation of women has uniquely defied the human capacity to progress from what is to what might, or ought to, be. The subordination of women 'is the primitive state of slavery lasting on, through successive mitigations and modifications occasioned by the same causes which have softened the general manners, and brought all human relations more under the control of justice and the influence of humanity' (ibid. 7). 'The social subordination of women thus stands out as an isolated fact in modern social institutions; a solitary breach of what has become their fundamental law' (ibid. 21).

But while Mill needs to argue against the existing state of affairs, he is also a good utilitarian thinker who must ground his theory firmly in the world: he cannot make an argument based solely upon abstract justice or rational principle in an idealist sense. How can he argue against the existing state of affairs and remain true to his empiricist training? (One way of interpreting this methodological dilemma is psychoanalytically: how can he remain true to his father's philosophical method while advocating a political agenda more compatible with his wife's philosophy?) He accomplishes this logical feat in the best tradition of social-scientific method: he advocates an empirical test. Mill suggests *trying* the equality of women to see how it works in practice. Drawing upon classical economics, he proposes a laissez-faire experiment: 'It is only asked that the present boundaries and protective duties in favor of men should be recalled' (ibid. 27).This experiment would provide the empirical evidence to enable society to decide whether women should be excluded from full participation or not. As things stand, 'Experience cannot possibly have decided between two courses, so long as there has only been the experience of one' (ibid. 21). Theory, without empirical evidence, is not to be relied upon. 'If it be said that the doctrine of the equality of the sexes rests only on theory, it must be remembered that the contrary doctrine also has only theory to rest upon' (ibid. 22). This move allows Mill to appear to withdraw his own involvement in the matter, arguing that there simply is not enough data to make a decision about whether or not women should be regarded as the equals of men. It also allows him to discard the trap of 'nature', which is often used politically to argue for the immutability of things. 'What is now called the nature of women is an eminently artificial thing—the result of forced repression in some directions, unnatural stimulation in others' (ibid. 22).

The experiment, however compatible with the methodology of liberal social science, and however compatible with the political substance of liberal individualism, in allowing individual women who can establish their qualifications to advance into the privileged male world, is riddled with problems that also characterize more generally the concept of liberal individualism. For, consider more closely what is involved in Mill's laissez-faire experiment. Who will make the decision about whether women are indeed 'as good as' men? Who will make the decision about which situation works best, equality or subordination? When will enough time have elapsed to permit the decision to be made with confidence? Does Mill believe women will quickly find their niches in the world, once they are legally permitted to try anything? Although enfranchising women would formally and legally include them in any future decisions about their status as equals, the issue of what would have to change culturally, educationally, and economically to permit women to make such a radical shift in consciousness and behaviour remains unaddressed. While the move may be politically well-intentioned, it suffers from the practical limitations also experienced by twentieth-century civil rights legislation. Is an affirmative action programme recommended? Or does Mill believe women's talents and abilities will immediately become evident, just as now 'nobody thinks it necessary to make a law that only a strong-armed man shall be a blacksmith. Freedom and competition suffice to make blacksmiths strong-armed men, because the weak-armed can earn more by engaging in occupations for which they are more fit' (ibid. 19)? Such an ahistorical view often characterizes the rationalist leanings of liberal theory, but Mill himself has dismissed it with his conviction about the artificiality of 'nature'. Knowing that 'nature' is in fact a reflection of experience, he ought to be able to anticipate that women, who have been excluded from competition with men for so long, simply will not be able to sail into battle with men and hold their own. Almost a century and a half after Mill produced his treatise, how much conflict still exists about the desirability of female muscular strength? If we still needed blacksmiths, strong-armed women would still be accused of a lack of femininity: they are either strong-armed, or women, but not both.

The problem here is not Mill's sincerity, but the methodological limitations of liberalism in general, and liberal feminism in particular. Social-scientific method is defined by prevailing standards of 'objectivity', and those standards historically have been male. Although Mill undoubtedly means to include educated, intelligent women, such as his wife, in his intellectual elite, in the view of many contemporary feminists the standards of objectivity and intellectual credibility is grounded in and dependent upon male standards.[10] When Mill suggests, a little further on, that men might learn a lot about women by studying their wives, the political limitations of the method are in full evidence. It becomes clear who controls the social experiment in women's equality: the experiment exists not *for women* but in order to provide a sufficient database by which men may arrive at a statistically significant decision about whether or not women are to be their equals. 'The most favorable use which a man can generally have for studying the character of a woman, is that of his own wife: for the opportunities are greater, and cases of complete sympathy are not so unspeakably rare. . . . But most men have not had the opportunity of studying in this way more than a single case' (ibid. 25). Whether or not he was conscious of the fact, Mill's stance presupposes that women must establish their excellence in terms of male standards, which will be used to evaluate their performance and decide whether the experiment in equality is working. One might argue that Mill is being politically shrewd and presenting a controversial position most delicately. In fact, I do not doubt the sincerity of Mill's conviction about the equality of women. But his methods, which are the methods of liberal social science, presuppose the existing standard as the norm, and expect a group with a history of exclusion and oppression to rise to the occasion and prove themselves worthy of inclusion in a game they had no part in creating. From the perspective of contemporary feminist theory, women will never be as good at being men as men will. The more difficult question is why the standards of excellence continue to be set on an entirely male model.

A parallel case in contemporary American politics is the dispute over affirmative action. Its critics claim that sufficient time has passed since its inception in the 1960s to prove that it 'doesn't work'. Affirmative action, they argue, is no more than special pleading for underqualified people. Or, sufficient quantities of minorities have gained access to positions of privilege to reverse the history of discrimination that once excluded them. Defenders argue that insufficient time has passed to be able to declare affirmative action a failure: centuries of historical exclusion cannot be overcome in two or three decades. Mill's proposal does not even go as far as affirmative action. He simply proposes eliminating laws that restrict women's choices in life. The political inadequacy of this proposal is also visible from the American civil rights analogy: in the *absence* of an affirmative action programme, how far would declaring the races legally equal have got? Indeed, how far did the post-Civil War legislation get the country on a path towards racial equality? Additional civil rights legislation was needed a century later, and then additional programmes such as affirmative action, in order to arrive at even the current deplorable state of racial inequality. To be fair, however, it must be admitted that this sort of legal inclusion as a means of rectifying injustice, while hardly utopian, can be regarded as a necessary precondition for equality—a first step, as it were. Without the concept of equal rights, the practical problems meant to be addressed by affirmative action do not even arise.

## Class politics and liberal feminism

Chapter 2 of *The Subjection* is a powerfully argued diatribe against the deplorable absence of legal rights for women. Mill comes close to anticipating the early contemporary women's movement slogan 'The personal is political' when he likens a wife's legal subservience to her husband to worse than abject slavery to a political sovereign. He notes that under the old laws of England a man could murder his wife with impunity, whereas if a woman should kill her husband she was charged with petty treason and could be punished more cruelly than if she had committed high treason against the state: the penalty was being burned alive. Yet this impassioned discussion concludes on a note so disappointing and at odds with the rest of Mill's prescient feminism that it has been noticed by every contemporary feminist writing about Mill as an indication of the inadequacy of Mill's argument. He acknowledges the importance of women's potential for earning their own wages, and states, 'The *power* of earning is essential to the dignity of a woman, if she has not independent property' (*Subjection*, 48). But he concludes by accepting the conventional division of labour in the household, never considering that a woman's earning power might be related to a redistribution of household and child-care duties, when he states,

> Like a man when he chooses a profession, so, when a woman marries, it may in general be understood that she makes choice of the management of a household, and the bringing up of a family, as the first call upon her exertions, during as many years of her life as may be required for the purpose; and that she renounces, not all other objects and occupations, but all which are not consistent with the requirements of this. (ibid. 48)

Never is there the equivalent assumption that a man might have to choose between family and occupation, between love and intimacy on the one hand and satisfying, creative work on the other.

This failure of imagination on Mill's part reveals a more serious bias in his feminist treatise, which may in fact reveal critical limitations in traditional liberalism as a vehicle for social liberation. Mill tacitly assumes the norm to be middle-class and property-holding. Thus, the enlightenment he assumes conducive to feminism is more characteristic of the well-to-do and educated than of working-class and poor people. He notes, for example, 'I readily admit (and it is the very foundation of my hopes) that numbers of married people even under the present law (in the higher classes of England probably a great majority), live in the spirit of a just law of equality. Laws never would be improved, if there were not numerous persons whose moral sentiments are better than the existing laws' (ibid. 45). While celebrating the moral superiority of the higher classes, he bemoans the fact that 'The clodhopper exercises or is to exercise, his share of the power equally with the highest nobleman,' and that

> The vilest malefactor has some wretched woman tied to him, against whom he can commit any atrocity except killing her, and if tolerantly cautious, can do that without much danger of the legal penalty. And how many thousands are there among these lowest classes in every country, who, without being in a legal sense malefactors in any other respect, because in every other quarter their aggressions meet with resistance, indulge the utmost habitual excesses of bodily violence towards the unhappy wife. (ibid. 35)

This view is compatible with the class prejudice that 'rough' working-class men are more prone to domestic violence and abuse than 'respectable' middle- and professional-class men. It also utterly neglects the working-class women who did not have the luxury of choosing between a 'satisfying' career, or even back-breaking, mind-dulling industrial labour, and domestic chores. Working women have always been expected to begin their 'second shift' of domestic work for their husband and family when finished with their day's wage labour.

The fact is that, in spite of Mill's efforts to transcend stereotypes, and to avoid associating how things are with any concept of 'nature', he slips into confusing the conventional with the natural so often that it must be considered central to the very logic of his argument. In the remaining two chapters of his book he considers whether women themselves are capable of contributing as much in the way of genius as men to society, and what society might stand to gain from a full utilization of women's talents. Both chapters rely upon empirical evidence about women, as they are (or were in Mill's day). In both, we witness the collapse of the hopefulness of Mill's early agnosticism about feminine 'nature'.

## Persistence of the concept of nature

Chapter 3 begins with the acknowledgement that the empirical evidence on women's ability to participate fully in public life is not yet in. The concept of nature begins to intrude in a vague way when Mill declares, 'Let us first make entire abstraction of all psychological considerations tending to show, that any of the mental differences supposed to exist between women and men are but the natural effect of the differences in their education and circumstances, and indicate no radical difference, far less radical inferiority, of nature' (*Subjection*, 53). 'Nature' is used in this sentence twice, once to refer to the effects of education and circumstances, and again to refer to something like innate qualities. The second sense is the one often used to lock women into characteristics that seem unchangeable, and, as Mill himself acknowledges, 'inferior'. But what can the 'natural effect' of education and circumstances mean? The context suggests that Mill intends *natural* in this sense to imply 'inevitable', and here particularly *logically* inevitable or necessary.

In spite of his best efforts, Mill continues to capitulate to the stereotypes endemic to relying upon 'evidence' from the empirical world about women, 'as they already are, or as they are known to have been; and the capacities which they have already shown. What they have done, that, at least, if nothing else, it is proved that they can do' (ibid. 54). What he finds, not surprisingly, is thoroughly compatible with prevailing gender-biased stereotypes. Women are more practical than men, so that 'the special nature of the mental capacities' of a woman of talent are 'all of a kind which fits them for practice, and makes them tend towards it'. He finds a 'gravitation of women's minds to the present, to the real, to the actual fact'. He finds that 'A woman seldom runs wild after an abstraction.' He never uses the term 'nature' to refer to masculine traits, and yet it turns out that women's penchant for practicality is a welcome corrective to the male penchant for speculation and abstraction. 'The principal and most characteristic aberration of speculative minds as such, consists precisely in the deficiency of this lively perception and ever-present sense of objective fact. . . . Women's thoughts are thus as useful in giving reality to those of thinking men, as men's thoughts in giving width and largeness to those of women' (ibid. 59). What escapes Mill's notice is the inherent bias of his stance: women are regarded as capable of equality because their stereotypically defined 'nature' will prove a useful complement to men's natural qualities.

This line of thinking, this objectification of both women and men, is in full flower in the final chapter, which opens with the question 'would mankind be at all better off if women were free? If not, why disturb their minds, and attempt to make a social revolution in the name of an abstract right?' (ibid. 79). His list of the utilitarian benefits to society that would result from the emancipation of women begins with his suggestion that the 'mass of mental faculties available for the higher service of humanity' would double if women were to be educated and taken seriously. The sympathetic reader might be inclined to defend Mill's intentions at this point, with the thought that Mill is, after all, making a genuine effort to include women in society, which is better than simply assuming that society is defined by its men. But thinking in terms of benefit to society cannot help but be a euphemism for thinking in terms of benefit to men because Mill cannot, given his epistemology, consider that women might have active needs and preferences that could change society. Mill wants predictable results from liberating women. But this entails changing their role according to specifications of his own choosing. Women remain objects to be manipulated by Mill, here specifically for what he regards as their benefit. He cannot maintain the empirical utility of freeing women (or any other oppressed group) and allow the group real subjectivity, taking a chance on letting them define the terms of both their own needs and the needs of society.

When Mill turns to a discussion of the cultural advantages women's liberation would bring men, the one-sidedness of his perspective is glaring. He is reduced to applauding stereotypes that are the result of women's history of oppression. He applauds 'the influence of mothers on the early character of their sons, and the desire of young men to recommend themselves to young women', which 'have in all recorded times been important agencies in the formation of character' (ibid. 84). He believes that 'the moral influence of women has had two modes of operation': a softening influence, as well as an inspirational influence urging men towards 'courage, and the military virtues generally, which have at all times been greatly indebted to the desire which men felt of being admired by women' (ibid. 85). He adds, 'The chivalrous ideal is the acme of the influence of women's sentiments on the moral cultivation of mankind' (ibid. 85). Here, unexpectedly, the liberal Mill expounds the favourite sentiments of the conservative Edmund Burke. Concluding his tribute to the aristocratic traits encouraged by women, Mill notes, 'The influence of women counts for a great deal in two of the most marked features of modern European life—its aversion to war, and its addiction to philanthropy' (ibid. 87).

Once again, we see the limitations of the empiricist methodology of liberal utilitarianism. The hidden class biases of Mill's perspective are revealed in his approval of chivalrous young men seeking the approval of women, who remain in their time-honoured role of audience to men's exploits. They may, in Mill's scenario, be intelligent equals, but their equality is useful primarily as inspiration to morally commendable stances such as philanthropy and pacifism. Meanwhile, the educated middle-class gaze that sees the working classes only as uneducated brutes remains intact. It becomes evident that Mill is concerned only with women and men of a particular, enlightened class and race. It might even be argued that he is advocating full participation of an elite group of women in political life in order to counteract the rising influence of uneducated working-class men upon the politics of his day. The notion of bolstering a besieged elite with the inclusion of 'sisters'—the women of elite ranks—rather than permitting one's class to be overrun by barbarians from the lower classes is not without historical precedent. The American Progressive Party at the turn of the twentieth century was also more supportive of women's suffrage than the lower classes and immigrants tended to be. Some factions of the nineteenth-century women's suffrage movement in the United States, despite its origins in anti-slavery, flirted with racists, and specifically southern racists, who would rather have seen educated white women vote than lower-class men of any ethnic origin, but especially freed African Americans.

## Mill's significance to contemporary feminists

In spite of the class bias, methodological limitations, and political incompleteness of Mill's feminist work, Mill's authorial skill in presenting the case for the liberation of women must be acknowledged. No theorist of his time, including Karl Marx, as well as a host of nineteenth-century feminist activists on both sides of the Atlantic, has provided a more enduring or highly respected work devoted exclusively to the political plight of women. Yet while the importance of *The Subjection of Women* must be acknowledged, the ensuing century of plodding, incomplete progress towards forging a world where women are regarded as fully human must lead us to question its efficacy as a political tract. Where does Mill's treatise 'fit' in the context of twenty-first century feminist theory?

In her classic volume *Women in Western Political Thought* Susan Moller Okin focuses on the utilitarian aspects of Mill's essay, regarding it as a 'valuable opportunity to see how he applied his central idea. The emancipation of women to a level of equality with men was not for Mill aimed solely at the increased happiness of women themselves, although this was an important part of it. It was also a very important prerequisite for the improvement of mankind.'[11] Okin acknowledges the contradictions that I have identified as methodological, noting that Mill 'regards what women have achieved as conclusive proof of what they can do but refuses to treat what they have not so far achieved as conclusive proof of anything at all'.[12] However, she is more interested in inconsistencies that undermine the political coherence of his essays, such as 'Mill's acceptance of traditional sex roles within the family',[13] and the fact that 'Mill's feminist writings are implicitly concerned only with middle- and upper-class women, and it is the bourgeois family that is his model.'[14] She notes that, in spite of his fervent efforts to 'apply the principles of liberation to women', he failed to see the institutionalization of male privilege that was the result of traditional gender roles within the family. 'His refusal to question the traditional family and its demands on women set the limits of his liberal feminism.'[15]

But on the whole Okin is appreciative of both the significance of Mill's contribution to feminist theory and his originality. He was the first political theorist since Plato to argue that moral excellence must be regarded as the same in a woman as in a man. In that conviction he dared to challenge the prevailing wisdom, upheld by Western political philosophers from Aristotle to Rousseau, that the moral qualities required in women are different from those required in men. 'It may not seem remarkable that Mill's conception of morality and excellence was uniform for the two sexes—until one realizes how vast a weight of historical opinion had asserted the opposite. Mill was the first major philosopher since Plato to have argued that goodness was the same in a woman as in a man.'[16]

Jean Bethke Elstain regards the discrepancy between Mill's treatment of women in public and private life as more damaging to the coherence of his theory. She observes, in *Public Man, Private Woman*, that Mill's acceptance of 'the principle of utility', along with his 'rather abstract view of persons', undermined the role of power and passion in his political theory and 'impoverished his understanding of the full power and texture of intimate human social relationships'. This sterility in his thinking weakens Mill's analysis of the public and the private, Elshtain's point of focus, in all of his work, including *The Subjection of Women*. Nonetheless, Elshtain believes, *The Subjection* 'remains one of the clearest and most intelligent statements of liberal feminism'.[17] The central problem Elshtain identifies in *The Subjection* is the inconsistency between public laws Mill is prepared to pass for women and the private roles that remain limited. His solution to the conflict between public liberation and private traditionalism was 'a grant of equality of citizenship and civil liberty, together with a formal grant of the *right* to public power to women, knowing full well that the structure of social arrangements forbade the implementation of these rights'.[18] That is, Elshtain has doubts about the depth of Mill's commitment to women's freedom.

Mary Lyndon Shanley and Carole Pateman have a different take on Mill's contribution and its shortcomings. While Elshtain and Okin concentrate on the discrepancies between the legal rights Mill is prepared to give women, and his apparent acceptance of conventional gender roles within the family, Shanley and Pateman believe that Mill's political originality lies in his advocacy of 'spousal friendship'. They are in agreement with Okin that Mill was the first Western philosopher since Plato to argue that moral excellence in men and women is identical: 'Mill . . . as early as 1833 had expressed his belief that "the highest masculine and the highest feminine" characters were without any real distinction.'[19] But, Shanley and Pateman continue, his real contribution was not legal equality, but his advocacy of the desirability of real partnership between the sexes. Legal equality was but a means to the idealistic end of friendship. 'Mill's final prescription to end the subjection of women was not equal opportunity but spousal friendship; equal opportunity was a means whereby such friendship could be encouraged. The theoretical force of Mill's condemnation of domestic hierarchy has not yet been sufficiently appreciated.'[20]

Thus the central conflict in Mill's argument identified by Shanley and Pateman is not the contradiction between gender roles within the family and in the public world per se, but the fact that Mill fails to see that, if the goal of his treatise is to create the opportunity not so much for individual female achievement but for the mutual benefits of intimate friendships between partners in marriage, he must still provide the public opportunity for women to develop as human beings.

> The most interesting shortcomings of Mill's analysis are thus not found in his belief in the efficacy of equal opportunity, but rather in his blindness to what other conditions might hinder or promote marital friendship. In his discussion of family life, for example, Mill seemed to forget his own warnings that women could be imprisoned not only 'by actual law' but also 'by custom equivalent to law'.[21]

His underlying assumption is that human relationships between equals are of a more valuable order than those between unequals. 'Mill's belief that equality was more suitable to friendship than inequality was as unalterable as his conviction that democracy was a better system of government than despotism.' In Shanley and Pateman's view, Mill's belief in the equality of the sexes is profound, consistent, and radical. His recommendations about how such equality might be achieved were not as profound as his vision of equality, but also not as central to *The Subjection of Women*, since the mechanics of equality were to be worked out empirically. Shanley and Pateman are convinced that 'Had Mill discovered that managing the household to the exclusion of most other activity created an impediment to the friendship of married women and men . . . [he] would have altered his view of practical domestic arrangements, but not his commitment to the desirability of male–female friendship in marriage.'[22] This is an original and convincing perspective, and casts Mill's feminism in a more radical light. The issue of class bias remains troubling, however.

## Concluding thoughts

*The Subjection of Women* is a major statement, a classic treatise of liberal feminism, useful as an indication of the difficulty of achieving even a modicum of change in women's condition, as well as of the inadequacy of the reforms advocated by liberal feminism itself. Liberal feminism views equality for women in terms of a male-defined model: women can, and should, achieve all the public benefits and privileges men have garnered in liberal capitalist society. However, liberal capitalist society is dependent upon social hierarchies and class privilege; equality at the top presupposes inequalities below. Women successful in this world of individual achievement may need to sacrifice roles that have been defined as traditionally female, although a stalwart few 'superwomen' can 'have it all'—career, husband, children, childcare. In the eyes of many contemporary feminists, this vision is inadequate because it so uncritically accepts the desirable life for women as essentially male. The particular needs of a woman's biological life are ignored for the purposes of public policy or corporate advancement: juggling pregnancies along with a career curve is each woman's private responsibility. But rarely is it intimated that a successful professional man might be shirking his responsibility as a father to his preoccupation with professional advancement. Equally overlooked is the inherent class bias in the liberal version of the emancipation of women: the childcare, the housekeeping, the 'take-out' meals, no matter how gourmet, are usually provided by members of the working class, and, at that, the notoriously underpaid members of the female working class, often members of racial minorities or recently arrived immigrants. The psychoanalytic association of women with nurturing remains unchallenged.[23]

Nonetheless, as members of liberal capitalist society, we often tend to think of equality for women in these terms, forgetting upon whose backs such equality is built. We think individually, in terms of what we ourselves can achieve, in terms of incremental reform rather than radical change, and we settle, however begrudgingly, for the glacier-like pace of the progress towards regarding women as definitive of humanity in as fundamental a way as men. John Stuart Mill's *The Subjection of Women* stands as a prescient manifesto pointing to an unfulfilled political agenda. His voice must still be considered significant among those dedicated to the achievement of the promise contained in that agenda.

## FURTHER READING

Elshtain, Jean Bethke, *Public Man, Private Woman: Women in Social and Political Thought* (Princeton: Princeton University Press, 1981).

Mazlish, Bruce, *James and John Stuart Mill: Father and Son in the Nineteenth Century* (New York: Basic Books, 1975).

Okin, Susan Moller, *Women in Western Political Thought* (Princeton: Princeton University Press, 1979).

Ring, Jennifer, *Modern Political Theory and Contemporary Feminism: A Dialectical Analysis* (Albany: State University of New York Press, 1991).

Ryan, Alan, *J. S. Mill* (London: Routledge & Kegan Paul, 1974).

Shanley, Mary Lyndon, and Pateman, Carole, *Feminist Interpretations and Political Theory* (University Park: Pennsylvania State University Press, 1991).

## NOTES

1. See, for examples, Susan Moller Okin, *Women in Western Political Thought* (Princeton: Princeton University Press, 1979), Jean Bethke Elshtain, *Public Man, Private Woman: Women in Social and Political Thought* (Princeton: Princeton University Press, 1981), and Mary Lyndon Shanley and Carole Pateman, *Feminist Interpretations and Political Theory* (University Park: Penn State University Press, 1991).
2. See Jennifer Ring, *Modern Political Theory and Contemporary Feminism: A Dialectical Analysis* (Albany: State University of New York Press, 1991).
3. Bruce Mazlish, *James and John Stuart Mill: Father and Son in the Nineteenth Century* (New York: Basic Books, 1975). The actual caption on the enclosed blank space is 'Harriet Burrow Mill (1782?–1854). There is no surviving portrait of Harriet Mill, John's mother. Symbolically, this accords with the fact that he never once mentions her in his published *Autobiography* . . .'. Mazlish's book is a psychoanalytic biography of the two Mills. His discussion of Mill's mother is lengthy, and kinder than any of the other works I have read. Mazlish notes, 'From Mill's *Autobiography*, one would think that he was also brought up without a mother. The truth, of course, is different, and the lack of public mention of his mother . . . gives testimony to intense feelings. One does not offer a new version of the immaculate conception, with only the father and a book at the birth, without having extraordinary emotions about one's mother. This is especially so if one goes on to be a pioneer in the feminist movement!' (p. 152). Mazlish refers to Mill's statement, on the first page of his *Autobiography*: 'I was born in London, on the 20th of May 1806, and was the eldest son of James Mill, the author of the History of British India.'
4. Wendell Robert Carr, 'Introduction', in John Stuart Mill, *The Subjection of Women* (Cambridge, Mass.: MIT Press, 1982), p. ix.
5. John Stuart Mill, *Autobiography*, ed. Jack Stillinger (Boston: Houghton Mifflin, 1969).
6. See Aileen S. Kraditor, *The Ideas of the Women's Suffrage Movement* (New York: Norton, 1981), 45 and 46. Kraditor discusses the theoretical basis of the women's suffrage movement from the first generation of American suffragists, throughout the 19th century. The early leader Elizabeth Cady Stanton, as an old woman, gave an address in 1892 entitled 'The Solitude of Self', in which she makes reference to the 'individuality of each human soul', 'individual conscience and judgment', and 'individual citizenship', claiming that women are 'an equal factor in civilization' and that 'her rights and duties are still the same; individual happiness and development'. The younger leader of the second generation of women's rights activists in the United States Carrie Chapman Catt quipped that she 'did not know what it [suffrage] was, a right, a duty or a privilege', but 'whatever it is, the women want it'. Stanton also wrote a pamphlet in 1894 entitled *Suffrage a Natural Right*.
7. The demand for women's suffrage was the only one in the Declaration of Sentiments not approved unanimously at the 1848 Seneca Falls Convention.

Elizabeth Cady Stanton insisted on it; Lucretia Mott feared it would make the women 'look ridiculous', but Frederick Douglass, freed slave, eloquent abolitionist, and publisher of the anti-slavery newspaper the *North Star*, supported it, and volunteered to second the motion from the floor, after Stanton read it from the list of demands. See Eleanor Flexner, *Century of Struggle: The Women's Rights Movement in the United States* (Cambridge, Mass.: Harvard University Press, 1975), 76.

8. Flexner, *Century of Struggle*, 259. It should be mentioned that the Pankhursts were more involved with the leaders of the English working-class women's movement than were the leaders of the American women's movement involved with working-class women of the United States. Christabel Pankhurst was arrested along with factory worker Annie Kenney, after being thrown out of a meeting where they had heckled the leader of the Liberal Party, Sir Edward Grey. In the street they were physically maltreated by both police and bystanders, and then arrested. The public uproar that followed this incident led them to utilize the tactic of deliberately provoking violent public reprisals as a regular part of their political arsenal.
9. Alan Ryan describes the scandal created by *The Subjection*, the inevitable comparison with *On Liberty*, and speculations about the influence of Harriet Taylor in these terms: 'Mill deliberately kept the focus of *The Subjection of Women* as narrow as possible, in order not to alienate more readers than necessary. To reveal the full extent of his unorthodoxy on sexual and marital arrangements would have served the cause of emancipation very badly. A second obvious difference lies in the reception of the two books. *Liberty* was an instant classic; eminent men declared that it had made them better people. . . . Mill's most savage critics could not deny that *Liberty* possessed a certain nobility. *The Subjection of Women* was another matter altogether. It was a failure in purely commercial terms—the only book on which Mill's publisher ever lost money. It was said by Fitzjames Stephen to verge on the indecent in daring to discuss the details of relations between the sexes at all. . . . There is, however, no evidence . . . of Harriet's contribution to the detail of the argument, and Mill's literary remains do not allow us to work out Harriet's contribution from manuscript sources or from her letters to him. All imputations of influence, therefore, have to be speculative and inferential . . .' (Alan Ryan, *J. S. Mill* (London: Routledge & Kegan Paul, 1974), 125).
10. On the persistence, often virtually unnoticed because it appears to be neutral, of male standards as definitive of legal and scientific objectivity, see Catharine MacKinnon, *Toward a Feminist Theory of State* (Cambridge, Mass.: Harvard University Press, 1989); Naomi Scheman, 'The Mind's Eye', in Sandra Harding and Merrill B. Hintikka (eds.), *Discovering Reality* (Dordrecht: Reidel, 1983); Sandra Harding, *The Science Question in Feminism* (Ithaca, NY: Cornell University Press, 1986); and Evelyn Fox Keller, *Reflections on Science and Gender* (New Haven: Yale University Press, 1985).
11. Okin, *Women in Western Political Thought*, 203.
12. Ibid. 224.
13. Ibid. 228.
14. Ibid. 226.
15. Ibid. 230.
16. Ibid. 219 and 220.
17. Elshtain, *Public Man, Private Woman*, 135.
18. Ibid. 145.
19. Mary Lyndon Shanley and Carole Pateman, *Feminist Interpretations and Political Theory* (University Park: Penn State University Press, 1991), 173.
20. Ibid. 175.
21. Ibid.
22. Ibid.
23. See e.g. Nancy Chodorow, *The Reproduction of Mothering* (Berkeley: University of California Press, 1978), and Dorothy Dinnerstein, *The Mermaid and the Minotaur* (New York: Colophon, 1977).

PART IV

# The counter-Enlightenment

# 21 Burke

David Boucher

## Contents



## Chapter guide

The chapter begins by discussing the three main interpretations of Burke: first, as a utilitarian; secondly, in relation to natural law; and the third which attempts to bring together the two antithetical interpretations. It is suggested that even though Burke has elements of utilitarianism in his thought, and although he subscribes to natural law and universal principles, both somehow have to coincide in the traditions and institutional practices of a community. It is through association that the rules and manners which govern conduct arise, and not from abstract principles. Although Burke may be described as an absolutist on the question of sovereignty, it is suggested that, like Pufendorf, he steers a course between Hobbes and Althusius. Supreme sovereignty is able to accommodate constitutional constraints. On the question of political obligation, although he uses the language of contract, it is clear that Burke does not subscribe to its central tenets. Obligation for him rests upon the notions of prescription, presumption, and prejudice. The collective reason embodied in practices that have existed since time immemorial must be presumed superior to the critical reason of one mind. It is suggested that Burke was concerned not only with the effect that the French Revolution may have on the internal affairs of England, but just as importantly with its effect upon the common heritage of Europe, which for him constituted one large commonwealth with a shared inheritance resting on the principles of a gentleman and of religion.

## Biography

Edmund Burke was born in Dublin on 12 January 1729 and died in London 9 July 1797. He graduated from Trinity College Dublin in 1748 and went to London to study law at the Inns of Court. He turned away from his studies in law in order to pursue a literary career. In 1756 he wrote *A Vindication of Natural Society*, a satire in the style of Bolingbroke which took as its target the rationalist principles of the Enlightenment. So convincing was his satirical defence of the natural basis of society and religion that it was genuinely mistaken to have been the work of Bolingbroke. In 1757 Burke wrote a treatise on aesthetics which gives considerable psychological insight into his abhorrence of revolution. Burke became a Member of Parliament and was closely associated with the Rockingham Whigs. He served as the Paymaster of the Forces under the Rockingham administration of 1782 and the Charles James Fox administration of 1783. Burke was primarily a politician with considerable rhetorical powers. He put them to good use in championing the cause of the Irish Catholics against the popery laws, the Americans against the British imposition of arbitrary taxation, and the Indians against the arbitrary and ruthless rule of Warren Hastings and the East India Company. His denunciation of the French revolutionaries and their English supporters alienated Burke from many of his allies and precipitated his break with Fox. In his final years Burke saw his efforts to impeach Warren Hastings come to nothing, and England, after entering into a war with France, sue for peace with what Burke termed the 'Regicide Directory'. His principles were, nevertheless, consistent, and while they are not presented systematically as a philosophy, they do constitute a philosophical outlook capable of being applied to different political situations.

## Key texts

*A Philosophical Inquiry into the Origin of our Ideas of the Sublime and Beautiful* (1756)
*Speech on Moving Resolutions for Conciliation with the Colonies* (1775)
*Speeches on the Impeachment of Warren Hastings* (1789–94)
*Reflections on the Revolution in France* (1790)
*Letters on a Regicide Peace* (1795–6)

## Main texts used

*Select Works of Edmund Burke* (1974–8), ed. E. J. Payne, 4 vols. (Indianapolis: Liberty Fund, 1999) (*SW*).

Additional material used comes from:

*Speeches on the Impeachment of Warren Hastings*, 2 vols. (Delhi: Discovery, 1987).

*The Works of Edmund Burke*, World's Classics, 6 vols. (London: Humphrey Milford, Oxford University Press, 1906).

## Key ideas

**Civil social person**: while Burke acknowledges basic universal natural characteristics, he thought that a human being's second nature and the manners to which he or she subscribed the product of circumstance. **Natural rights**: Burke famously denounces abstract natural rights, emphasizing the importance of usage and experience. One calls for the doctor when one is ill, not the metaphysician. **Prejudice**: by this Burke means settled habits of thinking and a presumption in favour of the tried and tested. For him it has a non-pejorative meaning. **Revolution**: Burke was not against revolution per se. He supported the Glorious and Bloodless Revolution because it restored some of the principles that James II had perverted. He also supported the American Revolution because England was in the wrong in denying Americans the basic rights of Englishmen, such as no taxation without representation. **Tradition**: the longer an institution has lasted the more we should give it the benefit of the doubt that it must contain some sediment of collective reason. **Vicinity**: the law of vicinity in relation to domestic affairs which prevents the construction of nuisances on one's property equally applied in the international sphere in which France was seen to construct a monstrosity.

---

## Interpretations of Burke

During the latter part of the eighteenth century and the early part of the nineteenth the principal work for which Burke was admired, despite his championing of the cause of the oppressed in Ireland, America, and India, and his defence of the Glorious and Bloodless Revolution of 1688, was his vehement attack upon the principles of the French Revolution and the practices of the French revolutionaries. Burke provided the antidote to the French disease and was hailed as the conservative par excellence. Although this interpretation fell into abeyance and was eclipsed in the nineteenth century by the utilitarian liberal Burke, whose *Reflections* were dismissed as a mere aberration, the conservative Burke steeped in the natural law tradition was revived in the 1950s and 1960s. What I want to suggest is that Burke consciously tried to steer a path between utilitarian pragmatism and the absolutism of natural law by developing a view of the civil social person who was neither motivated wholly by self-interest, nor dependent upon an other-worldly criterion of conduct neglectful of his or her interests. Burke's emphasis upon prejudice, presumption, and prescription provides the basis for anchoring morality and political obligation to the collective wisdom of a community, and not to empirical rational calculation or abstract principles.

### Burke the utilitarian liberal

It was H. T. Buckle who first gave prominence to the idea that Burke was a liberal utilitarian by suggesting that general principles and truth did not loom large in the Irishman's conception of politics. Instead, his characterization of the political was purely empirical and governed by grand views of expediency.[1] William Lecky echoed this rather crude interpretation by arguing that for Burke Church and State have their foundations in expediency and are defended purely in terms of their usefulness or utility.[2] John Morely, a leading nineteenth-century Benthamite liberal, enlarged upon this interpretation by suggesting that for Burke utility was the practical standard of government, not based upon prudence and expediency alone, but often tempered by appeal 'to the widest and highest sympathies'.[3]

Burke was first and foremost a patriot who believed that one's obligations and sympathies belong to a community. Love of one's country was second only to the natural instinct of love of one's family. Patriotism was for him more natural than humanitarianism. (*Warren Hastings*, i. 141[4]). A state has a duty of care to itself. This was a matter of expedience and prudence. Prudence was for Burke the highest of the virtues, and 'the director, the regulator, the standard of them all' ('Appeal from the New to the Old Whigs', in *Works*, v. 20[5]). Because of their imprecision rules of prudence can never be universal (*Regicide Peace*, in *SW* iii. 69[6]). A state must have regard for its interests in formulating policy, but should not be dictated to by the merely parochial and short-term. Nothing in morality or politics can be asserted as universal. There are always exceptions that call for modification, not by the application of logic, 'but by the rules of prudence' ('Appeal from the New to the Old Whigs', in *Works*, v. 20).

The British government, he contended, should not be guided by abstract principles. Irrespective of whether the British Parliament had the right to tax the American colonies,[7] it was not expedient for it to do so. Commercial and practical considerations should influence governmental decisions, leaving abstract theorizing to the metaphysicians and philosophers ('Speech on American Taxation', in *SW* i. 215). Britain's interests were simply not being served by refusing to repeal the tea tax in America.

When Burke condemns Irish persecution and pleads for toleration and the extension of civil liberties to Catholics, he appeals to civic not universal justice, and political utility. His argument against persecution is not based on natural right. He contended that no good reason could be given in justification of penalizing loyal citizens. It was in the interests of the state to court the support of its citizens and reward the Irish Catholics, on the grounds of expediency, for their loyalty during the American Revolution.[8] For strategic reasons Ireland was an important part of the empire and nothing should be done to precipitate political instability. Voluntary cooperation would lead to much greater stability in the empire than continued oppression, which was not so much unjust as futile.[9] It was now a matter of prudence to be just in the light of the dramatic effect on British affairs of the American Revolution ('Speech at Bristol Previous to the Election in that City, 1780', in *Works*, iii. 33). Necessity and expedience force institutions to adapt to circumstances. Modifications are rarely the result of the application of a theory. Indeed, theories are themselves derived from experience (*Reflections*, in *SW* ii. 297).

If Burke is to be viewed as a realist and a pragmatist, he would need to have more in common with its exponents than the exhibition of some elements of expedience. We would expect him, for example, to subscribe to the doctrine of *raison d'état*, and to regard religion as purely instrumental. We would also expect him to deny the existence of universal moral rules. It cannot be stated categorically that Burke subscribed to any of these positions.

*Raison d'état* may be justifiable in order to conceal the true motive or ground for a public action. 'In that case silence is manly and it is wise' (*Letters on a Regicide Peace* I, in *SW* iii. 148). In other words, public disclosure may not always be the reasonable thing to do. The 'great interests of a state' must occasionally take precedence over all considerations (ibid., *SW* iii. 86). It is sometimes unavoidable that truth becomes a casualty in the avoidance of unwelcome political consequences, including war ('Speech on the Acts of Uniformity', in *Works*, iii. 299). While deceit and delusion cannot be condoned, a certain economy with the truth may in some circumstances be wise. He could be economical with the truth himself when it was to his political advantage.

Burke's qualified and circumspect realism could not in any way compare with that of Machiavelli. In fact, Burke criticizes him by allusion in the satire on Bolingbroke, *A*

*Vindication of Natural Society*, and explicitly in the *Speech on Fox's East India Bill.* In the former he refers to Machiavelli as 'this great political Doctor' for suggesting that a prince consider times of peace as breathing spaces in which to prepare for the next war (*Vindication*, in *Works*, i. 12). In sending-up Bolingbroke, who admires the Florentine, Burke feigns sympathy for Machiavelli in having to 'bear the iniquities of those whose maxims and rules of government he published' (ibid. 23). In his *Speech on Fox's East India Bill* Burke explicitly criticizes Machiavelli for corrupting the minds of readers by not expressing disapproval of the 'horrible and detestable proceedings' he describes (*Miscellaneous*, in *SW* iv. 126). In the *Reflections* Burke is even more hostile towards Machiavelli: 'where men follow their natural impulses, they would not bear the odious maxims of a Machiavellian policy, whether applied to the attainment of monarchical or democratic tyranny' (*SW* iii. 175).

There could be no rigid principle where cases of necessity arise, and he was prepared to acknowledge that on occasions things may have to be done of which we would not morally approve. Such necessities could not be taken as precedents: 'Because we have done one humiliating act, we ought with infinite caution to admit more acts of the same nature' (*Regicide Peace*, *SW* iii. 143–4). Burke's most vehement denunciations of the principle of *raison d'état* are made in his attacks on Warren Hastings.

Hastings was accused of vicious, unprincipled, and criminal conduct against the Indian people. Burke maintained that he exceeded the authority vested in him by the British government and the East India Company, deliberately subverting the traditional laws of India which Britain held in trust when it entered into a virtual act of union with the Indian people. He also charged Hastings with conduct at variance with the fundamental principles of humanity (*Warren Hastings*, i. 14, 15, 40, 44, 60, 61, 92, 93, 231, 486; ii. 2–3) Hastings defended himself by arguing that India was throughout its history subject to arbitrary rule, and that he had merely inherited that style of governance from the Moguls. European standards of morality were inapplicable to a country to which they were so alien (ibid. i. 94, 97, 99, 104, 107, 485). His despotic conduct was not for personal gain, but to safeguard the interest and financial security of the government. In other words Hastings justified his methods by appeal to the principle of *raison d'état*, 'in the Time of the most pressing Necessity'.[10]

Burke's case against Hastings demonstrates the extent to which he was not prepared to separate the realms of politics and morality. In his view, the rule of law is a principle that can never justifiably be subverted because 'it is the security of the people of England, it is the security of the people of India, it is the security of every person that is governed, and of every person that governs' (ibid. 504). Hastings substituted will for law, government by force for justice and authority (ibid. 103, 486). All power, Burke contends, 'is limited by law, and ought to be guided by discretion and not by arbitrary will' (ibid. ii. 2). Hastings had no right to make 'his own will the sole rule of his government' (ibid. 4). No legal code or constitution could rationally sanction the exercise of arbitrary power in place of the rule of law (ibid. i. 105 and ii. 4). He challenges Hastings to state to what code of law he claims to be subject and by what law, if any, he can justify his conduct (ibid. i. 107).

The subversion of the rule of law by the exercise of arbitrary will could never be justified by the doctrine of *raison d'état*, even though it may be used in certain circumstances for concealing the true grounds of a policy. The account that Burke gave of *raison d'état* was considerably circumscribed; he was certainly presenting us with a severely qualified account of the legitimacy of *raison d'état*. He does not condone any of its classic formulations because he refuses to identify the will of the sovereign with law; nor does he condone the fundamental maxim of the doctrine, namely, that the end justifies the means.

## Burke and the natural law

It is no coincidence that the revival of Burke as a conservative thinker, and the attribution of a substantive natural law content to his principles, arose at the height of the cold war. He was appropriated as the defender of all that was decent, honest, and universal against the abstract theorizing and dogmatism of Soviet communism. Russell Kirk, for example, contends that 'great nations have fallen into what Burke called "the antagonistic world of madness, discord, vice, confusion, and unavailing sorrow"; and many of those men and women who hope to preserve some measure of order, justice, and freedom now find in Burke the moral and political imagination our age seems to require'.[11] Peter Stanlis and Burleigh T. Wilkins are responsible for the accommodation of Burke into the natural law tradition. Stanlis argues that 'far from being an enemy of Natural Law, Burke was one of the most eloquent and profound defenders of Natural Law morality and politics in Western civilisation'.[12] Burke's rejection of abstract metaphysical natural rights is accounted for by associating him with the ancient theological tradition of natural law, which has strong links with Aquinas, Pufendorf, Grotius, and Vattel. The natural right school, in Stanlis's view, is the unfortunate offspring of Hobbes, Locke, and Rousseau, and it is this bastardization of the tradition of which Burke is critical.

Burke certainly appeals to a universal moral law particularly in his discussions of the subjection of Irish Catholics and Indians to the arbitrary oppression of English misrule. In his fragmentary *Tracts on the Popery Laws* Burke portrays the penal laws against Catholics as the principal cause of Ireland's discontents. By systematically imposing hardship on the bulk of the population the laws depressed both morals and industry. Burke argues that they are at variance with the principles of natural justice from which no human positive law should deviate. In this respect he contends that human laws are strictly speaking not made, but are declaratory. They make explicit, and have no power to alter, 'the substance of original justice'.[13]

Burke's speeches against Warren Hastings often invoke a higher authority than the laws and customs of India and England. He probably realized that he could win a legal victory, but he was determined to win the moral argument. In appealing to the principle of trusteeship for the governance of India Burke frequently invokes God's universal and immutable laws of morality as criteria in terms of which Hastings should be judged. Was Burke a natural law theorist as many of his modern-day commentators suggest? He certainly wished to refute Hastings's appeal to moral relativism in justification of his conduct. In defiance of the principle of 'geographical morality' Burke contends that 'the laws of morality are the same everywhere; and that there is no action, which would pass for an act of extortion, of peculation, of bribery, and of oppression in England, that is not an act of extortion, of peculation, of bribery, and oppression in Europe, Asia, Africa, and all the world over' (*Warren Hastings*, i. 94).[14] The source of all authority is God, and those who exercise it are subject to 'the eternal laws of Him that gave it, with which no human authority can dispense' (ibid. 99). Human positive laws are declaratory in so far as they mirror the eternal laws of justice, humanity, and equity, which are primeval (ibid. 14, 99, 101, 231, 504; ii. 410, 439). These laws of justice are our birthright, placed in our breasts as guides to conduct. They are immutable, independent of human design, preexist society, and are destined to survive its destruction (ibid. i. 14, 99; ii. 410).

These references to a higher law have enabled commentators to put Burke on the side of a common humanity against the totalitarian excesses of Hitler and Stalin,[15] and which prompted Cobban to dissociate Burke altogether 'from the immoralism of the school . . . whose principle, whether derived from theoretical Machiavellianism or from practical expediency, was *raison d'état*'.[16] In Burke the separation between morality and politics, effected by Machiavelli, or the equation of morality with expediency, effected by Hobbes, were, the natural law interpreters tell us, firmly rejected in subordinating politics to 'the universal law of reason and justice ordained by God'.[17]

Burke's appeal to natural law is, however, puzzling. In fact, although there is no reason to accuse him of disbelief, his attitude to religion in general is very like that of Thucydides, Machiavelli, and Hobbes.[18] It was its social and political utility rather than its truth that interested them all. For Burke, religion is a source of energy in the people and is the foundation of society. Religion is, he tells us, 'our boast and comfort, and one great source of civilisation amongst us, and among other nations' (*Reflections*, in *SW* ii. 186). Religion promises salvation to the victims of injustice and is a source of happiness and consolation. In this respect it acts as an opiate. Social stability and cohesiveness require freedom of conscience and religious toleration.[19] Our natures are God-given. God willed the existence of the state for the perfection of our virtuous natures (ibid. 194–5). The state and religion are therefore inseparable. Toleration is a matter of political expedience, whereas atheism must be suppressed with the full weight of the law because it strikes at the very foundation of the state (ibid. 186).[20] He was nevertheless attuned to the dangers of religious fanaticism to the stability of the state.

In sum, Burke had an instrumental view of Christianity. It was politically and socially useful, irrespective of its theological truth. Similarly, he uses natural law for political ends. His appeals to a higher authority are often for rhetorical impact to reinforce principles that in different circumstances might be supported by prescription. He is quite happy, for example, to let the authority of the British constitution rest on prescription when advocating extreme caution in parliamentary reform, but the same ground could with difficulty be extended to India and the conduct of Warren Hastings. In this instance prescription is reinforced with the rhetorical weight of natural law. Burke genuinely believed that God sets us out on our journey in the world, but that the destination is of our own choosing. Man is, then, 'in a great degree a creature of his own making' (ibid. 188). God, in Burke's writings, is shrouded in mystery. He is the 'Governor of the universe' (*Warren Hastings*, i. 94), and 'the mysterious Governor of the World' (*Regicide Peace*, in *SW* iii. 160), who Burke often invokes, to explain the inexplicable. Burke contends that we cannot rely upon God's interventions and dispensations, for example, mysteriously to rescue a nation from ruin, in 'defiance of the rules of prudence' (ibid. 2, 160). It is folly to ignore the rules of prudence on the expectation that God will intervene to rectify our mistakes.

In their attempts to assimilate Burke to the natural law tradition commentators tend to underplay the extent to which individual reason is the vehicle through which it is known. Although traditional natural law theorists such as Aquinas, Grotius, and Pufendorf acknowledge the imperfections of reason, and the power of the passions to corrupt, they nevertheless believe that some people are better able than others to apprehend the eternal truths through the exercise of reason. The power of individual reason was a central tenet in postulating a transcendental and transhistorical code of conduct. The Enlightenment belief that right reason can discover the true principles upon which to base our laws and institutions without the slightest regard for historical precedent or traditional practices was merely an extension of the rationalism of the natural law theorists.[21] Burke, however, was contemptuous of such reliance upon individual reason, and unceremoniously rejected the applicability of abstract principles like the so-called rights of man to concrete political situations. He contended that 'The individual is foolish. The multitude, for the moment, is foolish when they act without deliberation; but the species is wise, and when time is given to it, as a species, it almost always acts right' ('Speech on the Reform of Representation', in *Miscellaneous*, *SW* iv. 21).

Burke always maintained that it was sheer folly and potentially dangerous to deduce practical policies from abstract principles in the guidance of human affairs. Irrespective of what they may think metaphysicians and abstract speculative philosophers, with whom he is little impressed, derive their theories from experience. It is therefore fallacious to think that experience conforms to the principles deduced, and then to criticize governments for not corresponding to them (ibid. 23). Although his denunciation of abstract natural rights is commonly associated with his writings on the French Revolution, he thought his comments universally applicable, whether it be in England in the name of rational dissent, or in America in the name of the rights of man. No rational person, he contends, could presume to direct his or her affairs by 'abstractions and universals' ('Speech on the Second Reading of a Bill for the Relief of Protestant Dissenters, 1773', in *Works*, iii. 316). The rights of man may be abstractly perfect, but that in fact is their practical defect. As Burke contemptuously asserts, 'The prattling about the rights of men will not be accepted in payment for a biscuit or a pound of gunpowder' (*Reflections*, in *SW* ii. 358). Politics is an eminently practical activity requiring an enormous amount of experience, more than one man can acquire in a lifetime, it is therefore extremely reckless to dismantle an established constitution or replace it on the basis of the metaphysical rights of man. These 'pretended rights', Burke tells us, 'are all extremes: and in proportion as they are metaphysically true, they are morally and politically false' (ibid. 154).

Right reason was not the only way in which the natural law could to discovered. Grotius, for example, contended that there were two ways of coming to know natural law. The first by means of the exercise of right reason a priori and the second by the a posteriori method. In the case of the second, beliefs that are held by all of civilized mankind must be assumed to be derived from the same source, namely God. Burke's occasional appeals to natural law are clearly of this second order, and the fact that he rejected abstract reasoning cannot therefore be taken as unequivocal evidence that he rejected a universal moral order. What differentiates Burke in this respect from Grotius is that Burke does not contend that the confirmation of natural law is its deduction from indubitable principles through logically certain reasoning.

## The middle way

In formulating a criterion of moral conduct Burke wished to depart from both utilitarian expediency and the abstract certainties of natural law. The tension between these two elements in his thought has long been evident to commentators. Sir Leslie Stephen, the late nineteenth-century positivist, describes Burke as a theological utilitarian because of the juxtaposition of expediency with appeals to God-given universal moral principles.[22] Charles E. Vaughan clearly sees Burke in a different league from Hume and the Utilitarians. Vaughan argues that Burke refused to equate expediency with morality and would not countenance the separation of morals and politics. However, the appeal to universal principles in quasi-metaphysical language is dismissed by Stephen as an aberration, and by Vaughan as a rhetorical device rather than 'an expression of the author's deliberate and reasoned judgement'.[23]

I want to suggest that Burke self-consciously departed from utilitarian expediency and the abstract moral certainty of natural law and tried to overcome their deficiencies by developing a criterion whose foundation is social and historical.[24] The self-consciousness of Burke's synthesis is recognized by W. H. Greenleaf, following Michael Oakeshott, and by David Cameron and Dante Germino.[25]

Burke was aware that the multiplicity of discrete actions required a manifold of principles, otherwise there 'would be only a confused jumble of particular facts and details, without the means of drawing out any sort of theoretical or practical conclusions' ('On a Motion for Leave to Bring in a Bill to Repeal and Alter Certain Acts Respecting Religious Opinions, May 11, 1792', in *Works*, iii. 317). On the other hand, it is madness to be guided solely by principles. Abstractly speaking liberty is good, but abstract liberty is nowhere to be found ('Speech on Conciliation with America', in *The Two Speeches on America*, in *SW* i. 237). It should not be inferred from Burke's strictures against metaphysical theories of abstract rights that he was against theory as such. This was not his position at all: to deny theory was to deny reason, and he had no wish to do that. He was against ill-founded theories, theories that had little basis in fact. The test of a good theory was its conformity with practice. It seemed ludicrous to him that a theory derived from the actual working of government should acquire the status of having informed the institution of the government from which it was derived, and in turn be used to criticize the government for not conforming with it ('Reform of the Representation of the Commons in Parliament', in *Miscellaneous*, in *SW* iv. 23).

'The circumstances', Burke tells us, 'are what render every civil and political scheme beneficial or noxious to mankind' (*Reflections*, in *SW* ii. 93). These circumstances give rise to infinite variations, and nothing can be settled among them by the application of 'any abstract rule' (ibid. 152). What is needed is a combination of the two extremes. This is surely what Burke is suggesting when he says that 'A statesman, never losing sight of principles, is to be guided by circumstances' ('A Motion . . . Respecting Religious Opinions', in *Works*, iii. 317), and when he contends that the rights of man are not to be found in a pre-societal state of nature, or the abstract speculations of metaphysicians, but 'in a sort of *middle*, incapable of definition but not impossible to be discerned' (*Reflections*, in *SW* ii. 154). What this means is that the principles and rules that guide conduct are to be discerned in the historical process itself, that is, the process from which they emanated and in which our individual and national characters are formed.

Hindson and Gray mislead us when they suggest that Burke believed human nature to be transhistorical and permanently fixed.[26] Only in its most basic characteristics is this the case. Because of his emphasis upon history and circumstance Burke saw human nature, that is, our socially produced second natures, as at once historically and geographically variable. Burke does have a conception of a universal human nature, particularly in relation to experience of the sublime and the beautiful, but his political insights are almost exclusively directed at the accommodation of our second natures.[27]

The 'civil social man' (ibid. 151) about which Burke speaks is the product both of our own making and of circumstance. The societies in which we live are not physical, but moral, entities. They are the products, not of nature, but of the human mind. Human beings are interdependent within the context of specific societies, and their actions invariably have a bearing upon the lives of others. In other words, the social relationships into which we enter have implicated in them certain degrees of responsibility for one's conduct. The conventions and constraints that modify our behaviour arise out of our social relations. Burke argues that 'the *situations* in which men relatively stand produce the rules and principles of that responsibility, and afford directions to prudence in exacting it' (*Regicide Peace*, in *SW* iii. 133). This is why Burke prefers to talk, not of the rights of man, but of the rights of Englishmen who enjoy them as an inheritance from their forefathers to which they are entitled 'without any reference whatever to any other more general or prior right' (*Reflections*, in *SW* ii. 121). If the civil social man differs according to circumstance, then the type of government appropriate to his character will not be the same everywhere and anywhere. There can be no ideal form of government to which all states should conform, 'the circumstances and habits of every country, which it is always perilous and productive of the greatest calamities to force are to decide upon the form of its government' (*Regicide Peace*, in *SW* iii. 134).

Similarly, it is the character of states, their common heritage, perceived affinities, and resemblances, which lead them to associate, and which in turn give rise to the constraints which they feel obliged to acknowledge. Common sympathies rather than formal legal requirements determine the nature of the historical relationships among states. We should not, Burke contends, rely too heavily in our international relations upon the abstractions embedded in formal treaties and agreements. It is also unwise to rely upon the interests of states as guarantees of their formal commitments. Interests and passions are just as likely to render useless those formal undertakings: 'Entirely to trust to either, is to disregard our own safety, or not to know mankind' (ibid. 132). In other words, Burke is resorting to a middle way in formulating a standard of state conduct:

> Men are not tied to one another by papers and seals. They are led to associate by resemblances, by conformities, by sympathies. It is with nations as with individuals. Nothing is so strong a tie of amity between nation and nation as correspondence in laws, customs, manners, and habits of life. They have more than the force of treaties in themselves. They are obligations written in the heart. They approximate men to men, without their knowledge, and sometimes against their intentions. The secret, unseen, but irrefragable bond of habitual intercourse holds them together, even when their perverse and litigious nature sets them to equivocate, scuffle, and fight about the terms of their written obligations. (ibid.)

The title to authority is not power, nor divine sanction, but prescription. Its ground, or the reason why we obey the authority, is presumption. We prefer the certainty of a time-honoured and settled form of government, or set of arrangements, to the uncertainty of untried projects. The constitution of a country or the relations in which nations stand with each other are not the result of the choice of one day, or one generation of people, but are 'made by the peculiar circumstances, occasions, tempers, dispositions, and moral, civil, and social habitudes of the people, which disclose themselves only in a long space of time' ('Speech on the Reform of Representation 1782', in *Miscellaneous*, in *SW* iv. 21). Prescription, and not abstract philosophizing, establishes our rights, the authority of government, and our political obligations.

## Sovereignty and constitutionalism

What needs to be emphasized is that, while Burke clearly understands a constitution to be the work of human artifice, he is not positing a distinction between nature and convention. Because he takes human beings to be social beings the constitution of a nation, although variable from place to place, has nevertheless to be in conformity with the needs of human nature. Any theory about government has to be assessed in terms of its compatibility with human nature in general, and with that nature as modified by practices and habits ('Speech on the Reform of Representation', in *Miscellaneous*, in *SW* iv. 23).

Burke's rejection of abstract natural rights entailed rejecting the corollary doctrines of the state of nature, natural liberty, and the social contract as irrelevant to his understanding of political obligation. Burke never explicitly denied the existence of a pre-social state of nature, nor that its inhabitants may have had original rights. The idea of individualistic liberty, however, was anathema to his whole idea of the civil social person. What he was concerned with was civil liberty, which he defined as 'not solitary, unconnected, individual, selfish liberty, as if every man was to regulate the whole of his conduct by his own will. The liberty I mean is *social* freedom. It is that state of things in which liberty is assured by the equality of restraint . . . . This kind of liberty is, indeed, but another name for justice.'[28]

Because of the religious foundation to Burke's thought he did not need recourse to the standard social contract theory, based on consent and the protection of individual liberty. Because human beings are social in nature society, although an artifice, is consistent with that nature. Societies are not instituted; they arise and develop in social interaction, and not as a result of design. This does not mean that he totally rejected the idea of a social contract in his understanding of political obligation. He simply had quite a different image of it which he connects to the idea of Order, or the Great Chain of Being, in which everything has its place. The institutions of a society are related to religion, which gives sanctity to the state and fosters due reverence.

Traditionally the idea of social contract took a variety of forms. In Hobbes it is a compact among inhabitants of the state of nature which at once created society and government. In Locke the state of nature is already a social condition in which each individual exercises executive power. The compact is among heads of families, women being consigned to the private realm of the family, to institute political society, and then a further step is taken to establish government. For Rousseau the people transform themselves into the sovereign body. It is the elevation of the subject to the status of citizen whose real or general will is the will of the whole. Burke certainly subscribes to some notion of a general will when he suggests that the collective rationality of a people must count for much more that individual reason, which is often flawed and subject to the pressures of the moment.

The contract of which Burke speaks is, nevertheless, very different. He first conceives the state as a whole encompassing every form of human relation, including arts, sciences, commerce, morals, and religion, but it is also a historically dynamic conception in which notions of intergenerational justice play a considerable part. In what we do now we have past, present, and future responsibilities to weigh. His idea of a social contract does not imply a voluntary association with determinate goals and purposes towards the attainment of which the laws are instrumental. It is a permanent association in which social cohesion is based not on consent, but instead on moral relations of association pertaining to one's station and its duties. Society is a moral essence exhibiting both continuity and gradation: continuity in the sense that the past inheritance permeates the present, and gradation in the sense that society is hierarchically structured. An aristocratic class was for him the necessary corollary of every society in

Europe, the function of which was to act as a safeguard against tyrannical monarchy and despotic democracy. The revolutionary doctrine of natural rights constituted a threat to the stability of Europe because it would sweep away the moderating force in politics and expose all societies to excesses. This is how Burke describes the social contract:

> Society is indeed a contract. Subordinate contracts for objects of mere occasional interest may be dissolved at pleasure—but the state ought not to be considered as nothing better than a partnership agreement in a trade of pepper and coffee, calico or tobacco, or some other such low concern, to be taken up for a little temporary interest, and to be dissolved by the fancy of parties. It is to be looked on with other reverence; because it is not a partnership in things subservient only to gross animal existence of a temporary and perishable nature. It is a partnership in all science; a partnership in all art; a partnership in every virtue, and in all perfection. As the ends of such a partnership cannot be obtained in many generations, it becomes a partnership not only between those who are living, but between those who are living, those who are dead, and those who are to be born. Each contract of each particular state is but a clause in the great primeval contract of eternal society, linking the lower with the higher natures, connecting the visible and invisible world, according to fixed compact sanctioned by the inviolable oath which holds all physical and all moral natures, each in their appointed place. This law is not subject to the will of those, who by an obligation above them, and infinitely superior, are bound to submit their will to that law. The municipal corporations of that universal kingdom are not morally at liberty at their pleasure, and on their speculation of a contingent improvement, wholly to speculate and tear asunder the bands of their subordinate community, and to dissolve it into an unsocial, uncivil, unconnected chaos of elementary principles. (*Reflections*, in *SW* ii. 192–3)

A number of individuals have no collective capacity and can claim no rights from nature, and in particular no natural right to resistance. Rights can only belong to a group of people as a result of political society. These people are conceived as a corporation, individuals collectively united in a single body, the creation not of nature but of human artifice. It is therefore perverse to suggest that such a corporation has a natural right to resist sovereign authority. The natural rights of which the French revolutionaries spoke, and about which Paine theorized, were those of self-determination in a state of nature, which were said to be carried over into civil society and purportedly gave men the right to govern themselves, or to be governed by people of their choice. For Burke, nothing could be further from the truth. Burke contended that 'And as to the share of power, authority, and direction which each individual ought to have in the management of the state, that I must deny to be amongst the direct original rights of man in civil society; for I have in my contemplation the civil social man, and no other. It is a thing to be settled by convention' (ibid. 151).

It has been suggested by Richard Bourke that Thomas Hobbes's conception of absolute sovereignty, designed partially to deny that the people had a natural right of resistance against established political authority, provided both the argument and the vocabulary for Edmund Burke's own conception of sovereignty.[29] In my view, Burke does not reproduce Hobbes's argument, but instead, like Samuel von Pufendorf, steers a course between Hobbes and Althusius. In Pufendorf's view it is not incompatible with the nature of sovereignty that it conform 'to a certain manner of procedure', in other words, that it may be procedurally limited. Supreme sovereignty, for Pufendorf, merely denotes that there is no superior or equal authority in the state.[30] Limited sovereignty, like absolute, is a species of the genus supreme sovereignty and may be constrained by constitutional arrangements regarding conformity to 'certain basic laws', or in accordance with specified procedures, such as consultation with a senate or council whose consent may be required.[31] In equating limited sovereignty with procedural constraints Pufendorf believes that the supremacy of sovereignty is not undermined.

Burke was certainly not an advocate of divided sovereignty, either in internal or in imperial affairs. Nor could he be said to favour absolute sovereignty over limited sovereignty. His idea of constitutional government is perfectly compatible with the idea of supreme sovereignty. It is what Pufendorf called limited sovereignty in that rule is not arbitrary but practised in accordance with established procedures.

## Political obligation

Burke makes his case in refuting what he takes to be the three central claims of Richard Price's sermon, namely that the English have a natural right to choose their own rulers, to bring them to account for misconduct, and to institute a government for themselves. Burke contends that none of these rights has a basis in the British constitution, nor does the necessary and aberrant deviation from the hereditary title in 1688 institute such revolutionary notions. Indeed, the Glorious and Bloodless Revolution sought to preserve the rights of Englishmen which are embodied in the traditional heritage of their ancestors. None of the rights which Englishmen claim are in need of prior title; they have existed since time immemorial and are embodied in the Ancient Constitution. The constitution is based on the principle of inheritance, in the monarchy, aristocracy, and the privileges which the House of Commons enjoys. This principle ensures conservation without excluding improvement or change (*Reflections*, in *SW* ii. 101–22). Burke contended elsewhere that 'our Constitution is a prescriptive Constitution; it is a Constitution, whose sole authority is, that it has existed time out of mind' (*Miscellaneous*, in *SW* iv. 20). 'Prescription is the most solid of all titles, not only to property, but, which is to secure that property, to Government' (ibid. 20–1). And again in the *Reflections* he contends that 'We procure reverence to our civil institutions on the principle upon which nature teaches us to revere individual men; on account of their age; and on account of those from whom they are descended' (*SW* ii. 123).

What this means in practical terms is that the origin of a title or practice has little or no bearing on the justification of its continuing relevance. The title of property that has been passed down from generation to generation rests on prescription, and its authority is unaffected by claims that the original title may have resulted from fraud or violence. Similarly, the authority of a government which has organized the affairs of a nation from time immemorial derives its legitimacy from prescription and is impervious to attacks which invoke natural rights of individual self-determination that we are said to have possessed in the state of nature. 'It is accompanied with another ground of authority in the constitution of the human mind, presumption. It is a presumption in favour of any settled scheme of government against any untried project, that a nation has long existed and flourished under it' (*Miscellaneous*, in *SW* iv. 20–1).

'Custom is to be regarded with great deference especially if it be an universal Custom; even popular notions are not always to be laughed at. There are some general principles operating to produce Customs, that is a more sure guide than our Theories. They are followed indeed often on odd motives, but that does not make them less reasonable or useful.'[32] We should look favourably, then, upon institutions that have stood the test of time because, irrespective of whether the reason or rationale is apparent, they must have served some useful social purpose. This is what Burke calls prejudice. Prejudice, for him, did not have the pejorative connotation that it has today. If prejudices are formed as a result of familiarity with social practices over long periods of time, or an inherited tradition, they may be well founded. Individual reason is notoriously fallible and a very poor test against which to measure the efficacy of established institutions. We cherish that which we have inherited, and cherish it all the more the longer its lineage, knowing that it embodies the collective wisdom of the ages or nation. Prejudice is superior to individual reason because it embraces not only reason, but also emotions and sentiment. Burke maintains that 'Prejudice is of ready application in the emergency; it previously engages the mind in a steady course of wisdom and virtue, and does not leave the man hesitating in the moment of decision, sceptical, puzzled, and unresolved. Prejudice renders a man's virtue his habit; and duty becomes a part of his nature' (*Reflections*, in *SW* ii. 182).

Religion was the source of all good and comfort in civil society, and to avoid the dire consequences of blind prejudice the state itself has been consecrated, so that any change is approached with the utmost caution, with no unnecessary deviations or uncharacteristic breaks. The state and society are things of beauty, and change has to comply not only with rational but also with aesthetic criteria. Things of beauty, Burke claims, are never angular. Angular objects never continue in the same straight line for long, and their sudden changes of direction jolt the senses. In contrast, surfaces that continually change, but almost imperceptibly, in that no point of beginning or end can be discerned, are most pleasing to the eye. A dove, for example, 'is smooth and downy: its parts are (to use that expression) melted into one another; you are presented with no sudden protuberance through the whole, and yet the whole is continually changing' (*A Philosophical Inquiry into the Origins of our Ideas of the Sublime and Beautiful*, in *Works*, i. 163). The same principle applies in politics. Even at his most radical, as for example, advocating the abolition of slavery long before it became a popular cause, Burke's proposals envisage a gradual phasing out of the practice rather than an abrupt end to the trade. Whereas abstract principles might dictate the immediate abolition of such an immoral trade, practical circumstances require its regulation and gradual cessation on the grounds that slave owners in the West Indies would almost certainly carry on the trade illicitly and unregulated if forced by abrupt abolition to find a substitute for its slave labour ('Sketch of the Negro Code', in *Miscellaneous*, in *SW* iv. 253–82).

## The community of states

Although most commentaries on Burke emphasize domestic politics, and the domestic implications of external relations, he had a much larger vision of international relations and the place of Britain within them. He saw Britain, first, as a member of a European family of nations and, secondly, as having imperial responsibilities to its colonies. Colonial relations were part and parcel of the delicate European balance of power which relied upon war as the instrument for securing justice in the international realm. Burke was certainly a theorist of just war, and the justification could have two sources. A country that deviated so violently from its traditional heritage and adopted practices so different from those of its neighbours as to constitute a palpable threat to peace would by its actions invite war. Secondly, any attempt to disrupt the balance of power in Europe by unprovoked aggression on a neighbour, as France had done by attacking Holland, constituted grounds for interference.

Too much emphasis upon the *Reflections* tends to obscure the fact that the spectre of revolutionary France became much more daunting for Europeans following its publication. By the summer of 1793 all of the major powers were at war with France, but the coalition failed to achieve its objectives and dissolved. The popularity of the war soon waned within Britain, and petitions urging peace negotiations were received from commercial centres all over the country. By October 1795 only England and Austria remained at war with France. With the establishment of the Directory in France the way now seemed open to court peace without losing face. The Directory, many believed, was not tainted with the Regicide epithet of the Convention. Burke, however, viewed the Directory as little more than a committee of the Convention, and the fact that no one could become a Director unless he had voted in the Convention for the death of the king was justification enough to implicate them in the regicide. Burke could not accept that France had renounced the errors of her Jacobin ways and still, in his view, constituted a threat to the stability of Europe. His pessimism was justified as France once again, in the name of defence, went on the offensive, making significant gains in the Netherlands, Germany, and Italy. At Basle and Berlin Britain made overtures for peace only to be rebuffed by the French. Such humiliation did not deter Britain from making a third attempt in Paris during 1796. Opponents of the attempted reconciliation hoped that France would continue in her arrogance and so inflame British public opinion that new vigour would be injected into the war. It is in this context that Burke, both privately and publicly, voiced his concern at the overtures for peace, and published his *Letters on a Regicide Peace*. Although the letters are often intemperate, they are more considered than the *Reflections* and draw out much more lucidly the implications of the government in France for the settled norms of the continent of Europe. E. J. Payne goes as far as to call the letters 'the writer's masterpiece' (introduction to *Letters on a Regicide Peace*, in *SW* iii. 57).

Burke's views elaborate more systematically some of the principles that he had espoused elsewhere. There was, in his view, a common law of Europe, to which both England and France were subject. European civilization, its customs and manners, rest upon two time-honoured principles: 'the sprit of a gentleman and, the spirit of religion' (*Reflections*, in *SW* iii. 173). Men of high breeding and men of the cloth kept learning alive even in the most adverse circumstances of war and famine. From the same source, commerce, trade, and manufacture flourished. Fundamentally the states of Europe constitute 'virtually one great state' because in manners, religion, and law they are all basically the same with slight variations. So much so that no one could feel an exile in any part of it (*Letters on a Regicide Peace*, in *SW* iii. 133).

In adopting an alien system of government, practising regicide, Jacobinism, and atheism, France committed a 'violent breach of the community of Europe' (ibid. 134). By her actions, Burke argued, France was 'to be considered as expunged out of the system of Europe' ('On the Army Estimates', in *Works*, iii. 274). France constituted a menace to the common law of Europe, which for Burke included the delicate balances of power that prevailed in the different regions. What was happening in France was a pestilence or a plague that should be quarantined with the severest of embargoes (*Reflections*, in *SW* ii. 184). The means of maintaining the delicate balance and of ensuring international justice was in the last resort the instrument of war. War could only be justified, however, if it was resorted to as a matter of necessity, and could only be a necessity if all other avenues had been explored and failed. Even then, if the effects of war were likely to cause more harm than good, it could not be justified. War against France was justified on the grounds that resistance to the decimation of the crowns of Europe was perfectly legitimate, and to prefer the reign of religion to that of irreligion, 'life without dignity, and death without hope', was sufficient reason to stand firm against the regicide regime. Furthermore, the war was just because the system of France stood as a menace to political and national independence, liberty, life, and honour (*Letters on a Regicide Peace*, in *SW* iii. 122).

In his speeches on Warren Hastings Burke had sought to refute the Jacobin claim that states had no right to interfere in the internal affairs of other states. We must be careful to distinguish between internal dissensions of a rebellious and seditious nature, and actually participating in the divisions once they are fully formed. In the first case it is difficult to justify intervention because of the nascent character of the opposition, but in the second, precedent and treaties support the principle of interference to the extent that it may be said to form the foundation of the public law of Europe. Of course, a great deal of circumspection must be exercised, taking into account principles of justice and the policy of one's own country, as well as the general interest of Europe, but an abstract principle forbidding interference is not supported by authorities on the law of nations, by the law of nations itself, by the practice of Great Britain, nor by any other nation considered to be civilized. Burke contends that

> A more mischievous idea cannot exist, than that any degree of wickedness, violence, and oppression may prevail in a country, that the most abominable, murderous, and exterminating rebellions may rage in it, or the most atrocious and bloody tyranny may domineer, and that no neighbouring power can take cognisance of either, or afford succour to the miserable sufferers. (*Warren Hastings*, ii. 481)

Because states are members of the larger family of states what they do cannot go unheeded by their neighbours. In other words, what happens within the borders of one state cannot be a matter of indifference to another. Applying the common law notion of vicinity to the wider context of international relations Burke argues that just as a man does not have the right to erect any monstrous construction on his property without due regard for the effect it may have on his neighbours, a country cannot erect a form of government so out of keeping with the traditional inheritance of Europe that it constitutes a danger or significant threat to the safety of its neighbours (*Regicide Peace*, in *SW* iii. 135–6). The government of France, in Burke's view, was equivalent to a gang of robbers forcibly taking over the house of one's neighbour. France was a 'Colossus', a 'system' with an 'armed doctrine' that constituted a threat to every state in Europe (ibid. 76). France not only renounced its former treaties, but also flouted the law of nations, and by doing so declared itself to be an outlaw.

In all respects France had showed hostility towards the fundamental principles of European civilization. It flagrantly exhibited establishment regicide, Jacobinism, and atheism. Any authority that is not democratic is declared a usurper. This, of course, is a denial of the monarchical character of Europe. Jacobinism, in the sense that new young and enterprising talents form themselves into associations to assault established property rights in order to redistribute wealth to the propertyless class. This violates the very laws that are at the heart of the pre-existing institutions of Europe. And atheism in the sense that the state refuses to acknowledge the existence of God, confiscates Church property, and persecutes the clergy, instituting in their place 'impious, blasphemous, indecent theatric rites, in honour of their own corrupted and bloody Republick' (ibid. 126). All this, he claims, has been compounded by the corruption of manners: 'Manners are what vex or sooth, corrupt or purify, exalt or debase, Barbarise or refine us, by consent, steady, uniform, insensible operation, like that of the air we breathe in. They give their whole form and colour to our lives. According to their quality, they aid morals, they supply them, or they totally destroy them' (ibid.).

## Colonialism

Burke's view of colonialism was far from the aggressive economic view that came to prevail in the nineteenth century, and much less exploitative than, for example, the social imperialism of Cecil Rhodes, in which the exploitation of the lower nations was justified on the grounds that it benefited the lower orders in Britain and served to quell potential social unrest. His attitude is best described as paternalistic. Following Grotius and Montesquieu Burke believed that the colonization of a country, by conquest or consent, did not confer a right to impose arbitrary rule. Colonies were under the tutelage of the mother country, and should be encouraged to grow and mature into the best that its traditions intimate. He acknowledged that each nation has a character peculiar to itself, and that it should be respected in all of England's dealings with it. Even in the governance of colonies every effort should be made to adhere to the time-honoured traditions either of the colonizers, as was the case in America, who could justifiably claim the rights of Englishmen, or of both the colonizers and the indigenous peoples, as in the case of India. In both cases there is the additional consideration of universal principles, arrived at through experience rather than abstract reasoning.

There could be no question in Burke's mind of trying to impose a uniform system of government over an empire. Government is a practical matter designed to further the happiness of humanity. It is not meant to gratify the visionary schemes of politicians in their symmetry and uniformity. 'I never was', Burke argues, 'wild enough to conceive, that one method would serve for the whole' of the empire (*Letter to the Sheriffs of Bristol*, in *Works*, ii. 272). In relation to his concern for conciliation with America he emphasizes the fact that distance weakens government. There are considerable delays between the enactment of orders and their execution, and, where clarification is needed on certain points, the whole system is exacerbated. It is foolish to rule with an iron hand in such circumstances because, on the analogy of nature, blood flows less vigorously at the extremities of the body than at its centre. Burke believed that the British government's handling of the American War of Independence lacked sensitivity to the 'American Spirit', which was characterized by 'a fierce spirit of liberty' ('Speech on Conciliation with the Colonies', in *SW* i. 237, 243). Any statesman ought to be persuaded to use what power he has to give due weight to the American cause whose liberties have been fired in the kiln as those of Englishmen, and who equally love their religion. American liberty was 'liberty According to English ideas, and on English principles. Abstract liberty, like other mere abstractions, is not to be found' (ibid. 237). The use of force in suppressing the American spirit could only do harm to both Britain and America.

Even though Burke valued the dignity and spirit of nations, he was, then, not averse to empire as long as the ruling country took due heed of the spirit of the people over whom it ruled and was faithful to their traditions and mindful of allowing them a degree of relative autonomy.

In its relationship with India Great Britain had entered into a virtual Act of Union and was bound to promote the common good of the Indian people by preserving the rights laws and liberties which their natural original sovereign would have supported. In practice, India was subject to the tyranny of the East India Company, which 'in Asia is a state in the disguise of a merchant. Its whole service is a system of public offices in the disguise of a counting-house' (*Warren Hastings*, ii. 23). As early as 1883 Burke highlighted the gross injustices perpetrated in India in the name of the British state. Young men, who were little more than boys, governed there with no more sensitivity to local practices and traditions than if they still resided in England. Their concern was not the welfare of the people, but with making their fortune (*Speech on Mr Fox's East India Bill*, in *Miscellaneous*, in *SW* iv. 124). Burke argued that Warren Hastings blatantly disregarded the British statutes that delegated authority to him, the Indian laws, customs, and rights that he was entrusted to respect, and the universal principles of conduct applicable to all men. Hastings is accused of governing according to his own arbitrary will (*Warren Hastings*, ii. 3).

In defending himself Hastings claimed that he acted as he did in order to safeguard and advance the interests of the British state. In other words, he claimed reason of state as his defence. Burke maintained that no governmental powers could be exercised arbitrarily and that there must be limits on what a government can do in the name of necessity and reason of state. Governments as well as citizens must be judged against well-grounded moral standards and justifiably condemned if they are in violation. Power is limited by law, and its use is a matter of discretion directed to the good of those over whom it is exercised, rather than a matter of arbitrary will.

Burke argued that on all possible grounds Hastings's resort to arbitrary rule could not be justified. What, however, were the grounds of Burke's objections? Hastings's claim to have been delegated, or to have inherited, arbitrary power could not rest upon prescription. The British constitution was, for Burke, prescriptive. Arbitrary power was never any part of this constitution, and therefore could not have been delegated to Hastings.[33] Furthermore, it was never any part of the 'Mohamedan' constitution, sanctioned by law and the Koran, nor the Institutes of Genghis Khan or Tamerlane (ibid. i. 104–14 and ii. 4). In other words, Hastings could derive no prescriptive right from the constitutions of Asia to rule by arbitrary will.

---

## FURTHER READING

Fennessy, R. R., *Burke, Paine and the Rights of Man* (The Hague: Martinus Nijhoff, 1963).

Freeman, Michael, *Edmund Burke and the Critique of Political Radicalism* (Oxford: Basil Blackwell, 1980).

Macpherson, C. B., *Burke* (Oxford: Oxford University Press, 1980).

O'Gorman, Frank, *Edmund Burke: His Political Philosophy* (London: Allen & Unwin, 1973).

Waldron, Jeremy (ed.), *Nonsense upon Stilts: Bentham, Burke and Marx on the Rights of Man* (London: Methuen, 1990).

## NOTES

1. H. T. Buckle, *History of Civilisation in England* (London: Longmans Green, 1869).
2. William Lecky, *A History of England in the Eighteenth Century* (London: Longmans Green, 1887), vol. v.
3. John Morely, *Burke* (London: Macmillan, 1879), 211.
4. Burke, *Speeches on the Impeachment of Warren Hastings*, 2 vols. (Delhi: Discovery, 1987).
5. *The Works of Edmund Burke*, World's Classics, 6 vols. (London: Humphrey Milford, Oxford University Press, 1906).
6. *Select Works of Edmund Burke* (1874–8), ed. E. J. Payne, 4 vols. (Indianapolis: Liberty Fund, 1999) (hereafter *SW*).
7. Burke did not for a moment question this right; it was a mere metaphysical abstraction not worthy of consideration in relation to pressing practical matters. He was prepared to accept the policy if it could be shown to be reasonable, a matter of common sense, or 'the means of attaining some useful end' (Burke, 'Speech on American Taxation 1774', in *SW* i. 170).
8. See R. R. Fennessy, *Burke, Paine and the Rights of Man* (The Hague: Martinus Nijhoff, 1963), 58–9.
9. Frank O'Gorman, *Edmund Burke: His Political Philosophy* (London: Allen & Unwin, 1973), 90; also see p. 82.
10. Cited by W. H. Greenleaf, 'Burke and State Necessity: The Case of Warren Hastings', in R. Schnur (ed.), *Staatsrason* (Berlin: Duncker & Humblot, 1975), 358.
11. Russell Kirk, 'Foreword', in Peter J. Stanlis, *Edmund Burke: The Enlightenment and Revolution* (New Brunswick, NJ: Transaction, 1991), p. ix.
12. P. J. Stanlis, *Edmund Burke and the Natural Law* (Ann Arbor: University of Michigan Press, 1958), p. ix. Also see Burleigh T. Wilkins, *The Problem of Burke's Political Philosophy* (Oxford: Clarendon Press, 1967).
13. Cited in Stanlis, *Edmund Burke: The Enlightenment and Revolution*, 18.
14. Burke confessed that a conviction was unlikely, but that his reputation had to be defended for posterity. See P. J. Marshall 'Introduction', in *The Writings and Speeches of Edmund Burke*, vol. vi: *1786–1788* (Oxford: Clarendon Press, 1991), 1–2.
15. See Stanlis, *Edmund Burke and the Natural Law*, and Russell Kirk, *Edmund Burke: A Genius Reconsidered* (New Rochelle, NY: Arlington House, 1967). Cf. J. G. A. Pocock, 'Introduction', in Edmund Burke, *Reflections on the Revolution in France* (Indianapolis: Hackett, 1987), p. xlviii, and Conor Cruise O'Brien, 'Introduction', in Edmund Burke, *Reflections on the Revolution in France* (Harmondsworth: Penguin, 1969), 56–62.
16. Alfred Cobban, *Edmund Burke and the Revolt against the Eighteenth Century* (London: Allen & Unwin, 1960), 48.
17. Ross Haffman and Paul Levack, 'Introduction', in Haffmon and Levack (eds.), *Burke's Politics* (New York: Alfred Knopf, 1949), p. xv.
18. Conor Cruise O'Brien suggests that Burke's association with the Church of England was an attachment of convenience, for which he showed no theological enthusiasm. His family background made him better disposed to Catholicism than it was politic to admit in the late 18th century. 'Introduction', in Burke, *Reflections on the Revolution in France*, 29–30.
19. See Michael Freeman, *Edmund Burke and the Critique of Political Radicalism* (Oxford: Basil Blackwell, 1980), 142.
20. '. . . atheism is against, not only our reason, but our instincts' (ibid. and Fennessy, *Burke, Paine and the Rights of Man*, 59).
21. David Cameron suggests that the essence of the Enlightenment's conception of natural law is 'its belief in the individual's rational capacity to discern the rights of nature' (*The Social Thought of Rousseau and Burke* (London: Weidenfeld & Nicolson, 1973), 58–9).
22. Leslie Stephen, *English Thought in the Eighteenth Century* (London: John Murray, 1881), ii. 225–6.
23. Charles E. Vaughan, *Studies in the History of Political Philosophy before and after Rousseau* (Manchester: Manchester University Press, 1925), vol. ii. 37.
24. See my 'The Character of the History of the Philosophy of International Relations and the Case of Edmund Burke', *Review of International Studies*, 17 (1991), 140–1.
25. W. H. Greenleaf, 'Hume, Burke and the General Will', *Political Studies*, 20 (1972), 131–40; Cameron, *The Social Thought of Rousseau and Burke*; Dante Germino, *From Machiavelli to Marx* (Chicago: University of Chicago Press, 1969).
26. P. Hindson and T. Gray, *Burke's Dramatic Theory of Politics* (Aldershot: Avebury, 1988), 177.
27. S. K. White, *Edmund Burke: Modernity, Politics and Aesthetics* (Newberry Park, Calif.: Sage, 1994), 35.

28. Burke, letter to Depont, cited in Fennessy, *Burke, Paine, and the Rights of Man*, 97.
29. Richard Bourke, 'Sovereignty, Opinion and Revolution in Edmund Burke', *History of European Ideas*, 25 (1999), 99.
30. Samuel von Pufendorf, *On the Law of Nature and Nations* (Oxford: Clarendon Press, 1934), VII. vi. 7 and 10.
31. Ibid. VII. vi. 10 and 12. It should be noted that Pufendorf's discussion is not entirely consistent. He begins by distinguishing between absolute and limited sovereignty, and then makes a distinction between absolute and supreme sovereignty as if they are quite distinct. The confusion is somewhat allayed if limited and absolute sovereignty are seen to be types of supreme sovereignty.
32. Cited in Fennessy, *Burke, Paine and the Rights of Man*, 64–5.
33. '*He* have arbitrary power! My lords, the East-India Company have not arbitrary power to give him; the king has no arbitrary power to give him; your lordships have not; nor the Commons; nor the whole legislature' (*Warren Hastings*, i. 99).

# 22 Hegel

Alan Patten

## Contents



## Chapter guide

Hegel is a very difficult author, whose work is marked by both a high density of unfamiliar terminology and jargon and a theoretical structure and strategy that is not easy for the casual or first-time reader to appreciate. The chapter aims to give readers a few of the tools they will need in approaching Hegel's political thought. With this in mind, it offers an overview of some of the central themes and theses of Hegel's most important work of political philosophy, the *Philosophy of Right* (1821). The chapter also discusses several basic elements in his thought: his concept of freedom, and his ideas of spirit and dialectic.

A further aim of the chapter is to develop a specific interpretation of some of the main arguments of the *Philosophy of Right*, focusing in particular on his crucial and controversial claim that freedom is most fully realized in the state. In doing so, the chapter proposes a distinctive account of Hegel's thought, one in which the problem of consolidating the promise and principles of the French Revolution emerges as central to Hegel's political theory.

## Biography

Georg Wilhelm Friedrich Hegel was born on 27 August 1770 in the German city of Stuttgart. Both his parents came from Protestant, middle-class backgrounds, and his father served as a civil servant in the state of Württemberg. An exceptionally precocious child, Hegel had studied the works of many contemporary and classical authors by the time he became a student at the Protestant seminary in Tübingen in 1788. His classmates and close friends in Tübingen included Friedrich Hölderlin and Friedrich Schelling, both of whom would go on to make major contributions to German intellectual life. During the Tübingen years Hegel and his friends were introduced to the ideas of Kant and Fichte, and observed—initially with great enthusiasm—the unfolding events of the French Revolution.

By 1793 Hegel had decided to pursue a career in philosophy rather than the Protestant ministry. For the next fourteen years he held a variety of teaching positions, starting off as a private tutor for well-to-do families in Berne and Frankfurt, and eventually gaining an appointment to the position of lecturer (but not yet professor) at the University of Jena. During this period Hegel wrote a serious of essays and lectures on theological, historical, ethical, political, and eventually metaphysical themes and subjects. The culmination of this early phase of his career was the publication in 1807 of the *Phenomenology of Spirit*. In this ambitious, extraordinarily original, but in places dense and impenetrable, masterpiece Hegel introduced many of the central themes of his mature philosophical system, including spirit, dialectic, history, and freedom.

Although the *Phenomenology* brought Hegel considerable fame and reputation, it was not until 1816 that he secured his first full university position as a professor at Heidelberg. Shortly thereafter, in 1818, he moved to Berlin to take up a prestigious and influential professorship in philosophy, which he held until his death in 1831. By the 1820s Hegel had become one of Germany's best-known intellectuals. His books were widely read and discussed, and his lectures attracted students from around Europe.

After lecturing on political philosophy for several years, Hegel published the *Philosophy of Right* in 1821, as a book intended to accompany the lectures. Throughout his tenure in Berlin the political situation in Prussia was tense and delicate. Many of his core political beliefs were developed during a period of reform and liberalism in Prussia that began in 1807. But shortly after his arrival in Berlin the reforms came abruptly to an end and the ascendant, reactionary regime imposed censorship on academic publications and a witch-hunt for 'demagogues' from the universities. In this environment Hegel was forced to tone down some of his reformist sympathies and even (in the Preface to the *Philosophy of Right*) to flatter the authorities in various ways. He has been regarded by some as the 'state philosopher' of Prussian authoritarianism, but this is not really accurate. Hegel was concerned to keep his position, and could be timid and cautious by disposition, and so did not wish to antagonize the authorities unnecessarily. But he found subtle ways to communicate his reformist leanings, and even expressed his ongoing commitment to the ideals of the French Revolution with an annual toast, among friends, on Bastille Day.

Hegel is both one of the most influential and one of the most difficult political theorists in the history of Western thought. His difficulty no doubt accounts for the very wide range of different ways in which his political theory has been received. It also means that his name is invoked more often than his work is carefully studied. Even professional political theorists sometimes seem unembarrassed by the confession that they can make little sense out of Hegel's writings and see little point in trying.

My first and most important aim in this chapter will be to give readers a few of the tools needed to tackle Hegel's political thought for themselves. With this in mind, I offer an overview of some of the central themes and theses of Hegel's most important work of political philosophy, the *Philosophy of Right*. I also discuss several basic elements in his thought: his concept of freedom, and his ideas of spirit and dialectic.

A second aim is to develop a specific interpretation of some of the main arguments of the *Philosophy of Right*, focusing in particular on his crucial and controversial claim that freedom is most fully realized in the state. In doing so, I try to offer a distinctive account of Hegel's thought, one in which the problem of consolidating the promise and principles of the French Revolution emerges as central to Hegel's political theory.

## Key texts

*Hegel's Lectures on the History of Philosophy* (1805–30; first pub. 1833–6)
*Phenomenology of Spirit* (1807)
*Elements of the Philosophy of Right* (1821)
*Lectures on the Philosophy of History* (1822–31; first pub. 1840)

## Main texts used

*Elements of the Philosophy of Right*, ed. Allen W. Wood, trans. H. B. Nisbet (Cambridge: Cambridge University Press, 1991).
*Hegel's Lectures on the History of Philosophy*, trans. Elizabeth Haldane, 3 vols. (Lincoln: University of Nebraska Press, 1995).
*Lectures on the Philosophy of World History: Introduction*, trans. H. B. Nisbet (Cambridge: Cambridge University Press, 1975).
*Phenomenology of Spirit*, trans. A. V. Miller (Oxford: Oxford University Press, 1977).
*The Philosophy of History*, trans. J. Sibree (New York: Dover, 1956).

## Key ideas

**Dialectic**: the characteristic, logical structure of everything in reality and the method by which we come to a full, scientific knowledge of reality. To say that everything in reality—including the social and political world—has a dialectical structure is to say that all phenomena are constituted by both contradiction and the resolution of contradiction. The thesis that reality is best understood dialectically amounts to the claim—central to Hegel's philosophy—that the best way to understand some particular phenomenon is by working through the sequence of contradictions and resolutions that make that phenomenon what it is. **Freedom**: the *will* is free when its ends are 'its own', so that it is self-determining. The *will* is self-determining, in turn, when two conditions are satisfied: one 'subjective', the other 'objective'. The subjective condition requires that the *will* reflect on its ends and endorse them on the basis of its given desires and goals. The objective condition requires that the *will* pursue ends and goals that are rational. So the *will* is self-determining and free if and only if it pursues ends that are its own, both (1) in the subjective sense that they are grounded in its reflectively endorsed desires and evaluations, and (2) in the objective sense that they are grounded in its own true goals and purposes as a rational being. **History**: a series of stages in the development of *spirit*. The process in which individuals, cultures, and God develop and extend their powers of intellect and *will*. **Spirit**: a term used by Hegel to designate three levels of reality that are central to his philosophy: (1) the individual human being, who possesses a mind and is capable of agency; (2) a human group that possesses a culture; (3) God. Spirit develops itself in a series of 'stages'. In the early stages the individual's powers of intellect and *will* are only partially realized, a culture that encourages the exercise of intellect and *will* is only partially articulated, and God has only partly realized himself in the world. In the later stages the individual's powers of agency are fully extended, in a public culture that is fully supportive of intellect and *will*, and God achieves a fully realized self-consciousness through the vehicle of the human world. **Will**: the practical, active part of the *spirit* or mind. That which exerts agency and enjoys *freedom* in Hegel's philosophy.

## Introduction

The Preface to the *Philosophy of Right* sets out the main aim of the book and some of Hegel's views about reason, actuality, and philosophy. The task of philosophy, according to Hegel, is to identify and display the reason contained in the actual institutions and practices of the social world. In successfully accomplishing this task, the philosopher can help his readers and followers to achieve a state of reconciliation with the world in which they live. Hegel is notoriously confident that philosophy *will* be able to find reason in the institutions of the social world he inhabits. 'What is rational is actual', he announces, 'and what is actual is rational' (p. 20).[1] Hegel witheringly dismisses philosophers who devote their energies to imagining a world as it ought to be rather than looking for reason in the here and now. The gaze of philosophy, he maintains, is always backwards-looking: 'The owl of Minerva begins its flight only with the onset of dusk' (p. 23).

The systematic development of the book's argument begins in the Introduction. The Introduction announces, as central to the argument, the theme of freedom, and indicates the method and structure of what is to follow. As the title already suggests, the *Philosophy of Right* will be about the idea of 'right'. By this Hegel means not just 'rights' in the narrow sense in which the term is often understood (as in 'legal rights' or 'human rights'), but the entire normative domain: that part of reality that relates to duties, obligations, prohibitions, permissions, principles, virtues, and so on. Right, in turn, is always, for Hegel, about freedom (§29). To show that something involves right—to show, for instance, that it is the ground of a duty or the basis for some virtue—is always to show that it is a condition or expression of freedom. The main task of the *Philosophy of Right* is to demonstrate that the 'system of right' represents a 'realm of actualised freedom' (§4). In this way, Hegel thinks he can encourage a sense of reconciliation with the various demands of that system and the institutions and practices that make those demands.

Hegel divides this task into two parts. The first part, tackled in the Introduction itself, consists of an investigation into what freedom is: an exposition of what Hegel sometimes terms the 'concept of freedom'. The second part, to which the main body of the *Philosophy of Right* is devoted, explores the objective conditions under which freedom is fully actualized. Here Hegel seeks to show that various institutions and practices, together with the norms and values that hold them together, must be in place if freedom is to be realized in a community of people. Confusingly, this second part of the task also involves an exposition of what freedom is. Hegel holds that the true nature of freedom is best discovered in the very process of working out the institutions and practices that give actuality to freedom. As with any concept in Hegel's philosophy, the concept of freedom only fully reveals itself to the philosopher through a dynamic interrelationship with the various modes of reality in which it achieves existence.

After the Introduction the remainder of the *Philosophy of Right* is divided into three sections, entitled 'Abstract Right', 'Morality', and 'Ethical Life'. Each section is constructed around a distinct understanding of the free agent: the 'person' is the agent of Abstract Right; the 'subject' the agent of Morality; and the 'member' the agent of Ethical Life. With the transition from one understanding of the agent to the next the previous one is never discarded. Thus, the subject of Morality is also a person, and the member of Ethical Life is a bearer of both personality and subjectivity. Each section consists, not only in an explication of a particular understanding of free agency, but also in an account of the different institutions and practices which give existence to freedom so understood.

## Freedom

Freedom, as Hegel understands it, is a variant of what Isaiah Berlin has termed 'positive freedom'.[2] It does not consist in the *absence* of obstacles or impediments—this is what Berlin means by 'negative freedom'—but in the *presence* of a certain kind of relationship or connection between the agent and his activity. I am free in this positive sense when I am shaping and controlling my own life—when, to use the language Hegel favours, I am *self-determining*.

Positive liberty occupies an important place in our moral and political outlook. It is valuable for individuals to be self-determining, and one goal of political activity—although not necessarily the only goal—is to establish and protect the social conditions of self-determination. At the same time it is easy to be sceptical about Hegel's interpretation of self-determination and about a politics grounded in Hegelian freedom.

Freedom, according to Hegel, consists in 'being with oneself in an other' (§7A). I cannot become free by avoiding otherness, by refusing to commit myself to any activity or relationship with others. But even if I do engage with otherness in some way, it does not follow that I am necessarily free. I must be 'with myself' in the action or relationship in which I engage: it must be an expression of my self-determination. For this state of being with myself to be achieved, Hegel thinks that two distinct conditions must be satisfied. I must be both (i) subjectively free, and (ii) objectively free with respect to my end (§258). When these conditions are both satisfied, then I am with myself in my end or 'concretely' (subjectively + objectively) free.

Hegel's idea of subjective freedom tracks to a considerable degree an intuitive understanding of freedom. An individual enjoys subjective freedom, according to Hegel, when he reflects on his ends (rather than blindly acting on authority or trust, or unquestioningly following the conventions and traditions of his community) and when he can endorse those ends on the basis of his own particular desires and ambitions. The idea of objective freedom, by contrast, is rather less familiar. An agent is objectively free when he has the ends and motives that reason prescribes. Putting these different elements together, Hegel thinks that an agent is self-determining and free if and only if his ends are his own both in the subjective sense that they are grounded in his reflectively endorsed desires and evaluations and in the objective sense that they are grounded in his own true goals and purposes as a rational being.

Most of the controversy over Hegel's conception of freedom can be traced back to his claim that freedom has an objective dimension. Freedom as it is ordinarily understood is not tied to any specific ends but is open-ended: its content is not restricted or predetermined by anything but the agent's own empirically given goals and ambitions. Hegel's insistence that freedom has an objective dimension, by contrast, implies that an agent is only fully free when he has specific ends and adopts certain codes of conduct.

Hegel's conception of freedom not only competes with a common-sense conception, but also seems to rely on a problematic picture of the human self as divided into several parts—what Berlin calls the 'empirical' self and the 'real' self.[3] According to Hegel, merely acting on my own empirically given desires and motives, whatever they might be, is not enough for self-determination. I am only *self*-determining (both subjectively *and* objectively free) if my desires and motives coincide with those that are prescribed by reason. In the light of this claim it has seemed to Berlin and others that Hegel is creating an artificial and highly dubious division between the actual or empirical self and the 'real' self of reason. And why, these critics ask, should we accept this bipartite picture of the self? Supposing for the sake of argument that the picture is accepted, why think that reason is a more authentic part of the self than empirically given desires and ambitions?

Another apparent problem with Hegel's view—again emphasized by Berlin—is the ideological danger implicit in understanding freedom as having an objective dimension. The claim that full freedom requires the adoption of certain specific ends leads inevitably, it is argued, to the grossly illiberal view that it is possible to force someone to be free. If the wise and virtuous were better able to identify the prescriptions of reason than ordinary people, then what would stop them from forcing, coercing, or manipulating those people into adopting the right ends in order to make them free? The concept of freedom can normally be deployed rhetorically *against* such efforts, but Hegel's view seems, perversely, to have the opposite implication. Hegel's claim that full freedom is achieved only in the context of the state simply reinforces this worry about his position.

Of course Hegel is hardly the first philosopher to oppose freedom and desire or to identify freedom with reason and with specific codes of conduct. Rousseau famously proclaims that 'to be driven by appetite alone is slavery',[4] and Kant argues that autonomy is a property of an agent's will only to the extent that the will is able to abstract completely from all of its empirically given determinations and find a basis for action in the ends and duties to which it is committed just in virtue of its freedom and rationality.[5] What is puzzling, however, given the apparent similarity of his own view, is how forcefully Hegel objects to the accounts of both Rousseau and Kant. Rousseau is rebuked for failing to get beyond a mere aggregate of particular wills to a truly general will, and Kant's own solution to the problem of freedom—the Categorical Imperative—is dismissed as an 'empty formalism' and an 'empty rhetoric of duty for duty's sake' (§135). In light of these criticisms of his predecessors, it is far from clear how Hegel himself proposes to generate content for freedom.

One of Hegel's key claims about freedom is that it involves both abstraction and particular content (§§5–7). The free will, he says, is the unity of two elements: an element of 'pure indeterminacy' or 'absolute abstraction' and an element of 'determination' or 'particularization'. A closer look at what he has in mind here can help shed some light on how he might respond to some of the criticisms and puzzles sketched above.

The claim that abstraction is essential to freedom is, in effect, a claim about the kind of practical reasoning and deliberation that is appropriate for a free agent. The claim is that I am not free if I simply accept some externally given command or impulse as a decisive reason-for-action that I could subject to the critical scrutiny of my own thought and reason. To be free, I must *stand back* from the given command or impulse and reflect on whether it constitutes a sufficient reason to act in some particular way. Hegel associates this idea of standing back with the Protestant Reformation, which he thinks was a great advance in freedom. He credits Luther with challenging the doctrine that a person could obtain salvation by unquestioningly obeying the instructions and prescriptions of the Church. For Luther, true spirituality is a matter, not just of the individual's outer actions and performances, but also of his inner faith and understanding.[6] In the same way that freedom is opposed to unreflective acceptance of authority, it is also, Hegel thinks, opposed to uncritical reliance on one's desires and inclinations as a guide to action. An unquestioning acceptance of the promptings of the social and natural environment that generates one's desires and inclinations is, on this view, no more a mark of freedom than is an uncritical obedience to authority.

At the same time freedom is not just about abstraction; it also involves having some particular end and motive. As was noted earlier, Hegel denies that freedom is achieved by simply refusing to act at all (indeed he seems to suggest that a refusal to act at all is itself a kind of action). But this presents a difficulty, albeit a fruitful, one in Hegel's view. For how could a will be *both* totally abstracted from every given desire and purpose *and* have particular content? Imagine, for instance, asking some agent why he acted as he did and his answering with an appeal to some desire or authority. We then ask him why he takes that desire or authority to be a good reason-for-action and he responds by citing some further desire or authority. And so on. Eventually, the agent may simply put a stop to this chain of reason-giving by insisting that some desire or authority constitutes his bedrock reason-for-action. If he does this, however, then he would be violating freedom's abstraction requirement: he would simply be accepting some externally generated prompting that he could subject to his own thought and reason. On the other hand, if he does not stop his deliberations in some way, then his reasoning would extend ad infinitum. Either way, it seems there is a contradiction between the two elements of freedom, one which casts doubt on whether anyone could actually achieve freedom in the full Hegelian sense.

For Hegel, the key to understanding freedom is finding a resolution to this contradiction. Unfortunately, the details of Hegel's solution are not as clear as they might be, but the general thrust of his position is not difficult to grasp. His key claim is that, when an agent abstracts away from all his contingently given desires and goals, he will eventually arrive at a set of rational norms and duties that he finds himself committed to just in virtue of being a free agent. Being committed to these norms and duties is part of what it is to be a free agent and thus they do not themselves call for further abstraction. It is because abstraction leads back to these rational norms and duties (and no further) that Hegel thinks that freedom has an objective dimension—that full freedom involves commitment to the ends and motives that reason prescribes. The agent who rejects these ends prescribed by reason is, so Hegel thinks, ultimately not deciding for himself but is letting whatever external processes determine his particular desires and goals decide for him. If he does follow the ends prescribed by reason, on the other hand, then his activity is an expression of norms and duties he is committed to just in virtue of being a free agent.

Once Hegel's conception of freedom is fleshed out in this way, it is possible to see how he might reply to the criticisms sketched earlier. To the objection that his view conflicts with the common-sense understanding of freedom, Hegel can point to at least one intuitive feature of his own account: the idea that freedom is opposed to authority and so involves abstraction. It is the abstraction requirement, pushed to its logical conclusion, that generates the idea that freedom has an objective dimension. He can refer to the same abstraction requirement in responding to the charge that his view rests on an untenable bipartite picture of the self. Freedom is not a matter of the right *part* of the self ruling but of *the* self deliberating about its ends and motives in the right kind of way: freedom means that the self does not unquestioningly act on the promptings of desire or authority where it could subject those promptings to the scrutiny of its own thought and reason. The idea of an opposition between freedom and authority also suggests how he might respond to the worry that his theory licenses forcing people to be free. Just as spirituality for Luther requires inner reconciliation with God, and not just outward performances, the same, Hegel thinks, is true of freedom. Concrete freedom requires, not just performing the actions prescribed by reason, but also having the right motives and perceiving that those actions are reasonable: it requires not only objective freedom but also subjective freedom.

The most difficult issue, and the one that brings us back to Hegel's disagreements with Rousseau and Kant, concerns reason. Why think that abstraction eventually leads to some set of rational norms and duties? And, supposing that it does lead there, what is the content of these norms and duties? Hegel criticizes Kant for failing to answer the first of these questions—Kantian freedom, he says, is just 'the negative of everything else'[7]—and for giving an answer to the second of these questions—the famous Categorical Imperative—that is itself an 'empty formalism'. But these charges just raise the bar as far as Hegel's own view is concerned. Why should we think that Hegel's view of freedom and reason has a positive and non-empty content?

Hegel's position on these issues is very hard to make out, and not surprisingly a number of different interpretations have been proposed. According to one influential interpretation, most elegantly developed by Charles Taylor, it is at this point in the argument that Hegel falls back on a metaphysical theory of spirit to generate content for freedom.[8] For Taylor, the key to Hegel's alternative to Kant is the idea that the main agent of, and provider of content for, freedom and reason is *spirit*, where this refers not just to the individual human being but also, ultimately, to God. On a different reading, Hegel's alternative to Kant involves an appeal to an essentially historical idea of reason: the content of freedom and rationality is not determined by some transcendental, universal formula but is settled by the practices and understandings of a concrete community that is the product of the progressive unfolding of history.[9]

Although there are certainly important metaphysical and historicist themes running throughout Hegel's work (as we shall see shortly), it is arguably not obvious how either of these interpretations solves the problem of reason in a way that is consistent with the structure or key formulations of the *Philosophy of Right*.[10] Instead, let me suggest a third possible interpretation, which, although consistent with recognizing important metaphysical and historical themes in Hegel's thought, does not make them central to his account of the rational content of freedom.

Hegel insists that the will that abstracts from all of its contingently given desires and purposes does remain committed to one end: the end of establishing and maintaining its own freedom. 'The will in its truth', he says, 'is such that what it wills, i.e. its content, is identical with the will itself, so that freedom is willed by freedom' (§21A). This claim is repeated in a number of places and suggests a standard of reason that Hegel appeals to in generating content for freedom. If an end in some way contributes to the establishment and maintenance of the conditions of the agent's own freedom, then, in committing himself to that end, the agent can think of himself as willing his own freedom and therefore as fully free. As we shall see later in this chapter, understanding Hegel's account of freedom in this way helps to make sense of why he identifies the state as the highest locus of freedom. It is in the state that the individual dedicates himself to the good of the community as a whole and thereby to one of the essential conditions of his own freedom.

Of course, it might still be wondered how the end of establishing and maintaining one's own freedom resolves the conflicting requirements of abstraction and particularization in Hegelian freedom. Why shouldn't the free agent also abstract from *this* end? Hegel's answer is that one could not be a free agent without being committed to this end; or, to put this differently, being committed to this end is the basis of free agency and thus no limitation on it. Unless an agent had a commitment to becoming and remaining free, he would never engage in the kind of radical reflection and abstraction that sets up the problem of identifying content for freedom in the first place.

Hegel was greatly impressed by the Protestant Reformation and the principle of subjectivity which he took to be at its core. He thought that the French Revolution represented the extension into the social and political realm of this same principle, and he admired Rousseau and Kant for giving philosophical expression to the principle. At the same time, he worried that, on its own, subjectivity could be a terribly destructive force: it could negate and undermine authorities, traditions, structures, and so on, and leave nothing in their place. He even suggested that the Terror was a logical outcome of the French Revolution (§§5, 258). However, the solution, in Hegel's view, is not to reject subjectivity or even to find ways to limit it. Rather, it is to perceive that subjectivity is itself ultimately an individual, social, and historical achievement which depends on individuals being committed to particular ends and duties. These conditions of subjectivity are what provide the content of objective freedom. The standard of reason to which the objective dimension of freedom refers is ultimately the one that is implicit in subjectivity itself. When individuals are committed to this standard, they enjoy both objective and subjective free and so are fully free in Hegel's account.

## Spirit and dialectic

An understanding of Hegel's conception of freedom is one prerequisite for following the main argument of the *Philosophy of Right*. Another is an appreciation of the structure and method of the book. As was noted earlier, the main text of the *Philosophy of Right* is divided into three sections, each of which presents a distinct conception of agency and a corresponding set of institutions and practices. It is in the process of working through this sequence of models that the conception of freedom I have been examining gets fleshed out. More generally, the development of this sequence constitutes Hegel's attempt to reconcile his readers to the modern social world by showing it to be a 'realm of actualized freedom'. A central problem in approaching Hegel's political philosophy is to get a handle on the character and argumentative force of this developmental or sequential way of proceeding.

Addressing this issue requires that we confront two difficult but key elements of Hegel's philosophical outlook: (1) his concept of *spirit*, and (2) his idea of *dialectic*. Towards the end of the Introduction to the *Philosophy of Right* Hegel refers to the elements in the sequence to be developed in the book as 'stages of spirit' (§30), and it is clear from Hegel's other philosophical works that spirit is a crucial, if not *the* crucial, concept in his whole philosophical system. Hegel also says in the Introduction that the method whereby the different stages of spirit are to be developed is what he calls 'dialectic' (§31). Anyone with even a nodding acquaintance with Hegel's thought will be aware that dialectic (or, as Hegel sometimes calls it, 'speculative logic') occupies a central place in Hegelian philosophy. To understand the method and structure of the *Philosophy of Right*, then, we need to come to terms with the suggestion that the book develops in a dialectical fashion a series of determinations of spirit.

Hegel does not explain his concept of spirit, or *Geist*, in the *Philosophy of Right* but does discuss it in a number of other places. One of the clearest and most accessible expositions can be found in his *Lectures on the Philosophy of History*.[11] In those lectures Hegel makes it clear that spirit can assume three quite different kinds of shapes. He refers to: (1) spirit when it 'assumes the shape of a human individual'; (2) to the spirit of a group, especially a people or nation (*Volksgeist*); and (3) the 'world spirit', which he closely associates with 'absolute spirit' and with God.

To talk of individual human beings as bearers of spirit is, most basically, to call attention to the individual human mind. Indeed the word *Geist*, which I am translating here as 'spirit', is occasionally (and somewhat misleadingly) translated as 'mind'. Individuals are spiritual in this initial sense of having minds in so far as they possess self-consciousness, thought, and agency. Thinking of spirit in this way helps to make sense of Hegel's assertion that the will is one part of spirit: to possess a will is to be an agent, someone who can translate thought into action (§4).

The idea of spirit in the group sense is rather more difficult, since Hegel does not literally think that groups can have minds. A group can, however, be sensibly thought of as the bearer of a culture: it is a locus of ideas, perspectives, traditions, and intellectual problems and controversies, and a corresponding set of institutions and practices. We have something like this idea of spirit in mind when we talk of the 'spirit of the age'. A group can also be thought of as achieving a kind of freedom and self-consciousness, so long as we remain clear that it does so through the vehicle of its members. A group enjoys freedom and self-consciousness through its public institutions and practices of deliberation, intellectual inquiry, artistic achievement, and religious worship, and, more basically, through the vocabularies and modes of discourse in which these institutions and practices express themselves. A group also achieves freedom and self-consciousness by encouraging these qualities of agency in its members and making and protecting spaces in which its members can exercise them.

Most difficult of all is Hegel's idea of a world spirit. The key idea here, as far as Hegel's social and political thought is concerned, is that a collective practice of freedom is only possible in virtue of a particular historical inheritance. A public culture of freedom does not create itself *ex nihilo* but is always, at least in part, the product of a historical process of development that draws, in a progressive fashion, on previous cultures and ways of living. If we think of this growth and progression, from one *Volksgeist* to the next, as the development of a single agency (rather like an individual who develops from infancy to adulthood), then we have something like Hegel's concept of world spirit. Again it is important to avoid the temptation of thinking that such a world spirit literally has agency or consciousness: its progress and flourishing is always achieved through the vehicle of particular collective practices of freedom, which themselves are made up of ordinary, reflective human agents. As noted earlier, Hegel identifies this world spirit with God. The story of the world spirit's development, through increasingly sophisticated practices of freedom, is the story of God's progress towards freedom, self-consciousness, and self-completion, through the vehicle of human individuals and their cultures.

Although Hegel's use of the term 'spirit' to refer to three apparently quite different levels of reality—the individual, the social, and the divine in history—can be rather confusing, it is essential to his philosophical outlook that spirit has this multivalent character. In part this is because he identifies spirit with freedom and self-consciousness and wants to draw attention to three different levels at which freedom and self-consciousness might be realized. In addition, however, he thinks that there are certain significant connections between the different shapes of spirit, connections that are so important that it becomes hard to talk of one level of spirit without, at the same time, talking of the others.

The most theoretically interesting and significant of these connections holds between spirit in the individual and collective senses. According to Hegel, spirit in the collective sense provides a social context that conditions the development and outlook of the individual spirit. Hegel's thesis is that an individual can develop the capacities, attitudes, self-understandings, and so on that make him 'spiritual' only in the context of a collective practice of freedom. It is this paradox—that the free individual is the product of a particular sort of social environment—that is overlooked, in Hegel's view, by social contract thinkers. In insisting that all political legitimacy is grounded in individual consent, contractarians ignore the role played by social and political settings in constituting free individuals in the first place.[12]

This thesis, in turn, is backed up by an argument about the importance of *recognition* to the development and outlook of the free individual—a theme that is exposed in the famous account of the 'struggle for recognition' given in Hegel's *Phenomenology of Spirit*.[13] In Hegel's view it is only possible to develop and sustain the *sense* of oneself as free that is crucial to *being* free through a practice of mutual recognition involving other free individuals. It is only in the context of a public culture of freedom, one in which certain ideas, practices, and self-understandings prevail, and certain pathways of mutual recognition are established, that the capacities and attitudes involved in individual free agency are fostered and nourished. Hegel has this thesis in mind in the *Phenomenology* when he offers the often-quoted definition of spirit as an '"I" that is "We" and "We" that is "I"'.[14]

In thinking about the role of spirit in Hegel's social and political thought we should always keep its multivalent character in mind. At one level the *Philosophy of Right* develops a sequence of shapes of spirit in the sense that it presents a series of different conceptions of agency. At another, its different shapes of spirit each involve a distinctive picture of a collective practice of freedom, a practice in which individual agency is developed and sustained. And at a third level the modern social world developed in the *Philosophy of Right* is tinged with the divine. It develops an account of the conditions under which God achieves completion and self-realization in history through the medium of a collective practice of freedom and the free individuals that participate in that practice.

Like the concept of spirit, the idea of dialectic is not systematically discussed in the *Philosophy of Right* itself but is assumed to be familiar to readers from Hegel's other works. The details of Hegel's dialectical logic, as expounded in his books on logic, are dense, jargon-laden, and extremely difficult, but the basic idea is reasonably clear and that is all we need in approaching the *Philosophy of Right*.

Hegelian dialectic involves both an ontological thesis about the nature of reality and an epistemological thesis about how reality is best understood. Both theses rely on ideas of contradiction and resolution of contradiction. The ontological thesis holds that a given piece of reality is always constituted by both contradiction and the resolution of contradiction. The epistemological thesis affirms that the best way to understand some piece of reality is by working through the sequence of contradictions and resolutions that make that reality what it is.

To say that some area of life is afflicted by contradiction is, for Hegel, to say that the very success of that reality at fulfilling the purpose to which it is dedicated will eventually bring about its own demise. Marx's prediction that the capitalist would sell the rope with which he is eventually hanged (and his more general view that the very success of capitalism at developing the forces of production would eventually bring about the conditions of its own destruction) is perhaps the most vivid illustration of this Hegelian idea. The resolution of contradiction (the German word is *Aufhebung*) involves both the cancellation of the contradiction and the preservation of what is essential about the reality that is afflicted by the contradiction. Again Marx clearly illustrates this notion of *Aufhebung* with his suggestion that communism would resolve the contradictions of capitalism. According to Marx, communism would cancel what is contradictory about capitalism (its polarization of humanity into two warring classes, its failure to promote the human development of the majority, proletarian class, etc.) while at the same time preserving what is essential about it (for instance, its marshalling of tremendous human ingenuity and productivity).

Hegelian dialectic always begins from some extremely minimal and abstract characterization of the reality that is being considered and works towards richer and more complexly articulated characterizations. The initial, abstract picture of reality is shown to be self-defeating and incapable of subsisting on its own. This picture is then enriched or transformed by the introduction of some additional element which seeks to cancel the contradiction undermining the initial picture while preserving what is essential about it. The new, richer characterization is then shown to be self-undermining and a further element is introduced, and so on. Eventually, a complex and highly differentiated final characterization is arrived at, one which resolves the various contradictions out of which it is generated but which is itself reasonably self-sufficient. This final determination has the character that it has in virtue of being the result of a specific process of negation and resolution. And the best way to understand it is by reconstructing the sequence of stages from which it results.

The sequence of stages of spirit developed in the *Philosophy of Right* proceeds in exactly this dialectical fashion. It starts by specifying an extremely minimal and abstract model of what a collective practice of freedom must be like. The model is minimal in the sense that it assumes only a very basic conception of free agency and a very limited institutional and normative articulation of this conception. The argument then proceeds to show how the features of this initial picture are indispensable for a collective practice of freedom but also, on their own, self-undermining, unless a new element is introduced with a new set of features. Since the features of the initial picture are indispensable for a successful collective practice of freedom, and they turn out to depend on the richer, more complexly articulated features of the new picture for their possibility, these further features can be regarded as indispensable as well. The argument then examines whether the newly characterized collective practice of freedom would, on its own, be self-sufficient, and so on.

The result, if Hegel can pull it off, is a rich and highly differentiated picture of the necessary structure and content of a social world of freedom—one that he thinks would correspond in its essentials with the modern European social world in which he lives. If we are willing to affirm the first, simple model as a necessary part of any successful practice of freedom, then we have reason to affirm and feel reconciled with our own social world as well.

Overall, then, two features of the structure and method of the *Philosophy of Right* are essential to the argument Hegel seeks to make. The book presents a series of shapes of spirit, and it does so in a dialectical fashion. The focus on spirit forces us to keep three distinct balls in the air at once. It requires that we see the argument of the *Philosophy of Right* as, at once, an analysis of individual agency, of the collective practices of freedom which make possible individual agency, and of the institutional and practical settings in which God achieves self-realization in history through the human world. The use of dialectic means that we have to appreciate the developmental character of Hegel's argument. The argument starts out from a basic and minimal picture of individual agency, collective practice, and God's presence in the human world, and fills out a richer and more concrete picture by showing how further determinations are conditions of the possibility of the initial one.

## From property to state

The central assumption of part I of the *Philosophy of Right*, entitled 'Abstract Right', is that the agents, or wills, who make up the social world are *persons*. This assumption distinguishes the social world of abstract right from the worlds of morality and ethical life, where agents are assumed not only to be persons but also subjects and members respectively.

Personality, in Hegel's vocabulary, represents the most abstract, immediate, and minimal possible conception of free agency. To be a person is to recognize both that one is confronted by a set of givens—a given natural and social environment—*and* that one is independent of those givens, that they do not fully determine one's being or activity. It is, in effect, to think of oneself as a maker of choices, capable of imposing one's own will on a given situation.

'Abstract Right' has two main aims relating to its assumption of personality—one positive, the other negative. The positive aim is to determine what institutional shape a collective practice of freedom must take, given the premiss that agents in that world are persons. Hegel's methodological assumption here is that, if we acknowledge the importance of personality, then the argument he makes should give us good reasons to feel reconciled to the institutions and practices in question. The second, negative aim of 'Abstract Right' is to show that a collective practice of freedom involving only persons, and the institutions and practices grounded in personality, would not be viable: unless agents possess subjectivity and membership in addition to personality, their practice of freedom would be self-undermining and even their personality would be at risk.

Hegel addresses the positive task by giving an account of the institutions of property and contract. His analysis of property revolves around two main assertions (§45). The first is that the person is an object to himself—he 'looks' at himself—in his property. The second claim is that it is this experience of being an object to himself that allows him to 'become an actual will'. It is through looking at himself in his property that he develops and reinforces the capacities and self-understandings that make up personality.

In his property, Hegel is arguing, a person can see evidence of his own agency and choices. He makes certain choices and, to the extent that his property is undisturbed by others, his property registers the effects of those choices in a way that is clearly discernible both to him and to others. In this way, he sees himself as someone who does not, and need not, take his situation as given, but who can impose his own will and agency onto his surroundings. This perception of his independence and agency, in turn, helps the individual to develop and sustain his personality itself—helps him to 'become an actual will'. The objective confirmation from his surroundings encourages the sense of himself as free that is integral to being free. This sense is further encouraged by the recognition of others—mediated by the institution of contract—made possible by the person's self-presentation through his property. Overall, then, Hegel's position is that it is important for individuals to have property because it is important that they develop and sustain their personalities. Property helps to do this because it gives the individual and others a concrete perception of the individual's independence, a perception that confirms (directly and through the recognition of others) the sense of himself as independent that is an essential part of being a person.

This argument for property is, as far as I know, unique in the history of political thought. It does not rely on the controversial ideas of labour-mixing or desert that are familiar from Locke, nor does it appeal to considerations of need or utility. Instead the argument posits a *developmental* connection between property and freedom: having at least some minimal amount of property is crucial for developing and maintaining the capacities involved in free agency. Ironically, Hegel's argument probably finds its greatest echo, not in subsequent theories of property, but in Marx's alienation-based critique of capitalist property relations. For Marx, workers are alienated under capitalism because their predominant mode of interaction with the material world is not one in which their capacities for free personality are given any objective confirmation.

Although the institutions of property and contract are necessary conditions of the development of free agency, Hegel thinks that they represent just one particularly 'abstract' stage in that development. The full actualization of freedom, he maintains, calls for a 'richer', 'more concrete', 'more truly universal' set of institutions and practices, including the family, civil society, and the state. From the previous section we have some idea of what is involved with this development from abstract to concrete. The abstract stages—however necessary they may be—lack self-sufficiency. They are subject to dialectical reversals and internal contradictions, and must be redeemed and made viable by the introduction of new, more concrete determinations.

Why might a collective practice of freedom lack self-sufficiency in this sense? One reason is that an institutional structure operates effectively only if the established rules of conduct that partly constitute it are generally accepted and followed. If, for example, a system of private property is to be established and maintained that has the beneficial consequences for individual development anticipated by Hegel, then people must, in general, respect the property and person of others, keep their contracts, and so on. Following such rules of conduct, however, often means accepting burdens and sacrifices or at least forbearing from actions that are in one's immediate self-interest. One major reason why an institutional structure may lack self-sufficiency, this suggests, is if it fails to imbue people with the disposition to accept the burdens and sacrifices needed for its own maintenance and effective operation.

In the latter part of 'Abstract Right' Hegel argues that property and contract imbue people with motivations and dispositions that lead them to act in ways which actually undermine the institutions of property and contract (§81A). As we know, these institutions encourage agents to think of themselves as independent of their given situations and capable of making choices for themselves. The problem arises because a person as such could choose *any* particular course of action: the notion of personality is neutral with respect to the content of an agent's ends. This is a problem because, as we have seen, the effective operation and survival of the institutions of property and contract depend on agents having certain ends and not having others: they must keep their contracts and not violate the property of others. If agents are only persons, and have no further incentives, or possess no deeper self-understanding, then it is contingent whether they will actually will the ends necessary for the survival of the institutions required to maintain their personality. In this sense, the very success of a social structure consisting of property and contract at turning agents into persons seems to guarantee its own demise.

This argument is one particular instantiation of a persistent theme in Hegel's social and political thought: the idea that a culture of independent personality and subjectivity has potentially destabilizing implications for the established institutions and practices of a society. In his lectures on history, for instance, Hegel argues that the Presocratic Greeks enjoyed a harmonious social existence in which they habitually fulfilled the tasks and functions that allowed their social order continuously to reproduce itself. It was only when the Sophists introduced the principle of critical reflection, and this principle gradually permeated Greek culture, that the maintenance of the social order was threatened. When individuals began to consult their own particular beliefs and convictions about what to do, rather than reflexively following the customs and conventions of their community, their willingness to accept the burdens and sacrifices needed to keep the community going could no longer be counted on. Hegel goes so far as to read Plato's *Republic* as a profound philosophical attempt to describe what his community would have to do (e.g. banning private property, occupational choice, and the family) in order to forestall the development of the principle of independent personality which threatens it with disintegration (§185).

Hegel's own project, however, is not the Platonic one of finding ways of stifling individuality and subjectivity. Quite to the contrary, his concern is to identify what features of the modern social world make a spirit of independent personality and subjectivity realizable in a stable and self-sustaining way. Indeed, one way of understanding the structure of the remainder of the *Philosophy of Right* is as an attempt to develop a solution to the contradiction set up by the institutions of property and contract. Property and contract are necessary conditions of the development of free agency, but on their own they are self-undermining and so some further elaboration of the institutional structure needed for freedom is required.

One institution introduced by Hegel to this end is punishment: punishment is supposed to orient individuals away from certain ends and towards others by expressing society's condemnation of wrongdoing. Hegel thinks that this is part of the solution to the contradiction he identifies in 'Abstract Right' but not the whole story: so long as agents possess only personality, and not some deeper self-understanding as well, punishment will remain indistinguishable from revenge, and destabilizing conflict will be impossible to avoid (§102).

With its idea of the subject, part II of the *Philosophy of Right*, 'Morality', proposes a quite different sort of corrective to the self-sufficiency problem introduced by property and contract. It suggests that the problem of stabilizing the institutional structure needed to develop free personality could be solved if agents possessed not just personality but also subjectivity (§§103–6). The subject wills ends that are distinctively his own. He has purposes, intentions, and a conscience, and he is a subject only to the extent that his activity is an expression of this inner dimension of his agency. As a bearer of purposes, we can hold the subject responsible. As someone with intentions, we can think of him as enjoying more or less welfare. And as a possessor of a conscience, the subject is related to an idea of the good, which he tries to bring about through his activity. In 'Morality' we have a picture of a social world in which agents interact with each other not just as persons through the institutions of property, contract, and punishment, but also as subjects, who have their own distinctive ends and a corresponding framework of responsibility, welfare, and goodness. Hegel's thought is that, if the fundamental self-understanding and disposition of individuals is not just one of independent personality but also revolves around willing certain specific ends, then the contradiction afflicting 'Abstract Right' could be resolved.

As with punishment, however, Hegel holds that morality and subjectivity are part of the resolution to that contradiction but not the complete solution. There are two separate problems with the attempt to resolve the contradiction in the way suggested by 'Morality': one concerns the *content* of conscience, the other the *motivation* of individuals. The content problem is simply the problem of whether the ends and duties which individuals find they are committed to after searching their consciences really will be the ones that provide support for the institutional structure needed for the development and maintenance of personality and subjectivity (§§135–41). The motivation problem concerns whether individuals will be disposed to follow their consciences or whether they will prefer to pursue their own personal interests and satisfaction instead. Hegel claims that, on its own, morality is unable to provide either of these guarantees needed to lend self-sufficiency to the institutions he has introduced. In 'Morality', as in 'Abstract Right', it is entirely contingent whether individuals will have the specific ends and motives needed to secure the development of freedom.

Underlying this argument is the assumption that an individual's deepest convictions, values, and motivations are shaped by the social practices and institutions in which he participates. Thus we might expect that given the 'right' social environment individuals would find the 'right' ends in their consciences and the motivation to follow those ends. The problem, however, is that morality, as Hegel understands it, makes no assumptions at all about social practices and institutions (except for property and contract, which introduced the contradiction in the first place). Morality is in effect an attempt to resolve the contradiction arising in 'Abstract Right' in a non-institutional way but is for this very reason bound to fail. Unless certain institutions are in place, there is no reason to suppose that individuals searching their consciences and considering their motives will make decisions that work to stabilize the institutional structure that has been established by the argument so far.

Hegel's third conception of agency is discussed in 'Ethical Life', the lengthiest section of the *Philosophy of Right*. Here agents are conceived of, not merely as persons and subjects, but also as members of certain social institutions: the family, civil society, and the state. These institutions impose various duties on those who occupy the roles they define—the duties, for instance, of parents, of association members, of public officials, and of citizens. They also socialize their members into having the subjective dispositions to support and affirm these duties. 'Ethical Life' is a sphere of virtue, because ethical institutions impose duties on their members and imbue in them the inclination to perform those duties.

The accounts of civil society and the state are among Hegel's best-known contributions to political philosophy. In the discussion of civil society he identifies a realm of market relations, policing and regulatory institutions, and associational life that has profound implications for the social life of a community but which had hardly been acknowledged or theorized in traditional political philosophy. This realm, Hegel argues, has a logic and dynamic of its own that is importantly distinct from those of the isolated individual or family, on the one hand, and the state, on the other. Hegel is particularly impressed by how market activity and associational life are spheres in which the agent consciously pursues his own satisfaction while, at the same time, unconsciously and indirectly serving the interests of others and realizing some of the conditions of his own freedom.

In contrast to civil society, the state, in Hegel's vocabulary, refers to the set of institutions and practices that are consciously and directly geared around the universal—around, that is, realizing for all citizens the higher good of freedom. The state is made up of sovereign, executive, and legislative powers that have the maintenance of the conditions of freedom for the whole community as the object of their deliberation and knowledge, and make, implement, and apply decisions on this basis. It is also a sphere in which the fundamental dispositions of individuals and officials are other-regarding ones, including civic virtue and patriotism.

Hegel's account of the state is remarkable in several respects. Most strikingly, and notoriously, he lavishes praise on the state, claiming that 'freedom enters into its highest right' (§258) in the state and even asserting that 'the state consists in the march of God in the world' (§258A). In Hegel's view, the state represents the apex of the system of right he has developed throughout the *Philosophy of Right*. It is crucial for the full actualization of freedom, not just that individuals belong to ethical institutions in general, but that they be good citizens of the rational state.

The other notable feature of Hegel's discussion of the state is his account of what exactly constitutes a *rational* state. The state, as Hegel presents it, is a constitutional monarchy with a powerful civil service and a bicameral legislature. Like Plato, Hegel's chief concern is to ensure that those with superior knowledge and virtue occupy key positions of power. He describes a civil service that is specially selected on the basis of merit and then thoroughly trained and socialized into a knowledge of, and commitment to, the universal. To prevent corruption, various institutional checks and balances are introduced. These include cross-cutting memberships of key bodies, as well as the monitoring of public officials from above by the appointed ministers of the monarch and from below by the legislature. Hegel argues against direct legislative elections on the grounds that they give too much free play to the untutored opinions of atomized individuals. But he does think that the views of ordinary people can be appropriately structured and channelled through participation in the communities and associations of civil society, and he argues that a lower house of the legislature should be made up of deputies elected by groups in civil society. These deputies can play an important role, not just in exposing official corruption, but in mediating between the demands and expectations of civil society, on the one hand, and the decisions and laws of the state, on the other.

According to Hegel, the full actualization of freedom can be achieved only if individuals are members of ethical institutions. Freedom is actualized in the ethical life because the institutions and practices of modern ethical life are an integral part of the minimum self-sufficient social setting in which agents can develop and reinforce the capacities for free agency. Ethical life is an indispensable part of such a setting because it is the only environment in which individuals can be reliably expected to acquire the other-regarding ends and dispositions that will encourage them to accept the burdens and sacrifices presupposed by a self-reproducing social order that is hospitable to personality and subjectivity. Hegel's response to the ancients' worries about the destabilizing effects of subjectivity is thus to argue that a social order *can* tolerate a high degree of independent personality and subjectivity but only if a crucial condition is met. Its citizens must be members of ethical institutions that imbue them with goals, values, convictions, and so forth, such that, when they consult their own opinions and consciences about what to do, the answers they arrive at reinforce that order rather than ripping it apart, as happened, so Hegel thinks, in the ancient world and as recently as the French Revolution.

The claim that the Hegelian state is a necessary part of this structure amounts to the proposition that the ties of sentiment and affection that characterize the family, and those of mutual advantage and collegiality that are found in civil society, are not on their own sufficient to guarantee that people will accept the sacrifices and burdens needed to support a freedom-developing institutional structure. The model of the family is not generalizable because the bonds of affection and sentiment only extend as far as one's close relations and friends, whereas the maintenance of the required institutional structure requires some willingness to accept burdens and sacrifices on behalf of the countless strangers with whom one shares a community. Mutual advantage, the principle of civil society, can have a tremendous integrative effect within the context of an established market economy, but it is much less able to support the background norms, rules, and institutions that make such an economy possible in the first place. The ties of camaraderie and collegiality characteristic of associational life do come closer to stabilizing and unifying a social order hospitable to subjectivity, and so Hegel views it as a transitional institution between the market economy and the state. Still, Hegel thinks that associations are not, on their own, sufficient to stabilize a social order conducive to subjectivity. Because their ends remain 'limited and finite' (§256) and involve only '*particular* common interests' (§288), there are forms of conflict and instability that they will not be able to address.

It is only when a social order seeking to accommodate and promote subjectivity includes as its central and overarching institution the Hegelian state that Hegel expects it to be stable and self-sufficient. The Hegelian state performs this function because its central institutions—the sovereign, executive, and legislative powers—effectively and reliably pursue the universal interest: the interest that all have in living in a stable and self-reproducing setting that develops, nourishes, and respects individual subjectivity. These institutions are *effective* in the sense that they have the capacity to stabilize and preserve a social order hospitable to subjectivity against a range of destabilizing shocks and deprivations of both an internal and external nature. The institutions of the Hegelian state are *reliable* in the sense that they do tend to exercise this capacity rather than abusing their power and authority by promoting their own particular interests.

So Hegel thinks that starting from a basic commitment to free personality one is led inevitably, and via a number of familiar ideas and institutions, to a reconciliation with the modern state. If one accepts the minimal idea that the social world should actualize individuals' powers of free personality, then one must also endorse the full set of institutions, practices, and modes of being free that Hegel introduces, because these further determinations are conditions of the possibility of the first.

With the reconstruction of Hegel's argument that I have just sketched, we get a clearer idea of why he associates freedom with specific codes of conduct and, indeed, with good citizenship in the rational state. More open-ended conceptions of freedom are not, on their own, self-sufficient. Unless individuals are oriented to specific duties and virtues—culminating in the virtues of the good citizen—a social order geared around freedom would not be stable and self-reproducing. When an individual realizes the virtues of the good citizen, he is working to protect and preserve the social and political setting needed for his own freedom to be possible. He is willing his own freedom and, in this sense, enjoys objective as well as subjective freedom.

## Hegel's significance

Within a few years of Hegel's death his legacy was already a matter of fierce dispute. For many, Hegel's essential commitment was to an accommodation of the status quo. His claims in the Preface about the rationality of the actual, and his disparaging comments about philosophers who imagine a world as it ought to be, encouraged readers to view the *Philosophy of Right* as a straightforward defence of existing European social life. Over time, and in the context of new political and historical events, this 'right-Hegelian' reading was stretched even further. Hegel was identified as a glorifier of the state, a spokesman for authoritarianism, and even a precursor to twentieth-century Fascism and totalitarianism.

From the start, however, there was also a 'left-Hegelian' reception of Hegel's thought. The left Hegelians emphasized his distinction between 'actuality' and 'existence' (it is only the former that is claimed to be rational, and not all existing social life qualifies as 'actual' in Hegel's sense) and pointed to the many details of the Hegelian state that were not in fact instantiated in the Prussian state of the 1820s. According to some left-Hegelian readings, Hegel was a cautious, liberal reformer, who sought to modernize the Prussia of his time by introducing into its political life as many of the French revolutionary principles as it could digest. In this tradition, numerous post-Second World War scholars have detailed the distortions and anachronisms involved in associating Hegel's name with authoritarian, let alone totalitarian, politics.

Beyond this debate over his place along the conservatism–reformism spectrum, Hegel's influence has shown itself in a number of other areas of social and political thought as well. Marx and Kierkegaard are only the most obvious examples of the generations of European intellectuals that have defined their own projects in opposition to Hegel's. Marx is clearly the most influential of Hegel's followers. Although Marx is strongly critical of Hegel's idealism (dismissing it at times as 'mysticism'), and of his inversion of civil society and state, he acknowledges important debts as well. He takes over Hegel's idea that history displays a rational, progressive character, and shares Hegel's commitment to understanding social reality using the tools of dialectic. As I suggested in the previous section, his early critique of alienation also seems to start from the Hegelian idea that the actualization of an individual's powers of freedom and agency depends on achieving certain forms of interaction with the material and human surroundings.

In contemporary political theory Hegel's name is probably most often associated with communitarianism. His critical engagement with Kant is seen as a forerunner of the contemporary communitarian critique of Rawlsian liberalism. He is credited with exposing the abstract, atomistic character of modern liberalism and with puncturing its universalist pretensions. Present-day communitarians take themselves to be reaching back to Hegel in arguing for a textured, context-oriented, anti-foundationalist political theory focused on the traditions and shared understandings of concrete communities.

Although there is probably a measure of truth in all of these different ways of engaging with Hegel's thought, arguably none of them does full justice to what he was trying to achieve. Least adequate of all is the suggestion that Hegel was some kind of proto-totalitarian glorifier of Prussian authoritarianism. The social and political arrangements laid out in the *Philosophy of Right* bear a much closer resemblance to the Prussia sought by pre-1820 reformers than to the existing Prussian state of the 1820s (let alone twentieth-century Fascism). At the philosophical level Hegel's outlook is even more at odds with the authoritarian tradition. For Hegel, a social order is only worthy of reconciliation if it actualizes freedom, and this means that such an order must respect and promote both subjective and objective freedom.

The communitarian reception of Hegel's thought also risks distorting an essential element in his political theory. Although Hegel does assign an important role to the shared norms and understandings of ethical life in guiding everyday practical reason, he does not simply leave it at that, as some communitarians suggest we should. Hegel also seeks to be show—indeed it is a major task of the *Philosophy of Right*—that ethical life is an essential part of the actualization of freedom.

The picture of Hegel as a liberal reformer is an improvement on these assessments of his thought, but it fails to capture what is striking and distinctive about Hegel's political theory. As I have tried to bring out in this chapter, one of Hegel's major preoccupations is with the *fragility* of collective practices of freedom. Influenced by the civic humanist tradition in political thought, he is attuned to the vulnerability of those practices to the individualism, egoism, and indifference of those who participate in them. The constant danger is that the social and political settings that encourage freedom will disintegrate into anarchy and chaos or easily be supplanted by oppressive and authoritarian regimes.

For Hegel, however, there is no turning back to a pre-reflective state of social harmony. Once individuality and subjectivity have made their entrance in world history, their claims cannot be denied. The challenge is to discover what features of modern social life allow individuality and subjectivity to flourish in a stable and self-reproducing way. How can a social order realize the principles of the French Revolution without generating the Terror and Napoleon as well? In working through the tensions and ambiguities in Hegel's political outlook—between reformism and conservatism, between liberalism and communitarianism—it is helpful to bear in mind Hegel's preoccupation with this consolidation problem. In the wake of 1989 this is no less a problem for us than it was for the generation that witnessed 1789.

## FURTHER READING

Avineri, Shlomo, *Hegel's Theory of the Modern State* (Cambridge: Cambridge University Press, 1972).

Berlin, Isaiah, *Four Essays on Liberty* (Oxford: Oxford University Press, 1969).

Hardimon, Michael, *Hegel's Social Philosophy: The Project of Reconciliation* (Cambridge: Cambridge University Press, 1994).

Kant, Immanuel, *The Moral Law*, trans. H. J. Paton (London: Unwin Hyman, 1948).

Patten, Alan, *Hegel's Idea of Freedom* (Oxford: Oxford University Press, 1999).

Pippin, Robert, *Idealism as Modernism: Hegelian Variations* (Cambridge: Cambridge University Press, 1997).

Rousseau, Jean-Jacques, *The Social Contract*, trans. G. D. H. Cole, rev. J. H. Brumfitt and John C. Hall (London: J. M. Dent & Sons, 1973).

Taylor, Charles, *Hegel* (Cambridge: Cambridge University Press, 1975).

Wood, Allen W, *Hegel's Ethical Thought* (Cambridge: Cambridge University Press, 1991).

## NOTES

1. Unless indicated otherwise, all parenthetical page and paragraph references are to Hegel, *Elements of the Philosophy of Right*, ed. Allen W. Wood, trans. H. B. Nisbet (Cambridge: Cambridge University Press, 1991). An 'A' following a paragraph number indicates a reference to one of the 'additions' included in all editions of the *Philosophy of Right* since the 1830s.
2. Isaiah Berlin, *Four Essays on Liberty* (Oxford: Oxford University Press, 1969).
3. Ibid. 132.
4. Jean-Jacques Rousseau, *The Social Contract*, trans. G. D. H. Cole, rev. J. H. Brumfitt and John C. Hall (London: J. M. Dent & Sons, 1987), book I, ch. viii.
5. Immanuel Kant, *The Moral Law*, trans. H. J. Paton (London: Unwin Hyman, 1948), 101, 107–8.
6. Hegel, *The Philosophy of History*, trans. J. Sibree (New York: Dover, 1956), 377–422.
7. *Hegel's Lectures on the History of Philosophy*, trans. Elizabeth Haldane, 3 vols. (Lincoln: University of Nebraska Press, 1995), iii. 460.
8. Charles Taylor, *Hegel* (Cambridge: Cambridge University Press, 1975), ch. xiv.
9. Robert Pippin, *Idealism as Modernism: Hegelian Variations* (Cambridge: Cambridge University Press, 1997), ch. 4.
10. Alan Patten, *Hegel's Idea of Freedom* (Oxford: Oxford University Press, 1999), 16–34.
11. *Lectures on the Philosophy of World History: Introduction*, trans. H. B. Nisbet (Cambridge: Cambridge University Press, 1975), 47–53.
12. Patten, *Hegel's Idea of Freedom*, ch. 4.
13. Trans. A. V. Miller (Oxford: Oxford University Press, 1977), 104–19.
14. Ibid. 110.

# 23 The early Marx

Lawrence Wilde

## Contents



## Chapter guide

The chapter focuses on the work of Marx prior to 1846. The dominant theme is the concept of alienation, which also implies a human essence from which we are alienated. Although Marx borrows heavily from Hegel and from Feuerbach, his background in the philosophy and culture of ancient Greece is an important factor in his early essentialism. The early Marx rejects Hegel's theory that the state represents an ethical community. For Marx, not even a democratic state can produce human emancipation, for the state always represents particular class interests. Only when private property is replaced and classes abolished can human freedom be achieved. Communism is seen as the movement of the exploited workers struggling to free themselves, and, in the process, liberate the whole of humanity so that they can freely develop their human essence of social creativity.

## Biography

Karl Marx was born into a middle-class family in Trier in Germany in 1818 and educated at the Universities of Bonn and Berlin, where he mixed in radical circles. He espoused communism in 1843 and, with the help of Friedrich Engels, developed a theory of history later known as historical materialism, emphasizing the key role played by the economic structure in determining social and political life. *The Manifesto of the Communist Party* (1848) portrayed history as a succession of class struggles leading eventually to the victory of the international working class and the abolition of capitalism. Exiled to London following the revolutions of 1848, he worked mainly on political economy, but only the first volume of *Capital*, his critical analysis of capitalism, was published in his lifetime (1867). He predicted the spread of capitalism throughout the globe, the development of monopolies, and recurring economic crises. He played a leading role in the International Working Men's Association from 1864 to 1872, but it was not until after his death in 1883 that major socialist parties espousing his ideas developed throughout Continental Europe. In the twentieth century his name was used in support of dictatorial communist regimes in Russia, China, and eastern Europe, conveniently ignoring his commitment to radical democracy.

### Key texts

*The Economic and Philosophic Manuscripts* (1844)
*Manifesto of the Communist Party* (1848)
*The Eighteenth Brumaire of Louis Bonaparte* (1852)
*Capital* (1867)

### Main texts used

The most important early writings are found in vol. iii of Karl Marx and Frederick Engels, *Collected Works* (London: Lawrence & Wishart, 1975).

### Key ideas

**Alienation**: a condition of oppression arising from loss of control over productive activity. **Political emancipation**: the achievement of a democratic constitution. **Human emancipation**: the achievement of freedom through the abolition of exploitation and oppression in **communist society**. **Communism**: the movement of the international **proletariat** struggling against capitalism.

---

## Introduction

The essence of the political thought of the early Marx is to be found in the concept of essence itself, or, more specifically, in the concept of human essence. When Marx, at the age of 26, endorses communism as the appropriation of the human essence 'by and for man' and as 'the complete return of man to himself as a social being' (*Works*, iii. 295–6[1]), his language reflects not only the humanism of the left-Hegelian movement with which he associated, but also the wider influence of the philosophy and culture of ancient Greece on German intellectual life. In his grand quest for human freedom the early Marx first embraces the cause of political democracy and then concludes that in itself it offers only political freedom. We need to examine why and how Marx developed his commitment to communism as the movement that could emancipate the world. More particularly, we need to look at how he conceived the relationship between state and civil society in his critical encounters with Hegel and the Young Hegelians. In virtually all periodizations of Marx's work, the manuscript written in the winter of 1845–6, *The German Ideology*, is regarded as a significant breakthrough, as it sets down for the first time his general theory of historical development and resolves on a more empirical approach towards understanding the origins and structure of socio-economic power. The concern of this chapter is therefore with his political thought prior to *The German Ideology*, although the crucial question of the continuity between the phases of his intellectual development will be addressed in the concluding remarks.

Marx gives a succinct account of his early intellectual development in the famous 1859 Preface to *A Contribution to the Critique of Political Economy*, in which he admits that his studies in philosophy and history at the University of Berlin left him at a disadvantage when it came to tackling social issues in his first paid employment as editor of the *Rheinische Zeitung* (*Works*, xxix. 262). Using the collapse of the newspaper as an opportunity to try to remedy the deficiencies in his knowledge, he returned to the study of Hegel, whose philosophy he had first got to grips with some six years earlier (*Works*, i. 19). The immanent critique of Hegel's justification of the Prussian political system, *A Contribution to the Critique of Hegel's Philosophy of Right*, written towards the end of 1843 but unpublished in his lifetime, marks a major theoretical stride forward. This 'critical re-examination' convinces him that legal relations or political forms can be properly understood neither within their own terms nor in terms of the general development of ideas. The underlying causes of legal and political phenomena had to be sought in civil society, which he describes as the totality of the material conditions of life. Furthermore, the 'anatomy' of this civil society is to be uncovered by the science of political economy (*Works*, xxix. 262).

By the end of 1843 he had announced his commitment to communism and even nominated the social class that would lead the way to human emancipation. In the Introduction to his critique of Hegel's *Philosophy of Right*, written after the critique itself, he identifies the proletariat as the class with the unique capacity to liberate the whole of society through the act of liberating itself. In modern society it represents 'the complete loss of man', and it could liberate itself only through the 'complete re-winning of man' (*Works*, iii. 186). Marx proceeds to amplify the relationship between civil society and the state in *On the Jewish Question* before moving on to his first encounters with political economy in the Paris Manuscripts of 1844, including the *Comments on James Mill* and the *Economic and Philosophic Manuscripts*, writings that remained unpublished until 1932. In these writings Marx is chiefly concerned with the alienation suffered by the workers in the modern industrial system and its wider implications for society as a whole. These themes are reiterated in *The Holy Family*, written with the assistance of Friedrich Engels, in which they finally set down detailed criticisms of the limitations of their erstwhile *confrères* among the Young Hegelians.

Before looking more carefully at Marx's philosophical development during this period we might pause to consider other factors which might throw light on his dramatic trajectory from constitutional democracy to communism. Certainly his upbringing, as the son of a Jewish lawyer in the Rhineland, was a liberal one.[2] Although the Rhineland had been absorbed into Prussia just before Marx's birth, its population retained great sympathy with the ideals of the French Revolution. The oppression suffered by European Jewry may well have contributed to Marx's outrage against all oppression, but there appears little evidence to suggest that Marx's political philosophy was in any way influenced by Jewish theology. In terms of his own experience, the practical problems he experienced in his work with the *Rheinische Zeitung* from May 1842 to March 1843 most certainly pushed him to a more radical position.[3] This involved not only looking at particular examples of class oppression, such as the debate on the law of theft from woods and the impoverishment of the Mosel wine-growers, but also facing the constant threat of censorship by the Prussian authorities. Accused of providing publicity to communists, Marx was moved to defend publicly the right to open discussion of communist ideas while privately bemoaning the quality of some of the allegedly communist contributions to his newspaper (*Works*, i. 215–21, 393–4). In short, what we see here is an intense confrontation with social reality following years of immersion in academic work, and, as Riazanov has noted, he left the paper 'a completely transformed man'.[4]

It was during his time in the editor's chair of the *Rheinische Zeitung* that Marx first met Friedrich Engels, but their association began to blossom the following year when the latter contributed 'Outlines of a Critique of Political Economy' to Marx's new journal, the *Deutsch-französiche Jahrbücher*. In his engagement with British political economy Engels exposes its callous disregard for the social cost of the inexorable advance of capitalism, but he goes further than that, seeing that the progress of the system erodes its own foundations and paves the way for its transformation. Private property will eventually be superseded by a more rational system which heralds the 'reconciliation of mankind with nature and with itself' (*Works*, iii. 424–6). He concludes by lambasting the 'despicable immorality' of the system and the brazen hypocrisy of the economists (ibid. 443). With its analysis of the irresistible yet contradictory dynamic of capitalism, its treatment of the coercive nature of the exchange process, and its emphasis on the dehumanizing nature of the system and the work of its apologists, Engels's brilliant article showed Marx the way to go.[5] It was only a few weeks later that Marx revealed his own commitment to communism, and the stage was set for his analysis of the alienation inherent in the process of modern commodity production.

## Human essence and its alienation

Marx was convinced that capitalism carries the threat of the complete 'loss of man', but who is this 'man' who has been lost and needs to be rewon? The great theme running through the writings of 1844–5 is the theme of alienation (*Entaüsserung*) or estrangement (*Entfremdung*), terms that may be used interchangeably, as both have descriptive and normative meanings. That is to say, they involve description of a process of separation or distantiation and also carry the connotation that the loss of control experienced by workers wrongly deprives them of something. According to Marx, four forms of alienation are experienced by the modern worker (*Works*, iii. 272–7). First, alienation from the product of labour, which belongs not to the worker but to the employer. Secondly, alienation from the act of production within the labour process, since the work is forced labour and is experienced as suffering and weakness. Thirdly, alienation from species-being (*Gattungswesen*), a term borrowed from Feuerbach which refers to that which makes us distinctively human. Marx refers frequently to the dehumanization of the worker, with the implication that this system of production denies them something which is their due as human beings (ibid. 137, 212, 284, 303, 308). He uses the simile of man's reduction to a machine three times in as many pages in the *Manuscripts* (ibid. 237–8). The fourth aspect of alienation, a consequence of the other three, is the alienation of 'man from man'. It follows that we are estranged from each other 'in every relationship', and the alienated situation of the worker is generalized through society at large (ibid. 277–8). Marx draws the conclusion that the emancipation of the workers contains 'universal human emancipation' because the whole of human servitude is involved in the process of production (ibid. 280).

In illustrating the first and second aspects of alienation Marx bemoans the fact that work is experienced as deadening compulsion, with the worker feeling free only in functions such as eating, drinking, and making love, which, taken abstractly, are animal functions (ibid. 275). The fact that these functions are shared with animals does not mean that they are not also human needs which are being met, but clearly for Marx there must be more to human life than this. In discussing alienation from species-being Marx enlarges on the difference between humans and animals. 'Conscious life activity' distinguishes humans from animals, according to Marx, for whereas animals are 'one' with their life activity, humans make their life activity the object of their will and consciousness. This emphasis on 'activity' is followed by a sharper focus on production, the ability people have to create products for each other in a consciously planned way: 'In creating a world of objects by his practical activity, in his work upon inorganic nature, man proves himself a conscious species being . . . animals also produce . . . but an animal only produces what it immediately needs for itself or its young. It produces one-sidedly, whilst man produces universally' (ibid. 276). Truly human production, then, transcends the instinctive response to immediate physical needs, and we are able to create things in accordance with the standards of other species and imbue our products with aesthetic qualities. The cave paintings of early *Homo sapiens* provide a good illustration of Marx's conception, for they were created beyond the requirements for physical survival and they often depict the struggle for survival in our relationships with other animals. It has been objected that Marx oversimplifies the difference in the productive capacities between humans and other animals,[6] yet it is difficult to deny that there is such a difference and, furthermore, that it is a qualitative one.[7]

As Marx insists that the individual is always a social being (ibid. 299), it is probably most accurate to characterize his view of the human essence as 'social creativity'. Full realization of this essence would involve free cooperation between equals, but historically, cooperation in labour has often been imposed by external discipline, whether it be by coercion, as in the building of the pyramids, or by contract, as in the modern factory system in which the workers have no creative input. In Marx's view, alienated labour transforms our human essence into a mere means to our existence. Marx talks about the workers losing their freedom 'in the service of greed' and of being 'depressed spiritually and physically to the condition of a machine' (ibid. 237–8). This perversion of human potential is brought about through the medium of money, which, when raised to omnipotence, accomplishes the 'confounding and confusing of all natural human qualities' and turns the world upside down (ibid. 326). For Marx, production under private property dulls the senses. The 'care-burdened, poverty stricken man has no *sense* for the finest play', he writes, and the dealer in minerals is interested only in their commercial value rather than their beauty (ibid. 302). Private property has made us so 'stupid and one-sided' that we think of an object as ours only when we have it, only through possession, rather than appreciating it as 'social, *human* object' (ibid. 300–1).

How can humanity progress from alienation to full freedom? The answer for Marx lies in the dynamism of historical development. Even at this early stage of his understanding of political economy, he argues that the expansion of the money economy produces a social class that will be compelled to resist it. Although the modern industrial system denies freedom to the mass of producers, it nevertheless exhibits the immense capacity of human creativity. He conceives the development of industry in dialectical terms, as presenting both the 'open book of man's essential powers' and the simultaneous perversion of that essence through alienation. The development of technology opens the way for human emancipation by offering the prospect of material abundance, but its immediate effect is the 'furthering of the dehumanisation of man' (ibid. 302–3). The achievements of modern production testify to our creative capability and provide the material basis for a life without scarcity, but for those who live by the sale of their labour power there is little or no experience of creativity or freedom. Only through the abolition of private property can we achieve the 'complete emancipation of all human senses and qualities' (ibid. 300). The movement to facilitate this transformation is communism, which involves the 'positive transcendence of private property as human self-estrangement', through which the human essence is no longer in strife with its existence (ibid. 296).

Many of the arguments developed in the *Manuscripts* reappear in the 1845 publication of *The Holy Family*, the first product of the Marx–Engels collaboration. Its main purpose was to criticize the approach of the Young Hegelians, who are now denounced as the most dangerous enemy of 'real humanism' in Germany because of their aridity and abstractness (*Works*, iv. 7). The alienation theme is restated, and here it is acknowledged that the propertied class as well as the proletariat suffer from the same alienation. However, whereas the former feel strengthened and at ease with this alienation, the 'inhuman' condition of the workers is presented as a 'contradiction between its human nature and its condition of life, which is the outright, resolute and comprehensive negation of that nature' (ibid. 36–7). Once again the plight of the proletariat is described as the loss of humanity, recoverable only by revolution, which will resolve the inhuman conditions of the life of the entire society.

Where, philosophically, do we locate Marx's humanism in the period just prior to the development of his theory of historical development? Do we accept, as Althusser suggests, that Marx's thought of this period is dominated by his attachment to Ludwig Feuerbach's communalist humanism?[8] There are certainly many reasons for accepting this view. Feuerbach had gained renown on the strength of his famous 'inversion' of Hegel's philosophy and his critique of religion. He argued that the subject–object relationship in Hegel's idealism needed to be inverted, so that rather than seeing human progress as the self-movement of Reason, we see it as the conscious striving of real human beings. In *The Essence of Christianity*, published in 1841, Feuerbach presented the personality of God as the 'projected personality of man', an ideological construction which meets pressing psychological needs based on humanity's deep-seated fears and aspirations.[9] Marx accepts this analysis of the role of religion, describing it as the fantastic realization of the human essence because that essence has no true reality. Religion, he argues, persists as an expression of distress and a protest against that distress, and should be understood as the 'sigh of the oppressed creature, the heart of a heartless world . . . the *opium* of the people' (*Works*, iii. 175). The powerful impact of Feuerbach's work on radicals in Germany in the early 1840s was recalled many years later by Engels, who comments that enthusiasm was universal and that 'we were all Feuerbachians for a moment' (*Works*, xxvi. 364). We have on record Marx's fulsome admiration of Feuerbach in two letters to him, written in October 1843 and August 1844, although the second letter, in which Feuerbach is credited with providing a philosophical basis for socialism, shows that Marx is already making different connections from his mentor (*Works*, iii. 349–51, 354–7).

The terms and language of Marx's humanism in the 1843–5 period are straightforwardly Feuerbachian. In the *Manuscripts* he praises Feuerbach's achievement in exposing philosophical idealism as a form of religious thinking and a manifestation of the 'estrangement of the essence of man' (ibid. 328). The discussion of the distinction between animals and humans in the *Manuscripts* follows closely the terms as Feuerbach's treatment of the issue in *Principles of the Philosophy of the Future* (1843), including the claim that only the human being is a universal being.[10] In addition, Marx shares Feuerbach's view that 'the essence of man is contained only in the community and unity of man with man'.[11] However, by now Marx's primary concern is with the plight of workers who, in advanced forms of private property, are obliged to live in 'disastrous isolation from this essential nature' (ibid. 204–5, 217). This focus on the material basis of alienation and the potential for humanity to break free of its shackles means that even when he is closest to Feuerbach's philosophy he is also in the process of going beyond it.

Ironically, although Marx's rejection of idealism owed much to Feuerbach's critique of Hegel's philosophy, the latter was of vital importance for Marx in his attempt at 'comprehending the action of world history' (ibid. 336). In his discussion of Hegel's *Phenomenology* in the *Economic and Philosophic Manuscripts* Marx makes the somewhat controversial claim that Hegel's outstanding achievement lay in grasping the self-creation of man as a process, involving alienation and its transcendence through labour, with labour being the essence of man (ibid. 332–3 and 339). Hegel's philosophy, according to Marx, opens up the possibility of human emancipation through the cooperative action of all mankind, and only as the result of history (ibid. 333). However, Marx objects that the only labour which Hegel knew was 'abstractly mental labour' and that the only resolution of the problem of alienation offered by Hegel is through purely philosophical self-confirmation. In Marx's view this resolution remains in the realm of abstract thought, and, as such, actually confirms the alienation it purports to supersede (ibid. 342). Marx's criticism turns on the formal and abstract procedure of Hegel's philosophy, although he stands accused of underestimating its powerful realism.[12] Nevertheless, what is important for Marx's own intellectual development is his approval of the Hegelian dialectic, which, he claims, in its depiction of alienation, contains 'all the elements of criticism, already prepared and elaborated in a manner rising far above the Hegelian standpoint' (ibid. 332). Marx had already expressed his disagreements with Hegel's conception of the structure of an ethical community, but the idea of achieving an ethical community of a different kind is embedded in his vision of communist society.

In concentrating on the Feuerbachian and Hegelian roots of Marx's thought there is a danger of neglecting the wider German intellectual milieu in which they all operated. German humanism as a whole was fixated on the philosophy and culture of ancient Greece. As Horst Mewes has argued, the ancient Greeks, and particularly the Athenians, were looked upon as the discoverers of the universal human essence, though lacking the practical means to realize that essence on a truly universal basis.[13] Allen Wood rightly points out that for Hegel 'the paradigm of "ethical life" is his nostalgic image of ancient Greek culture'.[14] Feuerbach's work on species and species consciousness bears great similarity to Aristotle's *De Anima*,[15] which was translated into German by Marx in 1840.[16] As for Marx, he was steeped in Greek and Latin culture at school and later at university,[17] and his doctoral dissertation focused on the differences between the natural philosophy of Democritus and Epicurus. Shortly before declaring his commitment to communism he comments that the feeling for freedom had vanished from the world with the Greeks, but can 'again transform society into a community of human beings united for their highest aims, into a democratic state' (*Works*, iii. 137). Marx revered Aristotle as a philosopher, and a strong similarity in their vision of the realization of human essence has been noted by a number of scholars in recent years.[18] In Aristotle's view, all things derive their essential character from their function and their capacity, and if that capacity is not fulfilled they are not complete or proper.[19] Aristotle argues that what distinguishes humans from other animals is our capacity to reason, to perceive good and evil, but although the perfected human is the best of animals, when isolated from law and justice 'he is the worst of all'.[20] For both Aristotle and Marx our sociality and rationality are elements of our human essence, and the exercise of these capacities must be the proper function of a human being. Aristotle is concerned with the virtuous self-development of citizens, who, ultimately, must have the opportunity to engage in the contemplation of truth to achieve *eudaemonia*, or happiness and integrity.

As we have seen, Marx's view of what constitutes our essence goes further than specifying our capacity to reason, for he stresses that the proof of our distinctiveness lies in our production, in our social creativity. He views the full realization of human essence as the end or *telos* of historical development, achievable only through the abolition of private property and its replacement by communist society based on free cooperation. It may be asked why he thinks history is heading in that direction, and why the human essence ought to be realized. At this stage, prior to any detailed analysis of capitalist accumulation, Marx's conviction about the communist 'solution' is based largely on the expectation of the emergence of a massive class of exploited workers whose interests will be logically in opposition to private property. Marx clearly thinks that human emancipation can only and *ought* to take place through the abolition of private property. Essentialism of this sort is open to the charge that it falls into the trap of the naturalistic fallacy, deriving a normative commitment from a factual premiss. However, as Alasdair MacIntyre points out, values are often built into premisses, particularly when the premisses are of a functional kind.[21] Aristotle, for example, couches his ethical theory in functional terms—the relationship of 'man' to 'living well' is likened to a harpist playing the harp well. Marx's conception of human essence as social creativity implies the need to develop our potential, and, as such, the 'ought' is built into what it is to be human.[22] It is true that Marx's historicization of the idea of self-realization is not something that can be found in Aristotle's work, but the narrative of passing through bitter and violent stages before achieving completeness is present in the Homeric epics which Marx valued so highly.[23] This sense of completeness, which occupies a place of central importance in ancient Greek ethics,[24] shines through the conception of freedom held by Marx.

Unlike Hegel, Marx saw no prospect of the establishment of an ethical community within the existing political framework, or, for that matter, within the democratic state presaged by the great French Revolution. We need now to examine *why* Marx looked beyond the democratic state in his quest for human emancipation.

## The critique of the modern state

Towards the end of 1844 Marx sketched out a nine-point plan for a work on the origin of the modern state based on the experience of the great French Revolution. It refers to a number of the themes he had been working on for the best part of two years and begins by condemning the 'self-conceit' of the political sphere for mistaking itself for the ancient state (*Works*, iv. 666). Behind this complaint is his conviction that there is a contradiction between, on the one hand, the claim of the modern state to represent all the people and, on the other, the reality of its function as an expression of the interests of the dominant class. However, he notes the logical progress of the state from being a constitutional representative state to a democratic representative state and sees the struggle for universal suffrage as the 'fight for the abolition of bourgeois society' (ibid. 666). In other words, the contradiction between state and civil society can be resolved only by the development of communist society. At this stage (and subsequently) Marx remains vague when it comes to telling us what a stateless, self-regulated society would look like, but we shall return to this issue presently.

Marx's view that the modern state was structurally bound to represent particular interests rather than universal ones was developed in his critique of Hegel's *Philosophy of Right*, which, as Avineri has rightly argued, is both original and crucial to the development of Marx's political philosophy.[25] Marx rejects Hegel's defence of the monarchy, instead lauding democracy as the 'solved riddle of all constitutions' (*Works*, iii. 29). He criticizes Hegel's idealist method for starting from the abstract idea of the state and proceeding to view the individual as the 'subjectified state', whereas democracy makes the citizens the authors of the constitution. However, a democratic constitution does not in itself equate with an emancipated society; rather it provides the arena for the open political expression of social conflict. Marx appreciates Hegel's perception of the relationship between political and civil society as a contradiction, but dismisses his attempts to show that the institutions of the existing Prussian state offer any sort of adequate resolution or 'mediation'. For Marx, the representative constitution is a great advance, not because it resolves all social problems, but because it permits the frank and undistorted expression of the modern condition of the state, which he dubs an 'unconcealed contradiction' (ibid. 75). This distinction between political emancipation through democracy and full human emancipation through social revolution becomes central for Marx in his polemic with Bruno Bauer, *On the Jewish Question*.

Bauer had argued that the Jews were wrong to demand equal political rights, since this would serve to legitimize the existing system, a condition of oppression. Jews, in his view, could be emancipated only by renouncing their religion and joining in the general struggle for a secular democratic state. Marx's criticism turns on Bauer's failure to examine the relationship between political emancipation and human emancipation. Why, asks Marx, does a commitment to political emancipation give the right to demand from the Jew the abolition of Judaism, or from man the abolition of religion (ibid. 149–50)? When Bauer argues that the Jews cannot claim the rights of man since they identify themselves as separate from other men, Marx retorts that the rights of man, as set down in the great French Revolution, were precisely the rights of egoistic man, the 'right of the restricted individual' (ibid. 163). Marx claims that the political revolution, in destroying the civil associations set up in the feudal era, such as the guilds, abolished the political character of civil society, rendering it completely materialistic and devoid of 'even the *semblance* of a universal content' (ibid. 166). Here, as in the *Critique of Hegel's Philosophy of Right*, Marx characterizes modern civil society by using Hobbes's term *bellum omnium contra omnes* ('the war of every man against every man') (ibid. 155; cf. p. 42). The conclusion to this article is shocking because Marx summarizes the essence of modern Jewry as the worship of money and the business of huckstering. According to

Marx, the *social* emancipation of the Jew is the emancipation of society from Judaism through the abolition of private property, not through the renunciation of race or religion (ibid. 170–4). Marx apparently takes for granted the reader's awareness that many Jews in western and central Europe had secured a social position through usury, although he does not make it clear that this was because a range of occupations had been legally denied them at the same time that usury was proscribed for Christians. Jews were the only group eligible to perform this function, which became vital for commercial life in the early modern period. Yet even when Marx complains that Bauer looks at Jewry theologically rather than looking at the 'everyday Jew', he reproduces a social stereotype which ignores the life situations of the vast majority of Jews, who lived in the east of the continent.[26] The fact that both Bauer and Marx speak of 'the Jew' is symptomatic of the sort of social stereotyping on which antisemitism feasted.

The arguments against Bauer are reproduced in *The Holy Family*, one of the few early writings to be published at the time. Although the bulk of the text is written by Marx, it is co-authored with Engels and in the Foreword their position is declared as one of *real humanism* (*Works*, iv. 7). Marx reiterates the view that Bauer confuses political emancipation with human emancipation, and insists that religious toleration rather than freedom from religion should prevail in a state of political freedom (ibid. 88, 106). States that do not give political freedom to Jews are regarded by Marx as 'under-developed' (ibid. 110). Marx complains that the contradictions which Bauer perceives in his examination of the constitutional debates during the great French Revolution are contradictions of constitutionalism in general rather than society in general. In other words, the constitutional problems can be resolved by the introduction of a democratic representative state, dubbed 'the perfected modern state', but it is erroneous to conclude that this means rising from the 'political to the human essence' (ibid. 114–15). On the contrary, the modern state stands in contradiction to civil society, so that when the former is perfected and privilege is legally destroyed, the latter is 'free' to reproduce 'fully developed slavery and inhumanity' (ibid. 116). This is a trenchant criticism of the liberal conception of freedom, which appears to offer the greatest freedom and independence to the individual, no longer curbed by common bonds, but also necessarily involves atomization and alienation as consequences of the functioning of the market economy. Marx extends this criticism to the high ideals of Robespierre and Saint-Just, which he characterizes as stemming from their reverence for ancient democratic Athens. They had confused the ancient democracy, based on slavery, with the modern democracy, based on the 'emancipated slavery' of bourgeois society:

> What a terrible illusion it is to have to recognise and sanction in the *rights of man* modern bourgeois society, the society of industry, of universal competition, of private interest freely pursuing its aims, of anarchy, of self-estranged natural and spiritual individuality, and at the same time to want afterwards to annul the *manifestations of the life* of this society in particular individuals and simultaneously to want to model the *political head* of that society in the manner of *antiquity*. (ibid. 122)

It is not the vision of a modern participatory society perfecting the flawed model of Athenian democracy that Marx disapproves, but the idea that it might be actualized in a society based on the unfettered power of private property. Although there have been strong disagreements about what the 'mature' Marx retains from his early work, it is undeniable that this distinction between political emancipation and human emancipation is held consistently, as is the view that human freedom is achievable only when capitalism has been transcended. In this sense the scope of his vision is immense, and, as Hannah Arendt has observed, it is the culmination of a particularly Germanic attempt to realize the civic ideal of ancient Athens.[27]

## The communist alternative

Marx is notoriously vague when it comes to fleshing out his ideas on the nature of communist society and how it might be achieved. He was to remain cautious on these issues throughout his life, not wishing to anticipate circumstances which might take generations to develop. In a letter to Arnold Ruge in the autumn of 1843 he contends that they had no business in 'constructing the future and settling everything for all times', adding that he was not in favour of raising any dogmatic banner (*Works*, iii. 142). He wished to avoid the utopianism of writers such as Etienne Cabet, who conjured pictures of ideal alternative societies without dealing with the central question of how progress could be made from the reality that confronted them. Despite these reservations, Marx outlines some ideas about the nature of the communist movement and the character of the future communist society. We can examine these remarks under four headings: first, his rejection of 'crude' communism; secondly, his projection of communism as a movement driven by and at the same time taking hold of historical development; thirdly, his designation of the working class as the agent of universal human emancipation; fourthly, his projection of the future communist society as one of undistorted communication and exchange in which a revolution in values has taken place.

At the beginning of his discussion of communism in the third manuscript of the *Economic and Philosophic Manuscripts* Marx distances himself from 'crude' communism (ibid. 294–5). He refers to forms of egalitarianism of the early modern period which were ascetic in nature and regarded 'levelling down' to a basic minimum as the ideal. In particular he was affronted at the suggestion of polygamy, wherein a woman was treated as the 'communal and common property'. Marx considered that these egalitarians had not risen above the mentality of private property, in the sense that their convictions were based on greed and envy. They wanted all men (as opposed to women) to become possessors of everything, and simultaneously to turn all people into workers instead of doing away with the category of 'worker' and the thraldom it implies. He concludes that this 'crude' communism is merely a 'manifestation of the vileness of private property' (ibid. 296). Marx was probably referring to the Anabaptist sects in Germany in the sixteenth century, although different elements of his model appear in the utopias of Thomas More, Tomasso Campanella, and Valentin Andreae.[28]

It follows from his rejection of crude communism that Marx favours a communism that can develop as a necessary part of historical progress, thereby 'embracing the entire wealth of previous development' (ibid. 296). It also follows that communism as a movement must carry with it a transcendence of the values of private property, declaring a new way of living in the world. The dialectic which carries communism forward is the dialectical contradiction between labour and capital, a dynamic relationship 'driving towards resolution' (ibid. 293–4), although it is sometimes thought that the young Marx had no such conception.[29] He is at pains to emphasize that the development of communism does not imply the subjugation of the individual to directly communal activities, or that society is somehow seen to be superior to the individual. The individual, for Marx, is a social being, which means that as well as being particular and unique, the person is the 'ideal totality', in that his or her actions are compatible with the full freedom of all others in the society (ibid. 298–9). Marx goes further, following up his criticism of the values of the crude communists by pointing to the need to transcend the outlook of private property. He laments the way in which our relationship to things and other people is governed by a psychology of possession, a fixation on *having* (ibid. 300). He criticizes political economy for its praise of self-renunciation, so that 'the less you *are*, the less you express your own, the more you *have*, i.e. the greater is your alienated life' (ibid. 309). Only with the positive transcendence of private property, with the appropriation 'for and by man of the human essence', will people be able to properly develop their senses and satisfy their needs (ibid. 299–300).

As noted above, Marx first designates the working class as the agent of human emancipation late in 1843. He does so when comparing the social and political development of the Germans with the French, and, in anticipating the eventual revolutionary success of the proletariat of his own country, he notes that in the process they will be emancipated from being specifically *Germans* into universal *human beings* (ibid. 187). From the outset, then, his vision transcends the limitations of national identity. He had little contact with workers until his sojourn to Paris in 1844. In the *Manuscripts* he enthuses about French socialist workers meeting together to discuss theory and propaganda, in the process creating a new need, the need for society, expressed in the comradeship which gives a reality to the idea of the brotherhood of man. Romantically, Marx comments that 'the nobility of man shines upon us from their work-hardened bodies' (ibid. 313). In *The Holy Family* he chides unspecified socialist writers for regarding the workers as gods, for this idealizes their position instead of seeing them as real people driven by necessity. In reality, he argues, even a semblance of humanity is almost completely denied to workers, and it is only through necessity that they are driven to revolt against this condition of inhumanity. What is important is not what the individual worker or even the working class as a whole considers to be the final goal, but rather what they will be historically compelled to do, and, somewhat optimistically, he claims that a large part of the French and English working class has already developed a consciousness of its historic emancipatory task (*Works*, iv. 36–7; cf. pp. 52–3). He characterizes the English and French socialism and communism of his day as representing 'materialism coinciding with humanism in the practical domain' (ibid. 125).

Marx has grasped the inexorable nature of capitalist development and the social forces which it unleashes. However, while his prediction of a mass social movement is sure-footed, his prediction of an emancipatory consciousness emerging from a condition of degradation is problematic because it ignores the endless variations through which class antagonisms can be managed and assuaged, economically and ideologically. In the process of attacking a form of idealism in the Young Hegelians, he leans towards a form of historical determinism which is fraught with difficulty. Later in *The Holy Family* he moves in the opposite direction, arguing against treating 'history' as an abstract determinant, stating that history does not use man to achieve its own aims but rather is nothing but 'the activity of man pursuing his aims' (ibid. 93). However, this sits uneasily with the earlier formulation which subordinates the aims of the workers to activity compelled by their historical situation. As Marx moves closer to a theory of history emphasizing structural conditioning, he is anxious to affirm that the structures themselves are the result of contestable social interaction. Nevertheless, there is clearly a theoretical tension between determinism and voluntarism, a tension not easily resolved.

In Marx's vision of communist society there is a strong sense that human beings will exchange and communicate transparently in ways undistorted by possessiveness and acquisitiveness. In the passages concluding the *Comments on James Mill* he laments that under capitalism human communication was conducted through the 'estranged language of material values', so that if people express their needs honestly it is regarded by the asker as a humiliation and by the listener as an impudence. He considers what it would look like if we carried out production as human beings, that is, if we produced things for use rather than for profit in a human-centred economy. The products would be 'so many mirrors in which we saw reflected our essential nature', a reciprocal relationship in which work would be a 'free manifestation of life' (*Works*, iii. 227). The influence of Charles Fourier (1772–1837) can be seen here, with his vision of *travail attractif*.[30] Marx was familiar with Fourier's work and followed him in deeming the relationship between men and women to be the supreme yardstick by which to gauge the extent to which a real humanism has emerged. In the *Economic and Philosophic Manuscripts* Marx writes that in modern society the position of women as the 'spoil and handmaid of communal lust' reflects the 'infinite degradation' of human existence (ibid. 295–6; cf. iv. 195–6). The real humanization of the relationship between men and women, when it is experienced as both 'natural' and 'human', is *the* criterion for judging humanity's whole level of development. Only when it is achieved can it be said that 'the human essence in him has become a *natural* essence' and that man in his individual existence become a social being. This is a remarkable passage, for it fixes on the treatment of women as sex objects as the starkest manifestation of man's alienation and presupposes the possibility of a new freedom in which sexual difference is valued on the basis of mutual respect.

## Conclusion

The political philosophy of the young Marx centres on his conviction that the human essence of social creativity is hideously alienated in the emerging capitalist system of production, and that this alienation must, of necessity, be challenged by the emerging working class. The struggle for democracy is regarded as progressive, but democracy itself offers only political emancipation, not the full human emancipation to which Marx was dedicated. In order to achieve the latter, nothing short of a social revolution is needed, involving the transcendence of private property and the distorted values which accompany it. In communist society classes would no longer exist and the sources of major antagonism would disappear as, for the first time, humanity as a whole assumes control of its own affairs. Ironically, we find support for this interpretation of the young Marx from the most famous critic of Marxist humanism, Louis Althusser: 'For the young Marx, "Man" was not just a cry denouncing poverty and slavery. It was the theoretical principle of his world outlook and of his practical attitude. The "Essence of Man" . . . was the basis for a rigorous theory of history and for a consistent political practice.'[31]

For Althusser, of course, this young Marx is a second-rate 'ideological' overture to the 'scientific' splendour of his mature work; *The German Ideology* marks a rupture in his thought rather than a development of it which encompasses the early philosophy. In this account of the young Marx, so far I have avoided making forward linkages with his later work in order to avoid smuggling in a 'continuity' thesis. However, from the time of Herbert Marcuse's appraisal of the newly discovered early writings in the 1930s[32] a long line of scholars have argued that the alienation thesis which dominates Marx's early writings also permeates his mature political economy.[33] The arguments that run through the *Grundrisse* (the preparatory notebooks of 1857–8) and the first chapter of volume i of *Capital*, particularly the part dealing with the fetishism of commodities, are shot through with the radical humanism of those early years. The philosophical foundations for Marx's analysis of capitalist production were already in place before *The German Ideology*.

## FURTHER READING

Avineri, Shlomo, *The Social and Political Thought of Karl Marx* (Cambridge: Cambridge University Press, 1968).

Carver, Terrell, *Marx and Engels: The Intellectual Relationship* (Brighton: Harvester, 1983).

McLellan, David, *Karl Marx: His Life and Thought* (London: Macmillan, 1973).

Marcuse, Herbert, *Reason and Revolution* (Boston: Beacon Press, 1969).

Ollman, Bertell, *Alienation: Marx's Critique of Man in Capitalist Society* (Cambridge: Cambridge University Press, 1971).

## NOTES

1. Karl Marx and Friedrich Engels, *Collected Works* (London: Lawrence & Wishart, 1975–••), vols. i and iii (1975), vol. xxvi (1990), vol. xxix (1987).
2. David McLellan, *Karl Marx: His Life and Thought* (London: Macmillan, 1973), chs. 1 and 2.
3. Heinz Lubasz, 'Marx's Initial Problematic: The Problem of Poverty', *Political Studies*, 24 (1976), 24–42.
4. David Riazanov, *Karl Marx and Friedrich Engels: An Introduction to their Lives and Work* (New York: Monthly Review Press, 1973).
5. Terrell Carver, *Marx and Engels: The Intellectual Relationship* (Brighton: Harvester, 1983).
6. Ted Benton, *Natural Relations: Ecology, Animal Rights and Social Justice* (London: Verso, 1993), ch. 2, and Jon Elster, *Making Sense of Marx* (Cambridge: Cambridge University Press, 1985), 62–8.
7. Lawrence Wilde, *Ethical Marxism and its Radical Critics* (Basingstoke: Macmillan, 1998), 131–8.
8. Louis Althusser, *For Marx* (London: Verso, 1977).
9. Ludwig Feuerbach, *The Essence of Christianity* (New York: Harper & Row, 1957).
10. Ludwig Feuerbach, *Principles of the Philosophy of the Future* (Indianapolis: Hackett, 1986), 69.
11. Ibid. 71.
12. Ian Fraser, *Hegel and Marx: The Concept of Need* (Edinburgh: Edinburgh University Press, 1998).
13. Horst Mewes, 'Karl Marx and the Influence of Greek Antiquity on Eighteenth-Century German Thought', in George E. McCarthy (ed.), *Marx and Aristotle: Nineteenth-Century German Social Theory and Classical Antiquity* (Savage, Md.: Rowman & Littlefield, 1992), 23.
14. Allen W. Wood, 'Hegel's Ethics', in Frederick Beiser (ed.), *The Cambridge Companion to Hegel* (Cambridge: Cambridge University Press, 1993), 215.
15. Marx Wartofsky, *Feuerbach* (Cambridge: Cambridge University Press, 1977), 224, 374, and 423.

16. Scott Meikle, *Essentialism in the Thought of Karl Marx* (London: Duckworth, 1985), 58.
17. S. S. Prawer, *Karl Marx and World Literature* (Oxford: Clarendon Press, 1976), 1–4.
18. e.g. Meikle, *Essentialism in the Thought of Karl Marx*; Philip J. Kain, *Marx and Ethics* (Oxford: Oxford University Press, 1991); McCarthy (ed.), *Marx and Aristotle*; Michel Vadée, *Marx: Penseur du possible* (Paris: Méridiens Klincksieck, 1992); Jonathan E. Pike, *From Aristotle to Marx: Aristotelianism in Marxist Social Ontology* (Aldershot: Ashgate, 1999).
19. Aristotle, *Politics*, ed. and trans. Ernest Barker (Oxford: Oxford University Press, 1969), 6.
20. Ibid. 6–7.
21. Alasdair MacIntyre, *After Virtue: A Study in Moral Theory* (London: Duckworth, 1981), 54–6.
22. Kain, *Marx and Ethics*, 29–32.
23. Wilde, *Ethical Marxism and its Radical Critics*, 31–41.
24. Julia Annas, *The Morality of Happiness* (Oxford: Oxford University Press, 1993), ch. 1.
25. Shlomo Avineri, *The Social and Political Thought of Karl Marx* (Cambridge: Cambridge University Press, 1968), 5.
26. Ilan Halevi, *A History of the Jews: Ancient and Modern* (London: Zed Books, 1987), 129–33.
27. Hannah Arendt, *Between Past and Present* (New York: Viking, 1968), 19.
28. Marie Louise Berneri, *Journey through Utopia* (London: Freedom Press, 1982), ch. 2.
29. Jon Elster, *Logic and Society: Contradiction and Possible Worlds* (Chichester: John Wiley, 1978), 65 n.
30. Charles Fourier, *The Utopian Vision of Charles Fourier*, ed. J. Beecher and R. Bienvenu (London: Cape, 1975), sect 6.
31. Althusser, *For Marx*, 233.
32. Herbert Marcuse, *Reason and Revolution* (Boston: Beacon Press, 1969), and id., 'The Foundations of Historical Materialism', in his *From Luther to Popper* (New York: Verso, 1988).
33. Erich Fromm, *Marx's Concept of Man* (London: Continuum, 1992); McLellan, *Karl Marx*; István Mészáros, *Marx's Theory of Alienation* (London: Merlin, 1970); Bertell Ollman, *Alienation: Marx's Critique of Man in Capitalist Society* (Cambridge: Cambridge University Press, 1971).

# 24 Marx and Engels

Paul Thomas

## Contents



## Biography

Engels was the son of a wealthy family of factory owners from the Rhineland in Germany. He was born in 1820. As a young man he chose not to go to university, and instead left school at 16 to take up a position in the family firm. He was attracted to the bohemian youthful literary nationalism of the 1830s, and at 17 was a published poet. At 18 he made some impact as a social critic by accusing the mill owners of his home town of being hypocritical in professing to be Christians while mercilessly exploiting those who worked for them and lived in the most squalid conditions. He met Marx for the first time in travelling to England in 1842, but made little impression upon him until the fruits of Engels's work on Chartism and social conditions in England came to Marx's attention. On Engels's return to Germany in 1844 the two agreed to collaborate on *The Holy Family*, published in 1845. They immediately travelled to England and became close friends, collaborating once again on *The German Ideology*, posthumously published in 1932. Their friendship lasted until Marx's death in 1883, but Engels continued faithful to their intellectual relationship by assuming the role of literary executor. Collaboration was anything but uniform. Its main period was the 1840s, when *The Holy Family* was published under Marx and Engels's joint imprint and the two of them together completed the unpublished manuscript of *The German Ideology* and the unsigned *Manifesto of the Communist Party*. In *The Holy Family* Marx and Engels each signed separate chapters; in the instance of the *Manifesto* Marx revised and recast an earlier draft by Engels, which had taken the form, now abandoned, of a revolutionary catechism. Thereafter significant theoretical collaboration ceased, though the two friends jointly composed a few addresses and articles, corresponded voluminously, on political matters among others, and worked together in the International Working Men's Association. Engels's busiest period on Marx's behalf was between Marx's death in 1883 and his own in 1895, a period when he laboured prodigiously as Marx's literary executor and set his own seal on the development of Marxism as a doctrine and a political movement.

## Chapter guide

The chapter examines Marx's relationship to Engels and characterizes their joint works of the 1840s as well as those works each theorist published separately. Marx is regarded as Engels regarded him, that is as the more important of the two, both as a theorist and as a political activist in the First International. Marx's contributions are then dealt with under the headings of ideology; the critique of political economy; Marx's concepts of use value, exchange value, and surplus value; the 'fetishism of commodities' as this is outlined in the first volume of *Capital*; forces and relations of production as these are outlined in Marx's 1859 Preface to *A Contribution to the Critique of Political Economy*; Marx's sketches of western European history; and his theory of the state.

## Key texts

*'Theses' on Feuerbach* (1845)
*The Holy Family* (1845)
*The German Ideology* (1845–6)
*The Poverty of Philosophy* (1846–7)
*The Manifesto of the Communist Party* (1848)
*The Class Struggles in France* (1850)
*The Eighteenth Brumaire of Louis Bonaparte* (1852)
*Grundrisse* (1857–8)
*Contribution to the Critique of Political Economy (1859)*
*Capital*, vol. i (1867)
*The Civil War in France* (1871)
*The Critique of the Gotha Programme* (1975)
*Anti-Dühring* (1878)
*Socialism, Utopian and Scientific* (1880)
*Capital*, vol. ii (1885)
*Capital*, vol. iii (1894)

## Main texts used

*Capital*, trans. Ben Fowkes (Harmondsworth: Marx Library; London: Penguin and New Left Review; New York: Random House/Vintage and Monthly Review, 1976).
*Early Writings*, trans. Rodney Livingstone and Gregor Benton (Harmondsworth: Marx Library; London: Penguin and New Left Review; New York: Random House/Vintage and Monthly Review, 1975).

*Grundrisse*, trans. Martin Nicolaus (Harmondsworth: Marx Library; London: Penguin and New Left Review; New York: Random House/Vintage and Monthly Review, 1973).

Karl Marx *The Poverty of Philosophy: Reply to 'The Philosophy of Poverty of M. Proudhon'* (Moscow: Foreign Languages Publishing House, 1968).

*Selected Writings*, ed. David McLellan (Oxford: Oxford University Press, 1977).

*The German Ideology*, trans. Sala Ryanskaya (London: Lawrence & Wishart, 1964).

*Marx-Engels Werke* (Berlin: Dietz, 1966), vol. xxix.

*Selected Correspondence* (Moscow: Progress Publishers, 1975).

Karl Marx and Frederick Engels *Selected Writings in Two Volumes* (Moscow: Foreign Languages Publishing House, 1962).

### Key ideas

**Forces of production**: how products get produced, technologically. **Relations of production**: how those producing these products relate socially (the class system). **Modes of production**: social systems (feudalism, capitalism) that themselves relate forces (the technological content) to relations (the social form) of production. **Commodity**: the form taken by the product under capitalism, entailing displacement of use value (usefulness, which characterizes products and commodities alike) by exchange value (exchangeability, which characterizes commodities alone). **Fetishism of commodities**: how commodities take on a 'life' of their own under capitalism. **Ideology**: a body of thought that is (systematically, but not always intentionally) slanted towards one class or group in society.

---

## Introduction

Marxism as it has come down to us is commonly supposed to have been the product of an intellectual partnership between Marx and Engels, though the coordinates of this partnership are impossible to pin down with precision. Engels's contribution to what has come down to us as Marxism is treated separately below.

It should not be supposed that the partnership of Marx and Engels was one between equals. At the theoretical level Engels was the first to award pride of place to Marx and the role of 'second fiddle' to himself. There is no good reason not to take him at his word. In the broadest terms, it is to Marx rather than Engels that we owe an entire political vocabulary, consisting of proletariat, including dictatorship of the proletariat; class, including class struggle, class warfare, and class consciousness; ideology; alienation, including the fetishism of commodities; use value, exchange value, surplus value, the falling rate of profit, and the theory of capitalist crisis.

In short, we owe to Marx the main elements of the method Engels termed 'historical materialism' or 'the materialist interpretation of history'. Even elements in this compound that were not, strictly speaking, originally Marx's at all—we would have had capitalism, revolution, socialism, communism, and the labour theory of value if he had not written a word—nonetheless were elements on which Marx left his own, distinctive imprint; so much so, that to this day it is hard to think about any of these without invoking Marx. His central convictions that 'the production of material life', the organization of productive activities, should have pride of place in the investigation of social structures and historical development, and that 'the mode of production of material life conditions the social, political and intellectual life process in general', have been of monumental importance to the study of history. Without Marx's detailed investigations into labour, commodities, value, wages, and exploitation, twentieth-century economics, as well as social science and history, might have taken a very different direction.

## The *Manifesto of the Communist Party*

The *Manifesto of the Communist Party* is the most widely read product of Marx and Engels, but it can still provoke and surprise the open-minded and receptive reader in the present day. In a document intended to create the conditions of its own, revolutionary success, Marx and Engels openly and with no small flourish declared their commitment to the nascent revolutionary proletariat, which was itself to eschew secret, conspiratorial forms of organization and publish its views, its character as the wave of the future, openly and brazenly to the world. The *Manifesto*'s ostensibly surprising insistence that 'the Communists turn their attention chiefly to Germany' (Marx and Engels, *Selected Writings*, i. 65[1]), a country where the proletariat was in 1848 not yet numerically strong, is an indication of Marx and Engels's belief that numerical inferiority can be compensated by theoretical sophistication and clear-headedness, which the *Manifesto* itself was designed to help provide. Marx in *The Poverty of Philosophy* (1847) had already distinguished a 'class in itself', defined objectively in terms of its placement within society, from a 'class for itself', which defines itself subjectively (*Poverty of Philosophy*, 166[2]). Its members, that is to say, are conscious of belonging to the class in question and of possessing agency by virtue of this class consciousness. Marx's *The Eighteenth Brumaire of Louis Bonaparte* (1852) was to depict the nineteenth-century French peasants as having had what were not internal bonds among its constituent members so much as features in common, defined by the peasants' purely objective position within French society. Marx's depiction culminated in words that are chilling for some classes but not for others. The peasants, who form a class 'much as potatoes in a sack form a sack of potatoes . . . cannot represent themselves; they must be represented' (Marx and Engels, *Selected Writings*, i. 334). The *Manifesto* portrays the urban proletariat very differently, and much more projectively.

As to the proletariat's enemy, the capitalist class, one of the *Manifesto*'s surprises is that within it Marx and Engels seem to have come not to bury the bourgeoisie but to praise it. 'The bourgeoisie', they insist, 'historically has played a most revolutionary part'; it 'has been the first to show what man's activity has brought about'. It has 'accomplished wonders that far surpass Egyptian pyramids, Roman aqueducts, Gothic cathedrals' and has 'conducted expeditions that put all former migrations of nations and crusades in the shade'. The *Manifesto* unashamedly celebrates the bourgeoisie's genius for activity, the 'conjuring up of whole populations out of the ground'—migrations which the bourgeoisie has inspired, subsidized, enforced, and exploited for profit. The things or material objects the bourgeoisie creates and utilizes are but residues or traces of processes and powers; even their inventions and technological innovations are but epiphenomena of this same kinetic energy and creativity.

The *Manifesto*'s paean is nevertheless fraught with historical dramatic irony. The bourgeoisie is obliged to close itself off from its own possibilities, even though these possibilities are the richest that human history has to offer. The bourgeoisie have created 'more massive, more colossal productive forces than all preceding generations together', yet cannot reap the benefit. The only mode of activity that matters to the bourgeoisie themselves is the prosaic one of making money and accumulating capital. All bourgeois enterprise is but a means to this end. The bourgeoisie may have 'created a world in their own image' (Marx and Engels, *Selected Writings*, i. 36–8); they may have proved what concerted human action can accomplish; but they are constrained to shrink from the implications of their own achievement. Others can properly look down the vistas bourgeois activity has opened up; the 'revolutionary activity, practical-critical activity' that will, we are assured, overthrow bourgeois rule is in one way but an extension of the kind of activistic energy the bourgeoisie has unleashed and set in motion for the first time in human history. It is the virtues for which the *Manifesto* praises the bourgeoisie that will bury it in the end.

In revising for publication Engels's catechism, Marx added an imagery that was distinctively his own, and which links significantly with that of his own later writings. It is an imagery of alchemy and necromancy.[3] 'Modern bourgeois society,' we read, 'a society that has conjured up such mighty means of production, is like the sorcerer who can no longer control the powers of the underworld that he has called up by his spells.' The bourgeoisie has 'conjur[ed] up . . . whole populations out of the ground', and has conjured up the 'specter of communism [that] is haunting Europe' (Marx and Engels, *Selected Writings*, i. 39, 33). Marx's evokes the spirits of a dark medieval past the bourgeoisie prides itself on having laid to rest once and for all. Its members see themselves as sober, no-nonsense, matter-of-fact rationalists. But there are depths to what these self-styled men of the moment are up to that they are bound to deny.[4] That capitalists in effect conjure up dark, irrational forces they then prove unable to control is also, as we shall see, a leitmotif of Marx's *Capital*, most particularly of the chapter in volume i on the 'fetishism of commodities'.

## Ideology

More immediately, however, the *Manifesto of the Communist Party* moves beyond *The German Ideology* in one crucial respect, when it identifies 'law, morality, religion' as being to the communist 'so many bourgeois prejudices, behind which lurk in ambush just as many bourgeois interests' (Marx and Engels, *Selected Writings*, i. 44). *The German Ideology* had proffered a view of ideology as 'speculative idealism', the German ideologists having believed that consciousness is an autonomous realm that admits of being studied and explained in its own terms, independently of social relations. Marx and Engels held that ideology as speculative idealism inverts the relationship between the human subject and consciousness and presents the world in a topsy-turvy manner: 'in ideology men and their circumstances appear upside down as in a camera obscura' (*The German Ideology*, 37[5]). Ideology here means idealism rather than apology, but in Marx's later works bias and apology become defining features of ideology. In the political writings (*The Class Struggles in France, The Eighteenth Brumaire of Louis Bonaparte*, and *The Civil War in France*) the 'ideological representatives of the bourgeoisie' are straightforward apologists for bourgeois interests. The economic writings (the *Grundrisse*, *Capital*, and *Theories of Surplus Value*) tend to distinguish between such open, unashamed advocacy and the work of honest, disinterested investigators who might unintentionally idealize, justify, or absolutize something. These latter universalize their points of view or forms of thought not because it is in their interest to do so but because they find them 'natural' or self-evident. Bias need not be intentional or self-interested, but (if the bias is ideological) will be slanted towards, and will thus defend, legitimize, or speak for, one group or class rather than another or others.

This does not mean that ideology is the same as justification. Marx justified capitalism in the *Manifesto*, in that he was prepared to admit its positive features, but he was not an apologist for capitalism in the way that the 'political economists' (Adam Smith, David Ricardo, and others) were. Nor is ideology defined simply by falsity or mendaciousness. An idea may be false without being ideological, and illusions have no necessary ideological function. Ideologies are rather always appropriate to those who proffer them, whether or not these persons do so with the intent to deceive or mislead. Nor again are ideologies necessarily imposed on people; they may be accepted by people, quite freely—as in the famous early characterization of religion as 'the opium of the people'. Opium, after all, is taken, and not as a rule administered. Ideologies must be intelligible and appear to 'make sense' to those who accept them as well as to those who disseminate them. But to the extent that ideologies are not instances of 'speculative idealism' but systematically biased bodies of thought favouring some group or class over another or others, their mere intellectual inversion will not suffice to dislodge their hold.[6]

## The critique of political economy

It is Marx's desire to engage with and undermine an ideological mode of argument that helps explain 'the critique of political economy' he characterized as his life's work and which he gave as the subtitle to his *magnum opus, Capital*. The 'work in question', Marx said in 1858, 'is the critique of economic categories or . . . the system of bourgeois economy critically presented. It is the presentation of the system and, at the same time, through the presentation, its critique' (*Selected Correspondence*, 96[7]). It was in other words to take the form of a critical outline of capitalism alongside a critique of the concepts, the theoretical frameworks that were said to justify, legitimize, or be appropriate to capitalism. Marx thought that unmasking the political economists' precepts, which conceal as well as reveal, would lay bare the real workings of the economy. Marx's *Economic and Philosophic Manuscripts* of 1844 already provided a prolegomenon.

> Just as we have found the concept of private property by analysis from the concept of estranged, alienated labor, in the same way every category of political economy can be evolved with the help of these two factors [private property and alienated labor]; and we shall find again in each category, e.g. trade, competition, capital, money, only a definite and developed expression of these first foundations. (*Marx, Early Writings*, 333[8])

And find this expression Marx did—not because of error or bias on the part of any particular political economist, but because of political economy's basic concepts and presuppositions, all of which bore a special relationship to the capitalist form of production. It is in this sense that 'the anatomy of bourgeois society may be sought in political economy' (Marx, *Selected Writings*, 388[9]).

Political economy understands the common life of man, the self-activating human essence and mutual reintegration towards generic and truly human life, in the form of exchange and commerce. Society, says Destutt de Tracy, is a series of multilateral exchanges. It is constituted by this movement of multilateral integration. Society, says Adam Smith, is a commercial enterprise. Each of its members is a merchant. It is evident that political economy establishes an alienated form of social intercourse as the essential, original and definitive human form. (Marx, *Early Writings*, 266)

Most modern economists' accounts of what they call 'Marxian economics' centre upon the view that Marx vitiated his economic analysis by virtue of having inherited, uncritically, a labour theory of value from the classical political economists. The logical consistency and strength of Marx's subsequent analysis is then generally admitted. From the labour theory of value and his concept of the commodity Marx derived his concepts of use value and exchange value. From the distinction between these two concepts he derived the concept of surplus value, which in turn he distinguished from profit, which forms but a part of surplus value. Surplus value in turn accounts for capital accumulation; for changes over time in the 'organic composition' of capital (once machine labour or automation begins to displace or dislodge human labour in the production process); and for the tendential law of the 'falling rate of profit' (rate being distinguished from amount) which will lead—other countervailing tendencies to one side—to periodic crises in production, crises that will generally fall short of being catastrophic for capitalism at large.[10]

This conventional account of Marx's procedure rightly allows that Marx's argument is logically consistent and also takes on board Marx's own admission of countervailing tendencies (technological innovation, separation of control over the forces of production from ownership of them) that may stave off, for a while, the demise of capitalism. Even so, Marx's ostensible premiss, the labour theory of value he is said to have adopted uncritically from the political economists, is regarded either as a puzzle or as being inherently assailable.

Few modern economists would spend time worrying, as Marx did, about what a commodity is. They would simply set about analysing the production, distribution, and exchange of goods, bracketing the question—which was central to Marx—of why, with the onset of capitalism, such products became identified as commodities in the first place. Similarly, few modern economists would expend much effort thinking about what value is. (Many of them, indeed, would regard value as a 'metaphysical' concept having no analytical purchase in the 'real world'.) As far as modern economists are concerned, the price of goods on the market has to do simply with supply and demand, and a well-formed economic statement about this or any other figuration is one that can be formulated in exact, mathematical terms.

Such an approach, which was given formulation, we should remember, by Sir Stanley Jevons (whose *Theory of Political Economy* was first published in 1871) and others within Marx's lifetime, seemed to Marx to raise a lot of important questions. If indeed we are to be exact, what are we to be exact *about*? Value was a category the political economists had worried over before connecting it (as they all did) with labour. The starting point of Marx's analysis was not at all an uncritical espousal of this same connection, but the recognition that value *cannot* be regarded as a simple expression of labour, because labour could be regarded much more straightforwardly as the source of wealth, and wealth, like labour, is a much older category than capital or capitalism. Value on the other hand is a historically specific expression of a historically specific *form* of labour. As a social convention that is specific to capitalism, value is a particular form of wealth that is materialized in the commodity. How and why the old concept of wealth got displaced or countermanded by the new, originary concept of value is an important question to Marx. So is the question of why this substitution took place *when* it took place and at no other time. If these questions are not raised, capitalism cannot be understood genetically, as it emerged at a particular historical juncture. If capitalism is not understood as it arose, its own historical specificity cannot be accounted for, and capitalism will be falsely, and uncritically, understood as the universal norm and standard by which all earlier modes of production should be judged. It is then likely that these earlier modes of production will be falsely, and uncritically, regarded as though they were nothing but early, immature, faltering approximations of capitalism itself. This indeed is the trap into which the political economists themselves duly fell. While it is unlikely that more modern economists will themselves, by extension, fall into this same trap in the same way, the trap itself—the trap, that is, of falsely absolutizing capitalism as the be-all and end-all of human existence—has widened considerably over the span of time that separates us from Marx. All the more reason why Marx should still throw down, or cast across this span, his own particular gauntlet.

## 'Use value' and 'exchange value'

Marx's economic analysis employs the concepts of use value, exchange value, and surplus value. Briefly put, use value or demand is in no way specific to commodity production or to capitalism, whereas exchange value (which Marx sometimes, confusingly, calls 'value') is specific to them in a particular way. Anything produced for purposes of exchange will have exchange value, which does not displace or annul use value, but complements or augments it. Anything having exchange value must also have use value, otherwise it would be unsaleable. But the reverse is not the case: exchange value characterizes capitalism in particular (though, like money, it may exist in the interstices of earlier modes of production too) and not production in general. Exchange value, that is to say, cannot be derived from use value, only superadded to it. But exchange value can, all the same, effectively displace use value. This is what happens under capitalism. Commodities, in order to meet demand (or 'realize' their use values) must first be exchanged against or in terms of other commodities. Exchange value then becomes the fulcrum or pivot of any transaction and the determining motive of economic activity at large.

The ultimate commodity, as Marx had already suggested in the *Economic and Philosophic Manuscripts* of 1844, is money. Since it cannot be directly consumed, money has no use value at all apart from its exchange value. Even so, money vastly extends and enhances the scope of exchange. Under capitalist conditions it serves both as an index of the value of all other commodities and as capital, that is as self-expanding exchange value. Yet exchange value throughout remains a purely conventional attribute of a commodity, having nothing to do with what that commodity is supposed to be *for*. Exchange value refers not to the nature or being or use of a commodity but simply to its social form. Even so, the production of more exchange value, and not the production of more goods, is privileged under capitalism. The productive forces expand, and use values get realized, to be sure, but these things happen indirectly, adventitiously, and in a manner that increases suffering and alienation among the working population. This means that a severe reversal has set in, and will continue to be self-reinforcing, like the accumulation of capital itself—unless the chain of causality can be broken, as Marx thinks it can. Human relationships have in the meantime become phenomena of the market, which is itself subject to no conscious social control. Humanity, as in the 1844 *Manuscripts*, is busily, indeed obsessively, defeating its own purpose(s).

To approach the phenomenon of value from another direction, the political economists had recognized that it is the character of labour that gives the clue to the character of value, for value has no other source. What Marx now throws into the mix is crucial. Abstract, undifferentiated labour, labour that is fundamentally meaningless, what Marx calls 'labor in general, labor *sans phrase*', is the only possible source of exchange value. It is important to the capitalist labour process that the worker be able to turn himself to a variety of different tasks without undue difficulty, that he be able to move easily and unproblematically from one occupational slot to any other. What could make work personal or distinctive is, like use value, no longer of any economic importance. What *is* of economic importance is that each and every act of labour be measurable against any other act of labour, by the clock, or in terms of units of output per unit of time. What Marx calls 'labour power', thus defined (or reduced), tells us as much about any labourer as horsepower tells us about any particular horse.

Just as exchange value abstracts from the specific qualities or characteristics of goods and products, treating these, as 'commodities', in an abstract quantitative ratio, so too labour power (which Marx, confusingly, sometimes calls 'labour') will express nothing about the personalities, gifts, aptitudes, inclinations, or preferences of any individual worker. (In Plato's *Republic* the division of labour means that people who are differently endowed have appropriately different functions to perform; in the capitalist division of labour, which is in reality a division of tasks, differently endowed people all do the same thing.) The parallelism between exchange value and labour power would be complete, and labour would be a commodity just like any other, but for one thing (which ironically was Marx's very starting point): the uniquely generative power of human labour as such. Labour generates something beyond itself even under the most alienating of conditions. It creates and re-creates the power by which its own further exploitation is made possible and (under capitalism) likely. Humanity in the capitalist epoch has lost control of its own evolution, its own standing in the natural world.[11]

## The 'fetishism of commodities'

In a society where people produce and exchange them, commodities as it were take on a life of their own and constrain those who produce them. To explain this, Marx makes an analogy to 'the misty realm of religion [where] the products of the human brain appear as autonomous figures endowed with a life of their own . . . [they appear as] independent forms standing in relations among themselves [as well as] with men. So it is in the commodity world with the products of the human hand . . .'. The fetish-character of commodities derives from the 'peculiar social character of the labor that produces them' (*Capital*, i. 165[12])—peculiar in that producers relate significantly with other producers only through the exchange of the commodities they produce. Commodities are produced in the first instance not because of their usefulness but primarily for the sake of exchange against other commodities, and this gives objects something important in common over and above the uses to which they may be put. It gives them exchangeability, a common value-character which comes to manipulate products and producers alike.

The commodity is in no way a self-explanatory concept, but it gives us an essential clue to the nature of economic reality. If human beings relate significantly only as their commodities relate, then human relations are reduced to the continuum of exchange relationships. 'Under capitalism the relations of production appear to individuals as what they are, material relations between persons and social relations between things' (ibid. 166). Marx saw in the production and exchange of commodities an important manifestation of alienation in capitalist society.

*Capital* is chock-a-block with references to phenomena that are invisible, concealed, or veiled, to symbols, secrets, fantasies, enigmas, riddles, most prominent among which is the commodity itself, which is variously described as mysterious or hieroglyphic. Its need for decipherment stems in part from the commodity's character as a concept, which refers to real, tangible objects but does so in a particular way. If commodities and their value are intangible, they are not for this reason purely symbolic or imaginary. They affect the way we act and think and are, like ideology itself, in this way practical concepts. Products of labour, things, objects, become and are treated as commodities, 'sensuous things that are at the same time supersensible or social' (ibid. 165). Without this operative, enabling assumption the capitalist economy could not and (Marx hastened to add) would not persist.

The 'fetishism of commodities' is designed to tell us something about the commodity, that it is mysterious and conventional at the same time. It is also designed to tell us something about fetishism, the attribution of human attributes to inanimate objects: that this will be exploitative and oppressive unless we can shake ourselves free from its hold. The state, law, the Church, the commodity—all can in principle operate as fetishes, unless they are unmasked practically. Things attain a life of their own and control their makers' lives, if and only if their makers remain content with adapting themselves, and making themselves relevant to a world they have created—a world whose revolutionary overthrow will also, at the same time, be an act of conscious reappropriation of what humanity had unconsciously alienated away.

## 'Forces' and 'relations' of production

In 1959 Marx summarized what we would now call his 'methodology' in a 'Preface' whose importance ranks alongside that of his "*Theses*" *on Feuerbach* (which, like *The German Ideology*, remained unpublished during his lifetime). The central paragraph of this Preface deserves quoting at length.

The general result at which I arrived and which, once won, served as the guiding thread for my studies, can be briefly formulated as follows: In the social production of their life, men enter into definite relations that are indispensable and independent of their will, relations of production which correspond to a definite stage of development of their material productive forces. The sum total of these relations of production constitutes the economic structure of society, the real foundation, on which arises a legal and political superstructure and to which correspond definite forms of social consciousness. The mode of production of material life conditions the social, political and intellectual life process in general. It is not the consciousness of men that determines their being but, on the contrary, their social being that determines their consciousness. At a certain stage of their development, the material productive forces of society come into conflict with the existing relations of production, or—what is but a legal expression for the same thing—with the property relations within which they had been at work hitherto. From forms of development of the productive forces these relations turn into their fetters. Then begins an epoch of social revolution. With the change of the economic foundations the entire immense superstructure is more or less rapidly transformed. In considering such transformations a distinction should always be made between the material transformation of the economic conditions of production, which can be determined with the precision of natural science, and the legal, political, religious, aesthetic, or philosophic—in short, ideological forms in which men become conscious of this conflict and fight it out. Just as our opinion of an individual is not based on what he thinks of himself, so can we not judge of such a period of transformation by its own consciousness; on the contrary, this consciousness must be explained rather from the contradictions of material life, from the existing conflict between the social productive forces and the relations of production . . . (Marx, *Selected Writings*, 388–91)

Marx's 1859 Preface to *A Contribution to the Critique of Political Economy* has often been misinterpreted. It is as difficult a short text as Marx ever produced, not because it takes the form of cryptic aphorisms (as the *'Theses' on Feuerbach* had) but because of the compressed nature of the summary he provides. Because it is compressed and telescoped, each sentence is self-contained in relation to its surrounding sentences; at the same time, however, all Marx's categories ('economic structure', 'real foundations', 'economic conditions of production', the 'social basis of production', 'social being', and so forth) are near-synonymous and overlap with one another. Each category refers to the others. All of the above-listed categories (in parentheses) include the social *relations* of production (the class structure) *and* the (material and technological) *forces* of production or productive forces. All these taken together constitute the 'base', which is then related to the 'superstructure' of society. The 'economic structure of society', its 'real basis', is not a material category; it contains social relations of production—relations among human beings—as well as forces of production, which are in large measure inanimate objects. A *mode* of production (feudalism, capitalism) is a relationship between forces of production and relations of production, a relationship between material and technological content and social form. Capitalism as a mode of production constantly revolutionizes the forces of production, but these expanding forces are going to clash with the (absolutely or relatively) contracting relations of production. Capacity to produce expands; ownership of the means of production contracts. The result is asymmetry, maladjustment, and this is not accidental but built-in. Relations of production, if these are to endure, must promote, and not hinder, the development of productive forces, and this is what capitalist relations of production cannot do. Forces here contradict relations by outstripping them, and relations become confining or restraining, a 'fetter' or 'integument' which is then 'burst asunder'. The distinction between forces and relations of production enables Marx to deny that physical production and material growth depend upon the maintenance or furthering of capitalism. Marx's distinction also gives content to phenomena other people had noticed but were unable to explain: the disparity between the capacity of capitalist society to produce, and the inability of people in that society to consume; the social organization of production in the factory, and individual ownership of and control over the means of production; concentration of wealth and power in the hands of a few, and dispersion of ill-paid, alienated labour into the hands of the many.

The Preface gives voice, as most of Marx's other writings gave voice, to his sense of the enormous promise, and the actual depravity, of capitalism, and does so without either lapsing into a purely moralistic critique or subscribing to the romantic attitude that capitalism had disrupted a pre-industrial idyll. The pre-industrial worker could not conceive of rejecting his conditions of life, for he understood himself only as part of these conditions; the modern proletarian, by contrast, stands in a detached, alienated relation with his conditions of life. But it *is* a relation (*Capital*, i. 162). If unity with the production process has been sacrificed, this can signify a gain in autonomy, not a loss to be lamented. Capitalism socializes the productive process, collectivizes labour, and develops the productive capabilities of the human species. Even if these make only an alienated appearance, even if the outcome of their productive activities confronts human beings as alien and inimical, the possibility of further developing productive potential is at least raised by these developments. If pre-capitalist artisan labour represents an undifferentiated unity between the worker and his work, proletarianized labour under capitalist conditions signifies differentiation without unity. Once capitalist relations of production have been surpassed, the prospect is thus of differentiated unity, though Marx, who rejected in principle the possibility of 'writing . . . recipes for the cook-shops of the future' (*Capital*, i. 99), left vague the details of this unity.

Marx intended his 1859 schema not as a social ontology but as a 'guiding thread', a guide to further research that lays out provisionally the questions to ask when seeking to explain why societies change or fail to change. The starting point of analysis should not be the political or legal organization of society, should not be ideology or consciousness, and should not be the level of technology attained by the society in question. (Marxism is not technological determinism. Technology functions within a social context; its ultimate source is human labour and inventiveness, but what makes it count is the character of the production process.) Marx is setting out his priorities and indicating the direction research should take. He wishes to investigate 'the material conditions of life' and dig beneath its surface manifestations in order to lay bare 'the anatomy of civil society' in the bourgeois epoch. All of Marx's various forays into broader historical questions were subsidiary, if complementary, to this aim.

## History

*The German Ideology* had listed three kinds of class society based upon three successive forms of private property, and restricted to a broadly defined western Europe: ancient society, based on slavery; feudal society, based on serfdom; and capitalist society, based on formally free wage labour. Marx's *Grundrisse* of 1858 features not the inclusion within but the addition to this sequence of a fourth type of society, the 'Asiatic' mode of production, and the 1859 Preface follows suit, listing 'the Asiatic, the ancient, the feudal and the bourgeois methods of production as so many epochs in the progress of the economic formation of society'. The

'Asiatic' mode of production has a peculiar relationship to the other three stages. It stands apart from them. Feudalism grows out of ancient society; capitalism grows out of feudal society; and communism will grow out of capitalist society (or its forcible overthrow). The 'Asiatic' mode of production by contrast appears to have no internal dynamic at all. It continuously rectifies its own *status quo ante* instead of generating any significant internal change. Any modification of the 'Asiatic' mode, which is not a stage but a condition, must by extension be introduced from without, which explains (without justifying) Marx's (limited but notorious) defence of British colonialism in India (Marx and Engels, *Selected Writings*, i. 345–58). Even though the notion of a (singular) 'Asiatic' mode of production is indefensible and is an embarrassment to the modern reader, it can still help make mincemeat of the claim that Marx's 'stage theory' was intended to be universal or 'global' in character.

Marx frequently advised his correspondents, prominently Vera Zasulich in Russia, that he had not attempted to proffer a series of 'progressive' or successive stages through which all societies without exception must pass, in sequence and in order. His ancient–feudal–capitalist–communist sequence was not supposed to provide a historical mould into which any specific society would perforce have to be squeezed. Nor did Marx try to deduce from any general or transhistorical 'law' of social evolution or historical development an inevitable necessity for any one type of society to be transformed 'progressively' into a more 'developed' one. Even within western Europe classical antiquity, for instance, far from progressing, actually regressed and made room for what was on most measurements a more primitive form of social organization, that of early feudalism. It in no sense 'evolved' to a 'higher' level.

What Marx itemized summarily in his 1859 Preface as a kind of principle by which historical change can be judged, measured, or identified, that is tension between the forces and relations of production, is a very different *kind* of principle. It is in no way invariant from mode of production to mode of production, and is never said by Marx to yield a 'law' by which any specific historical outcome could be predicted in principle. He did of course believe that tension between forces and relations of production was reaching a breaking point in the case of nineteenth-century capitalism, but this tension is best understood not as one particular expression of a general 'law' but as providing the objective preconditions for revolutionary change in that society, preconditions that would still have to be acted upon if the revolutionary change in question were not to be abortive or still-born. There is in Marx's writings, which have been misunderstood on this point, no general 'law' formulated by abstraction from the principle of interaction between forces and relations of production. Marx indeed denied the possibility, let alone the desirability of any such 'law', though it is not clear, as we shall see below, that Engels followed him on this point. Marx was nonetheless adamant. General statements that sum up the results of empirical observation 'in themselves, apart from real history, have no value whatsoever'. They might help arrange historical materials, 'to indicate the sequence of its separate strata . . . but they can by no means afford a recipe for neatly trimming the epochs of history' (*The German Ideology*, 38). Marx responded in print to a Russian reviewer of the first volume of *Capital* in similar terms:

He [N. K. Mikhailovsky] feels he absolutely must metamorphose my historical sketch of the genesis of capitalism in Western Europe into a historico-philosophic theory of the general path every people is fated to tread, whatever the historical circumstances in which it finds itself, in order that it might ultimately arrive at the form of economy which ensures, together with the greatest expansion of the productive powers of social labor, the most complete development of man. But I beg his pardon. (He is both honoring and shaming me too much.) . . . By studying each [separate form] of evolution separately and then comparing them one can easily find the clue to this phenomenon, but one will never arrive there by using as one's master-key a general historico-philosophical theory, the supreme virtue of which consists in being super-historical . . . (Marx, *Selected Writings*, 572)

## Revolutionary politics and the state

Marx was, as Engels said at his graveside, 'first and foremost a revolutionist' (Marx and Engels, *Selected Writings*, i. 168). He wrote nothing after the *Manifesto* that did not follow from its revolutionary precepts. In his own account of his intellectual development, the 1859 Preface, he singled out political concerns and grievances, not philosophical ones, as having impelled him to write. Most biographical accounts separate Marx's intellectual works from his political work, treating the latter as a mere framework for the production of the former. Such an approach is less than appropriate. It ill accords with what Marx himself considered he was up to. Marx's was the least disembodied of theories ['I am working madly through the night,' we find him writing to Engels in 1857, 'so that before the deluge, I should at least have the outlines clear' (*Marx-Engels Werke*, 225[13]). This may be one of the most extraordinary statements about theorizing ever uttered]. We should remember that Marx was the first theorist in the history of Western political theory to have spent the greater part of his life as a stateless political exile, hounded by all European authorities except the indifferent British. We should not lose sight of the fact that Marx was active, though sometimes uncomfortable, in the revolutionary politics of his day. After the first publication of the *Manifesto* Marx and Engels were actively engaged in German revolutionary agitation, and Marx was put on trial in Cologne for treason. There was a political impulse behind Marx's detailed investigations of French politics, *The Class Struggles in France, The Eighteenth Brumaire of Louis Bonaparte*, and *The Civil War in France*. The first two were designed to account for the set-backs suffered by the revolutionary *quarante-huitards* as a result, first, of the dashing of revolutionary hopes in 1848 and, secondly, of the *coup d'état* of Louis Bonaparte which inaugurated the Second Empire. *The Civil War in France* is of particular interest. I have argued elsewhere that Marx argues about the state and politics in two distinct ways.[14] Only one of these seems straightforwardly instrumental. In the words of the *Manifesto*, 'Political power, properly so-called, is merely the organized power of one class for oppressing another.' It follows that 'the executive of the modern state is but a committee for managing the common affairs of the whole bourgeoisie'. But it also follows, again in the words of the *Manifesto*, that with the overcoming of the state so defined, 'in place of the old bourgeois society and its classes and class antagonisms, we shall have an association in which the free development of each is the condition of the free development of all.' (Marx and Engels, *Selected Writings*, i. 36, 54). It is this more expansive understanding of politics that is also given expression in *The Civil War in France*'s characterization of the nature and actions of the 1871 Paris Commune, which provided 'the political form, at last discovered, under which to work out the economic emancipation of labor' (ibid. 522). *The Civil War in France* is important also because of the circumstances of its composition. Marx by 1871 had come to occupy a position of some prominence on the General Council of the International Working Men's Association (WMA; known later as the First International), a position he deliberately jeopardized by writing *The Civil War in France* and by issuing it in the name of a General Council many of whose other members were not of a revolutionary disposition and regarded the supposed excesses of the Commune with horror. Marx for his part evidently felt that his own hard-won standing on the General Council and the consequent political complexion of the IWMA at large were of less moment than the practical example of working-class rule set by the French *fédérés*, an example that deserved, and duly received, Marx's commemoration.

This leads to a point of considerable importance. The establishment of the IWMA in 1864 was no more Marx's personal initiative than the Commune was to be. Nevertheless, once invited to participate on the General Council of the former, Marx accepted with alacrity. The reasons for his eagerness are evident from his letters, among them letters to Engels, who thought Marx's time would have been better spent getting *Capital* into print. Having long been involuntarily isolated from the 'real forces' of the workers of any country, Marx was quick to applaud an independent, non-sectarian initiative in working-class internationalism (*Early Writings*, 137); 'it involved a matter where it was possible to do some important work' (*Selected Correspondence*, 65). The work with which Marx subsequently busied himself does not divide neatly into theoretical work, on the one hand, and practical, political activity, on the other. These were complementary, not mutually exclusive; the International provided Marx not with a distraction but with a forum. It meant that theoretical work could have some practical effect. In particular, the first volume of *Capital* was published in 1867 not despite the demands the IWMA made on Marx's time, but because of what it signified: a resurgence of working-class politics of the kind that might prove receptive to *Capital*'s doctrines. What prompted Marx to put his thoughts into shape was not enforced isolation but intense political involvement.

Conversely, however, the period stretching from the de facto demise of the IWMA in 1872 until Marx's death in 1883, a period of political inactivity and retrenchment, was also a period of enforced isolation when Marx's theoretical output dropped off precipitously. This period was theoretically barren because it was politically bleak. Marx's revolutionary hopes, dashed by the brutal suppression of the Paris Commune, a suppression that was disastrous for the workers' movement, were never effectively revived; his career as a revolutionist was never crowned with the practical success for which he had hoped and worked. Even his *Critique of the Gotha Programme* of 1875, a blisteringly critical attempt to ground the fledgling German Social Democratic Party in Marxian principles traceable back to the *Manifesto*, fell largely on deaf ears and was suppressed.

## Engels's contribution to Marxism

It is into this breach that Engels, as Marx's literary executor, leaped after 1883, expending a massive amount of energy rehabilitating his friend's reputation, seeing into print writings Marx had left unpublished during his lifetime (particularly the second (1885) and third (1894) volumes of *Capital* and Marx's *'Theses' on Feuerbach*), and writing updated introductions to new editions of works Marx had published (*The Poverty of Philosophy*, *Wage Labour and Capital*, *The Communist Trial in Cologne*, *The Class Struggles in France*, *The Eighteenth Brumaire of Louis Bonaparte*, and *The Civil War in France*). Into the bargain, Engels updated earlier writings of his own (*Anti-Dühring, Socialism, Utopian and Scientific*) and saw into print several new ones: *The Peasant War in Germany* (history), *The Origin of the Family, Private Property and the State* (anthropology, like the manuscript 'Labour in the Transition from Ape to Man'), and *Ludwig Feuerbach and the End of Classical German Philosophy* (an early philosophical 'Marxology').

Throughout these various endeavours Engels showed a penchant for publicity that Marx himself, with his weakness for overblown, turgid satires, had not always displayed. Engels's contribution to Marx's reputation was enormous, but difficult to assess. One of the difficulties stems from the fact that there was, during Marx's lifetime, so little real collaboration between the two friends after the 1840s. Another difficulty stems from the character of Engels's own work on Marx's behalf and on his own after Marx's death. There can be little doubt that Engels effectively set his own seal on the subsequent reception of Marx's doctrines—not just among the German Social Democrats but also, far less intentionally, among Russian Marxists prior to a Bolshevik Revolution in 1917 that neither he nor Marx foresaw or predicted. In both arenas Marx was remembered and commemorated very much as Engels wanted him to be remembered and commemorated.

One large example must suffice here. 'Just as Darwin discovered the law of development of organic nature,' said Engels at Marx's graveside, 'so Marx discovered the law of development of human history' (Marx and Engels, *Selected Writings*, 167). But if indeed he did 'discover' such a 'law', Marx seems to have been remarkably reticent about expressing it. He also refrained from equating any such laws with the 'laws' of matter in motion, which are said by the later Engels (and not by Marx) to cover even the 'laws' of thought. That human history and thought are but special fields of play for nature's general laws of motion and development is an idea of Engels's that appears to owe little (if anything at all) to Marx. Even so, it is an idea that came strongly to influence Soviet 'dialectical materialism' in the twentieth century.

The extent to which Engels's Marx (if I may so characterize him) really corresponded to Marx as a historical figure is still disputed, and the question may well be irresolvable. Even so, it is more than likely that Engels in his own writings, including the posthumously published *Dialectics of Nature*, departed from Marx in important respects, making of Marxism the kind of systematic materialist metaphysics that Marx (whose central concern had been the much more finite 'critique of political economy') had singularly failed to provide.[15]

## FURTHER READING

Avineri, Shlomo, *The Social and Political Thought of Karl Marx* (Cambridge: Cambridge University Press, 1970).

Berman, Marshall, *All that is Solid Melts into Air: The Experience of Modernity* (New York: Simon & Schuster, 1982).

Carver, Terrell, *Marx's Social Theory* (Oxford: Opus Books and Oxford University Press, 1982).

Mészáros, István, *Alienation: Marx's Conception of Man in Capitalist Society* (London: Merlin; New York: Harper & Row, 1972).

Suchting, W. A., *Marx: An Introduction* (Brighton: Harvester; New York: New York University Press, 1983).

Thomas, Paul, *Karl Marx and the Anarchists* (London: Routledge & Kegan Paul, 1985).
Weeks, John, *Capital and Exploitation* (London: Edward Arnold; Princeton, Princeton University Press, 1981).
Wood, Alan W., *Karl Marx* London: Routledge & Kegan Paul, 1981).

## NOTES

1. Marx and Engels, *Selected Writings in Two Volumes* (Moscow: Foreign Languages Publishing House, 1962).
2. Marx, *The Poverty of Philosophy: Reply to 'The Philosophy of Poverty of M. Proudhon'* (Moscow: Foreign Languages Publishing House, 1968).
3. Marshall Berman, *All that is Solid Melts into Air: The Experience of Modernity* (New York: Simon & Schuster, 1982), 87–129.
4. Ibid. 87–129.
5. Marx and Engels, *The German Ideology*, trans. Sala Ryanskaya (London: Lawrence & Wishart, 1965).
6. See Parekh Bhikhu, *Marx's Theory of Ideology* (London: Croom Helm; Baltimore, Md.: Johns Hopkins University Press, 1982), *passim*.
7. Marx and Engels, *Selected Correspondence* (Moscow: Progress Publishers, 1975).
8. Marx, *Early Writings*, trans. Rodney Livingstone and Gregor Benton (Harmondsworth: Marx Library; London: Penguin and New Left Review; New York: Random House/Vintage and Monthly Review, 1975).
9. Marx, *Selected Writings*, ed. David McLellan (Oxford: Oxford University Press, 1977).
10. Anthony Giddens, *Capitalism and Modern Social Theory: An Analysis of the Writings of Marx, Durkheim and Weber* (Cambridge: Cambridge University Press, 1971), 46–64.
11. See Paul Thomas, 'Nature and Artifice in Marx', *History of Political Thought*, 9 (1988), 485–503.
12. Marx, *Capital*, trans. Ben Fowkes (Harmondsworth: Marx Library; London: Penguin and New Left Review; New York: Random House/Vintage and Monthly Review, 1976).
13. Marx and Engels, *Marx-Engels Werke* (Berlin: Dietz, 1966), vol. xxix.
14. Paul Thomas, *Alien Politics: Marxist State Theory Retrieved* (London: Routledge, 1994), *passim*.
15. See Paul Thomas, 'Engels and "Scientific Socialism"', in Manfred Steger and Terrell Carver (eds.), *Engels after Marx* (University Park: Penn State University Press, 1999), 215–31.

# 25 Nietzsche

Nathan Widder

## Contents



## Chapter guide

This chapter analyses Nietzsche's claim that the 'death of God' marks the advent of nihilism in our modern age. This analysis explains the significance of Nietzsche's subsequent thought for political theory by situating it against the Platonist and Christian traditions that dominate political philosophy and with contemporary attempts to develop a new political theory of difference and pluralism. The second section outlines Nietzsche's genealogical method. The next three sections take the reader through the three essays of Nietzsche's *On the Genealogy of Morals*, detailing his attempt at a 'revaluation of values' through both a criticism of the values of our Judaeo-Christian legacy and the outline of another way of thinking and acting that strives 'beyond good and evil'. The final section looks at contemporary interpretations of Nietzsche's relation and relevance to political theory and practice, and argues that it is most fruitful to press Nietzsche's philosophy towards a 'politics of difference' by drawing on his rethinking of the friend–enemy relation and his call for the spiritualization of enmity.

## Biography

Friedrich Nietzsche was born on 15 October 1844 to Franziska Nietzsche and Karl Ludwig Nietzsche, a Lutheran minister. He was educated at Pforta, Bonn, and Leipzig University, and served as a lance corporal in the army before taking up a professorship in philology at the University of Basel in 1869. He resigned his chair and left the university in 1879 owing to ill health. Despite migraine headaches that made it extremely difficult to read and write, Nietzsche produced an extensive corpus, publishing his first book, *The Birth of Tragedy*, in 1872 and continuing to write until 1888. In early 1889 he collapsed and fell into insanity, an event that is generally accepted to have been caused by syphilis. During the remaining years of his life until his death on 25 August 1900 he progressively lost the capacity to communicate with others and his mentality became that of a child. Though he had not been read widely before, in his illness Nietzsche gained a kind of cult following, many people believing he had attained a higher, spiritual level of being. This cult following, together with his sister, Elisabeth Foerster's, obtaining control of his yet unpublished writings—including a set of notes recovered from Nietzsche's waste basket that became the infamous *Will to Power*—paved the way for Nietzsche to gain a reputation as a proto-Nazi and to be widely and inaccurately quoted by the Nazi regime. Post-war Nietzsche scholarship has rescued him from this reputation, at least within academic circles, and today he is widely studied. Nietzsche's influence can be felt on almost every important form of philosophy in the twentieth century, including existentialism, phenomenology, critical theory, and post-structuralism. In recent years Nietzsche has even been increasingly deployed in political theory in the service of calls for a 'politics of difference'.

## Key texts

*The Birth of Tragedy* (1872)
*Untimely Meditations* (1873–6)
*Human, All Too Human* (1878)
*The Wanderer and his Shadow* (1879)
*Daybreak* (1881)
*The Gay Science* (1882)
*Thus Spoke Zarathustra* (1883–5)
*Beyond Good and Evil* (1886)
*On the Genealogy of Morals* (1887)
*The Case of Wagner* (1888)
*Twilight of the Idols* (1889)
*The Anti-Christ* (1895)
*Nietzsche vs. Wagner* (1895)
*Ecce Homo* (1908)

## Main texts used

*The Anti-Christ*, trans. R. J. Hollingdale (Harmondsworth: Penguin Books, 1968, 1990) (*AC*).

*Beyond Good and Evil: Prelude to a Philosophy of the Future*, trans. Walter Kaufmann (New York: Vintage Books, 1966) (*BGE*).

*Daybreak*, trans. R. J. Hollingdale (Cambridge: Cambridge University Press, 1982) (*D*).

*The Gay Science*, trans. Walter Kaufmann (New York: Vintage Books, 1974) (*GS*).

*Human, All Too Human: A Book for Free Spirits*, trans. R. J. Hollingdale (Cambridge: Cambridge University Press, 1986) (*HH*).

*On the Genealogy of Morals*, trans. Walter Kaufmann and R. J. Hollingdale (New York: Vintage Books, 1967) (*GM*).

*Thus Spoke Zarathustra*, trans. Walter Kaufmann (New York: Viking Press, 1954, 1966) (*Z*).

*Twilight of the Idols*, trans. R. J. Hollingdale (Harmondsworth: Penguin Books, 1968, 1990) (*TI*).

*The Will to Power*, trans. Walter Kaufmann and R. J. Hollingdale (New York: Vintage Books, 1967) (*WP*).

## Key ideas

**Eternal return:** though not discussed in this chapter, this is a key Nietzschean idea. Interpretation of the doctrine of the eternal return is split between those who see it as a belief that all events will repeat themselves eternally and others who see it as an eternal return of mutation and overcoming. The first view fits Nietzsche's more straightforward statements about the doctrine; the second is more in line with the critique of identity found throughout his work. **Genealogy:** a quasi-historical and quasi-psychological approach that seeks to locate the origin of our contemporary values. **Nihilism:** the belief in nothing. Nietzsche believes that our modern values, born from a Judaeo-Christian and Platonist tradition, ultimately devalue themselves because they are grounded in nothing. **The overman:** a key figure in Nietzsche's thought, although few details are provided of what this overman will be. Man, Nietzsche says, must be overcome, and this is precisely what the overman will accomplish. ***Ressentiment*:** the French word for resentment is used regularly by Nietzsche and is retained in translations of his work into English. **Will to power:** Nietzsche calls the will to power the fundamental driving force of life and nature and opposes it to the Darwinian principle of self-preservation. All beings, Nietzsche says, seek to discharge their power and to dominate—though, importantly, this can mean self-domination as much as domination of others. The will to power always encounters resistance and seeks to overcome resistance.

## Introduction: God is dead and we have killed him

The aphorism of the madman (*GS* §125[1]) is probably Nietzsche's most famous. A madman enters the marketplace seeking after God, and those who do not believe in God laugh at him. 'Whither is God?' he cries; 'I will tell you. *We have killed him*—you and I. All of us are his murderers.' The aftermath of this deed, he continues, is catastrophic: we have 'wipe[d] away the entire horizon', 'unchained this earth from its sun', and sent it 'plunging continually . . . Backward, sideward, forward, in all directions . . . Is there still any up or down?' Our world has become colder, and we humans, 'the murderers of all murderers', are left with no way to cleanse ourselves. But when the madman finishes his speech, the crowd stares at him in astonishment, and he declares: 'I have come too early . . . my time is not yet . . . This deed is still more distant from them than the most distant stars—*and yet they have done it themselves*.'

Encapsulated in this aphorism is Nietzsche's appraisal of the modern condition. The contemporary reader would certainly be forgiven if s/he did not share his gloomy outlook. On its better days, at least, our modern age does not seem quite so desperate and the empirical evidence suggests that we are not spinning into an infinite abyss. Despite the blunt rhetoric, however, Nietzsche's analysis is in fact quite subtle. The madman does not say that God's existence has been disproved, or that we can or do no longer believe in a Supreme Being—as Nietzsche says, 'God is dead; but given the way of men, there may still be caves for thousands of years in which his shadow will be shown' (*GS* §108). The danger we face comes not from our lack of belief in God but rather the continuance of this belief in a form that seems compatible with Western Enlightenment but is in fact destructive of it.

The Western Enlightenment began, according to Nietzsche, with a seemingly innocuous move: we separated the truth of the world from the idea that God created it; we placed truth on the side of science, and God on the side of belief. After this move, it is still possible to believe in both God and truth, but even within this continuity something fundamental has changed. This change can be glimpsed in the fact that the people in the marketplace laugh at the madman's initial question, 'Whither is God?' For in an earlier time, Nietzsche says, when events and things in the world were understood as created by God, the meaning of any phenomenon referred back to a divine voice that spoke through it. Thus, comets were signs from God, as were floods, famines, and even the madman's talk. One need only note the role of the fool in Shakespeare plays, speaking a truth that the other characters cannot see; the other characters ignore the madman at their own peril. It is not that madness today has no truth. Rather, its truth is not a matter of the madman, like all creatures, being created by God. Whatever truth now attaches to madness comes from its being 'medicalized' and renamed 'insanity', an object of scientific study and treatment. The defining claim of Enlightenment rationalism is that it forgoes any appeal to faith, resting instead on reason, empirical evidence, and experiment. Once we moderns forgo this faith and disenchant the world, the entire colour of things changes even if their shape does not: 'We no longer understand altogether how the ancients experienced what was most familiar and frequent—for example, the day and waking . . . "Truth" was experienced differently, for the insane could be accepted formerly as its mouthpiece—which makes *us* shudder or laugh' (*GS* §152). Ironically, laughing at the madman confirms his claim: laughing is a sign that the world of signs, the world where madness carried a meaning instilled by God, is no more.

So we have separated the truth of things from the idea that God created them, Nietzsche says, and the result is that we can continue to believe in both God and truth, but they will shine in a world that has become darker. And the reason for this, Nietzsche maintains, is that truth, now reconfigured as scholarship or science, still carries residues of the theological and metaphysical conceptions it claims to leave behind. These residues appear in a continuing reliance on judgements that are merely aesthetic: that truth is simple; that it is pure; that the truth of something is that which remains constant over time, unchanging and universal; that truth is good, and that what is good is true. These judgements reflect a legacy of Platonism and Christian philosophy that must be challenged. In such philosophies, what is valued as good is also held to be true, pure, universal, useful, and beautiful, while what is bad or evil is held to be the simple opposite of these terms. These valuations were previously grounded in a transcendent source—a Form of the Good or God—that modern science rejects as mere belief. Through this rejection, however, science and rationalism delegitimize themselves, since they continue to hold to these valuations. Science can never raise itself above the level of mere belief because its own values refer back to philosophies that it declares to be no more than beliefs. Here modern science continues to carry the will to truth that drove its predecessors. The will to truth, Nietzsche says, does not seek after truth but instead demands that the world conform to ideals of purity and universality associated with a particular conception of truth. The problem, as Nietzsche sees it, is that these ideals can no longer sustain themselves once we have disconnected this conception of truth from the divine source that had grounded it.

The result of all this is modern nihilism, the internal devaluation of our highest values, which shows these values to be grounded in nothingness. Like the death of God, nihilism does not mean we cannot continue to espouse these values, but they cannot be lifted above being mere espousals that, perhaps, even their advocates no longer really believe. Thus even while modern life finds numerous defenders, the malaise of the times continues to be felt. It is felt in the way we celebrate the wonders of technological progress even while worrying about the environmental damage caused; in the way we hold democracy to be the best political system while routinely lamenting that all politicians are the same; in the way we still state our belief in human progress even after Auschwitz and the bomb; in how history has 'ended' with liberalism having seen off its evil enemy, communism, and yet no one seeming to be any happier. In all these cases we continue to idealize purity, progress, and truth even while it becomes harder to take them seriously.

The dangers here are as much political as they are social or cultural. On the one hand, the realization that the world fails to live up to the ideals still demanded by modern reason can lead to the denigration of this world as valueless: 'the untenability of one interpretation of the world, upon which a tremendous amount of energy has been lavished, awakens the suspicion that *all* interpretations of the world are false' (*WP* §1[2] ). On the other, the realization itself may be suppressed through a vigorous and even violent reinforcement of purity and the insistence that this purity is natural and good. The nationalism and xenophobia that Nietzsche regularly attacks in the new Reich is only the most overt form of this dangerous politics and is a consequence of what he calls the 'herd mentality'. A more subtle form of this politics is found in the way even liberal societies approach various forms of otherness. As the works of a twentieth-century Nietzschean, Michel Foucault, make clear, our scientific and social institutions continue to approach the difference between the sane and the insane, the law-abiding citizen and the criminal delinquent, heterosexuals and homosexuals, according to a schema of purity and corruption. In all these cases what is enforced is the purity of an *identity* through the characterization of anything that threatens to undermine its claim to purity as its polar opposite. The demand to sustain purity can license the greatest forms of cruelty and immorality precisely because this sought-after purity is so fragile. Our Judaeo-Christian morality offers little help here, Nietzsche says, because its condemnation of cruelty rests on the same problematic idealization of purity. As will be seen, Nietzsche holds this morality to carry within it a secret hatred towards what is different, compelling it to label such differences as the opposite of purity, evil.

Consequently, Nietzsche calls for a rethinking and *revaluation* of identity and opposition. He repeatedly argues that opposition itself is a fiction, a 'frog perspective' (*BGE* §2[3]; see also *HH* §1[4] ) used to make clear-cut, binary divisions in a world that remains, morally and otherwise, ambiguous. Identity and opposition, like the rest of our conceptual apparatuses, are merely human constructs rather than representations of some extra-human truth. Although we may find them necessary in order to live, this necessity 'does not prove them. Life is no argument. The conditions of life might include error' (*GS* §121). If we are going to take the 'death of God' seriously, we must approach our categories and valuations more critically. We must ask why we still think of evil as the opposite of goodness and falsity as the opposite of truth. Moreover, we must question why we seem to hold unambiguously to the goodness and usefulness of truth, 'if truth and untruth constantly proved to be useful, which is the case', and 'especially if it should seem—and does seem!—as if life aimed at semblance, meaning error, deception, simulation, delusion, self-delusion' (*GS* §344). Most importantly, we must critically assess the value of identity, be it personal, religious, national, or other identity. For if identity is not truly necessary, its claims to purity always risk necessitating the condemnation of that which might threaten it. At stake here politically is the question of what kind of pluralism we can and should have today. Can this be only a pluralism that tolerates different individuals and groups by maintaining a rational neutrality among them and their values, as advocated by contemporary liberals? Or must these differences be brought into harmony in some higher form of community, as advocated by communitarians? There is another possibility that has been taken up by much contemporary political theory: an affirmation of difference coming from the way that this difference puts identity and opposition into question. Moving in this direction means striving to go 'beyond good and evil'. It may seem strange that Nietzsche should be a prominent figure in this type of pluralism, given the way his name has in the past been associated with Nazism. Nonetheless, the Nazi misappropriation of Nietzsche's writings not only suppressed his harsh criticisms of German anti-Semitism and nationalism but enlisted his thought in the very idealization of purity that he sought to challenge. Consequently, though it may seem initially counterintuitive, Nietzsche's appropriation in the name of a pluralist politics that emphasizes the contamination of all identities is not the product of mere fancy.

## The genealogical approach

The revaluation of oppositional categories requires first a determination of how these categories have become hegemonic. In other words, we need a *genealogy* of oppositions, and of the opposition of good and evil in particular. Genealogy may appear to be a historical account, and Nietzsche does refer to historical groups and events in his analysis, but this is a superficial portrayal of his approach. This is not simply because if it were historical Nietzsche could easily and rightly be accused of inaccuracy, bias, and simplification. Rather, it is because such a historicism displays the very will to truth whose origin is being sought (see *GM* 3.26[5] ). It is more accurate to see Nietzsche's genealogical account as something akin to the state of nature of thinkers like Hobbes and Rousseau—that is, as a thought experiment or foil used to explain our present circumstances. Even better, genealogy can be compared with Hegel's master–slave dialectic, which abstracts from history a struggle implicated throughout history and presents this struggle in narrative form. Nietzsche himself suggests this understanding of genealogy when he states that the story it recounts of Judaeo-Christian slaves overturning a pre-Christian nobility underpins history and culture as such (*GM* 1.11) and when he holds that the struggle of noble and slave still occurs within the individual self (*GM* 1.12, 1.16). This indicates that genealogy provides an *ontological* rather than merely historical account, one that explores the nature of the human self as such rather than simply how the self appears at particular historical junctions.

What makes Nietzschean genealogy distinctive is the context in which it places the self. Like Hobbes, Locke, and Rousseau, Nietzsche maintains that there is no natural order but rather only chaos. However, unlike these state of nature theorists, Nietzsche does not see natural equality as the correlate to chaos, because such a view is another remnant of the Platonist legacy. In the *Republic* Plato attacks democracy on grounds that, because it treats all opinions as equal, it creates chaos in the city and the soul. For Plato, then, order means hierarchy: an ordered system is one in which one thing is placed over another. Early modern state of nature theorists continue this Platonism and simply invert the analysis: chaos means no hierarchy, so that the question for political theory becomes how naturally equal humans can agree to become unequal, creating an artificial political order by some submitting to others (cf. Rousseau's wicked or evil contract outlined in the *Discourse on the Origin of Inequality*). Against all this, Nietzsche takes the view that chaos implies inequality, but an inequality that is always in flux. This disequilibrium means, on the one hand, that there is inequality of power and hence an interplay of domination and submission. On the other hand, there is also resistance to any dominating force that is capable of overcoming domination—the weak may always defeat the strong. What is crucial, however, is that, because of this inherent inequality, the resistance of the weak always takes a form different from what it resists—the physically weak, for example, resist the physically strong not through any physical power but through a power of some other kind. Hence Nietzsche will say that even when the weak defeat the strong they do not cease being weak.

There is another difference with the natural chaos of state of nature theorists: although these thinkers develop their ideas of the human self in conjunction with their theorizations of the state of nature, they do not treat the context of chaos as *constitutive* of this self, but rather see the self as naturally independent. For Nietzsche, however, the self and, more specifically, its *will to power* are formed through these unequal relations. There are many dimensions to the concept of the will to power, and Nietzsche makes clear that it does not refer solely or even primarily to the human will (the world itself, he says, is will to power), but here it suffices to define the will to power as *an expression of power that follows from the position of the self in unequal relations*. It expresses not only the power of the self but also its judgement of the world and its moral and aesthetic outlook. The will to truth, for example, expresses judgements concerning purity, order, and universality, and augments the feeling of power of those who will it by holding that the world is ultimately knowable. Some interpreters crudely portray the will to power as a will to seek power over others, but in fact this is only one of its possible manifestations. In unequal relations the strong are able to act immediately, and consequently they express their power in immediate action, their morality following from this expression; those who are too weak to act are forced into inaction, and their corresponding will to power and moral view must take a different form. Ironically, it is the weak who seek power over others, although they will ascribe this desire to the strong. Regardless of the mode of expression, however, Nietzsche holds it to be a fundamental rule that the will to power must express itself in some way. If need be, it will even express itself in the form of nihilism: 'the human will . . . will rather will *nothingness* than *not* will' (*GM* 3.1).

The genealogical question now becomes clear: to understand the origin of the opposition between good and evil we must ask what sort of being wills that the world conform to this moral dualism. This means asking what relations of domination and submission constitute this being and its perspective and how this perspective governs its way of thinking and acting. While this may appear to be only a psychological exercise, Nietzsche's genealogy of the self is something more—it is an ontological rather than an existential analysis. Nietzsche is not trying to demonstrate, say, what sort of childhood experiences lead individuals to see the world in terms of good and evil, or even what social conditions lead to entire societies thinking in this way. Rather, he is trying to *evaluate* this morality that dominates Western culture, providing an overall assessment of its being by locating its essential nature. Given that our morality is not given to us by God, where, Nietzsche asks, does it come from? His answer is that it comes from slavishness—it is an expression of weakness and so must have its origin not in the weakness of particular individuals or groups who might perpetuate it but in the perspective of weakness itself. Nonetheless, by showing that this morality reflects a certain perspective, genealogy shows that it is just that—a limited viewpoint, which by its restricted nature implies the existence of other ways of being and acting. Nietzsche's genealogy thus examines how the will to moral opposition is created and how it dominates, but at the same time it uncovers another perspective that has been forgotten. It is this other perspective that can take us 'beyond' the opposition of good and evil, a direction required to overcome our nihilistic attachment to identity.

Nietzsche's *Genealogy of Morals* is structured in three interrelated essays. The first examines the genesis of the moral opposition of good and evil, which defines the good as pure, innocent, and selfless and evil as its antithesis. The second explores the origin of the moral subject and its sense of guilt. This is a corollary to the logic of good and evil, but also an extension of it that Nietzsche says accounts for this morality's universality. The final essay examines the ideal of purity—asceticism—as it appears in aesthetics, philosophy, religion, and science. Here Nietzsche shows how the moralistic and religious thought of good and evil continues to infect our purportedly secular, enlightened age, leading to nihilism.

## Good and bad; good and evil

In a world of chaos and strife, who would will that goodness be defined in terms of purity? Or, put differently, who would affirm as good that which is uncontaminated by such strife? The answer Nietzsche gives is: only a being unable to affirm strife, or *unable to affirm itself in relations of strife*—in other words, a being that is weak, slavish, helpless, and dominated. This is a being that cannot act and so can be only a recipient of action. But the recipient's position also implies the existence of another type that can act and so enforces its actions on others. Nietzsche calls this a noble or warrior type and maintains that because it is powerful enough to flourish in a world of strife, it affirms this strife as the condition needed to express its strength. These two perspectives—and Nietzsche makes clear that they are not the only two possibilities—define the noble morality of 'good and bad' and the slavish morality of 'good and evil'.

It may appear that the strong seek to dominate the weak, but this is not the case. Since a noble uses strife as a mechanism to affirm himself, he must engage in agonistic conflicts with a worthy opponent—another noble. This other noble need not be 'the same' as the first—the two need not share some common identity—but need only be sufficiently strong to offer a challenge. In this way, however, the other, even in his difference, is also affirmed as good: 'How much reverence has a noble man for his enemies!—and such reverence is a bridge to love.—For he desires his enemy for himself, as his mark of distinction; he can endure no other enemy than one in whom there is nothing to despise and *very much* to honor!' (*GM* 1.10) Those who are too weak to offer a challenge are labelled 'bad', but are otherwise ignored. A certain restraint is thereby part of noble morality inasmuch as those unable to fight are left alone. All this gives the noble morality of good and bad a non-oppositional character, not only because the nobles affirm their opponents but also because their affirmation of themselves does not operate through a comparison with what they call bad. There is certainly an opposition between good and bad in this morality, but it is not the case that 'good' is defined in contradistinction to 'bad'. Hence Nietzsche says that the nobles' affirmation follows from their high station—'It was out of this *pathos of distance* that they first seized the right to create values and to coin names for values' (*GM* 1.2)—but not from any comparison with what they stand above. Moreover, noble morality is not based on the attainment of identity. The nobles do not affirm the purity of their identity but instead seek challenges that allow them to transcend their limits and *overcome* themselves. This is why they need worthy adversaries as their mark of distinction. In this way, the name 'good' *identifies* the noble, but does not establish his *identity*.

Clearly those who do not act cannot affirm themselves in action. The slaves can therefore call themselves good only retrospectively, after first labelling another as evil. While the nobles do not concern themselves with the slaves caught beneath the fray, the slaves remain fixated on the nobles who compel them into passivity. Suffering from this weakness and driven by a perverse paranoia, they declare the nobles to be evil beings who *intentionally* cause their suffering. The weak can then affirm themselves in opposition to the strong: they are evil; we are not like them; therefore we are good. This is the creative moment of slave morality and constitutes the slave revolt of morality. It reflects the will to power of the weak that must express itself in some way and is the product, Nietzsche says, of *ressentiment*, a bitterness or resentment that festers in those who are forced by their weakness into inaction. Those able to discharge their frustrations must certainly think and feel differently than those with no such opportunity, in whom *ressentiment* accumulates as a toxin (*GM* 1.10). This leads the slaves to affirm what does not engage in conflict—goodness becomes what does not harm and thereby remains innocent, meek, and pure, while evil becomes intentional corruption. Nietzsche calls this the priestly mode of valuation, maintaining that it is with the priests that '"pure" and "impure" confront one another for the first time as designations of station' (*GM* 1.6). Through these designations, slave morality calls virtuous the very behaviour enforced upon them: weakness becomes meritoriousness, impotence becomes goodness of heart, lowliness becomes humility, and subjection to others becomes obedience (*GM* 1.14). Moreover, the priestly valuation establishes not only opposition but identity by construing noble overcoming as evil. The slaves not only establish an identity for themselves but also force one on the nobles, thereby extinguishing the ambiguity of the noble valuation of good that allowed it to be extended to what is different:

> That lambs dislike great birds of prey does not seem strange: only it gives no ground for reproaching these birds of prey for bearing off little lambs. And if the lambs say among themselves: 'these birds of prey are evil; and whoever is least like a bird of prey, but rather its opposite, a lamb—would he not be good?' there is no reason to find fault with this institution of an ideal, except perhaps that the birds of prey might view it a little ironically and say: '*we* don't dislike them at all, these good little lambs; we even love them: nothing is more tasty than a tender lamb'. (*GM* 1.13)

Through the idea of intentional harm, slave morality invents the moral subject responsible for its actions. Now, instead of each being acting in accordance with its unequal relations to others, it is held to have a choice in how it acts. The doer is separated from its deed: 'popular morality . . . separates strength from expressions of strength, as if there were a neutral substratum behind the strong man, which was *free* to express strength or not to do so' (ibid.). This implies that the strong are weak because they do not refrain from action and, for the same reason, that those who do not act are in fact strong (ibid.). Yet while all of this is a product of *ressentiment* and hatred towards strength, this source is concealed. In their ultimate gesture the slaves invent a God who is the infinite embodiment of purity and who ensures their revenge through his promise of a final Judgement. This allows them to continue to proclaim their love for those they despise. Christianity is the most obvious embodiment of this spirit of revenge, but it must be remembered that genealogy is not history. Although Nietzsche does align slave morality with the Jews, Christians, and Buddhists and noble morality with the likes of Napoleon, as well as 'Roman, Arabian, Germanic, Japanese nobility, the Homeric heroes, the Scandinavian Vikings' (*GM* 1.11), he later repudiates these classifications when he writes, 'consider how regularly and universally the ascetic priest appears in almost every age; he belongs to no one race; he prospers everywhere; he emerges from every class of society' (*GM* 3.11). Furthermore, as previously noted, the struggle between noble and slave moralities continues today within the individual self, 'born as one is to a subterranean life of struggle' (*GM* 1.12) so that 'there is perhaps no more decisive mark of a "*higher nature*," a more spiritual nature, than that of being divided in this sense and a genuine battleground of these opposed values' (*GM* 1.16).

Nonetheless, our modern society and values have their roots in slavishness, and a corresponding hatred of strength and action. Here, noble morality provides a counterpoint to the value we place on identity and purity. Some interpreters argue that Nietzsche unambiguously prefers the noble morality of good and bad, but this overlooks Nietzsche's portrayal of the nobles as brutish and stupid and his claim that 'Human history would be altogether too stupid a thing without the spirit that the impotent have introduced into it' (*GM* 1.7). It is with the rise of the priestly type, Nietzsche says, 'that man first became *an interesting animal*, that only here did the human soul in a higher sense acquire *depth* and become *evil*—and these are the two basic respects in which man has hitherto been superior to other beasts!' (*GM* 1.6) Still, despite their shortcomings, the nobles offer a morality that is inherently pluralist and that achieves this pluralism through a displacement and overcoming of identity.

## The victory of slave morality: bad conscience

With the idea of a subject that chooses its actions, slave morality creates the concept of moral culpability or guilt. The dominance of this concept can be glimpsed, Nietzsche says, in the way we moderns see the purpose of punishment as awakening the sense of guilt and remorse in the convicted criminal even though, more often than not, punishment only motivates the criminal to commit his crimes better in the future to avoid being caught (*GM* 2.14–15). There is no reason to think, however, that this is the only possible way in which a subject or self can be understood and ethically appraised. The second essay of the *Genealogy* explores another possibility while tracing the origin of the concept of the guilty subject or the subject of *bad conscience*.

Nietzsche defines conscience, bad or otherwise, simply as the right to make promises. One may make promises and be punished if those promises are broken without any reference to whether there was intent to break the promise, which indicates that the concept of guilt is not necessary to the idea of conscience. The question then is what is required to make a being with the right to make promises, and here the answer is very straightforward: force and cruelty. Just as the world for Nietzsche is chaotic, the human self is by nature flighty, disorganized, and forgetful, composed of an 'underworld of utility organs working with and against one another' (*GM* 2.1). This means that 'The task of breeding an animal with the right to make promises evidently embraces and presupposes as a preparatory task that one first *makes* man to a certain degree necessary, uniform, like among like, regular, and consequently calculable' (*GM* 2.2). Above all, a power of memory is to be 'burned in' (*GM* 2.3) so that men have a sense of both future and past. To unify the self sufficiently so that it can make and keep promises, it must be traumatized into this form: 'Man could never do without blood, torture, and sacrifices when he felt the need to create a memory for himself; the most dreadful sacrifices and pledges (sacrifices of the first-born among them), the most repulsive mutilations (castration, for example), the cruelest rites of all the religious cults (and all religions are at the deepest level systems of cruelties)—all this has its origin in the instinct that realized that pain is the most powerful aid to mnemonics [memory aids]' (ibid.).

That such violence is present is obvious given Nietzsche's view of a world of strife and conflict, but the genealogical approach indicates that the effects of violence are tied to the place of the self in its unequal relations. The strong suffer, Nietzsche argues, but also endure, without indignation or *ressentiment* towards existence, resulting in a particular form of conscience. At a time 'when mankind was not yet ashamed of its cruelty' (*GM* 2.7), the right to make promises, which is formed through force and violence, becomes the privilege of a free and sovereign being whose 'mastery over himself also necessarily gives him mastery over circumstances, over nature, and over all more short-willed and unreliable creatures' (*GM* 2.2). In this noble form of conscience the right to make promises is a consequence of the self-control of the strong.

Here punishment is a consequence of breaking promises, but it is dispensed to the promise-breaker on the basis not of his culpability but rather of the debt he owes, 'independently of any presupposition concerning freedom or non-freedom of the will' (*GM* 2.4). Punishment functions solely as retribution, as the right to inflict pain in order to compensate for unpaid debts (*GM* 2.5–6), which indicates that the cruelty of punishing must provide pleasure to the victimized party: 'Without cruelty there is no festival . . . and in punishment there is so much that is *festive*!' (*GM* 2.6) However, just as noble morality is restrained in so far as it does not seek out conflict with those who are too weak to provide a challenge, so too there are factors that moderate punishing. The first of these comes from the fact that intention is not a consideration in punishment, only that punishment should be equal to the unpaid debt: the strong punish 'as parents still punish their children, from anger at some harm or injury, vented on the one who caused it—but this anger is held in check and modified by the idea that every injury has its *equivalent* and can actually be paid back, even if only through the *pain* of the culprit' (*GM* 2.4). Moreover, the pleasure of punishment will be greatest for those who stand lowest on the social ladder—in other words, for the slavish one who only rarely 'participates in a *right of the masters*' and who, in punishing, 'may experience for once the exalted sensation of being allowed to despise and mistreat someone as "beneath him" ' (*GM* 2.5). But those who are truly masters can, because of their strength, afford the 'noblest luxury' (*GM* 2.10) of allowing those who harm them to go unpunished. Justice—the demand for equity—gives way to mercy, and so 'ends, as does every good thing on earth, by *overcoming itself*' (ibid.).

Mercy *through* strength is Nietzsche's answer to the apparent mercy that slave morality uses to hide its spirit of revenge. It is a mercy that comes from the refusal to strictly separate intent from accident in determining punishment (*GM* 2.4) and to be ashamed of aggressive instincts. From this comes a different understanding of the function of law. Instead of being a tool for revenge, the law of a strong society operates in 'the struggle *against* the reactive feelings . . . Wherever justice is practiced and maintained one sees a stronger power seeking a means of putting an end to the senseless raging of *ressentiment* among the weaker powers that stand under it' (*GM* 2.11). Law as a partial restriction on aggression and the spirit of revenge serves strength—this is the creed of the strong; conversely, when law seeks to eliminate all struggle and strife, it becomes 'a principle *hostile to life*' (ibid.).

Through all this Nietzsche shows how conscience, punishment, mercy, and law can be dissociated from the ideas of intentional evil and guilt. But it must still be asked how conscience succumbs to guilt—how does the slave revolt in morality create *bad conscience*? It is not simply through the turning of aggressive instincts back onto the self—a consequence of man's becoming social (*GM* 2.16)—for this is a quality of conscience generally. What is further necessary is that this turning back is associated with purity and beauty, so that man takes delight in self-torture (*GM* 2.18), and this indicates a further *moralization* of the creditor–debtor relation. This moralization is what makes guilt different from debt. Every civilization, Nietzsche says, feels a sense of debt to its ancestors, which can be seen, for example, in the use of sacrifice in primitive societies as a form of repayment (*GM* 2.19). As the civilization grows in strength the debt necessarily increases, leading to the deification of the founders and then beyond, so that 'the advance toward universal empires is always also an advance toward universal divinities' (*GM* 2.20). If debt and guilt were the same, then the establishment of the infinite God of Christianity would be 'accompanied by the maximum feeling of guilty indebtedness on earth' (ibid.). It would then follow, however, that with secularization bringing about the death of this infinite creditor, the indebtedness would dissipate (*GM* 2.20–1) and this has clearly not occurred.

This is because a strange inversion has taken place in the economy of debt, one designed 'to preclude, pessimistically, once and for all, the prospect of a final discharge' (*GM* 2.21): the supreme creditor has sacrificed himself to his debtors—a move symbolized by the image of God on the cross. Guilt is then forced on strong and weak alike and all humanity comes to suffer from a debt that can never be repaid: 'God himself sacrifices himself for the guilt of mankind, God himself makes payment to himself, God as the only being who can redeem man from what has become unredeemable for man himself—the creditor sacrifices himself for his debtor, out of *love* (can one credit that?), out of love for his debtor!' (ibid.) The sacrifice of the strong for the weak can only be a slavish idea. It is invented by a weak being 'in order to hurt himself after the *more natural* vent for this desire to hurt had been blocked' (*GM* 2.22). It establishes a mechanism that universalizes guilt and that does not even require belief in God to perpetuate itself, for its central tenet is not that we must struggle to repay a divine being but rather that we are born irremediably guilty. It embodies a self-hatred of mankind in which the difference between theism and atheism is irrelevant, embodying 'the *will* of man to find himself guilty and reprehensible to a degree that can never be atoned for' (ibid.) that continues to inhabit even a secular age.

Guilt is not simply a debt that is unrepayable because it is infinitely high. Just as today the stain of guilt follows the released convict even after he has paid his debt to society for his crime, so too do we all stand guilty according to slave morality. Whereas in the first essay the origin of slave morality was traced to the *ressentiment* that led the weak to label the strong as evil, the second essay shows how the dominance of slave morality requires it to go beyond this:

in order to become hegemonic, slave morality declares all humanity to be corrupt and guilty. *Ressentiment* is therefore directed not only at another, but back into the self as well. The consequence is that the weak do not simply valorize purity but embark on an impossible and endless task of self-purification, with every failure to achieve purity reproducing the very guilt that spawns the project. But again, the noble conception of conscience provides a glimpse of another attitude towards the self. As Nietzsche notes near the end of the second essay, the ancient gods took responsibility for human actions onto themselves. The Greek gods in particular reflect aristocratic men 'in whom *the animal* in man felt deified and did *not* lacerate itself, did *not* rage against itself!' (*GM* 2.23) This allowed pre-Socratic Greeks to treat the misdeeds of men not as intentional sins but rather as the result of foolishness or delusion by a god. The openness towards difference embodied in this morality appears in the way 'the gods served in those days to justify man to a certain extent even in his wickedness, they served as the originators of evil—in those days they took upon themselves, not the punishment but, what is *nobler*, the guilt' (ibid.).

## The ascetic ideal and the nihilism of modern secularism

Not all asceticisms express the ascetic ideal, which takes purity as its goal and is a product of the will to power of the weak. The strong, Nietzsche argues, express a different kind of asceticism, which is a condition of their mastery. Just as the forms of agonistic conflict, justice, mercy, and law discussed in the first two essays demonstrated the moderation and restraint of noble morality, noble ascetic practices display a restraint that is not a good in itself but a means to a healthy strength:

> The three great slogans of the ascetic ideal are familiar: poverty, humility, chastity. Now take a close look at the lives of all the great, fruitful, inventive spirits: you will always encounter all three to a certain degree. *Not*, it goes without saying, as though these constituted their 'virtues'—what has this kind of man to do with virtues!—but as the most appropriate and natural conditions of their *best* existence, their *fairest* fruitfulness. It is quite possible that their dominating spirituality had first to put a check on an unrestrained and irritable pride or a wanton sensuality, or that it perhaps had a hard job to maintain its will to the 'desert' against a love of luxury and refinement or an excessive liberality of heart and hand. But it did, precisely because it was the dominating instinct whose demands prevailed against those of all the other instincts—it continues to do it; if it did not do it, it would not dominate. Thus is there nothing of 'virtue' in this. (*GM* 3.8)

Locating the source of ascetic ideals, where their meaning is most clearly expressed, is therefore a complicated task. In so far as ascetic purity is tied to beauty, it seems that art would hold the key to its meaning. Yet art, Nietzsche says, is always capable of employing irony and parody, mimicking the ascetic ideal in order to undermine it (*GM* 3.3). This transgressive power means that in the case of artists, ascetic ideals mean either nothing or too many things (*GM* 3.1, 3.5). But since the artist has historically never stood independently, but always in the service of philosophy or religion (*GM* 3.5), it is towards the latter that the investigation must focus.

Because philosophy since Plato has been wary of the excessive power of art, it seems to be a prime candidate for the source of ascetic ideals. The philosopher has always sought to escape sensuality in order to contemplate, and consequently has held to an aesthetic conception of beauty as that 'which gives us pleasure *without interest*' (*GM* 3.6). This hatred of the sensual could only issue from a slavish perspective. Nonetheless, Nietzsche maintains that philosophy still retains much that is transgressive in its bent to question, criticize, doubt, and analyse (*GM* 3.9). Precisely because it was dangerous, philosophy in its early days was forced to hide itself behind a mask. It had to appear, Nietzsche says, like the contemplative type that was already socially and morally accepted—the religious man (*GM* 3.10). Even today this mask has not been fully removed (ibid.). Nonetheless, this finally indicates where the meaning of ascetic ideals is to be found: with the ascetic priest, who leads his flock in practices of purification. With the priest, asceticism is never a product of strength, only of weakness, and it is always posited specifically as an *ideal*.

The ascetic priest juxtaposes life, nature, and the world and its physicality to another mode of existence from which life is excluded unless it turns against itself. He posits a higher world that is pure in order to condemn the impurities of the world of experience. The physical world is treated as an error, and life itself is devalued as a mistaken turn. Life is opposed to itself by being compelled to purify itself in order to accord with this higher world. Religions such as Judaism, Christianity, Buddhism, and Hinduism all contain similar aspirations for redemption (*GM* 3.17). Similarly, philosophy, and particularly Platonism, posits an objective 'true world' that stands above all perspectives (*GM* 3.12). This world may be knowable through reason (i.e. Plato's world of Forms) or may be beyond the powers of reason (i.e. Kant's noumenal realm). In every case, however, the denial of perspective displays a will to clear-cut certainties that characterizes the slavish will to power.

Priestly asceticism would seem to work against life, but this does not explain its dominance (*GM* 3.11). Rather, Nietzsche argues, the ascetic ideal sustains life, but at its weakest level, working in the service of the impotent. Everything produced by the slave revolt is magnified and manipulated by the priest. Those who are forced into inaction are progressively poisoned by *ressentiment*. This *ressentiment* could eventually explode outwards at those the slaves call evil, but the priest prevents this, forcing it back onto the self. This provides a relief for the suffering but at the cost of greater sickness, because priestly medication works as a narcotic. Every sufferer 'instinctively seeks a cause for his suffering; more exactly, an agent; still more specifically, a *guilty* agent who is susceptible to suffering—in short, a living thing upon which he can, on some pretext or other, vent his affects, actually or in effigy' (*GM* 3.15). This is a defensive manoeuvre meant to prevent further injury, but it also functions 'to *deaden*, by means of a more violent emotion of any kind, a tormenting, secret pain that is becoming unendurable' (ibid.). As they are unable to react against others, the priest tells his dominated flock: 'Quite so, my sheep! someone must be to blame for it: but you yourself are this someone, you alone are to blame for it—*you alone are to blame for yourself!*' (ibid.) This strategy has often worked—'*in countless cases they have really freed* themselves from that profound psychological depression' (*GM* 3.17)—but it has simultaneously made the weak a threat to the strong: 'The sick represent the greatest danger for the healthy; it is *not* the strongest but the weakest who spell disaster for the strong' (*GM* 3.14). Here lies the answer to the question of how the weak defeat the strong while remaining weak. It is not that the weak, by combining together, form a greater physical force than the strong; rather, their resistance takes a different form. The weak, Nietzsche argues, defeat the strong by displaying their repugnance. This provokes a 'profound *nausea*' and 'great *pity*' (ibid.) that disables strength by making all action seem worthless in this sickly world. When nobility is drawn into the orbit of the priest, it falls into the trap of nihilism. The priest thus universalizes slave morality and becomes a universal figure himself. All are implicated: 'probably, we, too, are still victims of and prey to this moralized contemporary taste and ill with it, however much we think we despise it—probably it infects even *us*' (*GM* 3.20).

The priest exploits the self-hatred of his followers to establish ascetic practices of self-discipline and self-surveillance. In the first instance, these practices work to eliminate stimulus—obviously something coveted by those who are too weak to affirm the sensual. Related tactics include the use of regular, mechanical practices (what Foucault calls 'disciplinary practices'); the prescription of small pleasures in the form of 'good deeds' that are performed to provide a feeling of superiority and so always carry *ressentiment*; relief through a feeling of belonging—and in this way the weak are organized into a herd, living by the principle of 'love thy neighbour' at the expense of those who are different; and the occasional release of an orgy of violent emotion, which is then transformed into feelings of guilt, reinforcing the desire for redemption and purification and thus the need for further ascetic practices (*GM* 3.17–20). The circle of treatment thereby begins anew. The effect of all of these practices is to give a sickly life a meaning sufficient to keep it going.

As shown by the second essay, the priest's creation remains long after he loses his hegemony. What today seems opposed to the religious ascetic ideal in fact continues to develop it. As already seen, when the ascetic ideal is philosophized, it is raised to the status of truth. Modern science and scholarship may deny the higher world of religion and philosophy, but it still idealizes the philosophical-religious conception of truth in the purity of its objective, rational, unchanging laws and mechanisms. It is not that such scholarship has no value—'the last thing I want is to destroy the pleasure these honest workers take in their craft: for I approve of their work' (*GM* 3.23)—but it demonstrates its hypocrisy by denying it rests on faith while still holding to a faith in truth. That science maintains this 'faith in a *metaphysical* value, the absolute value of truth' (*GM* 3.24) follows from the fact that there is nothing in existence which proves that truth is unconditionally good. Science does no better than philosophy or religion in laying out a critique of truth itself—that is, an assessment of its *value*. What is required, Nietzsche says, is that 'the value of truth must for once be experimentally *called into question*' (ibid.).

In this project Nietzsche suggests that art, when freed from the constraints of aesthetics, is an important tool: 'art, in which precisely the *lie* is sanctified and the *will to deception* has a good conscience, is much more fundamentally opposed to the ascetic ideal than is science' (*GM* 3.25). What is required against the ascetic ideal are 'comedians of this ideal—for they arouse mistrust of it' (*GM* 3.27). But the downfall of the will to truth is in fact instituted by this will itself. Carried to its extreme, the will to truth forbids the possibility of lying to itself even at the cost of its own survival. It was because of this will that the Western Enlightenment separated the truth of the world from the idea that God created it; now, this same will to truth will not be able to lie to itself about the faith that it rests upon and the source of this faith in *ressentiment*. It was Christian morality, Nietzsche says, that killed the Christian God through its insistence on intellectual cleanliness at any price (ibid.) and this morality will in turn destroy itself by exposing the fact that it rests on nothing: 'As the will to truth thus gains self-consciousness—there can be no doubt about that—morality will gradually *perish* now: this is the great spectacle in a hundred acts reserved for the next two centuries in Europe—the most terrible, most questionable, and perhaps also the most hopeful of all spectacles' (ibid.).

Nietzsche begins and ends the third essay by stating the meaning of ascetic ideals: that the human will would 'rather will *nothingness* than *not* will' (*GM* 3.1, 3.28). In tracing the path to self-destruction traversed by the ideal, however, the fundamental truth underpinning the entire genealogy becomes clear. Genealogy sought to account for the genesis of the oppositional logic of good and evil, the linkage between goodness and purity, the belief in responsible agency, and the will for a higher, true world. All of these were determined to be the products of a weak and dominated will driven by hatred of the strife and suffering of life—and yet, 'it is and remains a *will*!' (*GM* 3.28) This will would rather will the fictions of identity, opposition, purity, and the true world than cease to will at all. Yet in willing these fictions, it is in fact willing nothing at all.

## The revaluation of values and the politics of difference: the friend and the enemy

There is no consensus on Nietzsche's relation to politics and political theory. His most overtly political statements are crude and illiberal and suggest a nostalgia for an earlier time of forceful rule by the strong. Nietzsche insists that the only purpose of politics can be to breed a superior being, an overman, which 'has exited often enough already: but as a lucky accident, as an exception, never as *willed*' (*AC* §3[6]). This requires a society of rank and slavery, where the distance felt between the highest and lowest social orders can instil a desire to transcend one's own limits (*BGE* §257). Moreover, this politics can only be instituted by an overman himself, who, through his superior will to power, legislates in this direction for all humanity. In light of this goal of breeding perfect beings, liberal democracy and revolutionary socialism can only be rejected as symptoms of a weak will that demands equality. At other times, Nietzsche seems to counsel a retreat from politics altogether: the strong should not seek to conquer the weak and establish dominion over them, but rather 'the healthy should be *segregated* from the sick, guarded even from the sight of the sick, that they may not confound themselves with the sick' (*GM* 3.14). Furthermore, his teachings, he says, are for 'free spirits' whose superior autonomy does not need the attachments of the herd and its politics. Politics and perfectionism are, in this way, incompatible.

Many interpreters, sometimes motivated to protect Nietzsche from his own sentiments, take this second route and declare his thought to be apolitical. Walter Kaufmann,[7] for example, takes Nietzsche's philosophy to be one of purely private self-creation. Richard Rorty[8] holds that Nietzsche *must* be treated as a private thinker because his philosophy is disastrous when introduced into the political sphere. Nietzsche's use to contemporary political theory, according to Rorty, comes in the way his thought can help contemporary, liberal societies recognize the groundlessness and contingency of their values and their existence. In affirming personal autonomy, however, Nietzsche shares with liberalism the ideal of the vibrant individual, which in liberal theory underpins a dynamic, free society. Indeed, liberal politics, Rorty argues, is the one form that can accommodate Nietzsche's demands, as its private sphere can enable personal freedom and experimentalism to flourish.

Others refuse to disconnect Nietzsche's calls for individual overcoming from his more overtly political pronouncements. Bruce Detwiler[9] gives a fairly standard portrayal, arguing that Nietzsche's aristocratic politics advocates the sacrifice of the many for the sake of a minority of radically autonomous higher individuals who stand above all moral restraints. This kind of reading ignores statements by Nietzsche that call the ideal of autonomy into question (when, for example, he holds that free spirits could not exist without the Church (*GM* 1.9) ), but it matches Nietzsche's more straightforward claims. Alisdair MacIntyre[10] holds that Nietzsche's vicious politics is nothing more than the logical conclusion of modern individualism and the atomistic society of everyone against everyone else it produces. Nietzsche's thought thereby demonstrates the bankruptcy of liberal political theory and the Enlightenment project of rationality, both of which undermine the communal bases for morality. Although he seeks to defend the Enlightenment project and many aspects of modern liberal societies, Jürgen Habermas[11] still sees Nietzsche's philosophy as a dead end brought about by a certain strain of Enlightenment thought itself. Habermas argues that Nietzsche's critique of the Enlightenment is incomplete and merely destructive, which is why the only alternative to modern politics that Nietzsche can propose is the barren and irrational one of a conquering overman.

In its normal sense, political theory involves the justification and legitimation of a social order, through either an ideal to which real societies should aspire, a set of abstract, rational rules that should govern the distribution of power and rights, or mechanisms that can bring about a more inclusive community of mutual respect and recognition of different identities. Given this focus, it would appear that Nietzsche could only be classified as apolitical or aristocratic in his politics, leading to the subsequent interpretative problem of determining how either of these positions can be of value today. Nietzsche's thought, however, cannot easily be subsumed in this way. His political thought certainly affirms hierarchy, yet he also levels criticisms at traditional social hierarchies, just as he attacks the metaphysical hierarchies of Platonism and Christianity. He speaks of 'ages when men . . . simply refused to acknowledge the element of accident, role, and caprice . . . [and] managed to erect those monsters of social pyramids that distinguished the Middle Ages' (*GS* §356). Against such rigid orders, which did have the virtue of 'durability' (ibid.), is the inequality in flux that characterizes Nietzsche's conception of chaos and governs his genealogical study of morality. And against the desire for settlement expressed in standard political theory are Nietzsche's attacks on the idealization of purity and the binary opposition of good and evil that arises with it. The idealization of identity and purity and the corresponding denigration of difference as evil certainly have political import, yet these aspects of Nietzsche's philosophy are often not considered political because they are not standard themes in political theory.

Recent Nietzsche scholarship has developed another line of interpretation and use of his thought. Taking its lead from writings by Gilles Deleuze and Michel Foucault, which have argued that Nietzsche's philosophy is essentially pluralist,[12] it has incorporated Nietzsche's thought into a politics and ethics of difference. Of key concern in this political theory is the *politicization* of identity itself—demonstrating how no identity is natural or pre-given but is instead always contingent and, moreover, constructed through a binary opposition between the goodness of that identity and the evil of that which would problematize it. Just as Nietzsche worried about the nationalist politics of his day, this theory focuses on those forms of politics that seek to build themselves upon stable identities deemed to be pure and good. The problem with standard political theory is that it remains committed to identity: liberalism, seeking neutral rules to guarantee equal rights for all identities, takes no account of the politics through which these identities are constituted; communitarianism, seeking to foster reciprocal recognition among different identities, ignores the way the politics of identity demands that others be seen as 'the same' in order to be recognized. It should be noted here that on the occasions that Nietzsche does speak positively about democracy, it is always to oppose a democratic demand for equality with the way democratic freedom can allow the unique and superior to flourish: ages are truly democratic, he says, when they foster experimentalism and improvisation (*GS* §356). This has meant that Nietzsche has become most salient in political theories and practices that have sought to contest the exclusionary nature of identity-based politics—ironically, Nietzsche, the aristocratic, misogynist theorist of the will to power, has become a key figure in feminism, gay and lesbian politics, post-Marxism, and New Left politics and political theory generally.

Nietzsche shows that the demand for stable identity issues from a particular perspective grounded in *ressentiment.* Moreover, as has been seen already in many arguments in the *Genealogy*, the revaluation of values that Nietzsche executes against this perspective does not simply assert the unrestrained power of the strong against the weak. Revaluation does not mean rejecting all moral values, or positing an overman who stands above all moral restraints, but rather removing these values from the *ressentiment* from which they have grown:

> It goes without saying that I do not deny—unless I am a fool—that many actions called immoral ought to be avoided and resisted, or that many called moral ought to be done and encouraged—but I think the one should be encouraged and the other avoided *for other reasons than hitherto*. We have to *learn to think differently*—in order at last, perhaps very late on, to attain even more: *to feel differently*. (*D* §103[13])

What this means above all is using the contingent nature of identity to press beyond traditional oppositions. Nietzsche provides an example of this in his rethinking of the meaning of 'friend' and 'enemy'. The friend is one who intervenes between the 'I' and 'me' to prevent the fall into the abyss of self-identity, of the nothingness that such an identity entails:

> I and me are always too deep in conversation: how could one stand that if there were no friend? For the hermit the friend is always the third person: the third is the cork that prevents the conversation of the two from sinking into the depths. (*Z* 1.14[14])

The friend resides within as the force that compels one to overcome oneself and one's identity, opening the self to what is different. This is the fundamental experience of noble morality, which affirms itself in strife and agonism. For this very reason, however, the friend is also an enemy: 'In a friend one should have one's best enemy' (ibid.). The friend is no longer the one who is closest, while the enemy is the furthest away. Against the Christian exhortation to love thy neighbour, Nietzsche proclaims: 'It is those farther away who must pay for your love of your neighbor; and even if five of you are together, there is always a sixth who must die . . . My brothers, love of the neighbor I do not recommend to you: I recommend to you love of the farthest' (*Z* 1.16). And against the Church's desire to destroy its enemies, he calls for the 'spiritualization of *enmity*. It consists in profoundly grasping the value of having enemies: in brief, in acting and thinking in the reverse of the way in which one formerly acted and thought. The Church has at all times desired the destruction of its enemies: we, we immoralists and anti-Christians, see that it is to our advantage that the Church exist' (*TI*, 'Morality as Anti-Nature', §3[15]). This spiritualization is not merely personal, but is also the key to the forbearance requisite to any 'grand politics' (ibid.). This politics, then, is not solely concerned with creating great individuals, but with overcoming the politics that is fixated on enemies. It retains the strife and conflict with the 'enemy'—and the 'friend'—but no longer in the brute form of opposition.

This is only one aspect of the alternative way of thinking and feeling that defines the overman, but it is a crucial one for the politics and ethics of difference for which Nietzsche has been employed. It is the first step in the thinking of a politics that moves beyond the need to create 'evil enemies'. Given that so much of our political and philosophical heritage comes from Platonist philosophy and Christian theology, which sustains a logic of identity and opposition, it is not surprising that Nietzsche can only point to alternative ideas that have political implications but do not add up to a political theory in the ordinary sense of a worked-out ideal of society—ideas such as conceptions of law and mercy that serve life, the affirmation of an agonism that compels self-overcoming, and the opening up of the self to difference by putting into question the moral opposition of good and evil.

Here Nietzsche offers a challenge to traditional approaches in political theory by showing how their demands for an ideal of settlement or order and the oppositions they establish between good and evil, friend and enemy, are the product of a limited perspective permeated with *ressentiment*. Exposing the politics of identity formation, he opens up the possibility of affirming difference precisely because this difference can call identity into question. Genealogy is central to this affirmation of pluralism because it outlines a noble way of being and acting that is no longer tied to identity. The genesis of oppositional thought indicates what must supersede it and this excess is another will to power that seeks not identity but overcoming.

## FURTHER READING


Ansell Pearson, Keith, *An Introduction to Nietzsche as a Political Thinker: The Perfect Nihilist* (Cambridge: Cambridge University Press, 1994).

Connolly, William, *Identity/Difference: Democratic Negotiations of Political Paradox* (Ithaca, NY and London: Cornell University Press, 1991).

Connolly, William, *Political Theory and Modernity*, 2nd edn. (Ithaca, NY: Cornell University Press, 1993).

Conway, Daniel, *Nietzsche and the Political* (London: Routledge, 1996).

Deleuze, Gilles, *Nietzsche and Philosophy*, trans. Hugh Tomlinson (London: Athlone Press, 1983).

Detwiler, Bruce, *Nietzsche and the Politics of Aristocratic Radicalism* (Chicago and London: University of Chicago Press, 1990).

Foucault, Michel, 'Nietzsche, Genealogy, History', in Paul Rabinow (ed.), *The Foucault Reader* (New York: Pantheon Books, 1984), 76–100.

Habermas, Jürgen, *The Philosophical Discourse of Modernity*, trans. Christian Lenhardt (Cambridge, Mass.: MIT Press, 1987).

Kaufmann, Walter, *Nietzsche: Philosopher, Psychologist, Antichrist*, 4th edn. (Princeton: Princeton University Press, 1974).

MacIntyre, Alasdair, *After Virtue* (Notre Dame, Ind.: Notre Dame University Press, 1984).

McIntyre, Alex, *The Sovereignty of Joy: Nietzsche's Vision of Grand Politics* (Toronto and London: University of Toronto Press, 1997).

Rorty, Richard, *Contingency, Irony, and Solidarity* (Cambridge: Cambridge University Press, 1989).

## NOTES

1. *The Gay Science*, trans. Walter Kaufmann (New York: Vintage Books, 1974) (hereafter *GS*).
2. *The Will to Power*, trans. Walter Kaufmann and R. J. Hollingdale (New York: Vintage Books, 1967) (hereafter *WP*).
3. *Beyond Good and Evil: Prelude to a Philosophy of the Future*, trans. Walter Kaufmann (New York: Vintage Books, 1966) (hereafter *BGE*).
4. *Human, All too Human: A Book for Free Spirits*, trans. R. J. Hollingdale (Cambridge: Cambridge University Press, 1986).
5. *On the Genealogy of Morals*, trans. Walter Kaufmann and R. J. Hollingdale (New York: Vintage Books, 1967) (hereafter *GM*); references are to essay and section number.
6. *The Anti-Christ*, trans. R. J. Hollingdale (Harmondsworth: Penguin Books, 1968, 1990).
7. Walter Kaufmann, *Nietzsche: Philosopher, Psychologist, Anti-Christ*, 4th edn. (Princeton: Princeton University Press, 1974).
8. Richard Rorty, *Contingency, Irony, and Solidarity* (Cambridge: Cambridge University Press, 1989).
9. Bruce Detwiler, *Nietzsche and the Politics of Aristocratic Radicalism* (Chicago and London: University of Chicago Press, 1990).
10. Alasdair MacIntyre, *After Virtue* (Notre Dame, Ind.: Notre Dame University Press, 1984) chs. 9, 18.
11. Jürgen Habermas, *The Philosophical Discourse of Modernity*, trans. Christian Lenhardt (Cambridge, Mass.: MIT Press, 1987), 51–74, 83–105.
12. Gilles Deleuze, *Nietzsche and Philosophy*, trans. Hugh Tomlinson (London: Athlone Press, 1983); Michel Foucault, 'Nietzsche, Genealogy, History', in Paul Rabinow (ed.), *The Foucault Reader* (New York: Pantheon Books, 1984), 76–100.
13. *Daybreak*, trans. R. J. Hollingdale (Cambridge: Cambridge University Press, 1982).
14. *Thus Spoke Zarathustra*, trans. Walter Kaufmann (New York: Viking Press, 1954, 1966); references are to book and section number.
15. *Twilight of the Idols*, trans. R. J. Hollingdale (Harmondsworth: Penguin Books, 1968, 1990).

# PART V

# The twentieth century: four approaches

# 26 Oakeshott

David Boucher

## Contents



## Chapter guide


The chapter begins by suggesting that Oakeshott's well-known scepticism is integrally related to the background theory of British idealism that informs all aspects of his philosophy. Following Bradley he took philosophy to be the uncovering and questioning of the postulates upon which all our forms of understanding rest. Typically, Oakeshott examined what was implied in the subject matter he explored, and either convicted it of failing to maintain what it asserted, or attempted to bring out in a clearer and more precise form something that was exhibited in its unsettled surface. He has been characterized as a conservative, a liberal, and an ideologist. He was neither conservative nor liberal in any party political sense, and in so far as the least we may expect of an ideology is a guide to political action, he steadfastly refused to give one because he wished at all times to maintain a strict logical separation between theory and practice, between theorizing and human conduct. The rationalist in politics was, for Oakeshott, a typical ideologist who completely misconceived the nature of the activity in which he was engaged. Principally, his characterization of the modern European state was as an amalgam of enterprise and civil association, and of the rule of law being intrinsic to the latter. This distinction enabled him to maintain that acknowledging the authority of law is categorially different from questioning its desirability, and that therefore ruling is an activity quite distinct from politics.

## Biography

Michael Joseph Oakeshott was born 11 December 1901 to a Fabian socialist Inland Revenue inspector who voted Liberal, and to a trained nurse who devoted her life to charitable work. Oakeshott became acquainted with the philosophy of Kant and Hegel at St. George's School, Harpenden, where the headmaster, the Revd Cecil Grant, spoke on philosophical subjects in his sermons, and instructed his charges in metaphysics on walking trips. Oakeshott took history at Gonville and Caius College, Cambridge, but studied two courses in history of political thought, and McTaggart's introduction to philosophy for non-philosophy students. He went on to study philosophy in Germany, and after a brief spell as a schoolteacher obtained a fellowship in his old college in 1927. He was a contemporary of Russell, Moore, and Wittgenstein at Cambridge, but chose not to participate in their philosophical discussions. The philosophers he knew at Cambridge were McTaggart and Sorley, both personal idealists, while Oakeshott himself not only rejected Cambridge realism, but also allied himself with Oxford idealism in adopting much of the spirit of F. H. Bradley's absolute idealism. He served in the army during the Second World War, rising to the rank of captain. He returned to Cambridge, and spent a brief interlude in Nuffield College, Oxford, before succeeding Harold Laski to the chair of government at the London School of Economics in 1951. He became a fellow of the British Academy in 1966. He retired in 1968, but continued to participate in the famous history of political thought M.Sc. seminar until the early 1980s. He was a man of immense learning, and wrote on a wide variety of subjects, but his reputation rests principally upon his writings in political philosophy. He wrote forceful condemnations of a style of politics he called rationalism, which were taken to be thinly veiled criticisms of the newly elected Attlee Labour government. He is generally casually associated with conservatism, and was indeed adopted by Margaret Thatcher as the foremost living conservative philosopher, but he declined her invitation to accept a knighthood. Her brand of conservatism was as rationalist and as alien to him as the politics of the Labour Party. Oakeshott died on 19th December 1990.

## Key texts

*Experience and its Modes* (1933)
*Rationalism in Politics and Other Essays* (1963), new expanded edn. ed. Tim Fuller (1991)
*On Human Conduct* (1975)
*On History and Other Essays* (1983)

## Main texts used

*Experience and its Modes* (Cambridge: Cambridge University Press, 1933) (*EM*).
*Hobbes on Civil Association* (Oxford: Basil Blackwell, 1975).
*On History and Other Essays* (Oxford: Basil Blackwell, 1983) (*OH*).
*On Human Conduct* (Oxford: Clarendon Press, 1975) (*OHC*).

*Rational in Politics and Other Essays* (London: Methuen 1963); new expanded edn. ed. Tim Fuller (Indianapolis: Liberty, 1991) (*RP*).

*The Voice of Liberal Learning*, ed. Timothy Fuller (New Haven: Yale University Press, 1989).

Posthumously published books:

*Morality and Politics in Modern Europe*, ed. Shirley Letwin (New Haven: Yale University Press, 1993).

*The Politics of Faith and the Politics of Scepticism*, ed. Timothy Fuller (New Haven: Yale University Press, 1996).

*Religion, Politics and the Moral Life*, ed. Timothy Fuller (New Haven: Yale University Press, 1993).

### Key ideas

**Rationalism**: a misconceived style of politics that believes itself to be starting from first principles and which constructs plans for society in accordance with them. It is the politics of perfection and the politics of certainty. **Modes**: a term typically used to denote self-subsistent ways of understanding experiences, such as history, poetry, and science, or forms of association such as **enterprise** and **civil association**. The former mode of association is composed of instrumental rules designed to achieve a common substantive purpose and in conceiving the state in such terms is denoted as *societas*, while the latter is composed of procedural rules acknowledged and recognized by the associates in pursuing their own substantive goals. Oakeshott calls this *universitas*. **Rule of law**: a moral relationship comprising a system of rules that are valid and authentic and in which differences of interpretation have authoritative procedures for settlement.

---

## Introduction

Michael Oakeshott was the philosophical sceptic par excellence of the twentieth century. F. H. Bradley defines scepticism as 'an attempt to become aware of and to doubt all preconceptions'.[1] This is exactly what Oakeshott takes scepticism to be. For the theorist, like himself, it is the determination constantly to be en route without ever hoping to arrive, but which does not exclude enjoying and even holidaying in the scenery on the way. The sceptic knows that he or she must doubt all preconceptions, but not all at the same time. Some things have to be accepted or taken for granted, if only temporarily, so that others may be interrogated.

## Philosophical idealism as the background theory

Interest in Oakeshott's political philosophy has tended to distract attention from the extent to which he consciously saw himself as the exponent of a particular type of philosophy completely opposed to the prevailing realism and positivism of the times. His first book was his philosophical statement, from which he deviated only in detail and with modest changes of emphasis. Philosophical idealism remained the background theory in all his writings, and the scepticism and anti-rationalism for which he is famous cannot be fully appreciated except in relation to the philosophical principles that he so clearly expressed at the age of 32.

The logical positivism of Rudolph Carnap, Otto Neurath, and Moritz Schlick, and the Cambridge analytic philosophy of Bertrand Russell, G. E. Moore, the early Wittgenstein, and L. S. Stebbing formed the philosophical context against which Oakeshott rebelled. He was much more comfortable with the philosophy that these schools of thought rejected, namely idealism. Oakeshott abjured certain aspects of idealism. He deviated from Hegel significantly in, for example, rejecting speculative philosophy of history, the idea that in history we can retrospectively discern a logic or pattern that reveals, to take an instance, the gradual revelation of freedom in the world.

Philosophical idealism, in all its forms, for the Logical Positivists of the Vienna Circle, was the enemy. They saw it as lacking rigour, confused and ambiguous, and as being mystical in its emphasis upon mind and spirit instead of upon science and logic. It was the importance of applying scientific method to philosophy that unified the Vienna Circle. The Logical Positivists, as they became known, argued that the logical rigour of science would be of great benefit to philosophy. This was in contrast with Cambridge realism, from which logical positivism derived inspiration, where it was held that philosophy had much to teach science. The powerful appeal of the Cambridge School and of the Vienna Circle to young philosophers such as A. J. Ayer was the lesson learned from David Hume that factual propositions are references to sense-experience. Philosophical thinking, they believed, entailed reformulating complex and puzzling statements more simply and clearly in order to reveal their underlying logic. The ideas of the Vienna Circle were also attractive because of their appeal to the simple and basic creed that there were only two types of valid statement: analytic statements that are true by definition, exemplified, for example in the deductive reasoning of the syllogism; and empirical statements, derived from observation—inductive and subject to the verification principle that determines the truth or falsity of a statement. A statement such as 'The world is flat', although false, is meaningful because it is open to verification. All other statements, such as 'There is a transcendent God', or 'There is a non-empirical world of values', are meaningless because they are matters of opinion and non-verifiable.

It was common among the idealists to assume that every aspect of experience is an invitation to relate it to a wider context in which it becomes more intelligible, and that the context itself belongs to a wider whole that endows it with meaning. Philosophy had to 'reveal its true position and relations with reference to all else that man can do and can know'.[2] Although in most other respects Bernard Bosanquet and Oakeshott were quite different, their conceptions of philosophy were expressed in similar terms. They addressed the question 'What is implied in a philosophical theory?' and contended that everyone knows that a flower is a different thing when understood by the botanist, chemist, or artist, and philosophy cannot hope to compete with these specialists on their own ground. Instead, it takes the flower and determines its significance in the totality of experience.[3] The idea of the modes of experience being self-subsistent and having a limited integrity of their own and of being arrests of the 'timeless and complete actuality' was something that Oakeshott could have found in one of his favourite books, H. H. Joachim's *The Nature of Truth*.[4] Whereas logical positivism assumed an external reality that could be invoked to verify empirical propositions, idealists rejected this correspondence theory of truth. For the idealists there is no external reality independent of the thinking mind; nature, for example, is intelligible to mind, and not independently of it. The truth of any proposition about experience depends upon its consistency with the coherence of the world of ideas, or mode of experience, to which it belongs: the more coherent that world, the greater the degree of truth the statement attains. The principles of coherence and non-contradiction are the criteria of truth.

When Oakeshott considered the possibility of ranking the modes of experience in terms of the degree of coherence attained, he admitted that is was a difficult task to accomplish, but it was not because of its difficulty that he rejected it. Instead, it was because it depended upon a misconception of the legitimate aims of philosophy. He did not deny that each mode may exhibit a different degree of abstraction, but, from the point of view of philosophy, it is an irrelevance, because what matters is the fact of abstraction, defect, and shortcoming, not the degree. For philosophy it is not necessary to measure the extent of the defect inherent in the different worlds of ideas: 'it is necessary only to recognise abstraction and to overcome it' (*EM* 84). In so far as the modes were coequal in relation to each other, and 'arrests' in relation to experience as a whole, Oakeshott undermined the reverence for natural science characteristic of logical positivism and Cambridge analytic philosophy. He argued that

> it is scarcely to be expected, in these days, that we should not be tempted to take up the idea of philosophy as, in some sense, 'the fusion of the sciences', 'the synthesis of the sciences' or the *scientia scientiarum*. Yet, what are the sciences that they must be accepted as the datum, and as a datum not to be changed, of valid knowledge? And if we begin with the sciences, can our conclusions be other or more than merely scientific? (*EM* 11)

## Interpretations of Oakeshott

### The conservative

Oakeshott is predominantly described as a conservative, and it is a self-description with which he seemed to be happiest. He was even cultivated and exploited by the first Thatcher government to give reflected philosophical gravitas, or epistemic authority, to a doctrine that had largely lost a clear identity. He gave no public endorsement of the Conservative government, and indeed he did not identify himself with party politics, all of which, as we shall see, had a tendency to pervert the type of non-managerial state he captured and saw reflected in the idea of the rule of law. To his great credit he did not compromise his distaste and disdain for politicians by accepting a knighthood, nor did he attempt to make capital out of declining the offer made to him by Margaret Thatcher on 4 December 1981. It was Oakeshott's heavy reliance upon the idea of tradition in his earlier characterizations of politics that led many critics to label him conservative. Freedom, for example, in Oakeshott's view, is not an inspired intuition or abstract idea, but is presupposed in every manner of concrete activity. Bernard Crick acknowledges that there is much truth in what Oakeshott says, but it is expressed in such general terms that it cannot act as a 'guide to political conduct'.[5]

Although he was not a party ideologue or party hack, Oakeshott was nevertheless a conservative by disposition. Gertrude Himmelfarb, for example, talks of his conservative 'imagination', which like disposition conveys 'a temper of mind rather than a set of ideas, a spirit rather than a philosophy or political creed'.[6] Most people tend to miss the irony in his argument, and think that he is advocating the adoption of a conservative disposition, whereas what he is actually saying is that in general most people of a certain age are inclined towards conservatism because they prefer certainty to uncertainty, the familiar as opposed to the unfamiliar. Greenleaf pointed out long ago that if Oakeshott was a conservative at all, it was with a small 'c', and that he explicitly rejected most of the doctrines upon which modern conservatism stood, such as a religious belief of some kind in a God-given order, and a right to private property based on natural law. Most modern conservative politicians differed only in degree from socialist social engineers and rationalists.[7] Anthony Quinton denies that religion played as large a logical part in the conservative conclusions of even the most overtly religious thinkers, such as Hooker and Burke. Quinton claims that the 'wisdom of our ancestors' in Oakeshott's reorchestrated conservatism 'appears, not as the constitution, but as a tradition of behaviour'.[8] Nevertheless, there is no getting away from the fact that for Oakeshott modern Conservative Party politics exhibited a style or tendency of politics that he very much regretted, that of the rationalist, the conduct of political activity with reference to a guiding creed or ideology, purporting to be premeditated in advance of the activity itself. Is he, then, best described as a liberal in politics?

## The liberal

Himmelfarb has made the interesting observation that Oakeshott rarely speaks of liberals or of liberalism in his writings. She speculates that he probably has too high a regard for liberty and freedom 'to apply those horrific labels to his antagonists'.[9] Those who cannot bear to see a commodity without a label maintain that, if Oakeshott is not to be branded a conservative, then he has to be a liberal. In Oakeshott's view, however, even though he is a philosopher of freedom and liberty, he saw in liberalism a strong tendency towards abstract individualism, the pursuit of half-baked ideals in the name of progress and the perfectibility of man. Indeed, Oakeshott is extremely harsh on liberalism in the introduction to his collection *The Social and Political Doctrines of Contemporary Europe*. There he accused liberalism of having become so dominant that it was scarcely short of despotism, and having become so commonplace that it had become intellectually boring.[10] Oakeshott preferred instead to talk of the tradition of representative democracy. It is a tradition because the doctrine changes, is ambiguous, and does not constitute a system of ideas. Two of its most important elements, in his view, were government by law, that is government as the administration of justice and not by arbitrary rule, and a recognition of the importance of nationality, or common sympathies.[11]

This was of no consequence because, for the revisionist, Oakeshott's repudiation of abstract individualism, characteristic of liberalism from Hobbes to Nozick, and of the free market economism that seemed to underpin the liberal moral ideal from Locke to Milton Friedman, clearly implied a restatement of liberalism because he was still concerned with liberty, appreciated individuality, and defended the rule of law.[12] Whereas Oakeshott repudiated the label because it had become too porous and allowed almost any ambiguous doctrine to seep in, the revisionists want to make the concept even more ambiguous in order to appropriate the favourable evaluative connotations of the ideas that it is said to encompass.

## The republican

He purposely alienates himself further from Anglo-American contemporary political philosophy by rejecting its vocabulary. In his view, the vocabulary has become so amorphous and misleading that Roman terms such as *respublica* and *lex* are more preferable and less encumbered with ideological baggage. In this respect, should he be assimilated to the republican tradition? It emphasizes the rule of law, where everyone is equal before the law and no one is above it. Its conception of freedom as non-dependence and the love of one's homeland are recognizable features of Oakeshott's political philosophy. Oakeshott could endorse Viroli's view that 'a republic is not a profit-seeking corporation but a way of living in common that aims to ensure the dignity of its citizens'.[13] He differs from republicans, however, in departing from the self-conscious design of creating and educating virtuous citizens, passionately proud of their institutions, who are willing and enthusiastic participators in civic life. Oakeshott, while acknowledging the importance of an inherited way of life, is almost contemptuous of practical politics and especially of politicians. In his article 'The Claims of Politics' he explicitly addresses the question of whether everyone has an obligation to take a more extended and active part in politics beyond keeping informed and exercising the vote. It would be an obligation, he suggests, if either of these two conditions were met: first, 'If political activity were the only adequate expression of a sensibility for the communal interests of a society of mankind', and, secondly, 'if it were incomparably the most important and most effective expression of such a sensibility'.[14] Such a view elevates and separates one aspect of the communal life of society above the rest, and denies the communal character of others, relegating them to so-called private life. The truth is, Oakeshott argues, the communal life encompasses everything we do, and the activity of a music hall entertainer is no less connected to the communal life than that of the prime minister. The choice, then, is not between public and private life, 'but between a life which has its place here or there in the common life, a life which touches the life and interests of our society either in this way or in that'.[15]

## The ideologue

Of course, the term 'ideology' encompasses a plethora of vices and virtues, and is used in its most innocuous form to describe political ideas in general. In this sense it is simply a generic term for the sets of beliefs that people have about politics. This is called the inclusive conception of ideology because everyone unavoidably has one. On the other hand, the exclusive conception is normally pejorative, and it is this conception that is usually levelled at philosophers. The exclusive conception contends that ideology is a somewhat corrupt way of looking at the world, providing distorted and often insidious images. In Marx's famous description ideology is false consciousness. Oakeshott himself adhered to this exclusive interpretation of ideology. As we shall see, Oakeshott believed that the ideologist is committed to a certain style of politics that abstracts or pillages from a tradition favoured elements that are privileged at the expense of others. The ideologist purports to start from first principles that can be used to guide political action. Because of Marx's emphasis upon the primary nature of the mode of economic production, the explanation of the superstructure in terms of the substructure, he would for Oakeshott typically be an ideologist, despite his insistence that he had avoided false consciousness by starting his philosophy in the material conditions of life.

Oakeshott is probably one of the most misunderstood modern political philosophers because he persistently refused to draw the political implications of his own inquiries, infuriating his critics, and delighting his disciples, who have been much less reluctant to express their political opinions than the softly spoken, modest, and retiring doyen of the English right. The right–left continuum, he thought, grossly mischaracterized modern politics and was more of a hindrance than a help in exploring political activity. Because *Rationalism in Politics* (1962), a collection including essays written in the period from 1947, was generally taken to be a thinly veiled attack on the Labour government, Oakeshott was widely taken to be an ideologue and political reactionary. Whereas, because of the context, the Labour Party might be taken to be the reference of Oakeshott's criticisms, the irony is that the book is an attack on all ideological politics, a tendency he calls rationalism, which had so perniciously tainted parties across the political spectrum in the British political tradition. One of the least things that we would expect an ideology to do is to provide a guide to political action, and this is what Oakeshott steadfastly refuses to do. In his view, to theorize an activity, such as politics, is conceptually and categorially different from prescription and injunction.

## Theory and practice

Among British Idealists philosophy had become a weapon in the social and political debates of late Victorian and early Edwardian Britain. It aspired to provide a practical guide to life. The very title of Henry Jones's book *Idealism as a Practical Creed* betrayed the relation in which, for him, philosophy and practical life stood.[16] On the other hand, J. M. E. McTaggart, Oakeshott's teacher, maintained that a person's views on practical matters were largely unaffected by his or her metaphysical beliefs.[17] For Oakeshott, practice was a distinct mode of experience that admitted of no theoretical intrusions from science, history, or philosophy. Both Bradley, from whom Oakeshott derived his scepticism, and Oakeshott argued that it is the business of philosophy to understand what is. Philosophy has no positive contribution to make to any other categorially distinct activity, including practical life. Moral philosophy has to understand morals, and has no business to manufacture them or offer a blueprint for manufacturing them.[18]

Oakeshott, like Hegel, maintained a distinction between theory and practice. Where both Hegel and Oakeshott may appear to be engaged in recommendation, at these points they may be said to be distracted from the engagement of philosophy. The political philosopher has no recipes for success to offer the politician, nor the student of politics. In his famous inaugural lecture at the London School of Economics Oakeshott contended that political philosophy cannot be expected to improve our chances of success in political activity, nor enable us to identify good and bad political projects. It cannot give direction in pursuing the intimations of a society's traditions (*RP* 65[19]). D. D. Raphael took exception to Oakeshott's distinction between explanation (or what Oakeshott later called theorizing) and recommendation, and suggested that very few philosophers of the first rank desisted from commendation and recommendation.[20] In reply Oakeshott stated that it is something very different to explain an action—historically, scientifically, psychologically, or what have you—and to recommend a course of action, and by extension both are very different from approving or disapproving of an action performed. To notice that Aquinas, Hobbes, or anyone else engaged in both explanation and recommendation does not suggest that they misjudged their task, or that Raphael is right in thinking that there is something akin to an amalgamation of explanatory and practical activity. It suggested to Oakeshott that these philosophers, like most other people, were both philosophers and preachers.[21] It needs to be emphasized, then, that to learn the language and skills of politics is to equip oneself for the vocation of political activity. But the academic or intellectual concern with the world of politics is not in the acquisition of its vocabulary for use; it is the designation of an area of activity as an appropriate subject matter for explanation. The concern, then, is not with participation but with explanation. The language of explaining an engagement such as politics is irrelevant to the practice of politics itself. In other words, an explanation of the presuppositions of performing actions 'is never a component of the knowledge which constitutes the performance'.[22]

### Practical life and politics

Practical life is a distinct mode of experience, injunctive rather than explanatory. The aspect of the mind engaged in this activity is the will. Practice posits two worlds: the world of what is, or existence, and the world of what ought to be. Practical activity is the attempt to make the former conform to the latter, to make the what is into the what ought to be by an act of will or volition (*EM* 358). This does not imply that we change things for the sake of changing them, or that the here and now is entirely discrepant with the there and then. The implication is that we see what ought to be as a 'not yet' or 'not here' and as in some way more coherent than what is. The world of practical facts is an unstable world. What is a practical act today may be nothing at all tomorrow. In practical life, as in other modes, the thing, or the individual, is designated and presupposed, not defined. The criterion of the designation is not completeness, or self-completion, but what is separate and self-contained. The practical self is the creature of practical thought and presupposed in all action. This self is presupposed to be self-determining, and the freedom entailed requires no demonstration, because it belongs to the practical self by definition. To deny it is to undermine the world of practice, and the principle upon which it is built, namely, the 'separateness and uniqueness' of the individual. The individual in practical life is just as much an abstraction, an arrest or modification of experience, as the individual, or thing, presupposed in all the other modes (*EM* 268–74). Politics is an aspect of practical life, and the work of the politician is, according to an idea, sometimes ossified into an ideology, to change what is into what ought to be.

## The rationalist in politics

Modern politicians in particular have fallen prey to a form of error whose consequences are potentially catastrophic. Rationalism in politics is, for Oakeshott, the great heresy of modern times. Its greatest fallacy is to think that it can wipe the slate clean and start from first principles. For the rationalist, the mind is a tabula rasa onto which a creed, blueprint, or plan can be imprinted. The rationalist assumes that the principles he, or she, promotes exist in advance of political activity, and can be applied independently of experience to the 'problem', and can provide the solution. The rationalist believes that there are right answers to political problems, and that these answers spring from a premeditated creed. It is the politics of certainty and the politics of perfection: certain because the formula generates the right answer, perfect because the most rational and efficient solution is to be implemented. The sovereignty of reason is in fact the sovereignty of technique. This self-understanding of the rationalist is in Oakeshott's view a misunderstanding because the rationalist fails to comprehend what is involved in the pursuit of any activity. Technical knowledge, which is what the rationalist's creed offers, is not in itself an adequate guide to action. Anyone who has ever picked up a motor car manual with the intention of saving some money on mechanics' bills will be aware that the technical advice it offers assumes, like all manuals, including the cookery book, some practical knowledge with which to put the technical knowledge into practice. This is why, Oakeshott tells us, such a clever man as Machiavelli did not merely offer his advice book for princes to Lorenzo de Medici, he also offered his own services, without which the technical knowledge formulated in precepts would be of little use.

The rationalist denies that practical knowledge is knowledge at all, and, in effect, is asserting that technical knowledge is the only form of knowledge. The rationalist worships certainty, and certainty is for him inseparable from technical knowledge. It is the appearance of the exercise of reason producing certainty and complete knowledge from the basis of pure ignorance that makes the idea of technical knowledge attractive to the rationalist. But this is an illusion because, in Oakeshott's view, 'as with every other sort of knowledge, learning a technique does not consist in getting rid of pure ignorance, but in reforming knowledge which is already there' (*RP* 17). The problem with modern European politics is that it has become increasingly more rationalistic in its manner. The danger is that a society infected by rationalist politics can easily slip into rationalist education where only the dominant ideology is taught. Thus the worship of technique and the politics of certainty lead a society to renounce its traditional heritage in favour of rationalist ideology.

D. D. Raphael was unconvinced by Oakeshott's alarmist portrait of the rationalist and argued that more modest rationalists are at work continually clarifying principles of justification within a tradition. These are what Raphael called the rational grounds that, for example, a scientist, moral agent, or politician would take to be the justifications of what they have done. Raphael accused Oakeshott of offering no principles in terms of which to choose between competing intimations within a tradition. The rationalist who thinks in terms of justifications does address this question, and whereas he or she may often go wrong, at least the right questions are being addressed. To approach what the tradition intimates in a historical frame of mind gives no clue to what should be followed. All that can be ascertained is what has been done. If questions of justification and explanation are approached historically, the conclusion would have to be 'that whatever is, is right'.[23] Raphael argued that even one so close in temperament and reverence for tradition as Lord Devlin in defending the unanimity rule in trial by jury for criminal cases uses a principle in deciding between the different intimations. Devlin's argument is not simply based on an ingrained rule of unanimity in the British legal tradition, but takes into account the view that the introduction of a majority verdict might lead the British public to think that the principle of the absence of reasonable doubt was being violated.[24]

Oakeshott's riposte was wounding. In relation to all of the beliefs, maxims, and conflicting opinions that face us in a tradition it is to be expected that there will be competing norms or intimations that cry out for recognition. In choosing between them, however, unlike what Raphael appears to suggest, it is not possible to apply a norm that stands above the fray. The higher norm one uses for abridging the essential principles in the tradition would itself stand in need of justification in terms of a higher norm. The Devlin example, Oakeshott contended, does not illustrate the appeal to some universal principle or norm in defence of the unanimity rule. Oakeshott argued:

> Lord Devlin solves his problem, not by appealing to some universal 'principle' or self-evident axiom, but by invoking *one* of our common beliefs about the administration of justice, and by suggesting that this belief, rather than any other (of which we have many), should weigh with us in this matter. He is not pointing to an inherent difference between civil and criminal proceedings as such; he is pointing to something *we* are apt to believe, and it is not difficult to imagine a society in which it would be considered more important to have stringency in civil than in criminal verdicts or one in which no such distinction was observed. Lord Devlin does not appeal to an incontestable 'principle'; his argument is persuasive because the principle (that is, the current belief) he invokes is familiar to us and is appropriate enough to be capable of engaging our sympathy while we listen to him expounding its bearing upon the proposal being considered. Like all arguments about what to do, it cannot be refuted; but it may be rebutted by showing (for example) that some other belief, pointing to some other conclusion, provides, in the circumstances, a more relevant aid to reflection, or that, in spite of its merits, the probable consequences of the proposal would be other than those intended and plausibly undesirable.[25]

Ideology and rationalism are, for Oakeshott, closely related concepts. An ideology is a rationalist formulation of related abstract principles that have been arrived at through the exercise of pure reason, what Oakeshott calls the sovereignty of reason. In other words, an ideology is composed of a set of principles believed to have been formulated by wiping the slate clean and starting from a position unhindered by prejudice or tradition. The ideology acts to guide empirical politics; that is, it gives direction to what otherwise would be a pragmatic and random set of impulses to the solution of immediate problems. However, an understanding of politics in terms of an ideology guiding political action is, as far as Oakeshott was concerned, a ridiculous conception. An ideology is simply not what it purports to be. It believes itself to be the product of intellectual premeditation owing nothing to the political tradition, yet offering itself as a guide to the direction of political conduct.

Ideology, in Oakeshott's view, is not like this at all. Ideology, far from guiding political conduct, is itself derived from it. As Oakeshott maintained, 'The pedigree of every political ideology shows it to be the culture, not of premeditation in advance of political activity, but of meditation upon a manner of politics. In short, political activity comes first and a political ideology follows after' (*RP* 51). An ideology is an abbreviation of a political tradition; it selects some aspects of political behaviour as being the most significant and ignores others. Those deemed significant are elevated above all others and form the basis of the ideological creed. The problem is that the pursuit of these principles without regard for a society's political inheritance and traditions can lead to the ignorance of blind certainty. The unrelenting adherence to principles, in disregard of the unpleasant unintended consequences, in pursuit of a certain end can bring disaster to a community.

What distinguishes the conservative sceptic from the rationalist of any political persuasion is that the rationalist holds to a creed, a political crib to guide conduct, and is perpetually pursuing what reason dictates. The pursuit of perfection leads him or her to see imperfection in everything. The conservative, however, has a disposition rather than a creed. It is a sceptical disposition that leads him or her to take pleasure in the moment, to enjoy what is. Steering a course between James Branch Cabell's optimist who thinks this the best of all possible worlds, and the pessimist who fears that it is true, the conservative sceptic subscribes to Bradley's aphorism that 'the world is the best of all possible worlds and everything in it is a necessary evil'. Oakeshott quotes this approvingly in his inaugural lecture, 'Political Education'. What makes rationalism so dangerous in Oakeshott's view is that the rationalist views the state almost wholly as an enterprise for mutual benefit, and understands its role as the management of this enterprise towards the achievement of substantive goals. This is only one aspect of the character of the modern European state, and what Oakeshott is trying to do is to temper the predominant understanding with one that has always coexisted with the other, namely, civil association.

## Modes of association

One of the great questions in political philosophy is to reconcile personal freedom with the collective constraints that society necessarily posits. This was a question that both Rousseau and Hegel explicitly addressed, and their answers were deemed to be intellectual sleights of hand in moving from a negative to a positive conception of freedom. To do as one wanted or desired to do was not freedom at all, but instead a form of slavery to those desires and an exhibition of an inability to apprehend what one really wants. Freedom becomes transformed into the liberty to do what is right in conformity with the general or real will. Oakeshott takes this same question of reconciling freedom and constraint without resort to a collective or substantive goal to which individuals were subordinate. Like Rousseau and Hegel Oakeshott rejected a purely empirical criterion and a transcendental or abstract criterion of political activity. If individuality were not to be compromised, then civil association had to be conceived in terms different from the politics of the felt need, that is, acting in accordance with a purely empirical criterion, waking up on impulse and acting upon it. Such action is impossible because there must always be a connection between such impulses, a manifold that holds them together. Similarly, he rejected abstract principles, either in the form of laws deemed to be derived from natural law bestowed upon us by a creator, or laws said to be derived from first principles. Both are divorced from experience and incapable of achieving what they purport to offer, guides to conduct independent of experience. What Oakeshott was self-consciously looking for, like Rousseau and Hegel, was a way of synthesizing the empirical and transcendental criteria of political conduct. The way in which he tried to bring these two criteria together was to suggest that political activity always took place within a tradition. The immediate demands of empiricism and the long-term ends of rationalism were dependent upon a tradition of political activity. The immediate problems we encounter and the solutions we offer are limited by the traditions of a society. Political activity can take no other form than 'the amending of existing arrangements by exploring and pursuing what is intimated in them'

(*RP* 56). Women, he suggested, gained the vote in British society, not because of any abstract arguments concerning natural law or justice, but because of the standing they had already achieved in other respects. They had taken a great deal of responsibility during and after the First World War, and their already increased stature in society intimated that a change towards enfranchisement was desirable. There was, in Oakeshott's terms, an incoherence in society, and the act of enfranchising women was an attempt to repair the incoherence.

Oakeshott was not for one moment recommending that politics are the pursuit of intimations, or that politicians see themselves as doing so, nor was he attributing such an idea as their motive for acting. What he was saying was that irrespective of what they believed they were doing, what politicians actually did was to pursue intimations inherent in a tradition of political and social behaviour. Such an understanding of politics was most vehemently denied by those who took civil association almost exclusively to be an enterprise for mutual benefit in which goals are set and rules designed as instruments to achieve them.

## Enterprise association

The most rudimentary form of relationship among individuals is a transactional relationship. Here more than one individual is related with others solely in terms of wants, most notably buyer and seller, but also, for example, entertainers and their audiences. It is a relationship of power in which each person attempts to attain substantive satisfactions by responding to each other's offers or refusals to enter into bargains. Collectively this mode of association may signify individuals joined in a common pursuit for mutual advantage, not to satisfy individual wants but to attain common goals as comrades or partners. Here power is assembled from the resources of its members in order to pursue the chosen end, and some form of organization is likely to be constituted to facilitate the pursuit, rather than just merely the common recognition of the goal.

This relationship involves the making of decisions concerning what course of action needs to be taken in achieving the goals. Thus a policy is formulated and needs to be under the direction of a 'management'. This management can be by unanimous or majority decisions of the associates, or by a small group of the associates, or by one person empowered to make such decisions on behalf of the associates. If the association is to have long-term objectives, then it may lay down rules, create offices, formulate procedures by which these offices are to be filled, and specify the conditions for withdrawing from such an enterprise association. Such enterprise associations may take the form of a business, a horse-racing syndicate, a charitable organization, or any other enterprise where individuals are associated in pursuit of a common goal.

The form of relationship known as enterprise association is exclusively concerned with the satisfaction of wants and desires. The rules that regulate the association are subordinate to the goals pursued by it. They are judged in terms of their ability to help or hinder the goal pursued. The rules are seen to be instrumental in attaining the common goals. This form of association, appropriate for satisfying substantive needs, has often been mistaken for the form of association that pertains within a state.

This view of the state arises from the belief that the people stand in need of deliverance from whatever evil may have befallen them, whether it be poverty, immorality, or subjugation. The government formulates the goals and manages the direction society takes in attaining them. The laws which the government enacts are instrumental to achieving the common purpose. Instrumental rules, or precepts, are prudential and urged in terms of their consequences. They are related to the achievement of substantive ends and the avoidance of unwanted outcomes. In this respect, as advice for conduct, their validity and desirability are indistinguishable because the criterion used is the same, namely, the utility of the outcome. Thus both people and laws within a state, understood as an enterprise association, are instruments in the enslavement of a common purpose. In such a society, for example, where the purpose might be 95 per cent transfer of transport from road to rail over five years, a large number of laws and a huge amount of resources would be harnessed to achieve this goal. Universities would teach degree courses on transport studies directly relevant to this goal; those that did not have a direct bearing on the collective purpose would become undersubscribed and ultimately abandoned.

In illustration of this conception of the state as an enterprise association Oakeshott retells the story of the Tower of Babel. All the resources and all the energies of the inhabitants of Babel were directed to Nimrod's plan of building a tower to heaven in order to conduct an assault to obtain its riches. All university courses were vocational relating to some form of building studies. The dream soon turned into a nightmare as clay for bricks ran out, and the buildings of the town were demolished for bricks to complete the project. People lived in tents in the interests of the common goal, and as the tower grew narrower at the top, fewer bricklayers were needed, resulting in large-scale unemployment. The people became suspicious of Nimrod's prolonged periods in the tower, and they feared that he may be planning an assault on heaven without them. When one day he did not emerge, the inhabitants of Babel panicked and surged up the tower, putting tremendous strain on its structure. The tower began to sway and eventually collapsed under them: 'What had been designed as a stairway to paradise had become the tomb of an entire people' (*OH* 193[26]).

## Civil association and the rule of law

The mode of association, or type of relationship, posited by civil association is association in terms of the rule of law. The conditions of this relationship are solely and exclusively laws formulated by fellow human beings. It is a distinctive type of relationship immediately distinguishable from the most obvious and rudimentary, transactional relations that are characteristic of enterprise association. This should not be confused with the playing of a game in which competitors are joined together in the pursuit of a substantive purpose, namely winning. There may, of course, be strategies and game plans, developed and enunciated by a coach, but they are not strictly speaking rules. They are tactics and precepts designed to facilitate a win. The rules of a game are constitutive and not instrumental. They do not command a player to do or forbear from doing. They are adverbial qualifications imposed upon the actions performed by competitors, namely the skills they employ in attempting to win. For example, in attempting to achieve the object of the game of rugby union—the scoring of tries—the rules relating to the forward pass, off-side, and knock-on adverbially qualify the actions employed to achieve the objective. A try is scored if the ball is touched down over the goal line and none of these rules are infringed. Like all rules they have a dual character: their authenticity and their desirability. To play the game is to subscribe to the rules in acknowledgement that they have been promulgated by the appropriate governing body. Questions of their desirability, whether they hinder the playing of the game, are entirely separate considerations that have no bearing upon whether the rule should be obeyed during the playing of the game itself.

There are two forms of association operative in a game. They are what Oakeshott calls 'categorially' distinct modes of association. The one entailing the pursuit of a common purpose on a given occasion, which is terminated or exhausted on that occasion. When the game is finished, the players cease to be engaged in the common purpose and are no longer bound by the constitutive rules. This is an *actual* relationship of fixed duration at a given time and place. The other relationship is *ideal*, in that the game subsists or exists in advance of every occasion upon which it is played on account of the rules being acknowledged as authentic and constitutive of the game. This second relationship offers us a glimpse of what is entailed in association in terms of the rule of law.

A rule, in the sense in which Oakeshott urges us to understand it as non-instrumental, is concerned not with the expediency of conduct, but with its propriety. The validity of a rule is not in its success in achieving substantive outcomes, but in its authenticity.

The rule of law, Oakeshott argues, is a form of moral association. Moral association entails human beings related in terms of their mutual recognition of the conditions that specify right and wrong, and assumes these same persons are related transactionally in the pursuit of substantive wants, the attainment of which is qualified by certain conditions that are neither instrumental in attaining those wants nor have a purpose of their own (*OH* 132). A morality is a practice into which we become inducted, and while we do not experience it as a set of rules and precepts, it may be abridged in this way, but it cannot be reduced solely to rules. In Oakeshott's view a legal order is a moral practice that has become a system of rules with all that it implies, namely, procedures for identifying valid or authentic rules, for invoking them in appropriate circumstances, and for settling differences of interpretation. When offices arise to legislate, amend, or revise, when judges determine what the rules mean in particular cases, and when rulers attend to such rules, a moral practice has become institutionalized into a system of law.

The rule of law is association solely in terms of the recognition of rules and the obligations prescribed. It is a relationship that does not entail doing or enjoying the rewards of doing, but is a relationship of procedural conditions, laws, that adverbially qualify and constrain doing (*OH* 148). Recognition of the laws entails the acknowledgement of the authenticity of their source. The rule of law, then, postulates a proper procedure or process, the sovereign legislative process, that must be followed in order to endow a rule with authenticity (*OH* 138). Acknowledgement of this authenticity does not imply approval of the content of the law. This does not exclude rules that have an origin outside the legislative process, such as those of the common law, as long as their 'authenticity derives from a presumption, namely, that it cannot resist appropriation, rejection or emendation in a legislative enactment' (*OH* 139).

The obvious point of comparison in modern legal theory is H. L. A. Hart. Hart characterizes law as a combination of primary rules of obligation, and secondary rules for determining, amending, and invoking the obligations. Like Hart, Oakeshott wants to maintain that considerations about the legitimacy or authority of law are conceptually different from those about its moral worth. Also, like H. L. A. Hart, Oakeshott rejects Austin's command theory of law. A rule, Oakeshott argues, is not a command because a command is directed towards an identifiable agent and is a response to a particular situation, and is exhausted by that situation.

Unlike rules, commands are injunctions to perform substantive actions and require obedience. Furthermore, John Austin, like many before him, including Bentham, failed to distinguish between the authority of law and its truth or desirability. This was because he understood the state not as a civil association but instead as an enterprise association whose purpose was to maximize the general happiness. His theory suggests that the authority of rules of law rests upon their relation to accurate information about their capacity to conduce to the general happiness. Acknowledgement of their authority rests upon due deference to the legislator's supposedly superior knowledge of the result of the inductive science of legislation, which in fact, due to its relative newness, was only marginally better than that of the subject (*OHC* 171[27]). The most significant difference between Oakeshott and Hart, however, quite markedly separates them. Hart's theory of law is consequentialist and is at bottom utilitarian. He does not recognize Oakeshott's important and crucial distinction between instrumental and non-instrumental rules and the types of association to which they are appropriate.[28] Oakeshott does acknowledge, however, that both Bentham and Hart make the logical distinction between what a law is and what it ought to be. On the question of the justice of a law, for example, Bentham regards it as a logically different question from what makes a law what it is. The role of the censor, or utilitarian judgement, relates to its justice.[29]

This does not mean that there is no relation between morality and law. Even though they both deny that traditional natural law doctrines can provide criteria for the validity of law, they do not think that law can have any arbitrary content as long as it fulfils the formal requirements of law. In Hart's case, there are certain minimum considerations about the human condition which, although they may be logically contingent, nevertheless need to be satisfied if law is genuinely to be legitimate. This is what he called the minimum content of natural law. This content is derived from the simple fact of the desire for human survival. Hart's minimum conception of natural law is categorially ruled out by Oakeshott because nothing about the content of law or its justness can be inferred from so-called facts about human nature. Oakeshott's view needs qualification. Hart certainly talks of the minimum content of natural law in that laws serve a minimal purpose of providing security. This is a justification external to the practice of law itself, and is an answer to the question 'What good does the practice of law serve?' It is a sociological question distinct from the analytic content of law. All three accept that what makes the practice of law of value is that it sustains social relations of a certain kind. It is, however, contingent and not intrinsic to the logical character of law, nor a necessary component of its justification.[30]

There are, nevertheless, certain moral considerations integral to law that have affinities with one of Hart's severest critics, Lon Fuller. They both maintain that a legal order cannot be maintained without intrinsic standards, such as its indifference to particular persons and interests, equality before the law, the exclusion of privilege, and the prohibition of secret and retroactive laws.[31] Complicity with a law that is not public can only be by chance, and a law that is systematically ignored undermines the character of civil association which relies upon the acknowledgement of the authority of non-instrumental laws, and where this acknowledgement implies obligation. In contradistinction to Hobbes, Oakeshott maintained that laws may be unjust if they fail to comply with the general character of law, but they may also be unjust on the basis of wider considerations: 'considerations in terms of which a law may be recognised, not merely as properly enacted, but as proper or not improper to be or to have been enacted' (*OH* 141). They are considerations, not in relation to an abstract and absolute natural law, but in relation to the developed historical moral sensibilities of its citizens: 'the prescriptions of the law should not conflict with a prevailing educated moral sensibility capable of distinguishing between the conditions of "virtue", the conditions of moral association ("good conduct"), and those which are of such a kind that they should be imposed by law ("justice")' (*OH* 160).

The mere proclamation and enforcement of law do not, however, satisfy the conditions of a law being known and on the whole observed. To be aware of the general considerations which the law promulgates when choosing to act leaves undetermined 'what will count as an adequate or acceptable subscription in a contingent situation' (*OHC* 130). There must be not only sanctions but a way of settling disputes about whether contingent compliances are faithful to the law. This is the office of adjudication related to a court of law. It is not merely a matter of applying laws to situations, because all law is underdetermined in the sense that it does not specify 'how a prescribed norm of conduct stands in relation to a contingent situation' (*OHC* 133). Adjudications are amplifications of law, specifying what was unspecific in the general conditions, which do not try to anticipate their relation to every contingent situation. Such amplifications are not merely the judges' subjective musings. They must necessarily make reference to the law, not as a deduction from or exemplification of it, but almost always as a novel illustration of it. The purpose of adjudication is to amplify the meaning of law as it relates to the specific contingent circumstances where it is invoked. It follows, for Oakeshott, that 'civil association is necessarily relationship in terms of the accumulated meanings of *lex* which emerge in the adjudication of disputes' (*OHC* 137).

The idea of the rule of law cannot be divorced from the justice of law, the *jus* of *lex*, and the criterion that has often been applied is some absolute standard to which law must conform or approximate, such as the precepts of the law of nature or of God. Alternatively the justice of law may be claimed to be in its conformity to fundamental values, inviolable liberties, or human rights. What is implied in the application of these criteria is that the justice of law lies in the promotion, or at least the non-hindrance, of the substantive values and outcomes that the criteria prescribe. Such a view, however, denies to law its non-instrumental character, and assumes the character of an enterprise association.

The rule of law postulates a distinction between the justice of law and the procedural considerations that determine it authenticity. Furthermore, it acknowledges, 'it recognizes the formal principles of a legal order which may be said to be themselves principles of "justice"' (*OH* 143). In order to determine the justice of law, what is required in this mode of association is not an abstract set of criteria, but 'an appropriately argumentative form of discourse in which to deliberate the matter' (*OH* 143). The focus of such discourse is not right and wrong generally in conduct, but more restrictively considers what kinds of conditional obligations are appropriate for law to impose, undistracted by questions of substantive outcomes, or the pleadings of minorities for special treatment. The justice of law, or *jus* in *lex*, is in fact its faithfulness to the principles inherent in the law itself. These include its non-instrumental character, neutrality between persons and interests, and exclusion of outlawry and privilege (*OH* 159). Beyond this faithfulness to the formal character of law, deliberating the justice of law entails something else: not recourse to moral absolutes, a fundamental code, or natural rights to which law must be faithful, right or wrong motives for action, but 'the negative and limited consideration that the prescriptions of the law should not conflict with a prevailing educated moral sensibility capable of distinguishing between the conditions of "virtue", the conditions of moral association ("good conduct"), and those which are of such a kind that they should be imposed by law ("justice")' (*OH* 160).

When Oakeshott calls his delineation of the postulates of the rule of law an ideal characterization, what he means is that the relationship that he identifies as the rule of law is intimated or glimpsed throughout early modern European history, not that it provides a portrait of the modern European state. Indeed, there have been many factors that have worked against the full realization of the rule of law. As states emerged in medieval Europe, they began to claim the 'exclusive custody' of their laws, and any conception of the non-instrumental character of law had to compete with the hesitation of governments to relinquish any of the managerial functions they inherited from their predecessors. The idea of the rule of law also had to compete with fanatical and short-lived attempts to create sovereign communities of believers, or the imposition of a religious community on the state whose leaders had direct access to the laws of God and whose purpose was to direct the actions of its subjects according to them.

The most serious impediment to the flourishing of the rule of law was the Baconian, or technological, conception of the state. Associates are joined together in a common enterprise of exploiting natural resources for their common benefit. The office of governments was conceived as nothing more that the custody and direction of the enterprise by enlightened technocrats. Surprisingly, as the inevitability of this conception became promoted by its advocates, the emergence of another factor made the development of the modern state in terms of the rule of law almost submerged. Political parties have more often than not served to organize interests, whatever they may be, and commit themselves to promoting or pursuing those interests when they gain office. This in itself is at odds with the idea of the rule of law, which is neither concerned to facilitate nor hinder particular interests. Indeed, a party would have to compromise or reject its character in order to 'acquire the *persona* of a legislator' (*OH* 154). The virtue of party politics in Europe is that it served to qualify the managerial conception of the state by making office temporary and competitive. Party politics had done nothing, however, to promote the rule of law. This is one of the reasons why Oakeshott contended that 'when properly understood the rule of law *cannot*, without qualifications, characterize a modern European state' (*OH* 155).

## Politics and law

Where, then, do politics fit into all this? Oakeshott's view of what constitutes political activity has become refined over the years. Politics is an eminently practical undertaking concerned with the language of persuasion and injunction, as opposed to explanation or theorizing. Within the practical mode we view the world in relation to ourselves. We look at objects in terms of their use for future action, and we formulate our purposes and pursue our desires. The practical mode is a world of wants and the satisfaction of wants. But in this world wants are never ultimately satisfied. The practical self is always seeking to change what is into what ought to be. We are always seeking those things that we believe to be valuable. What is valued is not whatever I happen to think and want. These desires are formulated within a community of other selves. In recognition of this fact our desires are modified. The forms of accommodation, or agreement, reached may be temporary or take a more permanent form. Certain aspects of practical life become well established, such as laws, customs, institutions, and traditions. In order to be successful in practical life we need to learn the skills associated with particular activities. We take the given in practical experience and try to change the what is into the what ought to be. But the attempt to reconcile these two worlds, the what is and what ought to be, is never finally achieved because, as soon as it is achieved in one area, tensions break out in another, which press for change. Thus practical life has this permanent division between what exists and what is valued. The vocabulary of politics is one of persuasion and preference; it has to do with practical concerns about what is desirable and what is not desirable. It takes as its object the present condition of things and thinks in terms of how it can be preserved or changed.

Oakeshott defines politics in a number of ways. In an unpublished paper, 'The Character of Modern British Politics', written for a Political Studies Association Conference, Oakeshott defined politics as the 'activity and utterance connected with government'. The definition is extended by arguing that politics is 'the activity of attending to the general arrangements of a set of people whom chance or choice have brought together' and who, 'in respect of their common recognition of a manner of attending to [their] arrangements, compose a single community' (*RP* 44 and 56). Mostly famously, as we have seen, he defined politics as 'the pursuit of intimations'. In these characterizations there is little attempt to distinguish governing or ruling from the activity of politics itself. In *On Human Conduct* his understanding of politics is refined by his further exploration of civil association and the rule of law. Politics is identified there as 'categorially distinguished from ruling'. Ruling is the ongoing activity of those who occupy governmental offices, and whose utterances are authoritative rather than persuasive. Political activity relates not to the recognition of the authority of laws, but to the desirability of the conditions that the laws prescribe. Rulers may, of course, engage in politics, but when they do they are doing something categorially distinct from ruling (*OHC* 166–7). Politics relates to the activity of approval and disapproval of the laws enacted, and of somehow desiring or imagining them to be different from what they are. It can also be the activity of resisting changes in the law, that is, of expressing approval of a law and disagreeing with any moves to replace or amend it. The proposed rules that are recommended in the activity of politics are not instrumental to a common purpose. They relate to no one in particular, yet to everyone in general. He maintains that 'Politics, then, is concerned with an imagined and wished-for condition of *respublica*, a condition in some respect different from its current condition and alleged to be more desirable' (*OHC* 168).

Recognition of the authority of rules and the deliberations concerning their desirability are, then, two distinct activities. Politics understood as the deliberation of the desirability of the conditions of what Oakeshott calls *respublica* must for him exclude certain types of consideration. Whereas proposals may arise from the substantive interests and desires of a group, they must lose this self-interested character before acquiring the demeanour of a serious political proposal. The rules or amendments proposed have to be general and non-instrumental in nature, imposing no desired substantive purposes on the associates. Politics, to use his famous phrase, is a 'boundless and bottomless sea' with no ultimate end or final destination, whose purpose is to keep the ship afloat rather than steer it towards an imagined utopia (*RP* 60). Politics is characterized by deliberation and argument, the purpose of which is to persuade others, especially those who have authority to make and alter law, of their merits. This is not to say that much else beside its ideal character as politics may grace itself with the title, and substantive ends may be proposed as a result of considering the desirability of the conditions of civil association. Such considerations extrinsic to political activity should not, however, be confused with it.

## Conclusion

We have seen that Oakeshott, rather unusually in modern political philosophy, formulated a non-consequentialist theory of the ideal character of civil association and the rule of law. The conclusions he reached were as a result of careful deliberations arising from a sceptical manner of thinking associated with his own brand of philosophical idealism. Philosophically he was determined to uncover and question the postulates of all activities and forms of relationship in order to exhibit their idea character. Because he contended that there is a logical distinction between theory and practice, he claimed to be not recommending political precepts, but merely attempting to offer less confused understandings of them. In examining rationalism in politics, for example, he explored the rationalist's self-understanding of his own activity, and exposed it as self-deception. Technical knowledge could not be separated from practical knowledge; the two together were present in every manner of activity. Thus, for instance, the French Bill of Rights was not the result of independent premeditation, but merely the abridgement of the traditional rights of Englishmen. Similarly, he was not recommending that we become conservative; he was arguing that by disposition we are all inclined to be conservative. Principally, his characterization of the modern European state as an amalgam of enterprise and civil association, and of the rule of law being intrinsic to the latter, enabled him to maintain that acknowledging the authority of law is categorially different from questioning its desirability, and that therefore ruling is an activity quite distinct from politics.

### FURTHER READING

Greenleaf, W. H., *Oakeshott's Philosophical Politics* (London: Longmans, 1966).

Franco, Paul, *The Philosophy of Michael Oakeshott* (New Haven: Yale University Press, 1990).

Gerencser, S. A., *The Skeptic's Oakeshott* (London: Macmillan, 2000).

Grant, Robert, *Oakeshott* (London: Claridge, 1990).

Nardin, Terry, *The Philosophy of Oakeshott* (University Park: Penn State University Press, 2001).

### NOTES

1. F. H. Bradley, *Appearance and Reality* (Oxford: Oxford University Press, 1930), p. viii.
2. Bernard Bosanquet, *The Philosophical Theory of the State* (London: Macmillan, 1899), 2.
3. Ibid. and Oakeshott, *Experience and its Modes* (Cambridge: Cambridge University Press, 1933), 2 (hereafter *EM*).
4. H. H. Joachim, *The Nature of Truth* (Oxford: Oxford University Press, 1906), 176.

5. Bernard Crick, *In Defence of Politics*, 4th edn. (London: Penguin, 1993), 117.
6. Gertrude Himmelfarb, 'The Conservative Imagination', *American Scholar*, 44 (1975), 405.
7. W. H. Greenleaf, *Oakeshott's Philosophical Politics* (London: Longmans, 1966), 82.
8. Anthony Quinton, *The Politics of Imperfection* (London: Faber & Faber, 1978), 96.
9. Himmelfarb, 'The Conservative Imagination', 410.
10. Michael Oakeshott (ed.), *The Social and Political Doctrines of Contemporary Europe*, American edn., 6th printing (New York: Macmillan, 1948), p. xii.
11. Ibid. 231.
12. Paul Franco, 'Michael Oakeshott as Liberal Theorist', *Political Theory*, 18 (1990), 411.
13. Maurizio Viroli, *Republicanism* (New York: Hill & Wang, 2002), 67.
14. Michael Oakeshott, 'The Claims of Politics', *Scrutiny*, 8 (1939–40), 146.
15. Ibid. 147.
16. Henry Jones, *Idealism as a Practical Creed* (Glasgow: Maclehose, 1909).
17. J. McTaggart Ellis McTaggart, 'Dare to be Wise', in his *Philosophical Studies*, ed. S. V. Keeling (London: Arnold, 1934), 38.
18. F. H. Bradley, *Ethical Studies* (1872), 2nd edn. (Oxford: Clarendon Press, 1927), 193.
19. Michael Oakeshott, *Rationalism in Politics and Other Essays* (London: Methuen, 1963); new expanded edn. ed. Tim Fuller (Indianapolis: Liberty, 1991) (hereafter *RP*); page numbers refer to the 1991 edn.
20. D. D. Raphael, 'Professor Oakeshott's *Rationalism in Politics*', *Political Studies*, 12 (1964), 208–9.
21. Michael Oakeshott, '*Rationalism in Politics*: A Reply to Raphael', *Political Studies*, 13 (1965), 89.
22. Michael Oakeshott, 'Learning and Teaching', in R. S. Peters (ed.), *The Concept of Education* (London: Routledge & Kegan Paul, 1970), 166–7.
23. Raphael, 'Professor Oakeshott's *Rationalism in Politics*', 213.
24. Ibid. 215.
25 Oakeshott, '*Rationalism in Politics*: A Reply to Raphael', 92.
26. Michael Oakeshott, *On History and Other Essays* (Oxford: Basil Blackwell, 1983) (hereafter *OH*).
27. Michael Oakeshott, *On Human Conduct* (Oxford: Clarendon Press, 1975) (hereafter *OHC*).
28. Cf. David Boucher, 'Oakeshott and the Non-Economic Character of Civil Association', in David Boucher and Andrew Vincent, *British Idealism and Political Theory* (Edinburgh: Edinburgh University Press, 2000). Also see Terry Nardin, *The Philosophy of Oakeshott* (University Park: Penn State University Press, 2001), 194–5.
29. I owe this qualification to Paul Kelly.
30. I am grateful to Paul Kelly for alerting me to this similarity.
31. Lon Fuller, *The Morality of Law*, rev. edn. (New Haven: Yale University Press, 1972), 176.

# 27 Habermas

Kenneth Baynes

## Contents



## Chapter guide

The German philosopher, sociologist, and social theorist Jürgen Habermas is one of the most influential figures in contemporary political theory. His influence spans the normally closed worlds of European social theory and Anglophone political theory. In his later work he has begun to expand the normative political implications of his work in social theory and philosophy culminating in his influential *Between Facts and Norms*. That said, his published output is daunting. Consequently this chapter sets out to provide an overview of Jürgen Habermas's major contributions to social and political thought. After a brief sketch of his earlier work, especially his influential study on the transformation of the liberal or bourgeois public sphere, more attention is devoted to his theory of communicative action (or action based on mutually supposed validity claims) and his subsequent attempt, in *Between Facts and Norms*, to develop an account of deliberative politics based on it. This is his major contribution to normative political theory. Central to this account is the idea that political legitimacy is ultimately based on a process of public reasoning focused on what individuals can reasonably be expected to share as free and equal citizens. The chapter concludes with a brief outline of cosmopolitanism. This forms the direction of the future development of his account of deliberative politics and has already had a considerable influence on contemporary political theory.

## Biography

Jürgen Habermas, a German philosopher and social theorist, was born in Düsseldorf in 1929. He studied in Göttingen, Zurich, and Bonn, completing a dissertation on Schelling's philosophy of nature in 1954. He served for a short while as Theodor Adorno's research assistant at the Institute for Social Research in Frankfurt, and in 1961 he completed his habilitation entitled 'The Structural Transformation of the Public Sphere'. He held professorships in Heidelberg and Frankfurt and, from 1971 to 1981, he was co-director of the Max Planck Institute in Starnberg. In 1981 he returned to Frankfurt, where he remained as Professor of Philosophy and Sociology until his retirement in 1994. His two-volume *The Theory of Communicative Action* (1981) is a major contribution to social theory, in which he locates the origins of the various political, economic, and cultural crises confronting modern society in a one-sided process of rationalization steered more by the media of money and administrative poser than by forms of collective decision-making based on consensually grounded norms and values. He is the author of more than thirty volumes, including *Knowledge and Human Interests*, *The Theory of Communicative Action*, *The Philosophical Discourse of Modernity*, and *Between Facts and Norms: A Discourse Theory of Law and Democracy*.

## Key texts

*Knowledge and Human Interests* (1968), trans. Jeremy Shapiro (Boston: Beacon Press, 1971) (*KHI*).

*Theory and Practice* (1963), trans. John Viertel (Boston: Beacon Press, 1973).

*Legitimation Crisis*, trans. Thomas McCarthy (Boston: Beacon Press, 1975).

*The Theory of Communicative Action* (1981), trans. Thomas McCarthy, 2 vols. (Boston: Beacon Press, 1984–7).

*The Philosophical Discourse of Modernity*, trans. Frederick Lawrence (Cambridge, Mass.: MIT Press, 1987).

*The Structural Transformation of the Public Sphere* (1962), trans. Thomas Burger (Cambridge, Mass.: MIT Press, 1989).

*Moral Consciousness and Communicative Action*, trans. Christian Lenhardt and Shierry Weber Nicholsen (Cambridge, Mass.: MIT Press, 1990).

*Between Facts and Norms* (1992), trans. William Rehg (Cambridge, Mass.: MIT Press, 1996).

*The Inclusion of the Other*, trans. Ciarin Cronin and Pablo de Grieff (Cambridge, Mass.: MIT Press, 1998).

*The Postnational Constellation*, trans. Max Pensky (Cambridge, Mass.: MIT Press, 2001).

## Key ideas

**Autonomy**: the capacity for freedom or self-governance; Habermas distinguishes further between 'private autonomy' (roughly, the set of private liberties or 'liberty of the moderns') and 'public autonomy' (roughly, the idea of self-governance as found in the 'liberty of the ancients'). **Civil society** (*bürgerliche Gesellschaft*): the broad domain of private associations distinguished from both the political state and the market economy, in which citizens form various 'public opinions' about their common interests. **Communicative action**: social action that is both based on and oriented to mutually supposed validity claims about shared interpretations of the world; Habermas contrasts this basic type of action with 'strategic action' or action that is primarily aimed at influencing others. **Deliberative politics**: in contrast to an 'aggregative' model, a view of the political process that promotes the search for reasoned agreement about the citizen's common good. **Mutual understanding** (*Verständigung*): the agreement on world-interpretations and their underlying validity claims that actors share and/or attempt to establish in the process of 'communicative action'. **Public reason**: the collective reasoning of citizens that strives to base itself on what citizens can reasonably be expected to share (such as a view of themselves as free and equal) rather than on private (sectarian) views, about which they will differ. **Public sphere**: like the closely related idea of civil society, the broad domain of 'private' (non-governmental) associations in which citizens form, debate, and revise variously shared interpretations of the world and its 'meaning'; some of these interpretations will be shared among all citizens, but many others will be more sectarian in character.

## Early writings (prior to *The Theory of Communicative Action*)

In his first book, *The Structural Transformation of the Public Sphere* (1962), Habermas traces the emergence of a bourgeois public sphere which, at least for a time, offered the prospect of a domain that would mediate between state and society. Rooted in the social and economic conditions of liberal capitalism, the 'bourgeois public sphere' refers to those sociocultural institutions that arose in the eighteenth century in opposition to the absolutist powers of the state—private clubs and coffee-houses, learned societies and literary associations, publishing houses, journals, and newspapers. Taken as a whole these institutions constituted a 'public realm of reasoning private persons' that was secured in part through the enactment of various constitutional rights and liberties. In theory and (to a more limited extent) in practice, this public sphere was distinct both from the private sphere of the market and the family and from the political authority of the state. It designated a sphere that comes about whenever private persons reason collectively about their common interests, and its function was both to restrain and legitimize the political power exercised by the administrative state.

Habermas's thesis, however, is that this idea of the public sphere had a very limited lifespan. At the level of theory, the idea of a 'reasoning public' was treated with suspicion by conservatives and progressives alike and, in liberal theory, the defence of a public sphere was often limited to the formal guarantee of a narrow set of so-called 'natural' civil and political rights. As a historical phenomenon, the bourgeois public sphere suffered an equally unfortunate fate. In connection with what he refers to as the 'refeudalization' of civil society during the latter part of the nineteenth century, Habermas traces the commercialization of civil society, the bureaucratization of political and non-political authority, and the growth of a manipulative or propagandistic mass media. A 'repoliticized social sphere' erodes the real distinction between state and society that is a necessary social condition for the bourgeois public sphere, and a society oriented to consumption and a politics based on the competition and bargaining between interest groups emerges in the place of a public sphere formed by an enlightened citizenry. Although Habermas never abandons the normative claims expressed in the bourgeois ideal, the conclusion of *The Structural Transformation of the Public Sphere* is extremely cautious about the possibility for a renewed public sphere under the altered conditions of late capitalist society. Only thirty years later in *Between Facts and Norms* (1992) does Habermas return, on a more optimistic note, to the prospects for democracy in complex, pluralist societies.

In the 1960s and 1970s Habermas pursued a number of related issues. He sharply criticized the 'scientization of politics' and increase in 'technocratic consciousness' he discerned in contemporary societies. For Habermas the growth of technocracy was not inevitable but the result of a failure to preserve (albeit by other means) the classical distinction between theory and practice, and between practical wisdom (*phronesis*) and technical skill (*techne*). In a series of influential essays, many of which are collected in *Theory and Practice* (1963), he traced the loss of these distinctions in modern political theory (from Hobbes to Hegel) as well as in Marx, whose own concept of *praxis* blurred a related and equally important distinction between labour (*Arbeit*) and modes of social interaction based on shared interpretations of the world. Thus, contra Marx, Habermas argues that the end of alienated labour does not alone ensure social emancipation.

During this same period Habermas also pursued a more systematic critique of positivism, found in his contributions to the so-called 'positivist dispute' in German sociology and in his popular study *Knowledge and Human Interests* (1968). The latter work traces the 'dissolution of epistemology' from its origin as a critical enterprise with Kant to its status as a relatively uncritical 'theory of science' in the first half of this century. Positivism (or scientism), for Habermas, is the insistence that only the sciences constitute genuine knowledge together with the belief that science does not need any further critical analysis or justification. It refers less to the practice of the sciences than to their 'scientistic self-misunderstanding'. Habermas challenges this view (which was still popular at the time) and attempts to secure an independent basis for critique by arguing that all forms of knowledge are rooted in fundamental human interests. He identifies three 'quasi-transcendental' or 'anthropologically deep-seated' cognitive interests with reference to which distinct forms of knowledge can be delineated: The natural sciences correspond to a technical interest; the historical–hermeneutic sciences, to a practical interest; and the critical sciences (e.g. Marxism and psychoanalysis when each is freed from its own 'scientistic self-misunderstanding'), to an emancipatory interest. Thus, through a kind of continuation of epistemology by social theory, Habermas sought to complete a critique of positivism and provide a 'prolegomena' for a critical social theory. Though he quickly became dissatisfied with the anthropological underpinnings of this initial attempt, there are already hints of the 'linguistic turn' in his later theory, evident, for example, in his remark that 'the human interest in autonomy and responsibility is not mere fancy, for it can be apprehended a priori. What raises us out of nature is the only thing whose nature we can know: *language*' (*KHI* 314[1]).

## The Theory of Communicative Action

*The Theory of Communicative Action* (1981), Habermas's *magnum opus*, is a major contribution to social theory which in its aim and structure resembles Max Weber's *Economy and Society* and Talcott Parsons's *The Structure of Social Action*. Like those works, it presents both metatheoretical reflections on the basic concepts of social theory along with observations on the methodology of the social sciences and quasi-empirical hypotheses about modernization as a process of societal rationalization. However, in contrast particularly to Weber, Habermas regards rationalization not as a process that inevitably culminates in the loss of meaning and freedom in the world, but as an ambivalent process that also opens up a potential for societal learning and new levels of human emancipation.

Like Weber and Parsons, Habermas begins with a set of metatheoretical reflections that yields a typology of action. His basic distinction is between 'consent-oriented' (or communicative) and 'success-oriented' (or purposive–rational) actions; within the latter class he distinguishes further between strategic and instrumental action. Instrumental actions are goal-oriented interventions in the physical world. They can be appraised from the standpoint of efficiency and described as the following of technical rules. Strategic action, by contrast, is action which aims at influencing others for the purpose of achieving some end. It too can be appraised in terms of its efficiency and analysed with the tools of game theory and theories of rational choice. Many instrumental actions can also be strategic, and some forms of strategic action may be instrumental. Communicative action, however, constitutes an independent and distinct type of social action. The goal, or *telos*, of communicative action is expressed or realized not in an attempt to influence others, but in the attempt to reach an agreement or mutual understanding (*Verständigung*) with one or more actors about something in the world. Thus, while all action is teleological or goal-oriented in a broad sense, in the case of communicative action any further ends the agent may have are subordinated to the goal of achieving a mutually shared definition of the agent's lifeworldly situation through a cooperative process of interpretation. In acting communicatively, individuals more or less naively accept as valid the various claims raised with their utterance or action and mutually suppose that each is prepared to provide reasons for them should the validity of those claims be questioned. In a slightly more technical (and controversial) sense, and one tied more specifically to modern structures of rationality, Habermas also holds that individuals who act communicatively and self-reflectively aim at reaching understanding about something in the world by relating their interpretations to three general types of validity claims that are constitutive for three basic types of speech-acts: a claim to truth raised in constative speech-acts, a claim to normative rightness raised in regulative speech-acts, and a claim to truthfulness raised in expressive speech-acts (*TCA* i. 319–20[2]).

At a methodological level this analysis of social action underscores the need for an interpretive, or *Verstehende*, approach in the social sciences. The requirement of *Verstehen* arises because the objects that the social sciences study—actions and their products—are embedded in 'complexes of meaning' (*Sinnzusammenhänge*) that can be understood by the social inquirer only as he or she relates them to his or her own pre-theoretical knowledge as a member of the lifeworld. This, in turn, gives rise to the 'disquieting thesis' that the interpretation of action cannot be separated from the interpreter's taking a position on the validity of the claims explicitly or implicitly connected with the action. The process of identifying the reasons for an action unavoidably draws one into the process of assessment in which the inquirer must adopt the perspective of an (at least virtual) participant. Understanding the reasons for action requires taking a position on the validity of those reasons according to our own lights, and that means (at least initially) setting aside an external or 'third-person' perspective in favour or an internal or 'first-person' perspective in which both actor and interpreter belong to the same 'universe of discourse'. It is in this way that Habermas is able to connect the notion of rationality generally with his more specific claim that reason is a capacity to test validity claims.

However, despite his emphasis on social (or communicative) rationality with its ties to criticizable validity claims, Habermas does not think that society can be viewed as a sort of large-scale debating club. On the one hand, actors' interpretations are generally taken for granted and form part of an implicit background of knowledge and practices that constitute what he calls (following Edmund Husserl and Alfred Schutz) the 'lifeworld'. On the other hand, social integration can also be achieved in large measure by relegating tasks of action coordination to social institutions that operate, so to speak, 'behind the backs' of social actors. In fact, Habermas's distinction between society as lifeworld and society as system reflects a trend towards differentiation that is yet another feature of modern societies.

Beyond these metatheoretical and methodological concerns, *The Theory of Communicative Action* presents an interpretation of modern society as the outcome of a process of rationalization and societal differentiation. Rationalization, like Weber, refers most generally to the extension of calculation, methodical treatment, and systematic ordering to ever more aspects of social life (e.g. science, law, business, and even religion and the arts). Differentiation in modern societies is reflected, first, in a (functional) separation of the economic and political subsystems from society as a whole and, secondly, within the lifeworld, in the division among institutional complexes devoted, respectively, to the tasks of the transmission of knowledge and interpretative patterns (culture), social integration ('society' in the narrower sense of normative orders), and socialization (personality). Finally, within culture one can also trace a differentiation among the three values spheres of science and technology, law and morality, and art and aesthetic criticism as each becomes independent of the other and develops its own internal standards of critique and evaluation. This interpretation of modern society as a process of rationalization is, of course, not new. However, in contrast to the classical theorists who generally viewed it as a threat to social life—Weber's 'iron cage', Marx's thesis of reification, Durkheim's analysis of anomie—Habermas emphasizes the potential for emancipation also made available. Thus, social pathologies are not an inevitable consequence of rationalization per se but result rather from a one-sided process in which the market and administrative state invade the lifeworld, displacing modes of integration based on communicative reason with their own form of functional rationality. Habermas dramatically describes this as the 'colonization of the lifeworld'. The primary task of a critical theory is to draw attention to this process of colonization and indicate the ways in which various social movements are a response to it.

## *Between Facts and Norms* and later political essays

In *Between Facts and Norms: Contributions to a Discourse Theory of Law and Democracy* (1992) Habermas returns again to his earlier interests in political theory and, in particular, to the question of the democratic possibilities of late capitalist society. However, he does this not only with thirty years of hindsight (including the 1989 'revolutions' in the countries of eastern Europe and Russia), but also with the normative framework developed in *The Theory of Communicative Action* and his writings on discourse ethics. *Between Facts and Norms* thus presents his most sustained and developed reflections on these questions. One overarching question guides his inquiry: has the ancient (and still radical) idea of democracy—the idea of a self-governing society of free and equal citizens—been rendered obsolete by the complexity of modern societies, so that the best we may hope for is a highly restricted version of that ideal (as suggested, for example, by the 'elite' theorists of democracy such as Joseph Schumpeter) or is at least the normative core of this ancient ideal still relevant today? Habermas predictably—though not without some shift from his earlier diagnosis in *The Structural Transformation of the Public Sphere*—answers this question affirmatively, and *Between Facts and Norms* is his attempt to indicate how this is so.

## Discourse theory, the principle of democracy, and the system of rights

Habermas first takes up the centrally important question of the legitimacy of law: what makes legal authority legitimate? In effect, Habermas advocates a sophisticated version of consent theory (one that depends strictly, however, on neither actual nor hypothetical consent, but one in which the legal–political order retains roots in processes of communicative association in principle open to all). He rejects the legal positivist position, advocated as well by Luhmann, that law is legitimate if it has been enacted in accordance with established legal procedures. At the same time, however, appeal to natural law theory is precluded on the basis of his own commitment to radical democracy. As Habermas puts it, 'Nothing is given prior to the citizen's practice of self-determination other than the discourse principle, which is built in the conditions of communicative association in general, and the legal medium as such' (pp. 127–8[3]). His strategy, in brief, is to show that legitimacy of law is based on a rationality immanent to law, even though that rationality draws upon dimensions of (communicative) reason that reach beyond the legal medium. 'In modern societies, too, the law can fulfill the function of stabilizing expectations only if it preserves an internal connection with the socially integrative force of communicative action' (p. 84).

Habermas approaches the question of the legitimacy of legality through a central difficulty in Kant's political thought frequently discussed in the secondary literature. The difficulty is reflected in the question whether Kant is best understood as a natural rights theorist or a social contract theorist. In a provocative and original reading Habermas suggests that the tension between these two interpretations arises from an ambiguity in Kant's concept of autonomy or self-rule. As Kant took over this notion from Rousseau, it suggests the idea of both individual *and* collective self-legislation: 'a person is subject to no laws other than those that he (either alone or at least jointly with others) gives to himself'.[4] For Kant, the concept of individual autonomy is almost synonymous with morality, while the notion of collective self-determination is identified with the idea of the social contract. However, in so far as Kant's argument for the establishment of civil society (or the state) relies solely on the universal principle of right, which guarantees equal subjective liberty for all, the notion of collective self-determination is subordinated to a moral principle (or natural right). As Habermas argues, this sets off an internal dialectic in the tradition of legal dogmatics between legal positivism (objective law as the command of the sovereign) and natural law (which stresses subjective liberties) in which the notion of collective self-determination is gradually effaced. However, so doing fails to account for the legitimacy of law for it ultimately removes law from the process of democratic lawmaking and/or deprives the right to subjective liberty of any relation to a conception of public autonomy (p. 88). It fails, in other words, to reconcile the public and private autonomy of citizens in a manner that could in turn secure the legitimacy of legality.

Of course, Habermas is not interested in Kant's system of rights only for historical reasons. He uses the problematic in Kant to clarify the basic structure of his own discourse theory and to respond to some earlier criticisms of it. He now insists, for instance, on a sharper delineation between the principle of discourse—'Only those action norms are valid to which all those possibly affected could agree as participants in rational discourses' (p. 108)—and its specification as a rule of *moral* argumentation, that is, as a principle of universalizability (or Principle U).[5] The principle of discourse is now conceived as a more general principle that applies to all action norms prior to any distinction between moral and legal norms. Principle U is then introduced *simultaneously* with the principle of democracy—roughly equivalent to Kant's idea of the social contract—that specifies a general procedure for legitimate lawmaking. The principle of democracy states: 'Only those juridical statutes may claim legitimacy that can meet with the assent of all citizens in a discursive law-making process that in turn has been legally constituted' (p. 110). Though distinct, the two principles are not hierarchically ordered as in Kant; rather, they are complementary and, in important ways, the principle of democracy (as a principle of legitimation for positive law) supplements various 'deficits' that necessarily accompany a post-conventional rational morality (e.g. cognitive indeterminacy and/or motivational weakness) (see pp. 112–13).

Even more important than this complementary relation between the basic moral principle and a principle for legitimate lawmaking is Habermas's parallel claim that the principle of democracy is not subordinate to a system of rights. On the contrary, Habermas claims that they are 'equiprimordial' or 'co-original' (*gleichursprünglich*; p. 122) and 'reciprocally explain each other' (p. 94). The system of rights is the 'reverse side' (p. 94) of the principle of democracy, and 'the principle of democracy can only appear as the heart of a system of rights' (p. 122). These remarks indicate Habermas's commitment to a reconciliation of democracy with other political values, especially a system of basic rights and liberties. His basic strategy is to recall attention to 'the intersubjective sense' of legally granted subjective liberties (p. 88). Echoing Hegel as well as Kant, he emphasizes the fact that rights are not primarily things individuals possess but relations that have their basis in a form of mutual recognition—however circumscribed and artificial.

> *At a conceptual level*, rights do not immediately refer to atomistic and estranged individuals who are possessively set against one another. On the contrary, as elements of the legal order they presuppose collaboration among subjects who recognize one another, in their reciprocally related rights and duties, as free and equal consociates under law. This mutual recognition is constitutive for a legal order from which actionable rights are derived. In this sense 'subjective' rights emerge equiprimordially with 'objective' law, to use the terminology of German jurisprudence. (pp. 88–9)

Basic rights do not exist in a determinate form in a pre-political state of nature. They are something individuals mutually confer on one another in so far as they undertake to regulate their common life via positive law and thus to regard one another as free and equal consociates under law.

More specifically, Habermas's claim is that the system of rights (together with the principle of democracy) can be developed from the 'interpenetration' (*Verschränkung*) of the discourse principle and the legal form (p. 121). As I understand it, this 'derivation'—Habermas speaks of a 'logical genesis' (*logische Genese*)—of a system of rights occurs in two stages. First, the notion of law cannot be limited to the semantic features of general and abstract norms. Rather, bourgeois formal law has always been identified with the guarantee of an equal right to subjective liberty. This is reflected in Kant's universal principle of right (*Recht*) as well as Rawls's first principle, both of which call for the greatest amount of liberty compatible with a like liberty for all. For Habermas this link between positive law and individual liberty means that, in so far as individuals undertake to regulate their common life through the legal form—something for which he argues in modern societies there is no practicable alternative—they must do so in a way that grants to each member an equal right to liberty.

However—and this is the second step—although the legal form is conceptually linked to the idea of subjective rights, it alone cannot ground any specific right (p. 128). A system of rights can be developed only if and when the legal form is made use of by the political sovereign in an exercise of the citizens' public autonomy. This public autonomy in the last analysis refers back to the discourse principle which implies the 'right' to submit only to those norms one could agree to in a discourse. Of course, in connection with the principle of discourse this 'right' has only the 'quasi-transcendental' status of a communicative act and does not carry with it any coercive authorization. It can acquire a coercive authorization only when, as the principle of democracy, it is realized in the legal medium together with a system of rights.

> The principle of discourse can assume through the medium of law the shape of a principle of democracy only insofar as the discourse principle and the legal medium interpenetrate and *develop* into a system of rights that brings private and public autonomy into a relation of mutual presupposition. Conversely, every exercise of political autonomy signifies both an interpretation and specific elaboration of these fundamentally 'unsaturated' rights by a historical law-giver. (p. 128)

Habermas hopes in this way to have reconciled democracy and individual rights in a manner that does not subordinate either one to the other. 'The system of rights can be reduced neither to a moral reading of human rights [as in Kant and the tradition of natural rights] nor to an ethical reading of popular sovereignty [as in Rousseau and some communitarians] because the private autonomy of citizens must neither be set above nor made subordinate to their political autonomy' (p. 104). Rather, the co-originality or 'equiprimordiality' of the system of rights and the principle of democracy, which also reflects the mutual presupposition of citizens' public and private autonomy, is derived from this 'interpenetration' of the legal form and the 'quasi-transcendental' discourse principle that 'must' occur if citizens are to regulate their living together by means of positive law. According to Habermas, this strategy yields not a determinate set of basic rights but rather a kind of formal scaffolding or categorical frame that must be 'filled in' by the legislative. Nonetheless, this scaffolding does present something close to the basic rights and liberties found, for example, in Rawls's principle of equal liberty or in the first amendments to the US Constitution, together with a guarantee of welfare and other social conditions necessary for their effective exercise.

Two final observations on this system of rights are worth noting. First, Habermas claims that the system of rights is universal not in the sense that it specifies a pre-given set of natural rights, but in the sense that it presents a general schema or 'unsaturated placeholder' (p. 126) that legal subjects must presuppose if they want to regulate their living together by positive law. It is thus constitutive of the legal medium, yet at the same time it is not fixed or determinate. The system of rights must be 'developed in a politically autonomous manner' by citizens in the context of their own particular traditions and history (see pp. 128–9).

Secondly, Habermas acknowledges that there is a paradox involved in the 'juridification' of communicative liberty (p. 120). The rights guaranteeing public autonomy, like those guaranteeing private autonomy, must assume the form of subjective liberties. This means that it is up to citizens themselves to exercise their communicative liberty. 'Legally granted liberties entitle one to *drop out of* communicative action, to refuse illocutionary obligations; they ground a privacy freed from the burden of a reciprocally acknowledged and expected communicative freedoms' (p. 120). At the same time, however, this juridification of communicative liberty also reveals the fact that the legitimacy of legality is not guaranteed by the legal form alone but depends on sources beyond its control, namely the realization of a rational public opinion and will-formation in an autonomous public sphere.

With his derivation of the system of rights that secures the private and public autonomy of citizens, Habermas claims to have accounted for the legitimacy of legality. It is based neither on the legal form alone (as maintained by positivists) nor on its conformity to an extra-legal set of natural rights or natural law. Rather, the legitimacy of law derives from the fact that it has a rationality of its own, secured in the mutual guarantee of the private and public autonomy of citizens, that ultimately refers back to the bonding–binding illocutionary force inherent in communicative reason and action.

## Procedural democracy, and 'weak' and 'strong' publics

If the legitimacy of law depends on the fact that it preserves 'an internal connection with the socially integrative force of communicative action' (p. 84), then the system of rights (including the rights of public autonomy) must be institutionalized, and the communicative power that comes about whenever, in Hannah Arendt's phrase, people act in concert must be mobilized and effectively secured within the legal medium itself. This requirement reveals still another aspect of the internal tension between facticity and validity: to become socially effective law requires a centralized political power with the capacity to enforce collectively binding decisions; at the same time, however, law is the sole medium through which the communicative power of citizens can be transformed into administrative power.

Habermas first introduces a set of 'principles of the constitutional state' (*Rechtsstaat*) that specify general institutional guidelines for both the *generation* of communicative power (through the institutionalization of the system of rights) and the *exercise* of power (by ensuring a connection between communicative power and administrative power). These include the principle of popular sovereignty, the guarantee of legal protection, the legality of administration, and the separation of state and society (pp. 168 ff.). Habermas's discussion attempts to locate these classical doctrines within the framework of his own discourse theory. Taken together, the principles should explain the idea of the constitutional state by showing how 'legitimate law is generated from communicative power and the latter in turn is converted into administrative power via legitimately enacted law' (p. 169).

Although his discussion cannot be adequately summarized here, it is clear that Habermas wishes to establish two general points. First, in contrast to Arendt, the notion of communicative power should not be understood too substantively as the (more or less spontaneous) expression of a common will but rather should be understood as the product of an overlapping and intermeshing of a variety of (more and less institutionalized) pragmatic, ethical–political, and moral discourses (p. 168). Communicative power neither presupposes a shared ethical–political self-understanding nor orients itself to the ideal of a rational consensus in the manner constitutive (for Habermas) of moral argumentation. Rather, it is identified with the realization of a rational public opinion and will-formation in a process of lawmaking that comprises a complex network of processes of reaching understanding *and* bargaining (p. 180). This interpretation of communicative power should also warn against an overly hasty and too direct identification of moral argumentation (which aim at a consensus) with political discourse.

Secondly, the legitimate *exercise* of power can only occur through the medium of law but in a way that nonetheless remains tied to communicative modes of association: rule by the people must be a rule of law, but the rule of law must be joined to rule by the people, or, as Frank Michelman has expressed it, rooted in a 'jurisgenerative politics'.[6] A discourse-theoretical approach offers a way of understanding this connection between the rule of law and popular sovereignty without appealing to a 'transcendent' notion of reason or over-burdening citizens' capacities for public virtue. It also provides for a less concrete interpretation of the classical principle of the separation of powers in that the functions of the legislature, judiciary, and administration can now be differentiated according to various forms of communication and a corresponding potential for reasons:

> Laws can regulate the transformation of communicative power into administrative inasmuch as they come about according to a democratic procedure, ground a legal protection guaranteed by impartial courts, and shield from the implementing administration the sorts of reasons that support legislative and judicial decisionmaking. These normative reasons belong to a universe within which legislature and judiciary share the work of justifying and applying norms. An administration limited to pragmatic discourses must not disturb anything *in this* universe by its contributions; at the same time, it draws therefrom the normative premises that have to underlie its own empirically informed, purposive-rational decision-making. (p. 192)

This analysis of the principles of the constitutional state and their justification—which I have only been able roughly to indicate—is nevertheless one-sided unless it is accompanied by an account of the *process* by which citizens are to govern themselves or engage in a 'jurisgenerative politics'. It is at this point that the model of a 'procedural democracy' is introduced. Within the context of Anglo-American discussions, however, this label could be misleading since the term 'procedure' is not used in contrast to a 'substantive' conception of democracy (as it is, for example, in Ely's influential account).[7] Rather, as Habermas uses the term, it designates the attempt to realize the rights of public and private autonomy through an institutional design that incorporates various practical discourses. Procedural democracy is thus closer to what has recently been called a 'public reasons' approach.[8]

Habermas introduces his model of procedural democracy by way of a contrast between two highly stylized alternatives: liberal and republican (or communitarian). These have become familiar reference points in recent discussions. Cass Sunstein, for example, has summarized the liberal model well: 'Self-interest, not virtue, is understood to be the usual motivating force of political behavior. Politics is typically, if not always, an effort to aggregate private interests. It is surrounded by checks, in the form of rights, protecting private liberty and private property from public intrusion.'[9] By contrast, republicanism characteristically places more emphasis on the value of citizens' public virtues and active political participation. Politics is regarded more as a deliberative process in which citizens seek to reach agreement about the common good, and law is not seen as a means for protecting individual rights but as the expression of the common praxis of the political community.

Habermas's procedural democracy attempts to incorporate the best features of both models while avoiding the shortcomings of each. In particular, with the republican model, it rejects the vision of the political process as primarily a process of competition and aggregation of private preferences. However, more in keeping with the liberal model, it regards the republican vision of a citizenry united and actively motivated by a shared conception of the good life as unrealistic in modern, pluralist societies.[10] Since, as we have seen, political discourses involve bargaining and negotiation as well as moral argumentation, the republican or communitarian notion of a shared ethical–political dialogue also seems too limited (p. 285). 'According to discourse theory, the success of deliberative politics depends not on a collectively acting citizenry but on the institutionalization of the corresponding procedures and conditions of communication, as well as on the interplay of institutionalized deliberative processes with informally constituted public opinions' (p. 298). What is central is not a shared ethos, but institutionalized discourses designed for the formation of rational political opinion.

The idea of a suitably interpreted 'deliberative politics' thus lies at the centre of Habermas's procedural democracy. In a deliberative politics, attention shifts away from the final act of voting and the problems of social choice that accompany it.[11] The model attempts to take seriously the fact that often enough preferences are not exogenous to the political system, but 'are instead adaptive to a wide range of factors—including the context in which the preference is expressed, the existing legal rules, past consumption choices, and culture in general'.[12] The aim of a deliberative politics is to provide context for a transformation of preferences in response to the considered views of others and the 'laundering,' or filtering, of irrational and/or morally repugnant preferences in ways that are not excessively paternalistic.[13] For example, by designing institutions of political will-formation so that they reflect the more complex preference structure of individuals rather than simply register the actual preferences individuals have at any given time, the conditions for a more rational politics (that is, a political process in which the outcomes are more informed, future-oriented, and other-regarding) can be improved. One could even speak of an extension of democracy to preferences themselves since the question is whether the reasons offered in support of them are ones that could meet the requirements of public justification. What is important for this notion of deliberation, however, is less that everyone participate—or even that voting be made public—than that there is a warranted presumption that public opinion be formed on the basis of adequate information and relevant reasons and that those whose interests are involved have an equal and effective opportunity to make their own interests (and the reasons for them) known.

Two further features serve to distinguish Habermas's model of procedural democracy and deliberative politics from other recent versions. First, this version of deliberative politics extends beyond the more formally organized political system to the vast and complex communication network that Habermas calls 'the public sphere'.

> [Deliberative politics] is bound to the demanding communicative presuppositions of political arenas that do not coincide with the institutionalized will-formation in parliamentary bodies but rather includes the political public sphere as well as its cultural context and social basis. A deliberative practice of self-determination can develop only in the interplay between, on the one hand, the parliamentary will-formation institutionalized in legal procedures and programmed to reach decisions and, on the other, political opinion-formation along informal channels of political communication. (pp. 274–5)

The model suggests a 'two-track' process in which there is a division of labour between 'weak publics'—the informally organized public sphere ranging from private associations to the mass media located in 'civil society'—and 'strong publics'—parliamentary bodies and other formally organized institutions of the political system. In this division of labour 'weak publics' assume a central responsibility for identifying, interpreting, and addressing social problems: 'For a good part of the normative expectations connected with deliberative politics now falls on the peripheral networks of opinion-formation. The expectations are directed at the capacity to perceive, interpret, and present society-wide problems in a way both attention-catching and innovative' (p. 358). However, decision-making responsibility, as well as the further 'filtering' of reasons via more formal parliamentary procedures, remain the task of a strong public (e.g. the formally organized political system).

Secondly, along with this division of labour between strong and weak publics and as a consequence of his increased acknowledgement of the 'decentred' character of modern societies, Habermas argues that radical-democratic practice must assume a 'self-limiting' form. Democratization is now focused not on society as a whole, but on the legal system broadly conceived (p. 305). In particular, he maintains, it must respect the boundaries of the political–administrative and economic subsystems that have become relatively freed from the integrative force of communicative action and are in this sense 'autonomous'. Failure to do so, he believes, at least partially explains the failure of state socialism.[14] The goal of radical democracy thus becomes not the democratic organization of these subsystems, but rather a type of indirect steering of them through the medium of law. In this connection, he also describes the task of an opinion-forming public sphere as that of laying siege to the formally organized political system by encircling it with reasons without, however, attempting to overthrow or replace it.

This raises a number of difficult questions about the scope and limits of democratization. Given the metaphorical form often adopted in his discussion, it is not obvious what specific institutional designs for mediating between weak and strong publics would follow from his model. Further, in view of his own description of 'weak publics' as 'wild', 'anarchic', and 'unrestricted' (p. 308), the suspicion can at least be raised whether discursive procedures will suffice to bring about a rational public opinion. To be sure, he states that a deliberative politics also requires a 'rationalized lifeworld' (including a 'liberal political culture') 'that meets it halfway' (pp. 302, 358). But without more attention to the particular 'liberal virtues' that make up that political culture and give rise to some notion of shared purposes, it is difficult to see how this version of a deliberative politics will respond to the challenges raised by the more recent 'politics of identity' and the apparent loss of any notion of the common good or shared political community in the modern liberal state. Habermas's notion of 'constitutional patriotism'—that is, a patriotism centred not on the idea of a people's cultural or ethnic identity but on the principles and rights embedded in its common history—offers an important first step, but more elaboration on this model of a 'solidarity among strangers' is required.

## Democracy beyond the nation-state

The variety of phenomena that, taken together, have recently been grouped under the heading 'globalization' raise important questions about the possibility of achieving democracy within the limited framework of the nation-state. The increased number and expanding influence of multinational corporations, growing international flow in labour and capital, expanding population migration, and large-scale ecological threats challenge in new ways the nation-state's claim to legitimacy, even on the domestic front. In short, can the nation-state, given its apparently diminished capacity to act, maintain its legitimacy in the face of growing demands of its citizenry? At the same time, the widening (if fragile) recognition of human rights, the more active role of the United Nations and other international organizations, and a developing global 'civil society' (including worldwide informational media) make it meaningful at least to ask whether a 'post-national constellation' is not emerging in which the locus of democratization is no longer centred exclusively on the territorial nation-state. In several important essays published since *Between Facts and Norms* Habermas has joined the growing conversation concerning the possibility—and shape—of a cosmopolitan democracy. Indeed, there is much in his 'two-track' model of democracy sketched above that suggests why this might be so. On the one hand, there is no inherent reason why his idea of a weak public sphere cannot be interpreted in the context of a 'global civil society' and, on the other, there are also some reasons for extending his discursive account of strong publics—the formal institutions of decision-making—in connection with the idea of a more multi-layered and dispersed conception of sovereignty and the related idea of 'subsidiarity'.[15] Similarly, his claim that there has been at most only a historical (not a necessary) convergence between the political *demos* (or state) and a relatively homogenous nation or people (*Volk*) also supports the claim that the former need not be limited to the traditional (territorial) idea of the nation-state. In this context Habermas has voiced support for strengthening the role of the United Nations and creating an international criminal court with a mandate to prevent at least gross violations of human rights. At the same time, however, he is more cautious than some advocates of cosmopolitan democracy about the likelihood of achieving on a global scale the kind of 'civic solidarity' (as a 'solidarity among strangers') that, as we saw, is for him a necessary condition for a robust deliberative politics. In this respect, he reflects a limited agreement with some of his more civic republican critics such as Charles Taylor or Benjamin Barber. His own constructive proposal (in addition to his support for a European constitution) is for the development of what he calls 'international negotiating systems' in which various players (including nation-states, international governmental institutions, and non-governmental organizations) would fulfil the role of 'strong public' while citizens motivated by a cosmopolitan consciousness and active in various ways in a cosmopolitan civil society would constitute a 'weak public'.[16] As with the two-track model described at the level of the nation-state above, the challenge again is for imaginative institutional design leading to a more responsive and accountable 'strong public' than is possible today at the level of the nation-state alone. However, the basic structure of this proposal for cosmopolitan democracy remains the same: a dynamic division of labour between a free-wheeling public sphere that functions as a kind of 'receptor' for identifying and thematizing social problems—and ensuring that they are placed on the political agenda—and the more formally organized (though multi-layered and dispersed) strong publics responsible for 'translating' publicly generated reasons into socially effective policies via accountable administrative bodies. This is certainly an extremely abstract model of democracy and many of its more specific institutional details are missing, but, contrary to some of his critics, Habermas's vision of a renewed public sphere is by no means simply an abdication either to the triumph of liberalism as traditionally conceived or to capitalism in its latest 'global' phase.

## FURTHER READING

Bernstein, Richard (ed.), *Habermas and Modernity* (Cambridge, Mass.: MIT Press, 1985).

Calhoun, Craig (ed.), *Habermas and the Public Sphere* (Cambridge, Mass.: MIT Press, 1992).

McCarthy, Thomas, *The Critical Theory of Jürgen Habermas* (Cambridge, Mass.: MIT Press, 1978).

Rosenfeld, Michel, and Arato, Andrew (eds.), *Habermas on Law and Democracy: Critical Exchanges* (Berkeley: University of California Press, 1998).

Von Schomberg, René, and Baynes, Kenneth (eds.), *Discourse and Democracy: Essays on Habermas's 'Between Facts and Norms'* (Albany: State University of New York Press, 2002).

## NOTES

1. Habermas, *Knowledge and Human Interests* (1968), trans. Jeremy Shapiro (Boston: Beacon Press, 1971) (hereafter *KHI*).
2. Habermas, *The Theory of Communicative Action* (1981), trans. Thomas McCarthy, 2 vols. (Boston: Beacon Press, 1984–7) (hereafter *TCA*).
3. Page numbers refer hereafter to Habermas, *Between Facts and Norms: Contributions to a Discourse Theory of Law and Democracy* (1992), trans. William Rehg (Cambridge, Mass.: MIT Press, 1996).
4. Kant, *Metaphysik der Sitten* (Hamburg: Meiner, 1966), 223.
5. For Habermas's earlier formulation of the relation between the discourse principle and the principle of universalizability, see 'Discourse Ethics', in his *Moral Consciousness and Communicative Action*, trans. Christian Lenhardt and Shierry Weber Nicolsen (Cambridge, Mass.: MIT Press, 1990), 65–6.
6. Frank Michelman, 'Law's Republic', *Yale Law Journal*, 97 (1988), 1502.
7. See John Ely, *Democracy and Distrust* (Cambridge, Mass.: Harvard University Press, 1980), and Brian Barry's procedural conception in 'Is Democracy Special?': 'I follow . . . those who insist that "democracy" is to be understood in procedural terms. That is to say, I reject the notion that one should build into "democracy" any constraints on the content of outcomes produced, such as substantive equality, respect for human rights, concern for the general welfare, personal liberty and the rule of law' (in P. Laslett (ed.), *Philosophy, Politics, and Society* (Oxford: Basil Blackwell, 1979), 155–6). Habermas's model is not procedural in this sense since it draws upon the notion of communicative liberty, articulated in the public and private autonomy of citizens, implicit in the notion of communicative reason.
8. For examples of this 'public reasons' approach, which is influenced by the work of Rawls and Scanlon, see esp. Joshua Cohen, 'Deliberation and Democratic Legitimacy', in Alan Hamlin and Philip Pettit (eds.), *The Good Polity* (Oxford: Basil Blackwell, 1989), and several essays by Samuel Freeman, especially 'Constitutional Democracy and the Legitimacy of Judicial Review', *Law and Philosophy*, 9 (1990–1), 327–70, and 'Original Meaning, Democratic Interpretation, and the Constitution', *Philosophy and Public Affairs*, 21 (1992), 3–42.
9. Cass Sunstein, 'Preferences and Politics', *Philosophy and Public Affairs*, 20 (1991), 4.
10. Habermas cites Frank Michelman's 'Law's Republic' as an example of this sort of republicanism; he might also have referred to some of the writings of Charles Taylor. Habermas's own position seems closest, however, to the 'Madisonian' republicanism of Cass Sunstein; see Sunstein, 'Beyond the Republican Revival', *Yale Law Journal*, 97 (1988), 1539–90.
11. See also B. Manin, 'On Legitimacy and Political Deliberation', *Political Theory*, 15 (1987), 338–68, and the interesting comparison offered by David Miller in 'Deliberative Democracy and Social Choice', *Political Studies*, special issue, 40 (1992), 54–67.
12. Sunstein, 'Preferences and Politics', 5; see also Jon Elster, *Sour Grapes* (New York: Cambridge University Press, 1983).
13. See Robert Goodin, 'Laundering Preferences', in Jon Elster (ed.), *Foundations of Rational Choice Theory* (New York: Cambridge University Press, 1985), 75–101.

14. See Habermas, 'What does Socialism Mean Today?', *New Left Review*, 183 (1990), 3–21.
15. See esp. David Held, Anthony McGrew, David Goldblatt, and Jonathan Perraton (eds.), *Global Transformations* (London: Polity Press, 1999), and Neil MacCormick, *Questioning Sovereignty* (Oxford: Clarendon Press, 1999).
16. Habermas, *The Postnational Constellation*, trans. Max Pensky (Cambridge, Mass.: MIT Press, 2001), 119.

# 28 Rawls

Rex Martin

## Contents



## Chapter guide

The chapter begins by placing John Rawls's thought in the context of the philosophy and politics of the twentieth century. Two themes are struck here: the need for a philosophical justification of political liberalism and Rawls's belief that utilitarianism (the reigning philosophy at the time) wasn't up to the job. Rawls identified two principles which are central to political liberalism—the principle of equal basic rights and liberties and a principle of economic justice, which stresses equality of opportunity, reciprocal benefit, and egalitarianism—and then provides the main arguments for these two principles. What's distinctive about these arguments is that Rawls represents them as taking place ultimately in an ideal arena for decision-making, which he calls the 'original position'. The features of the original position (in particular, the so-called veil of ignorance and the requirements of publicity and unanimity) taken together provide a setting for structuring the competition between principles (for example, the Rawlsian two principles versus various forms of utilitarianism) in a fair and objective way and then for determining a preference, if possible, for one of the candidate principles of justice over the others.

In time, Rawls came to have some dissatisfaction with this approach and he began to reconfigure his basic theory in new and interesting ways. He loosened things up in two distinct ways. First, he moved the focus away from his own two principles and towards a 'family' of liberal principles (which included his two principles as one possible option). And, secondly, he developed a background theory of justifying this family of principles that did not require people to come to any sort of unanimous foundational agreement. In short, people didn't have to hold one and the same basic moral theory or profess one and the same religion in order for the family of liberal principles to be conclusively justified;

rather, the issue of justification could be approached from a number of different angles, and this would work out all right, he argued, if a sufficient overlapping consensus developed over time. Rawls thought that this new theory solved the main problem he had seen in his own earlier theory of justice. It did so by taking account of the fact that in a free and open society there is very likely going to be an irreducible and continuing pluralism of ultimate moral and religious beliefs. Rawls then takes this new theory (which he calls political liberalism) and tries to outline a constructive place for it in the international order that emerged after the Second World War. This order is, like the international orders that came before it, a world of disparate peoples and of incommensurable values; but it also exhibits much more *worldwide* economic and even political integration than has ever been the case before. One notable example of this is the widespread human rights culture that has emerged since the UN's Universal Declaration of Human Rights (1948). The chapter concludes then with a discussion of the character and role and grounds of justification of human rights, in Rawls's view, in this new international order.

## Biography

John Rawls was born in Baltimore, Maryland, on 21 February 1921. He grew up in Baltimore, where his father was a lawyer. He attended secondary school in Connecticut (the Kent School) and then entered Princeton University in 1939 as an undergraduate. There he was first introduced to political philosophy by Norman Malcolm, a student of Ludwig Wittgenstein's. He wrote his senior thesis on the problem of evil. Upon graduating in January 1943, Rawls joined the US Army as a private in the infantry (1943–6) and saw active service in the Pacific. He then returned to Princeton, in 1946, to begin graduate studies in philosophy, receiving his Ph.D. degree in 1951. After teaching for two years at Princeton, Rawls had a Fulbright scholarship to Oxford University, where he was affiliated with Christ Church College (1952–3). At Oxford Rawls attended, and was especially influenced by, lectures by H. L. A. Hart on philosophy of law; he also attended seminars held by Isaiah Berlin and Stuart Hampshire.

After returning to the United States Rawls taught at Cornell (1953–9); then, after one year at Harvard, he took a post at the Massachusetts Institute of Technology for two years (1960–2). In 1962 he was offered a full professorship at Harvard, where he remained for the rest of his teaching career (retiring in 1991, but continuing to teach there until 1995). He occupied the John Cowles chair in Philosophy (1974–9) and, then, as successor to Nobel Laureate Kenneth Arrow, the James Bryant Conant University professorship (1979–91). Rawls received honorary doctorates from Oxford and Harvard. He was awarded the National Humanities Medal by President Clinton in 1999 and, that same year, the Rolf Schock Prize in Logic and Philosophy, in Stockholm.

Rawls married Margaret Warfield Fox, also of Baltimore, in 1949. Among the many portraits she painted (in her career as an artist) were several of John Rawls. They have two sons and two daughters.[1]

## Key texts

*A Theory of Justice* (1971; rev. 1999); *Political Liberalism* (1993, 1996); *The Law of Peoples with 'The Idea of Public Reason Revisited'* (1999); *John Rawls: Collected Papers*, ed. Samuel Freeman (1999).

## Main texts used

*John Rawls: Collected Papers*, ed. Samuel Freeman (Cambridge, Mass.: Harvard University Press, 1999).

*Justice as Fairness: A Restatement*, ed. Erin Kelly (Cambridge, Mass.: Harvard University Press, 2001). A publication of Rawls's lectures on political philosophy at Harvard during the 1980s. This book is based on the lecture set of 1989, as revised by Rawls in the early 1990s. The book constitutes, then, a sort of bridge between Rawls's *Theory of Justice* (1971) and his *Political Liberalism* (1993).

*The Law of Peoples with 'The Idea of Public Reason Revisited'* (Cambridge, Mass.: Harvard University Press, 1999) (*LP*).

*Lectures on the History of Moral Philosophy*, ed. Barbara Herman (Cambridge, Mass.: Harvard University Press, 2000).

*Political Liberalism* (New York: Columbia University Press, 1996) (*PL*). This paperback version is unchanged from the hardback version of 1993, except that it includes a second introd. and 'Reply to Habermas', *Journal of Philosophy*, 92 (1995), 132–80, as lecture IX.

*A Theory of Justice* (1971), rev. edn. (Cambridge, Mass.: Harvard University Press, 1999) (*TJ*).

## Key ideas

**Justice as fairness**: in his first book Rawls used this term as a shorthand way of describing the acceptable-to-all-perspectives and impartial procedures of the **original position**, suggesting that, whatever result came from using these procedures, it would be judged by all to have been a fairly decided one. In his second book (and thereafter) Rawls used the term to identify the expected (and, to him, the preferred) result of using such procedures (or some variant of them); here then 'justice as fairness' referred to the **two principles of justice** themselves and the main institutions required to embody them. **Utilitarianism**: this is the theory (stemming from Bentham and Mill) that made maximizing the overall or aggregate well-being of all human beings into the supreme principle of ethics and politics. One variant of this theory suggested that we should try to maximize, not the sum total of human welfare, but the *average* of such well-being. Rawls rejected both versions. He thought neither version took seriously the idea that ultimately people are individuals with distinctive projects and interests and affections, and their own lives to lead. He particularly disliked the idea that either version of utilitarianism would allow that the vital interests of some individuals could be sacrificed, so long as the total or the average of well-being was maximized. His theory of justice was designed to prevent this from ever happening. **The law of peoples**: this, of course, is the title of Rawls's third book. The law of peoples, about which this book is written, includes the traditional international relations view of states—that they have independence, sovereign status, territorial integrity, and formal equality with other states (the old Westphalian system, in short), but adds to it certain conditions or constraints on that traditional view. All these constraints derive from the post-Second World War settlement; the most important of them are the prohibition on waging war except in self-defence (or in collective defence), the idea that human rights are to be respected, and the claim that nations have a duty to provide economic and development aid to 'burdened societies'.

## Introduction

Immediately after graduating from Princeton University John Rawls entered the army and saw active combat service (in the Pacific theatre) in the Second World War. When the war ended, he returned to the United States to begin his postgraduate studies. By the time he had received his Ph.D. degree, a period of persistent tension had begun, marked by the spectre of nuclear war, between the NATO nations and the Soviet bloc; this 'cold war', as it was called, lasted until the demise of the Soviet Union in the early 1990s.

In short, from the time Rawls became an adult until his retirement from his university chair (in 1991), an ongoing and demanding challenge—physical as well as intellectual—threatened Western political institutions. The theoretical side of this challenge was advanced by Fascism/Nazism, on the one hand, and by Marxism, on the other. Though these theoretical challenges were significantly different from one another, they had certain points of agreement: they concurred in a deep contempt of parliamentary government and an intolerance for political controversy (disdaining the idea of a 'loyal opposition' or any acceptable difference of opinion from the official line); and they had no commitment to and no respect for the idea of the rights, human or constitutional, of individuals.

These challenges are the wellspring of Rawls's political thinking. He believed that they were not being effectively met by utilitarianism, the dominant political and moral theory in the Anglo-American world at the time he began his reflections. In the preface to the 1999 revised edition of his *Theory of Justice* (originally published in 1971), Rawls says that he 'wanted to work out a conception of justice that provides a reasonably systematic alternative to utilitarianism'. He continues,

> The primary reason for wanting to find such an alternative is the weakness . . . of utilitarian doctrine as a basis for the institutions of constitutional democracy. In particular, I do not believe that utilitarianism can provide a satisfactory account of the basic rights and liberties of citizens as free and equal persons, a requirement of absolutely first importance for an account of democratic institutions. (*TJ* (rev. edn.), pp. xi–xii[2])

Where did Rawls turn for the materials for this 'alternative to utilitarianism'? To three sources mainly: to the social contract tradition, as found in the writings of Locke and Rousseau and especially Kant; to the notion of liberalism as set forth most notably in Mill's *On Liberty*; and to the practice and theory of democratic politics.

These few remarks serve to locate Rawls within the tradition of modern political thought. What is not so clear, however, is the importance of his theory in the thirty or so years since the original publication of *Theory of Justice*. Quite simply put, the dominant philosophical theory of justice in the last thirty years of the twentieth century (as regards both political justice and economic justice), certainly in the English-speaking world and in much of western Europe, has been that of John Rawls. His theory will strike the reader, I trust, both as a novel and trenchant statement of political ideas, having peculiar contemporary resonance, and as a further voice in an ongoing dialogue of themes and theories long familiar.

The present chapter will first take up the main arguments for Rawls's ideas about justice; then it will discuss the 'original position', as Rawls called it; this a device for structuring these arguments and for determining a preference for Rawls's candidate principles of justice over utilitarian alternatives. After this is done, I want to indicate some grounds of dissatisfaction that Rawls and others have had with the *Theory of Justice* project. And, then, in the two sections after that, I hope to lay out the lines of Rawls's 'new theory' of justice (the one associated with his second book, *Political Liberalism* (1993, 1996) ) and to indicate how Rawls thought this new theory solved, with the idea of an overlapping consensus, the main problem he had seen in his own earlier theory of justice. The chapter concludes then with a section indicating what place Rawls thinks his new theory might have in the international arena.

## The first principle: equal basic liberties

Although Rawls intended his *Theory of Justice* to provide a 'convincing account of basic rights and liberties, and of their priority', Rawls admits he did not successfully achieve this objective until ten or so years later (*TJ* (rev. edn.), p. xii). Accordingly, I will draw on Rawls's 1980 Dewey Lectures and his 1982 Tanner Lecture as providing the best account of, and arguments for, his first principle of justice, the principle of equal basic liberties.

Rawls claims (in these lectures[3]) that for every individual citizen there are two fundamental capacities or powers and, correspondingly, two 'higher-order interests' in the realization of those capacities. Thus, each person has, over that person's entire life, (i) an interest in being able to formulate and live according to some particular conception of the good and (ii) an interest in exercising one's 'sense of justice' and being motivated by it, providing others do so as well. Let me amplify this second point a bit: each person has, over that person's entire life, an interest in living cooperatively with fellow citizens, on terms of mutual respect and reciprocal benefit, under a unified and stable scheme of basic political and economic institutions organized by a shared set of principles of justice which each citizen can affirm.

The notion of the two powers of the citizen is understood to include the idea that in a democratic society citizens are both equal and free. Here each person is conceived as having the two powers at a sufficient level to be able to be a fully contributing member of society over that person's entire adult life (or, at least, the working years). In having these powers at some such level, all the citizens are on the same footing. This, then, is the grounding idea behind Rawls's notion that the citizens are equal: they are equal in having reached what might be called this same *minimum* threshold level (see *TJ* (rev. edn.), sect. 77, and *PL* 19, 74, 79–80).

Rawls uses the idea of the two powers and the corresponding interests of the citizen to ground his elaboration of the concrete basic liberties that each citizen is to have equally. He identifies which 'liberties'—which ways of acting or of not being injured—should be among the basic constitutional rights, or among the most weighty such rights, by considering what he calls 'two fundamental cases'. Thus, those liberties that are part of or a means of achieving the *first* interest (the conception of the good interest) constitute the first of these cases and those that are a part of or a means of achieving the *second* (the sense of justice interest) constitute the second of the 'two fundamental cases'.

By way of illustration, Rawls offers liberty of conscience and freedom of personal association as examples of liberties justified under the *first* interest (the conception of the good interest). The argument here is simply that people would not be able to have or live according to their own particular determinate conception of the good, whatever it was, and in particular would not be able to *revise* any such conception, without liberty of conscience or freedom of personal association. He offers freedom of political speech and of assembly as examples under the *second* interest (the sense of justice interest). Rawls conceives this interest as being exercised in a democratic institutional context. The main argument here, then, is simply that people could not live cooperatively with fellow citizens, on terms of equality and mutual respect, under a unified and stable scheme of *democratic* political institutions without having a practice of free political speech in place there. And the same could be said about liberty of political association and assembly.

The basic liberties constitute, in effect, a determinate and well-defined set. For the most part, these liberties are rather standard civil rights, of the sort that would be found, for example, in the European Convention on Human Rights (1954) or the United Nations' Covenant on Civil and Political Rights (1966, entered into force in 1976), or on a list of important rights in current American constitutional law. As we have seen, most of the determinate liberties on this list would be justified in Rawls's schema as coming under either one or the other of the 'two fundamental cases'. Or they could be justified as falling under *both cases* (as all four of the liberties named in the previous paragraph presumably could be).

Finally, some liberties (or protections from injury) fall under neither case directly but are, nonetheless, necessary for the proper and adequate exercise of those that do so fall. For example, the due process rights to such things as fair trial or the rights to bodily integrity (rights that specify not being assaulted and possibly maimed, not being tortured, and so on) are justified as necessary to the full flourishing of the liberties justified in the 'two fundamental cases'.

For Rawls, then, all the liberties (and non-injuries) just specified should be counted among the basic constitutional rights. These basic liberties and rights, like the conception of the constitution of which they are a part, are not founded 'on basic (or natural) rights'. Rather, Rawls says, the 'foundation is in the conceptions of the person and of social cooperation most likely to be congenial to the public political culture of a modern democratic society' (*PL* 339).

Thus we arrive at Rawls's first principle of justice: 'Each person has an equal claim to a fully adequate scheme of equal basic rights and liberties, which scheme is compatible with the same scheme for all; and in this scheme the equal political liberties [e.g. the right to vote and to campaign], and only those liberties, are to be guaranteed their fair value' (*PL* 5).[4]

## The second principle: distributive economic justice

Unlike the case with his first principle, Rawls thought that the account and formulation of his *second* principle of justice, as found in *A Theory of Justice* (1971), was substantially sound. So I will confine myself to what he said there and to elaborations that he made over the next decade.

Rawls's account begins with the fact that people have different natural endowments and are born into and grow up in different social circumstances. No one can be said to be responsible for these factors in their *own* case. Nonetheless, factors such as natural endowment and initial social circumstance are not negligible; they powerfully affect a person's life prospects, advantageously for some and disadvantageously for others. Indeed, they may be the main sources of inequality between people.

Rawls's argument sets out from this point. He first develops the idea of 'democratic' equality of opportunity—conceived as (1) the taking of remedial steps, conscientiously, to reduce the *initial* differential in advantages that accrues to individuals, arbitrarily, from their starting points in life. State-supported primary and secondary education (of good quality and at no cost to the individual student) would be an example of such a step. The leading idea here is to try to make people somewhat less unequal at the point where they actually enter into adult life, as citizens and as workers. And to make sure that everyone there, so far as possible, has the basic capabilities required to be contributing members of society.

Rawls believes that an absolute equality of opportunity with respect to such *starting points* can never be achieved. And it is precisely where fundamental equality in starting points is not fully and strictly achieved, or cannot be, that concern for reducing the inequality of *resultant outcomes* is in order. Thus, Rawls introduces a further idea to complement equality of opportunity (point 1 above) and complete the line of argument. Rawls calls this new idea the 'difference principle'; it adds two further remedial steps to the picture; it adds (2) the principle of everyone's continual benefit, which in turn is constrained by the idea that, where there are several mutually improving (that is, efficient) options available, (3) we should choose that option which most reduces the resultant inequality in outcomes (as measured in terms of average income over a five-year period, say) between the topmost and bottom-most groups. The object of this three-step process is to reduce, ideally to *minimize*, the gap between persons by taking account of both starting points and end results.[5]

We can get to Rawls's final specification of the difference principle by repeatedly employing the set of ideas just sketched. The difference principle can be represented, then, as proceeding through a series of stages each one of which embodies a conscientious effort at achieving equality of opportunity and each one of which then repeats the same theme: first satisfy the standard of mutual benefit (or of efficiency) and then reduce differences in outcome between the topmost and the bottom-most group. This repeated pattern continues at each stage until we reach an optimum point, at which no further mutually improving moves are possible: at this point we have minimized the difference in question (without making any group worse off in the process), and those least well off (the bottom 20 per cent, say) have here their greatest benefit.[6]

I believe the argument just sketched becomes logically conclusive if we make certain simplifying assumptions. We must first assume, as does Rawls, that we are starting from a hypothetical point of strict equality between people. This 'zero point' does not, of course, describe the way things actually are; rather, it is used merely to orient and clarify our thinking. And, secondly, we must assume that so long as the benefit of the least well-off group could *possibly* be higher, that of the other groups could also be higher, right on up to the optimum or goal point. The object of this second assumption is to identify a zone or context in which the procedure (the repeated pattern described earlier) can operate, with full effect, to achieve its intended end.

With these two assumptions in place, we have completed our account of Rawls's argument for his second principle of justice, the principle of distributive economic justice. It remains now only to state that principle succinctly: 'Social and economic inequalities are to satisfy two conditions: first, they are to be attached to positions and offices open to all under conditions of fair equality of opportunity; and second, they are to be to the greatest benefit of the least advantaged members of society' (*PL* 6; see also *TJ* (rev. edn.), 72, 266).

The question we must next consider is, 'How would the arguments for each of Rawls's two principles fare as formal arguments? How would they do in the original position?'

## The original position

Rawls's contractarian method of justification is very complex. I will be able to mention only a few of its main features here. One feature that is often emphasized—and that Rawls continued to include even in his later writings—is that the 'parties' to the contract are placed (in what he calls the 'original position') behind a thick veil of ignorance. Here they are instructed in their subsequent reasoning to ignore their own *particular* traits (traits that distinguish them from most or, at least, many other people), to be unaware of (or to ignore) their actual place in society, to be unaware of their society's place in history or in institutional evolution, and so on. The point of the metaphor of the veil is to indicate that the parties should remove sources of bias and irrelevancy from their deliberations.

Other features are important as well. The parties understand that they are deciding about principles of justice (principles for distributing certain primary goods—such goods as liberties, opportunities, income, and wealth—to individuals) and that they will have to live, for their entire lives, under the principles they have selected. Accordingly, they would want the principles selected to be clear and intelligible to all, with nothing hidden from view and everything up front and accounted for. (This Rawls calls the 'publicity requirement'.) Such principles, when looked at from a variety of perspectives, ought to be acceptable to persons in *each* of those perspectives—this Rawls calls the 'unanimity requirement'. (Rawls's main discussion of the original position is found in *A Theory of Justice*, chapter 3, and a very helpful summary of its main features is found in *TJ* (rev. edn.), 126–7.)

In simplest terms the original position is an arena for deliberation and decision about principles of justice; its various features are meant to frame and constrain the debate about such principles. 'The idea of the original position is to set up a fair procedure so that any principles agreed to will be just' (*TJ* (rev. edn.), 118).

Rawls envisions two main roles for the original position. In its first role the original position is to serve as a screening device for the candidate principles, that is, principles taken from a short list of main, historically available theories of justice—such as Plato's republic, various versions of utilitarianism, and so on. Here the features of the original position serve as a checklist against which the candidate principles are to be measured and to be assessed.

Let me illustrate the force of this first role (screening) with an example, admittedly a rather extreme one. An avowedly racist principle would probably not pass through the filter afforded by the features of the original position. Thus, if people contemplated living in a multiracial society under that principle, it is clear that some of them would be seriously disadvantaged, indeed deeply harmed, by its operation. Everyone who took on, by hypothesis, the role of these injured parties would have to veto the racist principle; thus, it could not meet the unanimity requirement. Since anyone (given the veil of ignorance) could be in such a role, the racist principle would be decisively ruled out. For similar reasons it is likely that caste system principles or slavery principles would not survive the initial screening either.

In short, some principles (perhaps Plato's republic, with its endorsement of slavery, would be among them) would be filtered out, by the various features of the original position, and removed from any further consideration. But other principles, the various versions of utilitarianism, for example, might remain in contention after being examined under the conditions set by publicity, unanimity, the veil of ignorance, and so on. They have passed through the initial screening. This means simply that these principles can be formulated and argued for under the constraints of the original position. Unlike the discredited principles, these principles will have purchase there.

This brings us to the second main role of the original position: to *rank* the remaining eligible candidates, after the preliminary screening has been accomplished. (See *TJ* (rev. edn.), 16; also 'Basic Structure as Subject', 278,[7] for the point about ranking.) In performing this second role, of ranking, the parties rely on the balance of reasons (determined in light of assessments that could be reached in the original position) to decide which of the remaining eligible candidates is best. If they can do so unanimously, there should be no real doubt about *that* particular ranking.

Let us turn, then, to an examination of Rawls's two principles in the original position. We have already noted that one of the main features of the original position is the veil of ignorance. Thus, extreme uncertainty about starting points and outcomes for any given individual would characterize the deliberations in the original position, in which individuals are called upon to construct and then to choose the principles of justice that they would prefer to determine the basic structure of their society, in which they are to spend their entire lives.

Given this high degree of uncertainty, we find that Rawls's earlier straightforward argument for his second principle of justice fares rather well. For example, the transition from the idea that nobody is responsible for their *own* starting points in life to the idea that people should use their natural endowments and their social origins (where these things are advantageous) in such a way that everybody benefits would surely go more smoothly behind the veil of ignorance than it would where people were already aware of their own and others' natural endowments and social origins. This transition would certainly carry more conviction for the parties in the original position.

And, for a second example, the mutual benefit part of the earlier argument would gain strong endorsement behind the veil of ignorance, especially if we assumed a starting point of strict equality. The argument would go as follows: the parties would have no reason to give up this equality in their choice of principles unless there were benefits for each and all, or at least for some of them (and no losses).

Let me make the same argument now in somewhat different words. In the original position (as I have already indicated) a certain amount of role-playing is allowed; individuals are allowed to assume certain standpoints and then to consider how things would play out in the deliberations of the parties. One could assume, for example, that one was in a religious minority (see *TJ* (rev. edn.), sect. 33) or in the least well-off economic class (see ibid. 82–6). Now, where one took strict equality in starting points as a benchmark and remained behind the veil of ignorance, no one would prefer *disadvantageous* deviations, were they on the losing end, and hence would veto such deviations (for example, disadvantageous deviations from strict equality). Thus, only deviations advantageous to all would survive the veto (that is, only such *advantageous* deviations could achieve the unanimity required of conclusive deliberations in the original position construct). But it would be rational, in the eyes of each, to allow for mutually *beneficial* changes, where there were more benefits for each and all (or at least for some) and no losses.

Now, a third example. Where persons have an equal status (as parties to the deliberation) and each has equal claim to shares of primary goods, then the parties (as representing such persons in the original position) would prefer a mutually beneficial outcome that *reduced* the difference in income between the topmost and bottom-most group over one that increased that inequality. The idea is that, even after mutual benefit is assured, one should continue to use equal shares (of primary goods) as a standing constraint on beneficial options, as a tie-breaker of sorts. Here, among available options, that efficient and mutually beneficial outcome which reduces inequality is to be preferred.[8]

In sum, I think Rawls's straightforward arguments for each of his two principles would fare well in the original position construct; the arguments could be formulated and would hold up, under the constraints identified there. I have stressed, in this discussion, his arguments for the second principle, in particular.[9] I have done this for two reasons, to achieve economy and simplicity of presentation and to emphasize (by looking at a single sample case) how the screening function of the original position would proceed.

Now, let us turn to the second main function of the original position construct, to the ranking of the competing candidate principles that remain eligible after screening. Here we encounter the most memorable argument from *A Theory of Justice*, chapter 3 (the chapter devoted to the original position), the famous maximin argument. As should be expected, this argument actually presupposes and builds on the arguments allowed and the assessments reached, in the screening process, for the various candidate principles there.

We can put the line of reasoning in the maximin argument quickly and intuitively, as follows. Behind the veil of ignorance and given the high degree of uncertainty there, each individual thinks that, since they don't know how or where they might end up, they should set things up in the principles they select, each one having a veto, so that the worst controllable outcome for any one of them is the best of a bad lot, the best, that is, of the set of worst outcomes. This line of reasoning, which has its home in rational choice theory, is, as I have already indicated, sometimes called *maximin* reasoning, that is, reasoning literally on the principle of maximizing the minimum.

The outcomes, which the maximin argument ranges over, are in fact generated by the main competing principles under review—by justice as fairness (Rawls's own theory), on the one hand, and by its strongest competitor, the principle of maximizing average utility, on the other. It is these particular outcomes, sets of characteristic outcomes as determined by these competing principles, which the maximin argument then chooses between.

Rawls's view is that utilitarians and others, especially in the setting afforded by the original position, would allow the sacrifice or the serious weakening of some of the demands of justice as fairness, or would do so for some people at least. Here the argument focuses, in particular, on the loss of equal basic liberties of the sort enshrined in the *first* principle. (See *TJ* (rev. edn.), 135, 137; also p. xiv and sect. 49.) And it is this fact that marks the primary ground, in Rawls's view, for *preferring* the principles of justice as fairness over their presumed closest competitor. Thus, the maximin test provides what, in the context of the original position, is a compelling reason for ranking the two principles, as a set, above the principle of average utility.

Rawls's theory of justice (as developed in his 1971 book) is very complex, and the discussion

I have offered in this and the previous two sections merely scratches the surface. Nonetheless, the things we have looked at here—his two principles of justice and the arguments for them and for preferring them to alternative theories—have tended to dominate debate and to have had the lion's share of attention.

## Some problems in *A Theory of Justice*

The book has at least two main problems. Let me sketch the most significant of these problems, and then merely mention the other.

The complicated procedure whereby Rawls attempted to justify his two principles of justice—a procedure centring on the notion of an 'original position' for deciding about candidate principles of justice—has, I think, important defects. For one thing, Rawls's theory seemed to rule out from serious consideration certain rival candidates to his own two principles (especially those candidates, such as Platonic aristocracy or Nietzschean elitism, that did not take the equality or liberty of individuals as fundamental). Rawls had simply stacked the deck in the original position against these perfectionist theories. Arguably, the only principles of justice that could survive scrutiny by the 'parties'—by the body of fellow citizens (or their representatives), each one of them having equal status and an equal voice and full veto power—are principles that treat people as substantive equals.

The point, then, is that Rawls's theory is not, *on its own terms*, an acceptable or accredited theory of critical moral justification. For the screening procedure it employs does not satisfy its own goal: of wielding a set of *objectively* based considerations for fairly assessing rival principles of justice.[10]

A second criticism, a lesser one, is that Rawls never succeeds in making an adequate case for the priority of the first principle of justice over the second—of the equal basic liberties over elements in the second principle (elements that include policies designed to achieve fair equality of opportunity, in all its aspects, and to achieve maximization of the level of goods and services available to the least well-off income group).[11] Indeed, for that matter, we cannot say even that Rawls makes a satisfactory case for putting equal basic liberties over policies advancing corporate goods or other aggregate considerations.[12]

Of course, there have been many other criticisms of Rawls's book than the two I have mentioned, because the book has been widely discussed, both favourably and unfavourably.[13] Over the years Rawls responded to many of the criticisms. Indeed, Rawls appears to have become dissatisfied with the shape his theory had taken in 1971 and had retained for about a decade afterwards. He began to rethink that theory. Beginning with his Dewey Lectures in 1980, he began to reconfigure his entire justificatory account. A number of important changes have occurred as he has moved further from positions he had occupied in *A Theory of Justice*.

In his more recent writings Rawls seems especially concerned with the problem of assuring political stability in a pluralist or multicultural social environment. Rawls gives this current preoccupation—and his new theory of justice—its most complete elaboration in his second book, *Political Liberalism*.[14]

## Rawls's new theory

Perhaps, the most significant feature of this book is that Rawls takes the public political culture of a contemporary democratic society to be the deep background of the entire theory. Rawls says that the leading ideas out of which the political conception of justice is to be constructed and by reference to which it is to be justified are implicit in that culture (*PL* 13, 15, 175, 223).

Establishing terms for social cooperation for reciprocal benefit—principles for a fair distribution of certain primary goods (as he called them)—continues to be the main object of Rawls's new *political* conception (just as it had been in his earlier book, *A Theory of Justice*). But significant differences begin to appear as well. In the new account the principles of justice that emerge as preferred (from among a small set of historically available candidate principles) are the principles that are best supported by the background *democratic* ideas. The preferred principles are the principles most appropriate to the basic ideas there (ideas such as the two moral powers and the citizens' corresponding fundamental interests, and the importance of reciprocal benefit).[15] That is, they are the principles that, upon reflection and given the balance of reasons, are the most appropriate ones with respect to the democratic starting point itself, under the assumption that there is and is going to be, in a continuing free and open society, an irreducible pluralism of reasonable comprehensive moral and religious and philosophic doctrines.

Rawls thinks that the best-supported principles will be those of 'justice as fairness'—that is, they will be the two principles of justice, understood now as *political* principles. Or, to be precise, he thinks the preferred set will actually be a 'family' of principles, among which are included the two he emphasizes.

The members of this 'family' have three main features in common: (1) certain familiar rights, liberties, opportunities are to be singled out and specified and maintained; (2) a certain priority is to be given to these rights etc. over against 'the claims of the general good [understood aggregatively] and of perfectionist values'; (3) measures to help citizens make effective use of these rights etc., by having an adequate base of income and wealth, are to be set in place.[16]

In Rawls's account the justification of the political conception proceeds in two main stages (see *PL* 64–5, 140–1, 385–8). The first stage is the one I have focused on up to now. The main project here is to settle on that principle or set of principles for distributing primary goods which is most appropriate, given the fundamental democratic ideas from which we started. Thus, Rawls argues that the generic liberal principles (the family of principles in which are included his own preferred two principles) are well designed to specify an acceptable distribution of primary goods in the context of existing democratic political arrangements.

This first line of justification (justification from democratic principles in a democratic context) is said by Rawls to be 'freestanding', in the sense that it draws only on these background democratic ideas, presumably shared already to a large degree by fellow citizens.

What Rawls calls overlapping consensus is a second stage of political justification in which the already established 'freestanding' justification is endorsed from the respective points of view of a variety of comprehensive ethical doctrines, such as Kant's moral theory or Mill's utilitarianism, and religious doctrines, such as contemporary Catholic Christianity. On this view, the political conception (as supported by free-standing justification) is a common focal point—a 'module . . . that fits into and can be supported by various reasonable comprehensive doctrines that endure in the society regulated by it' (*PL* 12; see also pp. 145, 387). But the political conception need not be *presented* by reference to such support initially; rather it is established independently of direct consideration of any and all such doctrines.

At the second stage we contemplate the justification of the political conception from *within* the confines of a variety of comprehensive views. In some of these cases such justification will follow a deductive pattern; in others it will be a justification based on the claim that the political conception counts as a nearest practical approximation, or at least as a feasible real-world exemplification, of the comprehensive view in question; in yet others it will be a justification only in the very weak sense given by the notion of consistency—here the political conception is said merely to be compatible with the comprehensive doctrine in question. (See *PL* 11, 140, 160, 169–71, 242; also pp. 158–64.) In any event, where several different comprehensive doctrines can justify a single political conception in one of these ways, we say that there is an overlapping consensus among these comprehensive doctrines; each for its own reasons endorses the same political conception.

## Overlapping consensus

Is overlapping consensus a utopian notion (as some have claimed)? Rawls attempts to deal with this issue by showing how it is possible to move from a mere political modus vivendi to a consensus over a detailed set of constitutional essentials, the features of which 'all citizens may reasonably be expected to endorse' (*PL* 217).

In a mere modus vivendi, certain principles and practices are accepted as a way for people to live together without constant fighting and disruption. Such agreement is not wide (it covers only a fairly narrow range of institutions and of rights, for example, the right of religious toleration). It is not deep, in that the reasons offered for the desirability of these accepted arrangements do not go beyond the idea of establishing a modus vivendi. And it lacks focus: fellow citizens have no shared conception of a public political life that would take them beyond the status quo. In a modus vivendi they have, really, only one important idea in common: the fear of a worse alternative, the return to open war, as in the wars of religion in the past and in the present day.

The sort of political consensus Rawls had in view would come about as the agreed-upon area of rights and practices widens; it would come about as the ground under that area deepens, as convincing political reasons for having such arrangements, reasons that go beyond the mere utility of a modus vivendi, gain acceptance and are taken on board. And it would come about as a conception of public principles of justice, with these deeper reasons as justification and with greater focus and definition, gains widespread support.

Thus, a shared conception of a public order would be created as a given body politic goes beyond its starting point, in a mere modus vivendi, and moves in the direction of a broader, deeper, and more focused political consensus. When such a consensus has emerged, a *shared* political conception of justice becomes possible. A space has been created for citizenship, and in this new dimension there is a new role for political co-inhabitants, that of fellow citizens.

Now, let us assume that at some point a public political conception of this sort has been successfully achieved. An important degree of stability, based on this consensual support, is built into any such public political conception of justice (see *PL* 168).

An overlapping consensus would arise where the great bulk of citizens could affirm, upon reflection and given experience, that the governing principles and institutional essentials of the public political conception were compatible (or could be made so), in each of their respective cases, with the various comprehensive moral and religious and philosophical doctrines that they individually held to. (See *PL* 160; also pp. 187–8, 210.)

Such affirmation is not far-fetched, where we assume that the existing support for a given public political conception, or close-knit family of such conceptions, is already widespread and long-lived. And such affirmation would have great weight where we assumed that citizens are reflective within normal limits. This last point is crucial. If we assume that these citizens generally are as reflective as ordinary people can be expected to be, it follows that they don't, upon reflection, regard the perspectives they're individually coming from as *in*compatible, in general or in principle, with the institutional essentials there. And if this is true for a sizeable number of the citizens, then it's true for the variety of diverse perspectives, collectively held by the citizens, that these diverse views constitute, or can be regarded as constituting, an overlapping consensus upon a given set of institutional essentials.

Here it is not so much that various comprehensive doctrines (understood as 'isms') converge on a single public political conception of justice; rather, it is that a considerable bulk of citizens, coming from diverse perspectives, do. In this latter case we would, nonetheless, have an overlapping consensus, of a quite definite and interesting sort. Such an overlapping consensus would, of course, occur gradually; it would take time to gel (see *PL* 160 n. 25).

None of this shows, of course, that an overlapping consensus *will* occur; nothing is guaranteed. It shows merely that such a consensus plausibly could occur, in the way Rawls envisioned (see *PL*, pp. xlvii–xlviii). Its occurring in that way is not utopian.

The *shared* public political conception we are concerned with, given Rawls's starting point in democratic political culture, would belong to the 'family' of liberal conceptions. Rawls thinks that justice as fairness might well become the centrepiece in an evolving democratic public political conception. His view here is something like this: that, as a process of progressive narrowing goes on over time in the course of democratic debate, justice as fairness would continue to be *one* of the primary contending perspectives on political justice within the 'family' of liberal conceptions. Indeed, it would be at the 'center of the focal class' there (because it fits in well with the fundamental democratic ideas and is compatible with the developing pattern of democratic institutions).[17] The degree of internal stability of any family of liberal conceptions which had justice as fairness at its continuing centre would be quite considerable; such an order would be less likely to be overturned by divisive issues.

But if a democratic political conception, even with justice as fairness as its focus, is stable in the way indicated, one might well wonder what more an overlapping consensus of the various competing moral and religious doctrines alive at the same time could add to that rather high degree of stability. Very little, I would think.

What overlapping consensus provides is not political stability per se, but 'stability for the right reasons' (*PL*, pp. xxxix, xliii, 388 n. 21, 390, 391, 394; and 'The Idea of Public Reason Revisited' (1997), as reprinted in *John Rawls: Collected Papers*, ed. Freeman 589). By this Rawls meant the right moral reasons, the reasons of critical morality.

A public political conception, simply on its own, is always a consensus within and from public reasons, in the case at hand, the reasons appropriate to a liberal democratic society. As such it lacks a certain dimension: it lacks deep moral credentials of the sort afforded by a comprehensive critical moral theory. Thus, one goal, in Rawls's view, of critical moral justification would be to give freestanding political justification this particular kind of moral grounding, which it otherwise lacks.

The problem is, of course, that several different critical moral and religious doctrines can be drawn upon, at a given time, in a liberal society. Each of them is controversial, no one of them is accepted by everybody, and all of them are subject to endless and apparently unresolvable disputation. In so far as we are concerned, then, with anything like a *full* critical moral justification of the political conception, we must accept that the doctrines there admissible as premisses in *that* form of justification, doctrines such as the utilitarians' general happiness principle and Catholic natural law, are clearly *not* acceptable to all reasonable citizens but, rather, only to the adherents to those respective doctrines. The only form a full justification could take in a morally and religiously pluralistic society and still have authority outside a narrow circle of partisan sentiment would be as an overlapping consensus—with the public political conception as focus, of these various doctrines.

If it could be established as a matter of public fact (based on settled judgements of compatibility by the great bulk of citizens) that various of the main present-day comprehensive moral doctrines and religious faiths and philosophical world-views all endorsed, each for its own reasons, one and the same public political conception of justice, then that particular conception, a freestanding one, in Rawls's view, would be fully and publicly accredited by the standards of these various comprehensive doctrines.[18] Thus, even in the face of a continuing and very likely ineradicable pluralism, we would have achieved stability, as provided by a public political conception, *and* for the right reasons (as provided by an overlapping consensus, and not a mere compromise, among the various relevant critical moral doctrines).

It was this problem, of moral justification under conditions of pluralism, that *A Theory of Justice* had conspicuously failed to solve. And overlapping consensus, one of Rawls's new ideas in *Political Liberalism*, was called upon to repair this self-professed defect. Let me elaborate.

Rawls assumed in *A Theory of Justice* that, since his preferred principles of justice came out on top in the contest with utilitarianism and with perfectionist values, values such as Platonic aristocracy or Nietzschean elitism, these principles would in effect be endorsed by everybody and for the *same* reasons. Thus, these principles would become the moral theory or part of the moral theory of any well-ordered society whose principles of justice were constructed in the original position behind the veil of ignorance, subject to the constraints of publicity and unanimity. Ultimately, then, it is this almost universal convergence upon a single justifying moral theory that underwrites Rawls's account of stability in *A Theory of Justice*.[19]

Such uniform acceptance, Rawls now says, is inconsistent with the idea that a pluralism of reasonable comprehensive moral and religious doctrines is here to stay. The pluralism of moral principles is a continuing, indeed very likely an ineradicable, fact of modern political society, at least, in any society committed to free and open discussion. (See *PL*, pp. xvii–xx, xxvi, xlii, 4, 36–7, 129, 144.)

In Rawls's second book, *Political Liberalism*, the problem of political stability, in a world of moral pluralism, was tackled first and on its own, using political devices: constitutional consensus (or, more generally, what I have called public political conceptions) and the attendant idea of institutional essentials which all citizens 'may reasonably be expected to endorse'. The solution to the next problem, that of critical moral justification, was first tailored to confront the idea of a permanent and irresolvable pluralism of moral and religious doctrines and was then brought to bear, in the idea of overlapping consensus, on a 'freestanding' political conception of justice and on a pre-existing political solution to the problem of internal stability. The job of overlapping consensus is to provide an *independent* critical moral grounding for each, for the public political conception itself and for the inherent stability afforded by that conception.

This new solution, in *Political Liberalism*, is compatible with the moral pluralism that had infirmed the original *Theory of Justice* solution. Overlapping consensus (whatever marginal increase in stability it might afford) is directed by Rawls primarily at the issue, not of stability, but of critical moral justification.

## The law of peoples

It is this solution, then, that Rawls (in his third book, *The Law of Peoples* (1999) ) draws upon in attempting to situate the main lines of his theory within the international arena, a world of disparate peoples and of incommensurable values. Rawls, while accepting that a large number of societies in the world today are neither liberal nor democratic, argues here that many of them are nonetheless 'decent' societies. That is, they are or can be societies in which the values accepted by the majority—and often these are shared religious values—afford grounds for certain protections and securities for *all* the inhabitants in the country. Such societies can be conceived as subscribing to a 'common good' standard of justice for all inhabitants, based on religious values shared by most of them.[20]

This is not to say that they conform to anything like democratic norms (on a one person–one vote basis), but Rawls does regard the decent societies in question as all of them well ordered. Specifically, each one operates as a 'consultation hierarchy'. Here the basic decision procedure, though not democratic, is such that the governing person or governing council, nonetheless, makes a genuine effort to consult various *constituencies* on their interests and their view of the public interest, and to keep them informed. (See *LP* 68, 72, 78, 88, 92.) And these societies are non-aggressive towards their neighbours.

Accordingly, Rawls argues that both liberal societies and decent non-liberal societies would be able to agree to the same set of international conventions, as outlined and detailed in the articles of the post-Second World War law of peoples, as he calls it (see *LP* 37 for these articles). And this would include a shared commitment to a short list of human rights; among these would be 'the right to life (to the means of subsistence and security); to liberty (to freedom from slavery, serfdom and forced occupation, and to a sufficient measure of liberty of conscience to ensure freedom of religion and thought); to property (personal property); and to formal equality as expressed by the rules of natural justice (that is, that similar cases are to be treated similarly).'[21]

Human rights, on this conception, represent not only a standard for how a government treats its own inhabitants but also a standard for how it is willing to treat the inhabitants of other societies—in particular, the inhabitants of other societies that belong to the camp of liberal societies and decent non-liberal ones. But we must note two important things about the set of human rights Rawls has emphasized here. First, they constitute a rather reduced list of rights (when contrasted, say, with the rather robust array of active rights one finds in the European Convention on Human Rights or among the basic constitutional rights of a typical contemporary liberal democratic society). And, secondly, the pattern for justifying this short list of international human rights is markedly different, in Rawls's book *The Law of Peoples*, than was the pattern he used to justify the basic constitutional rights of a liberal democratic society (as set out in the section on equal basic liberties in this chapter). In concluding my discussion I want to turn to this second point.

The law of peoples is part of the conventions and practices of the international world order (as amended by the post-Second World War settlement). As such that law fits in with the *conventional* morality of both liberal and decent non-liberal societies, fits in, for example, with the fact of peace between democratic societies (see *LP* 51–4) and with the non-aggressiveness of decent non-liberal societies. One could add, of course, that this is as it should be. A notion of human rights and, more importantly, an active set of such rights (rights that are both specified and maintained on an international scale) should, in a multicultural world, be acceptable to societies other than simply liberal democratic ones.

There ought to be more to the justification of human rights (as part of the law of peoples) than just this one point. I think there is. If we took the brief sketch or list of human rights (from *LP* 65) as our primary example of international human rights today, then we could offer the following two claims as part of the justification for the rights on that list.

First, the rights here are something of a minimum (see *LP* 67) or, better, they constitute a list of the most urgent rights (basic liberties and non-injuries) that we, as individuals, have and should have against the greatest evils (see *LP* 79). Secondly, these ways of acting (liberties) and ways of being treated (non-injuries) are *necessary* conditions of social cooperation (see *LP* 81). These two justifying considerations go well beyond the merely conventional: they have a normative dimension (one that could be endorsed in a critical moral theory) and they have a universal reach (in that they could apply in *any* society).

Admittedly, Rawls also offers, as a third justifying consideration, that the human rights on the list (from *LP* 65) are a proper subset of liberal rights. And it could be said, equally truly, that they are a proper subset of established ways of acting and ways of being treated available to all persons, under a 'common good' conception of justice, in a decent, well-ordered hierarchical society. (See *LP* 81 for both these points). Now, this looks like a mere conventional argument (and, accordingly, a weak argument for a universal set of human rights).

But there are more than merely conventionalist considerations present even in this case. After all, the basic rights of a liberal society (of which the list of rights in *LP* 65 is a proper subset) are themselves justified by the background ideas latent in a democratic society (such ideas as that persons are free and equal); thus, they are rights peculiarly appropriate to a particular *kind* of society (democratic or liberal society). In turn, the liberal political conception, of which the basic rights are a part, can be justified from the perspective of a number of competing doctrinal perspectives, both moral and religious (in what is called an overlapping consensus). Thus, there is a normative argument pattern for these rights.

Similar considerations could be invoked for a decent non-liberal society. The basic rules of social conduct in such a society (of which the list of rights in *LP* 65 is a proper subset) are themselves justified as part of the 'common good' conception of justice applicable to all persons in that society (a conception capable of assigning rights and duties to those persons).

And, ultimately, this common good conception can be justified by reference to the comprehensive moral or religious doctrine (for example, a version of Islam) that the vast majority of citizens in that society accept. Thus, there is a normative argument pattern for these rights.

Ultimately, Rawls thinks that the basic rights endorsed in both these normative patterns (the liberal one and the decent non-liberal one) can be deployed and justified in something like an original position context, one in which the parties are the representatives of nations devising principles for an international order, rather than (as in the original original position) individual persons devising principles for a domestic political state (see *LP* 32–5, 39–42, 57, 69). These basic rights, and the other features of the law of peoples (see *LP* 37), have normative purchase because they can satisfy the standard that 'in proposing a principle to regulate the mutual relations between peoples, a people or their representatives must think not only that it is reasonable for them to propose it, but also that it is reasonable for other peoples to accept it' (*LP* 57; also p. 69). Since *all* peoples, or at least all peoples within the set of decent societies (liberal and non-liberal), could reasonably accept these rights and the other principles of the law of peoples, they become the standards of international public reason for these peoples. These points, if allowed, take us well beyond the conventional.[22]

Of course, it could be argued that none of the main justifying arguments are currently accepted or put into practice at an acceptable level by literally all peoples. Even so, these Rawlsian arguments have universal reach in principle: they can be accepted by societies that are other than liberal societies—by decent non-liberal societies right now; and potentially by all societies, if these societies are suitably amended over time. This is one of the main things Rawls's book *The Law of Peoples* is meant to show.

Whether these justifying arguments offer suitable grounds for intervention, in particular, forcible intervention, against societies (against peoples) that do not accept these justifications and, especially, against societies who engage regularly and unamendably in practices that are seriously unacceptable in the light of these arguments, is a difficult question.[23] Consider here (as examples of serious violations of human rights) genocide, slavery, and warlord-induced famine and starvation, all of them cases from our own day.

Of course, whatever answer is ultimately given, be it a general one or an answer in a particular case, the question asked has to be rethought and parsed over and over again. It is one of the fundamental and inescapable questions of our time.

## FURTHER READING


Barry, Brian, *The Liberal Theory of Justice* (Oxford: Clarendon Press, 1973).

Daniels, Norman (ed.), *Reading Rawls* (New York: Basic Books, 1975); rev. with updated bibliography and new editor's preface (Stanford, Calif.: Stanford University Press, 1989).

Davion, Victoria, and Wolf, Clark (eds.), *The Idea of a Political Liberalism: Essays on Rawls* (Lanham, Md.: Rowman & Littlefield, 2000).

Kukathas, Chandran, and Pettit, Philip, *Rawls: A Theory of Justice and its Critics* (Stanford, Calif.: Stanford University Press, 1990).

Martin, Rex, *Rawls and Rights* (Lawrence: University of Kansas Press, 1985).

Pogge, Thomas, *John Rawls* (Munich: Beck, 1994; incl. an interesting biography of Rawls and résumé of important dates in Rawls's life, and a useful bibliography).

Pogge, Thomas, *Realizing Rawls* (Ithaca, NY: Cornell University Press, 1989).

Sandel, Michael, *Liberalism and the Limits of Justice* (1982; 2nd edn. Cambridge: Cambridge University Press, 1996).

Wolff, Robert Paul, *Understanding Rawls* (Princeton: Princeton University Press, 1977).

## NOTES

1. This biographical note is taken from material provided to me by Samuel Freeman. I am grateful to him for this material and also to Thomas Pogge for the biographical details on Rawls in his book *John Rawls* (Munich: Beck, 1994).
2. Rawls, *A Theory of Justice* (1971), rev. edn. (Cambridge, Mass.: Harvard University Press, 1999) (hereafter *TJ* (rev. edn.) ).
3. The part of the Dewey Lectures we're concerned with is printed, in revised form, as lecture II of Rawls's *Political Liberalism* (1993; rev. New York: Columbia University Press, 1996) (references are to the 1996 edn., hereafter *PL*). And the Tanner Lecture is reprinted there, unrevised, as lecture VIII (see here *PL*, esp. sects. 5 and 6 of lecture VIII, and pp. 332–6, 358–9).
4. By 'fair value' Rawls means, I think, that these particular rights should make people substantively equal in the respect identified (by giving them an equal voice in voting and in campaigning). It should be noted that most of the important changes in Rawls's account and formulation of the first principle were made in response to criticisms put forward by H. L. A. Hart in an article originally published in 1973. See Hart in Norman Daniels (ed.), *Reading Rawls*, rev. edn. (Stanford, Calif.: Stanford University Press, 1989). For Rawls's original formulation of the first principle, see *TJ* (rev. edn.), 266.
5. The egalitarian motif—the motif of reducing, ideally of minimizing, differences in income between the topmost and the bottom-most group—is expressed most clearly in *A Theory of Justice* in sect. 17 (see esp. *TJ* (rev. edn.), 89–90). See also Rawls, 'Reply to Alexander and Musgrave' (1974), repr. in *John Rawls: Collected Papers*, ed. Samuel Freeman (Cambridge, Mass.: Harvard University Press, 1999), 246–7, incl. n. 7; and see Rawls, 'Social Unity and Primary Goods' (1982), repr. ibid. 374 n. 12.
6. The goal point of Rawls's difference principle can be stated in either of two distinctive ways: (i) as minimizing the difference (measured in terms of income or wealth) between the topmost and bottom-most group, consistent with the realization of everyone's continual betterment, or (ii) as achieving 'the greatest benefit of the least advantaged' (*TJ* (rev. edn.), 72, 266), that is, the greatest benefit for the least well-off group. Here we have a distinction without a difference; the two goal point formulations, (i) and (ii), say the same thing. (For a proof of this last contention, see the appendix in Rex Martin, *Rawls and Rights* (Lawrence: University of Kansas Press, 1985), 197–201.)
7. Rawls, 'Basic Structure as Subject' (1978), repr. in *PL*.
8. Rawls's statement of this line of argument, stressing (as a consideration in the original position) the continuing importance of the benchmark of equality in a condition of fundamental inequality in actual starting points, can be found in his writings at several points: in 'Kantian Conception of Equality' (1975), repr. in *John Rawls: Collected Papers*, ed. Freeman, 262–4; 'Reply to Alexander and Musgrave' (1974), repr. ibid. 246–7; 'Some Reasons for the Maximin Criterion' (1974), repr. ibid. 230–1; 'Distributive Justice: Some Addenda' (1968), repr. ibid. 164–6; and 'Basic Structure as Subject', 281–2.
9. For a brief and interesting look at Rawls's own view of the main arguments for his *first* principle, see *PL* 417–19.
10. Rawls regards the original position as an *objective* forum for making a definitive ranking among rival principles of justice, as provided by the short list of historical theories. See here *TJ* (rev. edn.), sect. 78, esp. p. 453, and sect. 87, esp. pp. 508–10; in addition, see his discussion of a *fair* decision procedure ibid. 118, as spelled out on pp. 74–5.
11. Rawls argues in *A Theory of Justice* that the first principle, the principle of equal basic liberties and rights, has priority over the second, the principle of distributive economic justice; and that the first part of the second principle, the fair equality of

opportunity part, has priority over the second or difference principle part. See *TJ* (rev. edn.), 53–4, 76–7, 267.

12. For elaboration of this second criticism, see Martin, *Rawls and Rights*, ch. 6, sect. 1.
13. Some of the most significant early criticisms can be found in Daniels (ed.), *Reading Rawls*.
14. For criticisms and discussion of Rawls's *Political Liberalism*, see e.g. the symposium in *Chicago–Kent Law Review*, 69 (1994), 549–842, and the essays in Victoria Davion and Clark Wolf (eds.), *The Idea of a Political Liberalism: Essays on Rawls* (Lanham, Md.: Rowman & Littlefield, 2000).
15. In his earlier writings Rawls typically spoke of *mutual* benefit, as we have seen; but in *PL* 16–18 (see esp. p. 17 n. 18), and also pp. 50, 54, Rawls distinguishes between 'mutual advantage' and 'reciprocity'. The former takes as its benchmark 'each person's present or expected future situation as things are [now]'; the latter takes as its fundamental point of comparison that 'everyone benefits judged with respect to an appropriate benchmark of equality defined with respect to that world' (for both passages quoted, see *PL* 17). If one does make a distinction between 'mutual advantage' and 'reciprocity', as Rawls is now inclined to do, it should be clear from earlier arguments in this chapter why Rawls would prefer the latter notion. A strict notion of mutual benefit is probably more at home in other theories, for example in the one advanced by David Gauthier in *Morals by Agreement* (Oxford: Oxford University Press, 1986).
16. See *PL* 6; also pp. xlviii, 7, 156–7, 375; Rawls, 'The Idea of Public Reason Revisited' (1997), repr. in *John Rawls: Collected Papers*, ed. Freeman, 581–2; and Rawls, *The Law of Peoples with 'The Idea of Public Reason Revisited'* (Cambridge, Mass.: Harvard University Press, 1999) (hereafter *LP*), 14, 49.
17. For the quoted phrase, see *PL* 168; also pp. xlviii, 164, 167–8, and Rawls, 'The Idea of Public Reason Revisited' (1997) reprinted in *John Rawls: Collected Papers*, ed. Freeman, 582 n. 27.
18. For discussion of what Rawls calls a 'full [moral] justification' and of 'public justification of the political conception by political society' (as both of them aspects of overlapping consensus), see *PL* 385–94, esp. pp. 385–8; also p. 67.
19. Rawls makes the point here (that his 'premiss' in *A Theory of Justice* was that there would be an almost universal convergence on a single comprehensive moral doctrine) quite explicit in his later writings. See *PL*, pp. xvii–xix, xlii, 388 n. 21; 'The Idea of Public Reason Revisited' (1997) reprinted in *John Rawls: Collected Papers*, ed. Freeman, 614–15.
20. For Rawls's account of these 'decent' non-liberal societies, see *LP*, sects. 8 and 9 (esp. p. 77) and p. 88. For the crucial idea of a 'common good' conception of justice, see *LP* 61, 64–7, 69, 83, and sect. 9.
21. See *LP* 65 for this list. For Rawls's discussion of human rights more generally, see *LP* 67, 68, 78–81, 83.
22. Actually, Rawls envisions two distinct stages for his international version of the original position. In the first stage the liberal societies agree on a set of principles to govern an international order conceived as comprising liberal peoples and liberal states. (Here one might regard the European Convention on Human Rights or the principles of the European Union as examples of a special case of such an order.) A similar first stage could be conceived for decent non-liberal societies, in which they lay out the terms of an international order conceived as comprising such societies. (See *LP*, sects. 6 and 8 for the respective cases.) The second stage is not so clear in Rawls's text, but it is there (see *LP*, sects. 11 and 12). Here both liberal and decent non-liberal societies agree on a set of principles to govern an international order conceived as comprising *all* such peoples. In my discussion here I have ignored the complication posed by having these two distinct stages and have gone directly to the idea of a *comprehensive* international version of the original position.
23. Rawls thinks that these arguments do allow forcible intervention against serious violators of human rights. See *LP* 93, esp. pp. 93–4 n. 6; also pp. 27, 80–1.

# 29 Foucault

Paul Patton

## Contents



## Chapter guide

Foucault described his work as a series of historico-philosophical critiques of aspects of present-day European society. He practised a form of criticism that combined archaeological and genealogical methods of writing history, and that purported to operate along three distinct axes corresponding to knowledge, power, and ethics in the distinctive senses that he gave to these terms. The first section outlines his conception of philosophy as the critique of the present. The next presents his archaeological approach to the study of systems of thought or discourse and outlines his historical approach to truth. The third section outlines his theory of power and freedom and discusses some criticisms. The next section surveys his sketches towards a history of conceptions of the nature and tasks of government. The fifth section discusses his concept of ethics as the forms of relation to the self by means of which individuals govern aspects of their behaviour, thereby making themselves ethical subjects of a certain kind. In conclusion, the chapter points to key dimensions of Foucault's influence on political thought.

## Biography

Michel Foucault (1926–84) was born in Poitiers. After preparation at the Lycée Henri IV in Paris he studied at the École normale supérieure, where he obtained *licences* in philosophy and psychology, before passing the *agrégation de philosophie* in 1951. Between 1952 and 1960 he took a diploma in psychopathology, taught at the University of Uppsala, and held positions at French institutes in Warsaw and Hamburg. He became Professor of Philosophy at the University of Clermont-Ferrand in 1962. From 1966 to 1968 he taught at the University of Tunis, returning to Paris after the events of May 1968 to become Head of the Philosophy Department at the University of Paris VIII (Vincennes). In 1969 he was elected to the Collège de France, where he chose as the title for his chair Professor of the History of Systems of Thought. He lectured widely in North America, Brazil, and Europe during the 1970s and 1980s. Throughout this period Foucault was active in a number of political movements, including the Groupe d'information sur les prisons, and protests in support of the radical newspaper *Libération*, immigrant workers, and gay liberation. He also took part in anti-racist campaigns and various actions on behalf of Soviet dissidents and the Solidarity movement in Poland.

## Key texts

*Folie et déraison: Histoire de la folie à l'âge classique* (1961); abridged as *Madness and Civilization*, trans. Richard Howard (New York: Pantheon, 1965).

*The Birth of the Clinic* (1963), trans. Alan Sheridan (London: Tavistock, 1973).

*The Order of Things: An Archaeology of the Human Sciences* (1966), trans. Alan Sheridan (London: Tavistock, 1970).

*The Archaeology of Knowledge* (1969), trans. Alan Sheridan (London: Tavistock, 1972).

*Discipline and Punish* (1975), trans. Alan Sheridan (London: Allen Lane/Penguin, 1977).

*The History of Sexuality*, vol. i: *An Introduction* (1976), trans. Robert Hurley (London: Allen Lane/Penguin, 1978).

*The Use of Pleasure, The History of Sexuality*, vol. ii (1984), trans. Robert Hurley (New York: Pantheon, 1985).

*The Care of the Self, The History of Sexuality*, vol. iii (1984), trans. Robert Hurley (New York: Pantheon, 1986).

*Essential Works of Foucault 1954–1984*, vol. i: *Ethics*, ed. Paul Rabinow, trans. Robert Hurley *et al.* (New York: New Press, 1997).

*The Politics of Truth*, ed. Sylvère Lotringer (New York: Semiotext(e), 1997).

*Essential Works of Foucault 1954–1984*, vol. ii: *Aesthetics, Method and Epistemology*, ed. James D. Faubion, trans. Robert Hurley *et al.* (New York: New Press, 1998).

*Essential Works of Foucault 1954–1984*, vol. iii: *Power*, ed. James D. Faubion, trans. Robert Hurley *et al.* (New York: New Press, 2000).

## Key ideas

Foucault's distinctive approach to the **history of systems of thought** relies upon his concept of **discourse**, which he defines in terms of rules governing the production of **statements** in a given empirical field at a given time. The study of these rules forms the basis of his **archaeology of knowledge**. He also developed a distinctive **genealogical** approach to the history of particular formations of **knowledge** and **power** such as criminality, sexuality, and forms of **governmentality**. These govern not only the ways in which **power** is exercised over individuals or groups, but also the ways in which subjects of delinquency, sexuality, or government are constituted. Finally, he outlines a distinctive concept of **ethics** understood in terms of the kinds of techniques and relations to the self through which individuals govern their own behaviour and make themselves into certain kinds of ethical subjects.

## Introduction: critique of the present

Foucault does not belong squarely within the tradition of normative political philosophy. He does not provide foundations for liberal political institutions or key political concepts such as justice, equality, or freedom. Unlike the classical modern theorists, he is not concerned with the justification of sovereign power by reference to the reason or consent of the governed. Instead, his analyses are directed at the objects, means, and materials of government, and at the explicit rationalities which inform different practices of government. While he locates his work in a critical tradition which extends from Kant and Hegel through Marx, Nietzsche, Weber, and the Frankfurt School, he does not develop systematic theories of history, modernity, or the political. He does outline grand theories of discourse and power, as well as an idiosyncratic concept of ethics understood as the forms of relation to the self which enable individuals to govern their conduct in certain ways. However, these theories are primarily intended to serve as methodological accompaniments to his critical-historical studies.[1]

Foucault wrote histories of the emergence of institutions such as asylums, hospitals, and prisons which were also histories of the forms of knowledge associated with their operation such as psychiatry, clinical medicine, and criminology. He wrote an archaeology of the eighteenth- and nineteenth-century proto-sciences of language, life, and labour, as well as several volumes of a projected history of European sexuality. In addition, he sketched a history of modern forms of political reason and gave numerous interviews on political issues of the day. He became a very public, critical intellectual who saw his role as one of assisting social transformations under way in the present. In particular, since the intellectual works in the sphere of thought, he suggested that his or her role is 'to see how far the liberation of thought can go toward making these transformations urgent enough for people to want to carry them out, and sufficiently difficult to carry out for them to be deeply inscribed in reality' ('So is it Important to Think?', 457[2]).

Commentators dispute the degree of overall coherence to be found in Foucault's œuvre. For some, he achieves a more or less unified form of historico-philosophical critique of the present. For others, while all of his books share a common critical relationship to aspects of the historical present such as sexuality, criminal punishment, or the history of the human sciences, their effectivity does not derive from a single methodology or theory but from the nature of the engagement with a particular field of problems.[3] In this chapter I argue that the unity of Foucault's work comes not from some fundamental intuition, methodology, or system of thought but from its recurrent efforts to undertake a certain kind of critical analysis of present forms of knowledge, power, and subjectivity. In each case, his historical studies are undertaken in relation to efforts to go beyond established ways of treating the insane or convicted criminals, or to think outside current conceptions of human nature, sexuality, or the task of government. In several versions of a lecture he gave near the end of his life Foucault sought to spell out this distinctive critical relationship to the present by comparing it with the approach adopted by Kant in a short newspaper article published in 1784 entitled 'What is Enlightenment?'[4] The analysis of Kant's text allows Foucault to characterize a novel kind of attitude towards the present which is really his own. He argues that this apparently minor work signals the appearance of new type of question for philosophy, namely one directed at the nature of the present in which the philosopher lives and writes: 'What is happening now?

And what is this "now" which we all inhabit?' ('Kant on Enlightenment and Revolution', 88). Averting his gaze from the remnants of teleology in Kant, Foucault describes his approach to the present historical moment as essentially negative, looking for a point of exit from or difference with respect to the past: 'It is in the reflection on "today" as difference in history and as motive for a particular philosophical task that the novelty of this text appears to me to lie' ('What is Enlightenment?', 309).

Foucault's distinctive contribution to political thought lies in his elaboration of this attitude or philosophical ethos of permanent criticism. As such, it must be understood in terms of the particular methods and focus of his historical studies. He identifies truth, power, and subjectivity as the recurrent axes of all his critical histories, even though one or the other took precedence in different periods. Thus, *The Birth of the Clinic* and *The Order of Things* are primarily concerned with forms of knowledge accepted as true in eighteenth-century medical science, theories of language, life, and wealth; *Discipline and Punish* and the *History of Sexuality*, volume i, are primarily concerned with normative practices governing behaviour, while *The Use of Pleasure* and *The Care of the Self* are primarily concerned with classical Greek and Roman forms of relation to the self. Throughout his career Foucault used the term 'experience' to characterize the object of these historical analyses, even if the precise sense of this term evolved from one period to the next. His doctoral thesis and first major book, *Folie et déraison: Histoire de la folie à l'âge classique*, was written under the influence of the conjuncture of phenomenology, Marxism, and conceptual history of science which prevailed in France after the Second World War.[5] It addressed what he called the 'experience' of madness characteristic of modern European society: how did this experience of madness come about? What kinds of knowledge and what practices of incarceration and treatment helped to define it? Much later, in a projected preface to volume ii of his *History of Sexuality*, he described the object of this history as 'a historically singular form of experience' (Preface to *The History of Sexuality*, ii. 199). Here he clarifies that by 'experience' he means a particular combination of certain kinds of relation to the self, certain normative rules governing conduct, and certain forms of thought, by which he meant not only the conceptual thought practised within philosophy and the human sciences, but also the forms of rationality embedded in the everyday practice of administrators, doctors, priests, and private individuals. In this sense, 'experience' implies no reference to an implicit subject but rather refers to the three axes of any system of human activity, namely the relation to things (knowledge), the relation to others (power), and the relation to self (ethics).

Foucault's ethos of criticism of the present must be further specified in relation to the choice of objects for historical analysis. What interests him above all is the potential for transformation of the present. As a result, his books are directed at those points of fragility at which things were beginning to change, such as the central role of the concept of 'man' in the contemporary human sciences which *The Order of Things* suggests is already beginning to wane, the apparent inevitability and obviousness of the prison which is questioned by *Discipline and Punish*, or the link between sexual subjectivity and questions of truth which is problematized by the successive volumes of *The History of Sexuality*. In this manner, Foucault seeks to connect his critical studies to movements for social change in one or other dimension of the present. Sometimes, he suggests, this a matter of anticipating faultlines in the present which only subsequently became sites of overt contestation, such as the psychiatric hospital in the mid-1950s. At other times it is a matter of responding to what has already become intolerable, such as the prison at the end of the 1960s and beginning of the 1970s, or the experience of sexuality in the decades which followed the social upheavals of the 1960s.[6]

Although he only became publicly involved in political causes during the 1970s, all of Foucault's historico-philosophical studies are intended to assist such movements by exposing the historical and contingent character of contemporary experience. It was not inevitable that madness be considered a mental illness and become caught up in the institutional and scientific apparatus of psychiatry. It was no more inevitable that judicial punishment, incarceration, and the techniques of corporeal discipline come together in the modern penal system. It was not inevitable that desire, concupiscence, and individual sexual behaviour become articulated in our contemporary manner of classifying sexualities as normal or perverse. On the one hand, these historical studies seek to undermine the obviousness of present practices and ways of thinking, providing indirect responses to questions such as the following: What else could we do with criminals but imprison and attempt to rehabilitate them? How can we understand the social relations between the sexes other than as the product of natural differences? How could we regulate our sexual behaviour other than by discovering and accepting the truth about our desire? On the other hand, they seek to render the given dimension of the present more fragile rather than less by retracing the strategies and conditions under which contemporary experience came into being, and by providing a context and a rationale for the transformations currently under way. Over and above the details of his critical histories of sexuality, prisons, hospitals, or the social-scientific and philosophical versions of humanism, the enduring legacy of Foucault's work lies in the critical ethos manifested in these studies.[7]

A further novelty of Foucault's critical approach lies in his refusal to identify the desired outcome of such transformations or to elaborate normative foundations for his criticism of the present. He shares with other French poststructuralist philosophers such as Deleuze and Derrida a suspicion of political utopias or grand revolutionary projects, preferring instead to focus on local transformations in specific domains of social experience. His failure to provide justification for his opposition to aspects of who we are, how we are governed, and what we take to be true sets him apart from much contemporary normative political philosophy and is the source of many of the criticisms directed at his work. His reasons for this refusal include a commitment to a more modest form of critical intellectual work, but also a commitment to a more critical conception of freedom, one which does not assume that present normative standards should be allowed to determine the limits of permissible criticism or experimentation. Although he prefers a relentlessly empirical exploration of the limits of the present to the deconstructive affirmation of the possibility of change, this enthusiasm for what he refers to as 'the undefined work of freedom' ('What is Enlightenment?', 316) is also something that Foucault shares with his poststructuralist contemporaries.

## History of systems of thought

Foucault acknowledges a series of debts to different aspects of Nietzsche's work at different stages of his career, but his commitment to the kind of historical philosophizing which seeks an explanation of phenomena in terms of their worldly origins remains constant throughout.[8] The title he chose for the chair he occupied at the Collège de France—the History of Systems of Thought—may not have been a direct allusion to Nietzsche's hypothesis that the greatest triumph of historical philosophy will one day be 'a history of the genesis of thought' (*Human, All too Human*, I, para. 18). Nevertheless, his inaugural course in 1971 embarked on a series of historical case studies and theoretical analyses the objective of which he described as a 'morphology of the will to knowledge' ('The Will to Knowledge', 11[9]). The morphological task is undertaken by means of what he called an archaeology of knowledge. This was the method associated with his early studies of the history of the human sciences, but also the method he both systematized and revised in *The Archaeology of Knowledge*. In its revised form, archaeological analysis seeks to uncover the systematicity peculiar to the assemblages of knowledge and power that inform what we think, say, and do in a given domain such as the treatment of madness or criminality. It does not seek universal structures of thought but rather aims to treat these complex assemblages of knowledge and power as so many historical singularities. In this sense, Foucault follows Nietzsche in regarding empirical truth as a human phenomenon which has its own history.

A primary concern of *Histoire de la folie*, which Foucault described in the preface as a work carried out 'under the sun of the great Nietzschean enquiry' (*Madness and Civilization*, p. v[10]), is to provide an account of the emergence of modern psychiatry. It shows how nineteenth-century psychopathology preserved even as it transformed certain elements of the classical view of madness as the result of a moral flaw which reduced human beings to mere animals. More generally, *Histoire de la folie* weaves together several interconnected narratives in the attempt to delineate the European experience of madness between the end of the Middle Ages and the early part of the nineteenth century. A secondary aim is to outline the political and economic circumstances under which those who previously were allowed to circulate freely within society began to be confined. Foucault argues that madness during this period was embedded within a broader category of 'unreason'. Not only were those who would later be identified as mentally ill confined but so too were beggars, freethinkers, offenders against sexual morality, and other indigent elements of the population. This broad category dissolved at the end of the eighteenth century once specialized treatments began to be applied to the poor, criminals, and the mentally ill. Finally, *Histoire de la folie* aims to bring to light one of the fundamental principles of exclusion within modern thought.[11] Early modern European culture harboured an ambivalence towards madness which represented both a dark, inexplicable underside of human existence but also a privileged relation to the truth. Madness in both guises was widely represented in the literature and painting of the period, in Shakespeare's plays as well as the paintings of Bosch, Brueghel, and Dürer. Because it was the result of all too human error, foolishness, or pride, madness was an ever present threat to human reason. By contrast, the classical age saw this cultural dialogue replaced by a silent opposition between reason and unreason. Foucault described the 'language' of modern psychiatry as a 'monologue of reason about madness'. Since this monologue could only be established only on the basis of a silence on the part of madness, he describes the project of *Histoire de la folie* as 'the archaeology of that silence' (*Madness and Civilization*, pp. x–xi).

Foucault's early work on the history of psychopathology and clinical medicine owes much to the conceptual history of science practised by Bachelard, Canguilhem, and other French philosopher–historians of science. His studies in the history of certain empirical sciences stress the variability over time of what was accepted and allowed to function as knowledge. In this sense, he later argued that each society 'has its regime of truth . . . that is, the types of discourse it accepts and makes function as true; the mechanisms and instances that enable one to distinguish true and false statements; the means by which each is sanctioned; the techniques and procedures accorded value in the acquisition of truth; the status of those who are charged with saying what counts as true' ('Truth and Power', 131[12]). In common with much post-Kuhnian philosophy of science, Foucault insists on the judgemental character of knowledge and rejects the idea of pure observation. He also rejects the idea that the history of knowledge is a more or less continuous process of the elimination of error, pointing to the sudden emergence of new ways of perceiving and describing natural phenomena which result from the creation of new concepts. For example, *The Birth of the Clinic* describes how, at the end of the eighteenth century, the medical language of humours was rendered obsolete by the emergence of an anatomical discourse about bodies and their diseases. *The Order of Things* describes two series of mutations in the forms of knowledge about language, wealth, and living beings since the end of the sixteenth century. What enabled the description of such discontinuities in the forms of empirical knowledge was the archaeological description of the underlying discursive structure of knowledge during the classical period. To the extent that it focused on higher-order conceptual conditions of possibility for knowledge across a number of empirical domains, Foucault's practice of archaeology amounts to a historically specific version of Kant's search for the transcendental conditions of all knowledge. Knowledge in the empirical domains of language, wealth, and life during the classical period rested upon a historical a priori which, Foucault suggests, 'delimits in the totality of experience a field of knowledge, defines the mode of being of the objects that appear in that field, provides man's everyday perception with theoretical powers, and defines the conditions in which he can sustain a discourse about things that is to be recognised as true' (*The Order of Things*, 157[13]).

Foucault's archaeology of the human sciences enabled him to outline a powerful critique of the philosophical humanism which exercised considerable sway over post-war European social thought. The crucial difference which separated seventeenth- and eighteenth-century knowledge in these domains from the nineteenth-century human sciences was the fact that, in classical thought, even though it provided knowledge of such distinctively human activities as speaking and exchanging goods, there was no place for a concept of man as the source or agent of the representation of nature. By contrast, throughout the modern period which endured until the second half of the twentieth century, 'man' was conceived in fundamentally irreconcilable ways both as the transcendental subject of knowledge and action and as the empirical object of the laws of philology, economics, and biology. The figure of man which defined the epistemological space of the nineteenth-century human sciences found its philosophical expression at the end of the eighteenth century in Kant's dual-aspect conception of human being. At the end of *The Order of Things*, in a phrase which encapsulated the theoretical anti-humanism associated with structuralist thought, Foucault suggested that this conceptual figure of 'man' was destined to disappear 'like a face drawn in sand at the edge of the sea' (*The Order of Things*, 387).

*The Archaeology of Knowledge* attempted to define the precise object and method of his archaeology in contrast to other approaches to the history of ideas or the sciences. Archaeology, it argued, sought to identify singular formations of discourse, where discourse was defined with reference to statements or 'things said' (*énoncés*). These were understood as events of a very particular kind, like speech-acts, at once tied to a historical context of utterance and yet capable of repetition. The regularities among statements, and between statements and non-discursive procedures, together define a given discursive formation such as clinical medicine or the mercantilist discourse on wealth. These regularities include the type of subject-position or 'enunciative modality' presupposed by a given type of utterance (who is entitled to say what, under what conditions, and in relation to which institutional sites?); the type of theoretical object to which they may refer (bodily humours? sexual desires? populations as objects of government?), and the empirical or institutional domains in relation to which such objects are formed (asylums, hospitals, prisons, or the territorial boundaries of the nation). The resulting 'rules of formation' which define a given discursive formation provide an elaborate theoretical apparatus with which to analyse the transformations which such formations may undergo. In this manner, for example, *Histoire de la folie* argued that it was against the background of the amorphous category of unreason that the concept of mental illness emerged in the nineteenth century. On the one hand, the theory of mental alienation represented a decisive break with the earlier systems of classification which saw various forms of mental aberration as the effects of bodily disorder. On the other hand, the forms of medico-moral treatment practised within the 'enlightened' asylums maintained certain normative elements of the earlier conception of madness as a physical and moral disorder.

In many respects, the theory of discourse outlined in *The Archaeology of Knowledge* only systematized the kind of analysis undertaken in Foucault's work prior to 1969. In others, it presaged the transition to the overtly genealogical analyses which followed. From 1970 onwards it is genealogical analysis which assumes the burden of providing critical histories of the present, where this entails identifying the multiple and contingent sources of a given domain of experience. *Discipline and Punish* is perhaps the most straightforwardly genealogical of Foucault's studies, by virtue of the manner in which it identifies disparate historical sources of the modern penal system: on the one hand, prisons were a solution to the economic and politico-juridical concerns of the eighteenth-century reform of penal codes; on the other hand, they represented a further step in the long history of disciplinary techniques being applied to collectivities of bodies in monasteries, armies, factories, and schools. Archaeology and genealogy are often described as contrasting methodologies which Foucault employed at different stages of his career. However, several chapters of *Discipline and Punish* are devoted to the reconstruction of the underlying rationality which governs the disciplinary exercise of power. Similarly, the genealogy of the modern experience of sexuality outlined in *The History of Sexuality*, volume i, includes as part of the project an archaeological analysis of the form in which modern knowledge of sex developed in the course of the nineteenth century. Foucault argues that, because it evolved out of religious discourse on sexual behaviour, knowledge of sex assigned a privileged role to confession. As a result, a number of theoretical postulates and transformations in the form of such confessional discourse were necessary before it could be adjusted to the norms of nineteenth-century science (*The History of Sexuality*, i. 65–7). Thus, far from being incompatible approaches, archaeological analysis of underlying systematicity and genealogical analysis of the events that gave rise to present experience are entirely complementary operations which Foucault successfully combines in his later work. He insists that the form of critical analysis that he identifies with the Kantian ethos of enlightenment will be 'genealogical in its design and archaeological in its method' ('What is Enlightenment?', 315). Its aim is to show that features of the present that have been considered universal, necessary, or obligatory are in fact only apparent limits. In this sense, it seeks to 'separate out, from the contingency that has made us what we are, the possibility of no longer being, doing, or thinking what are, do, or think' (ibid. 315–16).

Despite their methodological as well as thematic continuities, there are undeniable differences between the style of Foucault's work before and after 1970. Whereas in *The Order of Things* he had confined himself to describing the internal or conceptual conditions of truth within a given empirical domain, in *Discipline and Punish* he argues for a strong correlation between social and institutional processes and changes within the regime of truth. He rejects the idea that power and knowledge bear only external relations to one another, arguing instead that 'power and knowledge directly imply one another; that there is no power relation without the correlative constitution of a field of knowledge, nor any knowledge that does not at the same time presuppose and constitute power relations' (*Discipline and Punish*, 27[14]). His claim is that objects of social-scientific enquiry such as delinquency and criminality have not always existed, but that their historical conditions of possibility include the penal institutions and techniques of disciplinary power deployed in the early part of the nineteenth century. Similarly, *The History of Sexuality*, volume i, argues for an internal relation between the development of certain kinds of knowledge of sexuality and the increased political regulation of sexual conduct during the eighteenth and nineteenth centuries. Foucault's genealogies of particular forms of knowledge do not commit him to a generalized relativism. Nor do they imply that all sciences remain bound to the institutional and political conditions under which they first appeared, even though some clearly do. However, they do refuse both the idea of truth as independent of social and political forces and the idea that political interests have only distorting effects upon knowledge. Truth is understood not only to involve procedures for the 'production, regulation, distribution, circulation and operation of statements' but also to be 'linked in a circular relation with systems of power that produce and sustain it, and to effects of power which it induces and which extend it' ('Truth and Power', 132).

## Power and freedom

Foucault's practice of 'critique' both incorporates and exceeds the familiar Kantian sense of critique aimed at knowing what are the limits of empirical knowledge. To the concern to identify limits, he adds the positive and practical question of discerning paths beyond the contemporary limits of what it is possible to do, to say, and to be. His genealogies describe the singularity of present forms of thought and practice only in order to suggest that these are transformable. The Kantian concern with legitimacy which underpins so much of contemporary epistemology and political theory plays no part in Foucault's historical analyses. Just as his archaeological studies of systems of discursive 'knowledge' (*savoir*) leave aside the normative question of their status as knowledge, so his analyses of power and government are designed to circumvent the perspective of legitimation. To the extent that his genealogies of modern judicial punishment, sexuality, and practices of government involved detailed analyses of specific forms and technologies of power, they pursue a project analogous to that undertaken in relation to truth, namely a morphology of the will to power.

Foucault became increasingly preoccupied with the analysis of power during the 1970s, so much so that in 1976 he could claim that the point of his proposed six-volume history of sexuality lay in the re-elaboration of the theory of power ('The History of Sexuality', 187[15]). In contrast to the tradition of normative political theory, he insisted on a descriptive approach to the phenomenon of power. Instead of questions about the nature, limits, and legitimate exercise of power, he advocated a more concrete and positive approach oriented towards the question of *how* power is exercised. In contrast to the Marxism which informed much French political thought at this time, he drew attention to the relative autonomy and ubiquity of power relations. Whereas Marxism tended to treat social and institutional forms of power as superstructural phenomena, and to account for their political significance in terms of the extension of state power, Foucault famously recommended that, in political theory, 'we need to cut off the king's head' ('Truth and Power', 122; *History of Sexuality*, i. 88–9).

Initially, his reformulation of the theory of power took the form of a series of injunctions intended to free political thinking from the grip of what he called the 'juridico-discursive' conception of power: power is not a thing but a relation; power relations operate at all levels throughout society and not merely through the apparatuses of the state; power should be analysed from below; power is not always repressive but productive; wherever power is exercised there is the possibility of resistance; power must be understood in terms of strategies but without reference to a unique strategist; and so on.[16] While these rules were adequate for their intended purpose of setting out the methodological principles of his analyses of the technologies and strategies of power deployed in relation to prisons and sexuality, they were widely criticized for their failure to distinguish between different kinds of power relation and for their failure to provide normative foundations for the condemnation of certain kinds of power relation.[17] In the absence of explicit normative foundations, Habermas argued, Foucault's critical project faced incoherence by virtue of '(1) . . . the involuntary *presentism* of a historiography that remains hermeneutically stuck in its starting situation; (2) . . . the unavoidable *relativism* of an analysis related to the present that can understand itself only as a context-dependent practical enterprise; (3) . . . the arbitrary *partisanship* of a criticism that cannot account for its own normative foundations'.[18]

While much of this criticism only appeared after his death in 1984, Foucault did develop a more consistent account of the exercise of power which allowed him to distinguish between relations of power and relations of enslavement or domination. In an afterword to Dreyfus and Rabinow's influential commentary first published in 1982, he set out both a rationale for his focus on power and an analysis of the concept.[19] This clarification drew upon his discovery, in the course of his lectures in 1977–8, of the significance of the problem of government in early modern Europe. In the context of the weakening of feudal institutions and Reformation challenges to ecclesiastical authority from the fifteenth century onwards, there was a proliferation of discourses on the ecclesiastical, pedagogical, economic, and political arts of government. Foucault drew upon this early modern sense of 'government' to refer to all of the ways in which one could act upon the possibilities for action of others, by developing or hindering the capacities they acquire, by expanding or limiting the possible courses of action open to them. He took the concept of government to define the field of power relations properly so called, so that to govern 'is to structure the possible field of action of others' ('The Subject and Power', 341).

Unlike his earlier characterizations of power relations in *Discipline and Punish* and *The History of Sexuality*, volume i, which relied upon the terminology of bodies and forces, this definition makes it clear that power is only exercised over another in so far as the other is recognized and treated 'as a subject who acts'. In other words, Foucault's considered definition of power relations implies the freedom of the subject on whom power is exercised: 'Power is exercised only over free subjects, and only in so far as they are "free"' ('The Subject and Power', 342). This definition allows him to provide a reason for his earlier claims regarding the coextensivity of power and resistance, since it implies that there will always be a spectrum of possible responses to the exercise of power on the part of those over whom it is exercised, ranging from compliance to resistance or outright challenge. In this sense, he says, there is an 'agonism' at the heart of the power relation ('The Subject and Power', 344). While Foucault never responded directly to the Habermasian demand for universal criteria, others have argued that his characterization of genealogical criticism as a 'practice of freedom', along with the conception of freedom as internal to relations of power outlined in 'The Subject and Power', provides an indirect response to the charge that he lacks normative foundations. By performing an agonic engagement with particular limits of the present, his genealogies exemplify the very critical ethos which is supposed to require justification.[20]

In addition, whereas the earlier terminology of bodies and forces served to obscure important differences between the exercise of power over individuals and populations and the exercise of violence or the maintenance of structures of domination, this definition enabled him to distinguish clearly between possible forms of power relation. At one pole, there is a relatively free play of antagonistic actions and reactions in which neither side is assured of superiority since reversal is always a possibility. At the other, there are relatively fixed relations of domination and subordination where one party's room to manoeuvre is severely curtailed. In between these extremes lies the range of more or less effective ways of directing the conduct of others. This is the range in which particular techniques and strategies of government are deployed:

> It seem to me that we must distinguish between power relations understood as strategic games between liberties—in which some try to control the conduct of others, who in turn try to avoid allowing their conduct to be controlled or try to control the conduct of the others—and the states of domination that people ordinarily call 'power'. And between the two, between games of power and states of domination, you have technologies of government—understood, of course, in a very broad sense that includes not only the way institutions are governed but also the way one governs one's wife and children. The analysis of these techniques is necessary because it is very often through such techniques that states of domination are established and maintained. There are three levels to my analysis of power: strategic relations, techniques of government, and states of domination. (*The Ethics of the Concern for Self as a Practice of Freedom*, 299[21])

## Governmentality

Much of Foucault's work during the 1970s dealt with what he called 'micro-political' techniques of bodily coercion, control, and training. These were increasingly deployed in a variety of European state and non-state institutions from the sixteenth century onwards: in workshops and factories as well as armies, schools, reformatories, and prisons. *Discipline and Punish* provided a meticulous analysis of the various spatial, temporal, and developmental techniques of disciplinary power. In terms of the tripartite distinction above, these were technologies of government deployed in such a way as to ensure the domination of inmates. Bentham's Panopticon provided a model of such mechanisms for controlling the conduct of others: the asymmetrical structure of visibility which is the key to its architectural design maps onto the asymmetrical distribution of power which defines every system of domination. However, these disciplinary techniques by no means exhaust the modern ways of exercising power over others. The seventeenth and eighteenth centuries also saw the development of a series of new techniques for the political government of territories and populations, along with new forms of knowledge of these objects. At the end of *The History of Sexuality*, volume i, Foucault contrasted the medieval exercise of sovereign power, which relied on the capacity to inflict death on rebellious or recalcitrant subjects, with a modern form of 'bio-power' which was exercised over populations and over individuals in so far as they were living beings.

In his 1978 lectures he outlined a new project intended to trace the emergence of the modern conception of the object and art of government.[22] This would be a genealogical history of governmental rationality or 'governmentality', by which Foucault meant the kinds of rationality which have informed the exercise of European state power since the sixteenth century and which continue to delineate the objectives and methods of modern political government. Consistent with his aversion to the question of legitimacy, his concern was not with normative foundations for the institutions of government but with the ways in which its practice was conceptualized. The doctrine of *reason of state* was especially important for the emergence of a specifically modern art of government. This doctrine gave expression, for the first time, to an autonomous art of political government which was no longer subject to the requirements of a divine order or to the particular interests of a monarch. Henceforth, the state, 'like nature, has its own proper form of rationality' ('Governmentality', 213[23]). Whereas earlier forms of the art of government took as their object the territory and its inhabitants conceived as subjects of the sovereign, the eighteenth century saw the discovery of population as an entity in its own right, with its own regularities, rates of death and disease, and cycles of scarcity and abundance. With the identification of the population as the proper object and end of government, the science of government was fully liberated from the constraints of sovereignty: 'in contrast to sovereignty, government has as its purpose not the act of government itself, but the welfare of the population, the improvement of its condition, the increase of its wealth, longevity, health and so on; and the means the government uses to attain these ends are themselves, all in some sense, immanent to the population; it is the population itself on which government will act' (ibid. 217). Such action upon populations required a knowledge of their forces and capacities. For this reason, the development of this new art of government was intimately bound up with the emergence of new sciences of political statistics and political arithmetic ('*Omnes et singulatim*', 317[24]).

The doctrine which laid out the means of enhancing the power of the state by attending to all aspects of the welfare of its population was the seventeenth- and eighteenth-century science of police. This was considered to be a branch of political economy, which complemented other means of enhancing the forces of the state: diplomatic alliances and military force, and the circulation of money and goods through commerce. According to classic texts such as De Lamare's *Treatise on the Police* and von Justi's *Elements of Police*, the state must concern itself with all aspects of the lives of its citizens, not only roads, public safety, health, and supplies but also religion, morals, and the liberal arts. Police government was also an individualizing power in so far as it was concerned with the welfare and well-being of each citizen. Foucault traced the origins of this individualizing tendency of modern government to a pastoral form of power, modelled on Hebrew society's conception of the relationship of shepherd and flock. Introduced into European culture by Christian techniques for the government of souls, this paradoxical form of power individualized by granting 'as much value to a single one of the sheep as to the entire flock' ('Security, Territory, Population', 68[25]). While the Church's exercise of this pastoral power has declined since the eighteenth century, Foucault suggests that elements of the shepherd–flock relationship remain in the modern state's responsibility for the welfare of individuals. Western societies, he suggests, are unique in their reliance upon this 'strange technology of power treating the vast majority of men as a flock with a few as shepherds' ('*Omnes et singulatim*', 303).

In his 1979 lectures devoted to the theme of 'biopolitics', Foucault turned to the analysis of liberalism as a specific form of governmental rationality. In some respects, liberalism represented a significant departure from the accepted principles of reason of state. In other respects, it was an immensely fruitful form of economic governmental rationality. Whereas the science of police operated on the assumption that there is never enough regulation, liberalism embraced the principle that there is always too much government. Thus, against the idea that the population was an object in need of detailed and constant regulation, liberalism advanced a conception of society and the economy as naturally self-regulating systems. Government should leave these self-regulating systems alone, or at least confine itself to setting in place mechanisms of security which sustain and facilitate natural regulation. In the event, Foucault argued, these 'mechanisms or modes of state intervention whose function is to assure the security of those natural phenomena, economic processes and the intrinsic processes of population' became 'the basic objective of liberal governmental rationality'.[26] Foucault regards liberalism less as a theory or even a coherent practice of government than 'a form of critical reflection on governmental practice' ('The Birth of Biopolitics', 77[27]). Since the eighteenth century it has provided a framework for both the criticism of techniques of government and the reinvention of those techniques. In the interest of further demonstrating the utility of this form of analysis of governmental reason, he devoted several lectures to the examination of two schools of twentieth-century neo-liberalism: the Ordo-liberalism which inspired the post-war reconstruction of a market economy in the German Federal Republic and the American neo-liberalism associated with the Chicago School. These represented contrasting approaches to the role of the market and the kinds of government intervention required to sustain it. Where the Ordo-liberals saw the need for support in the form of social government designed to sustain competitive market operations, American neo-liberals sought to extend the rationality of the market into previously non-economic areas of social life such as the family or crime prevention. Ultimately, they envisaged the extension of market principles to the entire range of individuals' purposive conduct in the management of their 'human capital'.

Foucault's analyses of pastoral power, police science, and liberalism amount to an archaeological analysis of the forms of rationality implicit in different arts of government. While he does not provide a systematic account of the relations between these distinct rationalities of government, much less of their precise resonance in the present, these studies nevertheless suggest some elements of a genealogy of modern government. They imply a displacement of the central role often assigned to the state, even by its harshest critics. Foucault suggests that the central political problem of the present is not the state but the forms of power which have made the state what it is today. In contrast to state theory, Foucault argues that 'it is the tactics of government that make possible the continual definition and redefinition of what is within the competence of the state and what is not, the public versus the private, and so on. Thus the state can only be understood in its survival and its limits on the basis of the general tactics of governmentality' ('Governmentality', 221). The appropriate response to this problem is not an anarchic rejection of political power but a rejection of certain ways of being governed. The earliest manifestations of such rejection were almost coextensive with the early modern invention of the art of political government. Foucault identified this 'art of not being governed, or the art of not being governed like that and at this price' ('What is Critique?', 384) with the critical attitude which he claims to share with Kant. His own studies of the forms of political rationality may be seen as exemplifying this art of not being governed, to the extent that, as he says, resistance cannot be content with the denunciation of violence, reason in general, or the state as such, but must 'question the very forms of political rationality' ('*Omnes et Singulatim*', 324).

## Subjectivity and ethics

In the final years of his life Foucault sought to reposition subjectivity as the overall objective of his work, suggesting that it is not power but the subject that forms the general theme of his research ('The Subject and Power', 327). In part this was simply a redescription of his earlier studies which emphasized their common concern with the different ways in which human beings are made subjects: subjects of knowledge, subjects of power, and subjects of certain kinds of relation to oneself. It was certainly a less radical turn in Foucault's theoretical trajectory than is often believed, since there is considerable overlap between the three possible axes along which genealogies of present experience might be pursued: the forms of truth, the manner in which we exercise power over others and over ourselves, and the ways in which we are constituted as subjects.

All three are present, if not always clearly distinguished, throughout Foucault's work from *Histoire de la folie* to the later volumes of the *History of Sexuality*. In *Discipline and Punish* and *The History of Sexuality*, volume i, he advanced the thesis that power creates subjects. In the first place, this thesis refers to the way in which particular educative, therapeutic, or training procedures may be applied to bodies in order to make them into certain kinds of subjects. Like Nietzsche, Foucault rejects the idea that there is a universal human nature or subjectivity on which power relations are superimposed, even though he admits the existence of a distinctively human body endowed with historically constituted capacities for action. It is, he argues, 'one of the prime effects of power that certain bodies, certain gestures, certain discourses, certain desires come to be identified and constituted as individuals. The individual, that is, is not the *vis-à-vis* of power; it is, I believe, one of its prime effects' ('Two Lectures', 98[28]). In this sense, neither delinquents nor habitual criminals existed before the penal institutions and criminal anthropologies of the nineteenth century produced them as identifiable modes of social being. Conversely, the advent of new categories and new ways of describing human actions opens up new possibilities for action. Human action is, by definition, intentional and therefore presupposes the existence of frameworks for self-interpretation. The systems of knowledge and rationalities of government which Foucault studied in relation to mental illness, punishment, and sexuality are elements of the interpretative frameworks within which Europeans have acted upon themselves and upon others. In this sense, the advent of new descriptions of actions and kinds of subject changes what it is possible for individuals to do or to become in a given historical context.

In the terms of his redefinition of power in terms of government, the thesis that power creates subjects amounts to the claim that certain ways of being a subject are created by means of particular techniques for the government of others, such as the disciplinary techniques for producing docile subjects or the ways in which the policing of sexual behaviour produced the masturbating child as a problem. But in the light of Foucault's insistence that power is only exercised over free subjects, the claim that power creates subjects refers not only to the manner in which new political technologies and new forms of knowledge bring into existence new ways of being constituted as a subject, but also to the ways in which these give rise to new possibilities for choice on the part of individuals. While some forms of subjectivity, such as madness or delinquency, require only minimal cooperation on the part of the subject, others require the exercise of power over the self by the self. Different kinds of relation of the self to the self were already apparent in Foucault's discussion of the manner in which power creates individuals as subjects of a sexuality. Consider the practice of confession: this was a technique through which the Church sought to govern the souls of its flock, but it was also a technique which obliged individuals to give an account of themselves. It thus established the kind of critical and hermeneutic relation of the self to the self which became a focus of the second and third volumes of *The History of Sexuality*. These are concerned above all with the techniques of self described in texts relating to classical Greek sexual ethics and Greek and Roman practices of care for the self during the first and second centuries AD. These techniques of self-reflection and self-government enable individuals to transform themselves in particular ways in order to satisfy certain aesthetic and moral criteria.

Thus, the hypothesis which informs the study of the Greek ethics of moderation and self-mastery in volume ii, *The Use of Pleasure*, is that 'there is a whole rich and complex field of historicity in the way the individual is summoned to recognise himself as an ethical subject of sexual conduct' (*The Use of Pleasure*, 32). In order to analyse this field, Foucault proposes a novel conception of ethics as the form of the relation of the self to the self practised within a given style of moral life. There are four aspects to this relation: the part of the self or its actions that is relevant for ethical judgement (ethical substance); the manner in which the self relates to moral rules and obligations (mode of subjection); the kinds of activity undertaken on the self by the self (ethical work); and finally the goal or type of being the self aspires to become (*telos*). In a given period, change may occur at different rates along some or all of these levels. For example, while ancient Greek and Christian asceticisms involve similar kinds of ethical work upon the self, the substance, mode of subjection, and the *telos* of the activity are quite different ('On the Genealogy of Ethics: An Overview of Work in Progress', 263–8[29]).

This concept of ethics enables the description of continuities and changes in the forms of relation to the self in a manner which parallels the descriptive analysis of transformations in discursive formations proposed in *The Archaeology of Knowledge*. At the same time, it enabled Foucault to attempt to reconcile and redescribe his political passions, his private life, and his practice of philosophy as an exercise in self-creation.[30] His interest in the history of the different ways in which individuals governed their own behaviour was not unrelated to problems which he saw in contemporary styles of homosexual life and in other efforts to redefine sexual ethics. The idea that sexuality was an object of knowledge, or that we might understand our true nature by analysing our desires, was an entrenched feature of the modern experience of sexuality which Foucault sought to dislodge by recourse to the Greek experience. His cautious advocacy of the Greek practice of an 'ethics of existence' might be read as a proposal for a different economy of power with respect to our sexual being. Like the ancient ethic of moderation, this would be a non-universalizable ethic and therefore different from the modern form of regulation of sexual conduct by means of legal obligations and truths about sexuality. But it would also be different from the ancient ethic in so far as this was practised by Greek men for whom self-mastery and moderation were both conditioned by and predicated upon relations of domination over others.

Foucault's account of the manner in which our freedom is embedded within relations of power implies an inescapable responsibility towards others as well as towards the self in the exercise of that freedom. Conversely, his archaeological excavation of the ancient arts of caring for the self reminds us that, even as subjects of power and forms of subjectivity imposed from without, we are nevertheless free to question present limits and to experiment with ways of going beyond them. For political thought, the interest of Foucault's genealogy of ethics lay in the manner in which it opened up the possibility of transforming all kinds of ways in which we constitute ourselves as ethical, social, or political subjects. The subject is not a substance, he argues, but a form. Moreover, it is a form that is not 'primarily or always identical to itself', since it can sustain a variety of different kinds of relation to itself in the course of engaging in different social, sexual, or political practices ('The Ethics of the Concern for Self as a Practice of Freedom', 290). In response to his diagnosis of the character of modern government and his suggestion that many of the political struggles of our present were directed against this individualizing power, Foucault suggested that 'maybe the target nowadays is not to discover what we are but to refuse what we are' ('The Subject and Power', 336). In this sense, the problem addressed by the genealogy of ethics is not that of formulating the moral norms that accord with our present moral constitution, but rather the Nietzschean problem of suggesting ways in which we might become other than what we are.

## Conclusion

Foucault's impact upon political thought in the two decades since his untimely death in 1984 has been extraordinarily wide-ranging. His influence has been felt throughout the social and political sciences, from legal and international-relations theory to accountancy and environmentalism.[31] While some commentators consider him to be one of the most significant twentieth-century diagnosticians of modernity, in the tradition of Marx, Nietzsche, and Weber,[32] the most obvious and immediate effects of his work have been in relation to topics on which he wrote, such as asylums, prisons, the relations between power and knowledge, and the history of governmental rationalities. His largely unpublished lectures on different forms of governmental rationality have given rise to a 'governmentality school' in contemporary political theory.[33] His quasi-empirical approach to the study of power and the manner in which it is exercised offers an influential alternative to the tradition which considers political power as a function of consent.[34] His writings on sexuality and the constitution of identities have been widely taken up within feminist, gay, and queer theory.[35] And even though he wrote very little about race and colonialism, his work has inspired new approaches to the study of these issues.[36]

While the significance of these developments is beyond doubt, they do suggest the possibility that Foucault's importance will fade as interest in these particular questions wanes and other issues come to the foreground of political consciousness. Something like this fate appears to be implied by his conception of philosophy as a form of critical engagement with the present. However, it has yet to materialize. In part, this is due to the degree to which elements of his diagnoses of the present, such as his remarks about the medicalization of human life or the emergence of biopolitics, have become even more pertinent since 1984.[37] In part, it is due to the untapped resources in his work for which other theorists continue to find new applications.[38] More importantly, it is due to the manner in which, over and above the particular topics which he addressed, Foucault invented a new way to practise critical political philosophy. His focus on power, knowledge, and their role in the constitution of subjectivity has contributed to a broader understanding of what counts as political. Some theorists draw consequences from this for central issues in normative political theory, such as the relations between democracy, justice, and deep diversity within and between contemporary cultures. Others take him to provide a model for a new practice of political philosophy which is oriented towards freedom rather than justice or equality.[39] As many have suggested, Foucault's enduring contribution to political philosophy lies in his reformulation of the concept of freedom and his contribution to a new form of critical-theoretical activity applicable to the entire range of present practices of governance.[40]

## FURTHER READING

Ashenden, S., and Owen, D. (eds.), *Foucault contra Habermas* (London: Sage, 1999).

Clifford, Michael, *Political Genealogy after Foucault: Savage Identities* (New York: Routledge, 2001).

Moss, J. (ed.), *The Later Foucault: Politics and Philosophy* (London: Sage, 1998).

Ransom, John S., *Foucault's Discipline: The Politics of Subjectivity* (Durham, NC: Duke University Press, 1997).

Simons, J., *Foucault and the Political* (London: Routledge, 1995).

## NOTES

1. Foucault's theory of discourse is outlined in *The Archaeology of Knowledge*, esp. pts. II and III. His approach to power is discussed in *Discipline and Punish, The History of Sexuality*, vol. i, and in some of the interviews reprinted in Colin Gordon (ed.), *Michel Foucault: Power/Knowledge: Selected Interviews and Other Writings 1972–1977* (Hemel Hempstead: Harvester Wheatsheaf, 1980), and in *Essential Works of Foucault 1954–1984*, vol. iii: *Power*, ed. James D. Faubion, trans. Robert Hurley *et al.* (New York: New Press, 2000). His concept of ethics appears in the introduction to *The Use of Pleasure, The History of Sexuality*, vol. ii (1984), trans. Robert Hurley (New York: Pantheon, 1985), 25–32.
2. In *Essential Works*, vol. iii.
3. G. Gutting writes, 'his analyses are effective precisely because they are specific to the particular

terrain of the discipline he is challenging, not determined by some general theory or methodology' ('Introduction: A User's Manual', in id. (ed.), *The Cambridge Companion to Foucault* (Cambridge: Cambridge University Press, 1994), 3). Dreyfus and Rabinow provide an example of a systematic reading of Foucault's work, describing it as an 'interpretive analytics' of present social practices; see Hubert L. Dreyfus and Paul Rabinow, *Michel Foucault: Beyond Structuralism and Hermeneutics*, 2nd edn. (Chicago: University of Chicago Press, 1983).

4. 'What is Critique?' was presented to the Société française de philosophie on 27 May 1978 and published in the *Bulletin de la Société Française de Philosophie*, 84 (1990), 35–63. It is translated in J. Schmidt (ed.), *What is Enlightenment?* (Berkeley and Los Angeles: University of California Press, 1996). 'Kant on Enlightenment and Revolution' was part of the first lecture in Foucault's 1983 course at the Collège de France. It appeared under the title 'Un Cours inédit' in the *Magazine Littéraire*, 207 (May 1984), 35–9, and is translated by Colin Gordon in *Economy and Society*, 15/1 (1986), 88–96. 'What is Enlightenment?' was first published in P. Rabinow (ed.), *The Foucault Reader* (New York: Pantheon, 1984); citations are from *Essential Works*, vol. i: *Ethics*, ed. Paul Rabinow, trans. Robert Hurley *et al.* (New York: New Press, 1997).
5. Foucault describes this conjuncture in his introduction to the English translation of George Canguilhem's *The Normal and the Pathological* (New York: Zone, 1989). A modified version of this essay appears as 'Life: Experience and Science', in *Essential Works of Foucault 1954–1984*, vol. ii: *Aesthetics, Method and Epistemology*, ed. James D. Faubion, trans. Robert Hurley *et al.* (New York: New Press, 1998).
6. In relation to the anticipation of faultlines in the present, Foucault suggests that 'the game is to try to detect those things which have yet been talked about, those things that, at that present time, introduce, show, give some more or less vague indications of the fragility of our system of thought, in our way of reflecting, in our practices' ('What Our Present Is', in *The Politics of Truth*, ed. Sylvère Lotringer (New York: Semiotext(e), 1997), 159). For further comments on the manner in which *Histoire de la folie* contributed to the emergence of a critical community around the treatment of mental illness, see 'Polemics, Politics, and Problematizations: An Interview with Michel Foucault', in *Essential Works*, i. 114–15. For his views on 'the intolerable', see A. Glucksmann, 'Michel Foucault's Nihilism', in *Michel Foucault: Philosopher*, ed. and trans. T. Armstrong (London: Routledge, 1992), 336–9.
7. James Tully, 'Political Philosophy as a Critical Activity', *Political Theory*, 30/4 (Aug. 2002), 525–47.
8. The tragic experience of existence, genealogical history, and the concept of power were all identified as significant Nietzschean influences at different times, while in his last interview he said: 'I am simply a Nietzschean, and try as far as possible, on a certain number of issues, to see with the help of Nietzsche's texts' ('The Return of Morality', trans. John Johnston, in Sylvère Lotringer (ed.), *Foucault Live* (New York: Semiotext(e), 1989), 327).
9. In *Essential Works*, vol. i.
10. Trans. Richard Howard (New York: Pantheon, 1965); until now only this heavily abridged version of the original 600-page work has been translated into English.
11. Foucault suggests that Descartes's dismissal of the possibility of madness as a ground of error at the beginning of the *Meditations* parallels the social and institutional exclusion of the unreasoning elements of the population. These remarks became the focus of a critical review of *Histoire de la folie* by Derrida in which he challenges Foucault's reading of Descartes. Derrida also denounces the aspiration to presence implied by Foucault's allusions to the possibility of an unmediated experience of madness, of the kind which is occasionally glimpsed in the work of artists such as Goya or writers such as Nietzsche and Artaud ('Cogito and the History of Madness', in his *Writing and Difference*, trans. Alan Bass (Chicago: University of Chicago Press, 1978) ). Foucault later dissociates himself from any ambition to write a history of 'madness itself', and replied in detail to Derrida's reading of Descartes ('My Body, this Paper, this Fire', in *Essential Works*, vol. ii). For a detailed discussion of this exchange which gave rise to a considerable secondary literature, see R. Boyne, *Foucault and Derrida: The Other Side of Reason* (London: Unwin Hyman, 1990).
12. In *Essential Works*, vol. iii.
13. *The Order of Things: An Archaeology of the Human Sciences*, trans. Alan Sheridan (London: Tavistock, 1970).
14. Trans. Alan Sheridan (London: Allen Lane/Penguin, 1977).
15. In Gordon (ed.), *Michel Foucault: Power/Knowledge.*

16. *Discipline and Punish*, 26–8; *History of Sexuality*, i. 92–102; 'Powers and Strategies', in Gordon (ed.), *Michel Foucault: Power Knowledge* 142.
17. Criticisms of Foucault along these lines are put forward by I. Hacking, D. C. Hoy, M. Walzer, and H. L. Dreyfus and P. Rabinow, in D. C. Hoy (ed.), *Foucault: A Critical Reader* (Oxford: Basil Blackwell, 1986). Nancy Fraser summarizes the criticism that Foucault lacks normative foundations as follows: 'Because Foucault has no basis for distinguishing, for example, forms of power that involve domination from those that do not, he appears to endorse a one-sided, wholesale rejection of modernity as such . . . Clearly, what Foucault needs, and needs desperately, are normative criteria for distinguishing acceptable from unacceptable forms of power' ('Foucault on Modern Power: Empirical Insights and Normative Confusions', in her *Unruly Practices* (Minneapolis: University of Minnesota Press, 1989), 32–3, 40).
18. J. Habermas, *The Philosophical Discourse of Modernity*, trans. Frederick G. Lawrence (Cambridge, Mass.: MIT Press, 1987), 276. Further discussion of Habermas's criticism and responses from a Foucauldian perspective may be found in D. C. Hoy and T. McCarthy, *Critical Theory* (Oxford: Basil Blackwell, 1994); M. Kelly (ed.), *Critique and Power: Recasting the Foucault/Habermas Debate* (Cambridge, Mass.: MIT Press, 1994); M. Passerin d'Entrèves and S. Benhabib, *Habermas and the Unfinished Project of Modernity* (Cambridge: Polity Press, 1996); S. Ashenden and D. Owen (eds.), *Foucault contra Habermas* (London: Sage, 1999).
19. See 'The Subject and Power', in Hubert L. Dreyfus and Paul Rabinow, *Michel Foucault: Beyond Structuralism and Hermeneutics* (Chicago: University of Chicago Press, 1982); repr. in *Essential Works*, vol. iii. For discussion of the extent to which this essay responds to some of the criticisms mentioned above, see Paul Patton, 'Foucault's Subject of Power', in J. Moss (ed.), *The Later Foucault: Politics and Philosophy* (London: Sage, 1998).
20. See David Owen, 'Genealogy as Exemplary Critique: Reflections on Foucault and the Imagination of the Political', *Economy and Society*, 24 (1995), 489–506; id., 'Orientation and Enlightenment: An Essay on Critique and Genealogy', in Ashenden and Owen (eds.), *Foucault contra Habermas*. See also James Tully, 'To Think and Act Differently: Foucault's Four Reciprocal Objections to Habermas' Theory', in Ashenden and Owen (eds.), *Foucault contra Habermas*.
21. In *Essential Works*, vol. i.
22. With the exception of 'Governmentality', '"*Omnes et Singulatim*": Towards a Critique of Political Reason', and the course summaries published in *Essential Works*, vol. i, much of this material is yet to be published. Other essays in which Foucault discusses the history of governmentality include 'What is Critique?' and 'The Subject and Power'.
23. In *Essential Works*, vol. iii.
24. In *Essential Works*, vol. iii.
25. In *Essential Works*, vol. i.
26. Foucault, lecture at the Collège de France, 5 Apr. 1978; quoted in Colin Gordon 'Governmental Rationality: An Introduction', in G. Burchell, C. Gordon, and P. Miller (eds.), *The Foucault Effect: Studies in Governmentality* (Hemel Hempstead: Harvester Wheatsheaf, 1991), 19.
27. In *Essential Works*, vol. i.
28. In Gordon (ed.), *Michel Foucault: Power/Knowledge.*
29. In *Essential Works*, vol. i.
30. Alexander Nehamas, *The Art of Living: Socratic Reflections from Plato to Foucault* (Berkeley and Los Angeles: University of California Press, 1998), 175–80.
31. See e.g. Kimberly Hutchings, 'Foucault and International Relations Theory', in M. Lloyd and A. Thacker (eds.), *The Impact of Michel Foucault on the Social Sciences and the Humanities* (Houndsmills, Basingstoke: Macmillan, 1997); Anthony G. Hopwood and Peter Miller (eds.), *Accounting as Social and Institutional Practice* (Cambridge: Cambridge University Press, 1994); Éric Darier (ed.), *Discourses of the Environment* (Oxford: Basil Blackwell, 1999).
32. David Owen, *Maturity and Modernity: Nietzsche, Weber, Foucault and the Ambivalence of Reason* (London: Routledge, 1994); John S. Ransom, *Foucault's Discipline: The Politics of Subjectivity* (Durham, NC: Duke University Press, 1997).
33. See Burchell *et al.* (eds.), *The Foucault Effect*; N. Barry, T. Osborne, and N. Rose (eds.), *Foucault and Political Reason: Liberalism, Neo-Liberalism and Rationalities of Government* (London: UCL Press, 1996); M. Dean and B. Hindess (eds.), *Governing Australia: Studies in Contemporary Rationalities of Government* (Cambridge: Cambridge University Press, 1998); Mitchell Dean, *Governmentality: Power and Rule in Modern Society* (London: Sage, 1999); Nikolas Rose, *Powers of Freedom: Reframing Political Thought* (Cambridge: Cambridge University Press, 1999).

34. Barry Hindess points to the manner in which Foucault dispels the confusion between power as capacity and power as right which has bedevilled modern political theory since Hobbes and Locke, in *Discourses of Power: From Hobbes to Foucault* (Oxford: Basil Blackwell, 1996), 96–136.
35. See Irene Diamond and Lee Quinby (eds.), *Feminism and Foucault: Reflections on Resistance* (Boston: Northeastern University Press, 1988); Judith Butler, *Gender Trouble: Feminism and the Subversion of Identity* (New York: Routledge, 1990); Jana Sawicki, *Disciplining Foucault: Feminism, Power and the Body* (New York: Routledge, 1991); Lois McNay, *Foucault and Feminism: Power, Gender and the Self* (Cambridge: Polity Press, 1992); David M. Halperin, *Saint Foucault: Towards a Gay Hagiography* (New York: Oxford University Press, 1995).
36. Robert J. C. Young comments on the paradox that 'despite the absence of explicit discussions of colonialism, Foucault's work has been a central theoretical reference point for postcolonial analysis. It provided the theoretical basis for what has effectively become the founding disciplinary text for contemporary postcolonial theory, Edward Said's *Orientalism* (1978)' ('Foucault on Race and Colonialism', *New Formations*, 25 (1995), 57–65). See also Ann Laura Stoler, *Race and the Education of Desire: Foucault's History of Sexuality and the Colonial Order of Things* (Durham, NC: Duke University Press, 1995).
37. François Ewald, 'Foucault and the Contemporary Scene', *Philosophy and Social Criticism*, 25 (1999), 81–91.
38. For example, Michael Clifford argues that, contrary to the tendency among commentators to overlook Foucault's remarks on enunciative modalities, this aspect of his theory of discourse is potentially fruitful for the study of modern forms of political subjectivity. On this basis, he sketches a genealogical account of the subject positions characteristic of American political identity, such as the rugged individual formed by the encounter with the frontier between civilization and savagery, the citizen of a nation endowed with a manifest destiny, etc. See his *Political Genealogy after Foucault: Savage Identities* (New York: Routledge, 2001), 54–62.
39. Tully, 'Political Philosophy as a Critical Activity', 543.
40. See William Connolly, 'Beyond Good and Evil: The Ethical Sensibility of Michel Foucault', *Political Theory*, 21 (1993), 365–89. Reprinted in J. Moss (ed.) *The Later Foucault: Politics and Philosophy*. Thomas L. Dumm, *Michel Foucault and the Politics of Freedom* (London: Sage, 1996); Duncan Ivison, *The Self at Liberty: Political Argument and the Arts of Government* (Ithaca, NY: Cornell University Press, 1997); Clifford, *Political Genealogy after Foucault.*

# Index

## C

## D



## E



## F

## G



## H

## I

## M

## N

## O



## P

## W



## X



## Y

Political Thinkers

# Political Thinkers

## From Socrates to the Present

Edited by
David Boucher and Paul Kelly

OXFORD
UNIVERSITY PRESS

Great Clarendon Street, Oxford OX2 6DP

Oxford University Press is a department of the University of Oxford.
It furthers the University's objective of excellence in research, scholarship, and education by publishing worldwide in

Oxford New York

Auckland Cape Town Dar es Salaam Hong Kong Karachi
Kuala Lumpur Madrid Melbourne Mexico City Nairobi
New Delhi Shanghai Taipei Toronto

With offices in

Argentina Austria Brazil Chile Czech Republic France Greece
Guatemala Hungary Italy Japan Poland Portugal Singapore
South Korea Switzerland Thailand Turkey Ukraine Vietnam



Published in the United States
by Oxford University Press Inc., New York



First published 2003
Reprinted 2003, 2004, 2005, 2006



British Library Cataloguing in Publication Data

Data available

Library of Congress Cataloging in Publication Data

Data available

ISBN-13: 978-0-19-878194-3
ISBN-10: 0-19-878194-6

10 9 8 7 6

Typeset by SNP Best-set Typesetter Ltd., Hong Kong
Printed in Great Britain by
Antony Rowe Ltd
Chippenham, Wilts